T0328717

Economic Dynamics
Phase Diagrams and Their Economic Application
Second Edition

This is the substantially revised and restructured second edition of Ron Shone's successful undergraduate and graduate textbook *Economic Dynamics*.

The book provides detailed coverage of dynamics and phase diagrams including: quantitative and qualitative dynamic systems, continuous and discrete dynamics, linear and nonlinear systems and single equation and systems of equations. It illustrates dynamic systems using *Mathematica*, *Maple* and spreadsheets. It provides a thorough introduction to phase diagrams and their economic application and explains the nature of saddle path solutions.

The second edition contains a new chapter on oligopoly and an extended treatment of stability of discrete dynamic systems and the solving of first-order difference equations. Detailed routines on the use of *Mathematica* and *Maple* are now contained in the body of the text, which now also includes advice on the use of *Excel* and additional examples and exercises throughout. The supporting website contains a solutions manual and learning tools.

RONALD SHONE is Senior Lecturer in Economics at the University of Stirling. He is the author of eight books on economics covering the areas of microeconomics, macroeconomics and international economics at both undergraduate and postgraduate level. He has written a number of articles published in *Oxford Economic Papers*, the *Economic Journal*, *Journal of Economic Surveys* and *Journal of Economic Studies*.

Economic Dynamics

Phase Diagrams and Their Economic Application

Second Edition

RONALD SHONE
University of Stirling

CAMBRIDGE
UNIVERSITY PRESS

CAMBRIDGE UNIVERSITY PRESS
Cambridge, New York, Melbourne, Madrid, Cape Town, Singapore, São Paulo

Cambridge University Press
The Edinburgh Building, Cambridge CB2 8RU, UK

Published in the United States of America by Cambridge University Press, New York

www.cambridge.org
Information on this title: www.cambridge.org/9780521816847

First published 2002

A catalogue record for this publication is available from the British Library

Library of Congress Cataloguing in Publication data

Shone, Ronald.
Economic dynamics/Ronald Shone. – 2nd ed.
    p.   cm.
Includes bibliographical references and index.
ISBN 0-521-81684-X – ISBN 0-521-01703-3 (pbk.)
1. Economics, Mathematical.   2. Phase diagrams.   3. Statics and dynamics (Social
sciences)   I. Title.
HB135 .S485   2002
330'.01'51 – dc21   2002022270

ISBN 978-0-521-81684-7 hardback
ISBN 978-0-521-01703-9 paperback

Transferred to digital printing 2007

Contents

Preface to the second edition

I was very encouraged with the reception of the first edition, from both staff and students. Correspondence eliminated a number of errors and helped me to improve clarity. Some of the new sections are in response to communications I received.

The book has retained its basic structure, but there have been extensive revisions to the text. Part I, containing the mathematical background, has been considerably enhanced in all chapters. All chapters contain new material. This new material is largely in terms of the mathematical content, but there are some new economic examples to illustrate the mathematics. Chapter 1 contains a new section on dimensionality in economics, a much-neglected topic in my view. Chapter 3 on discrete systems has been extensively revised, with a more thorough discussion of the stability of discrete dynamical systems and an extended discussion of solving second-order difference equations. Chapter 5 also contains a more extensive discussion of discrete systems of equations, including a more thorough discussion of solving such systems. Direct solution methods using *Mathematica* and *Maple* are now provided in the main body of the text. Indirect solution methods using the Jordan form are new to this edition. There is also a more thorough treatment of the stability of discrete systems.

The two topics covered in chapter 6 of the first edition have now been given a chapter each. This has allowed topics to be covered in more depth. Chapter 6 on control theory now includes the use of *Excel's Solver* for solving discrete control problems. Chapter 7 on chaos theory has also been extended, with a discussion of Sarkovskii's theorem. It also contains a much more extended discussion of bifurcations and strange attractors.

Changes to part II, although less extensive, are quite significant. The mathematical treatment of cobwebs in chapter 8 has been extended and there is now a new section on stock models and another on chaotic demand and supply. Chapter 9 on dynamic oligopoly is totally new to this edition. It deals with both discrete and continuous dynamic oligopoly and goes beyond the typical duopoly model. There is also a discussion of an R&D dynamic model of duopoly and a brief introduction to Schumpeterian dynamics. Chapter 11 now includes a discussion of deflationary 'death spirals' which have been prominent in discussions of Japan's downturn. Cagan's model of hyperinflations is also a new introduction to this chapter.

The open economy was covered quite extensively in the first edition, so these chapters contain only minor changes. Population models now include a consideration of age classes and Leslie projection matrices. This material is employed in chapter 15 to discuss culling policy. The chapter on overlapping generations modelling has been dropped in this edition to make way for the new material. Part of the reason for this is that, as presented, it contained little by the way of dynamics. It had much more to say about nonlinearity.

Two additional changes have been made throughout. *Mathematica* and *Maple* routines are now generally introduced into the main body of the text rather than as appendices. The purpose of doing this is to show that these programmes are 'natural' tools for the economist. Finally, there has been an increase in the number of questions attached to almost all chapters. As in the first edition, the full solution to all these questions is provided on the Cambridge University website, which is attached to this book: one set of solutions provided in *Mathematica* notebooks and an alternative set of solutions provided in *Maple* worksheets.

Writing a book of this nature, involving as it does a number of software packages, has become problematic with constant upgrades. This is especially true with *Mathematica* and *Maple*. Some of the routines provided in the first edition no longer work in the upgrade versions. Even in the final stages of preparing this edition, new upgrades were occurring. I had to make a decision, therefore, at which upgrade I would conclude. All routines and all solutions on the web site are carried out with *Mathematica 4* and *Maple 6*.

I would like to thank all those individuals who wrote or emailed me on material in the first edition. I would especially like to thank Mary E. Edwards, Yee-Tien Fu, Christian Groth, Cars Hommes, Alkis Karabalis, Julio Lopez-Gallardo, Johannes Ludsteck and Yanghoon Song. I would also like to thank Simon Whitby for information and clarification on new material in chapter 9. I would like to thank Ashwin Rattan for his continued support of this project and Barbara Docherty for an excellent job of copy-editing, which not only eliminated a number of errors but improved the final project considerably.

The author and publishers wish to thank the following for permission to use copyright material: Springer-Verlag for the programme listing on p. 192 of *A First Course in Discrete Dynamic Systems* and the use of the Visual D Solve software package from *Visual D Solve*; Cambridge University Press for table 3 from *British Economic Growth 1688–1959*, p. 8.

The publisher has used its best endeavours to ensure that the URLs for external websites referred to in this book are correct and active at the time of going to press. However, the publisher has no responsibility for the websites and can make no guarantee that a site will remain live or that the content is or will remain appropriate.

March 2002

Preface to the first edition

The conception of this book began in the autumn semester of 1990 when I undertook a course in Advanced Economic Theory for undergraduates at the University of Stirling. In this course we attempted to introduce students to dynamics and some of the more recent advances in economic theory. In looking at this material it was quite clear that phase diagrams, and what mathematicians would call qualitative differential equations, were becoming widespread in the economics literature. There is little doubt that in large part this was a result of the rational expectations revolution going on in economics. With a more explicit introduction of expectations into economic modelling, adjustment processes became the mainstay of many economic models. As such, there was a movement away from models just depicting comparative statics. The result was a more explicit statement of a model's dynamics, along with its comparative statics. A model's dynamics were explicitly spelled out, and in particular, vectors of forces indicating movements when the system was not in equilibrium. This led the way to solving dynamic systems by employing the theory of differential equations. Saddle paths soon entered many papers in economic theory. However, students found this material hard to follow, and it did not often use the type of mathematics they were taught in their quantitative courses. Furthermore, the material that was available was very scattered indeed.

But there was another change taking place in Universities which has a bearing on the way the present book took shape. As the academic audit was about to be imposed on Universities, there was a strong incentive to make course work assessment quite different from examination assessment. Stirling has always had a long tradition of course work assessment. In the earlier period there was a tendency to make course work assessment the same as examination assessment: the only real difference being that examinations could set questions which required greater links between material since the course was by then complete. In undertaking this new course, I decided from the very outset that the course work assessment would be quite different from the examination assessment. In particular, I conceived the course work to be very 'problem oriented'. It was my belief that students come to a better understanding of the economics, and its relation to mathematics, if they carry out problems which require them to explicitly solve models, and to go on to discuss the implications of their analysis.

This provided me with a challenge. There was no material available of this type. Furthermore, many economics textbooks of an advanced nature, and certainly the published articles, involved setting up models in general form and carrying out very tedious algebraic manipulations. This is quite understandable. But such algebraic manipulation does not give students the same insight it may provide the research academic. A compromise is to set out models with specific numerical coefficients. This has at least four advantages.

It allowed the models to be *solved explicitly*. This means that students can get to grips with the models themselves fairly quickly and easily.

Generalisation can always be achieved by replacing the numerical coefficients by *unspecified parameters*. Or alternatively, the models can be solved for different values, and students can be alerted to the fact that a model's solution is quite dependent on the value (sign) of a particular parameter.

The dynamic nature of the models can more readily be *illustrated*. Accordingly concentration can be centred on the economics and not on the mathematics.

Explicit solutions to saddle paths can be obtained and so students can explicitly graph these solutions. Since it was the nature of saddle paths which gave students the greatest conceptual difficulty, this approach soon provided students with the insight into their nature that was lacking from a much more formal approach. Furthermore, they acquired this insight by explicitly dealing with an economic model.

I was much encouraged by the students' attitude to this 'problem oriented' approach. The course work assignments that I set were far too long and required far more preparation than could possibly be available under examination conditions. However, the students approached them with vigour during their course work period. Furthermore, it led to greater exchanges between students and a positive externality resulted.

This book is an attempt to bring this material together, to extend it, and make it more widely available. It is suitable for core courses in economic theory, and reading for students undertaking postgraduate courses and to researchers who require to acquaint themselves with the phase diagram technique. In addition, it can also be part of courses in quantitative economics. Outside of economics, it is also applicable to courses in mathematical modelling.

Finally, I would like to thank Cambridge University Press and the department of economics at Stirling for supplying the two mathematical software programmes; the copy editor, Anne Rix, for an excellent job on a complex manuscript; and my wife, Anne Thomson, for her tolerance in bringing this book about.

January 1997

PART I

Dynamic modelling

CHAPTER 1

Introduction

1.1 What this book is about

This is *not* a book on mathematics, nor is it a book on economics. It is true that the over-riding emphasis is on the economics, but the economics under review is specified very much in mathematical form. Our main concern is with *dynamics* and, most especially with phase diagrams, which have entered the economics literature in a major way since 1990. By their very nature, phase diagrams are a feature of dynamic systems.

But why have phase diagrams so dominated modern economics? Quite clearly it is because more emphasis is now placed on dynamics than in the past. Comparative statics dominated economics for a long time, and much of the teaching is still concerned with comparative statics. But the breakdown of many economies, especially under the pressure of high inflation, and the major influence of inflationary expectations, has directed attention to dynamics. By its very nature, dynamics involves time derivatives, dx/dt, where x is a continuous function of time, or difference equations, $x_t - x_{t-1}$ where time is considered in discrete units. This does not imply that these have not been considered or developed in the past. What has been the case is that they have been given only cursory treatment. The most distinguishing feature today is that dynamics is now taking a more central position.

In order to reveal this emphasis *and* to bring the material within the bounds of undergraduate (and postgraduate) courses, it has been necessary to consider dynamic modelling, in both its continuous and discrete forms. But in doing this the over-riding concern has been with the economic applications. It is easy to write a text on the formal mathematics, but what has always been demonstrated in teaching economics is the difficulty students have in relating the mathematics to the economics. This is as true at the postgraduate level as it is at the undergraduate level. This linking of the two disciplines is an art rather than a science. In addition, many books on dynamics are mathematical texts that often choose simple and brief examples from economics. Most often than not, these reduce down to a single differential equation or a single difference equation. Emphasis is on the mathematics. We do this too in part I. Even so, the concentration is on the mathematical concepts that have the widest use in the study of dynamic economics. In part II this emphasis is reversed. The mathematics is chosen in order to enhance the economics. The mathematics is applied to the economic problem rather than the (simple) economic problem being applied to the mathematics. We take a number of major economic areas and consider various aspects of their dynamics.

Because this book is intended to be self-contained, then it has been necessary to provide the mathematical *background*. By 'background' we, of course, mean that this must be mastered *before* the economic problem is reviewed. Accordingly, part I supplies this mathematical background. However, in order not to make part I totally mathematical we have discussed a number of economic applications. These are set out in part I for the first time, but the emphasis here is in illustrating the type of mathematics they involve so that we know what mathematical techniques are required in order to investigate them. Thus, the Malthusian population growth model is shown to be just a particular differential equation, if population growth is assumed to vary continuously over time. But equally, population growth can be considered in terms of a discrete time-period model. Hence, part I covers not only differential equations but also difference equations.

Mathematical specification can indicate that topics such as *A, B* and *C* should be covered. However, *A, B* and *C* are not always relevant to the economic problem under review. Our choice of material to include in part I, and the emphasis of this material, has been dictated by what mathematics is required to understand certain features of dynamic *economic* systems. It is quite clear when considering mathematical models of differential equations that the emphasis has been, and still is, with models from the physical sciences. This is not surprising given the development of science. In this text, however, we shall concentrate on economics as the *raison d'être* of the mathematics. In a nutshell, we have taken a number of economic dynamic models and asked: 'What mathematics is necessary to understand these?' This is the emphasis of part I. The content of part I has been dictated by the models developed in part II. Of course, if more economic models are considered then the mathematical background will inevitably expand. What we are attempting in this text is dynamic modelling that should be within the compass of an undergraduate with appropriate training in both economics *and* quantitative economics.

Not all dynamic questions are dealt with in this book. The over-riding concern has been to explain phase diagrams. Such phase diagrams have entered many academic research papers over the past decade, and the number is likely to increase. Azariades (1993) has gone as far as saying that

> Dynamical systems have spread so widely into macroeconomics that vector fields and phase diagrams are on the verge of displacing the familiar supply–demand schedules and Hicksian crosses of static macroeconomics. (p. xii)

The emphasis is therefore justified. Courses in quantitative economics generally provide inadequate training to master this material. They provide the basics in differentiation, integration and optimisation. But dynamic considerations get less emphasis – most usually because of a resource constraint. But this is a most unfortunate deficiency in undergraduate teaching that simply does not equip students to understand the articles dealing with dynamic systems. The present book is one attempt to bridge this gap.

I have assumed some basic knowledge of differentiation and integration, along with some basic knowledge of difference equations. However, I have made great pains to spell out the modelling specifications and procedures. This should enable a student to follow how the mathematics and economics interrelate. Such knowledge can be imparted only by demonstration. I have always been disheartened by the idea that you can teach the mathematics and statistics in quantitative courses, and you can teach the economics in economics courses, and by some unspecified osmosis the two areas are supposed to fuse together in the minds of the student. For some, this is true. But I suspect that for the bulk of students this is simply *not* true. Students require knowledge and experience in how to relate the mathematics and the economics.

As I said earlier, this is more of an art than a science. But more importantly, it shows how a problem excites the economist, how to then specify the problem in a formal (usually mathematical) way, and how to solve it. At each stage ingenuity is required. Economics at the moment is very much in the mould of problem solving. It appears that the procedure the investigator goes through[1] is:

(1)   Specify the problem
(2)   Mathematise the problem
(3)   See if the problem's solution conforms to standard mathematical solutions
(4)   Investigate the properties of the solution.

It is not always possible to mathematise a problem and so steps (2)–(4) cannot be undertaken. However, in many such cases a verbal discussion is carried out in which a 'story' is told about the situation. This is no more than a heuristic model, but a model just the same. In such models the dynamics are part of the 'story' – about how adjustment takes place over time. It has long been argued by some economists that only those problems that can be mathematised get investigated. There are advantages to formal modelling, of going beyond heuristics. In this book we concentrate only on the formal modelling process.

1.2   The rise in economic dynamics

Economic dynamics has recently become more prominent in mainstream economics. This influence has been quite pervasive and has influenced both microeconomics and macroeconomics. Its influence in macroeconomics, however, has been much greater. In this section we outline some of the main areas where economic dynamics has become more prominent and the possible reasons for this rise in the subject.

1.2.1   Macroeconomic dynamics

Economists have always known that the world is a dynamic one, and yet a scan of the books and articles over the past twenty years or so would make one wonder if they really believed it. With a few exceptions, dynamics has been notably absent from published works. This began to change in the 1970s. The 1970s became a watershed in both economic analysis and economic policy. It was a turbulent time.

[1] For an extended discussion of the modelling process, see Mooney and Swift (1999, chapter 0).

Economic relationships broke down, stagflation became typical of many Western economies, and Conservative policies became prominent. Theories, especially macroeconomic theories, were breaking down, or at best becoming poor predictors of economic changes. The most conspicuous change was the rapid (and accelerating) rise in inflation that occurred with rising unemployment. This became a feature of most Western economies. Individuals began to expect price rises and to build this into their decision-making. If such behaviour was to be modelled, and it was essential to do so, then it inevitably involved a dynamic model of the macroeconomy. More and more, therefore, articles postulated dynamic models that often involved inflationary expectations.

Inflation, however, was not the only issue. As inflation increased, as OPEC changed its oil price and as countries discovered major resource deposits, so there were major changes to countries' balance of payments situations. Macroeconomists had for a long time considered their models in the context of a closed economy. But with such changes, the fixed exchange rate system that operated from 1945 until 1973 had to give way to floating. Generalised floating began in 1973. This would not have been a problem if economies had been substantially closed. But trade in goods and services was growing for most countries. Even more significant was the increase in capital flows between countries. Earlier trade theories concentrated on the current account. But with the growth of capital flows, such models became quite unrealistic. The combination of major structural changes and the increased flows of capital meant that exchange rates had substantial impacts on many economies. It was no longer possible to model the macroeconomy as a closed economy. But with the advent of generalised floating changes in the exchange rate needed to be modelled. Also, like inflation, market participants began to formulate expectations about exchange rate movements and act accordingly. It became essential, then, to model exchange rate expectations. This modelling was inevitably dynamic. More and more articles considered dynamic models, and are still doing so.

One feature of significance that grew out of *both* the closed economy modelling and the open economy modelling was the stock-flow aspects of the models. Keynesian economics had emphasised a flow theory. This was because Keynes himself was very much interested in the short run – as he aptly put it: 'In the long run we are all dead.' Even growth theories allowed investment to take place (a flow) but assumed the stock of capital constant, even though such investment added to the capital stock! If considering only one or two periods, this may be a reasonable approximation. However, economists were being asked to predict over a period of five or more years. More importantly, the change in the bond issue (a flow) altered the National Debt (a stock), and also the interest payment on this debt. It is one thing to consider a change in government spending and the impact this has on the budget balance; but the budget, or more significantly the National Debt, gives a stock dimension to the long-run forces. Governments are not unconcerned with the size of the National Debt.

The same was true of the open economy. The balance of payments is a flow. The early models, especially those ignoring the capital account, were concerned only with the impact of the difference between the exports and imports of goods and services. In other words, the inflow and outflow of goods and services to and from an economy. This was the emphasis of modelling under fixed exchange rates. But a deficit leads to a reduction in the level of a country's *stock* of reserves. A surplus does the opposite. Repeated deficits lead to a repeated decline in a country's level of reserves and to the money stock. Printing more money could, of course, offset the latter (sterilisation), but this simply complicates the adjustment process. At best it delays the adjustment that is necessary. Even so, the adjustment requires *both* a change in the flows and a change in stocks.

What has all this to do with dynamics? Flows usually (although not always) take place in the same time period, say over a year. Stocks are at points in time. To change stock levels, however, to some desired amount would often take a number of periods to achieve. There would be stock-adjustment flows. These are inherently dynamic. Such stock-adjustment flows became highly significant in the 1970s and needed to be included in the modelling process. Models had to become more dynamic if they were to become more realistic or better predictors.

These general remarks about why economists need to consider dynamics, how-ever, hide an important distinction in the way dynamics enters economics. It enters in two quite different and fundamental ways (Farmer 1999). The first, which has its counterpart in the natural sciences, is from the fact that the present depends upon the past. Such models typically are of the form

$$y_t = f(y_{t-1}) \tag{1.1}$$

where we consider just a one-period lag. The second way dynamics enters macro-economics, *which has no counterpart in the natural sciences*, arises from the fact that economic agents in the present have expectations (or beliefs) about the future. Again taking a one-period analysis, and denoting the present expectation about the variable y one period from now by Ey_{t+1}, then

$$y_t = g(Ey_{t+1}) \tag{1.2}$$

Let us refer to the first lag as a *past lag* and the second a *future lag*. There is certainly no reason to suppose modelling past lags is the same as modelling future lags. Furthermore, a given model can incorporate both past lags and future lags.

The natural sciences provide the mathematics for handling past lags but has nothing to say about how to handle future lags. It is the future lag that gained most attention in the 1970s, most especially with the rise in rational expectations. Once a future lag enters a model it becomes absolutely essential to model expectations, and at the moment there is no generally accepted way of doing this. This does not mean that we should not model expectations, rather it means that at the present time there are a variety of ways of modelling expectations, each with its strengths and weaknesses. This is an area for future research.

1.2.2   Environmental issues

Another change was taking place in the 1970s. Environmental issues were becom-ing, and are becoming, more prominent. Environmental economics as a subject began to have a clear delineation from other areas of economics. It is true that environmental economics already had a body of literature. What happened in the 1970s and 1980s was that it became a recognised sub-discipline.

Economists who had considered questions in the area had largely confined themselves to the static questions, most especially the questions of welfare and cost–benefit analysis. But environmental issues are about resources. Resources have a stock and there is a rate of depletion and replenishment. In other words, there is the inevitable stock-flow dimension to the issue. Environmentalists have always known this, but economists have only recently considered such issues. Why? Because the issues are dynamic. Biological species, such as fish, grow and decline, and decline most especially when harvested by humans. Forests decline and take a long time to replace. Fossil fuels simply get used up. These aspects have led to a number of dynamic models – some discrete and some continuous. Such modelling has been influenced most particularly by control theory. We shall briefly cover some of this material in chapters 6 and 15.

1.2.3   The implication for economics

All the changes highlighted have meant a significant move towards economic dynamics. But the quantitative courses have in large part not kept abreast of these developments. The bulk of the mathematical analysis is still concerned with equilibrium and comparative statics. Little consideration is given to dynamics – with the exception of the cobweb in microeconomics and the multiplier–accelerator model in macroeconomics.

Now that more attention has been paid to economic dynamics, more and more articles are highlighting the problems that arise from nonlinearity which typify many of the dynamic models we shall be considering in this book. It is the presence of nonlinearity that often leads to more than one equilibrium; and given more than one equilibrium then only local stability properties can be considered. We discuss these issues briefly in section 1.4.

1.3   Stocks, flows and dimensionality

Nearly all variables and parameters – whether they occur in physics, biology, sociology or economics – have units in which they are defined and measured. Typical units in physics are weight and length. Weight can be measured in pounds or kilograms, while length can be measured in inches or centimetres. We can add together length and we can add together weight, but what we cannot do is add length to weight. This makes no sense. Put simply, we can add only things that have the same dimension.

DEFINITION
Any set of additive quantities is a **dimension**. A *primary dimension* is not expressible in terms of any other dimension; a *secondary dimension* is defined in terms of primary dimensions.[2]

---

[2] An elementary discussion of dimensionality in economics can be found in Neal and Shone (1976, chapter 3). The definitive source remains De Jong (1967).

To clarify these ideas, and other to follow, we list the following set of primary dimensions used in economics:

(1) Money [*M*]
(2) Resources or quantity [*Q*]
(3) Time [*T*]
(4) Utility or satisfaction [*S*]

Apples has, say, dimension [*Q*1] and bananas [*Q*2]. We cannot add an apple to a banana (we can of course add the number of objects, but that is not the same thing). The *value* of an apple has dimension [*M*] and the value of a banana has dimension [*M*], so we can add the value of an apple to the value of a banana. They have the same dimension. Our reference to [*Q*1] and [*Q*2] immediately highlights a problem, especially for macroeconomics. Since we cannot add apples and bananas, it is sometimes assumed in macroeconomics that there is a *single* aggregate good, which then involves dimension [*Q*].

For any set of primary dimensions, and we shall use money [*M*] and time [*T*] to illustrate, we have the following three propositions:

(1)   If $a \in [M]$ and $b \in [M]$ then $a \pm b \in [M]$
(2)   If $a \in [M]$ and $b \in [T]$ then $ab \in [MT]$ and $a/b \in [MT^{-1}]$
(3)   If $y = f(x)$ and $y \in [M]$ then $f(x) \in [M]$.

Proposition (1) says that we can add or subtract only things that have the same dimension. Proposition (2) illustrates what is meant by secondary dimensions, e.g., $[MT^{-1}]$ is a secondary or derived dimension. Proposition (3) refers to equations and states that an equation must be dimensionally consistent. Not only must the two sides of an equation have the same value, but it must also have the same dimension, i.e., the equation must be *dimensionally homogeneous.*

The use of time as a primary dimension helps us to clarify most particularly the difference between stocks and flows. A stock is something that occurs at a *point* in time. Thus, the money supply, *Ms*, has a certain value on 31 December 2001. *Ms* is a stock with dimension [*M*], i.e., $Ms \in [M]$. A stock variable is independent of the dimension [*T*]. A flow, on the other hand, is something that occurs over a *period* of time. A flow variable must involve the dimension $[T^{-1}]$. In demand and supply analysis we usually consider demand and supply per period of time. Thus, q^d and q^s are the quantities demanded and supplied per period of time. More specifically, $q^d \in [QT^{-1}]$ and $q^s \in [QT^{-1}]$. In fact, all flow variables involve dimension $[T^{-1}]$. The nominal rate of interest, *i*, for example, is a per cent per period, so $i \in [T^{-1}]$ and is a flow variable. Inflation, π, is the percentage change in prices per period, say a year. Thus, $\pi \in [T^{-1}]$. The real rate of interest, defined as $r = i - \pi$, is dimensionally consistent since $r \in [T^{-1}]$, being the difference of two variables each with dimension $[T^{-1}]$.

Continuous variables, such as $x(t)$, can be a stock or a flow but are still defined for a point in time. In dealing with discrete variables we need to be a little more careful. Let x_t denote a stock variable. We define this as the value at the *end of period t.*[3] Figure 1.1 uses three time periods to clarify our discussion: $t - 1$, t and

---

[3] We use this convention throughout this book.

Figure 1.1.

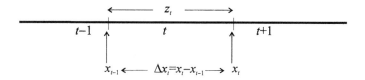

period $t+1$. Thus x_{t-1} is the stock at the end of period $t-1$ and x_t is the stock at the end of period t. Now let z_t be a flow variable *over* period t, and involving dimension $[T^{-1}]$. Of course, there is also z_{t-1} and z_{t+1}. Now return to variable x. It is possible to consider the change in x over period t, which we write as

$$\Delta x_t = x_t - x_{t-1}$$

This immediately shows up a problem. Let x_t have dimension $[Q]$, then by proposition (1) so would Δx_t. But this cannot be correct! Δx_t is the change *over* period t and must involve dimension $[T^{-1}]$. So how can this be? The correct formulation is, in fact,

(1.3)
$$\frac{\Delta x_t}{\Delta t} = \frac{x_t - x_{t-1}}{t - (t-1)} \in [QT^{-1}]$$

Implicit is that $\Delta t = 1$ and so $\Delta x_t = x_t - x_{t-1}$. But this 'hides' the dimension $[T^{-1}]$. This is because $\Delta t \in [T]$, even though it has a value of unity, $\Delta x_t / \Delta t \in [QT^{-1}]$.

Keeping with the convention $\Delta x_t = x_t - x_{t-1}$, then $\Delta x_t \in [QT^{-1}]$ is referred to as a **stock-flow variable**. Δx_t must be kept quite distinct from z_t. The variable z_t is a flow variable and has no stock dimension. Δx_t, on the other hand, is a difference of two stocks defined over period t.

Example 1.1

Consider the quantity equation $MV = Py$. M is the stock of money, with dimension $[M]$. The variable y is the level of real output. To make dimensional sense of this equation, we need to assume a single-good economy. It is usual to consider y as real GDP over a period of time, say one year. So, with a single-good economy with goods having dimension $[Q]$, then $y \in [QT^{-1}]$. If we have a single-good economy, then P is the money per unit of the good and has dimension $[MQ^{-1}]$. V is the income velocity of circulation of money, and indicates the average number of times a unit of money circulates over a period of time. Hence $V \in [T^{-1}]$. Having considered the dimensions of the variables separately, do we have dimensional consistency?

$$MV \in [M][T^{-1}] = [MT^{-1}]$$
$$Py \in [MQ^{-1}][QT^{-1}] = [MT^{-1}]$$

and so we do have dimensional consistency. Notice in saying this that we have utilised the feature that dimensions 'act like algebra' and so dimensions cancel, as with $[QQ^{-1}]$. Thus

$$Py \in [MQ^{-1}][QT^{-1}] = [MQ^{-1}QT^{-1}] = [MT^{-1}]$$

Example 1.2

Consider again the nominal rate of interest, denoted i. This can more accurately be defined as the amount of money received over some interval of time divided by the capital outlay. Hence,

$$i \in \frac{[MT^{-1}]}{[M]} = [T^{-1}]$$

Example 1.3

Consider the linear static model of demand and supply, given by the following equations.

$$\begin{aligned} q^d &= a - bp & a, b > 0 \\ q^s &= c + dp & d > 0 \\ q^d &= q^s = q \end{aligned} \qquad (1.4)$$

with equilibrium price and quantity

$$p^* = \frac{a - c}{b + d}, \qquad q^* = \frac{ad + bc}{b + d}$$

and with dimensions

$$q^d, q^s \in [QT^{-1}], \qquad p \in [MQ^{-1}]$$

The model is a flow model since q^d and q^s are defined as quantities per period of time.[4] It is still, however, a static model because all variables refer to time period t. Because of this we conventionally do not include a time subscript.

Now turn to the parameters of the model. If the demand and supply equations are to be dimensionally consistent, then

$$a, c \in [QT^{-1}] \qquad \text{and} \qquad b, d \in [Q^2 T^{-1} M^{-1}]$$

Then

$$a - c \in [QT^{-1}]$$

$$b + d \in [Q^2 T^{-1} M^{-1}]$$

$$p^* \in \frac{[QT^{-1}]}{[Q^2 T^{-1} M^{-1}]} = [MQ^{-1}]$$

Also

$$ad \in [QT^{-1}][Q^2 T^{-1} M^{-1}] = [Q^3 T^{-2} M^{-1}]$$

$$bc \in [Q^2 T^{-1} M^{-1}][QT^{-1}] = [Q^3 T^{-2} M^{-1}]$$

$$q^* \in \frac{[Q^3 T^{-2} M^{-1}]}{[Q^2 T^{-1} M^{-1}]} = [QT^{-1}]$$

Where a problem sometimes occurs in writing formulas is when parameters have values of unity. Consider just the demand equation and suppose it takes the

---

[4] We could have considered a stock demand and supply model, in which case q^d and q^s would have dimension $[Q]$. Such a model would apply to a particular point in time.

form $q^d = a - p$. On the face of it this is dimensionally inconsistent. $a \in [QT^{-1}]$ and $p \in [MQ^{-1}]$ and so cannot be subtracted! The point is that the coefficient of p is unity with dimension $[Q^2T^{-1}M^{-1}]$, and this dimension gets 'hidden'.

Example 1.4

A typically dynamic version of example 1.3 is the cobweb model

(1.5)
$$q_t^d = a - bp_t \qquad a, b > 0$$
$$q_t^s = c + dp_{t-1} \qquad d > 0$$
$$q_t^d = q_t^s = q_t$$

Here we do subscript the variables since now two time periods are involved. Although q_t^d and q_t^s are quantities per period to time with dimension $[QT^{-1}]$, they both refer to period t. However, $p \in [MQ^{-1}]$ is for period t in demand but period $t - 1$ for supply. A model that is specified over more than one time period is a dynamic model.

We have laboured dimensionality because it is still a much-neglected topic in economics. Yet much confusion can be avoided with a proper understanding of this topic. Furthermore, it lies at the foundations of economic dynamics.

1.4 Nonlinearities, multiple equilibria and local stability

Nonlinearities, multiple equilibria and local stability/instability are all interlinked. Consider the following simple nonlinear difference equation

(1.6)
$$x_t = f(x_{t-1})$$

An equilibrium (a fixed point) exists, as we shall investigate fully later in the book, if $x^* = f(x^*)$. Suppose the situation is that indicated in figure 1.2(a), then an equilibrium point is where $f(x_{t-1})$ cuts the 45°-line. But in this example three such fixed points satisfy this condition: x_1^*, x_2^* and x_3^*. A linear system, by contrast, can cross the 45°-line at only one point (we exclude here the function coinciding with the 45°-line), as illustrated in figures 1.2(b) and 1.2(c). It is the presence of the nonlinearity that leads to multiple equilibria.

If we consider a sequence of points $\{x_t\}$ beginning at x_0, and if for a small neighbourhood of a fixed point x^* the sequence $\{x_t\}$ converges on x^*, then x^* is said to be *locally asymptotically stable*. We shall explain this in more detail later in the book. Now consider the sequence in the neighbourhood of each fixed point in figure 1.2(a). We do this for each point in terms of figure 1.3. In the case of x_1^*, for any initial point x_0 (or x_0') in the neighbourhood of x_1^*, the sequence $\{x_t\}$ will converge on x_1^*. This is also true for the fixed point x_3^*. However, it is *not* true for the fixed point x_2^*, represented by point b. The fixed point x_2^* is locally asymptotically unstable. On the other hand both x_1^* and x_3^* are locally asymptotically stable.

Suppose we approximate the nonlinear system in the neighbourhood of each of the fixed points. This can be done by means of a Taylor expansion about the appropriate fixed point. These are shown by each of the dotted lines in figure 1.3.

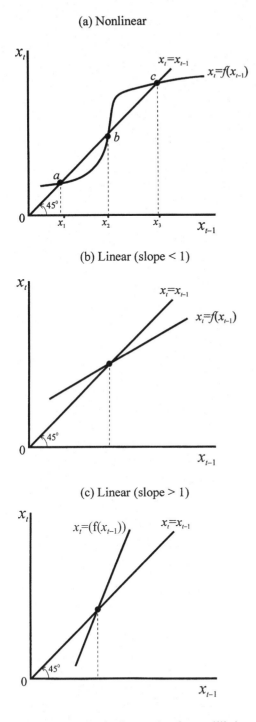

Figure 1.2.

(a) Nonlinear

(b) Linear (slope < 1)

(c) Linear (slope > 1)

Observation of these lines indicates that for equilibrium points x_1^* and x_3^* the linear approximation has a slope *less* than unity. On the other hand, the linear approximation about x_2^* has a slope greater than unity. It is this feature that allows us to deal with the dynamics of a nonlinear system – so long as we keep within a small neighbourhood of a fixed point.

Figure 1.3.

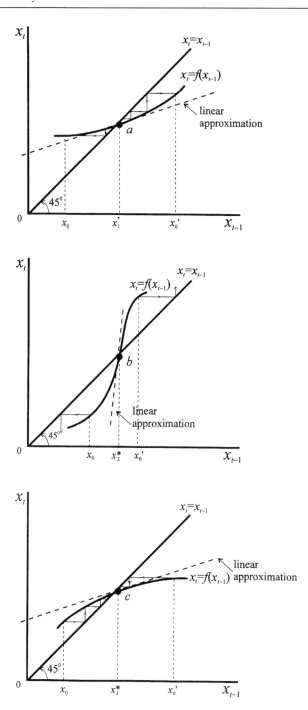

Although a great deal of attention has been given to linear difference and differential equations, far less attention has been given to nonlinear relationships. This is now changing. Some of the most recent researches in economics are considering nonlinearities. Since, however, there is likely to be no general solutions for nonlinear relationships, both mathematicians and economists have, with minor exceptions, been content to investigate the local stability of the fixed points to a nonlinear system.

The fact that a linear approximation can be taken in the neighbourhood of a fixed point in no way removes the fact that there can be more than one fixed point, more than one equilibrium point. Even where we confine ourselves only to stable equilibria, there is likely to be more than one. This leads to some new and interesting policy implications. In simple terms, and using figure 1.2(a) for illustrative purposes, the welfare attached to point x_1^* will be different from that attached to x_3^*. If this is so, then it is possible for governments to choose between the two equilibrium points. Or, it may be that after investigation one of the stable equilibria is found to be always superior. With linear systems in which only one equilibrium exists, such questions are meaningless.

Multiple equilibria of this nature create a problem for models involving perfect foresight. If, as such models predict, agents act knowing the system will converge on equilibrium, will agents assume the system converges on the *same* equilibrium? Or, even with perfect foresight, can agents switch from one (stable) equilibrium to another (stable) equilibrium? As we shall investigate in this book, many of the rational expectations solutions involve saddle paths. In other words, the path to equilibrium will arise only if the system 'jumps' to the saddle path and then traverses this path to equilibrium. There is something unsatisfactory about this modelling process and its justification largely rests on the view that the world is inherently stable. Since points off the saddle path tend the system ever further away from equilibrium, then the only possible (rational) solution is that on the saddle path. Even if we accept this argument, it does not help in analysing systems with multiple equilibrium in which more than one stable saddle path exits. Given some initial point off the saddle path, to which saddle path will the system 'jump'? Economists are only just beginning to investigate these difficult questions.

1.5 Nonlinearity and chaos

Aperiodic behaviour had usually been considered to be the result of either exogenous shocks or complex systems. However, *nonlinear* systems that are simple and deterministic can give rise to aperiodic, or chaotic, behaviour. The crucial element leading to this behaviour is the fact that the system is nonlinear. For a linear system a small change in a parameter value does not affect the qualitative nature of the system. For nonlinear systems this is far from true. For some small change (even very small) both the quantitative and qualitative behaviour of the system can dramatically change. Strangely, nonlinearity is the norm. But in both the physical sciences and economics linearity has been the dominant mode of study for over 300 years. Nonlinearity is the most commonly found characteristic of systems and it is therefore necessary for the scientist, including the social scientist, to take note of this. The fact that nonlinear systems can lead to aperiodic or chaotic behaviour has meant a new branch of study has arisen – **chaos theory**.

It may be useful to point out that in studying any deterministic system three characteristics of the system must be known (Hilborn 1994, p. 7):

(1)   the time-evolution values,
(2)   the parameter values, and
(3)   the initial conditions.

A system for which all three are known is said to be *deterministic*. If such a de-terministic system exhibits chaos, then it is very sensitive to initial conditions. Given very small differences in initial conditions, then the system will after time behave very differently. But this essentially means that the system is *unpredictable* since there is always some imprecision in specifying initial conditions,[5] and there-fore the future path of the system cannot be known *in advance*. In this instance the future path of the system is said to be *indeterminable* even though the system itself is *deterministic*.

The presence of chaos raises the question of whether economic fluctuations are generated by the 'endogenous propagation mechanism' (Brock and Malliaris 1989, p. 305) or from exogenous shocks to the system. The authors go on,

> Theories that support the existence of endogenous propagation mechanisms typ-ically suggest strong government stabilization policies. Theories that argue that business cycles are, in the main, caused by exogenous shocks suggest that gov-ernment stabilization policies are, at best, an exercise in futility and, at worst, harmful. (pp. 306–7)

This is important. New classical economics assumes that the macroeconomy is asymptotically stable so long as there are no exogenous shocks. If chaos is present then this is not true. On the other hand, new Keynesian economics assumes that the economic system is inherently unstable. What is not clear, however, is whether this instability arises from random shocks or from the presence of chaos. As Day and Shafer (1992) illustrate, in the presence of nonlinearity a simple Keynesian model can exhibit chaos. In the presence of chaos, prediction is either hazardous or possibly useless – and this is more true the longer the prediction period.

Nonlinearity and chaos is quite pervasive in economics. Azariadis (1993) has argued that much of macroeconomics is (presently) concerned with three rela-tionships: the Solow growth model, optimal growth, and overlapping generations models. The three models can be captured in the following discrete versions:

(i) $$k_{t+1} = \frac{(1 - \delta)k_t + sf(k_t)}{1 + n}$$

(1.7)   (ii) $$k_{t+1} = f(k_t) + (1 - \delta)k_t - c_t$$
$$u'(c_t) = \rho u'(c_{t+1})[f'(k_{t+1}) + (1 - \delta)]$$

(iii) $$(1 + n)k_{t+1} = z[f'(k_{t+1}) + (1 - \delta), w(k_t)]$$

The explanation of these equations will occur later in the book. Suffice it to say here that Azariadis considers that

> the business of mainstream macroeconomics amounts to 'complicating' one of [these] dynamical systems . . . and exploring what happens as new features are added. (p. 5)

---

[5] As we shall see in chapter 7, even a change in only the third or fourth decimal place can lead to very different time paths. Given the poor quality of economic data, not to mention knowledge of the system, this will always be present. The literature refers to this as the *butterfly effect*.

All these major concerns involve dynamical systems that require investigation. Some have found to involve chaotic behaviour while others involve multiple equilibria. All three involve nonlinear equations. How do we represent these systems? How do we solve these systems? Why do multiple equilibria arise? How can we handle the analysis in the presence of nonlinearity? These and many more questions have been addressed in the literature and will be discussed in this book. They all involve an understanding of dynamical systems, both in continuous time and in discrete time. The present book considers these issues, but also considers dynamic issues relevant to microeconomics. The present book also tries to make the point that even in the area of macroeconomics, these three systems do not constitute the whole of the subject matter. As one moves into the realms of policy questions, open economy issues begin to dominate. For this reason, the present book covers much more of the open economy when discussing macroeconomic issues. Of importance here is the differential speeds of adjustment in the various sectors of the economy. Such asymmetry, however, is also relevant to closed economy models, as we shall see.

1.6   Computer software and economic dynamics

Economic dynamics has not been investigated for a long time because of the mathematical and computational requirements. But with the development of computers, especially ready-made software packages, economists can now fairly easily handle complex dynamic systems.

Each software package has its comparative advantage. This is not surprising. But for this reason I would not use one package to do everything. Spreadsheets – whether *Excel*, *QuattroPro*, *Lotus 1-2-3*, etc. – are all good at manipulating data and are particularly good at displaying sequential data. For this reason they are especially useful at computing and displaying difference equations. This should not be surprising. Difference equations involve recursive formulae, but recursion is the basis of the **copy** command in spreadsheets, where entries in the cells being copied have relative (and possibly absolute) cell addresses. If we have a difference equation of the form $x_t = f(x_{t-1})$, then so long as we have a starting value x_0, it is possible to compute the next cell down as $f(x_0)$. If we copy down $n-1$ times, then x_n is no more than $f(x_{n-1})$. Equally important is the fact that $f(x_{t-1})$ need not be linear. There is inherently no more difficulty in copying $f(x_{t-1}) = a + bx_{t-1}$ than in copying $f(x_{t-1}) = a + bx_{t-1} + cx_{t-1}^2$ or $f(x_{t-1}) = a + b\sin(x_{t-1})$. The results may be dramatically different, but the principle is the same.

Nonlinear equations are becoming more important in economics, as we indicated in the previous section, and nonlinear difference equations have been at the heart of chaos. The most famous is the logistic recursive equation

$$x_t = f(x_{t-1}, \lambda) = \lambda x_{t-1}(1 - x_{t-1}) \tag{1.8}$$

It is very easy to place the value of λ in a cell that can then be referred to using an absolute address reference. In the data column all one does is specify x_0 and then x_1 is computed from $f(x_0, \lambda)$, which refers to the relative address of x_0 and

Figure 1.4.

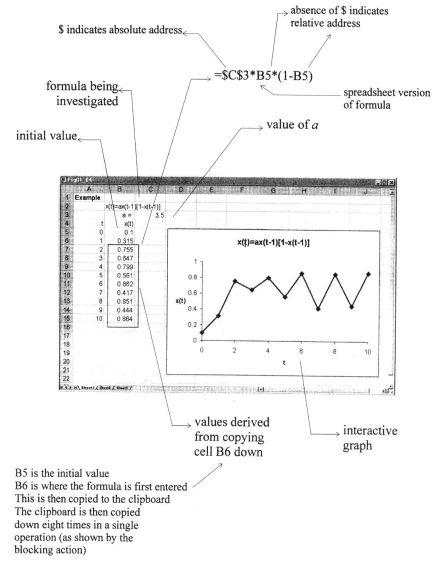

absence of $ indicates
relative address

$ indicates absolute address

formula being
investigated

=C3*B5*(1-B5)

spreadsheet version
of formula

value of *a*

initial value

values derived
from copying
cell B6 down

interactive
graph

B5 is the initial value
B6 is where the formula is first entered
This is then copied to the clipboard
The clipboard is then copied
down eight times in a single
operation (as shown by the
blocking action)

the absolute address of λ. This is then copied down as many times as one likes, as illustrated in figure 1.4.[6]

This procedure allows two things to be investigated:

(1)   different values for λ
(2)   different initial values (different values for x_0).

Equally important, x_t can be plotted against t and the implications of changing λ and/or x_0 can immediately be observed. This is one of the real benefits of the Windows spreadsheets. There is no substitute for interactive learning. In writing this

---

[6] In this edition, all spreadsheets are created in *Microsoft Excel*.

book there were a number of occasions when I set up spreadsheets and investigated the property of some system and was quite surprised by the plot of the data. Sometimes this led me to reinvestigate the theory to establish why I saw what I did. The whole process, sometimes frustrating, was a most satisfying learning experience.

The scope of using spreadsheets for investigating recursive equations cannot be emphasised enough. But they can also be used to investigate recursive *systems*. Often this is no more difficult than a single equation, it just means copying down more than one column. For example, suppose we have the system

$$x_t = ax_{t-1} + by_{t-1}$$
$$y_t = cx_{t-1} + dy_{t-1}$$

(1.9)

Then on a spreadsheet all that needs to be specified is the values for a, b, c and d and the initial values for x and y, i.e., x_0 and y_0. Then x_1 and y_1 can be computed with *relative* addresses to x_0 and y_0 and *absolute* addresses to a, b, c and d. Given these solutions then all that needs to be done is to copy the cells down. Using this procedure it is possible to investigate some sophisticated systems. It is also possible to plot trajectories. The above system is autonomous (it does not involve t explicitly) and so $\{x(t), y(t)\}$ can be plotted using the spreadsheet's x-y plot. Doing this allows the display of some intriguing trajectories – and all without any intricate mathematical knowledge.[7]

Having said this, I would not use a spreadsheet to do econometrics, nor would I use *Mathematica* or *Maple* to do so – not even regression. Economists have many econometrics packages that specialise in regression and related techniques. They are largely (although not wholly) for parameter estimation and diagnostic testing. *Mathematica* and *Maple* (see the next section) can be used for statistical work, and each comes with a statistical package that accompanies the main programme, but they are inefficient and unsuitable for the economist. But the choice is not always obvious. Consider, for example, the logistic equation

$$x_t = f(x_{t-1}) = 3.5x_{t-1}(1 - x_{t-1})$$

(1.10)

It is possible to compute a sequence $\{x_t\}$ beginning at $x_0 = 0.1$ and to print the 10th through to the 20th iteration using the following commands in *Mathematica*[8]

```
clear[f]
f[x_]:=3.5x(1-x);
StartingValue:.1;
FirstIteration=10:
LastIteration=20;
i=0;
y=N[StartingValue];
While[i<=LastIteration,
        If[i>=FirstIteration, Print[i, `` ``, N[y,8] ] ];
        y = f[y];
        i =i+1]
```

---

[7] See Shone (2001) for an introductory treatment of economic dynamics using spreadsheets.
[8] Taken from Holmgren (1994, appendix A1).

which would undoubtedly appeal to a mathematician or computer programmer. The same result, however, can be achieved much simpler by means of a spreadsheet by inputting 0.1 in the first cell and then obtaining $3.5x_0(1 - x_0)$ in the second cell and copying down the next 18 cells. Nothing more is required than knowing how to enter a formula and copying down.[9]

There are advantages, however, to each approach. The spreadsheet approach is simple and requires no knowledge of *Mathematica* or programming. However, there is not the same control over precision (it is just as acceptable to write N[y,99] for precision to 99 significant digits in the above instructions). Also what about the iteration from the 1000th through to 1020th? Use of the spreadsheet means accepting its precision; while establishing the iterations from 1000 onwards still requires copying down the first 998 entries!

For the economist who just wants to see the dynamic path of a sequence $\{x_t\}$, then a spreadsheet may be all that is required. Not only can the sequence be derived, but also it can readily be graphed. Furthermore, if the formula is entered as $f(x) = rx(1 - x)$, then the value of r can be given by an absolute address and then changed.[10] Similarly, it is a simple matter of changing x_0 to some value other than 0.1. Doing such manipulations immediately shows the implications on a plot of $\{x_t\}$, most especially its convergence or divergence. Such interactive learning is quick, simple and very rewarding.

The message is a simple one. Know your tools and use the most suitable. A hammer can put a nail in a plank of wood. It is possible to use a pair of pliers and hit the nail, but no tradesman would do this. Use the tool designed for the task.

I will not be dealing with econometrics in this book, but the message is general across software: use the software for which it is 'best' suited. This does beg the question of what a particular software package is best suited to handle. In this book we intend to answer this by illustration. Sometimes we employ one software package rather than another. But even here there are *classes* of packages. It is this that we concentrate on. Which package in any particular class is often less important: they are close substitutes. Thus, we have four basic classes of software:

(1)   Spreadsheets   *Excel, QuattroPro, Lotus 1-2-3*, etc.
(2)   Mathematics   *Mathematica, Maple, MatLab, MathCad, DERIVE*, etc.
(3)   Statistical   *SPSS, Systat, Statgraphics*, etc.
(4)   Econometrics   *Shazam, TSP, Microfit*, etc.

1.7   *Mathematica* and *Maple*

An important feature of the present book is the ready use of both *Mathematica* and *Maple*.[11] These packages for mathematics are much more than glorified calculators because each of them can also be applied to symbolic manipulation: they can expand the expression $(x + y)^2$ into $x^2 + y^2 + 2xy$, they can carry out differentiation and integration and they can solve standard differential equations – and much

---

[9] Occam's razor would suggest the use of the spreadsheet in *this* instance.
[10] We use r rather than λ to avoid Greek symbols in the spreadsheet.
[11] There are other similar software packages on the market, such as *DERIVE* and *MathCad*, but these are either more specialised or not as extensive as *Mathematica* or *Maple*.

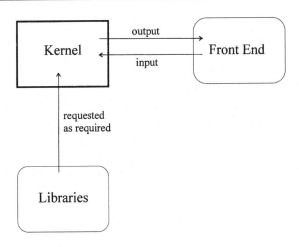

Figure 1.5.

more. Of course, computer algebra requires some getting used to. But so did the calculator (and the slide rule even more so!). But the gains are extensive. Once the basic syntax is mastered and a core set of commands, much can be accomplished. Furthermore, it is not necessary to learn everything in these software packages. They are meant to be tools for a variety of disciplines. The present book illustrates the type of tools they provide which are useful for the economist. By allowing computer software to carry out the tedious manipulations – whether algebraic or numeric – allows concentration to be directed towards the problem in hand.

Both *Mathematica* and *Maple* have the same basic structure. They are composed of three parts:

(1)   a *kernel*, which does all the computational work,
(2)   a *front end*, which displays the input/output and interacts with the user, and
(3)   a set of *libraries* of specialist routines.

This basic structure is illustrated in figure 1.5. What each programme can do depends very much on which version of the programme that is being used. Both programmes have gone through many upgrades. In this second edition we use *Mathematica for Windows* version *4* and *Maple 6* (upgrade 6.01).[12] Each programme is provided for a different platform. The three basic platforms are DOS, Windows and UNIX. In the case of each programme, the kernel, which is the heart of the programme, is identical for the different platforms. It is the front end that differs across the three platforms. In this book it is the Windows platform that is being referred to in the case of both programmes.

The front end of *Maple* is more user friendly to that of *Mathematica*, but *Mathematica*'s kernel is far more comprehensive than that of *Maple*.[13] Both have extensive specialist library packages. For the economist, it is probably ease of use

---

[12] *Mathematica* for Windows has been frequently upgraded, with a major change occurring with *Mathematica 3*. *Maple* was *Maple V* up to release 5, and then become *Maple 6*. Both packages now provide student editions.

[13] *Mathematica*'s palettes are far more extensive than those of *Maple* (see Shone 2001).

that matters most, and *Maple*'s front end is far more user friendly and far more intuitive than that of *Mathematica*. Having said this, each has its strengths and in this book we shall highlight these in the light of *applicability to economics*. The choice is not always obvious. For instance, although the front end of *Maple* is more user friendly, I found *Mathematica*'s way of handling differential equations easier and more intuitive, and with greater control over the graphical output. Certainly both are comprehensive and will handle all the types of mathematics encountered in economics. Accordingly, the choice between the two packages will reduce to cost and ease of use.

Having mentioned the front end, what do these look like for the two packages? Figure 1.6 illustrates the front end for a very simple function, namely $y = x^3$, where each programme is simply required to plot the function over the interval $-3 < x < 3$ and differentiate it. Both programmes now contain the graphical output in the same window.[14] In *Mathematica* (figure 1.6a) a postscript rendering of the graph is displayed in the body of the page. This can be resized and copied to the clipboard. It can also be saved as an Encapsulated Postscript (EPS), Bitmap (BMP), Enhanced Metafile (EMF) and a Windows Metafile. However, many more graphical formats are available using the **Export** command of *Mathematica*. To use this the graphic needs to have a name. For instance, the plot shown in figure 1.6 could be called plot16, i.e., the input line would now be

```
plot16=Plot [(x^3,{x,-3,3}]
```

Suppose we wish to export this with a file name Fig01_06. Furthermore, we wish to export it as an Encapsulated Postscript File (EPS), then the next instruction would be

```
Export[``Fig01_06.eps",plot16, ``EPS"]
```

In the case of *Maple* (figure 1.6b) the plot can be copied to the clipboard and pasted or can be exported as an Encapsulated Postscript (EPS), Graphics Interchange Format (GIF), JPEG Interchange Format (JPG), Windows Bitmap (BMP) and Windows Metafile (WMF). For instance, to export the *Maple* plot in figure 1.6, simply right click the plot, choose 'Export As', then choose 'Encapsulated Postscript (EPS) . . .' and then simply give it a name, e.g., Fig01_06. The 'eps' file extension is automatically added.

Moving plots into other programmes can be problematic. This would be necessary, for example, if a certain degree of annotation is required to the diagram. This is certainly the case in many of the phase diagrams constructed in this book. In many instances, diagrams were transported into *CorelDraw* for annotation.[15] When importing postscript files it is necessary to use *CorelDraw's* '.eps,*.ps (interpreted)' import filter.

In this book we often provide detailed instructions on deriving solutions, especially graphical solutions, to a number of problems. Sometimes these are provided in the appendices. Since the reader is likely to be using either *Mathematica* or *Maple*, then instructions for each of these programmes are given in full in the body

---

[14] This was not always the case with *Maple*. In earlier versions, the graphical output was placed in separate windows.

[15] *CorelDraw* has also gone through a number of incarnations. This book uses *CorelDraw 9.0*.

Figure 1.6.

(a) *Mathematica*

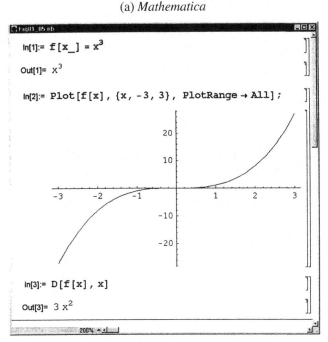

(b) *Maple*

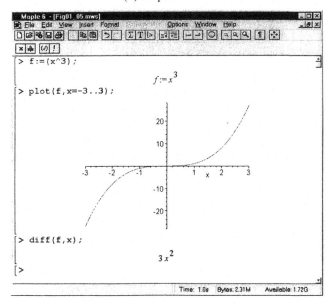

of the text for the most important features useful to the economist. This allows the reader to choose whichever programme they wish without having to follow instructions on the use of the alternative one, with which they are probably not familiar. Although this does involve some repeat of the text, it seems the most sensible approach to take. The routines contained here may not always be the most efficient – at least in the eyes of a computer programmer – but they are straightforward and can readily be reproduced without any knowledge of computer programming. Furthermore, they have been written in such a way that they can easily be adapted for any similar investigation by the reader.

1.8 Structure and features

This book takes a problem solving, learning by doing approach to economic dynamics. Chapters 2–5 set out the basic mathematics for continuous and discrete dynamical systems with some references to economics. Chapter 2 covers continuous single-equation dynamics, while chapter 3 deals with discrete single-equation dynamics. Chapter 4 covers continuous dynamical systems of equations and chapter 5 deals with discrete dynamical systems of equations. Chapters 6 and 7 cover two quite distinct dynamical topics that do not fit into the continuous/discrete categorisation so neatly. Chapter 6 deals with control theory and chapter 7 with chaos theory. Both these topics are more advanced, but can be taken up at any stage. Each deals with both continuous and discrete modelling. Chapters 1–7 constitute part I and set out the mathematical foundation for the economic topics covered in part II.

Part II contains chapters 8–15, and deals with problems and problem solving. Each subject intermingles continuous and discrete modelling according to the problem being discussed and the approach taken to solving it. We begin with demand and supply in chapter 8. Chapter 9 also deals with a topic in microeconomics, namely the dynamics of oligopoly. This chapter is new to this edition. We then introduce the basic modelling of macroeconomics in terms of closed economy dynamics, emphasising the underlying dynamics of the IS–LM model and extending this to the Tobin–Blanchard model. Next we consider the important topics of inflation and unemployment. Here we are more restrictive, considering just certain dynamic aspects of these interrelated topics. Chapters 12 and 13 deal with open economy dynamics, a much-neglected topic in macroeconomics until recently. Chapter 12 deals with the open economy under the assumption of a fixed price level, while Chapter 13 deals with open economy dynamics under the assumption of flexible prices. It will be seen that the modelling approach between these two differs quite considerably. In chapter 14 we consider population models, which can be considered a microeconomic topic. Not only does it deal with single populations, but it also considers the interaction between two populations. Finally, chapter 15 on fisheries economics also deals with a microeconomic topic that is a central model in the theory of environmental economics.

All the topics covered in part II are contained in core courses in economic theory. The main difference here is the concentration on the dynamics of these topics and the techniques necessary to investigate them.

All chapters, with the exception of this one, contain exercises. These not only enhance the understanding of the material in the chapter, but also extend the analysis. Many of these questions, especially in part II, are problem solving type exercises. They require the use of computer software to carry them out. Sometimes this is no more than using a spreadsheet. However, for some problems the power of a mathematical programme is required. It is in carrying out the exercises that one learns by doing. In a number of the exercises the answers are provided in the question. When this is not the case, answers to a number of the questions are supplied at the end of the book.

The present book has a number of features. The coverage is both up-to-date and deals with discrete as well as continuous models. The book is fairly self-contained, with part I supplying all the mathematical background for discussing dynamic economic models, which is the content of part II. Many recent books on dynamic economics deal largely with macroeconomics only. In this book we have attempted a more balanced coverage between microeconomics and macroeconomics. Part I in large part treats continuous models and discrete models separately. In part II, however, the economics dictates to a large extent whether a particular model is discrete or continuous – or even both. A feature of both part I and part II is a discussion of the phase diagram for analysing dynamic models.

A major emphasis is problem solving, and to this end we supply copious solved problems in the text. These range from simple undergraduate economic models to more sophisticated ones. In accomplishing this task ready use has been made of three software packages: *Mathematica*, *Maple* and *Excel*. The text has detailed instructions on using both *Mathematica* and *Maple*, allowing the reader to duplicate the models in the text and then to go beyond these. In order to reinforce the learning process, the book contains copious exercises. Detailed solutions using both *Mathematica* and *Maple* are provided on the Cambridge University website.

Additional reading

Additional material on the economic content of this chapter can be found in Azariades (1993), Brock and Malliaris (1989), Bullard and Butler (1993), Day and Shafer (1992), De Jong (1967), Farmer (1999), Mizrach (1992), Mooney and Swift (1999), Mullineux and Peng (1993), Neal and Shone (1976) and Scheinkman (1990).

Additional material on *Mathematica* can be found in, Abell and Braselton (1992, 1997a, 1997b), Blachman (1992), Brown, Porta and Uhl (1991), Burbulla and Dodson (1992), Coombes *et al.* (1998), Crandall (1991), Don (2001), Gray and Glynn (1991), Huang and Crooke (1997), Ruskeepaa (1999), Schwalbe and Wagon (1996), Shaw and Tigg (1994), Shone (2001), Skeel and Keiper (1993), Varian *et al.* (1993), Wagon (1991) and Wolfram (1999).

Additional material on *Maple* can be found in Abell and Braselton (1994a, 1994b, 1999), Devitt (1993), Ellis *et al.* (1992), Gander and Hrebicek (1991), Heck (1993), Kofler (1997), Kreyszig and Norminton (1994) and Nicolaides and Walkington (1996).

CHAPTER 2

Continuous dynamic systems

2.1 Some definitions

A **differential equation** is an equation relating:

(a)   the derivatives of an unknown function,
(b)   the function itself,
(c)   the variables in terms of which the function is defined, and
(d)   constants.

More briefly, a differential equation is an equation that relates an unknown function and any of its derivatives. Thus

$$\frac{dy}{dx} + 3xy = e^x$$

is a differential equation. In general

$$\frac{dy}{dx} = f(x, y)$$

is a general form of a differential equation.

In this chapter we shall consider *continuous dynamic systems of a single variable*. In other words, we assume a variable x is a continuous function of time, t. A **differential equation** for a dynamic equation is a relationship between a function of time and its derivatives. One typical general form of a differential equation is

(2.1)
$$\frac{dx}{dt} = f(t, x)$$

Examples of differential equations are:

(i) $\dfrac{dx}{dt} + 3x = 4 + e^{-t}$

(ii) $\dfrac{d^2x}{dt^2} + 4t\dfrac{dx}{dt} - 3(1 - t^2)x = 0$

(iii) $\dfrac{dx}{dt} = kx$

(iv) $\dfrac{\partial u}{\partial t} + \dfrac{\partial v}{\partial t} + 4u = 0$

In each of the first three examples there is only one variable other than time, namely x. They are therefore referred to as **ordinary differential equations**. When functions of several variables are involved, such as u and v in example (iv), such equations are referred to as **partial differential equations**. In this book we shall be concerned only with ordinary differential equations.

Ordinary differential equations are classified according to their order. The **order** of a differential equation is the order of the highest derivative to appear in the equation. In the examples above (i) and (iii) are first-order differential equations, while (ii) is a second-order differential equation. Of particular interest is the **linear differential equation**, whose general form is

$$a_0(t)\frac{d^n x}{dt^n} + a_1(t)\frac{d^{n-1}x}{dt^{n-1}} + \ldots + a_n(t)x = g(t) \tag{2.2}$$

If $a_0(t), a_1(t), \ldots, a_n(t)$ are absolute constants, and so independent of t, then equation (2.2) is a **constant-coefficient nth-order differential equation**. Any differential equation not conforming to equation (2.2) is referred to as a **nonlinear differential equation**. The nth-order differential equation (2.2) is said to be **homogeneous** if $g(t) \equiv 0$ and **nonhomogeneous** if $g(t)$ is not identically equal to zero. Employing these categories, the examples given above are as follows:

(i)   a linear constant-coefficient differential equation with nonhomogeneous term $g(t) = 4 + e^{-t}$
(ii) a second-order linear homogeneous differential equation
(iii) a linear constant-coefficient homogeneous differential equation.

In the present book particular attention will be directed to first-order linear differential equations which can be expressed in the general form

$$h(t)\frac{dx}{dt} + k(t)x = g(t)$$

by dividing throughout by $h(t)$ we have the simpler form

$$\frac{dx}{dt} + a(t)x = b(t) \tag{2.3}$$

The problem is to find all functions $x(t)$ which satisfy equation (2.3). However, in general equation (2.3) is hard to solve. In only a few cases can equation (2.1) or (2.3) be solved explicitly. One category that is sometimes capable of solution is **autonomous** or **time-invariant differential equations**, especially if they are linear. Equation (2.1) would be autonomous if $\partial f/\partial t = 0$ and nonautonomous if $\partial f/\partial t \neq 0$. In the examples of ordinary differential equations given above only (iii) is an autonomous differential equation.

A **solution** to a nth-order differential equation is an n-times differential function

$$x = \phi(t)$$

which when substituted into the equation satisfies it exactly in some interval $a < t < b$.

Example 2.1

Consider (iii) above. This is an autonomous first-order homogeneous differential equation. Rearranging the equation we have

$$\frac{dx}{dt}\frac{1}{x} = k$$

Integrating both sides with respect to t yields

$$\int \frac{dx}{dt}\frac{1}{x}dt = \int k\,dt$$

$$\ln x(t) = kt + c_0$$

where c_0 is the constant of integration. Taking exponentials of both sides yields

$$x(t) = ce^{kt}$$

where $c = e^{c_0}$. It is readily verified that this is indeed a solution by differentiating it and substituting. Thus

$$kce^{kt} = kx = kce^{kt}$$

which holds identically for any $a < t < b$.

Example 2.2

To check whether $x(t) = 1 + t + ce^t$ is a solution of $dx/dt = x - t$, we can differentiate x with respect to t and check whether the differential equation holds exactly. Thus

$$\frac{dx}{dt} = 1 + ce^t$$

$$\therefore \quad 1 + ce^t = 1 + t + ce^t - t$$

Hence $x(t) = 1 + t + ce^t$ is indeed a solution.

Example 2.3

Check whether

$$p(t) = \frac{ap_0}{bp_0 + (a - bp_0)e^{-at}}$$

is a solution to the differential equation

$$\frac{dp}{dt} = p(a - bp)$$

Differentiating the solution function with respect to t we obtain

$$\frac{dp}{dt} = -ap_0[bp_0 + (a - bp_0)e^{-at}]^{-2}(-a(a - bp_0)e^{-at})$$

$$= \frac{a^2p_0(a - bp_0)e^{-at}}{[bp_0 + (a - bp_0)e^{-at}]^2}$$

while substituting for p we obtain

$$ap - bp^2 = \frac{a^2 p_0}{bp_0 + (a - bp_0)e^{-at}} - b\left(\frac{ap_0}{bp_0 + (a - bp_0)e^{-at}}\right)^2$$

$$= \frac{a^2 p_0 (a - bp_0)e^{-at}}{[bp_0 + (a - bp_0)e^{-at}]^2}$$

which is identically true for all values of t.

Equation $x(t) = ce^{kt}$ is an **explicit solution** to example (iii) because we can solve directly $x(t)$ as a function of t. On occasions it is not possible to solve $x(t)$ directly in terms of t, and solutions arise in the implicit form

$$F(x, t) = 0 \qquad\qquad (2.4)$$

Solutions of this type are referred to as **implicit solutions**.

A **graphical solution** to a first-order differential equation is a curve whose slope at any point is the value of the derivative at that point as given by the differential equation. The graph may be known precisely, in which case it is a *quantitative* graphical representation. On the other hand, the graph may be imprecise, as far as the numerical values are concerned; yet we have some knowledge of the solution curve's general shape and features. This is a graph giving a *qualitative* solution.

The graph of a solution, whether quantitative or qualitative, can supply considerable information about the nature of the solution. For example, maxima and minima or other turning points, when the solution is zero, when the solution is increasing and when decreasing, etc. Consider, for example, $dx/dt = t^2$ whose solution is

$$x(t) = \frac{t^3}{3} + c$$

where c is the constant of integration. There are a whole series of solution curves depending on the value of c. Four such curves are illustrated in figure 2.1, with solutions

$$x(t) = \frac{t^3}{3} + 8, \qquad x(t) = \frac{t^3}{3} + 2, \qquad x(t) = \frac{t^3}{3}, \qquad x(t) = \frac{t^3}{3} - 3$$

$$x(t) = (t^3/3) + c$$

Figure 2.1.

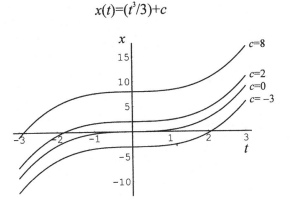

A **general solution** to a differential equation is a solution, whether expressed explicitly or implicitly, which contains all possible solutions over an open interval. In the present example, all solutions are involved for all possible values of c. A **particular solution** involves no arbitrary constants. Thus, if $c = 2$ then $x(t) = (t^3/3) + 2$ represents a particular solution. It is apparent that a second-order differential equation would involve integrating twice and so would involve two arbitrary constants of integration. In general the solution to an nth-order differential equation will involve n arbitrary constants. It follows from this discussion that general solutions are graphically represented by families of solution curves, while a particular solution is just one solution curve.

Consider further the general solution in the above example. If we require that $x = 0$ when $t = 0$, then this is the same as specifying $c = 0$. Similarly if $x = 2$ when $t = 0$, then this is the same as specifying that $c = 2$. It is clear, then, that a particular solution curve to a first-order differential equation is equivalent to specifying a point (x_0, t_0) through which the solution curve must pass (where t_0 need not be zero). In other words, we wish to find a solution $x = x(t)$ satisfying $x(t_0) = x_0$. The condition $x(t_0) = x_0$ is called the **initial condition** of a first-order differential equation. A first-order differential equation, together with an initial condition, is called a **first-order initial value problem**.

In many applications we find that we need to impose an **initial condition** on the solution. Consider the following first-order initial value problem

(2.5)
$$\frac{dx}{dt} = kx \qquad x(t_0) = x_0$$

Rearranging and integrating over the interval t_0 to t_1 we obtain

$$\int_{t_0}^{t_1} \frac{dx}{dt} \frac{1}{x} dt = \int_{t_0}^{t_1} k \, dt$$

$$[\ln x]_{t_0}^{t} = [k \, t]_{t_0}^{t}$$

$$\ln \left(\frac{x(t)}{x_0} \right) = k(t - t_0)$$

$$x(t) = x_0 e^{k(t-t_0)}$$

This is a particular solution that satisfies the initial condition.

We shall conclude this section with some applications taken from economics and some noneconomic examples. At this stage our aim is simply to set out the problem so as to highlight the type of ordinary differential equations that are involved, the general or specific nature of the solution and whether the solution satisfies some initial value.

Example 2.4

A simple continuous price-adjustment demand and supply model takes the form:

$$q^d = a + bp \qquad b < 0$$

(2.6)
$$q^s = c + dp \qquad d > 0$$

$$\frac{dp}{dt} = \alpha(q^d - q^s) \qquad \alpha > 0$$

$$p(t) = \frac{c-a}{b-d} + [p_0 - (\frac{c-a}{b-d})]e^{-\alpha(d-b)t}$$

Figure 2.2.

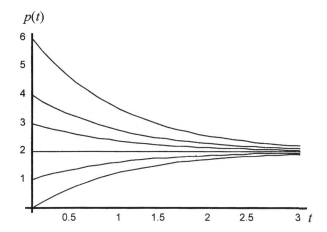

where quantities, q^d and q^s and price, p, are assumed to be continuous functions of time. Substituting the demand and supply equations into the price adjustment equation we derive the following

$$\frac{dp}{dt} - \alpha(b - d) = \alpha(a - c)$$

which is a first-order linear nonhomogeneous differential equation.

Using a typical software programme for solving differential equations, the solution path is readily found to be

$$p(t) = \frac{c - a}{b - d} + \left[p_0 - \left(\frac{c - a}{b - d} \right) \right] e^{-\alpha(d - b)t}$$

which satisfies the initial condition. For $d - b > 0$ the solution path for different initial prices is illustrated in figure 2.2

Example 2.5

Suppose we have the same basic demand and supply model as in example 2.4 but now assume that demand responds not only to the price of the good but also to the change in the price of the good. In other words, we assume that if the price of the good is changing, then this shifts the demand curve. We shall leave open the question at this stage of whether the demand curve shifts to the right or the left as a result of the price change. The model now takes the form

$$q^d = a + bp + f\frac{dp}{dt} \quad b < 0, f \neq 0$$

$$q^s = c + dp \qquad d > 0 \tag{2.7}$$

$$\frac{dp}{dt} = \alpha(q^d - q^s) \qquad \alpha > 0$$

This is effectively a stock-adjustment model. Stocks (inventories) change according to the difference between supply and demand, and price adjusts according to the accumulation–decumulation of stocks. Thus, if $i(t)$ denotes the inventory holding of stocks at time t, then

$$\frac{di}{dt} = q^s - q^d$$

$$i = i_0 + \int_0^t (q^s - q^d)dt$$

and prices adjust according to

$$\frac{dp}{dt} = -\alpha\frac{di}{dt} = -\alpha(q^s - q^d)$$

$$= \alpha(q^d - q^s) \quad \alpha > 0$$

which is the third equation in the model. Substituting the demand and supply equations into the price-adjustment equation results in the following first-order linear nonhomogeneous differential equation

$$\frac{dp}{dt} - \left[\frac{\alpha(b-d)}{1-\alpha f}\right]p = \frac{\alpha(a-c)}{1-\alpha f}$$

with solution

$$p(t) = \left(\frac{c-a}{b-d}\right) + \left[p_0 - \left(\frac{c-a}{b-d}\right)\right]e^{\frac{-\alpha(d-b)t}{1-\alpha f}}$$

which satisfies the initial condition $p(0) = p_0$. For this model there are far more varieties of solution paths, depending on the values of the various parameters. Some typical solution paths are illustrated in figure 2.3. We shall discuss the stability of such systems later.

Figure 2.3.

$$p(t) = \frac{c-a}{b-d} + [p_0 - (\frac{c-a}{b-d})]\,e^{\{-\alpha(d-b)t/(1-\alpha f)\}}$$

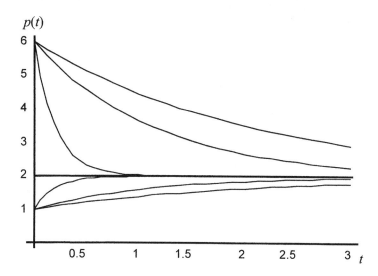

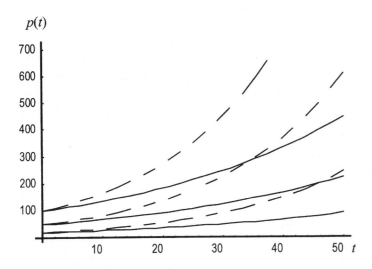

Figure 2.4.

Example 2.6

Assume population, p, grows at a constant rate k, where we assume that p is a continuous function of time, t. This means that the percentage change in the population is a constant k. Hence

$$\frac{dp}{dt}\frac{1}{p} = k \tag{2.8}$$

which immediately gives the first-order linear homogeneous differential equation

$$\frac{dp}{dt} - kp = 0$$

with solution

$$p(t) = p_0 e^{kt}$$

which satisfies the initial condition $p(0) = p_0$. Typical solution paths for this Malthusian population growth are illustrated in figure 2.4.

Example 2.7

In many scientific problems use is made of radioactive decay. Certain radioactive elements are unstable and within a certain period the atoms degenerate to form another element. However, in a specified time period the decay is quite specific. In the early twentieth century the famous physicist Ernest Rutherford showed that the radioactivity of a substance is directly proportional to the number of atoms present at time t. If dn/dt denotes the number of atoms that degenerate per unit of time, then according to Rutherford

(2.9)
$$\frac{dn}{dt} = -\lambda n \quad \lambda > 0$$

where λ is the decay constant of the substance concerned and n is a continuous function of time. This is a first-order linear homogeneous differential equation and is identical in form to the exponential population growth specified in example 2.6 above. We shall return to this example later when we consider its solution and how the solution is used for calculating the *half-life* of a radioactive substance and how this is used to authenticate paintings and such items as the Turin shroud.

Example 2.8

In this example we consider a continuous form of the Harrod–Domar growth model. In this model savings, S, is assumed to be proportional to income, Y; investment, I, i.e., the change in the capital stock, is proportional to the change in income over time; and in equilibrium investment is equal to savings. If s denotes the average (here equal to the marginal) propensity to save, and v the coefficient for the investment relationship, then the model can be captured by the following set of equations

(2.10)
$$S = sY$$
$$I = \dot{K} = v\dot{Y}$$
$$I = S$$

where a dot above a variable denotes the first-time derivate, i.e., dx/dt. Substituting, we immediately derive the following homogeneous differential equation

$$v\dot{Y} = sY$$
$$\dot{Y} - \left(\frac{s}{v}\right)Y = 0$$

with initial condition

$$I_0 = S_0 = sY_0$$

It also follows from the homogeneous equation that the rate of growth of income is equal to s/v, which Harrod called the 'warranted rate of growth'. The solution path satisfying the initial condition is readily established to be

$$Y(t) = Y_0 e^{(s/v)t}$$

Example 2.9[1]

It is well known that the Solow growth model reduces down to a simple autonomous differential equation. We begin with a continuous production function

---

[1] We develop this model in detail here because it has once again become of interest and is the basis of *new* classical growth models and real business cycle models. A discrete version of the model is developed in chapter 3.

$Y = F(K, L)$, which is twice differentiable and homogeneous of degree one (i.e. constant returns to scale). Let $k = K/L$ denote the capital/labour ratio and $y = Y/L$ the output/labour ratio. Then

$$\frac{Y}{L} = \frac{F(K, L)}{L} = F\left(\frac{K}{L}, 1\right) = F(k, 1) = f(k)$$

i.e. $y = f(k)$

with $f(0) = 0, f'(k) > 0, f''(k) < 0, k > 0$

We make two further assumptions:

1.   The labour force grows at a constant rate n, and is independent of any economic variables in the system. Hence

$$\dot{L} = nL \qquad L(0) = L_0$$

2.   Savings is undertaken as a constant fraction of output ($S = sY$) and savings equal investment, which is simply the change in the capital stock plus replacement investment, hence

$$I = \dot{K} + \delta K$$
$$S = sY$$
$$\dot{K} + \delta K = sY$$
$$K(0) = K_0$$

Now differentiate the variable k with respect to time, i.e., derive dk/dt,

$$\frac{dk}{dt} = \dot{k} = \frac{L\dfrac{dK}{dt} - K\dfrac{dL}{dt}}{L^2}$$

$$\dot{k} = \left(\frac{1}{L}\right)\frac{dK}{dt} - \left(\frac{K}{L}\right)\left(\frac{1}{L}\right)\frac{dL}{dt}$$

$$= \left(\frac{K}{L}\right)\left(\frac{1}{K}\right)\frac{dK}{dt} - \left(\frac{K}{L}\right)\left(\frac{1}{L}\right)\frac{dL}{dt}$$

$$= k\left(\frac{\dot{K}}{K} - \frac{\dot{L}}{L}\right)$$

But

$$\frac{\dot{K}}{K} = \frac{sY - \delta K}{K} = \frac{sY}{L}\left(\frac{L}{K}\right) - \delta = \frac{sf(k)}{k} - \delta$$

and

$$\frac{\dot{L}}{L} = \frac{nL}{L} = n$$

Hence

$$\dot{k} = sf(k) - \delta k - nk$$
$$= sf(k) - (n + \delta)k$$

(2.11)

with initial conditions

$$k(0) = \frac{K_0}{L_0} = k_0$$

We cannot solve equation (2.11) because the production function is not explicitly defined. Suppose we assume that the production function $F(K, L)$ conforms to a Cobb–Douglas, i.e., we assume

$$Y = aK^\alpha L^{1-\alpha} \quad 0 < \alpha < 1$$

$$\frac{Y}{L} = a\left(\frac{K}{L}\right)^\alpha$$

or

(2.12) $$y = f(k) = ak^\alpha$$

In this instance the capital/labour ratio grows according to

(2.13) $$\dot{k} = sak^\alpha - (n + \delta)k$$

The Solow growth model with a Cobb–Douglas production function therefore conforms to the following differential equation

$$\dot{k} + (n + \delta)k = sak^\alpha$$

This is a Bernoulli equation,[2] and can accordingly be solved by performing a transformation that results in a linear differential equation that is readily solvable. Given such a solution, then a solution can be found for the original variable.

To verify this, define the following transformation:

$$v = k^{1-\alpha}$$

$$\therefore \quad \frac{dv}{dt} = (1 - \alpha)k^{-\alpha}\frac{dk}{dt}$$

$$\text{or} \quad \dot{k} = \frac{k^\alpha}{(1 - \alpha)}\frac{dv}{dt}$$

Using these results we can derive the following

$$k^{-\alpha}\dot{k} + (n + \delta)kk^{-\alpha} = sa$$

$$k^{-\alpha}\dot{k} + (n + \delta)k^{1-\alpha} = sa$$

$$\left(\frac{k^{-\alpha}k^\alpha}{1 - \alpha}\right)\frac{dv}{dt} + (n + \delta)v = sa$$

$$\text{i.e.} \quad \frac{dv}{dt} + (1 - \alpha)(n + \delta)v = (1 - \alpha)sa$$

which is a linear differential equation in v with solution

$$v(t) = \frac{as}{n + \delta} + \left(v_0 - \frac{as}{n + \delta}\right)e^{-(1-\alpha)(n+\delta)t}$$

---

[2] A Bernoulli equation takes the general form

$$\frac{dy}{dt} + f(t)x = h(t)x^\alpha$$

See Giordano and Weir (1991, pp. 95–6).

Figure 2.5.

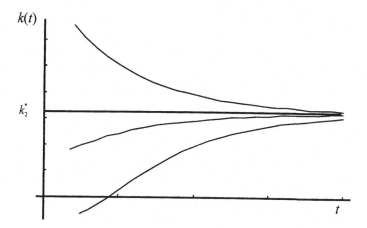

which satisfies the initial condition

$$v_0 = k_0^{1-\alpha}$$

This allows us to solve for $k(t)$ as follows

$$k^{1-\alpha} = \frac{as}{n+\delta} + \left(k_0^{1-\alpha} - \frac{as}{n+\delta} \right) e^{-(1-\alpha)(n+\delta)t}$$

i.e. $$k(t) = \left[\frac{as}{n+\delta} + e^{-(1-\alpha)(n+\delta)t} \left(k_0^{1-\alpha} - \frac{as}{n+\delta} \right) \right]^{\frac{1}{1-\alpha}}$$

The solution path for different initial values of k is illustrated in figure 2.5.

2.2   Solutions to first-order linear differential equations

Solutions to first-order linear differential equations are well discussed in the mathematical texts on differential equations (see Boyce and DiPrima 1997; Giordano
and Weir 1991). Here our intention is simply to provide the steps in obtaining a
solution. In doing this we shall suppose y is a function of t. This is useful since
most economic examples are of this type. The general form for a first-order linear
differential equation is then

$$\frac{dy}{dt} + p(t)y = g(t)$$

Notice that in this formulation both p and g are functions of time. This also allows
for the case where $p(t)$ and $g(t)$ are constants, in which case we have

$$\frac{dy}{dt} + by = a$$

The four-step procedure is as follows.

Step 1   Write the linear first-order equation in the standard form

$$\frac{dy}{dt} + p(t)y = g(t)$$

Step 2   Calculate the **integrating factor**

$$\mu(t) = e^{\int p(t)dt}$$

Step 3   Multiply throughout by the integrating factor, integrate both sides and add a constant of integration to the right-hand side

(a) $\mu(t)\left(\dfrac{dy}{dt} + p(t)y\right) = \mu(t)g(t)$

or

$$\dfrac{d}{dt}[\mu(t)y] = \mu(t)g(t)$$

(b) $\displaystyle\int \dfrac{d}{dt}[\mu(t)y]dt = \int \mu(t)g(t)dt + c$

Step 4   Write the general result

$$\mu(t)y = \int \mu(t)g(t) + c$$

Example 2.10

As an example, let us apply this four-step procedure to the equation

$$\dfrac{dy}{dt} = a + by$$

Step 1   We can write this in the standard form

$$\dfrac{dy}{dt} - by = a$$

Step 2   Calculate the integrating factor

$$\mu(t) = e^{\int (-b)dt} = e^{-bt}$$

Step 3   Multiply throughout by the integrating factor, integrate both sides and add a constant of integration to the right-hand side

(a) $e^{-bt}\left(\dfrac{dy}{dt} - by\right) = ae^{-bt}$ or $\dfrac{d}{dt}(e^{-bt}y) = ae^{-bt}$

(b) $\displaystyle\int \dfrac{d}{dt}(e^{-bt}y)dt = \int ae^{-bt}dt + c$

Step 4 $e^{-bt}y = \displaystyle\int ae^{-bt}dt + c$

or

$$e^{-bt}y = -\dfrac{ae^{-bt}}{b} + c$$

$$y = -\dfrac{a}{b} + ce^{bt}$$

Furthermore, if we have the initial condition that $y(0) = y_0$, then we can solve for c

$$y_0 = -\frac{a}{b} + c$$

$$c = y_0 + \frac{a}{b}$$

Hence, we have the solution to the initial value problem of

$$y(t) = -\frac{a}{b} + \left(y_0 + \frac{a}{b}\right) e^{bt}$$

Example 2.11

Suppose we have the initial value problem

$$\frac{dy}{dt} = 2y + 4t \quad y(0) = 1$$

Applying the four-step procedure we have

Step 1 $\quad \dfrac{dy}{dt} - 2y = 4t$

Step 2 $\quad \mu(t) = e^{\int -2dt} = e^{-2t}$

Step 3 $\quad e^{-2t}y = \displaystyle\int 4te^{-2t}\,dt + c$

Step 4 $\quad e^{-2t}y = -2te^{-2t} - e^{-2t} + c$

Or

$$y = -2t - 1 + ce^{2t}$$

Since $y(0) = 1$, then

$$1 = -1 + c$$
$$c = 2$$

Hence,

$$y(t) = -2t - 1 + 2e^{2t}$$

2.3 Compound interest

If an amount A is compounded annually at a market interest rate of r for a given number of years t, then the payment received at time t, P_t is given by

$$P_t = A(1 + r)^t \tag{2.14}$$

On the other hand if the same amount is compounded m times each year, then the payment received is given by

$$P_t = A\left(1 + \frac{r}{m}\right)^{mt} \tag{2.15}$$

If compounded continuously, then $m \to \infty$ and

$$P(t) = A \lim_{x \to \infty} \left(1 + \frac{r}{m}\right)^{mt} = Ae^{rt} \tag{2.16}$$

Looked at from the point of view of a differential equation, we can readily establish that

$$\frac{dP}{dt} = rP$$

with solution

$$P(t) = P_0 e^{rt}$$

Since P_0 is the initial payment, then $P_0 = A$ in this formulation of the problem.

We know that an initial deposit, P_0, compounded continuously at a rate of r per cent per period will grow to

$$P(t) = P_0 e^{rt}$$

Now assume that in addition to the interest received, rP, there is a constant rate of deposit, d. Thus

$$\frac{dP}{dt} = rP + d$$

The solution to this differential equation can be found as follows[3]

$$\frac{dP}{dt} = r[P + (d/r)]$$

$$\frac{dP/dt}{P + (d/r)} = r$$

then

$$\frac{d}{dt} \ln |P + (d/r)| = r$$

Integrating both sides

$$\int \frac{d}{dt} \ln |P + (d/r)| dt = \int r dt$$

which leads to

$$\ln |P + (d/r)| = rt + c_0$$

$$P + (d/r) = c e^{rt} \quad c = e^{c_0}$$

Therefore

$$P(t) = c e^{rt} - (d/r)$$

If $P(0) = P_0$, then

$$P_0 = c - (d/r)$$

and

(2.17)

$$P(t) = [P_0 + (d/r)] e^{rt} - (d/r)$$

$$= P_0 e^{rt} + (d/r)(e^{rt} - 1)$$

We know that $P_0 e^{rt}$ is the interest paid on the initial deposit of P_0, so $(d/r)(e^{rt} - 1)$ is the interest paid on the additional deposit rate, d.

---

[3] An alternative solution method is to use the one outlined in section 2.2.

2.4   First-order equations and isoclines

For many problems, especially in economics where fairly general equations are used in model construction, it may not be possible to find the *explicit* solution to a differential equation. Even if we can derive an *implicit* form, it still may not be possible to solve its explicit form. This does not mean that we can say nothing about the solution. On the contrary, it is possible to investigate information *about* the solution, i.e., we can investigate the *qualitative* properties of the solution. These properties can be obtained by studying features of the differential equation.

As an introduction to the study of the *qualitative* properties of differential equations let us begin by simply investigating the following differential equation. We shall use this example to define a number of terms that we shall use throughout this book

$$\frac{dy}{dx} = ax - by \qquad y(0) = \frac{a}{b} \qquad a, b > 0$$

With no more information we cannot solve this equation. Suppose, then, that

$$y = f(x)$$
$$\text{and} \quad f'(x) = ax - bf(x) \qquad f(0) = \frac{a}{b}$$

Since, by assumption, $f(x)$ is differentiable, then so is $f'(x)$. Thus

$$f''(x) = a - bf'(x)$$
$$= a - b[ax - bf(x)] = a - [abx - b^2 f(x)]$$

Since each derivative can be reduced to functions of x and $f(x)$, then so long as $f(x)$ is differentiable, all order differentials exist.

But why consider the existence of such differentials? The reason is that they give information about $f(x)$, the domain of x.

Now consider $y = f(x)$ for the range $x \geq 0$. Since $f(0) = a/b$

$$f'(0) = a.0 - \frac{ba}{b} = -a < 0$$

Then we know that $f(x)$ crosses the y-axis at a/b and for x near zero the function is decreasing. This decrease will continue until a turning point occurs. A turning point requires that $f'(x) = 0$. Let x^* denote the value of x at the turning point, then

$$f'(x^*) = ax^* - bf(x^*) = 0$$

$$\text{or} \quad \frac{ax^*}{b} = f(x^*)$$

i.e. where $f(x)$ cuts the line $y = ax/b$.

To establish whether the turning point at $x = x^*$ is a minimum or a maximum we turn to

$$f''(x^*) = a - [abx^* - b^2 f(x^*)]$$
$$= a - \left[abx^* - \frac{b^2 ax^*}{b} \right]$$
$$= a - [abx^* - abx^*]$$
$$= a > 0$$

Figure 2.6.

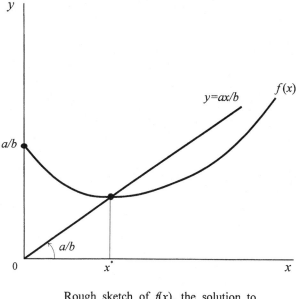

Rough sketch of *f*(*x*), the solution to
$$dy/dx = ax - by,$$
$$y(0)=a/b \text{ and } a,b>0$$

Hence, $f(x)$ reaches a minimum at $x = x^*$ where $f(x)$ cuts the line $y = ax/b$. It must follow, then, that for $x > x^*$, $f(x)$ is positively sloped. This can be verified immediately

$$f'(x) = ax - bf(x)$$
$$x > x^* \quad \text{implying} \quad \frac{ax}{b} > f(x) \text{ or } ax > bf(x)$$
$$\therefore \quad f'(x) > 0$$

All the analysis so far allows us to graph the properties, as shown in figure 2.6. The curve $f(x)$ cuts the y-axis at a/b, declines and reaches a minimum where $f(x)$ cuts the line $y = ax/b$, and then turns up.

Although we cannot identify $f(x)$ or the solution value of x^*, we *do* know that x^* is nonzero. But can we obtain additional information about the shape of $f(x)$? Yes – if we consider *isoclines*.

Isoclines and direction fields

Given

$$\frac{dy}{dx} = ax - by$$

then for every (x,y)-combination this equation specifies the slope at that point. A plot of all such slopes gives the *direction field* for the differential equation, and gives the 'flow of solutions'. (The slopes at given points can be considered as small lines, like iron filings, and if many of these are drawn the direction field is revealed – just like iron filings reveal magnetic forces.) However, it is

Figure 2.7.

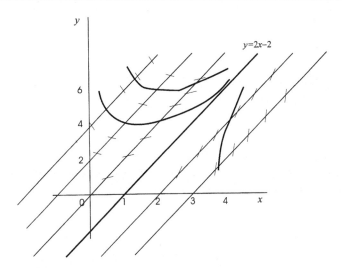

not possible to consider all points in the (x,y)-plane. One procedure is to consider the points in the (x,y)-plane associated with a fixed slope. If m denotes a fixed slope, then $f(x, y) = m$ denotes all combinations of x and y for which the slope is equal to m. $f(x, y) = m$ is referred to as an *isocline*. The purpose of constructing these isoclines is so that a more accurate sketch of $f(x)$ can be obtained.

For $dy/dx = ax - by = m$ the isoclines are the curves (lines)

$$ax - by = m$$
$$\text{or} \quad y = \frac{ax}{b} - \frac{m}{b}$$

These are shown in figure 2.7. Of course, the slope of $f(x, y)$ at each point along an isocline is simply the value of m. Thus, along $y = ax/b$ the slope is zero or inclination arctan$0 = 0°$. Along $y = (ax/b) - (1/b)$ the slope is unity or inclination arc tan$1 = 45°$; while along $y = (ax/b) - (2/b)$ the slope is 2 or inclination arc tan$2 = 63°$. Hence, for values of m rising the slope rises towards infinity (but never reaching it). We have already established that along $y = ax/b$ the slope is zero and so there are turning points all along this isocline. For m negative and increasing, the slope becomes greater in absolute terms. Consider finally $m = a/b$. Then the isocline is

$$y = \frac{ax}{b} - \left(\frac{a}{b}\right)\left(\frac{1}{b}\right) = \frac{ax}{b} - \left(\frac{a}{b^2}\right)$$

with intercept $-a/b^2$. Then along this isocline the slope of the directional field is identical to the slope of the isocline. Hence, the direction fields look quite different either side of this isocline. Above it the solution approaches this isocline asymptotically from above. Hence, the function $f(x)$ takes the shape of the heavy curve in figure 2.7. In general we do not know the intercept or the turning point. In this instance we consider the approximate *integral curves*, which are the continuous lines drawn in figure 2.7. Such integral curves can take a variety of shapes.

We can summarise the method of isoclines as follows:

(1)   From the differential equation

$$\frac{dy}{dx} = \phi(x, y)$$

determine the family of isoclines

$$\phi(x, y) = m$$

and construct several members of this family.

(2)   Consider a particular isocline $\phi(x, y) = m_0$. All points (x, y) on this isocline have the same slope m_0. Obtain the inclination

$$\alpha_0 = \arctan m_0 \qquad 0 \leq \alpha_0 \leq 180°$$

Along the isocline $\phi(x, y) = m_0$ construct line elements with inclination
α_0. (This establishes part of the direction field.)

(3)   Repeat step 2 for each isocline.

(4)   Draw smooth curves to represent the approximate integral curves indicated by the line elements of step 3.

It is apparent that this is a very tedious procedure. Luckily, a number of mathematical software packages now compute direction fields and can be used to construct isoclines (see appendices 2.1 and 2.2).

Example 2.12

$$\frac{dy}{dx} = 2x - y$$

In sections 2.11 and 2.12 we give the instructions on using software packages to solve this differential equation explicitly, and in appendices 2.1 and
2.2 we provide *Mathematica* and *Maple* instructions, respectively, for plotting solution curves along with the direction field. The result is shown in
figure 2.8

Throughout this book we shall provide a number of direction field diagrams
of differential equation systems. In some cases we can readily obtain the solution explicitly, as shown in figure 2.9(a) for the Malthusian population and figure
2.9(b) for the logistic growth curve,[4] which features prominently in the present
text.

In the previous section we derived a differential equation for the Solow growth
model under the assumption that production conformed to a Cobb–Douglas production function. Although we explicitly solved this using the Bernoulli equation,
its solution was not at all obvious. In such cases we can obtain considerable insight
into the solution paths by considering the direction field. Thus, in figure 2.10 we
illustrate this feature of the Solow growth model for three initial values of k, the

---

[4] See example 2.15 in section 2.5.

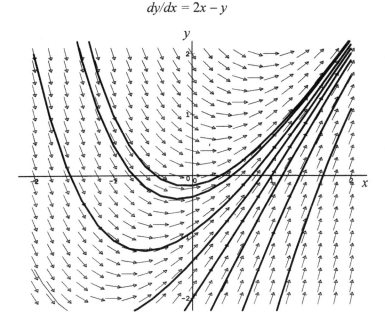

$$dy/dx = 2x - y$$

Figure 2.8.

capital/labour ratio: one below the equilibrium level, another equal to the equilibrium level and a third above the equilibrium level. It is quite clear from the solution paths and the direction field that the equilibrium k^* is locally stable (see exercise 14).

Direction fields can usefully be employed for two further areas of study. First, when considering nonlinear differential equations whose solution may not be available. In this case the qualitative features of the solution can be observed from the direction field. Second, in the case of simultaneous equation systems, the examples given so far refer to only one variable along with time. But suppose we are investigating a system of two variables, say x and y, both of which are related to time. In these cases we can observe much about the solution trajectories from considering the direction field in the plane of x and y – which later we shall refer to as the **phase plane**. We shall investigate such differential equation systems in detail in chapter 4.

2.5 Separable functions

Earlier we solved for the first-order linear homogeneous differential equation

$$\frac{dx}{dt} - kx = 0 \tag{2.18}$$

for the initial condition $x(0) = x_0$ (see equation (2.5)). We did this by first re-writing equation (2.18) in the form

$$\frac{dx}{dt}\frac{1}{x} = k$$

Figure 2.9.

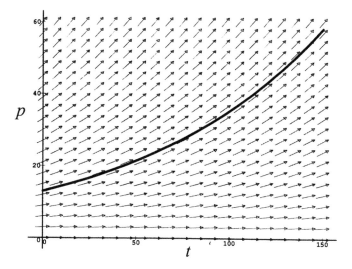

(a) Direction field for Malthusian population growth

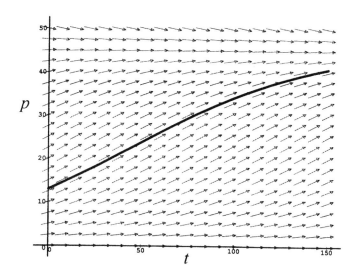

(b) Direction field for logistic population growth

Hence integrating both sides with respect to t gives

$$\int \frac{dx}{dt} \frac{1}{x} dt = \int k\, dt + c_0$$

$$\ln x = kt + c_0$$

$$x(t) = ce^{kt}$$

which gives the solution

$$x(t) = x_0 e^{kt}$$

In other words, we could solve $x(t)$ explicitly in terms of t.

Figure 2.10.

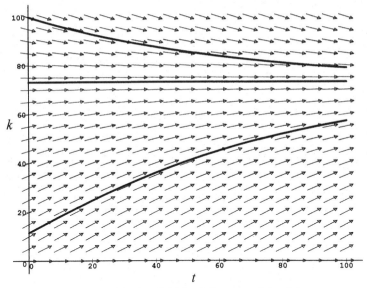

k

t

Direction field for Solow growth model

But equation (2.18) is just a particular example of a more general differential equation

$$\frac{dx}{dt} = \frac{g(t)}{f(x)} \qquad (2.19)$$

Any differential equation which can be written in terms of two distinct functions $f(x)$ and $g(t)$ is said to be a separable differential equation. Some examples are the following:

(i) $\quad \dfrac{dx}{dt} = \dfrac{1}{x^2}$

(ii) $\quad \dfrac{dx}{dt} = x(2 - x)$

(iii) $\quad \dfrac{dx}{dt} = \sqrt{\dfrac{1}{2xt}}$

Our interest in these particular differential equations is because they are often possible to solve fairly readily since we can write one side in terms of x and the other in terms of t. Thus, writing (2.19) in the form

$$f(x)\frac{dx}{dt} = g(t)$$

we can then integrate both sides with respect to t

$$\int f(x)\frac{dx}{dt}dt = \int g(t)dt + c_0$$

or $\quad F[x(t)] = \displaystyle\int g(t)dt + c_0$

where

$$F[x(t)] = \int f(x)dx$$

Using this equation we can solve for $x = x(t)$ which gives the general solution to equation (2.19).

Example 2.13 Radioactive decay and half-life

Equation (2.9) specified the differential equation that represented the radioactive decay of atomic particles. We can employ the feature of separability to solve this equation. Thus, if

$$\frac{dn}{dt} = -\lambda n \quad \lambda > 0$$

then we can re-write this equation

$$\frac{dn}{n} = -\lambda\, dt$$

Integrating both sides, and letting c_0 denote the coefficient of integration, then

$$\int \frac{dn}{n} = -\int \lambda\, dt + c_0$$

$$\ln n = -\lambda t + c_0$$

$$n = e^{-\lambda t + c_0} = ce^{-\lambda t} \qquad c = e^{c_0}$$

At $t = t_0$, $n = n_0$. From this initial condition we can establish the value of c

$$n_0 = ce^{-\lambda t_0}$$

$$c = n_0 e^{\lambda t_0}$$

$$n = n_0 e^{-\lambda t} e^{\lambda t_0} = n_0 e^{-\lambda(t - t_0)}$$

The **half-life** of a radioactive substance is the time necessary for the number of nuclei to reduce to half the original level. Since n_0 denotes the original level then half this number is $n_0/2$. The point in time when this occurs we denote $t_{1/2}$. Hence

$$\frac{n_0}{2} = n_0 e^{-\lambda(t_{1/2} - t_0)}$$

$$\frac{1}{2} = e^{-\lambda(t_{1/2} - t_0)}$$

$$-\ln 2 = -\lambda(t_{1/2} - t_0)$$

$$\therefore \quad t_{1/2} = t_0 + \frac{\ln 2}{\lambda} = t_0 + \frac{0.693}{\lambda}$$

Usually, $t_0 = 0$ and so

$$t_{1/2} = \frac{0.693}{\lambda}$$

These results are illustrated in figure 2.11.

Figure 2.11.

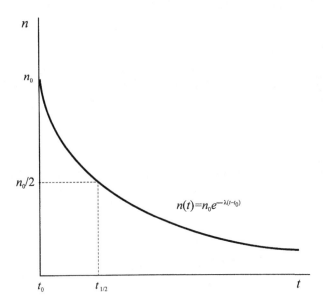

Example 2.14 Testing for art forgeries[5]

All paintings contain small amounts of the radioactive element lead-210 and a smaller amount of radium-226. These elements are contained in white lead which is a pigment used by artists. Because of the smelting process from which the pigment comes, lead-210 gets transferred to the pigment. On the other hand, over 90 per cent of the radium is removed. The result of the smelting process is that lead-210 loses its radioactivity very rapidly, having a half-life of about 22 years; radium-226 on the other hand has a half-life of 1,600 years (see example 2.7). For most practical purposes we can treat radium-226 emissions as constant. Let $l(t)$ denote the amount of lead-210 per gram of white lead at time t, and l_0 the amount present at the time of manufacture, which we take to be t_0. The disintegration of radium-226 we assume constant at r. If λ is the decay constant of lead-210, then

$$\frac{dl}{dt} = -\lambda l + r \qquad l(t_0) = l_0$$

with solution

$$l(t) = \frac{r}{\lambda}\left(1 - e^{-\lambda(t-t_0)}\right) + l_0 e^{-\lambda(t-t_0)}$$

Although $l(t)$ and r can readily be measured, this is not true of l_0, and therefore we cannot determine $t - t_0$.

We can, however, approach the problem from a different perspective. Assume that the painting of interest, if authentic, is 300 years old and if new is at the present time t. Then $t - t_0 = 300$. If we substitute this into the previous result and simplify we obtain

$$\lambda l_0 = \lambda l(t) e^{300\lambda} - r(e^{300\lambda} - 1)$$

---

[5] This is based on the analysis presented in Braun (1983, pp. 11–17).

It is possible to estimate λl_0 for an authentic painting. It is also possible to estimate λl_0 for the lead in the painting under investigation. If the latter is absurdly large relative to the former, then we can conclude that it is a forgery. A very conservative estimate would indicate that any value for λl_0 in excess of 30,000 disintegrations per minute per gram of white lead is absurd for an authentic painting aged 300 years. Using 22 years for the half-life of lead-210, then the value of λ is $(\ln 2/22)$ and

$$ e^{300\lambda} = e^{(300/22)\ln 2} = 2^{(150/11)} $$

To estimate the present disintegration rate of lead-210 the disintegration rate of polonium-210 is used instead because it has the same disintegration rate as lead-210 and because it is easier to measure.

In order, then, to authenticate the 'Disciples at Emmaus', purported to be a Vermeer, it is established that the disintegration rate of polonium-210 per minute per gram of white lead in this particular painting is 8.5 and that of radium-226 is 0.8. Using all this information then we can estimate the value of λl_0 for the 'Disciples at Emmaus' as follows:

$$ \lambda l_0 = (8.5)2^{150/11} - 0.8(2^{150/11} - 1) $$
$$ = 98{,}050 $$

which is considerably in excess of 30,000. We, therefore, conclude that the 'Disciples at Emmaus' is not an authentic Vermeer.

Example 2.15 The logistic curve

In this example we shall consider the logistic equation in some detail. Not only does this illustrate a separable differential equation, but also it is an equation that occurs in a number of areas of economics. It occurs in population growth models, which we shall consider in part II, and in product diffusion models. It is the characteristic equation to represent learning, and hence occurs in a number of learning models. We shall justify the specification of the equation in part II; here we are concerned only with solving the following growth equation for the variable x

(2.20)
$$ \frac{dx}{dt} = kx(a - x) $$

The differential equation is first separated

$$ \frac{dx}{(a - x)x} = k\,dt $$

Integrating both sides, and including the constant of integration, denoted c_0

$$ \int \frac{dx}{(a - x)x} = \int k\,dt + c_0 $$

However

$$ \frac{1}{(a - x)x} = \frac{1}{a}\left[\frac{1}{x} + \frac{1}{a - x}\right] $$

Hence

$$\frac{1}{a}\left[\int \frac{dx}{x} + \int \frac{dx}{a-x}\right] = \int k\,dt + c_0$$

$$\frac{1}{a}[\ln x - \ln|a-x|] = kt + c_0$$

$$\frac{1}{a}\ln\left|\frac{x}{a-x}\right| = kt + c_0$$

$$\ln\left|\frac{x}{a-x}\right| = akt + ac_0$$

Taking anti-logs, we have

$$\frac{x}{a-x} = e^{akt+ac_0} = e^{ac_0}e^{akt} = ce^{akt}$$

where $c = e^{ac_0}$. Substituting for the initial condition, i.e., $t = t_0$ then $x = x_0$, we can solve for the constant c, as follows

$$\frac{x_0}{a-x_0} = ce^{akt_0}$$

$$c = \left(\frac{x_0}{a-x_0}\right)e^{-akt_0}$$

Substituting, then

$$\frac{x}{a-x} = \left(\frac{x_0}{a-x_0}\right)e^{-akt_0}e^{akt}$$

$$= \left(\frac{x_0}{a-x_0}\right)e^{ak(t-t_0)}$$

Solving for x

$$x = \frac{a\left(\dfrac{x_0}{a-x_0}\right)e^{ak(t-t_0)}}{\left[1 + \left(\dfrac{x_0}{a-x_0}\right)e^{ak(t-t_0)}\right]}$$

Which can be further expressed[6]

$$x = \frac{ax_0}{(a-x_0)e^{-ak(t-t_0)} + x_0} \tag{2.21}$$

From the logistic equation (2.21) we can readily establish the following results, assuming that x_0 is less than a:

1. For $t = t_0$ then $x = x_0$
2. As $t \to \infty$ then $x \to a$

---

[6] The logistic growth equation is a particular example of the Bernoulli function and can be solved in a totally different way using a simple transformation. See n. 2 and exercise 6.

Figure 2.12.

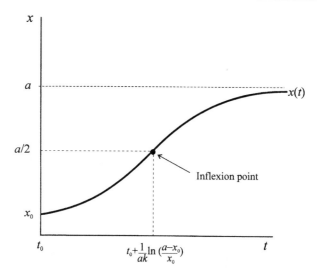

3.   An inflexion occurs at the point

$$t = t_0 + \frac{1}{ak} \ln \left(\frac{a - x_0}{x_0} \right)$$

$$x = \frac{a}{2}$$

The logistic curve is shown in figure 2.12.

Example 2.16 Constant elasticity of demand

Let a commodity x be related to price p with a constant elasticity of demand ε, then

$$\frac{dx}{dp} \frac{p}{x} = -\varepsilon \quad \varepsilon > 0$$

We can rearrange this as

$$\frac{dx}{x} = -\varepsilon \frac{dp}{p}$$

Integrating both sides and adding a constant of integration, then

$$\int \frac{dx}{x} = -\varepsilon \int \frac{dp}{p}$$

$$\ln x = -\varepsilon \ln p + c_0$$

$$= -\varepsilon \ln p + \ln c \quad \text{where } c_0 = \ln c$$

$$= \ln cp^{-\varepsilon}$$

Therefore

$$x = cp^{-\varepsilon}$$

which is the general expression for a demand curve with constant elasticity of demand.

2.6 Diffusion models

In recent years we have seen the widespread use of desktop computers, and more recently the increased use of the mobile phone. The process by which such innovations are communicated through society and the rate at which they are taken up is called **diffusion**. Innovations need not be products. They can just as easily be an idea or some contagious disease. Although a variety of models have been discussed in the literature (e.g. Davies 1979; Mahajan and Peterson 1985), the time path of the diffusion process most typically takes the form of the S-shaped (sigmoid) curve. Considering the mobile phone, we would expect only a few adoptions in the early stages, possibly business people. The adoption begins to accelerate, diffusing to the public at large and even to youngsters. But then it begins to tail off as saturation of the market becomes closer. At the upper limit the market is saturated.

Although this is a verbal description of the diffusion process, and suggests an S-shaped mathematical formulation of the process, it supplies no exact information about the functional form. In particular, the slope, which indicates the speed of the diffusion; or the asymptote, which indicates the level of saturation. Furthermore, such diffusion processes may differ between products.

The typical diffusion model can be expressed

$$\frac{dN(t)}{dt} = g(t)(m - N(t)) \tag{2.22}$$

where $N(t)$ is the cumulative number of adopters at time t, m is the maximum number of potential adopters and $g(t)$ is the coefficient of diffusion. $dN(t)/dt$ then represents the rate of diffusion at time t. Although we refer to the number of adopters, the model is assumed to hold for continuous time t. It is possible to think of $g(t)$ as the probability of adoption at time t, and so $g(t)(m - N(t))$ is the expected number of adopters at time t.

Although a number of specifications of $g(t)$ have been suggested, most are a special case of

$$g(t) = a + bN(t)$$

So the diffusion equation generally used is

$$\frac{dN(t)}{dt} = (a/m + bN(t))(m - N(t)) \tag{2.23}$$

If we divide (2.23) throughout by m and define $F(t) = N(t)/m$, with $\dot{F}(t) = \dot{N}(t)/m$, then

$$\frac{dF(t)}{dt} = (a + bF(t))(1 - F(t)) \tag{2.24}$$

This is still a logistic equation that is separable, and we can re-arrange and integrate by parts (see example 2.15) to solve for $F(t)$

$$F(t) = \frac{1 - e^{-(a+b)t}}{1 + (b/a)e^{-(a+b)t}} \tag{2.25}$$

This specification, however, is not the only possibility. The **Gompertz function** also exhibits the typical S-shaped curve (see exercise 2), and using this we can express the diffusion process as

$$\frac{dN(t)}{dt} = bN(t)(\ln m - \ln N(t))$$ (2.26)

or

$$\frac{dF(t)}{dt} = bF(t)(-\ln F(t))$$

Suppressing the time variable for convenience, then the two models are

$$\dot{F} = (a + bF)(1 - F)$$

and

$$\dot{F} = bF(-\ln F)$$

Pursuing the logistic equation, we can graph $\dot{F}$ against F. When $F = 0$ then $\dot{F} = a$ and when $\dot{F} = 0$ then $(a + bF)(1 - F) = 0$ with solutions

$$F_1 = -b/a \quad \text{and} \quad F_2 = 1$$

Since $\dot{F}$ denotes the rate of diffusion, then the diffusion rate is at a maximum (penetration is at its maximum rate) when $\ddot{F} = 0$, i.e., when $d^2F/dt^2 = 0$. Differentiating and solving for F, which we denote Fp (for maximum penetration rate), we obtain

$$Fp = \frac{1}{2} - \frac{a}{2b} \quad \text{implying} \quad Np = m \cdot Fp = m\left(\frac{1}{2} - \frac{a}{2b}\right) = \frac{m}{2} - \frac{am}{2b}$$

In order to find the time tp when $F(tp)$ is at a maximum penetration rate, we must first solve for $F(t)$. This we indicated above. Since we need to find the value of t satisfying $F(t) = Fp$, then we need to solve

$$\frac{1 - e^{-(a+b)t}}{1 + (b/a)e^{-(a+b)t}} = \frac{1}{2} - \frac{a}{2b}$$

for t, which we can do using a software package. This gives the time for the maximum penetration of

$$tp = \frac{\ln\left(\dfrac{b}{a}\right)}{a + b}$$ (2.27)

Since $d^2F/dt^2 = 0$ at Fp, then this must denote the inflexion point of $F(t)$.

The stylised information is shown in figure 2.13. Notice that the time for the maximum penetration is the same for both $F(t)$ and $N(t)$. Also note that $F(t)$ involves only the two parameters a and b; while $N(t)$ involves the three parameters a, b and m.

2.7　Phase portrait of a single variable

This book is particularly concerned with phase diagrams. These diagrams help to convey the dynamic properties of differential and difference equations – either single equations or simultaneous equations. To introduce this topic and to lay down some terminology, we shall consider here just a single variable. Let x denote

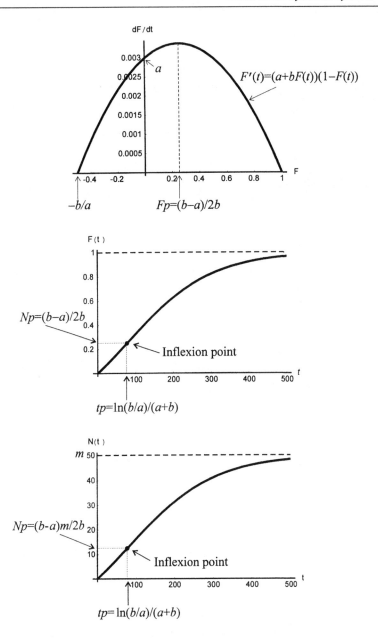

Figure 2.13.

a variable which is a continuous function of time, t. Let $x'(t)$ denote an autonomous differential equation, so that $x'(t)$ is just a function of x and independent of t. Assume that we can solve for $x'(t)$ for any point in time t. Then at any point in time we have a value for $x'(t)$. The path of solutions as t varies is called a **trajectory**, **path** or **orbit**. The x-axis containing the trajectory is called the **phase line**.

If $x'(t) = 0$ then the system is at rest. This must occur at some particular point in time, say t_0. The solution value would then be $x(t_0) = x^*$. The point x^* is referred to variedly as a **rest point**, **fixed point**, **critical point**, **equilibrium point** or **steady-state solution**. For the Malthusian population equation $p'(t) = kp$, there is

Figure 2.14.

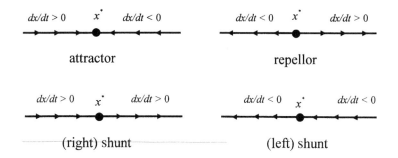

only one fixed point, namely $p^* = 0$. In the case of the logistic growth equation $x'(t) = kx(a - x)$ there are two fixed points, one at $x_1^* = 0$ and the other at $x_2^* = a$. In example 2.4 on demand and supply the fixed point, the equilibrium point, is given by

$$p^* = \frac{c - a}{b - d}$$

which is also the fixed point for example 2.5. For the Harrod–Domar growth model (example 2.8) there is only one stationary point, only one equilibrium point, and that is $Y^* = 0$. For the Solow growth model, in which the production function conforms to a Cobb–Douglas (example 2.9), there are two stationary values, one at $k_1^* = 0$ and the other at

$$k_2^* = \left(\frac{sa}{n + \delta} \right)^{-\left(\frac{1}{\alpha - 1}\right)}$$

Whether a system is moving towards a fixed point or away from a fixed point is of major importance. A trajectory is said to approach a fixed point if $x(t) \rightarrow x^*$ as $t \rightarrow \infty$, in this case the fixed point is said to be an **attractor**. On the other hand, if $x(t)$ moves away from x^* as t increases, then x^* is said to be a **repellor**. Fixed points, attractors and repellors are illustrated in figure 2.14. Also illustrated in figure 2.14 is the intermediate case where the trajectory moves first towards the fixed point and then away from the fixed point. Since this can occur from two different directions, they are illustrated separately, but both appear as a shunting motion, and the fixed point is accordingly referred to as a **shunt**.

Consider once again the logistic growth equation $x'(t) = kx(a - x)$, as illustrated in figure 2.15. Figure 2.15(a) illustrates the differential equation, figure 2.15(b) illustrates the phase line[7] and figure 2.15(c) denotes the path of $x(t)$ against time. The stationary points on the phase line are enclosed in small circles to identify them. The arrows marked on the phase line, as in figure 2.15(b), indicate the direction of change in $x(t)$ as t increases. In general, $x^* = 0$ is uninteresting, and for any initial value of x not equal to zero, the system moves towards $x^* = a$, as illustrated in figure 2.15(c). Even if x initially begins above the level $x^* = a$, the system moves over time towards $x^* = a$. In other words, $x^* = a$ is an attractor.

---

[7] Some textbooks in economics confusingly refer to figure 2.15(b) as a phase diagram.

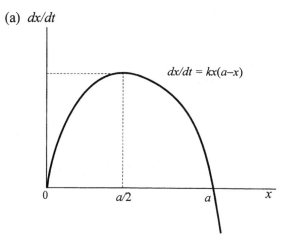

Figure 2.15.

(a) dx/dt

$dx/dt = kx(a-x)$

0 $a/2$ a x

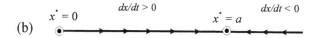

(b)

$dx/dt > 0$ $dx/dt < 0$

$\overset{\bullet}{x} = 0$ $\overset{\bullet}{x} = a$

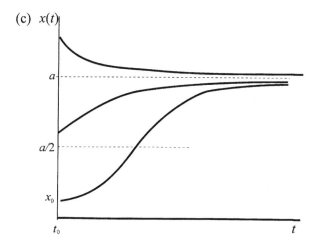

(c) $x(t)$

a

$a/2$

x_0

t_0 t

If any trajectory starting 'close to' a fixed point[8] stays close to it for all future time, then the fixed point is said to be **stable**. A fixed point is **asymptotically stable** if it is stable as just defined, and also if any trajectory that starts close to the fixed point approaches the fixed point as $t \to \infty$. Considering the logistic equation as shown in figure 2.15, it is clear that $x^* = a$ is an *asymptotically stable rest point*.

Figure 2.15 also illustrates another feature of the characteristics of a fixed point. The origin, $x^* = 0$, is a repellor while $x^* = a$ is an attractor. In the *neighbourhood* of the origin, the differential equation has a positive slope. In the *neighbourhood*

---

[8] We shall be more explicit about the meaning of 'close to' in section 4.2.

of the attractor, the differential equation has a negative slope. In fact, this is a typical feature of instability/stability. A fixed point is unstable if the slope of the differential equation in the neighbourhood of this point is positive; it is stable if the slope of the differential equation in the neighbourhood of this point is negative. If there is only one fixed point in a dynamic system, then such a fixed point is either **globally** stable or **globally** unstable. In the case of a **globally stable** system, for any initial value not equal to the fixed point, then the system will converge on the fixed point. For a **globally unstable** system, for any initial value not equal to the fixed point, then the system will move away from it.

Consider example 2.4, a simple continuous price-adjustment demand and supply model with the differential equation

$$\frac{dp}{dt} = \alpha(a - c) + \alpha(b - d)p \quad \alpha > 0$$

For a solution (a fixed point, an equilibrium point) to exist in the positive quadrant then $a > c$ and so the intercept is positive. With conventional shaped demand and supply curves, then $b < 0$ and $d > 0$, respectively, so that the slope of the differential equation is negative. The situation is illustrated in figure 2.16(a).

Figure 2.16.

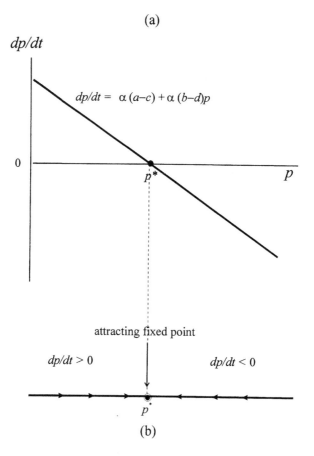

(a)

dp/dt

$dp/dt = \alpha(a-c) + \alpha(b-d)p$

0

p^*

p

attracting fixed point

$dp/dt > 0$

$dp/dt < 0$

$\overset{\cdot}{p}$

(b)

Given linear demand and supply then there is only one fixed point. The system is either globally stable or globally unstable. It is apparent from figure 2.16 that the fixed point is an attractor, as illustrated in figure 2.16(b). Furthermore, the differential equation is negatively sloped for all values of p. In other words, whenever the price is different from the equilibrium price (whether above or below), it will converge on the fixed point (the equilibrium price) over time. The same *qualitative* characteristics hold for example 2.5, although other possibilities are possible depending on the value/sign of the parameter f.

Example 2.6 on population growth, and example 2.7 on radioactive decay, also exhibit linear differential equations and are globally stable/unstable only for $p = 0$ and $n = 0$, respectively. Whether they are globally stable or globally unstable depends on the sign of critical parameters. For example, in the case of Malthusian population, if the population is growing, $k > 0$, then for any initial positive population will mean continuously increased population over time. If $k < 0$, then for any initial positive population will mean continuously declining population over time. In the case of radioactive decay, λ is positive, and so there will be a continuous decrease in the radioactivity of a substance over time.

The Harrod–Domar growth model, example 2.8, is qualitatively similar to the Malthusian population growth model, with the 'knife-edge' simply indicating the unstable nature of the fixed point. The Solow growth model, example 2.9, on the other hand, exhibits multiple equilibria. There cannot be *global* stability or instability because such statements have meaning only with reference to a single fixed point system. In the case of multiple fixed points, statements about stability or instability must be made in relation to a particular fixed point. Hence, with systems containing multiple equilibria we refer to **local** stability or **local** instability, i.e., reference is made only to the characteristics of the system in the *neighbourhood* of a fixed point. For instance, for the Solow growth model with a Cobb–Douglas production function homogeneous of degree one there are two fixed points

$$k_1^* = 0 \quad \text{and} \quad k_2^* = \left(\frac{sa}{n+\delta} \right)^{\left(\frac{1}{1-\alpha} \right)}$$

The first is locally unstable while the second is locally stable, as we observed in figure 2.10. The first fixed point is a repellor while the second fixed point is an attractor. The slope of the differential equation in the neighbourhood of the origin has a *positive* slope, which is characteristic of a repellor; while the slope of the differential equation in the neighbourhood of the second fixed point is *negative*, which is characteristic of an attractor. These characteristics of the slope of the differential equation in the neighbourhood of a system's fixed points and the features of the phase line are illustrated in figure 2.17.

2.8 Second-order linear homogeneous equations

A general second-order linear homogeneous differential equation with constant coefficients is

$$a\frac{d^2y}{dt^2} + b\frac{dy}{dt} + cy = 0 \tag{2.28}$$

Figure 2.17.

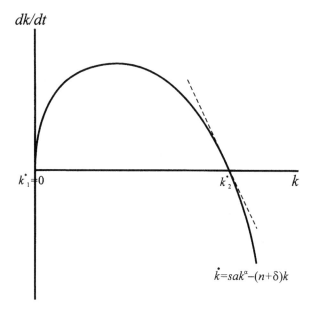

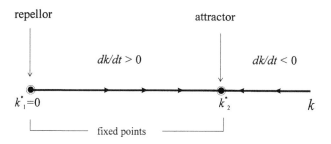

Or

$$ay''(t) + by'(t) + cy(t) = 0$$

If we can find two linearly independent solutions[9] y_1 and y_2 then the general solution is of the form

$$y = c_1y_1 + c_2y_2$$

where c_1 and c_2 are arbitrary constants. Suppose $y = e^{xt}$. Substituting we obtain

$$ax^2e^{xt} + bxe^{xt} + ce^{xt} = 0$$
$$e^{xt}(ax^2 + bx + c) = 0$$

Hence, $y = e^{xt}$ is a solution if and only if

$$ax^2 + bx + c = 0$$

---

[9] See exercises 9 and 10 for a discussion of linear dependence and independence.

which is referred to as the *auxiliary equation* of the homogeneous equation. The quadratic has two solutions

$$r = \frac{-b + \sqrt{b^2 - 4ac}}{2a}, \qquad s = \frac{-b - \sqrt{b^2 - 4ac}}{2a}$$

If $b^2 > 4ac$ the roots r and s are real and distinct; if $b^2 = 4ac$ the roots are real and equal; while if $b^2 < 4ac$ the roots are complex conjugate. There are, therefore, three types of solutions. Here we shall summarise them.

2.8.1 Real and distinct ($b^2 > 4ac$)

If the auxiliary equation has distinct real roots r and s, then e^{rt} and e^{st} are linearly independent solutions to the second-order linear homogeneous equation. The **general** solution is

$$y(t) = c_1 e^{rt} + c_2 e^{st}$$

where c_1 and c_2 are arbitrary constants.

If $y(0)$ and $y'(0)$ are the initial conditions when $t = 0$, then we can solve for c_1 and c_2

$$y(0) = c_1 e^{r(0)} + c_2 e^{s(0)} = c_1 + c_2$$
$$y'(t) = r c_1 e^{rt} + s c_2 e^{st}$$
$$y'(0) = r c_1 e^{r(0)} + s c_2 e^{s(0)} = r c_1 + s c_2$$

Hence

$$c_1 = \frac{y'(0) - s y(0)}{r - s}, \qquad c_2 = \frac{y'(0) - r y(0)}{s - r}$$

and the **particular** solution is

$$y(t) = \left(\frac{y'(0) - s y(0)}{r - s} \right) e^{rt} + \left(\frac{y'(0) - r y(0)}{s - r} \right) e^{st}$$

which satisfies the initial conditions $y(0)$ and $y'(0)$.

Example 2.17

Suppose

$$\frac{d^2 y}{dt^2} + 4 \frac{dy}{dt} - 5y = 0$$

Then the auxiliary equation is

$$x^2 + 4x - 5 = 0$$
$$(x + 5)(x - 1) = 0$$

Hence, $r = -5$ and $s = 1$, with the **general** solution

$$y(t) = c_1 e^{-5t} + c_2 e^t$$

If $y(0) = 0$ and $y'(0) = 1$, then

$$c_1 = \frac{1}{-5 - 1} = -\frac{1}{6}$$

$$c_2 = \frac{1}{1 - (-5)} = \frac{1}{6}$$

So the **particular** solution is

$$y(t) = -\left(\frac{1}{6}\right)e^{-5t} + \left(\frac{1}{6}\right)e^{t}$$

2.8.2   Real and equal roots ($b^2 = 4ac$)

If r is a repeated real root to the differential equation

$$ay''(t) + by'(t) + c = 0$$

then a **general** solution is

$$y(t) = c_1 e^{rt} + c_2 t e^{rt}$$

where c_1 and c_2 are arbitrary constants (see exercise 9). If $y(0)$ and $y'(0)$ are the two initial conditions, then

$$y(0) = c_1 + c_2(0) = c_1$$
$$y'(t) = rc_1 e^{rt} + rc_2 t e^{rt} + c_2 e^{rt}$$
$$y'(0) = rc_1 + c_2$$

Hence

$$c_1 = y(0), \qquad c_2 = y'(0) - ry(0)$$

So the **particular** solution is

$$y(t) = y(0)e^{rt} + [y'(0) - ry(0)]t e^{rt}$$

Example 2.18

$$y''(t) + 4y'(t) + 4y(t) = 0$$

Then the auxiliary equation is

$$x^2 + 4x + 4 = 0$$
$$(x + 2)^2 = 0$$

Hence, $r = -2$ and the **general** solution is

$$y(t) = c_1 e^{-2t} + c_2 t e^{-2t}$$

If $y(0) = 3$ and $y'(0) = 7$, then

$$c_1 = y(0) = 3$$
$$c_2 = y'(0) - ry(0) = 7 - (-2)(3) = 13$$

so the **particular** solution is

$$y(t) = 3e^{-2t} + 13te^{-2t}$$
$$= (3 + 13t)e^{-2t}$$

2.8.3   Complex conjugate ($b^2 < 4ac$)

If the auxiliary equation has complex conjugate roots r and s where $r = \alpha + i\beta$ and $s = \alpha - i\beta$ then

$$e^{\alpha t} \cos(\beta t) \qquad \text{and} \qquad e^{\alpha t} \sin(\beta t)$$

are linearly independent solutions to the second-order homogeneous equation (see exercise 10). The **general** solution is

$$y(t) = c_1 e^{\alpha t} \cos(\beta t) + c_2 e^{\alpha t} \sin(\beta t)$$

where c_1 and c_2 are arbitrary constants.

If $y(0)$ and $y'(0)$ are the initial conditions when $t = 0$, then we can solve for c_1 and c_2

$$y(0) = c_1 \cos(0) + c_2 \sin(0) = c_1$$
$$y'(t) = (\alpha c_1 + \beta c_2)e^{\alpha t} \cos(\beta t) + (\alpha c_2 - \beta c_1)e^{\alpha t} \sin(\beta t)$$
$$y'(0) = (\alpha c_1 + \beta c_2)e^0 \cos(0) + (\alpha c_2 - \beta c_1)e^0 \sin(0)$$
$$= \alpha c_1 + \beta c_2$$

i.e.

$$c_1 = y(0) \qquad \text{and} \qquad c_2 = \frac{y'(0) - \alpha y(0)}{\beta}$$

Hence, the **particular** solution is

$$y(t) = y(0)e^{\alpha t} \cos(\beta t) + \left(\frac{y'(0) - \alpha y(0)}{\beta} \right) e^{\alpha t} \sin(\beta t)$$

Example 2.19

$$y''(t) + 2y'(t) + 2y(t) = 0, \qquad y(0) = 2 \qquad \text{and} \qquad y'(0) = 1$$

The auxiliary equation is

$$x^2 + 2x + 2 = 0$$

with complex conjugate roots

$$r = \frac{-2 + \sqrt{4 - 4(2)}}{2} = -1 + i$$
$$s = \frac{-2 - \sqrt{4 - 4(2)}}{2} = -1 - i$$

The **general** solution is

$$y(t) = c_1 e^{-t} \cos(t) + c_2 e^{-t} \sin(t)$$

The coefficients are

$$c_1 = y(0) = 2$$

$$c_2 = \frac{y'(0) - \alpha y(0)}{\beta} = 3$$

Hence the **particular** solution is

$$y(t) = 2e^{-t}\cos(t) + 3e^{-t}\sin(t)$$

2.9   Second-order linear nonhomogeneous equations

A second-order linear nonhomogeneous equation with constant coefficients takes
the form

(2.29)
$$a\frac{d^2y}{dt^2} + b\frac{dy}{dt} + cy = g(t)$$

or

$$ay''(t) + by'(t) + cy(t) = g(t)$$

Let $L(y) = ay''(t) + by'(t) + cy(t)$ then equation (2.29) can be expressed as $L(y) = g(t)$. The solution to equation (2.29) can be thought of in two parts. First, there
is the homogeneous component, $L(y) = 0$. As we demonstrated in the previous
section, if the roots are real and distinct then

$$y_c = c_1e^{rt} + c_2e^{st}$$

The reason for denoting this solution as y_c will become clear in a moment.
Second, it is possible to come up with a particular solution, denoted y_p, which
satisfies $L(y_p) = g(t)$. y_c is referred to as the *complementary* solution satisfying
$L(y) = 0$, while y_p is the *particular* solution satisfying $L(y_p) = g(t)$. If both y_c
and y_p are solutions, then so is their sum, $y = y_c + y_p$, which is referred to as
the *general solution to a linear nonhomogeneous differential equation*. Hence,
the general solution to equation (2.29) if the roots are real and distinct takes the
form

$$y(t) = y_c + y_p = c_1e^{rt} + c_2e^{st} + y_p$$

The general solution $y(t) = y_c + y_p$ holds even when the roots are not real or
distinct. The point is that the complementary solution arises from the solution to
$L(y) = 0$. As in the previous section there are three possible cases:

(1)   Real and distinct roots

$$y_c = c_1e^{rt} + c_2e^{st}$$

(2)   Real and equal roots

$$y_c = c_1e^{rt} + c_2te^{rt}$$

(3)   Complex conjugate roots

$$y_c = c_1 e^{\alpha t} \cos(\beta t) + c_2 e^{\alpha t} \sin(\beta t)$$

In finding a solution to a linear nonhomogeneous equation, four steps need to be followed:

Step 1   Find the complementary solution y_c.

Step 2   Find the general solution y_h by solving the higher-order equation

$$L_h(y_h) = 0$$

where y_h is determined from $L(y)$ and $g(t)$.

Step 3   Obtain $y_q = y_h - y_c$.

Step 4   Determine the unknown constant, the *undetermined coefficients*, in the solution y_q by requiring

$$L(y_q) = g(t)$$

and substituting these into y_q, giving the particular solution y_p.

Example 2.20

Suppose

$$y''(t) + y'(t) = t$$

Step 1   This has the complementary solution y_c, which is the solution to the auxiliary equation

$$x^2 + x = 0$$

$$x(x + 1) = 0$$

with solutions $r = 0$ and $s = -1$ and

$$y_c = c_1 e^{0t} + c_2 e^{-t}$$
$$= c_1 + c_2 e^{-t}$$

Step 2   The differential equation needs to be differentiated twice to obtain $L_h(y_h) = 0$. Thus, differentiating twice

$$y^{(4)}(t) + y^{(3)}(t) = 0$$

with auxiliary equation

$$x^4 + x^3 = 0$$

with roots $0, -1, 0, 0$. Hence[10]

$$y_h = c_1 e^{0t} + c_2 e^{-t} + c_3 t e^{0t} + c_4 t^2 e^{0t}$$
$$= c_1 + c_2 e^{-t} + c_3 t + c_4 t^2$$

---

[10] We have here used the property that e^{rt}, te^{rt} and $t^2 e^{rt}$ are linearly independent and need to be combined with a root repeating itself three times (see exercise 9(ii)).

Step 3   Obtain $y_q = y_h - y_c$. Thus

$$y_q = (c_1 + c_2 e^{-t} + c_3 t + c_4 t^2) - (c_1 + c_2 e^{-t})$$
$$= c_3 t + c_4 t^2$$

Step 4   To find c_3 and c_4, the undetermined coefficients, we need $L(y_q) = t$. Hence

$$y_q''(t) + y_q'(t) = t$$

But from step 3 we can derive

$$y_q' = c_3 + 2c_4 t$$
$$y_q'' = 2c_4$$

Hence

$$2c_4 + c_3 + 2c_4 t = t$$

Since the solution must satisfy the differential equation identically for *all* t, then the result just derived must be an identity for all t and so the coefficients of like terms must be equal. Hence, we have the two simultaneous equations

$$2c_4 + c_3 = 0$$
$$2c_4 = 1$$

with solutions $c_4 = 1/2$ and $c_3 = -1$. Thus

$$y_p = -t + \tfrac{1}{2}t^2$$

and the solution is

$$y(t) = c_1 + c_2 e^{-t} - t + \tfrac{1}{2}t^2$$

It is also possible to solve for c_1 and c_2 if we know $y(0)$ and $y'(0)$.

Although we have presented the method of solution, many software packages have routines built into them, and will readily supply solutions if they exist. The economist can use such programmes to solve the mathematics and so concentrate on model formulation and model features. This we shall do in part II.

2.10   Linear approximations to nonlinear differential equations

Consider the differential equation

$$\dot{x} = f(x)$$

here f is nonlinear and continuously differentiable. In general we cannot solve such equations explicitly. We may be able to establish the fixed points of the system by solving the equation $f(x) = 0$, since a fixed point is characterised by $\dot{x} = 0$. Depending on the nonlinearity there may be more than one fixed point.

If f is continuously differentiable in an open interval containing $x = x^*$, then we approximate f using the Taylor expansion

$$f(x) = f(x^*) + f'(x^*)(x - x^*)$$
$$+ \frac{f''(x^*)(x - x^*)}{2!} + \ldots + \frac{f^n(x^*)(x - x^*)}{n!} + R_n(x, x^*)$$

where $R_n(x, x^*)$ is the remainder. In particular, a *first-order* approximation takes the form

$$f(x) = f(x^*) + f'(x^*)(x - x^*) + R_2(x, x^*)$$

If the initial point x_0 is sufficiently close to x^*, then $R_2(x, x^*) \simeq 0$. Furthermore, if we choose x^* as being a fixed point, then $f(x^*) = 0$. Hence we can approximate $f(x)$ about a fixed point x^* with

$$f(x) = f'(x^*)(x - x^*) \tag{2.30}$$

Example 2.21

Although we could solve the Solow growth model explicitly if the production function was a Cobb–Douglas by using a transformation suggested by Bernoulli, it provides a good example of a typical nonlinear differential equation problem. Our equation is

$$\dot{k} = f(k) = sak^\alpha - (n + \delta)k$$

This function has two fixed points obtained from solving

$$k[sak^{\alpha-1} - (n + \delta)] = 0$$

namely

$$k_1^* = 0 \qquad \text{and} \qquad k_2^* = \left(\frac{sa}{n+\delta}\right)^{-\left(\frac{1}{\alpha-1}\right)}$$

Taking a first-order Taylor expansion about point k^*, we have

$$f(k) = f(k^*) + f'(k^*)(k - k^*)$$

where

$$f'(k^*) = \alpha sa(k^*)^{\alpha-1} - (n + \delta)$$
$$\text{and} \quad f(k^*) = 0$$

Consider first $k^* = k_1^* = 0$, then

$$f'(k_1^*) = \lim_{k \to 0} f'(k) = \lim_{k \to 0} [\alpha sak^{\alpha-1} - (n + \delta)] = \infty$$

Next consider $k = k_2^* > 0$, then $f(k_2^*) = 0$ and

$$f'(k_2^*) = \alpha sa(k_2^*)^{\alpha-1} - (n + \delta) = \alpha sa \left[\left(\frac{sa}{n+\delta}\right)^{-\left(\frac{1}{\alpha-1}\right)}\right]^{\alpha-1} - (n + \delta)$$

$$= \alpha(n + \delta) - (n + \delta)$$
$$= -(n + \delta)(1 - \alpha)$$

Figure 2.18.

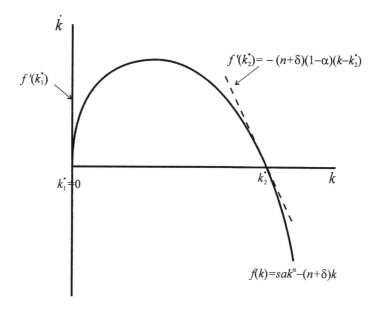

Hence

$$f(k) = -(n + \delta)(1 - \alpha)(k - k^*)$$

Since $0 < \alpha < 1$ and n and δ are both positive, then this has a negative slope about k_2^* and hence k_2^* is a locally stable equilibrium. The situation is shown in figure 2.18.

The first-order linear approximation about the non-zero equilibrium is then

$$\dot{k} = f(k) = -(n + \delta)(1 - \alpha)(k - k^*)$$

with the linear approximate solution

$$k(t) = k_2^* + (k(0) - k_2^*)e^{-(n+\delta)(1-\alpha)t}$$

As $t \to \infty$ then $k(t) \to k_2^*$.

What we are invoking here is the following theorem attributed to Liapunov

THEOREM 2.1

If $\dot{x} = f(x)$ is a nonlinear equation with a linear approximation

$$f(x) = f(x^*) + f'(x^*)(x - x^*)$$

about the equilibrium point x^*, and if x^* is (globally) stable for the linear approximation, then x^* is asymptotically stable for the original nonlinear equation.

Care must be exercised in using this theorem. The converse of the theorem is generally not true. In other words, it is possible for x^* to be stable for the nonlinear system but asymptotically unstable for its linear approximation.

Figure 2.19.

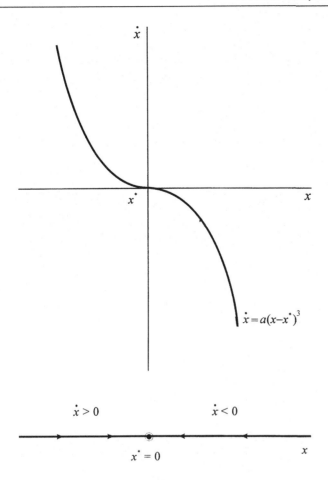

Example 2.22

Consider

$$\dot{x} = f(x) = a(x - x^*)^3 \qquad -\infty < x < \infty, \qquad a > 0$$

There is a unique equilibrium at $x = x^* = 0$ which is globally stable. This is readily seen in terms of figure 2.19, which also displays the phase line.

Now consider its linear approximation at $x = x^*$

$$f'(x) = 3a(x - x^*)^2$$
$$f'(x^*) = 0$$

and so

$$\dot{x} = f(x) = f(x^*) + f'(x^*)(x - x^*) = 0$$

which does not exhibit global stability. This is because for any $x_0 \neq x^*$ then $x = x_0$ for all t since $\dot{x} = 0$. Consequently, x_0 does not approach x^* in the limit, and so $x^* = 0$ cannot be asymptotically stable.

We shall return to linear approximations in chapter 3 when considering difference equations, and then again in chapters 4 and 5 when we deal with nonlinear *systems* of differential and difference equations. These investigations will allow us to use linear approximation methods when we consider economic models in part II.

2.11   Solving differential equations with *Mathematica*

2.11.1   *First-order equations*

Mathematica has two built in commands for dealing with differential equations, which are the **DSolve** command and the **NDSolve** command. The first is used to find a symbolic solution to a differential equation; the second finds a numerical approximation. Consider the following first-order differential equation

$$\frac{dy}{dt} = f(y, t)$$

In particular, we are assuming that y is a function of t, $y(t)$. Then we employ the **DSolve** command by using

```
DSolve[y'[t]==f[y[t],t],y[t],t]
```

Note a number of aspects of this instruction:

(1)   The equation utilises the single apostrophe, so $y'(t)$ denotes dy/dt
(2)   The function $f(y(t), t)$ may or may not be independent of t
(3) $y(t)$ is written in the equation rather than simply y
(4)   The second term, $y(t)$, is indicating what is being solved for, and t denotes the independent variable.

It is possible to first define the differential equation and use the designation in the **DSolve** command. Thus

```
Eq = y'[t]==f[y[t],t]
DSolve[Eq,y[t],t]
```

If *Mathematica* can solve the differential equation then this is provided in the output. Sometimes warnings are provided, especially if inverse functions are being used. If *Mathematica* can find no solution, then the programme simply repeats the input. The user does not need to know what algorithm is being used to solve the differential equation. What matters is whether a solution can be found. What is important to understand, however, is that a first-order differential equation (as we are discussing here) involves one unknown constant of integration. The output will, therefore, involve an unknown constant, which is denoted C[1].

Consider the examples of first-order differential equations used in various places throughout this chapter shown in table 2.1.

Mathematica has no difficulty solving all these problems, but it does provide a warning with the last stating: 'The equations appear to involve transcendental functions of the variables in an essentially non-algebraic way.' What is also illustrated by these solutions is that the output may not, and usually is not, provided in

Table 2.1 First-order differential equations with *Mathematica*

Problem		Input instructions
(i)	$\dfrac{dx}{dt} = kx$	`DSolve[x'[t]==kx[t],x[t],t]`
(ii)	$\dfrac{dx}{dt} = 1 + ce^t$	`DSolve[x'[t]==1+cExp[t],x[t],t]`
(iii)	$\dfrac{dp}{dt} - \alpha(b - d)p = \alpha(a - c)$	`DSolve[p'[t]-α (b-d)p[t]==α(a-c),p[t],t]`
(iv)	$\dfrac{dx}{dt} = kx(a - x)$	`DSolve[x'[t]==kx[t](a-x[t]),x[t],t]`
(v)	$\dot{k} = sak^\alpha - (n + \delta)k$	`DSolve[k'[t]==sak[t]ᵅ-(n+δ)k[t],k[t],t]`

Table 2.2 *Mathematica* input instructions for initial value problems

Problem		Input instructions
(i)	$\dfrac{dp}{dt} = p(a - bp), p(0) = p0$	`DSolve[{p'[t]==p[t](a-bp[t]),p[0]==p0},` `p[t],t]`
(ii)	$\dfrac{dn}{dt} = -\lambda n, n(0) = n0$	`DSolve[{n'[t]==-λn[t],n[0]==n0},n[t],t]`
(iii)	$\dfrac{dy}{dx} = x^2 - 2x + 1, y(0) = 1$	`DSolve[{y'[x]==x²-2x+1,y[0]==1},y[x],x]`

a way useful for *economic* interpretation. So some manipulation of the output is often necessary.

It will be noted that none of the above examples involve initial conditions, which is why all outputs involve the unknown constant C[1]. Initial value problems are treated in a similar manner. If we have the initial value problem,

$$\frac{dy}{dt} = f(y, t) \qquad y(0) = y0$$

then the input instruction is

`DSolve[{y'[t]==f[y[t],t],y[0]==y0},y[t],t]`

For example, look at table 2.2.

2.11.2 Second-order equations

Second-order differential equations are treated in fundamentally the same way. If we have the homogeneous second-order differential equation

$$a\frac{d^2y}{dt^2} + b\frac{dy}{dt} + cy = 0$$

Table 2.3 Mathematica input instructions for second-order differential equations

Problem		Input Instructions
(i)	$\dfrac{d^2y}{dt^2} + 4\dfrac{dy}{dt} - 5y = 0$	`DSolve[y''[t]+4y'[t]-5y[t]==0,y[t],t]`
(ii)	$y''(t) + 4y'(t) + 4y(t) = 0$	`DSolve[y''[t]+4y'[t]+4y[t]==0,y[t],t]`
(iii)	$y''(t) + 2y'(t) + 2y(t) = 0$	`DSolve[y''[t]+2y'[t]+2y[t]==0,y[t],t]`
(iv)	$y''(t) + y'(t) = t$	`DSolve[y''[t]+y'[t]==t,y[t],t]`

Table 2.4 Mathematica input instructions for initial value problems

Problem		Input instructions
(i)	$\dfrac{d^2y}{dt^2} + 4\dfrac{dy}{dt} - 5y = 0,$ $y(0) = 0, y'(0) = 1$	`DSolve[{y''[t]+4y'[t]-5y[t]==0,y[0]==0,` `y'[0]==1},y[t],t]`
(ii)	$y''(t) + 4y'(t) + 4y(t) = 0,$ $y(0) = 3, y'(0) = 7$	`DSolve[{y''[t]+4y'[t]+4y[t]==0,y[0]==3,` `y'[0]==7},y[t],t]`

then the input instruction is[11]

> `DSolve[ay''[t]+by'[t]+cy[t]==0,y[t],t]`

If we have the nonhomogeneous second-order differential equation

$$a\frac{d^2y}{dt^2} + b\frac{dy}{dt} + cy = g(t)$$

then the input instruction is

> `DSolve[ay''[t]+by'[t]+cy[t]==g[t],y[t],t]`

Of course, the solutions are far more complex because they can involve real and distinct roots, real and equal roots and complex conjugate roots. But the solution algorithms that are built into *Mathematica* handle all these. Furthermore, second-order differential equations involve two unknowns, which are denoted C[1] and C[2] in *Mathematica*'s output.

The *Mathematica* input instructions for some examples used in this chapter are shown in table 2.3.

Initial value problems follow the same structure as before (table 2.4).

2.11.3   NDSolve

Many differential equations, especially nonlinear and nonautonomous differential equations, cannot be solved by any of the known solution methods. In such cases a numerical approximation can be provided using the **NDSolve** command. In using **NDSolve** it is necessary, however, to provide initial conditions and the range for

---

[11] Do not use the double quotes in these equations; rather input the single quote twice.

the independent variable. Given the following initial value problem

$$\frac{dy}{dt} = f(y(t), t) \qquad y(0) = y0$$

the input instruction is

```
NDSolve[{y'[t]==f[y[t],t],y[0]==y0},
    y[t],{t,tmin,tmax}]
```

Mathematica provides output in the form of an **InterpolatingFunction** that represents an approximate function obtained using interpolation. This Interpolating-Function can then be plotted. Since it is usual to plot an InterpolatingFunction, then it is useful to give the output a name. For example, given the problem

$$\frac{dy}{dt} = \sin(3t - y) \qquad y(0) = 0.5, \qquad t \in [0, 10]$$

the instruction is

```
sol=NDSolve[{y'[t]==Sin[3t-y[t]],y[0]==0.5},
    y[t],{t,0,10}]
```

Although the output is named 'sol', the solution is still for the variable $y(t)$. So the plot would involve the input

```
Plot[y[t] /. sol, {t,0,10}]
```

Note that the range for t in the plot is identical to the range given in the **NDSolve** command.

Higher-order ordinary differential equations are treated in the same way. For example, given the initial value problem

$$\frac{d^2y}{dt^2} + 0.5\frac{dy}{dt} + \sin(y) = 0, \qquad y(0) = -1, y'(0) = 0, \qquad t \in [0, 15]$$

the input instruction is

```
sol=NDSolve[{y''[t]+0.5y'[t]+Sin[y[t]]==0,
    y[0]==-1,y'[0]==0}, y[t],{t,0,15}]
```

with plot

```
Plot[y[t] /. sol, {t,0,15}]
```

2.12 Solving differential equations with *Maple*

2.12.1 First-order equations

Maple has a built in command for dealing with differential equations, which is the **dsolve** command. This command is used to find a symbolic solution to a differential equation. The command **dsolve(..., numeric)** finds a numerical approximation. Consider the following first-order differential equation

$$\frac{dy}{dt} = f(y, t)$$

In particular, we are assuming that y is a function of t, $y(t)$. Then we employ the **dsolve** command by using

```
dsolve(diff(y(t),t)=f(y(t),t),y(t));
```

Note a number of aspects of this instruction:

(1)   The equation utilises diff($y(t)$, t) to denote dy/dt
(2)   The function $f(y(t), t)$ may or may not be independent of t
(3) $y(t)$ is written in the equation rather than simply y
(4)   The second term, $y(t)$, is indicating what is being solved for and that t is the independent variable.

It is possible to first define the differential equation and use the designation in the **dsolve** command. Thus

```
Eq:=diff(y(t),t);
dsolve(Eq,y(t));
```

If *Maple* can solve the differential equation then this is provided in the output. If *Maple* can find no solution, then the programme simply gives a blank output. The user does not need to know what algorithm is being used to solve the differential equation. What matters is whether a solution can be found. What is important to understand, however, is that a first-order differential equation (as we are discussing here) involves one unknown constant of integration. The output will, therefore, involve an unknown constant, which is denoted _C1.

Consider the following examples of first-order differential equations used in various places throughout this chapter (table 2.5). *Maple* has no difficulty solving all these problems. What is illustrated by these solutions is that the output may not, and usually is not, provided in a way useful for *economic* interpretation. So some manipulation of the output is often necessary.

It will be noted that none of the above examples involves initial conditions, which is why all outputs involve the unknown constant _C1. Initial value problems

Table 2.5 Maple input instructions for first-order differential equations

Problem		Input instructions
(i)	$\dfrac{dx}{dt} = kx$	`dsolve(diff(x(t),t)=k*x(t),x(t));`
(ii)	$\dfrac{dx}{dt} = 1 + ce^t$	`dsolve(diff(x(t),t)=1+c*exp(t),x(t));`
(iii)	$\dfrac{dp}{dt} - \alpha(b - d)p = \alpha(a - c)$	`dsolve(diff(p(t),t)-alpha*(b-d)*p(t)=` `    alpha*(a-c),p(t));`
(iv)	$\dfrac{dx}{dt} = kx(a - x)$	`dsolve(diff(x(t),t)=` `    k*x(t)*(a-x(t)),x(t));`
(v)	$\dot{k} = sak^\alpha - (n + \delta)k$	`dsolve(diff(k(t),t)=s*a*k(t)^alpha-` `    (n+delta)*k(t),k(t));`

Table 2.6 Maple input instructions for first-order initial value problems

Problem		Input instructions
(i)	$\dfrac{dp}{dt} = p(a - bp), p(0) = p0$	`dsolve({diff(p(t),t)=` `          p(t)*(a-b*p(t)),p(0)=p0},p(t));`
(ii)	$\dfrac{dn}{dt} = -\lambda n, n(0) = n0$	`dsolve({diff(n(t),t)=` `          -lambda*n(t),n(0)=n0},n(t));`
(iii)	$\dfrac{dy}{dx} = x^2 - 2x + 1, y(0) = 1$	`dsolve({diff(y(x),x)=` `          x^2-2*x+1,y(0)=1},y(x));`

are treated in a similar manner. If we have the initial value problem,

$$\frac{dy}{dt} = f(y, t) \qquad y(0) = y0$$

then the input instruction is

`dsolve({diff(y(t),t)=f(y(t),t),y(0)=y0},y(t));`

For example, look at table 2.6.

2.12.2 *Second-order equations*

Second-order differential equations are treated in fundamentally the same way. If we have the homogeneous second-order differential equation

$$a\frac{d^2y}{dt^2} + b\frac{dy}{dt} + cy = 0$$

then the input instruction is

`dsolve(a*diff(y(t),t$2)+b*diff(y(t),t)+c*y(t)=0,y(t));`

If we have the nonhomogeneous second-order differential equation

$$a\frac{d^2y}{dt^2} + b\frac{dy}{dt} + cy = g(t)$$

then the input instruction is

`dsolve(a*diff(y(t),t$2)+b*diff(y(t),t)+c*y(t)`
`      =g(t),y(t));`

Of course, the solutions are far more complex because they can involve real and distinct roots, real and equal roots and complex conjugate roots. But the solution algorithms that are built into *Maple* handle all these. Furthermore, second-order differential equations involve two unknowns, which are denoted _C1 and _C2 in *Maple*'s output.

The input instructions for some examples used in this chapter are shown in table 2.7.

Initial value problems follow the same structure as before (table 2.8).

Table 2.7 Maple input instructions for second-order differential equations

Problem		Input instructions
(i)	$\dfrac{d^2y}{dt^2} + 4\dfrac{dy}{dt} - 5y = 0$	`dsolve(diff(y(t),t$2)+4*diff(y(t),t)-` `5*y(t)=0,y(t));`
(ii)	$y''(t) + 4y'(t) + 4y(t) = 0$	`dsolve(diff(y(t),t$2)+4*diff(y(t),t)+` `4*y(t)=0,y(t));`
(iii)	$y''(t) + 2y'(t) + 2y(t) = 0$	`dsolve(diff(y(t),t$2)+2*diff(y(t),t)+` `2*y(t)=0,y(t));`
(iv)	$y''(t) + y'(t) = t$	`dsolve(diff(y(t),t$2)+diff(y(t),t)=` `t,y(t));`

Table 2.8 Maple input instructions for second-order initial value problems

Problem		Input instructions
(i)	$\dfrac{d^2y}{dt^2} + 4\dfrac{dy}{dt} - 5y = 0,$ $y(0) = 0, y'(0) = 1$	`dsolve({diff(y(t),t$2)+4*diff(y(t),t)-` `5*y(t)=0,y(0)=0,D(y)(0)=1},y(t));`
(ii)	$y''(t) + 4y'(t) + 4y(t) = 0,$ $y(0) = 3, y'(0) = 7$	`dsolve({diff(y(t),t$2)+4*diff(y(t),t)+` `4*y(t)=0,y(0)=3,D(y)(0)=7},y(t));`

2.12.3   dsolve(..., numeric)

Many differential equations, especially nonlinear and nonautonomous differential equations, cannot be solved by any of the known solution methods. In such cases a numerical approximation can be provided using the **dsolve(..., numeric)** command. In using the numerical version of the **dsolve** command, it is necessary to provide also the initial condition. Given the following initial value problem,

$$\frac{dy}{dt} = f(y(t), t) \qquad y(0) = y0$$

the input instruction is

`dsolve({diff(y(t),t)=f(y(t),t),y(0)=y0},y(t),numeric);`

Maple provides output in the form of a **proc function** (i.e. a procedural function) that represents an approximate function obtained using interpolation. This procedure can then be plotted. Since it is usual to plot such a procedural function, it is useful to give the output a name. Furthermore, since the plot is of a procedural function, it is necessary to use the **odeplot** rather than simply the **plot** command. In order to do this, however, it is first necessary to load the plots subroutine with the following instruction.

`with(plots):`

For example, given the problem

$$\frac{dy}{dt} = \sin(3t - y) \qquad y(0) = 0.5, \qquad t \in [0,10]$$

the instruction for solving this is

```
Sol1=dsolve({diff(y(t),t)=sin(3*t-y(t)),y(0)=0.5},
        y(t),numeric);
```

Although the output is named 'Sol', the solution is still for the variable $y(t)$. So the plot would involve the input

```
odeplot(Sol1,[t,y(t)],0..10);
```

Note that the range for t is given only in the odeplot instruction.

Higher-order ordinary differential equations are treated in the same way. For example, given the initial value problem,

$$\frac{d^2y}{dt^2} + 0.5\frac{dy}{dt} + \sin(y) = 0, \qquad y(0) = -1, y'(0) = 0, \qquad t \in [0,15]$$

the input instruction is

```
Sol2=dsolve({diff(y(t),t$2)+0.5*diff(y(t),
        t)+sin(y(t))=0, y(0)=-1,D(y)(0)=0},y(t),numeric);
```

with plot

```
odeplot(Sol2,[t,y(t)],0..15);
```

Appendix 2.1 Plotting direction fields for a single equation with *Mathematica*

Figure 2.8 (p. 45)

Given the differential equation

$$\frac{dy}{dx} = 2x - y$$

the direction field and isoclines can be obtained using *Mathematica* as follows:

Step 1 Load the **PlotField** subroutine with the instruction

```
<< Graphics`PlotField`
```

Note the use of the back-sloped apostrophe.

Step 2 Obtain the direction field by using the **PlotVectorField** command as follows

```
arrows=PlotVectorField[{1,2x-y},{x,-2,2},{y,-2,2}]
```

Note the following:
(a) 'arrows' is a name (with lower case a) which will be used later in the routine
(b) the first element in the first bracket is unity, which represents the time derivative with respect to itself
(c) if memory is scarce, the plot can be suppressed by inserting a semicolon at the end of the line.

Step 3   Solve the differential equation using the **DSolve** command (not available prior to version 2.0)

```
sol=DSolve[ y'[x]+y[x]==2x, y[x], x]
```

Note the double equal sign in the equation.

Step 4   Derive an arbitrary path by extracting out the second term in the previous result. This is accomplished with the line

```
path=sol[[1,1,2]]
```

Step 5   Derive a series of trajectories in the form of a table using the **Table** command.

```
trajectories=Table[sol[[1,1,2]]/.C[1]->a,{a,-2,2,.5}]
```

Note the following:

(a) the solution to the differential equation is evaluated by letting C[1], the constant of integration, take the value of *a*. This is accomplished by adding the term '/. C[1]->*a*'

(b) *a* is then given values between −2 and 2 in increments of 0.5.

Step 6   Plot the trajectories using the **Plot** and **Evaluate** commands

```
plottraj=Plot[ Evaluate[trajectories], {x,-2,2} ]
```

Note that it is important to give the domain for *x* the same as in the direction field plot.

Step 7   Combine the direction field plot and the trajectories plot using the **Show** command (not available prior to version 2.0)

```
Show[arrows,plottraj]
```

This final result is shown in figure 2.8.

Figure 2.9(a) (p. 46)

This follows similar steps as for figure 2.8, and so here we shall simply list the input lines, followed by a few notes.

(1)   Input   `<<Graphics`PlotField``
(2)   Input   `malthus[t_, k_,p0_]=p0 E^(k t)`
(3)   Input   `malthus[0,0.01,13]`
(4)   Input   `malthus[150,0.01,13]`
(5)   Input   `pop1=Plot[ malthus t,0.01,13 ], {t,0,150} ]`
(6)   Input   `arrows=PlotVectorField[{1, 0.01p},`
              `{t,0,150}, {p,0,60}]`
(7)   Input   `Show[pop1,arrows,`
              `AxesOrigin->{0,0},`
              `AxesLabel->{"t","p"} ]`

Input (2) and (3) are simply to check the initial population size and the final population size. Input (6) has {1, kp} (with *k* = 0.01) as the first element in the

PlotVectorField. Input (7) indicates some *options* that can be used with the **Show** command. These too could be employed in (a) above.

Figure 2.9(b) (p. 46)

Before we can plot the logistic function we need to solve it. In this example we shall employ the figures for a and b we derive in chapter 14 for the UK population over the period 1781–1931.

$$a = 0.02 \qquad \text{and} \qquad b = 0.000436$$

and with $p0 = 13$.

(1)   Input   `<<Graphics`PlotField``

(2)   Input   `DSolve[{p'[t]==(0.02-0.000436p[t])p[t],`
             `p[0]==13}, p[t], t ]`

(3)   Input   `logistic=%[[1,1,2]]`

(4)   Input   `logplot=Plot[logistic, {t,0,150} ]`

(5)   Input   `arrows=PlotVectorField[{1,0.02p-0.000436p^2},`
             `{t,0,150}, {p,0,50} ]`

(6)   Input   `Show[logplot, arrows,`
             `AxesOrigin->{0,0},`
             `AxesLabel->{"t","p"} ]`

Note again that the PlotVectorField has the first element in the form $\{1, (a - bp)p\}$ (with $a = 0.02$ and $b = 0.000436$).

Appendix 2.2 Plotting direction fields for a single equation with *Maple*

Figure 2.8 (p. 45)

Given the differential equation

$$\frac{dy}{dx} = 2x - y$$

the direction field and isoclines can be obtained using *Maple* as follows:

Step 1   Load the **DEtools** subroutine with the instruction

       `with(DEtools):`

       Note the colon after the instruction.

Step 2   Define the differential equation and a set of points for the isoclines.

       `Eq:= diff(y(x),x)=2*x-y`
       `Points:={[-2,2],[-1,1],[-1,0.5],[-0.5,-2],`
          `[0,-2],[0.5,-1.5],[0.5,-1],[1,-1],[1.5,-0.5]};`

Step 3   Obtain the direction field and the integral curves with the instruction

       `DEplot(Eq,y(x),x=-2..2,Points,y=-2..2, arrows=slim,`
          `linecolour=blue);`

Note that the direction field has six elements:

(i)   the differential equation
(ii) $y(x)$ indicates that x is the independent variable and y the dependent variable
(iii)   the range for the x-axis
(iv)   the initial points
(v)   the range for the y-axis
(vi)   a set of options; here we have two options:
        (a) arrows are to be drawn slim (the default is thin)
        (b) the colour of the lines is to be blue (the default is yellow).

Figure 2.9(a) (p. 46)

This follows similar steps as figure 2.8 and so we shall be brief. We assume a new session. Input the following:

```
(1)     with(DEtools):
(2)     equ:=p0*exp(k*t);
(3)     newequ:=subs(p0=13,k=0.01,equ);
(4)     inisol:=evalf(subs(t=0,newequ));
(5)     finsol:=evalf(subs(t=150,newequ));
(6)     DEplot(diff(p(t),t)=0.01*p,p(t),t=0..150,{[0,13]},
                p=0..60, arrows=slim,linecolour=blue);
```

Instructions (2), (3), (4) and (5) input the equation and evaluate it for the initial point (time $t = 0$) and at $t = 150$. The remaining instruction plots the direction field and one integral curve through the point (0, 13).

Figure 2.9(b) (p. 46)

The logistic equation uses the values $a = 0.02$ and $b = 0.000436$ and $p0 = 13$. The input instructions are the following, where again we assume a new session:

```
(1)     with(DEtools):
(2)     DEplot(diff(p(t),t)=(0.02-0.000436*p)*p,p(t),
                t=0..150,{[0,13]},p=0..50,arrows=slim,
                linecolour=blue);
```

Exercises

1.   Show the following are solutions to their respective differential equations

        (i) $\dfrac{dy}{dx} = ky \qquad y = ce^{kx}$

        (ii) $\dfrac{dy}{dx} = \dfrac{-x}{y} \qquad y = x^2 + y^2 = c$

        (iii) $\dfrac{dy}{dx} = \dfrac{-2y}{x} \qquad y = \dfrac{a}{x^2}$

2. Analyse the qualitative and quantitative properties of the **Gompertz equation** for population growth

$$\dot{p} = p'(t) = kp(a - \ln p)$$

3. Solve the following separable differential equations

(i) $\dfrac{dy}{dx} = x(1 - y^2)$ $\quad -1 < y < 1$

(ii) $\dfrac{dy}{dx} = 1 - 2y + y^2$

(iii) $\dfrac{dy}{dx} = \dfrac{y^2}{x^2}$

4. Solve the following initial value problems

(i) $\dfrac{dy}{dx} = x^2 - 2x + 1$ $\quad y = 1$ when $x = 0$

(ii) $\dfrac{dy}{dx} = \dfrac{(3x^2 + 4x + 2)}{2(y - 1)}$ $\quad y = -1$ when $x = 0$

5. Solve the following Bernoulli differential equations

(i) $\dfrac{dy}{dx} - y = -y^2$

(ii) $\dfrac{dy}{dx} - y = xy^2$

(iii) $\dfrac{dy}{dx} = 2y - e^x y^2$

6. Show that the logistic equation

$$\frac{dp}{dt} = p(a - bp)$$

can be represented as a Bernoulli function. Using a suitable transformation, solve the resulting linear differential equation; and hence show that

$$p(t) = \frac{ap_0}{(a - bp_0)e^{-at} + bp_0} \qquad \text{where } p(0) = p_0$$

7. In the Great Hall in Winchester hangs a round table on the wall that was purported to be King Arthur's famous original round table top. Wood contains carbon-14 with a decay-constant of 1.245×10^{-4} per year. Living wood has a rate of disintegration of 6.68 per minute per gram of sample. When the tabletop was inspected in 1977 the rate of disintegration was found to be 6.08 per minute per gram of sample. Given King Arthur was on the throne in the fifth century AD, demonstrate that the tabletop at Winchester was not that of King Arthur.

8. (Use information in exercise 7.) In 1950 the Babylonian city of Nippur was excavated. In this excavation there was charcoal from a wooden roof beam which gave off a carbon-14 disintegration count of 4.09 per minute

per gram. If this charcoal was formed during the reign of Hammurabi, what is the likely time of Hammurabi's succession?

9. (i) $f_1(x)$ and $f_2(x)$ are linearly dependent if and only if there exists constants b_1 and b_2 not all zero such that

$$b_1 f_1(x) + b_2 f_2(x) = 0$$

for every x. Suppose $b_1 \neq 0$, then $f_1(x) = -(b_2/b_1) f_2(x)$ and so $f_1(x)$ is a multiple of $f_2(x)$ and therefore the functions are linearly dependent. If the set of functions is *not* linearly dependent, then $f_1(x)$ and $f_2(x)$ are linearly independent. Show that $y_1 = e^{rt}$ and $y_2 = te^{rt}$ are linearly independent.

(ii) $f_1(x)$, $f_2(x)$ and $f_3(x)$ are linearly dependent if and only if there exist constants b_1, b_2 and b_3 not all zero such that

$$b_1 f_1(x) + b_2 f_2(x) + b_3 f_3(x) = 0$$

for every x. If the set of functions is *not* linearly dependent, then $f_1(x)$, $f_2(x)$ and $f_3(x)$ are linearly independent. Show that $y_1 = e^{rt}$, $y_2 = te^{rt}$ and $y_3 = t^2 e^{rt}$ are linearly independent.

10. For the second-order linear differential equation with complex conjugate roots $r = \alpha + \beta i$ and $s = \alpha - \beta i$, show that

$$y(t) = c_1 e^{rt} + c_2 e^{st}$$

is equivalent to

$$y(t) = c_1 e^{\alpha i} \cos(\beta t) + c_2 e^{\alpha i} \sin(\beta t)$$

by using Euler's identity that for the complex number $i\beta$

$$e^{i\beta} = \cos \beta + i \sin \beta$$

11. A principal P is compounded continuously with interest rate r.
     (i) What is the rate of change of P?
     (ii) Solve for P at time t, i.e., $P(t)$, given $P(0) = P_0$.
     (iii) If $P_0 = £2,000$ and $r = 7.5\%$ annually, what is P after 5 years?

12. If £1,000 is invested at a compound interest of 5%, how long before the investment has doubled in size, to the nearest whole year?

13. If $\dot{x} = x^2 + 2x - 15$
     (i) establish the fixed points
     (ii) determine whether the fixed points are attracting or repelling.

14. Given the following parameters for the Solow growth model

$$a = 4, \alpha = 0.25, s = 0.1, \delta = 0.4, n = 0.03$$

(i) use a software program to plot the graph of $k(t)$
(ii) plot the function

$$\dot{k} = sak^{\alpha} - (n + \delta)k$$

(iii) Linearise $\dot{k}$ about the equilibrium in (ii) and establish whether it is stable or unstable.

15. Given the differential equation

$$\dot{Y} - \left(\frac{s}{v}\right) Y = 0$$

for the Harrod–Domar growth model:
   (i) construct a diagram of $\dot{Y}$ against Y and establish the phase line for this model
   (ii) establish $Y(t)$ given $Y(0) = Y_0$.

16. From Domar (1944), assume income $Y(t)$ grows at a constant rate r. In order to maintain full employment the budget deficit, $D(t)$, changes in proportion k to $Y(t)$, i.e.,

$$\dot{D}(t) = kY(t)$$

   Show that

$$\frac{D(t)}{Y(t)} = \left(\frac{D_0}{Y_0} - \frac{k}{r}\right) e^{-rt} + \frac{k}{r}$$

17. At what nominal interest rate will it take to double a real initial investment of A over 25 years, assuming a constant rate of inflation of 5% per annum?

18. Table 2A.1 provides annual GDP growth rates for a number of countries based on the period 1960–1990 (Jones 1998, table 1.1).
   (a) In each case, calculate the number of years required for a doubling of GDP.
   (b) Interpret the negative numbers in the 'years to double' when the growth rate is negative.

19. In 1960 China's population was 667,073,000 and by 1992 it was 1,162,000,000.
   (a) What is China's annual population growth over this period?
   (b) How many years will it take for China's population to double?
   (c) Given China's population in 1992, and assuming the same annual: growth rate in population, what was the predicted size of China's population at the beginning of the new millennium (2000)?

20. An individual opens up a retirement pension at age 25 of an amount £5,000. He contributes £2,000 per annum each year up to his retirement at age 65. Interest is 5% compounded continuously. What payment will he receive on his retirement?

Table 2A.1 GDP growth rates, selected countries, 1960–1990

'Rich' countries	Growth rate	Years to double	'Poor' countries	Growth rate	Years to double
France	2.7		China	2.4	
Japan	5.0		India	2.0	
West Germany	2.5		Uganda	−0.2	
UK	2.0		Zimbabwe	0.2	
USA	1.4				

Source: Jones (1998, table 1.1).

Additional reading

For additional material on the contents of the present chapter the reader can consult: Arrowsmith and Place (1992), Berry (1996), Borrelli *et al.* (1992), Boyce and DiPrima (1997), Braun (1983), Burmeister and Dobell (1970), Davies (1979), Giordano and Weir (1991), Griffiths and Oldknow (1993), Jeffrey (1990), Lynch (2001), Mahajan and Peterson (1985), Percival and Richards (1982), Takayama (1994) and Tu (1994).

CHAPTER 3

Discrete dynamic systems

3.1 Classifying discrete dynamic systems

A discrete dynamic system is a sequence of numbers, y_t, that are defined recursively, i.e., there is a rule relating each number in the sequence to previous numbers in the sequence; we denote such a sequence $\{y_t\}$.

A first-order discrete dynamic system is a sequence of numbers y_t for $t = 0, 1, 2 \ldots$ such that each number after the first is related to the previous number by the relationship

$$y_{t+1} = f(y_t) \tag{3.1}$$

We shall refer to (3.1) as a **recursive equation**. The sequence of numbers given by the relationship

$$\Delta y_{t+1} \equiv y_{t+1} - y_t = g(y_t) \tag{3.2}$$

we shall refer to as a **first-order difference equation**.[1] Examples are

(i) $y_{t+1} = 2 + y_t$ implies $y_{t+1} - y_t = 2$
(ii) $y_{t+1} = 2y_t$ implies $y_{t+1} - y_t = y_t$

Given the discrete dynamic system $y_{t+1} = f(y_t)$, then if $f(y_t)$ is linear, the system is said to be **linear**; if $f(y_t)$ is nonlinear then the system is said to be **nonlinear**. Examples

(i) $y_{t+1} = 2 + 3y_t$ linear
(ii) $y_{t+2} - 2y_{t+1} - 3y_t = 5$ linear
(iii) $y_{t+1} = 3.2y_t(1 - y_t)$ nonlinear
(iv) $y_{t+1} = ry_t \ln(k/y_t)$ nonlinear

Consider the general discrete dynamic system

$$y_{t+1} = f(t, y_t) \tag{3.3}$$

For example

$$y_{t+1} = th(y_t)$$

---

[1] Often equation (3.1) and equation (3.2) are each referred to as a difference equation.

As in the case of differential equations, if the dynamic system depends not only on $h(y_t)$ but also on t itself, then the system is said to be **nonautonomous**. If, however, the dynamic system is independent of t, then it is said to be **autonomous**. Hence, $y_{t+1} = t + 2y_t$ is a nonautonomous dynamic system, while $y_{t+1} = 2y_t$ is autonomous.

Suppose we consider a linear first-order difference equation with all y-terms on the left-hand side, for example

$$y_{t+1} + ay_t = g(t)$$

If $g(t) \equiv 0$ for all t, then these equations are said to be **homogeneous**, otherwise they are **nonhomogeneous**. They are referred to as homogeneous difference equations because if a series $\{y_t\}$ satisfies the equation, then so does the series $\{ky_t\}$.

Of particular importance is the **order** of a dynamic system. The dynamic system (3.1) is a **first-order** system in which each number in the sequence depends only on the previous number. In general, an mth-order discrete dynamic system takes the form

(3.4) $$y_{t+m} = f(y_{t+m-1}, y_{t+m-2}, \ldots, y_t)$$

For instance, a second-order linear discrete dynamic system takes the general form

$$y_{t+2} + ay_{t+1} + by_t = g(t)$$

This would be a second-order linear homogeneous dynamic system if $g(t) \equiv 0$ for all t.

Examples are:

(i) $y_{t+1} - 2y_t = 0$ is first-order linear homogeneous
(ii) $y_{t+2} - 4y_{t+1} - 4y_t = 0$ is second-order linear homogeneous
(iii) $y_{t+1} - 2y_t = 5$ is first-order linear nonhomogeneous
(iv) $y_{t+2} - 4y_{t+1} - 4y_t = 6$ is second-order linear nonhomogeneous

All are also examples of autonomous systems. In this book we shall consider only autonomous systems.

3.2   The initial value problem

The **initial value problem** is the requirement of knowing certain initial values in order to solve the sequence of numbers. Thus, for $y_{t+1} = f(y_t)$

$$y_{t+2} = f(y_{t+1}) = f(f(y_t)) = f^2(y_t)$$

Hence, the sequence of numbers is defined only given some initial value for y_t. In the case of a second-order sequence, then we require to know two initial values. This is because, if

$$y_{t+2} = f(y_{t+1}, y_t)$$

then

$$y_{t+3} = f(y_{t+2}, y_{t+1}) = f(f(y_{t+1}, y_t), y_{t+1})$$

and so on. Hence, each number in the sequence ultimately depends on two initial values, y_{t+1} and y_t. This requirement generalises. For an m-order dynamic system m-initial values are generally required for its solution.

Let

$$y_{t+1} = f(y_t) \qquad y_0 \text{ at } t = 0$$

This represents a **recursive equation** and we can generate a sequence starting from the value y_0. The sequence would be

$$y_0, f(y_0), f(f(y_0)), f(f(f(y_0))), \cdots$$

Letting $f^n(y_0)$ denote the nth iterate of y_0 under f, then the sequence can be expressed

$$y_0, f(y_0), f^2(y_0), f^3(y_0), \cdots$$

The set of all (positive) iterates $\{f^n(y_0), n \geq 0\}$ is called the (positive) **orbit** of y_0.

3.3 The cobweb model: an introduction

To highlight the features so far outlined, and others to follow, consider the following typical cobweb model in which demand at time t, q_t^d, depends on the price now ruling on the market, p_t, while the supply at time t, q_t^s, depends on planting, which in turn was governed by what the price the farmer received in the last period, p_{t-1}. The market is cleared in any period, and so $q_t^d = q_t^s$. Assuming linear demand and supply curves for simplicity, the model is, then,

$$\begin{aligned} q_t^d &= a - bp_t & a, b &> 0 \\ q_t^s &= c + dp_{t-1} & d &> 0 \\ q_t^d &= q_t^s \end{aligned} \tag{3.5}$$

Substituting, we obtain

$$a - bp_t = c + dp_{t-1}$$

or

$$p_t = \left(\frac{a-c}{b}\right) - \left(\frac{d}{b}\right)p_{t-1} \tag{3.6}$$

which is a first-order nonhomogeneous dynamic system. It is also an autonomous dynamic system since it does not depend explicitly on t.

This model is illustrated in figure 3.1. The demand and supply curves are indicated by D and S, respectively. Because we have a first-order system, we need one initial starting price. Suppose this is p_0. This gives a quantity supplied in the *next* period of q_1, read off the supply curve, and indicated by point a. But since demand equals supply in any one period, this gives a demand of also q_1, while this demand implies a price of p_1 in period 1. This in turn means that supply in period 2 is q_2. And so the sequence continues.

We shall refer to this model frequently in this chapter.

Figure 3.1.

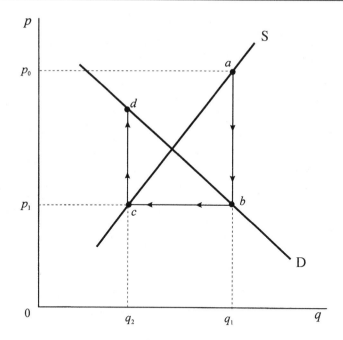

3.4   Equilibrium and stability of discrete dynamic systems

If $y_{t+1} = f(y_t)$ is a discrete dynamic system, then y^* is a **fixed point** or **equilibrium point** of the system if

(3.7)
$$f(y_t) = y^* \quad \text{for all } t$$

A useful implication of this definition is that y^* is an equilibrium value of the system $y_{t+1} = f(y_t)$ if and only if

$$y^* = f(y^*)$$

For example, in the cobweb model (3.6) we have,

$$p^* = \frac{a-c}{b} - \left(\frac{d}{b}\right)p^*$$

Hence

$$p^* = \frac{a-c}{b+d} \quad \text{where } p^* \geq 0 \text{ if } a \geq c$$

With linear demand and supply curves, therefore, there is only one fixed point, one equilibrium point. However, such a fixed point makes economic sense (i.e. for price to be nonnegative) only if the additional condition $a \geq c$ is also satisfied.

As with fixed points in continuous dynamic systems, a particularly important consideration is the stability/instability of a fixed point. Let y^* denote a fixed point for the discrete dynamic system $y_{t+1} = f(y_t)$. Then (Elaydi 1996, p. 11)

(i)   The equilibrium point y^* is **stable** if given $\varepsilon > 0$ there exists $\delta > 0$ such that

$$\left|y_0 - y^*\right| < \delta \qquad \text{implies} \qquad \left|f^n(y_0) - y^*\right| < \varepsilon$$

for all $n > 0$. If y^* is not stable then it is **unstable**.

(ii)   The equilibrium point y^* is a **repelling fixed point** if there exists $\varepsilon > 0$ such that

$$0 < \left|y_0 - y^*\right| < \varepsilon \qquad \text{implies} \qquad \left|f(y_0) - y^*\right| > \left|y_0 - y^*\right|$$

(iii)   The point y^* is an **asymptotically stable** (attracting) equilibrium point[2] if it is stable and there exists $\eta > 0$ such that

$$\left|y_0 - y^*\right| < \eta \qquad \text{implies} \qquad \lim_{t \to \infty} y_t = y^*$$

If $\eta = \infty$ then y^* is **globally asymptotically stable**.

All these are illustrated in figure 3.2(a)–(e).

In utilising these concepts we employ the following theorem (Elaydi 1996, section 1.4).

THEOREM 3.1
Let y^* be an equilibrium point of the dynamical system

$$y_{t+1} = f(y_t)$$

where f is continuously differentiable at y^*. Then

(i)   *if $\left|f'(y^*)\right| < 1$ then y^* is an asymptotically stable (attracting) fixed point*

(ii)   *if $\left|f'(y^*)\right| > 1$ then y^* is unstable and is a repelling fixed point*

(iii)   *if $\left|f'(y^*)\right| = 1$ and*
        (a) if $f''(y^*) \neq 0$, then y^* is unstable
        (b) if $f''(y^*) = 0$ and $f'''(y^*) > 0$, then y^* is unstable
        (c) if $f''(y^*) = 0$ and $f'''(y^*) < 0$, then y^* is asymptotically stable

(iv)   *if $f'(y^*) = -1$ and*
        (a) if $-2f'''(y^*) - 3[f''(y^*)]^2 < 0$, then y^* is asymptotically stable
        (b) if $-2f'''(y^*) - 3[f''(y^*)]^2 > 0$, then y^* is unstable.

The attraction and repulsion of a fixed point can readily be illustrated for a first-order system. Suppose $f(y_t)$ is linear for the first-order system $y_{t+1} = f(y_t)$. This is represented by the lines denoted L in figures 3.3(a) and (b), where y_{t+1} is marked on the vertical axis and y_t on the horizontal axis. The equilibrium condition requires $y_{t+1} = y_t$ for all t, hence this denotes a 45°-line, denoted by E in figures 3.3(a) and (b). The fixed point in each case, therefore, is y^*.

---

[2] Sometimes an asymptotically stable (attracting) equilibrium point is called a *sink*.

Figure 3.2.

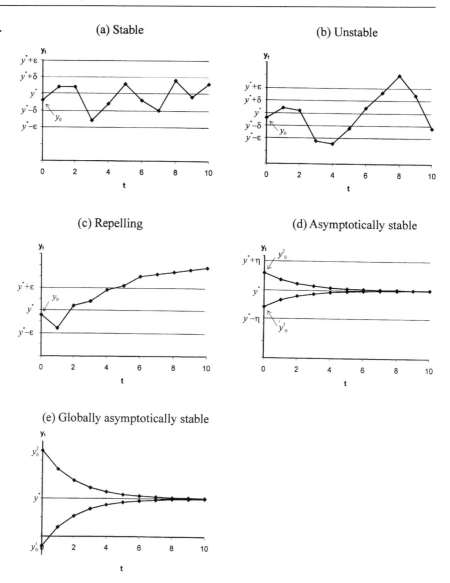

(a) Stable

(b) Unstable

(c) Repelling

(d) Asymptotically stable

(e) Globally asymptotically stable

Consider first figure 3.3(a). We require an initial value for y to start the sequence, which is denoted y_0. Given y_0 in period 0, then we have y_1 in period 1, as read off from the line L. In terms of the horizontal axis, this gives a value of y_1 as read off the $45°$-line (i.e. the horizontal movement across). But this means that in period 2 the value of y is y_2, once again read off from the line L. In terms of the horizontal axis this also gives a value y_2, read horizontally across. Regardless of the initial value y_0, the sequence converges on y^*, and this is true whether y_0 is below y^*, as in the figure, or is above y^*. Using the same analysis, it is clear that in figure 3.3(b), starting from an initial value of y of y_0, the sequence diverges from y^*. If y_0 is below y^* then the system creates smaller values of y and moves away from y^* in the negative direction. On the other hand, if y_0 is above y^*, then the sequence diverges from y^* with the sequence diverging in the positive direction. Only if

Figure 3.3.

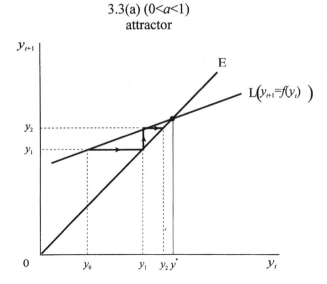

3.3(a) $(0<a<1)$
attractor

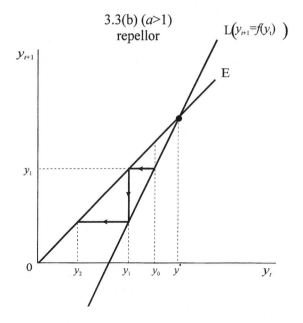

3.3(b) $(a>1)$
repellor

$y_0 = y^*$ will the system remain at rest. Hence, y^* in figure 3.3(a) is an attractor
while y^* in figure 3.3(b) is a repellor.

It is apparent from figure 3.2 that the essential difference between the two
situations is that the line in figure 3.3(a) has a (positive) slope less than 45°, while
in figure 3.3(b) the slope is greater than 45°.

Another feature can be illustrated in a similar diagram. Consider the following
simple linear dynamic system

$$y_{t+1} = -y_t + k$$

Given this system, the first few terms in the sequence are readily found to be:

$$y_{t+1} = -y_t + k$$
$$y_{t+2} = -y_{t+1} + k = -(-y_t + k) + k = y_t$$
$$y_{t+3} = -y_{t+2} + k = -y_t + k$$
$$y_{t+4} = -y_{t+3} + k = -(-y_t + k) + k = y_t$$

It is apparent that this is a repeating pattern. If y_0 denotes the initial value, then we have

$$y_0 = y_2 = y_4 = \ldots \qquad \text{and} \qquad y_1 = y_3 = y_5 = \ldots$$

We have here an example of a **two-cycle** system that oscillates between $-y_0 + k$ and y_0. There is still a fixed point to the system, namely

$$y^* = -y^* + k$$
$$y^* = \frac{k}{2}$$

but it is neither an attractor nor a repellor. The situation is illustrated in figure 3.4, where again the line L denotes the difference equation and the line E gives the equilibrium condition. The two-cycle situation is readily revealed by the fact that the system cycles around a rectangle.

Return to the linear cobweb model given above, equation (3.5). Suppose the slope of the (linear) demand curve is the same as the slope of the (linear) supply

Figure 3.4.

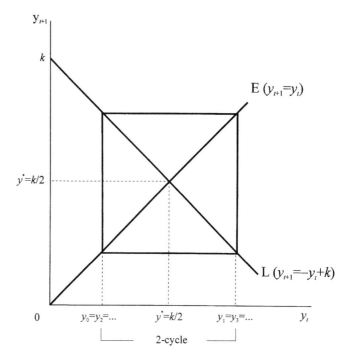

curve but with opposite sign. Then $b = d$ and

$$p_t = \frac{a-c}{d} - \left(\frac{b}{d}\right) p_{t-1}$$

$$= \left(\frac{a-c}{d}\right) - p_{t-1}$$

or

$$p_{t+1} = -p_t + k \text{ where } k = \frac{a-c}{d}$$

which is identical to the situation shown in figure 3.4, and must produce a two-cycle result.

In general, a solution y_n is **periodic** if

$$y_{n+m} = y_n$$

for some fixed integer m and all n. The smallest integer for m is called the period of the solution. For example, given the linear cobweb system

$$q_t^d = 10 - 2p_t$$
$$q_t^s = 4 + 2p_{t-1}$$
$$q_t^d = q_t^s$$

it is readily established that the price cycles between p_0 and $3-p_0$, while the quantity cycles between $4 + 2p_0$ and $10 - 2p_0$ (see exercise 12). In other words

$$p_0 = p_2 = p_4 = \dots \qquad \text{and} \qquad p_1 = p_3 = p_5 = \dots$$

so that $y_{n+2} = y_n$ for all n and hence we have a two-cycle solution.

More formally:

DEFINITION
If a sequence $\{y_t\}$ has (say) two repeating values y_1 and y_2, then y_1 and y_2 are called period points, *and the set $\{y_1, y_2\}$ is called a* periodic orbit.

Geometrically, a ***k*-periodic point** for the discrete system $y_{t+1} = f(y_t)$ is the y-coordinate of the point where the graph of $f^k(y)$ meets the diagonal line $y_{t+1} = y_t$. Thus, a three-period cycle is where $f^3(y)$ meets the line $y_{t+1} = y_t$.

In establishing the stability/instability of period points we utilise the following theorem.

THEOREM 3.2
Let b be a k-period point of f. Then b is

(i)   *stable if it is a stable fixed point of f^k*
(ii)   *asymptotically stable (attracting) if it is an attracting fixed point of f^k*
(iii)   *repelling if it is a repelling fixed point of f^k.*

In deriving the stability of a periodic point we require, then, to compute $[f^k(y)]'$, and to do this we utilise the chain rule

$$[f^k(y)]' = f'(y_1^*)f'(y_2^*)\ldots f'(y_n^*)$$

where $y_1^*, y_2^*, \ldots, y_k^*$ are the k-periodic points. For example, if y_1^* and y_2^* are two periodic points of $f^2(y)$, then

$$\left|[f^2(y)]'\right| = \left|f'(y_1^*)f'(y_2^*)\right|$$

and is asymptotically stable if

$$\left|f'(y_1^*)f'(y_2^*)\right| < 1$$

All other stability theorems hold in a similar fashion.

Although it is fairly easy to determine the stability/instability of linear dynamic systems, this is not true for nonlinear systems. In particular, such systems can create complex cycle phenomena. To illustrate, and no more than illustrate, the more complex nature of systems that arise from nonlinearity, consider the following quadratic equation

$$y_{t+1} = ay_t - by_t^2$$

First we need to establish any fixed points. It is readily established that two fixed points arise since

$$y^* = ay^* - by^{*2} = ay^*\left(1 - \frac{by^*}{a}\right)$$

which gives two fixed points

$$y^* = 0 \qquad \text{and} \qquad y^* = \frac{a-1}{b}$$

The situation is illustrated in figure 3.5, where the quadratic is denoted by the graph G, and the line E as before denotes the equilibrium condition. The two equilibrium points, the two fixed points of the system, are where the graph G intersects the line E.

Depending on the values for a and b, it is of course possible for the graph G to be totally below the line E, in which case only one equilibrium point exists, namely $y^* = 0$. Whether one or more equilibria exist, the question of interest is whether such a fixed point is stable or unstable. Suppose we attempt to establish which by means of a numerical example

$$y_{t+1} = 2y_t - y_t^2$$

The situation is illustrated in figure 3.6, where G denotes the graph of the difference equation, and the line E the equilibrium condition. The two equilibrium values are readily found to be $y^* = 0$ and $y^* = 1$.

As in the linear system, we need to consider a starting value, which we denote y_0, then $y_1 = 2y_0 - y_0^2$. But this is no more than the value as read off the graph G. In terms of the horizontal axis, this value is read off by moving horizontally across to the E-line, as shown more clearly in figure 3.7. Given y_1 then $y_2 = 2y_1 - y_1^2$ as read off the graph G, which gives y_2 on the horizontal axis when read horizontally

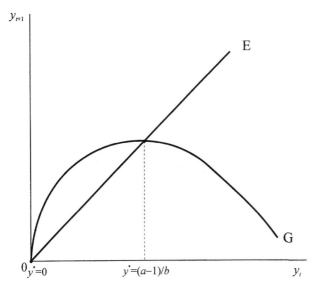

Figure 3.5.

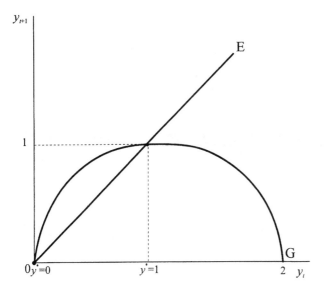

Figure 3.6.

off the E-line. And so on. It would *appear*, therefore, that $y^* = 1$ is an attractor. Even if y_0 is above $y^* = 1$, the system *appears* to converge on $y^* = 1$. Similarly, $y^* = 0$ *appears* to be a repellor.

It is useful to use a spreadsheet not only to establish the sequence $\{y_n\}$, but also to graph the situation. A spreadsheet is ideal for recursive equations because the relation gives the next element in the sequence, and for given initial values, the sequence is simply copied to all future cells. A typical spreadsheet for the present example is illustrated in figure 3.8, where we have identified the formulas in the initial cells.

Figure 3.7.

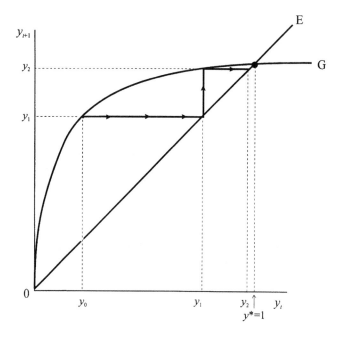

Figure 3.8.

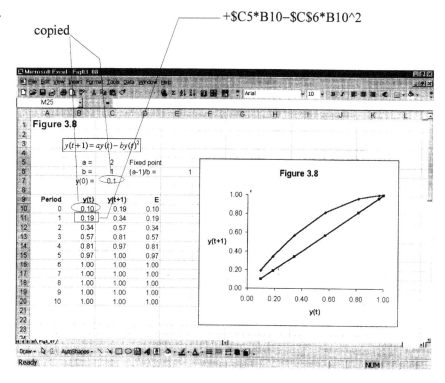

Given such a spreadsheet, it is possible to change the initial value y_0 and see the result in the sequence and on the various graphs that can be constructed.[3] For instance, considering

$$y_{t+1} = 3.2y_t - 0.8y_t^2$$

readily establishes that the equilibrium value is $y^* = 2.75$, but that this is not reached for any initial value not equal to it. For any initial value not equal to the equilibrium value, then the system will tend towards a two-cycle with values 2.05 and 3.20, as can readily be established by means of a spreadsheet. It is also easy to establish that for any value slightly above or slightly below 2.75, i.e., in the neighbourhood of the equilibrium point, then the system diverges further from the equilibrium. In other words, the equilibrium is locally unstable. What is not apparent, however, is why the system will tend towards a two-cycle result. We shall explain why in section 3.7.

Nor should it be assumed that only a two-cycle result can arise from the logistic equation. For instance, the logistic equation

$$y_{t+1} = 3.84y_t(1 - y_t)$$

has a three-cycle (see exercise 13).

We can approach stability/instability from a slightly different perspective. Consider the first-order difference equation $y_{t+1} = f(y_t)$ with fixed points satisfying $a = f(a)$. Let y denote y_{t+1} and x denote y_t, then the difference equation is of the form $y = f(x)$. Expanding this equation around an equilibrium point (a, a) we have

$$y - a = f'(a)(x - a)$$

or

$$y = a[1 - f'(a)] + f'(a)x$$

which is simply a linear equation with slope $f'(a)$. The situation is illustrated in figure 3.9.

This procedure reduces the problem of stability down to that of our linear model. There we noted that if the *absolute* slope of $f(x)$ was less than the 45°-line, as in figure 3.9, then the situation was stable, otherwise it was unstable. To summarise,

If $|f'(a)| < 1$ then a is an attractor or stable

If $|f'(a)| > 1$ then a is a repellor or unstable

If $|f'(a)| = 1$ then the situation is inconclusive.[4]

We can use such a condition for each fixed point.

---

[3] Many spreadsheets now allow graphics to be displayed within the spreadsheet, as shown here – especially those using the Windows environment. Hence, any change in initial values or parameter values results in an immediate change in the displayed graph. This is a very interactive experimentation.

[4] However, it is possible to utilise higher derivatives to obtain more information about the fixed point a, as pointed out in theorem 3.1 (p. 89).

Figure 3.9.

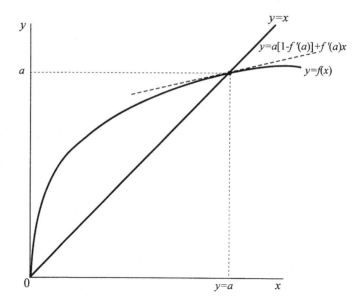

Example 3.1

$$y_{t+1} = 2y_t - y_t^2$$

The fixed points can be found from

$$a = 2a - a^2$$
$$a^2 - a = 0$$
$$a(a - 1) = 0$$
$$a = 0 \qquad \text{and} \qquad a = 1$$

To establish stability, let

$$y = f(x) = 2x - x^2$$

then

$$f'(x) = 2 - 2x$$
$$f'(0) = 2 \qquad \text{and} \qquad f'(1) = 0$$

Since

$$\left| f'(0) \right| > 1 \text{ then } a = 0 \text{ is unstable}$$

Since

$$\left| f'(1) \right| < 1 \text{ then } a = 1 \text{ is stable}$$

Example 3.2

$$y_{t+1} = 3.2y_t - 0.8y_t^2$$

The fixed points can be found from

$$a = 3.2a - 0.8a^2$$
$$0.8a^2 - 2.2a = 0$$
$$a(0.8a - 2.2) = 0$$
$$a = 0 \quad \text{and} \quad a = 2.75$$

To establish stability let

$$y = f(x) = 3.2x - 0.8x^2$$

then

$$f'(x) = 3.2 - 1.6x$$
$$f'(0) = 3.2 \quad \text{and} \quad f'(2.75) = -1.2$$

Since

$$|f'(0)| > 1 \text{ then } a = 0 \text{ is unstable}$$

Since

$$|f'(2.75)| > 1 \text{ then } a = 2.75 \text{ is unstable.}$$

Although $a = 2.75$ is unstable, knowledge about $f'(x)$ does not give sufficient information to determine what is happening to the sequence $\{y_n\}$ around the point $a = 2.75$.

3.5   Solving first-order difference equations

For some relatively simple difference equations it is possible to find *analytical solutions*. The simplest difference equation is a first-order linear homogeneous equation of the form

$$y_{t+1} = ay_t \tag{3.8}$$

If we consider the recursive nature of this system, beginning with the initial value y_0, we have

$$y_1 = ay_0$$
$$y_2 = ay_1 = a(ay_0) = a^2 y_0$$
$$y_3 = ay_2 = a(a^2 y_0) = a^3 y_0$$
$$\vdots$$
$$y_n = a^n y_0$$

The analytical solution is, therefore,

$$y_n = a^n y_0 \tag{3.9}$$

satisfying the initial value y_0. The properties of this system depend only on the value and sign of the parameter a. There is only one fixed point to such a system, $y^* = 0$. For positive y_0, if a exceeds unity, then the series gets larger and larger over time, tending to infinity in the limit. If $0 < a < 1$, then the series gets smaller

Figure 3.10.

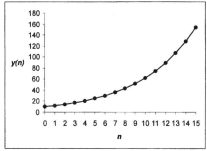

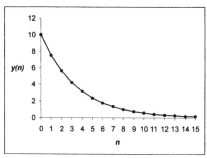

$$y(n)=10(-0.75)^n$$

$$y(n)=10(-1.2)^n$$

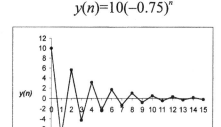

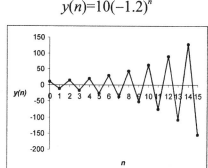

and smaller over time, tending to zero in the limit. If a is negative, then the series will alternate between positive and negative numbers. However, if $-1 < a < 0$ the values of the alternating series becomes smaller and smaller, tending to zero in the limit. While if $a < -1$, then the series alternates but tends to explode over time. The various solution paths are plotted in figure 3.10.

Example 3.3

A number of systems satisfy this general form. Consider the Malthusian population discussed in chapter 2, but now specified in discrete form. Between time t and $t + 1$ the change in the population is proportional to the population size. If p_t denotes the population size in period t, then $\Delta p_{t+1} = p_{t+1} - p_t$ is proportional to p_t. If k denotes the proportionality factor, then

$$\Delta p_{t+1} = kp_t$$

Or

$$p_{t+1} = (1+k)p_t$$

which has the analytical solution

$$p_t = (1+k)^t p_0$$

where p_0 is the initial population size. If population is growing at all, $k > 0$, then this population will grow over time becoming ever larger. We shall discuss population more fully in chapter 14.

Example 3.4

As a second example, consider the Harrod–Domar growth model in discrete time

$$S_t = sY_t$$
$$I_t = v(Y_t - Y_{t-1})$$
$$S_t = I_t$$

This gives a first-order homogeneous difference equation of the form

$$Y_t = \left(\frac{v}{v-s}\right)Y_{t-1}$$

with solution

$$Y_t = \left(\frac{v}{v-s}\right)^t Y_0$$

If $v > 0$ and $v > s$ then $v/(v-s) > 1$ and the solution is explosive and nonoscillatory. On the other hand, even if $v > 0$ if $s > v$ then the solution oscillates, being damped if $s < 2v$, explosive if $s > 2v$ or constant if $s = 2v$.

The analytical solution to the first-order linear homogeneous equation is useful because it also helps to solve first-order linear nonhomogeneous equations. Consider the following general first-order linear nonhomogeneous equation

$$y_{t+1} = ay_t + c \tag{3.10}$$

A simple way to solve such equations, and one particularly useful for the economist, is to transform the system into deviations from its fixed point, deviations from equilibrium. Let y^* denote the fixed point of the system, then

$$y^* = ay^* + c$$
$$y^* = \frac{c}{1-a}$$

Subtracting the equilibrium equation from the recursive equation gives

$$y_{t+1} - y^* = a(y_t - y^*)$$

Letting $x_{t+1} = y_{t+1} - y^*$ and $x_t = y_t - y^*$ then this is no more than a simple homogeneous difference equation in x

$$x_{t+1} = ax_t$$

with solution

$$x_t = a^t x_0$$

Hence,

$$y_t - y^* = a^t(y_0 - y^*)$$

or

(3.11) $$y_t = \frac{c}{1 - a} + a^t \left(y_0 - \frac{c}{1 - a} \right)$$

which clearly satisfies the initial condition.

Example 3.5

Consider, for example, the cobweb model we developed earlier in the chapter, equation (3.5), with the resulting recursive equation

$$p_t = \frac{a - c}{b} - \left(\frac{d}{b} \right) p_{t-1}$$

and with equilibrium

$$p^* = \frac{a - c}{b + d}$$

Taking deviations from the equilibrium, we have

$$p_t - p^* = -\frac{d}{b}(p_{t-1} - p^*)$$

which is a first-order linear homogeneous difference equation, with solution

$$p_t - p^* = \left(-\frac{d}{b} \right)^t (p_0 - p^*)$$

or

(3.12) $$p_t = \left(\frac{a - c}{b + d} \right) + \left(-\frac{d}{b} \right)^t \left[p_0 - \left(\frac{a - c}{b + d} \right) \right]$$

With the usual shaped demand and supply curves, i.e., $b > 0$ and $d > 0$, then $d/b > 0$, hence $(-d/b)^t$ will alternate in sign, being positive for even numbers of t and negative for odd numbers of t. Furthermore, if $0 < |-d/b| < 1$ then the series will become damped, and in the limit tend towards the equilibrium price. On the other hand, if $|-d/b| > 1$ then the system will diverge from the equilibrium price. These results are verified by means of a simple numerical example and solved by means of a spreadsheet, as shown in figure 3.11.

The examples we have just discussed can be considered as special cases of the following recursive equation:

(3.13) $$y_{n+1} = a_n y_n \qquad y_0 \text{ at } n = 0$$

The solution to this more general case can be derived as follows:

$$y_1 = a_0 y_0$$
$$y_2 = a_1 y_1 = a_1 a_0 y_0$$
$$y_3 = a_2 y_2 = a_2 a_1 a_0 y_0$$
$$\vdots$$
$$y_n = a_{n-1} a_{n-2} \ldots a_1 a_0 y_0$$

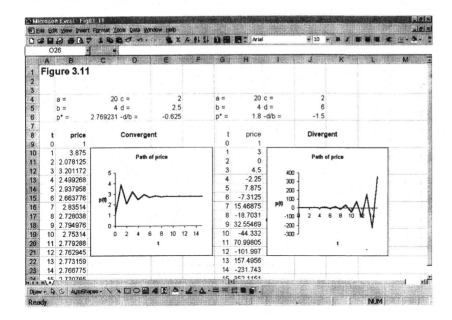

Figure 3.11.

or

$$y_n = \left[\prod_{k=0}^{n-1} a_k\right] y_0 \qquad (3.14)$$

Hence, if $a_k = a$ for all k, then

$$\left[\prod_{k=0}^{n-1} a_k\right] = a^n \qquad \text{and} \qquad y_n = a^n y_0$$

Consider an even more general case: that of the nonhomogeneous first-order equation given by

$$y_{n+1} = a_n y_n + g_n \qquad a_0, g_0, y_0 \text{ at } n = 0 \qquad (3.15)$$

Then

$$\begin{aligned}
y_1 &= a_0 y_0 + g_0 \\
y_2 &= a_1 y_1 + g_1 = a_1(a_0 y_0 + g_0) + g_1 \\
&= a_1 a_0 y_0 + a_1 g_0 + g_1 \\
y_3 &= a_2 y_2 + g_2 = a_2(a_1 a_0 y_0 + a_1 g_0 + g_1) + g_2 \\
&= a_2 a_1 a_0 y_0 + a_2 a_1 g_0 + a_2 g_1 + g_2 \\
&\vdots
\end{aligned}$$

with solution for y_n of

$$y_n = \left[\prod_{k=0}^{n-1} a_k\right] y_0 + \sum_{i=0}^{n-1} \left[\prod_{k=i+1}^{n-1} a_k\right] g_i \qquad (3.16)$$

We can consider two special cases:

$$Case\ A : a_k = a \text{ for all } k$$
$$Case\ B : a_k = a \quad \text{and} \quad g_k = b \text{ for all } k$$

Case A $a_k = a$ *for all k*
In this case we have

$$y_{n+1} = ay_n + g_n \qquad g_0,\ y_0 \text{ at } n = 0$$

Using the general result above, then

$$\prod_{k=0}^{n-1} a_k = a^n \qquad \text{and} \qquad \prod_{k=i+1}^{n-1} a_k = a^{n-i-1}$$

Hence,

(3.17)
$$y_n = a^n y_0 + \sum_{i=0}^{n-1} a^{n-i-1} g_i$$

Case B $a_k = a$ *and* $g_k = b$ *for all k*
In this case we have

$$y_{n+1} = ay_n + b \qquad y_0 \text{ at } n = 0$$

We already know that if $a_k = a$ for all k then

$$\prod_{k=0}^{n-1} a_k = a^n \qquad \text{and} \qquad \prod_{k=i+1}^{n-1} a_k = a^{n-i-1}$$

and so

$$y_n = a^n y_0 + b \sum_{i=0}^{n-1} a^{n-i-1}$$

This case itself, however, can be divided into two sub-categories: (i) where $a = 1$ and (ii) where $a \neq 1$.

Case (i) $a = 1$
If $a = 1$ then

$$\sum_{i=0}^{n-1} a^{n-i-1} = n$$

and so

$$y_n = y_0 + bn$$

Case (ii) $a \neq 1$
Let

$$S = \sum_{i=0}^{n-1} a^{n-i-1}$$

then

$$aS = \sum_{i=0}^{n-1} a^{n-i}$$

$$S - aS = (1 - a)S = 1 - a^n$$

$$S = \frac{1 - a^n}{1 - a}$$

and

$$y_n = a^n y_0 + b \left(\frac{1 - a^n}{1 - a} \right)$$

Combining these two we can summarise case B as follows

$$y_n = \begin{cases} y_0 + bn & a = 1 \\ a^n y_0 + b \left(\dfrac{1 - a^n}{1 - a} \right) & a \neq 1 \end{cases} \tag{3.18}$$

These particular formulas are useful in dealing with recursive equations in the area of finance. We take these up in the exercises.

These special cases can be derived immediately using either *Mathematica* or *Maple* with the following input instructions[5]:

Mathematica
```
RSolve[{y[n+1]==y[n]+b, y[0]==y0},y[n],n]
RSolve[{y[n+1]==a y[n]+b, y[0]==y0},y[n],n]
```
Maple
```
rsolve({y(n+1)=y(n)+b, y(0)=y0},y(n));
rsolve({y(n+1)=a*y(n)+b, y(0)=y0},y(n));
```

3.6   Compound interest

If an amount A is compounded annually at a market interest rate of r for a given number of years, t, then the payment received at time t, P_t, is given by

$$P_t = A(1 + r)^t$$

On the other hand, if it is compounded m times each year, then the payment received is

$$P_t = A \left(1 + \frac{r}{m} \right)^{mt}$$

If compounding is done more frequently over the year, then the amount received is larger. The actual interest rate being paid, once allowance is made for the compounding, is called the **effective interest rate**, which we denote re. The relationship between re and (r, m) is developed as follows

$$A(1 + re) = A \left(1 + \frac{r}{m} \right)^m$$

$$\text{i.e. } re = \left(1 + \frac{r}{m} \right)^m - 1$$

It follows that $re \geq r$.

---

[5] See section 3.13 on solving recursive equations with *Mathematica* and *Maple*.

Figure 3.12.

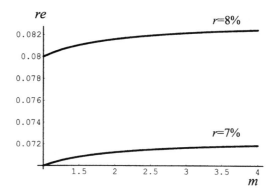

Example 3.6

A bank is offering a savings account paying 7% interest per annum, compounded quarterly. What is the effective interest rate?

$$re = \left(1 + \frac{0.07}{4}\right)^4 - 1 = 0.072$$

or 7.2%.

If we assume that m is a continuous variable, then given an interest rate of say, 7%, we can graph the relationship between re and m. A higher market interest rate leads to a curve wholly above that of the lower interest rate, as shown in figure 3.12.

Returning to the compounding result, if an amount is compounded at an annual interest rate r, then at time t we have the relationship $Y_t = (1 + r)Y_{t-1}$. If we generalise this further and assume an additional deposit (or withdrawal) in each period, a_t, then the resulting recursive equation is

$$Y_t = (1 + r)Y_{t-1} + a_{t-1}$$

Or more generally, we have the recursive equation

$$Y_t = a_{t-1} + bY_{t-1}$$

Many problems reduce to this kind of relationship. For example, population of a species at time t may be proportional to its size in the previous period, but predation may take place each period. Or, human populations may grow proportionally but immigration and emigration occurs in each period.

Solving the recursive equation can be achieved by iteration. Let the initial values be Y_0 and a_0, respectively, then

$$Y_1 = a_0 + bY_0$$
$$Y_2 = a_1 + bY_1 = a_1 + b(a_0 + bY_0) = a_1 + ba_0 + b^2 Y_0$$
$$Y_3 = a_2 + bY_2 = a_2 + b(a_1 + ba_0 + b^2 Y_0) = a_2 + ba_1 + b^2 a_0 + b^3 Y_0$$
$$Y_4 = a_3 + bY_3 = a_3 + b(a_2 + ba_1 + b^2 a_0 + b^3 Y_0)$$
$$= a_3 + ba_2 + b^2 a_1 + b^3 a_0 + b^4 Y_0$$

and so on. The general result emerging is

$$Y_t = a_{t-1} + ba_{t-2} + b^2 a_{t-3} + \cdots + b^{t-1} a_0 + b^t Y_0$$

or

$$Y_t = \sum_{k=0}^{t-1} b^{t-1-k} a_k + b^t Y_0$$

Having derived the general result two cases are of interest. The first is where $a_k = a$ for all k; the second is where $a_k = a$ and $b = 1$ for all k.

Case (i) $a_k = a$ for all k

In this case we have

$$Y_t = a + bY_{t-1}$$

with the general result

$$Y_t = a \sum_{k=0}^{t-1} b^{t-1-k} + b^t Y_0$$

or

$$Y_t = a \left(\frac{1 - b^t}{1 - b} \right) + b^t Y_0$$

It is useful for the economist to see this result from a different perspective. In equilibrium $Y_t = \bar{Y}$ for all t. So

$$\bar{Y} = a + b\bar{Y}$$

$$\bar{Y} = \frac{a}{1 - b}$$

Re-arranging the result for case (i), we have

$$Y_t = \frac{a}{1 - b} - \frac{ab^t}{1 - b} + b^t Y_0$$

$$Y_t = b^t \left(Y_0 - \frac{a}{1 - b} \right) + \frac{a}{1 - b}$$

It is clear from this result that if $|b| < 1$ then the series converges on the equilibrium. If $0 < b < 1$, there is steady convergence; while if $-1 < b < 0$, the convergence oscillates. If $|b| > 1$, the system is unstable.

Case (ii) $a_k = a$ and $b = 1$ for all k

In this case

$$Y_t = a + Y_{t-1}$$

with result

$$Y_t = a \sum_{k=0}^{t-1} (1)^{t-1-k} + Y_0$$

i.e.

$$Y_t = at + Y_0$$

Example 3.7

An investor makes an initial deposit of £10,000 and an additional £250 each year. The market interest rate is 5% per annum. What are his accumulated savings after five years? For this problem, $Y_0 = £10,000$, $a_k = £250$ for all k and $b = (1 + r) = 1.05$. Hence

$$Y_5 = 250 \left(\frac{1 - (1.05)^5}{1 - 1.05} \right) + (1.05)^5 (10000) = £14,144.20$$

3.7   Discounting, present value and internal rates of return

Since the future payment when interest is compounded is $P_t = P_0(1 + r)^t$, then it follows that the **present value**, PV, of an amount P_t received in the future is

$$PV = \frac{P_t}{(1 + r)^t}$$

and r is now referred to as the *discount rate*.

   Consider an annuity. An annuity consists of a series of payments of an amount A made at constant intervals of time for n periods. Each payment receives interest from the date it is made until the end of the nth-period. The last payment receives no interest. The future value, FV, is then

$$FV = A(1 + r)^{n-1} + A(1 + r)^{n-2} + \cdots + (1 + r)A + A$$

Utilising a software package, the solution is readily found to be

$$FV = A \left[\frac{(1 + r)^n - 1}{r} \right]$$

On the other hand, the present value of an annuity requires each future payment to be discounted by the appropriate discount factor. Thus the payment A received at the end of the first period is worth $A/(1 + r)$ today, while a payment A at the end of the second period is worth $A/(1 + r)^2$ today. So the present value of the annuity is

$$PV = \frac{A}{(1 + r)} + \frac{A}{(1 + r)^2} + \cdots + \frac{A}{(1 + r)^{n-1}} + \frac{A}{(1 + r)^n}$$

with solution

$$PV = A \left[\frac{1 - (1 + r)^{-n}}{r} \right]$$

Example 3.8

£1,000 is deposited at the end of each year in a savings account that earns 6.5% interest compounded annually.

(a)   At the end of ten years, how much is the account worth?
(b)   What is the present value of the payments stream?

(a) $\quad FV = A\left[\dfrac{(1+r)^n - 1}{r}\right] = 1000\left[\dfrac{(1+0.065)^{10} - 1}{0.065}\right] = £13494.40$

(b) $\quad PV = A\left[\dfrac{1 - (1+r)^{-n}}{r}\right] = 1000\left[\dfrac{1 - (1+0.065)^{-10}}{0.065}\right] = £7188.83$

Discounting is readily used in investment appraisal and cost–benefit analysis. Suppose B_t and C_t denote the benefits and costs, respectively, at time t. Then the present value of such flows are $B_t/(1+r)^t$ and $C_t/(1+r)^t$, respectively. It follows, then, that the **net present value**, NPV, of a project with financial flows over n-periods is

$$NPV = \sum_{t=0}^{n} \frac{B_t}{(1+r)^t} - \sum_{t=0}^{n} \frac{C_t}{(1+r)^t} = \sum_{t=0}^{n} \frac{B_t - C_t}{(1+r)^t}$$

Notice that for $t = 0$ the benefits B_0 and the costs C_0 involve no discounting. In many projects no benefits accrue in early years only costs. If $NPV > 0$ then a project (or investment) should be undertaken.

Example 3.9

Bramwell plc is considering buying a new welding machine to increase its output. The machine would cost £40,000 but would lead to increased revenue of £7,500 each year for the next ten years. Half way through the machine's lifespan, in year 5, there is a one-off maintenance expense of £5,000. Bramwell plc consider that the appropriate discount rate is 8%. Should they buy the machine?

$$NPV = -40000 + \sum_{t=1}^{10} \frac{7500}{(1+r)^t} - \frac{5000}{(1+r)^5}$$

The second term is simply the present value of an annuity of £7,500 received for ten years and discounted at 8%. The present value of this is

$$PV = A\left[\frac{1 - (1+r)^{-n}}{r}\right] = 7500\left[\frac{1 - (1+0.08)^{-10}}{0.08}\right]$$

Hence

$$NPV = -40000 + 7500\left[\frac{1 - (1.08)^{-10}}{0.08}\right] - \frac{5000}{(1.08)^5} = £6922.69$$

Since $NPV > 0$, then Bramwell plc should go ahead with the investment.

Net present value is just one method for determining projects. One difficulty, as the above example illustrates, is that it is necessary to make an assumption about the appropriate discount rate. Since there is often uncertainty about this, computations are often carried out for different discount rates. An alternative is to use the **internal rate of return** (*IRR*). The internal rate of return is the discount rate that leads to a zero net present value. Thus, the internal rate of return is the value of r satisfying

$$\sum_{t=0}^{n} \frac{B_t - C_t}{(1+r)^t} = 0$$

Although software programmes can readily solve for the internal rate of return, there is a problem in the choice of r.

$$\sum_{t=0}^{n} \frac{B_t - C_t}{(1+r)^t}$$

is a polynomial with the highest power of n, and so theoretically there are n possible roots to this equation. Of course, we can rule out negative values and complex values. For example, the choice problem for Bramwell plc involves r^{10} as the highest term and so there are ten possible solutions to the equation

$$-40000 + 7500 \left[\frac{1 - (1+r)^{-10}}{r} \right] - \frac{5000}{(1+r)^5} = 0$$

Eight solutions, however, are complex and another is negative. This leaves only one positive real-valued solution, namely $r = 0.1172$ or $r = 11.72\%$. Since such a return is well above the typical market interest rate, then the investment should be undertaken. The point is, however, that multiple positive real-valued solutions are possible.

3.8   Solving second-order difference equations

3.8.1   *Homogeneous*

Consider the following general second-order linear homogeneous equation

(3.19) $y_{n+2} = ay_{n+1} + by_n$

Similar to the solution for a first-order linear homogeneous equation, we can suppose the solution takes the form

$$y_n = c_1 r^n + c_2 s^n$$

for some constants r and s and where c_1 and c_2 depend on the initial conditions y_0 and y_1. If this indeed is correct, then

$$c_1 r^{n+2} + c_2 s^{n+2} = a(c_1 r^{n+1} + c_2 s^{n+1}) + b(c_1 r^n + c_2 s^n)$$

Re-arranging and factorising, we obtain

$$c_1 r^n (r^2 - ar - b) + c_2 s^n (s^2 - as - b) = 0$$

So long as r and s are chosen to be the solution values to the general quadratic equation

$$x^2 - ax - b = 0$$

i.e. $x = r$ and $x = s$, where $r \neq s$, then $y_n = c_1 r^n + c_2 s^n$ is a solution to the dynamic system. This quadratic equation is referred to as the *characteristic equation* of the dynamical system. If $r > s$, then we call $y_1 = c_1 r^n$ the *dominant solution* and r the dominant characteristic root.

Furthermore, given we have obtained the solution values r and s, and given the initial conditions, y_0 and y_1, then we can solve for the two unknown coefficients,

c_1 and c_2. Since

$$y_0 = c_1 r^0 + c_2 s^0 = c_1 + c_2$$
$$y_1 = c_1 r + c_2 s$$

then

$$c_1 = \frac{y_1 - sy_0}{r - s} \quad \text{and} \quad c_2 = \frac{y_1 - ry_0}{s - r}$$

The solution values r and s to the characteristic equation of the dynamic system are the solutions to a quadratic. As in all quadratics, three possibilities can occur:

(i)   distinct real roots
(ii)   identical real roots
(iii)   complex conjugate roots

Since the solution values to the quadratic equation are

$$r, s = \frac{-a \pm \sqrt{a^2 + 4b}}{2}$$

then we have distinct real roots if $a^2 > -4b$, identical roots if $a^2 = -4b$, and complex conjugate roots if $a^2 < -4b$.

Example 3.10 (real distinct roots)

Suppose

$$y_{n+2} = y_{n+1} + 2y_n$$

The characteristic equation is given by

$$x^2 - x - 2 = 0$$
$$\text{i.e. } (x - 2)(x + 1) = 0$$

Hence, we have two real distinct roots, $x = 2$ and $x = -1$, and the general solution is

$$y_n = c_1(2)^n + c_2(-1)^n$$

If we know $y_0 = 5$ and $y_1 = 4$, then

$$c_1 = \frac{y_1 - sy_0}{r - s} = \frac{4 - (-1)(5)}{2 - (-1)} = 3$$

$$c_2 = \frac{y_1 - ry_0}{s - r} = \frac{4 - (2)(5)}{(-1) - 2} = 2$$

Hence, the particular solution satisfying these initial conditions is given by

$$y_n = 3(2)^n + 2(-1)^n$$

As figure 3.13 makes clear, this is an explosive system that tends to infinity over time.

The limiting behaviour of the general solution $y_n = c_1 r^n + c_2 s^n$ is determined by the behaviour of the dominant solution. If, for example, r is the dominant

Figure 3.13.

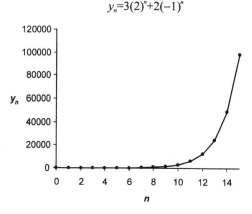

$$y_n = 3(2)^n + 2(-1)^n$$

characteristic root and $|r| > |s|$, then

$$y_n = r^n \left[c_1 + c_2 \left(\frac{s}{r} \right)^n \right]$$

Since $|s/r| < 1$, then $(s/r)^n \to 0$ as $n \to \infty$. Therefore,

$$\lim_{n \to \infty} y_n = \lim_{n \to \infty} c_1 r^n$$

There are six different situations that can arise depending on the value of r.

(1) $r > 1$, then the sequence $\{c_1 r^n\}$ diverges to infinity and the system is unstable

(2) $r = 1$, then the sequence $\{c_1 r^n\}$ is a constant sequence

(3) $0 \leq r < 1$, then the sequence $\{c_1 r^n\}$ is monotonically decreasing to zero and the system is stable

(4) $-1 < r \leq 0$, then the sequence $\{c_1 r^n\}$ is oscillating around zero and converging on zero, so the system is stable

(5) $r = -1$, then the sequence $\{c_1 r^n\}$ is oscillating between two values

(6) $r < -1$, then the sequence $\{c_1 r^n\}$ is oscillating but increasing in magnitude.

Identical real roots

If the roots are real and equal, i.e., $r = s$, then the solution becomes

$$y_n = (c_1 + c_2)r^n = c_3 r^n$$

But if $c_3 r^n$ is a solution, then so is $c_4 n r^n$ (see Chiang 1992, p. 580 or Goldberg 1961, p. 136 and exercise 14), hence the general solution when the roots are equal is given by

$$y_n = c_3 r^n + c_4 n r^n$$

We can now solve for c_3 and c_4 given the two initial conditions y_0 and y_1

$$y_0 = c_3 r^0 + c_4(0)r^0 = c_3$$
$$y_1 = c_3 r + c_4(1)r = (c_3 + c_4)r$$

Hence

$$c_3 = y_0$$

$$c_4 = \frac{y_1}{r} - c_3 = \left(\frac{y_1 - ry_0}{r}\right)$$

Therefore, the general solution satisfying the two initial conditions, is

$$y_n = y_0 r^n + \left(\frac{y_1 - ry_0}{r}\right) nr^n$$

Example 3.11 (equal real roots)

Let

$$y_{n+2} = 4y_{n+1} - 4y_n$$

This has the characteristic equation

$$x^2 - 4x + 4 = (x - 2)^2 = 0$$

Hence, $r = 2$.

$$y_n = c_3(2)^n + c_4 n(2)^n$$

Suppose $y_0 = 6$ and $y_1 = 4$, then

$$c_3 = y_0 = 6$$

$$c_4 = \frac{y_1 - ry_0}{r} = \frac{4 - (2)(6)}{2} = -4$$

Hence, the particular solution is

$$y_n = 6(2)^n - 4n(2)^n$$

which tends to minus infinity as n increases, as shown in figure 3.14.
In the case of the general solution $y_n = (c_3 + c_4 n)r^n$

(1)   If $|r| \geq 1$, then y_n diverges monotonically
(2)   If $r \leq -1$, then the solution oscillates
(3)   If $|r| < 1$, then the solution converges to zero

$$y_n = 6(2^n) - 4n(2^n)$$

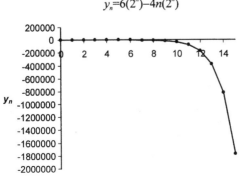

Figure 3.14.

Complex conjugate roots[6]

If the roots are complex conjugate then $r = \alpha + \beta i$ and $s = \alpha - \beta i$ and

$$R^n \cos(\beta t) \quad \text{and} \quad R^n \sin(\beta t)$$

are solutions and the general solution is

$$y_n = c_1 R^n \cos(\theta n) + c_2 R^n \sin(\theta n)$$

where

$$R = \sqrt{\alpha^2 + \beta^2},$$

$$\cos \theta = \frac{\alpha}{R} \quad \text{and} \quad \sin \theta = \frac{\beta}{R}$$

$$\text{or} \quad \tan \theta = \frac{\sin \theta}{\cos \theta} = \frac{\beta}{\alpha}$$

Example 3.12 (complex conjugate)

Consider

$$y_{n+2} - 4y_{n+1} + 16y_n = 0$$

The characteristic equation is

$$x^2 - 4x + 16 = 0$$

with roots

$$r, s = \frac{4 \pm \sqrt{16 - 64}}{2} = 2 \pm \left(\frac{\sqrt{48}}{2} \right) i$$

i.e.

$$r = 2 + \tfrac{1}{2}\sqrt{48}i \qquad \alpha = 2$$
$$s = 2 - \tfrac{1}{2}\sqrt{48}i \qquad \beta = \tfrac{1}{2}\sqrt{48}$$

and polar coordinates

$$R = \sqrt{2^2 + (\tfrac{1}{2}\sqrt{48})^2} = \sqrt{4 + 12} = 4$$

$$\cos \theta = \frac{\alpha}{R} = \frac{2}{4} = \frac{1}{2} \quad \text{and} \quad \sin \theta = \frac{\beta}{R} = \frac{\tfrac{1}{2}\sqrt{48}}{4} = \frac{\sqrt{3}}{2}$$

Implying $\theta = \pi/3$. Hence

$$y_n = c_1 4^n \cos\left(\frac{n\pi}{3} \right) + c_2 4^n \sin\left(\frac{n\pi}{3} \right)$$

---

[6] In this section the complex roots are expressed in polar coordinate form (see Allen 1965 or Chiang 1984).

Given y_0 and y_1, it is possible to solve for c_1 and c_2. Specifically

$$c_1 = y_0$$

$$c_2 = \frac{y_1 - y_0 4 \cos\left(\dfrac{\pi}{3}\right)}{4 \sin\left(\dfrac{\pi}{3}\right)}$$

If r and s are complex conjugate, then y_n oscillates because the cosine function oscillates. There are, however, three different types of oscillation:

(1) $R > 1$. In this instance the characteristic roots r and s lie *outside* the unit circle, shown in figure 3.15(a). Hence y_n is oscillating, but increasing in magnitude. The system is unstable.

(2) $R = 1$. In this instance the characteristic roots r and s lie *on* the unit circle, and the system oscillates with a constant magnitude, figure 3.15(b).

(3) $R < 1$. In this instance the characteristic roots r and s lie *inside* the unit circle and the system oscillates but converges to zero as $n \to \infty$, figure 3.15(c). The system is stable.

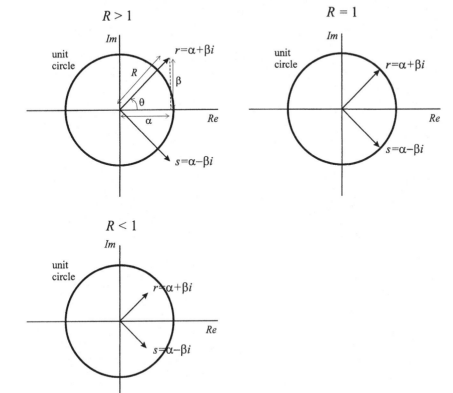

Figure 3.15.

3.8.2   *Nonhomogeneous*

A constant coefficient nonhomogeneous second-order difference equation takes the general form

(3.20)
$$y_{n+2} + ay_{n+1} + by_n = g(n)$$

If $g(n) = c$, a constant, then

$$y_{n+2} + ay_{n+1} + by_n = c$$

which is the form we shall consider here. As with second-order differential equations considered in chapter 2, we can break the solution down into a *complementary* component, y_c, and a *particular* component, y_p, i.e., the general solution y_n, can be expressed

$$y_n = y_c + y_p$$

The complementary component is the solution to the homogeneous part of the recursive equation, i.e., y_c is the solution to

$$y_{n+2} + ay_{n+1} + by_n = 0$$

which we have already outlined in the previous section.

Since $y_n = y^*$ is a fixed point for all n, then this will satisfy the particular solution. Thus

$$y^* + ay^* + by^* = c$$
$$y^* = \frac{c}{1 + a + b}$$

so long as $1 + a + b \neq 0$.

Example 3.13

$$y_{n+2} - 4y_{n+1} + 16y_n = 26$$

Then

$$y^* - 4y^* + 16y^* = 26$$
$$y^* = 2$$

Hence, $y_p = 2$. The general solution is, then

$$y_n = c_1 4^n \cos\left(\frac{\pi n}{3}\right) + c_2 4^n \left(\frac{\pi n}{3}\right) + 2$$

Example 3.14

$$y_{n+2} - 5y_{n+1} + 4y_n = 4$$

In this example, $1 + a + b = 0$ and so it is not possible to use y^* as a solution. In this instance we try a moving fixed point, ny^*. Thus

$$(n + 2)y^* - 5(n + 1)y^* + 4ny^* = 4$$

$$-3y^* = 4$$

$$y^* = -\frac{4}{3}$$

$$\therefore ny^* = \frac{-4n}{3}$$

For the complementary component we need to solve the homogeneous equation

$$y_{n+2} - 5y_{n+1} + 4y_n = 0$$

whose characteristic equation is

$$x^2 - 5x + 4 = 0$$

with solutions

$$r, s = \frac{5 \pm \sqrt{25 - 16}}{2} = \frac{5 \pm 3}{2}$$

i.e. $r = 4$ and $s = 1$. Hence

$$y_n = c_1 4^n + c_2 1^n - (4n/3) = c_1 4^n + c_2 - (4n/3)$$

Example 3.15

$$y_{n+2} + y_{n+1} - 2y_n = 12 \qquad y_0 = 4 \qquad \text{and} \qquad y_1 = 5$$

The particular solution cannot be solved for y^* (since $1 + a + b = 0$) and so we employ ny^*

$$(n + 2)y^* + (n + 1)y^* - 2ny^* = 12$$

$$(n + 2 + n + 1 - 2n)y^* = 12$$

$$y^* = \frac{12}{3} = 4$$

Hence, $ny^* = 4n = y_p$.

The complementary component is derived by solving the characteristic equation

$$x^2 + x - 2 = 0$$

$$(x + 2)(x - 1) = 0$$

giving $r = 1$ and $s = -2$. Giving the complementary component of

$$y_c = c_1 r^n + c_2 s^n$$

$$= c_1 (1)^n + c_2 (-2)^n$$

$$= c_1 + c_2 (-2)^n$$

Hence, the general solution is

$$y_n = y_c + y_p = c_1 + c_2 (-2)^n + 4n$$

Given $y_0 = 4$ and $y_1 = 5$, then

$$y_0 = c_1 + c_2 = 4$$
$$y_1 = c_1 - 2c_2 + 4 = 5$$

with solutions

$$c_1 = 3 \quad \text{and} \quad c_2 = 1$$

Hence, the general solution satisfying the given conditions is

$$y_n = 3 + (-2)^n + 4n$$

For the nonhomogeneous second-order linear difference equation

$$y_{n+2} + ay_{n+1} + by_n = c$$

$y_n \to y^*$, where y^* is the fixed point, if and only if the complementary solution, y_c, tends to zero as n tends to infinity; while y_n will oscillate about y^* if and only if the complementary solution oscillates about zero. Since the complementary solution is the solution to the homogeneous part, we have already indicated the stability of these in section 3.8.1.

In the case of the second-order linear difference equations, both homogeneous and nonhomogeneous, it is possible to have explicit criteria on the parameters a and b for stability. These are contained in the following theorem (Elaydi 1996, pp. 87–8).

THEOREM 3.3
The conditions

$$1 + a + b > 0, \qquad 1 - a + b > 0, \qquad 1 - b > 0$$

are necessary and sufficient for the equilibrium point of both homogeneous and nonhomogeneous second-order difference equations to be asymptotically stable.

3.9   The logistic equation: discrete version

Suppose

(3.21)
$$\Delta y_{t+1} = ay_t - by_t^2$$

where b is the competition coefficient.[7] Then

$$y_{t+1} = (1 + a)y_t - by_t^2$$

This is a nonlinear recursive equation and cannot be solved analytically as it stands. However, with a slight change we can solve the model.[8] Let

$$y_t^2 \simeq y_t y_{t+1}$$

---

[7] We shall discuss this coefficient more fully in chapter 14.
[8] This approximate solution is taken from Griffiths and Oldknow (1993, p. 16).

then

$$y_{t+1} = (1+a)y_t - by_t y_{t+1}$$

Solving we obtain

$$y_{t+1} = \frac{(1+a)y_t}{1+by_t}$$

This can be transformed by dividing both sides by $y_{t+1}y_t$

$$\frac{1}{y_t} = \frac{1}{y_{t+1}}\frac{1+a}{1+by_t}$$

i.e.

$$\frac{1}{y_{t+1}} = \frac{1+by_t}{(1+a)y_t} = \frac{1}{(1+a)}\frac{1}{y_t} + \frac{b}{1+a}$$

Let $x_t = 1/y_t$, then

$$x_{t+1} = \left(\frac{1}{1+a}\right)x_t + \frac{b}{1+a}$$

In equilibrium $x_{t+1} = x_t = \ldots = x^*$, hence

$$x^* = \left(\frac{1}{1+a}\right)x^* + \frac{b}{1+a}$$

Solving for x^* we obtain the fixed point

$$x^* = \frac{b}{a}$$

Subtracting the equilibrium equation from the recursive equation we obtain

$$x_{t+1} - x^* = \frac{1}{1+a}(x_t - x^*)$$

which has the general solution

$$x_t - x^* = \left(\frac{1}{1+a}\right)^t (x_0 - x^*)$$

or

$$x_t = \frac{b}{a} + (1+a)^{-t}\left(x_0 - \frac{b}{a}\right)$$

Substituting back $x_t = 1/y_t$ for all t

$$\frac{1}{y_t} = \frac{b}{a} + (1+a)^{-t}\left(\frac{1}{y_0} - \frac{b}{a}\right)$$

Hence,

$$y_t = \frac{1}{\left(\dfrac{b}{a}\right) + (1+a)^{-t}\left(\dfrac{1}{y_0} - \dfrac{b}{a}\right)}$$

or

$$y_t = \frac{ay_0}{by_0 + (1+a)^{-t}(a - by_0)} \tag{3.22}$$

Figure 3.16.

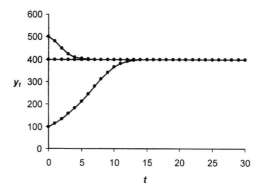

It is readily established that

$$\lim_{t \to \infty} y_t = \frac{a}{b}$$

Three typical plots are shown in figure 3.16, for $y_0 < a/b$, $y_0 = a/b$ and $y_0 > a/b$.
Return to the original formulation

$$y_{t+1} - y_t = ay_t - by_t^2$$

i.e.

$$y_{t+1} = (1+a)y_t - by_t^2$$

It is not possible to solve this nonlinear equation, although our approximation
is quite good (see exercise 6). But the equation has been much investigated by
mathematicians because of its possible chaotic behaviour.[9] In carrying out this
investigation it is normal to respecify the equation in its generic form

(3.23) $$x_{t+1} = \lambda x_t(1 - x_t)$$

It is this simple recursive formulation that is often employed for investigation
because it involves only a single parameter, λ.

The reader is encouraged to set up this equation on a spreadsheet, which is
very straightforward. If $\lambda = 3.2$ it is readily established that the series will, after
a sufficient time period, oscillate between two values: $a_1 = 0.799455$ and $a_2 =
0.513045$. This two-cycle is typical of the logistic equation for a certain range of λ.
To establish the range of λ is straightforward but algebraically tedious. Here we
shall give the gist of the solution, and leave appendices 3.1 and 3.2 to illustrate
how *Mathematica* and *Maple*, respectively, can be employed to solve the tedious
algebra.
Let

$$f(x) = \lambda x(1 - x)$$

then a two-cycle result will occur if

$$a = f(f(a))$$

---

[9] We shall investigate chaos in chapter 7.

where a is a fixed point. Hence

$$a = f[\lambda a(1-a)] = \lambda[\lambda a(1-a)][1 - \lambda a(1-a)]$$
$$= \lambda^2 a(1-a)[1 - \lambda a(1-a)]$$

It is at this point where *Mathematica* or *Maple* is used to solve this equation.

The range for a stable two-cycle is established by solving[10]

$$-1 < f'(a_1)f'(a_2) < 1$$

where a_1 and a_2 are the two relevant solutions. Since

$$f'(x) = \lambda(1-x) - \lambda x$$

then we can compute $f'(a_1)f'(a_2)$, which is a surprisingly simple equation of the form

$$4 + 2\lambda - \lambda^2$$

Hence, we have a stable two-cycle if

$$-1 < 4 + 2\lambda - \lambda^2 < 1$$

Discarding negative values for λ, we establish the range to be $3 < \lambda < 3.449$. Given we have already a_1 and a_2 solved for any particular value of λ, then we can find these two stable solutions for any λ in the range just established. Thus, for $\lambda = 3.2$ it is readily established using *Mathematica* or *Maple*, that $a_1 = 0.799455$ and $a_2 = 0.513045$, which are the same results as those established using a spreadsheet. For $\lambda < 3$ we have a single fixed point which is stable, which again can readily be established by means of the same spreadsheet. Finally, if $\lambda = 3.84$ the system converges on a three-cycle result with $a_1 = 0.149407$, $a_2 = 0.488044$ and $a_3 = 0.959447$ (see exercise 13).

Example 3.16

As an application of the logistic equation, different from its normal application in population models (see chapter 14), we turn to the issue of productivity growth discussed by Baumol and Wolff (1991). Let q_t denote the rate of growth of productivity *outside* of the research development industries; y_t the activity level of the information producing industry (the R&D industries); and p_t the price of information. The authors now assume three relationships:

(1)   Information contributes to productivity growth according to:

   (i) $y_{t+1} = a + by_t$

(2)   The price of information grows in proportion to productivity in the sector outside of the R&D industries, so:

   (ii) $\dfrac{p_{t+1} - p_t}{p_t} = vq_{t+1}$

---

[10] See theorem 3.2, p. 93 and Sandefur (1990, chapter 4).

(3)   Information demand has a constant elasticity, so:

(iii) $\dfrac{y_{t+1} - y_t}{y_t} = -\varepsilon \left(\dfrac{p_{t+1} - p_t}{p_t} \right)$

Substituting (i) into (ii) and the result into (iii), we obtain

$$\frac{y_{t+1} - y_t}{y_t} = -\varepsilon v(a + by_t)$$

Assume $\varepsilon v = k > 0$ then

$$\frac{y_{t+1} - y_t}{y_t} = -k(a + by_t)$$

i.e. $y_{t+1} = (1 - ak)y_t - kby_t^2$

which is no more than a logistic equation.
   In equilibrium $y_t = y^*$ for all t, hence

$$y^* = (1 - ak)y^* - kby^{*2}$$
$$y^*(ak + kby^*) = 0$$

and

$$y^* = 0 \text{ or } y^* = -\frac{a}{b}$$

   It is possible to consider the stability in the locality of the equilibrium. Since

$$y_{t+1} = (1 - ak)y_t - kby_t^2$$

let $y_{t+1} = y$ and $y_t = x$, then

$$y = (1 - ak)x - kbx^2 = f(x)$$
$$f'(x) = (1 - ak) - 2kbx$$

and

$$\left. \frac{dy}{dx} \right|_{y^* = -a/b} = \left. \frac{dy_{t+1}}{dy_t} \right|_{y^* = -a/b}$$
$$= (1 - ak) - 2kb(-a/b)$$
$$= 1 + ak$$

Hence the stability is very dependent on the sign/value of ak.
   Letting

$$y_{t+1} = Ay_t - By_t^2, \quad A = (1 - ak), B = kb$$

then using our earlier approximation (equation (3.22)) we have

$$y_t = \frac{Ay_0}{By_0 + (1 + A)^{-t}(A - By_0)}$$

i.e.

$$y_t = \frac{(1 - ak)y_0}{kby_0 + (2 - ak)^{-t}(1 - ak - kby_0)}$$

   Various paths for this solution are possible depending on the values of v and ε. For instance, if $v = 1$ and $\varepsilon \leq 2$, then $k = \varepsilon v \leq 2$, and if $a < 1$ then $ak < 2$, which is highly probable. Even with $ak < 1$, two possibilities arise:

(i)   if $a < 0$ then $ak < 2$
(ii)   if $0 < a < 1$ then $0 < ak < 2$

with various paths for y_t. This should not be surprising because we have already established that the discrete logistic equation has a variety of paths and possible cycles.

3.10   The multiplier–accelerator model

A good example that illustrates the use of recursive equations, and the variety of solution paths for income in an economy, is that of the multiplier–accelerator model first outlined by Samuelson (1939). Consumption is related to lagged income while investment at time t is related to the difference between income at time $t - 1$ and income at time $t - 2$.[11] In our formulation we shall treat government spending as constant, and equal to G in all periods. The model is then

$$C_t = a + bY_{t-1}$$
$$I_t = v(Y_{t-1} - Y_{t-2})$$
$$G_t = G \text{ for all } t$$
$$E_t = C_t + I_t + G_t$$
$$Y_t = E_t$$

which on straight substitution gives rise to the second-order nonhomogeneous recursive equation

$$Y_t - (b + v)Y_{t-1} + vY_{t-2} = a + G$$

The particular solution is found by letting $Y_t = Y^*$ for all t. Hence

$$Y^* - (b + v)Y^* + vY^* = a + G$$
$$\text{i.e. } Y^* = \frac{a + G}{1 - b}$$

In other words, in equilibrium, income equals the simple multiplier result.

The complementary result, Y_c, is obtained by solving the homogeneous component

$$Y_t - (b + v)Y_{t-1} + vY_{t-2} = 0$$

which has the characteristic equation

$$x^2 - (b + v)x + v = 0$$

with solutions

$$r, s = \frac{(b + v) \pm \sqrt{(b + v)^2 - 4v}}{2}$$

---

[11] Samuelson originally related investment to lagged consumption rather than lagged income.

Example 3.17

Determine the path of income for the equations

$$C_t = 50 + 0.75Y_{t-1}$$
$$I_t = 4(Y_{t-1} - Y_{t-2})$$
$$G = 100$$

The equilibrium is readily found to be $Y^* = 600$, which is the particular solution. The complementary solution is found by solving the quadratic

$$x^2 - (19/4)x + 4 = 0$$

i.e. $r = 3.6559$ and $s = 1.0941$

Since r and s are real and distinct, then the solution is

$$Y_t = c_1(3.6559)^t + c_2(1.0941)^t + 600$$

and c_1 and c_2 can be obtained if we know Y_0 and Y_1.

Of more interest is the fact that the model can give rise to a whole variety of paths for Y_t depending on the various parameter values for b and v. It is to this issue that we now turn.

From the roots of the characteristic equation given above we have three possible outcomes:

(i)   real distinct roots $(b + v)^2 > 4v$
(ii)   real equal roots $(b + v)^2 = 4v$
(iii)   complex roots $(b + v)^2 < 4v$

In determining the implications of these possible outcomes we use the two properties of roots

$$r + s = b + v$$
$$rs = v$$

It also follows using these two results that

$$(1 - r)(1 - s) = 1 - (r + s) + rs$$
$$= 1 - (b + v) + v$$
$$= 1 - b$$

and since $0 < b < 1$, then $0 < (1 - r)(1 - s) < 1$.

With both roots real and distinct, the general solution is

$$Y_t = c_1r^t + c_2s^t + Y^*$$

where r is the larger of the two roots. The path of Y_t is determined by the largest root, $r > s$. Since $b > 0$ and $v > 0$, then $rs = v > 0$ and so the roots must have the same sign. Furthermore, since $r + s = b + v > 0$, then both r and s must be positive. The path of income cannot oscillate. However, it will be damped if the largest root lies between zero and unity. Thus, a damped path occurs if $0 < s < r < 1$, which arises if $0 < b < 1$ and $v < 1$. Similarly, the path is explosive if the largest root exceeds unity, i.e., if $r > s > 1$, which implies $0 < b < 1$ and $rs = v > 1$.

With only one real root, r, the same conditions hold. Hence, in the case of real roots with $0 < b < 1$, the path of income is damped for $0 < v < 1$ and explosive for $v > 1$.

If the solution is complex conjugate then $r = \alpha + \beta i$ and $s = \alpha - \beta i$ and the general solution

$$Y_t = c_1 R^t \cos(t\theta) + c_2 R^t \sin(\theta t) + Y^*$$

exhibits oscillations, whose damped or explosive nature depends on the amplitude, R.

From our earlier analysis we know $R = \sqrt{\alpha^2 + \beta^2}$. But

$$\alpha = \frac{b+v}{2} \quad \text{and} \quad \beta = \frac{+\sqrt{4v - (b+v)^2}}{2}$$

Hence

$$R = \sqrt{\left(\frac{b+v}{2}\right)^2 + \frac{4v - (b+v)^2}{4}} = \sqrt{v}$$

For damped oscillations, $R < 1$, i.e., $v < 1$; while for explosive oscillations, $R > 1$, i.e., $v > 1$.

All cases are drawn in figure 3.17. The dividing line between real and complex roots is the curve $(b+v)^2 = 4v$, which was drawn using *Mathematica*'s **Implicit-Plot** command and annotated in *CorelDraw*. A similar result can be derived using *Maple*. The instructions for each software are:

Mathematica
```
<<Graphics`ImplicitPlot`
ImplicitPlot [(b+v)^2==4v, {v,0,5}, {b,0,1}]
```
Maple
```
with(plots):
implicitplot ((b+v)^2=4v, v=0..5, b=0..1);
```

On the other hand, the division between damped and explosive paths (given $0 < b < 1$) is determined by $v < 1$ and $v > 1$, respectively.

The accelerator model just outlined was utilised by Hicks (1950) in his discussion of the trade cycle. The major change was introducing an autonomous component to investment, I_0, which grows exogenously at a rate g. So at time t,

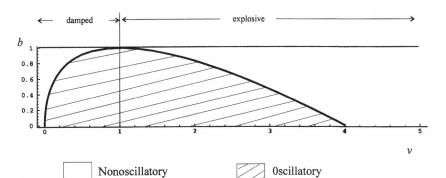

Figure 3.17.

the autonomous component of investment is $I_0(1 + g)^t$. Hicks' model can then be expressed

(3.24)
$$C_t = bY_{t-1}$$
$$I_t = I_0(1 + g)^t + v(Y_{t-1} - Y_{t-2})$$
$$Y_t = C_t + I_t$$

Substituting, we get

$$Y_t = bY_{t-1} + I_0(1 + g)^t + v(Y_{t-1} - Y_{t-2})$$
$$= (b + v)Y_{t-1} - vY_{t-2} + I_0(1 + g)^t$$

Since the model involves a moving equilibrium, then assume equilibrium income at time t is $\overline{Y}(1 + g)^t$ and at time $t - 1$ it is $\overline{Y}(1 + g)^{t-1}$, etc. Then in equilibrium

(3.25)
$$\overline{Y}(1 + g)^t - (b + v)\overline{Y}(1 + g)^{t-1} + v\overline{Y}(1 + g)^{t-2} = I_0(1 + g)^t$$

Dividing throughout by $(1 + g)^{t-2}$, then

$$\overline{Y}(1 + g)^2 - (b + v)\overline{Y}(1 + g) + v\overline{Y} = I_0(1 + g)^2$$

i.e.

(3.26)
$$\overline{Y} = \frac{I_0(1 + g)^2}{(1 + g)^2 - (b + v)(1 + g) + v}$$

Note that in the static case where $g = 0$, that this reduces down to the simple result $\overline{Y} = I_0/(1 - b)$.

The particular solution to equation (3.25) is then

$$Y_p = \overline{Y}(1 + g)^t = \frac{I_0(1 + g)^{t+2}}{(1 + g)^2 - (b + v)(1 + g) + v}$$

Since the homogeneous component is

$$\overline{Y}(1 + g)^t - (b + v)\overline{Y}(1 + g)^{t-1} + v\overline{Y}(1 + g)^{t-2} = 0$$

then the complementary function, Y_c is

$$Y_c = c_1 r^t + c_2 s^t$$

where

$$r, s = \frac{-(b + v) \pm \sqrt{(b + v)^2 - 4v}}{2}$$

The complete solution to equation (3.25) is then

$$Y_t = c_1 r^t + c_2 s^t + \frac{I_0(1 + g)^{t+2}}{(1 + g)^2 - (b + v)(1 + g) + v}$$

(3.27)
$$r = \frac{-(b + v) + \sqrt{(b + v)^2 - 4v}}{2}$$

$$s = \frac{-(b + v) - \sqrt{(b + v)^2 - 4v}}{2}$$

Once again the stability of (3.27) depends on the sign of $(b + v)^2 - 4v$, and the various possibilities we have already investigated.

3.11 Linear approximation to discrete nonlinear difference equations

In chapter 2, section 2.7, we considered linear approximations to nonlinear differential equations. In this section we do the same for nonlinear difference equations. A typical nonlinear difference equation for a one-period lag is

$$x_t - x_{t-1} = g(x_{t-1})$$
$$\Delta x_t = g(x_{t-1})$$

However, it is useful to consider the problem in the recursive form

$$x_t = g(x_{t-1}) + x_{t-1}$$
$$\text{i.e.} \quad x_t = f(x_{t-1})$$

because this allows a graphical representation. In this section we shall consider only *autonomous* nonlinear difference equations and so $f(x_{t-1})$ does not depend explicitly on time.

We have already established that a fixed point, an equilibrium point, exists if

$$x^* = f(x^*) \quad \text{for all } t$$

and that we can represent this on a diagram with x_{t-1} on the horizontal axis and x_t on the vertical axis. A fixed point occurs where $f(x_{t-1})$ cuts the 45°-line, as shown in figure 3.18, where we have three such fixed points. Since $f(x) = x^3$ then $y = f(y)$ and satisfies $y = y^3$ or $y(y^2 - 1) = 0$. This results in three values for y, $y = 0, -1$ and 1. It is to be noted that we have drawn $x_t = f(x_{t-1})$ as a continuous function, which we also assume to be differentiable.

We have also established that x^* is an attractor, a stable point, if there exists a number ε such that when $|x_0 - x^*| < \varepsilon$ then x_t approaches x^* in the limit, otherwise it is unstable. In the present illustration we can consider only local stability or

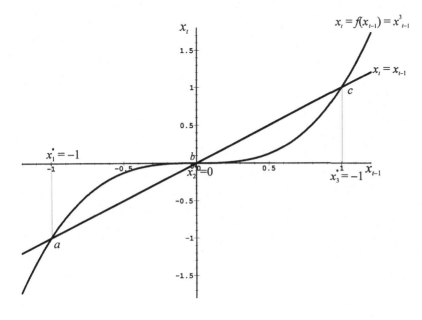

Figure 3.18.

instability, and so we take ε to be some 'small' distance either side of x_1^* or x_2^* or x_3^*.

In order to establish the stability properties of each of the equilibrium points, we take a Taylor expansion of f about x^*. Thus for a first-order linear approximation we have

$$f(x_{t-1}) = f(x^*) + f'(x^*)(x_{t-1} - x^*) + R_2(x_{t-1}x^*)$$

Ignoring the remainder term, then our linear approximation is

$$x_t = f(x^*) + f'(x^*)(x_{t-1} - x^*)$$

Furthermore, we have established that:

if $|f'(x^*)| < 1$ then x^* is an attractor or stable

if $|f'(x^*)| > 1$ then x^* is a repellor or unstable

if $|f'(x^*)| = 1$ then the stability of x^* is inconclusive.

Example 3.18

Consider

$$x_t = \sqrt{4x_{t-1} - 3}$$

This has two equilibria found by solving $x^2 - 4x + 3 = 0$, i.e., $x_1^* = 1$ and $x_2^* = 3$, and shown by the points a and b in figure 3.19.

The linear approximation is

$$x_t = f(x^*) + f'(x^*)(x_{t-1} - x^*)$$

Figure 3.19.

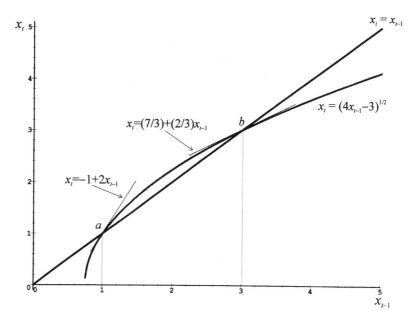

Take first $x_1^* = 1$, then

$$f(x_1^*) = 1$$
$$f'(x_1^*) = 2(4x_1^* - 3)^{-1/2} = 2$$

Hence

$$x_t = 1 + 2(x_{t-1} - 1) = -1 + 2x_{t-1}$$

which is unstable since $f'(x_1^*) = 2 > 1$.
  Next consider $x_2^* = 3$

$$f(x_2^*) = 3$$
$$f'(x_2^*) = 2(4x_2^* - 3)^{-1/2} = \frac{2}{3}$$

Hence

$$x_t = 3 + \left(\frac{2}{3}\right)(x_{t-1} - 3)$$
$$= 1 + \frac{2}{3}x_{t-1}$$

which is stable since $f'(x_2^*) = 2/3 < 1$.

Example 3.19

$$y_{t+1} = f(y_t) = 3.2y_t - 0.8y_t^2$$

Letting $y_t = y^*$ for all t we can readily establish two equilibria: $y_1^* = 0$ and $y_2^* = 2.75$. Considering the nonzero equilibrium, then

$$f(y_2^*) = 2.75$$
$$f'(y_2^*) = 3.2 - 1.6y_2^* = -1.2$$

Hence, the linear approximation is

$$y_{t+1} = 2.75 - 1.2(y_t - 2.75)$$
$$= 6.05 - 1.2y_t$$

The situation is shown in figure 3.20. The solution to this model is

$$y_{t+1} = 2.75 + (-1.2)^t(y_0 - 2.75)$$

which is oscillatory and explosive.
    Although the linear approximation leads to an explosive oscillatory equilibrium, the system in its nonlinear form exhibits a two-cycle with values 2.0522 and 3.1978.[12] What the linear approximation reveals is the movement *away* from $y^* = 2.75$. What it cannot show is that it will converge on a two-cycle. This example, therefore, illustrates the care required in interpreting the stability of nonlinear difference equations using their linear approximations.

---

[12] This can be established quite readily with a spreadsheet or as explained in appendices 3.1 and 3.2.

Figure 3.20.

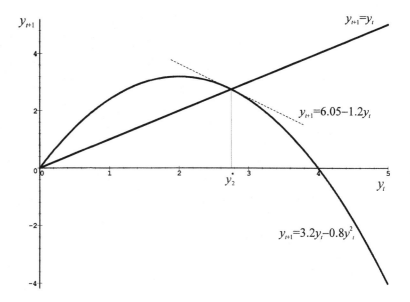

3.12 Solow growth model in discrete time

We have already established in chapter 2, example 2.9, that a homogeneous of degree one production function can be written $y = f(k)$, where y is the output/labour ratio and k is the capital/labour ratio. In discrete time we have[13]

$$y_t = f(k_{t-1})$$

where $y_t = Y_t/L_{t-1}$ and $k_{t-1} = K_{t-1}/L_{t-1}$. Given the same assumptions as example 2.9, savings is given by $S_t = sY_t$ and investment as $I_t = K_t - K_{t-1} + \delta K_{t-1}$, where δ is the rate of depreciation. Assuming saving is equal to investment in period t, then

$$sY_t = K_t - K_{t-1} + \delta K_{t-1} = K_t - (1 - \delta)K_{t-1}$$

Dividing both sides by L_{t-1}, then

$$\frac{sY_t}{L_{t-1}} = \frac{K_t}{L_{t-1}} - \frac{(1-\delta)K_{t-1}}{L_{t-1}}$$

$$= \frac{K_t}{L_t}\left(\frac{L_t}{L_{t-1}}\right) - (1-\delta)\frac{K_{t-1}}{L_{t-1}}$$

But if population is growing at a constant rate n, as is assumed in this model, then

$$\frac{L_t - L_{t-1}}{L_{t-1}} = n$$

i.e. $$\frac{L_t}{L_{t-1}} = 1 + n$$

---

[13] A little care is required in discrete models in terms of stocks and flows (see section 1.3). Capital and labour are stocks and are defined at the *end* of the period. Hence, K_t and L_t are capital and labour at the *end* of period t. Flows, such as income, investment and savings are flows *over a period of time*. Thus, Y_t, I_t and S_t are flows over period t.

Hence

$$sy_t = k_t(1+n) - (1-\delta)k_{t-1}$$

or

$$(1+n)k_t - (1-\delta)k_{t-1} = sf(k_{t-1})$$

which can be expressed

$$k_t = \frac{(1-\delta)k_{t-1} + sf(k_{t-1})}{1+n}$$

i.e. $k_t = h(k_{t-1})$

With constant returns to scale and assuming a Cobb–Douglas production function, then

$$y_t = f(k_{t-1}) = ak_{t-1}^\alpha \qquad a > 0, 0 < \alpha < 1$$

Example 3.20

This can be investigated by means of a spreadsheet, where we assume

$$a = 5, \qquad \alpha = 0.25, \qquad s = 0.1, \qquad n = 0.02, \qquad \delta = 0$$

and let $k_0 = 20$.

Alternatively, using a Taylor expansion about $k^* > 0$, then

$$k_t = h(k^*) + \frac{(1-\delta)(k_{t-1} - k^*) + \alpha sa(k^*)^{\alpha-1}(k_{t-1} - k^*)}{1+n}$$

$$= h(k^*) + \left[\frac{(1-\delta) + \alpha sa(k^*)^{\alpha-1}}{1+n}\right](k_{t-1} - k^*)$$

$$= k^* + \left[\frac{(1-\delta) + \alpha sa(k^*)^{\alpha-1}}{1+n}\right](k_{t-1} - k^*)$$

The situation is illustrated in figure 3.21.

3.13 Solving recursive equations with *Mathematica* and *Maple*

Both *Mathematica* and *Maple* come with a solver for solving recursive equations. **RSolve** in *Mathematica* and **rsolve** in *Maple*. They both operate in fundamentally the same way, and both can solve only linear recursive equations. While rsolve is built into the main kernel of *Maple*, the RSolve command of *Mathematica* is contained in the DiscreteMath package, and so must first be loaded with the following command.

```
Needs["DiscreteMath`RSolve`"]
```

(Note the back single-quote on RSolve.) These solvers are particularly useful for solving many difference equations. There are, however, some differences in the two

Figure 3.21.

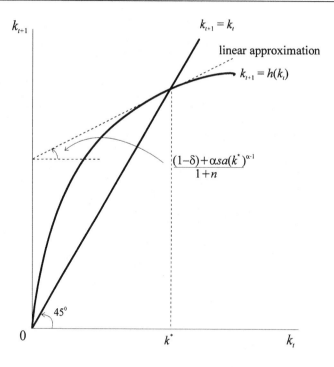

solvers. One difference is shown immediately by attempting to solve the recursive equation $x_t = ax_{t-1}$. The input and output from each programme is as follows.

> *Mathematica*
> ```
> RSolve[x[t]==ax[t-1],x[t],t]
> {{x[t]->a^{1+t}C[1]
> ```
> *Maple*
> ```
> rsolve(x(t)=a*x(t-1),x(t));
> x(0)a^t
> ```

While *Maple*'s output looks quite familiar, *Mathematica*'s looks decidedly odd. The reason for this is that *Mathematica* is solving for a 'future' variable. If the input had been

> ```
> RSolve[x[t+1]== ax[t],x[t],t]
> ```

Then the solution would be

> ```
> {{x[t]->a^tC[1]}}
> ```

which is what we would expect. Note also that while *Mathematica* leaves unsolved the unknown constant, which it labels C[1], *Maple* assumes the initial condition is $x(0)$ for $t = 0$. If attempting to solve $y_t = ay_{t-1} + by_{y-2}$ for example, then when using *Mathematica*, this should be thought of as $y_{t+2} = ay_{t+1} + by_t$ when solving for y_t. With this caveat in mind, we can explore the **RSolve** and **rsolve** commands in more detail.

When an initial condition is supplied the caveat just alluded to is of no consequence. Thus, if we wish to solve

$$x_t = ax_{t-1} \qquad x_0 = 2$$

then the instructions are:

> *Mathematica*
> `RSolve[{x[t]==ax[t-1],x[0]==2},x[t],t]`
> with result
> `{{x[t]->2aᵗ}}`
> *Maple*
> `rsolve({x(t)=a*x(t-1),x(0)=2},x(t));`
> with result
> `2aᵗ`

So no difference arises when initial conditions are supplied.

Using either the **RSolve** command of *Mathematica* or the **rsolve** command of *Maple*, we can readily check the following equations used in this chapter:

(i) $y_{t+1} = ay_t$

(ii) $p_{t+1} = (1 + k)p_t$

(iii) $Y_t = \left(\dfrac{v}{v + s}\right) Y_{t-1}$

(iv) $y_{t+1} = ay_t + c$

(v) $p_t = \left(\dfrac{a - c}{b}\right) - \left(\dfrac{d}{b}\right) p_{t-1}$

The following observations, however, should be borne in mind.

(1)   When using both *Mathematica* and *Maple* to solve the Harrod–Domar model, problem (iii), the recursive equation should be thought of as $Y_{t+1} = (v/(v + s))Y_t$ and solved accordingly.

(2)   On some occasions it is necessary to use additional commands, especially the **Simplify** command (*Mathematica*) or the **simplify** command (*Maple*).

(3)   *Mathematica* sometimes supplies 'If' conditions in the solutions, usually to do with $t \geq -1$ for example. This partly arises from the caveat mentioned above. Many of these can be avoided by writing the equations in terms of future lags, as in the case of the Harrod–Domar model.

(4)   A number of solutions involve complex output that is not always meaningful. This is especially true of general algebraic problems, such as solving $y_{t+2} = ay_{t+1} + by_t$.

(5)   Even when results have been simplified, it is not always possible to interpret the results in an economically meaningful way. For instance, in problem (v), it is impossible for a computer software package to 'know' that $(a - c)/(b + d)$ is the equilibrium price and that it is more economically meaningful to take the difference $(p_0 - (a - c)/(b + d))$. Economic insight is still a vital element.

Problems (i)–(v) are all recursive equations of the first-order. The same basic form is used to solve higher-order recursive equations. Given the recursive equation

$$y_{t+2} = ay_{t+1} + by_t$$

then this can be solved with the instructions:

Mathematica
```
RSolve[y[t+2]==ay[t+1]+by[t],y[t],t]
```
Maple
```
rsolve(y(t+2)=a*y(t+1)+b*y(t),y(t));
```

But because this is a general recursive equation the output in each case is quite involved. *Mathematica*'s output even more so, since it involves Binomial equations! What is revealed by the output is the need to know two initial conditions to solve such second-order recursive equations:

Solving $y_{t+2} = y_{t+1} + 2y_t$ with initial conditions $y(0) = 5$ and $y(1) = 4$, we have

Mathematica
```
RSolve[{y[t+2]==y[t+1]+2y[t],y[0]==5,y[1]==4},y[t],t]
```
with output
```
{{y[t]->2(-1)ᵗ + 3 2ᵗ}}
```
Maple
```
rsolve({r(t+2)=y(t+1)+2*y(t),y(0)=5,y(1)=4},y(t));
```
with output
```
2(-1)ᵗ + 3 2ᵗ
```

Furthermore, there is no difficulty with repeated roots, which occur in solving $y_{t+2} = 4y_{t+1} - 4y_t$. For initial conditions $y(0) = 6$ and $y(1) = 4$, we have solutions

Mathematica: $\{\{y[t]->-2^{1+t}\ (-3\ +\ 2t)\}\}$
Maple: $(-4t-4)2^t\ +\ 10\ 2^t$

Here we see that output in the two packages need not look the same, and often does not, yet both are identical; and identical to $6(2)^t - 4t(2)^t$ which we derived in the text.

Complex roots, on the other hand, are solved by giving solutions in their complex form rather than in trigonometric form.

The **RSolve** and **rsolve** commands, therefore, allow a check of the following equations in this chapter.

(i) $y_{t+2} = ay_{t+1} + by_t$
(ii) $y_{t+2} = y_{t+1} + 2y_t$ $y(0) = 5, y(1) = 4$
(iii) $y_{t+2} = 4y_{t+1} - 4y_t$
(iv) $y_{t+2} = 4y_{t+1} - 4y_t$ $y(0) = 6, y(1) = 4$
(v) $y_{t+2} = 4y_{t+1} - 16y_t$
(vi) $y_{t+2} = ay_{t+1} - by_t + c$
(vii) $y_{t+2} = 4y_{t+1} - 16y_t + 26$
(viii) $y_{t+2} = 5y_{t+1} - 4y_t + 4$
(ix) $y_{t+2} = -y_{t+1} + 2y_t + 12$ $y(0) = 4, y(1) = 5$
(x) $Y_t = (b + v)Y_{t-1} - vY_{t-2} + (a + G)$
(xi) $Y_t = 4.75Y_{t-1} + 4Y_{t-2} + 150$

Neither *Mathematica* nor *Maple*, however, can solve directly the logistic equation

$$y_{t+1} = \frac{(1+a)y_t}{1+by_t}$$

This is readily accomplished using the substitution provided in section 3.9.

It is worth pointing out that in the case of numerical examples, if all that is required is a plot of the sequence of points, then there is no need to solve the recursive (or difference) equation. We conclude this section, therefore, with simple instructions for doing this.[14]

The equation we use as an example is

$$p_t = 5.6 - 0.4p_{t-1} \qquad p_0 = 1$$

Mathematica
```
Clear[p];
p[0]=1;
p[t_]:=p[t]=5.6-0.4p[t-1];
data=Table[{t,p[t]},{t,0,20}];
ListPlot[data,PlotJoined->True,PlotRange->All];
```
Maple
```
t:='t':
p:='p':
p:=proc(t)option remember; 5.6-0.4*p(t-1)end:
p(0):=1:
data:=seq([t,p(t)],t=0..20)];
plot(data,colour=black,thickness=2);
```

Notice that the instructions in *Maple* require a 'small' procedural function. It is important in using this to include the option remember, which allows the programme to remember values already computed.

Higher-order recursive equations and nonlinear recursive equations are dealt with in exactly the same way. With discrete dynamic models, however, it is often easier and quicker to set the model up on a spreadsheet (see Shone 2001).

Appendix 3.1 Two-cycle logistic equation using *Mathematica*

THEOREM
The number a satisfies the equation

$$a = f(f(a))$$

if a is either a fixed point or is part of a two-cycle for the dynamical system

$$x_{n+1} = f(x_n)$$

---

[14] I am grateful to Johannes Ludsteck, Centre for European Economic Research (ZEW), for the method of computing tables from recursive equations in *Mathematica*, which is more efficient than the one I provided in the first edition.

Example (the generic logistic equation)

$$x_{n+1} = rx_n(1 - x_n)$$

```
In[1]:= f[x_]=rx(1-x)
```

$Out[1]= r (1-x) x$

```
In[2]:= eq1=f[f[x]]
```

$Out[2]= r^2 (1-x) x (1-r (1-x)x)$

```
In[3]:= sol1=Solve[eq1==x,x]
```

$Out[3]= \{\{x \to 0\}, \{x \to \frac{-1+r}{r}\}, \{x \to \frac{r+r^2-r\sqrt{-3-2r+r^2}}{2r^2}\},$

$\{x \to \frac{r+r^2+r\sqrt{-3-2r+r^2}}{2r^2}\}\}$

```
In[4]:= a1=sol1[[3, 1, 2]]
```

$Out[4]= \frac{r+r^2-r\sqrt{-3-2r+r^2}}{2r^2}$

```
In[5]:= a2=sol1[[4, 1, 2]]
```

$Out[5]= \frac{r+r^2+r\sqrt{-3-2r+r^2}}{2r^2}$

```
In[6]:= g[x_]=∂_x f[x]
```

$Out[6]= r(1-x)-rx$

```
In[7]:= eq2=Simplify[g[a1]g[a2]]
```

$Out[7]= 4+2r-r^2$

```
In[8]:= sol2=Nsolve[eq2==0,r]
```

$Out[8]= \{\{r \to -1.23607\}, \{r \to 3.23607\}\}$

```
In[9]:= rstar=sol2[[2, 1, 2]]
```

$Out[9]= 3.23607$

```
In[10]:= a1/.r → rstar
```

$Out[10]= 0.5$

```
In[11]:= a2/.r → rstar
```

$Out[11]= 0.809017$

```
In[12]:= a1/.r → 3.2
```

$Out[12]= 0.513045$

```
In[13]:= a2/.r → 3.2
```

$Out[13]= 0.799455$

```
In[14]:= Nsolve[-1==4+2r-r^2,r]
```

$Out[14]= \{\{r \to -1.44949\}, \{r \to 3.44949\}\}$

```
In[15]:= Nsolve[4+2r-r^2==1, r]
```

$Out[15]= \{\{r \to -1.\}, \{r \to 3.\}\}$

Considering only positive roots, we have:

$$r = 3 \quad \text{and} \quad r = 3.44949$$

Appendix 3.2 Two-cycle logistic equation using *Maple*

```
> f:=x->r* x* (1-x);
```
$$f := x \rightarrow rx(1-x)$$

```
>
```

```
> eq1:=f(f(x));
```
$$eq1 := r^2 x(1-x)(1-rx(1-x))$$

```
> sol1:=solve(eq1=x,x);
```
$$Sol1 := 0, \; \frac{-1+r}{r}, \; \frac{\frac{1}{2}r + \frac{1}{2} + \frac{1}{2}\sqrt{-3-2r+r^2}}{r},$$

$$\frac{\frac{1}{2}r + \frac{1}{2} - \frac{1}{2}\sqrt{-3-2r+r^2}}{r}$$

```
> a1:=sol1[3];
```
$$a1 := \frac{\frac{1}{2}r + \frac{1}{2} + \frac{1}{2}\sqrt{-3-2r+r^2}}{r}$$

```
> a2:=sol1[4];
```
$$a2 := \frac{\frac{1}{2}r + \frac{1}{2} - \frac{1}{2}\sqrt{-3-2r+r^2}}{r}$$

```
> g:=diff(f(x),x);
```
$$g := r(1-x) - rx$$

```
> eq2:=expand(subs(x=a1,g)*subs(x=a2,g));
```
$$eq2 := 4 + 2r - r^2$$

```
> sol2:=solve(eq2=0,r);
```
$$sol2 := 1 - \sqrt{5}, 1 + \sqrt{5}$$

```
> rstar:=sol2[2];
```
$$rstar := 1 + \sqrt{5}$$

```
> evalf(subs(r=rstar,a1));
```
$$.8090169946$$

```
> evalf(subs(r=rstar,a2));
```
$$.4999999997$$

```
> evalf(subs(r=3.2,a1));
```
$$.7994554906$$

```
> evalf(subs(r=3.2,a2));
```
$$.5130445094$$

```
> solve(eq2=-1,r);
```
$$1 - \sqrt{6}, 1 + \sqrt{6}$$

```
> evalf(%);
```
$$-1.449489743, 3.449489743$$

```
> solve(eq2=1,r);
```
$$-1, 3$$

Exercises

1. Classify the following difference equations:
    (i) $y_{t+2} = y_{t+1} - 0.5y_t + 1$
    (ii) $y_{t+2} = 2y_t + 3$
    (iii) $\dfrac{y_{t+1} - y_t}{y_t} = 4$
    (iv) $y_{t+2} - 2y_{t+1} + 3y_t = t$

2. Suppose you borrow an amount P_0, the principal, but you repay a fixed amount, R, each period. Formulate the general amount, P_{t+1}, owing in period $t + 1$, with interest payment $r\%$. Solve for P_n.

3. In question 2, suppose the repayment is also variable, with amount repaid in period t of R_t. Derive the solution P_n.

4. Establish whether the following are stable or unstable and which are cyclical.
    (i) $y_{t+1} = -0.5y_t + 3$
    (ii) $2y_{t+1} = -3y_t + 4$
    (iii) $y_{t+1} = -y_t + 6$
    (iv) $y_{t+1} = 0.5y_t + 3$
    (v) $4y_{t+2} + 4y_{t+1} - 2 = 0$

5. Consider
    $$y_{t+1} = y_t^3 - y_t^2 + 1$$
    (i) Show that $a = 1$ is a fixed point of this system.
    (ii) Illustrate that $a = 1$ is a *shunt* by considering points either side of unity for y_0.

6. Use a spreadsheet to compare
    $$y_{t+1} = (1 + a)y_t - by_t^2$$
    and
    $$y_{t+1} = \frac{(1 + a)y_t}{1 + by_t}$$
    using

(i) $a = 1.5$	$b = 0.1$	$y_0 = 1$
(ii) $a = 1.5$	$b = 0.1$	$y_0 = 22$
(iii) $a = 2.2$	$b = 0.1$	$y_0 = 1$
(iv) $a = 2.2$	$b = 0.1$	$y_0 = 25$
(v) $a = 1.8$	$b = 0.15$	$y_0 = 11.5$

7. Derive the cobweb system for the price in each of the following demand and supply systems, and establish whether the equilibrium price is (i) stable, (ii) unstable, or (iii) oscillatory.

(i) $q_t^d = 10 - 3P_t$ (ii) $q_t^d = 25 - 4P_t$ (iii) $q_t^d = 45 - 2.5P_t$
    $q_t^s = 2 + P_{t-1}$ $q_t^s = 3 + 4P_{t-1}$ $q_t^s = 5 + 7.5P_{t-1}$
    $q_t^d = q_t^s$ $q_t^d = q_t^s$ $q_t^d = q_t^s$

8. Suppose we have the macroeconomic model

$$C_t = a + bY_{t-1}$$
$$E_t = C_t + I_t + G_t$$
$$Y_t = E_t$$

where C and Y are endogenous and I and G are exogenous. Derive the general solution for Y_n. Under what conditions is the equilibrium of income, Y^*, stable?

9. Verify your results of question 8 by using a spreadsheet and letting $I = 10$, $G = 20$, $a = 50$, $Y_0 = 20$, and $b = 0.8$ and 1.2, respectively. For what period does the system converge on $Y^* - Y_0$ within 1% deviation from equilibrium? For the same initial value Y_0, is the period longer or shorter in approaching equilibrium the higher the value of b?

10. Given

$$q_t^d = a - bp_t$$
$$q_t^s = c + dp_t^e$$
$$p_t^e = p_{t-1} - e(p_{t-1} - p_{t-2})$$

(i) Show that if in each period demand equals supply, then the model exhibits a second-order nonhomogeneous difference equation for p_t.
(ii) Use a spreadsheet to investigate the path of price *and* quantity for the parameter values

$$a = 10 \quad c = 2 \quad e = 0.5$$
$$b = 3 \quad d = 1$$

11. In the linear cobweb model of demand and supply, demonstrate that the steeper the demand curve relative to the supply curve, the more damped the oscillations and the more rapidly equilibrium is reached.

12. Using a spreadsheet, verify for the linear cobweb model of demand and supply that whenever the absolute slope of the demand curve is equal to the absolute slope of the supply curve, both price *and* quantity have a two-period cycle.

13. Given the following logistic model

$$y_{t+1} = 3.84y_t(1 - y_t)$$

set this up on a spreadsheet. Set $y_0 = 0.1$ and calculate y_n for the first 100 elements in the series. Use the 100th element as the starting value and then re-compute the next 100 elements in the series. Do the same again, and verify that this system tends to a three-cycle with

$$a_1 = 0.149407 \quad a_2 = 0.488044 \quad a_3 = 0.959447$$

14. $f_1(x)$ and $f_2(x)$ are linearly dependent if and only if there exist constants b_1 and b_2, not all zero, such that

$$b_1 f_1(x) + b_2 f_2(x) = 0$$

for every x. If the set of functions is *not* linearly dependent, then $f_1(x)$ and $f_2(x)$ are linearly independent. Show that

$$y_1 = Y^* \qquad \text{and} \qquad y_2 = tY^*$$

are linearly independent.

15. Given the following version of the Solow model with labour augmenting technical progress

$$Y_t = F(K_t, A_t L_t)$$
$$K_{t+1} = K_t + \delta K_t$$
$$S_t = sY_t$$
$$I_t = S_t$$
$$\frac{L_{t+1} - L_t}{L_t} = n$$
$$A_t = \gamma^t A_0$$

(i) show that

$$\hat{k}_{t+1} = \frac{(1 - \delta)\hat{k}_t + sf(\hat{k}_t)}{\gamma(1 + n)}$$

where $\hat{k}$ is the capital/labour ratio *measured in efficiency units*, i.e.,

$$\hat{k} = (K/AL).$$

(ii) Approximate this result around $\hat{k}^* > 0$.

16. Given the model

$$q_t^d = a - bp_t \quad b > 0$$
$$q_t^s = c + dp_t^e \quad d > 0$$
$$p_t^e = p_{t-1}^e - \lambda(p_{t-1} - p_{t-1}^e) \quad 0 < \lambda < 1$$

(i) Show that price conforms to a first-order nonhomogeneous difference equation.
(ii) Obtain the equilibrium price and quantity.
(iii) Show that for a stable cobweb then

$$0 < \lambda < \frac{2b}{b + d}$$

17. A student takes out a loan of £8,000 to buy a second hand car, at a fixed interest loan of 7.5% per annum. She intends to pay off the loan in three years just before she graduates. What is her monthly payment?

18. A bacterial cell divides every minute. A concentration of this bacterium in excess of 5 million cells becomes contagious. Assuming no cells die, how long does it take for the bacteria to become contagious?

19.   Show that neither *Mathematica* nor *Maple* can solve the following difference equation

$$x_{t+1} = \frac{x_t}{1 + x_t}$$

Use either programme to generate the first elements of the series up to $t = 10$, and hence show that this indicates a solution.

20.   A Fibonacci series takes the form

$$x_n = x_{n-1} + x_{n-2} \quad x_0 = 1 \quad \text{and} \quad x_1 = 1$$

(i)   Use a spreadsheet to generate this series, and hence show that the series is composed of integers.

(ii)   Solve the recursive equation with a software package and show that all of its factors are irrational numbers but that it takes on integer values for all n, which are identical to those in the spreadsheet.

Additional reading

For additional material on the contents of this chapter the reader can consult Allen (1965), Baumol (1959), Baumol and Wolff (1991), Chiang (1984), Domar (1944), Elaydi (1996), Farmer (1999), Gapinski (1982), Goldberg (1961), Griffiths and Oldknow (1993), Hicks (1950), Holmgren (1994), Jeffrey (1990), Kelley and Peterson (2001), Samuelson (1939), Sandefur (1990), Shone (2001), Solow (1956) and Tu (1994).

CHAPTER 4

Systems of first-order differential equations

4.1 Definitions and autonomous systems

In many economic problems the models reduce down to two or more systems of
differential equations that require to be solved simultaneously. Since most economic models reduce down to two such equations, and since only two variables
can easily be drawn, we shall concentrate very much on a system of two equations.
In general, a system of two ordinary first-order differential equations takes the form

(4.1)

$$\frac{dx}{dt} = \dot{x} = f(x, y, t)$$

$$\frac{dy}{dt} = \dot{y} = g(x, y, t)$$

Consider the following examples in which x and y are the dependent variables
and t is an independent variable:

(i) $\quad \begin{aligned} \dot{x} &= ax - by - ce^t \\ \dot{y} &= rx + sy - qe^t \end{aligned}$

(ii) $\quad \begin{aligned} \dot{x} &= ax - by \\ \dot{y} &= rx + sy \end{aligned}$

(iii) $\quad \begin{aligned} \dot{x} &= ax - bxy \\ \dot{y} &= rx - sxy \end{aligned}$

Examples (i) and (ii) are **linear systems** of first-order differential equations
because they involve the dependent variables x and y in a linear fashion.
Example (iii), on the other hand, is a **nonlinear system** of first-order differential
equations because of the term xy occurring on the right-hand side of both equations
in the system. Examples (ii) and (iii) are **autonomous** systems since the variable
t does not appear explicitly in the system of equations; otherwise a system is said
to be **nonautonomous**, as in the case of example (i). Furthermore, examples (ii)
and (iii) are **homogeneous** because there is no additional constant. Example (i)
is **nonhomogeneous** with a variable term, namely ce^t.

A **solution** to system (4.1) is a pair of parametric equations $x = x(t)$ and $y =
y(t)$ which satisfy the system over some open interval. Since, by definition, they
satisfy the differential equation system, then it follows that the solution functions
are differentiable functions of t. As with single differential equations, it is often
necessary to impose initial conditions on system (4.1), which take the form

$$x_0 = x(t_0) \quad \text{and} \quad y_0 = y(t_0)$$

Our initial value problem is, then

$$\dot{x} = f(x, y, t)$$
$$\dot{y} = g(x, y, t) \tag{4.2}$$
$$x(t_0) = x_0, y(t_0) = y_0$$

Economic models invariably involve both linear and nonlinear systems of equations that are autonomous. It is, therefore, worth exploring the meaning of autonomous systems in more detail because it is this characteristic that allows much of the graphical analysis we observe in economic theory. In order to elaborate on the ideas we need to develop, consider an extremely simple set of differential equations.

Example 4.1

$$\dot{x} = 2x$$
$$\dot{y} = y \tag{4.3}$$
$$x(t_0) = 2, \qquad y(t_0) = 3$$

We can capture the movement of the system in the following way. Construct a plane in terms of x and y. Then the initial point is $(x_0, y_0) = (2,3)$. The movement of the system away from this initial point is indicated by the systems of motion, or transition functions, $x'(t)$ and $y'(t)$. If we can solve the system for $x(t)$ and $y(t)$, then we can plot the path of the system in the (x,y)-plane. In the present example this is easy to do. Here we are not so concerned with solving systems of autonomous equations, but rather in seeing how such solutions appear in the (x,y)-plane. The solutions are

$$x(t) = 2e^{2t} \qquad \text{and} \qquad y(t) = 3e^{t}$$

The path of the system in the (x,y)-plane is readily established by eliminating the variable t and expressing y as a function of x. Thus

$$y = \sqrt{\frac{9x}{2}}$$

which is defined for $x \geq 2, y \geq 3$. Over time, $x(t)$ increases beyond the initial value of $x(0) = 2$ and $y(t)$ increases beyond the initial value of $y(0) = 3$. Hence, the system moves along the trajectory shown in figure 4.1(a) and in the direction indicated by the arrows. More significantly, for any initial point (x_0, y_0) there is only one trajectory through this point. Put another way, no matter when the system begins to move, it will always move along the same trajectory since there is only one trajectory through point (x_0, y_0). In terms of figure 4.1(a), there is only one trajectory through the point $(2,3)$.

Example 4.2

But now consider a similar system of equations

$$\dot{x} = 2x + t$$
$$\dot{y} = y \tag{4.4}$$
$$x(0) = 2, \qquad y(0) = 3$$

Figure 4.1.

(a)

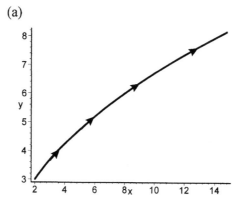

(b)

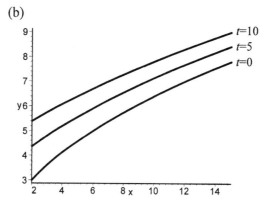

with solutions

$$x(t) = \frac{9e^{2t} - 1}{4} - \frac{t}{2}$$

$$y(t) = 3e^t$$

which clearly satisfy the initial conditions. Eliminating e^t, we can express the relationship between x and y as

$$y = \sqrt{1 + 4x + 2t} \qquad x \geq 2, y \geq 3$$

which clearly depends on t. This means that where a system is at any point in time in the (x,y)-plane depends on precisely the moment the system arrives at that point. For instance, in figure 4.1(b) we draw the system for three points of time, $t = 0, 5, 10$. There is no longer a single trajectory in the (x,y)-plane, but a whole series of trajectories, one for each point in time. The system is clearly time-dependent.

Autonomous systems are time-independent. One must be careful of the meaning here of being 'time-independent'. All that is meant is that the time derivatives are not changing over time (the transition functions are independent of time); however, the solution values for the dependent variables x and y will be functions of time, as we clearly saw from the above example. With autonomous systems there is only a single trajectory in the (x,y)-plane which satisfies the initial conditions. Of course, with different initial conditions, there will be different trajectories in the (x,y)-plane, but these too will be unique for a given initial condition.

4.2   The phase plane, fixed points and stability

In chapter 2 we introduced the *phase line*. This was the plot of $x(t)$ on the x-line. It is apparent that figure 4.1(a) is a generalisation of this to two variables. In figure 4.1(a) we have plotted the path of the two variables x and y. At any point in time we have a point such as $(x(t), y(t))$, and since the solution path is uniquely defined for some initial condition (x_0, y_0), then there is only one path, one function $y = \phi(x)$, which satisfies the condition $y_0 = \phi(x_0)$.

A solution curve for two variables is illustrated in figure 4.2(a), whose coordinates are $(x(t), y(t))$ as t varies over the solution interval. This curve is called a **trajectory, path** or **orbit** of the system; and the (x,y)-plane containing the trajectory is called the **phase plane** of the system. The set of all possible trajectories is called the **phase portrait**. It should be noted that in the case of autonomous systems as t varies the system moves along a trajectory (x, y) through the phase plane which depends only on the coordinates (x, y) and not on the time of its arrival at that point. As time increases, the arrows show the direction of movement along the trajectory. The same is true for an autonomous system of three variables, x, y and z. Figure 4.2(b) illustrates a typical trajectory in a three-dimensional phase plane which passes through the point (x_0, y_0, z_0). Again the arrows indicate the movement of this system over time.

Since for autonomous systems the solution curve is uniquely defined for some initial value, then we can think of y as a function of x, $y = \phi(x)$, whose slope is given by

$$\frac{dy}{dx} = \frac{dy/dt}{dx/dt} \tag{4.5}$$

and which is uniquely determined so long as dx/dt is not zero. For autonomous systems, this allows us to eliminate the variable t. To see this, return to example 4.1

$$\frac{dy}{dx} = \frac{dy/dt}{dx/dt} = \frac{y}{2x}$$

This is a separable equation and so can be solved by the method developed in chapter 2. Solving, and solving for the constant of integration by letting the initial conditions be $x_0 = 2$ and $y_0 = 3$, we find again that $y = \sqrt{9x/2}$ (see exercise 1).

If (x^*, y^*) is a point in the phase plane for which $f(x, y) = 0$ and $g(x, y) = 0$ simultaneously, then it follows that $dx/dt = 0$ and $dy/dt = 0$. This means that neither x nor y is changing over time: the system has a **fixed point**, or has an **equilibrium point**. For example 4.1 it is quite clear that the only fixed point is $(x^*, y^*) = (0, 0)$. In the case of example 4.2, although $y^* = 0$, $x^* = t/2$ and so x^* depends on the point in time the system arrives at x^*. Consider another example.

Figure 4.2.

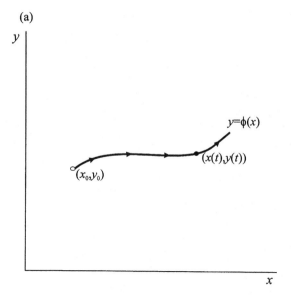

(a)

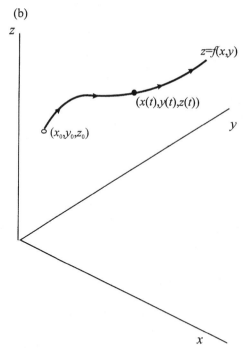

(b)

Example 4.3

We can establish the fixed point of the following simultaneous equation system

(4.6)
$$\dot{x} = x - 3y$$
$$\dot{y} = -2x + y$$
$$x_0 = 4, \, y_0 = 5$$

by setting $\dot{x} = 0$ and $\dot{y} = 0$, which has solution $x^* = 0$ and $y^* = 0$.

It should be quite clear from these examples that independent homogeneous linear equation systems have a fixed point at the origin. Also, there is only the one fixed point.

Having established that such a system has a fixed point, an equilibrium point, the next step is to establish whether such a point is stable or unstable. A trajectory that seems to approach a fixed point would indicate that the system was stable while one which moved away from a fixed point would indicate that the system was unstable. However, we need to be more precise about what we mean when we say 'a fixed point (x^*, y^*) is stable or unstable'.

A fixed point (x^*, y^*) which satisfies the condition $f(x, y) = 0$ and $g(x, y) = 0$ is **stable** or **attracting** if, given some starting value (x_0, y_0) 'close to' (x^*, y^*), i.e., within some distance δ, the trajectory stays close to the fixed point, i.e., within some distance $\varepsilon > \delta$. It is clear that this definition requires some measure of 'distance'. There are many ways to define distance, but the most common is that of Liapunov. In simple terms we define a ball around the fixed point (x^*, y^*) with radius δ and ε, respectively. Thus, define $B_\delta(x^*, y^*)$ to be a ball (circle) centred on (x^*, y^*) and with radius δ. Define a second ball, $B_\varepsilon(x^*, y^*)$ to be a ball (circle) centred on (x^*, y^*) and with radius $\varepsilon > \delta$. The situation is illustrated in figure 4.3(a) and (b). We have a starting value (x_0, y_0) 'close to' the fixed point (x^*, y^*), in the sense that (x_0, y_0) lies in the ball $B_\delta(x^*, y^*)$. The solution value (path) starting from (x_0, y_0) stays 'close to' the fixed point, in the sense that it stays within the ball $B_\varepsilon(x^*, y^*)$. The solution paths in figure 4.3(a) and (b) both satisfy this condition, and so are both stable.

But a careful consideration of the statement of stability will indicate that there is nothing within the definition that insists that the trajectory has to *approach* the fixed point. All that is required is that it stay within the ball $B_\varepsilon(x^*, y^*)$. A look at figure 4.3(b) will indicate that this satisfies the definition of stability just outlined. However, the solution path is periodic, it begins close to the fixed point (i.e. the starting point lies within the ball $B_\delta(x^*, y^*)$) but cycles around the fixed point while staying 'close to' the fixed point (i.e. stays within the ball $B_\varepsilon(x^*, y^*)$). Such a **limit cycle** is stable but not asymptotically stable. We shall find examples of this when we consider competing population models in chapter 14.

A fixed point that is not stable is said to be **unstable** or **repelling**.

A fixed point is **asymptotically stable** if it is stable in the sense just discussed, but eventually approaches the fixed point as $t \to \infty$. Thus to be asymptotically stable, it must start close to (x^*, y^*) (i.e. within δ), it must remain close to the fixed point (i.e. within ε), and must eventually approach (x^*, y^*) as $t \to \infty$. Hence, the situation shown in figure 4.3(a) is asymptotically stable. Also notice that the trajectory can move away from the fixed point so long as it stays within the ball $B_\varepsilon(x^*, y^*)$ and approaches the fixed point in the limit.[1]

Asymptotic stability is a stronger property than stability. This is clear because to be asymptotically stable then it must be stable. The limit condition on its *own* is not sufficient. A system may start 'close to' (x^*, y^*) (i.e. within $B_\delta(x^*, y^*)$) and approach the fixed point in the limit, but diverge considerably away from (go beyond the ball $B_\varepsilon(x^*, y^*)$) in the intermediate period.

---

[1] A fixed point that is stable but not asymptotically stable is sometimes referred to as **neutrally stable**. Figure 4.3(b) illustrates a periodic trajectory around the fixed point, which is accordingly neutrally stable. This type of system is typical of competing populations, as we shall illustrate in chapter 14.

Figure 4.3.

(a)

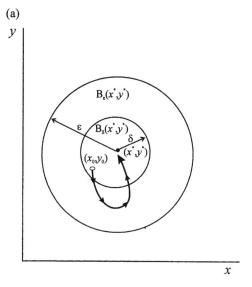

(b)

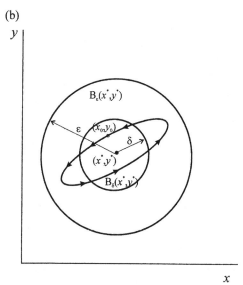

If a system has a fixed point (x^*, y^*) which is asymptotically stable, and if every trajectory approaches the fixed point (i.e. both points close to the fixed point and far away from the fixed point), then the fixed point is said to be **globally asymptotically stable**. Another way to consider this is to establish the initial set of conditions for which the given fixed point is asymptotically stable, i.e., the largest ball from which any entering trajectory converges asymptotically to the fixed point. This set of initial conditions is called the **basin of attraction**. A fixed point is **locally asymptotically stable** if there exists a basin of attraction, $B_\varepsilon(x^*, y^*)$, within which all trajectories entering this ball eventually approach the fixed point (x^*, y^*). If the basin of attraction is the whole of the (x,y)-plane, then the system is globally asymptotically stable about the fixed point (x^*, y^*).

Mathematicians have demonstrated a number of properties for the trajectories of autonomous systems. Here we shall simply list them.

(1)   There is no more than one trajectory through any point in the phase plane
(2)   A trajectory that starts at a point that is not a fixed point will only reach a fixed point in an infinite time period
(3)   No trajectory can cross itself unless it is a closed curve. If it is a closed curve then the solution is a periodic one.

4.3   Vectors of forces in the phase plane

We established in chapter 2, when considering single autonomous differential equations, that we could establish the direction of x when t varies from the sign of $\dot{x}$. In the case of a system of two differential equations we can establish the direction of x from the sign of $\dot{x}$ and the direction of y from the sign of $\dot{y}$. Such movements in x and y give us insight into the dynamics of the system around the equilibrium. In this section we shall pursue three very simple examples in some detail in order to investigate the dynamic properties of each system. Although each can be solved explicitly, this will not always be the case, and the qualitative dynamics we shall be developing will be particularly useful in such circumstances.

Example 4.4

This continues example 4.3, equation system (4.6), but we shall repeat it here. Consider the following first-order autonomous system with initial conditions

$$\dot{x} = x - 3y$$
$$\dot{y} = -2x + y \tag{4.7}$$
$$x_0 = 4, y_0 = 5$$

The solution to this system, which satisfies the initial values, is the following

$$x(t) = \frac{8e^{(1-\sqrt{6})t} + 5\sqrt{6}e^{(1-\sqrt{6})t} + 8e^{(1+\sqrt{6})t} - 5\sqrt{6}e^{(1+\sqrt{6})t}}{4}$$
$$\tag{4.8}$$
$$y(t) = \frac{15e^{(1-\sqrt{6})t} + \sqrt{96}e^{(1-\sqrt{6})t} + 15e^{(1+\sqrt{6})t} - \sqrt{96}e^{(1+\sqrt{6})t}}{6}$$

For the moment we are not concerned about how to derive these solutions, which we shall consider later, all we are concerned about here is to show that these are indeed the solution values that satisfy the initial conditions. We verify this by differentiating both x and y with respect to t and substituting into the system of equations. A rather tedious exercise, which can be accomplished with software packages like *Mathematica* or *Maple*. Doing so shows that each equation in the system is identically true. Hence the equations are indeed the solutions to the system.

It will be noted that the solution values are not straightforward. We could plot the solution values for x and y against time, as shown in figure 4.4. Alternatively, and much more informatively, we can plot the path of points $\{x(t), y(t)\}$ in the phase plane as the independent variable t varies over the solution interval. Generally, this will involve a phase portrait, which again can be done using *Mathematica*

Figure 4.4.

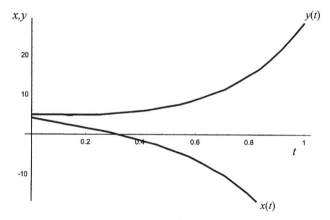

Figure 4.5.

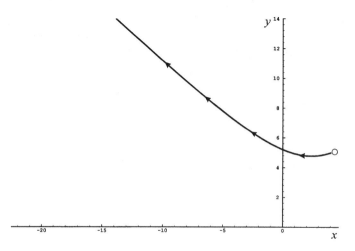

or *Maple.*[2] Such a solution path to the system in the (x,y)-plane is illustrated in figure 4.5. This is a specific solution since it satisfies the initial conditions.

But we want to know what is happening to the path in relation to the fixed point, the equilibrium point, of the system. We already know that a fixed point is established by setting $\dot{x} = 0$ and $\dot{y} = 0$. The fixed point is readily established by solving the simultaneous equations

$$0 = x - 3y$$
$$0 = -2x + y$$

which has solution $x^* = 0$ and $y^* = 0$. Another way to view the fixed point is to note that $0 = x - 3y$ is the equilibrium condition for the variable x; while $0 = -2x + y$ is the equilibrium condition for the variable y. The fixed point is simply where the two equilibrium lines intersect. The equilibrium lines are

$$y = \frac{x}{3} \qquad (\dot{x} = 0)$$
$$y = 2x \qquad (\dot{y} = 0)$$

---

[2] See section 4.12.

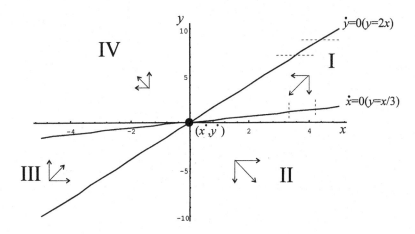

Figure 4.6.

Consider the first equilibrium line. Along this line we have combinations of x and y for which $\dot{x} = 0$. But this means that for any value of x on this line, x cannot be changing. This information is shown by the vertical dotted lines in figure 4.6 for any particular value of x. Similarly, for the line denoted

$$\dot{y} = 0 \qquad (y = 2x)$$

the value of y on this line cannot be changing. This information is shown by the horizontal dotted lines in figure 4.6 for any particular value of y.

Next consider points either side of the equilibrium lines in the phase plane. To the right of the x-line we have

$$y < \frac{x}{3} \qquad \text{implying} \qquad \dot{x} > 0$$

Hence, for any point at which x lies below the x-line, then x is rising. Two are shown in figure 4.6 by the *horizontal* arrows that are pointing to the right. By the same reasoning, to the left of the x-line we have

$$y > \frac{x}{3} \qquad \text{implying} \qquad \dot{x} < 0$$

Hence, for any point at which x lies above the x-line, then x is falling. Two are shown in figure 4.6 by the *horizontal* arrows pointing to the left.

By the same reasoning we can establish to the right of the y-line

$$y < 2x \qquad \text{implying} \qquad \dot{y} < 0, \text{ hence } y \text{ is falling}$$

while to its left

$$y > 2x \qquad \text{implying} \qquad \dot{y} > 0, \text{ hence } y \text{ is rising}$$

Again these are shown by the *vertical* arrows pointing down and up respectively in figure 4.6. It is clear from figure 4.6 that we have four quadrants, which we have labelled I, II, III and IV, and that the general direction of force in each quadrant is shown by the arrow between the vertical and the horizontal.

It can be seen from figure 4.6 that in quadrants I and III forces are directing the system towards the origin, towards the fixed point. In quadrants II and IV, however, the forces are directing the system away from the fixed point. We can immediately conclude, therefore, that the fixed point cannot be a stable point. Can we conclude that for any initial value of x and y, positioning the system in quadrants I or III, that the trajectory will tend over time to the fixed point? No, we cannot make any such deduction! For instance, if the system began in quadrant I, and began to move towards the fixed point, it could over time pass into quadrant IV, and once in quadrant IV would move away from the fixed point. In fact, this is precisely the trajectory shown in figure 4.5. Although the trajectory shown in figure 4.5 moves from quadrant I into quadrant IV, this need not be true of all initial points beginning in quadrant I. Depending on the initial value for x and y, it is quite possible for the system to move from quadrant I into quadrant II, first moving towards the fixed point and then away from it once quadrant II has been entered. This would be the situation, for example, if the initial point was $(x_0, y_0) = (4, 2)$ (see exercise 2). This complex nature of the solution paths can be observed by considering the direction field for the differential equation system. The direction field, along with the equilibrium lines are shown in figure 4.7. Why the dynamic forces seem to operate in this way we shall investigate later in this chapter.

Example 4.5

The following system of linear differential equations

$$\dot{x} = -3x + y$$
$$\dot{y} = x - 3y$$

with initial condition $x_0 = 4$ and $y_0 = 5$ has solution equations

$$x(t) = \frac{9e^{2t} - 1}{2e^{4t}} \quad \text{and} \quad y(t) = \frac{1 + 9e^{2t}}{2e^{4t}}$$

which gives rise to a trajectory which approaches the fixed point $(x^*, y^*) = (0, 0)$, as shown in figure 4.8. The path of $x(t)$ and $y(t)$, represented by the phase line, as t increases is shown by the direction of the arrows.

Figure 4.7.

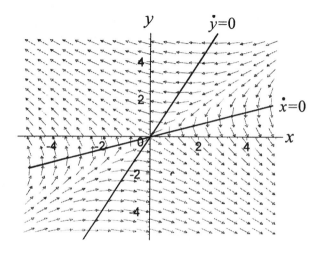

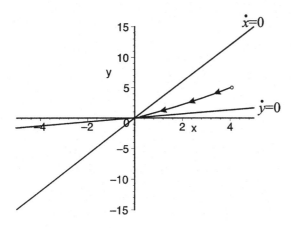

Figure 4.8.

No matter what the initial point, it will be found that each trajectory approaches the fixed point $(x^*, y^*) = (0, 0)$. In other words, the fixed point (the equilibrium point) is globally stable. Considering the vector of forces for this system captures this feature.

The equilibrium solution lines are

$$y = 3x \text{ for } \dot{x} = 0$$

$$y = \frac{x}{3} \text{ for } \dot{y} = 0$$

with a fixed point at the origin. To the right of the x-line we have

$$y < 3x \text{ or } -3x + y < 0 \qquad \text{implying} \qquad \dot{x} < 0 \text{ so } x \text{ is falling}$$

While to the left of the x-line we have

$$y > 3x \text{ or } -3x + y > 0 \qquad \text{implying} \qquad \dot{x} > 0 \text{ so } x \text{ is rising}$$

Similarly, to the right of the y-line we have

$$y < \frac{x}{3} \text{ or } 0 < -3y + x \qquad \text{implying} \qquad \dot{y} > 0 \text{ so } y \text{ is rising}$$

While to the left of the y-line we have

$$y > \frac{x}{3} \text{ or } 0 > -3y + x \qquad \text{implying} \qquad \dot{y} < 0 \text{ so } y \text{ is falling}$$

All this information, including the vectors of force implied by the above results, is illustrated in figure 4.9. It is clear that no matter in which of the four quadrants the system begins, all the forces push the system towards the fixed point. This means that even if the trajectory crosses from one quadrant into another, it is still being directed towards the fixed point. The fixed point must be globally stable. If the initial point is $(x_0, y_0) = (4, 5)$, then the trajectory remains in quadrant I and tends to the fixed point $(x^*, y^*) = (0, 0)$ over time. However, figure 4.9 reveals much more. If the system should pass from one quadrant into an adjacent quadrant, then the trajectory is still being directed towards the fixed point, but the movement

Figure 4.9.

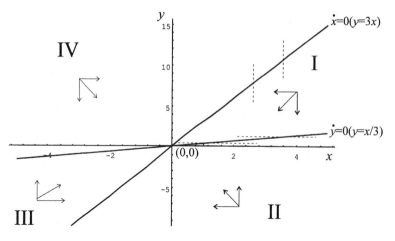

Figure 4.10.

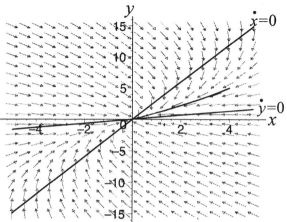

of the system is *clockwise*.[3] This clockwise motion is shown most explicitly by including the direction field on the equilibrium lines, as shown in figure 4.10.

Example 4.6

The two examples discussed so far both have fixed points at the origin. However, this need not always be the case. Consider the following system of linear

---

[3] The nature of the trajectory can be established by noting that

$$x^2 + y^2 = \frac{(9e^{2t} - 1)^2}{4e^{8t}} + \frac{(1 + 9e^{2t})^2}{4e^{8t}}$$

$$= \frac{81e^{4t} + 1}{2e^{8t}}$$

i.e. $x^2 + y^2 = \phi(t)$

This is a circle at any moment in time whose radius is governed by $\phi(t)$. But over time the limit of $\phi(t)$ is zero. Consequently, as time passes the radius must diminish. This means that the trajectory conforms to a spiralling path of ever-decreasing radius. Furthermore, the vector forces indicate that the spiral moves in a clockwise direction regardless of the initial value.

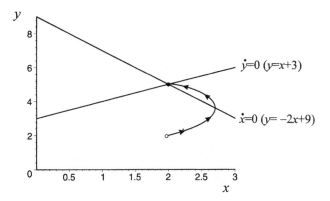

Figure 4.11.

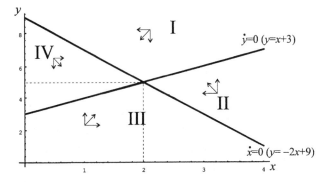

Figure 4.12.

nonhomogeneous autonomous differential equations

$$\dot{x} = -2x - y + 9$$
$$\dot{y} = -y + x + 3$$

The equilibrium lines in the phase plane can readily be found by setting $\dot{x} = 0$ and $\dot{y} = 0$. Thus

$$\dot{x} = 0 \quad \text{implying} \quad y = -2x + 9$$
$$\dot{y} = 0 \quad \text{implying} \quad y = x + 3$$

which can be solved to give a fixed point, an equilibrium point, namely $(x^*, y^*) = (2, 5)$. The solution equations for this system for initial condition, $x_0 = 2$ and $y_0 = 2$ are

$$x(t) = 2 + 2\sqrt{3}\sin(\sqrt{3}t/2)e^{-(3t/2)}$$
$$y(t) = 5 - (3\cos(\sqrt{3}t/2)) - \sqrt{3}\sin(\sqrt{3}t/2)e^{-(3t/2)}$$

The equilibrium lines along with the trajectory are illustrated in figure 4.11.

The analysis of this example is the same as for examples 4.4 and 4.5. In this case the fixed point is at $(x^*, y^*) = (2, 5)$. The vectors of force are illustrated in figure 4.12 by the arrows. What is apparent from this figure is that the system is globally stable, and the dynamic forces are sending the system towards the fixed point in a *counter-clockwise* motion. As we illustrated in figure 4.11, if the initial point is $(x_0, y_0) = (2, 2)$, then the system begins in quadrant III and tends to the fixed point over time in a counter-clockwise direction, passing first into quadrant

Figure 4.13.

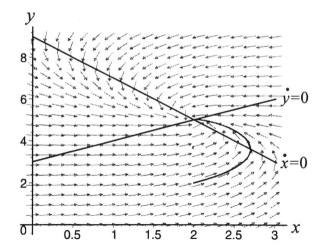

II and then into I as it moves towards the fixed point. A similar behaviour occurs if the initial point is $(x_0, y_0) = (3, 1)$ beginning in quadrant III (see exercise 4).

Once again the vector forces can be seen in terms of the direction field, which we show in figure 4.13, along with the equilibrium lines.

4.4 Matrix specification of autonomous systems

The examples so far discussed illustrate that even with simple linear autonomous systems, the type of dynamic behaviour is quite varied. In order to pursue the stability/instability aspects of systems of autonomous equations it is more convenient to specify the models in terms of matrices and vectors.

Example 4.4 can be written

(4.9)
$$\begin{bmatrix} \dot{x} \\ \dot{y} \end{bmatrix} = \begin{bmatrix} 1 & -3 \\ -2 & 1 \end{bmatrix} \begin{bmatrix} x \\ y \end{bmatrix}$$

example 4.5 as

(4.10)
$$\begin{bmatrix} \dot{x} \\ \dot{y} \end{bmatrix} = \begin{bmatrix} -3 & 1 \\ 1 & -3 \end{bmatrix} \begin{bmatrix} x \\ y \end{bmatrix}$$

while example 4.6 can be written

(4.11)
$$\begin{bmatrix} \dot{x} \\ \dot{y} \end{bmatrix} = \begin{bmatrix} -2 & -1 \\ 1 & -1 \end{bmatrix} \begin{bmatrix} x \\ y \end{bmatrix} + \begin{bmatrix} 9 \\ 3 \end{bmatrix}$$

In fact, we can readily generalise such linear autonomous systems with constant coefficients. Although we shall talk here of only two variables, it can readily be generalised to n.

Define the following vectors and matrices

(4.12)
$$\dot{\mathbf{x}} = \begin{bmatrix} \dot{x}_1 \\ \dot{x}_2 \end{bmatrix}, \qquad \mathbf{A} = \begin{bmatrix} a_{11} & a_{12} \\ a_{21} & a_{22} \end{bmatrix}, \qquad \mathbf{x} = \begin{bmatrix} x_1 \\ x_2 \end{bmatrix}, \qquad \mathbf{b} = \begin{bmatrix} b_1 \\ b_2 \end{bmatrix}$$

Then systems 4.4 and 4.5 are simply specific examples of the homogeneous linear system

$$\dot{\mathbf{x}} = \mathbf{A}\mathbf{x} \tag{4.13}$$

while system 4.6 is a specific example of the nonhomogeneous linear system

$$\dot{\mathbf{x}} = \mathbf{A}\mathbf{x} + \mathbf{b} \tag{4.14}$$

For linear homogeneous systems, if the determinant of $\mathbf{A}$ is not zero, then the only solution, the only fixed point, is $\mathbf{x}^* = \mathbf{0}$, i.e., $(x_1^* = 0$ and $x_2^* = 0)$. On the other hand, for nonhomogeneous linear systems, the equilibrium can be found, so long as $\mathbf{A}$ is nonsingular, from

$$\begin{aligned} \mathbf{0} &= \mathbf{A}\mathbf{x}^* + \mathbf{b} \\ \mathbf{x}^* &= -\mathbf{A}^{-1}\mathbf{b} \end{aligned} \tag{4.15}$$

When considering the issue of stability/instability it is useful to note that linear nonhomogeneous systems can always be reduced to linear homogeneous systems in terms of deviations from equilibrium if an equilibrium exists. For

$$\begin{aligned} \dot{\mathbf{x}} &= \mathbf{A}\mathbf{x} + \mathbf{b} \\ \mathbf{0} &= \mathbf{A}\mathbf{x}^* + \mathbf{b} \end{aligned}$$

subtracting we immediately have in deviation form

$$\dot{\mathbf{x}} = \mathbf{A}(\mathbf{x} - \mathbf{x}^*) \tag{4.16}$$

which is homogeneous in terms of deviations from the fixed point $\mathbf{x}^* = (x_1^*, x_2^*)$. There will be no loss of generality, therefore, if we concentrate on linear homogeneous systems.

The matrix $\mathbf{A}$ is of particular importance in dealing with stability and instability. Two important properties of such a *square* matrix are its trace, denoted tr($\mathbf{A}$), and its determinant, denoted det($\mathbf{A}$), where[4]

$$\operatorname{tr}(\mathbf{A}) = a_{11} + a_{22}$$

$$\det(\mathbf{A}) = \begin{vmatrix} a_{11} & a_{12} \\ a_{21} & a_{22} \end{vmatrix} = a_{11}a_{22} - a_{12}a_{21} \tag{4.17}$$

It should be noted that both the trace and the determinant are *scalars*. The matrix $\mathbf{A}$ is nonsingular if $\det(\mathbf{A}) \neq 0$.

There is another property of the matrix $\mathbf{A}$ that arises for special linear systems. Consider the following general linear system

$$\mathbf{y} = \mathbf{A}\mathbf{x}$$

This can be viewed as a transformation of the vector $\mathbf{x}$ into the vector $\mathbf{y}$. But suppose that $\mathbf{x}$ is transformed into a multiple of itself, i.e., $\mathbf{y} = \lambda\mathbf{x}$, where λ is a scalar of proportionality. Then

$$\mathbf{A}\mathbf{x} = \lambda\mathbf{x}$$

or

$$(\mathbf{A} - \lambda\mathbf{I})\mathbf{x} = \mathbf{0} \tag{4.18}$$

---

[4] See Chiang (1984) or any book on linear algebra.

But equation (4.18) will have a nonzero solution if and only if λ is chosen such that

(4.19) $$\phi(\lambda) = \det(\mathbf{A} - \lambda\mathbf{I}) = 0$$

The values of λ which satisfy equation (4.19) are called the **eigenvalues** of the matrix $\mathbf{A}$, and the solution to the system that are obtained using these values are called the **eigenvectors** corresponding to that eigenvalue. Let us clarify these concepts with a simple example.

Example 4.7

Let

$$\mathbf{A} = \begin{bmatrix} 1 & 1 \\ -2 & 4 \end{bmatrix}$$

then

$$\det(\mathbf{A} - \lambda\mathbf{I}) = \begin{vmatrix} 1 - \lambda & 1 \\ -2 & 4 - \lambda \end{vmatrix} = \lambda^2 - 5\lambda + 6 = 0$$

Let the two roots, the two eigenvalues, of this quadratic be denoted r and s, respectively. Then $r = 3$ and $s = 2$. In this example we have two distinct real roots.

To determine the eigenvectors, we must substitute for a particular value of λ in the equation

$$(\mathbf{A} - \lambda_i\mathbf{I})\mathbf{v}^i = \mathbf{0} \qquad (i = r, s)$$

With $\lambda = r = 3$ then

$$\mathbf{A} - 3\mathbf{I} = \begin{bmatrix} 1 & 1 \\ -2 & 4 \end{bmatrix} - \begin{bmatrix} 3 & 0 \\ 0 & 3 \end{bmatrix} = \begin{bmatrix} -2 & 1 \\ -2 & 1 \end{bmatrix}$$

whose determinant value is zero as required. Hence

$$\begin{bmatrix} -2 & 1 \\ -2 & 1 \end{bmatrix}\begin{bmatrix} v_1^r \\ v_2^r \end{bmatrix} = \begin{bmatrix} 0 \\ 0 \end{bmatrix}$$

which has the single condition $-2v_1^r + v_2^r = 0$, and v_2^r is determined in terms of v_1^r. Thus, if $v_1^r = c$, then $v_2^r = 2c$. Accordingly, the eigenvector, denoted $\mathbf{v}^r$ is

$$\mathbf{v}^r = c\begin{bmatrix} 1 \\ 2 \end{bmatrix}$$

Since c is an arbitrary constant this is usually normalised to unity, and so the eigenvector is simply denoted

$$\mathbf{v}^r = \begin{bmatrix} 1 \\ 2 \end{bmatrix}$$

Of course, this eigenvector was derived from the root $r = 3$, which is why we have labelled it $\mathbf{v}^r$. We also have a second eigenvector associated with the root $\lambda = s = 2$. Following through exactly the same procedure we find that

Figure 4.14.

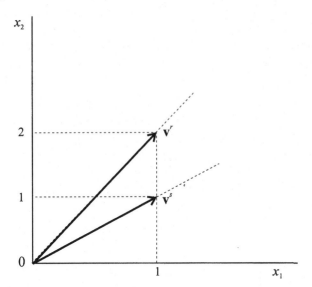

$-v_1^s + v_2^s = 0$ and hence

$$\mathbf{v}^s = \begin{bmatrix} 1 \\ 1 \end{bmatrix}$$

Figure 4.14 illustrates the two eigenvectors associated with the two eigenvalues.

Although this illustration had two distinct roots, it is quite clear that for any system of two dimensions, there will be two roots that correspond to one of the following possibilities:

(1)   real and distinct
(2)   real and equal
(3)   complex conjugate.

It is possible to relate these three possibilities to conditions imposed on the trace and determinant of the matrix $\mathbf{A}$. To see this let

$$\mathbf{A} = \begin{bmatrix} a & b \\ c & d \end{bmatrix}$$

Then

$$\det(\mathbf{A} - \lambda \mathbf{I}) = \begin{vmatrix} a - \lambda & b \\ c & d - \lambda \end{vmatrix} = \lambda^2 - (a+d)\lambda + (ad - bc) = 0$$

But $a + d = \text{tr}(\mathbf{A})$ and $ad - bc = \det(\mathbf{A})$. Hence the characteristic equation can be expressed

$$\lambda^2 - \text{tr}(\mathbf{A})\lambda + \det(\mathbf{A}) = 0 \tag{4.20}$$

with solutions

$$r = \frac{\text{tr}(\mathbf{A}) + \sqrt{\text{tr}(\mathbf{A})^2 - 4\det(\mathbf{A})}}{2}$$

$$s = \frac{\text{tr}(\mathbf{A}) - \sqrt{\text{tr}(\mathbf{A})^2 - 4\det(\mathbf{A})}}{2}$$

It follows immediately that the roots are:

(1)   real and distinct if $\text{tr}(\mathbf{A})^2 > 4\det(\mathbf{A})$
(2)   real and equal if $\text{tr}(\mathbf{A})^2 = 4\det(\mathbf{A})$
(3)   complex conjugate if $\text{tr}(\mathbf{A})^2 < 4\det(\mathbf{A})$.

4.5   Solutions to the homogeneous differential equation system: real distinct roots

Suppose we have an n-dimensional dynamic system

(4.21) $$\dot{\mathbf{x}} = \mathbf{A}\mathbf{x}$$

where

$$\dot{\mathbf{x}} = \begin{bmatrix} \dot{x}_1 \\ \dot{x}_2 \\ \vdots \\ \dot{x}_n \end{bmatrix}, \quad \mathbf{A} = \begin{bmatrix} a_{11} & a_{12} & \cdots & a_{1n} \\ \vdots & \vdots & \vdots & \vdots \\ a_{n1} & a_{n2} & \cdots & a_{nn} \end{bmatrix}, \quad \mathbf{x} = \begin{bmatrix} x_1 \\ x_2 \\ \vdots \\ x_n \end{bmatrix}$$

and suppose $\mathbf{u}^1, \mathbf{u}^2, \ldots, \mathbf{u}^n$ are n linearly independent solutions, then a linear combination of these solutions is also a solution. We can therefore express the *general solution* as the linear combination

$$\mathbf{x} = c_1\mathbf{u}^1 + c_2\mathbf{u}^2 + \ldots + c_n\mathbf{u}^n$$

where $c_1, c_2, \ldots, c_n$ are arbitrary constants. In the case of just two variables, we are after the general solution

$$\mathbf{x} = c_1\mathbf{u}^1 + c_2\mathbf{u}^2$$

In chapter 2, where we considered a single variable, we had a solution

$$x = ce^{rt}$$

This would suggest that we try the solution[5]

$$\mathbf{x} = e^{\lambda t}\mathbf{v}$$

where λ is an unknown constant and $\mathbf{v}$ is an unknown vector of constants. If we do this and substitute into the differential equation system we have

$$\lambda e^{\lambda t}\mathbf{v} = \mathbf{A}e^{\lambda t}\mathbf{v}$$

eliminating the term $e^{\lambda t}$ we have

$$\lambda\mathbf{v} = \mathbf{A}\mathbf{v}$$
$$\text{i.e. } (\mathbf{A} - \lambda\mathbf{I})\mathbf{v} = \mathbf{0}$$

For a nontrivial solution we require that

$$\det(\mathbf{A} - \lambda\mathbf{I}) = 0$$

---

[5] Here $\mathbf{u} = e^{rt}\mathbf{v}$.

We investigated this problem in the last section. What we wish to find is the eigenvalues of **A** and the associated eigenvectors. Return to the situation with only two variables, and let the two roots (the two eigenvalues) be real and distinct, which we shall again label as r and s. Let $\mathbf{v}^r$ be the eigenvector associated with the root r and $\mathbf{v}^s$ be the eigenvector associated with the root s. Then so long as $r \neq s$

$$\mathbf{u}^1 = e^{rt}\mathbf{v}^r \qquad \text{and} \qquad \mathbf{u}^2 = e^{st}\mathbf{v}^s$$

are independent solutions, while

$$\mathbf{x} = c_1 e^{rt}\mathbf{v}^r + c_2 e^{st}\mathbf{v}^s \tag{4.22}$$

is a general solution.

Example 4.8

Find the general solution to the dynamic system

$$\dot{x} = x + y$$
$$\dot{y} = -2x + 4y$$

We can write this in matrix form

$$\begin{bmatrix} \dot{x} \\ \dot{y} \end{bmatrix} = \begin{bmatrix} 1 & 1 \\ -2 & 4 \end{bmatrix} \begin{bmatrix} x \\ y \end{bmatrix}$$

The matrix **A** of this system has already been investigated in terms of example 4.7. Note, however, that $\det(\mathbf{A}) > 0$. In example 4.7 we found that the two eigenvalues were $r = 3$ and $s = 2$ and the associated eigenvectors were

$$\mathbf{v}^r = \begin{bmatrix} 1 \\ 2 \end{bmatrix}, \qquad \mathbf{v}^s = \begin{bmatrix} 1 \\ 1 \end{bmatrix}$$

Then the general solution is

$$\mathbf{x} = c_1 e^{3t} \begin{bmatrix} 1 \\ 2 \end{bmatrix} + c_2 e^{2t} \begin{bmatrix} 1 \\ 1 \end{bmatrix}$$

or, in terms of x and y

$$x(t) = c_1 e^{3t} + c_2 e^{2t}$$
$$y(t) = 2c_1 e^{3t} + c_2 e^{2t}$$

Given an initial condition, it is possible to solve for c_1 and c_2. For example, if $x(0) = 1$ and $y(0) = 3$, then

$$1 = c_1 + c_2$$
$$3 = 2c_1 + c_2$$

which gives $c_1 = 2$ and $c_2 = -1$. Leading to our final result

$$x(t) = 2e^{3t} - e^{2t}$$
$$y(t) = 4e^{3t} - e^{2t}$$

4.6 Solutions with repeating roots

In chapter 2 we used

$$ce^{\lambda t} \quad \text{and} \quad cte^{\lambda t}$$

for a repeated root. If $\lambda = r$ which is a repeated root, then either there are two independent eigenvectors $\mathbf{v}^1$ and $\mathbf{v}^2$ which will lead to the general solution

$$\mathbf{x} = c_1 e^{rt}\mathbf{v}^1 + c_2 e^{rt}\mathbf{v}^2$$

or else there is only *one* associated eigenvector, say $\mathbf{v}$. In this latter case we use the result

(4.23) $$\mathbf{x} = c_1 e^{rt}\mathbf{v}^1 + c_2(e^{rt}t\mathbf{v} + e^{rt}\mathbf{v}^2)$$

In this latter case the second solution satisfies $e^{rt}t\mathbf{v} + e^{rt}\mathbf{v}^2$ and is combined with the solution $e^{rt}\mathbf{v}^1$ to obtain the general solution (see Boyce and DiPrima 1997, pp. 390–6). We shall consider two examples, the first with a repeating root, but with two linearly independent eigenvectors, and a second with a repeating root but only one associated eigenvector.

Example 4.9

Consider

$$\dot{x} = x$$
$$\dot{y} = y$$

Then

$$\begin{bmatrix} \dot{x} \\ \dot{y} \end{bmatrix} = \begin{bmatrix} 1 & 0 \\ 0 & 1 \end{bmatrix} \begin{bmatrix} x \\ y \end{bmatrix}$$

where

$$\mathbf{A} = \begin{bmatrix} 1 & 0 \\ 0 & 1 \end{bmatrix}, \quad \det(\mathbf{A}) = 1, \quad \mathbf{A} - \lambda\mathbf{I} = \begin{bmatrix} 1 - \lambda & 0 \\ 0 & 1 - \lambda \end{bmatrix}$$

Hence, $\det(\mathbf{A} - \lambda\mathbf{I}) = (1 - \lambda)^2 = 0$, with root $\lambda = r = 1$ (twice).
Using this value of λ then

$$(\mathbf{A} - \mathbf{I}) = \begin{bmatrix} 0 & 0 \\ 0 & 0 \end{bmatrix}$$

Since $(\mathbf{A} - r\mathbf{I})\mathbf{v} = \mathbf{0}\,(r = 1)$ is satisfied for any vector $\mathbf{v}$, then we can choose any arbitrary set of linearly independent vectors for eigenvectors. Let these be

$$\mathbf{v}^1 = \begin{bmatrix} 1 \\ 0 \end{bmatrix} \quad \text{and} \quad \mathbf{v}^2 = \begin{bmatrix} 0 \\ 1 \end{bmatrix}$$

then the general solution is

$$\mathbf{x} = c_1 e^{rt} \begin{bmatrix} 1 \\ 0 \end{bmatrix} + c_2 e^{rt} \begin{bmatrix} 0 \\ 1 \end{bmatrix}$$

or

$$x(t) = c_1 e^{rt}$$
$$y(t) = c_2 e^{rt}$$

Example 4.10

Let

$$\dot{x} = x - y$$
$$\dot{y} = x + 3y$$

Then

$$\begin{bmatrix} \dot{x} \\ \dot{y} \end{bmatrix} = \begin{bmatrix} 1 & -1 \\ 1 & 3 \end{bmatrix} \begin{bmatrix} x \\ y \end{bmatrix}$$

with

$$\mathbf{A} = \begin{bmatrix} 1 & -1 \\ 1 & 3 \end{bmatrix}, \qquad \det(\mathbf{A}) = 4, \qquad \mathbf{A} - \lambda\mathbf{I} = \begin{bmatrix} 1 - \lambda & -1 \\ 1 & 3 - \lambda \end{bmatrix}$$

Hence, $\det(\mathbf{A} - \lambda\mathbf{I}) = \lambda^2 - 4\lambda + 4 = (\lambda - 2)^2$, with root $\lambda = r = 2$ (twice).
Using $\lambda = r = 2$

$$\mathbf{A} - r\mathbf{I} = \begin{bmatrix} -1 & -1 \\ 1 & 1 \end{bmatrix}$$

and

$$(\mathbf{A} - r\mathbf{I}) \begin{bmatrix} x \\ y \end{bmatrix} = \begin{bmatrix} -1 & -1 \\ 1 & 1 \end{bmatrix} \begin{bmatrix} x \\ y \end{bmatrix}$$

which implies $-x - y = 0$. Given we normalise x to $x = 1$, then $y = -1$. The first solution is then

$$e^{2t} \begin{bmatrix} 1 \\ -1 \end{bmatrix}$$

To obtain the second solution we might think of proceeding as in the single variable case, but this is not valid (see Boyce and DiPrima 1997, pp. 390–6). What we need to use is

$$e^{2t} t\mathbf{v} + e^{2t} \mathbf{v}^2$$

where we need to find the elements of $\mathbf{v}^2$.
Since we know $\mathbf{v}$, then the second solution $\mathbf{u}^2 = (x_2, y_2)$ is

$$\begin{bmatrix} x_2 \\ y_2 \end{bmatrix} = e^{2t} t \begin{bmatrix} 1 \\ -1 \end{bmatrix} + e^{2t} \begin{bmatrix} v_1 \\ v_2 \end{bmatrix}$$

i.e.

$$x_2 = e^{2t}(t + v_1)$$
$$y_2 = e^{2t}(-t + v_2)$$

Hence

$$\dot{x} = 2e^{2t}(t + v_1) + e^{2t} = e^{2t}(2t + 2v_1 + 1)$$
$$\dot{y} = 2e^{2t}(-t + v_2) + e^{2t} = e^{2t}(-2t + 2v_2 + 1)$$

Substituting all these results into the differential equation system we have

$$e^{2t}(2t + 2v_1 + 1) = e^{2t}(t + v_1) - e^{2t}(-t + v_2)$$
$$e^{2t}(-2t + 2v_2 - 1) = e^{2t}(t + v_1) + 3e^{2t}(-t + v_2)$$

Eliminating e^{2t} and simplifying, we obtain

$$v_1 + v_2 = -1$$
$$v_1 + v_2 = -1$$

which is a *dependent* system. Since we require only one solution, set $v_2 = 0$, giving $v_1 = -1$. This means solution $\mathbf{x}^2$ is

$$\mathbf{x}^2 = e^{2t}t \begin{bmatrix} 1 \\ -1 \end{bmatrix} + e^{2t} \begin{bmatrix} -1 \\ 0 \end{bmatrix}$$

Hence, the *general* solution is

$$\mathbf{x} = c_1 e^{2t} \begin{bmatrix} 1 \\ -1 \end{bmatrix} + c_2 \left(e^{2t}t \begin{bmatrix} 1 \\ -1 \end{bmatrix} + e^{2t} \begin{bmatrix} -1 \\ 0 \end{bmatrix} \right)$$

or

$$x = c_1 e^{2t} + c_2(t - 1)e^{2t}$$
$$y = -c_1 e^{2t} - c_2 t e^{2t}$$

4.7   Solutions with complex roots

For the system

$$\dot{\mathbf{x}} = \mathbf{A}\mathbf{x}$$

with characteristic equation $\det(\mathbf{A} - \lambda \mathbf{I}) = 0$, if $\mathrm{tr}(\mathbf{A})^2 < 4\det(\mathbf{A})$, then we have complex conjugate roots.

Return to our situation of just two roots, $\lambda = r$ and $\lambda = s$. Then

(4.24)
$$r = \alpha + \beta i$$
$$s = \alpha - \beta i$$

But this implies that the eigenvectors $\mathbf{v}^r$ and $\mathbf{v}^s$ associated with r and s, respectively, are also complex conjugate.

Example 4.11

Consider

$$\dot{x} = -3x + 4y$$
$$\dot{y} = -2x + y$$

Then

$$\begin{bmatrix} \dot{x} \\ \dot{y} \end{bmatrix} = \begin{bmatrix} -3 & 4 \\ -2 & 1 \end{bmatrix} \begin{bmatrix} x \\ y \end{bmatrix}$$

with

$$\mathbf{A} = \begin{bmatrix} -3 & 4 \\ -2 & 1 \end{bmatrix}, \qquad \det(\mathbf{A}) = 5, \qquad \mathbf{A} - \lambda \mathbf{I} = \begin{bmatrix} -3 - \lambda & 4 \\ -2 & 1 - \lambda \end{bmatrix}$$

and $\det(\mathbf{A} - \lambda\mathbf{I}) = \lambda^2 + 2\lambda + 5$, which leads to the roots

$$r = \frac{-2 + \sqrt{4 - 20}}{2} = -1 + 2i \quad \text{and} \quad s = \frac{-2 - \sqrt{4 - 20}}{2} = -1 - 2i$$

The associated eigenvectors are

$$(\mathbf{A} - \lambda\mathbf{I})\mathbf{v}^r = \begin{bmatrix} -2 - 2i & 4 \\ -2 & 2 - 2i \end{bmatrix} \mathbf{v}^r = \begin{bmatrix} 0 \\ 0 \end{bmatrix}$$

i.e.

$$-(2 + 2i)v_r^1 + 4v_2^r = 0$$
$$-2v_1^r + (2 - 2i)v_2^r = 0$$

Let $v_1^r = 2$, then $v_2^r = 2(2 + 2i)/4 = 1 + i$. Thus

$$\mathbf{u}^1 = e^{(-1+2i)t} \begin{bmatrix} 2 \\ 1 + i \end{bmatrix}$$

Turning to the second root. With $\lambda = s = -1 - 2i$ then

$$(\mathbf{A} - \lambda\mathbf{I})\mathbf{v}^s = \begin{bmatrix} -2 + 2i & 4 \\ -2 & 2 + 2i \end{bmatrix} \begin{bmatrix} v_1^s \\ v_2^s \end{bmatrix}$$

i.e.

$$(-2 + 2i)v_1^s + 4v_2^s = 0$$
$$-2v_1^s + (2 + 2i)v_2^s = 0$$

Choose $v_1^s = 2$, then $v_2^s = -(-2 + 2i)(2)/4 = 1 - i$. Hence the second solution is

$$\mathbf{u}^2 = e^{-(1+2i)t} \begin{bmatrix} 2 \\ 1 - i \end{bmatrix}$$

i.e. $\mathbf{v}^s$ is the complex conjugate of $\mathbf{v}^r$. Hence the general solution is

$$\mathbf{x} = c_1 e^{(-1+2i)t} \begin{bmatrix} 2 \\ 1 + i \end{bmatrix} + c_2 e^{-(1+2i)t} \begin{bmatrix} 2 \\ 1 - i \end{bmatrix}$$

These are, however, imaginary solutions. To convert them to real solutions we employ two results. One is Euler's identity (see exercise 10 of chapter 2), i.e.

$$e^{i\theta} = \cos\theta + i\sin\theta$$

The other employs the real elements of $\mathbf{v}^r$ (or $\mathbf{v}^s$). Let $\mathbf{v}^r$ generally be written

$$\mathbf{v}^r = \begin{bmatrix} u_1 + w_1 i \\ u_2 + w_2 i \end{bmatrix}$$

and define

$$\mathbf{b}_1 = \begin{bmatrix} u_1 \\ u_2 \end{bmatrix} \quad \text{and} \quad \mathbf{b}_2 = -\begin{bmatrix} w_1 \\ w_2 \end{bmatrix}$$

then the two solutions can be written in the form[6]

$$\mathbf{u}^1 = e^{\alpha t}(\mathbf{b}_1 \cos\beta t + \mathbf{b}_2 \sin\beta t)$$
$$\mathbf{u}^2 = e^{\alpha t}(\mathbf{b}_2 \cos\beta t - \mathbf{b}_1 \sin\beta t)$$

---

[6] See Giordano and Weir (1991, pp. 180–1).

with the general solution

(4.25) $\mathbf{x} = c_1\mathbf{u}^1 + c_2\mathbf{u}^2$

Continuing our example, where $\lambda = -1 + 2i$, i.e., $\alpha = -1$ and $\beta = 2$, then

$$\mathbf{v}^r = \begin{bmatrix} 2 \\ 1+i \end{bmatrix}, \quad \text{i.e. } \mathbf{b}_1 = \begin{bmatrix} 2 \\ 1 \end{bmatrix} \quad \text{and} \quad \mathbf{b}_2 = \begin{bmatrix} 0 \\ -1 \end{bmatrix}$$

Hence

$$\mathbf{u}^1 = e^{-t}\left(\begin{bmatrix} 2 \\ 1 \end{bmatrix}\cos 2t + \begin{bmatrix} 0 \\ -1 \end{bmatrix}\sin 2t\right)$$

$$\mathbf{u}^2 = e^{-t}\left(\begin{bmatrix} 0 \\ -1 \end{bmatrix}\cos 2t - \begin{bmatrix} 2 \\ 1 \end{bmatrix}\sin 2t\right)$$

and

$$\mathbf{x} = c_1\mathbf{u}^1 + c_2\mathbf{u}^2$$

or

$$x(t) = c_1 e^{-t}2\cos 2t - 2c_2 e^{-t}\sin 2t$$
$$= 2e^{-t}(c_1\cos 2t - c_2\sin 2t)$$

$$y(t) = c_1 e^{-t}\cos 2t - c_1 e^{-t}\sin 2t - c_2 e^{-t}\cos 2t - c_2 e^{-t}\sin 2t$$
$$= e^{-t}[(c_1 - c_2)\cos 2t - (c_1 + c_2)\sin 2t]$$

4.8 Nodes, spirals and saddles

Here we shall consider only a two-variable system of the general form

$$\dot{\mathbf{x}} = \mathbf{Ax}$$

which to have solutions of the form $\mathbf{x} = e^{\lambda t}\mathbf{v}$ must satisfy

$$(\mathbf{A} - \lambda\mathbf{I})\mathbf{v} = \mathbf{0}$$

and λ must be the eigenvalue and $\mathbf{v}$ the eigenvector associated with the matrix $\mathbf{A}$. We shall denote the two eigenvalues as $\lambda = r$ and $\lambda = s$ and the two associated eigenvectors $\mathbf{v}^r$ and $\mathbf{v}^s$, respectively. We have already discussed the general solution of the form

$$\mathbf{x} = c_1 e^{rt}\mathbf{v}^r + c_2 e^{st}\mathbf{v}^s$$

In this section we shall extract some geometric properties from the various possible solutions. First such a system will have a critical point, denoted $\mathbf{x}^*$, if $\mathbf{Ax} = \mathbf{0}$. If $\mathbf{A}$ is nonsingular, or $\det(\mathbf{A}) \neq 0$, then the only solution is $\mathbf{x}^* = \mathbf{0}$. The only critical point is at the origin. The solution function $\mathbf{x} = \phi(t)$ satisfies the differential equations, and this shows the solution path in the phase plane. In terms of vectors, the situation is illustrated in figure 4.15. The (x,y)-plane denotes the phase plane and the origin is a critical point, fixed point or equilibrium point. At time $t = 0$ we have $x(0) = x_0$ and $y(0) = y_0$. At time t there is a vector with coordinates $(x(t), y(t))$ and the movement of the system as time increases is indicated by the arrows along the solution path.

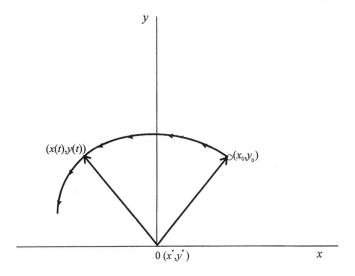

Figure 4.15.

Case 1 (Real distinct roots of the same sign)

Here we are considering the general solution

$$\mathbf{x} = c_1 e^{rt} \mathbf{v}^r + c_2 e^{st} \mathbf{v}^s$$

where r and s are real and distinct and are either both positive or both negative. We shall assume that r is the larger root in absolute value $|r| > |s|$. Suppose both roots are negative, then $r < s < 0$. Further, suppose the associated eigenvectors $\mathbf{v}^r$ and $\mathbf{v}^s$ are as shown in figure 4.16 by the heavy arrows. Thus it is quite clear that as $t \to \infty$, $e^{rt} \to 0$ and $e^{st} \to 0$, and so $\mathbf{x} \to \mathbf{0}$ regardless of the value of c_1 and c_2. Of particular significance is that if the initial point lies on $\mathbf{v}^r$, then $c_2 = 0$ and the system moves down the line through $\mathbf{v}^r$ and approaches the origin over time. Similarly, if the initial point lies on $\mathbf{v}^s$, then $c_1 = 0$ and the system moves down the line $\mathbf{v}^s$, approaching the origin in the limit. The critical point is called a **node**.[7] In the present case we have a *stable* node.

If r and s are both positive, then the system will move away from the fixed point over time. This is because both x and y grow exponentially. In this case we have an *unstable* node.

Example 4.12

Let

$$\dot{x} = -2x + y$$
$$\dot{y} = x - 2y$$

with

$$\mathbf{A} = \begin{bmatrix} -2 & 1 \\ 1 & -2 \end{bmatrix}, \qquad \det(\mathbf{A}) = 3, \qquad \mathbf{A} - \lambda \mathbf{I} = \begin{bmatrix} -2 - \lambda & 1 \\ 1 & -2 - \lambda \end{bmatrix}$$

---

[7] Sometimes called an *improper node*.

Figure 4.16.

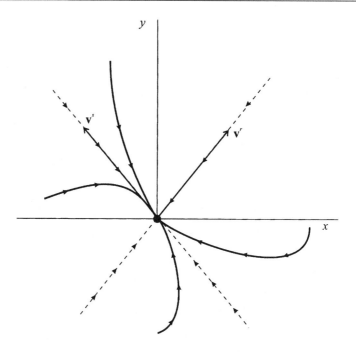

Hence $\det(\mathbf{A} - \lambda\mathbf{I}) = \lambda^2 + 4\lambda + 3 = (\lambda + 3)(\lambda + 1) = 0$, which leads to roots $\lambda = r = -3$ and $\lambda = s = -1$. Using these values for the eigenvalues, the eigenvectors are

$$\mathbf{v}^r = \begin{bmatrix} 1 \\ -1 \end{bmatrix} \quad \text{and} \quad \mathbf{v}^s = \begin{bmatrix} 1 \\ 1 \end{bmatrix}$$

which gives the general solution

$$\mathbf{x} = c_1 e^{-3t} \begin{bmatrix} 1 \\ -1 \end{bmatrix} + c_2 e^{-t} \begin{bmatrix} 1 \\ 1 \end{bmatrix}$$

or

$$x(t) = c_1 e^{-3t} + c_2 e^{-t}$$
$$y(t) = -c_1 e^{-3t} + c_2 e^{-t}$$

The solution is illustrated in figure 4.17,[8] where the solution paths are revealed by the direction field, indicating quite clearly that the origin is a stable node.

Case 2 (Real distinct roots of opposite sign)

Consider again

$$\mathbf{x} = c_1 e^{rt} \mathbf{v}^r + c_2 e^{st} \mathbf{v}^s$$

where r and s are both real but of opposite sign. Let $r > 0$ and $s < 0$. Suppose the eigenvectors are those as shown in figure 4.18. If a solution starts on the line

[8] Notice that the solution paths tend towards the eigenvector $\mathbf{v}^s$.

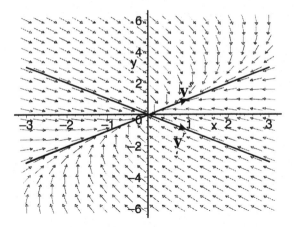

Figure 4.17.

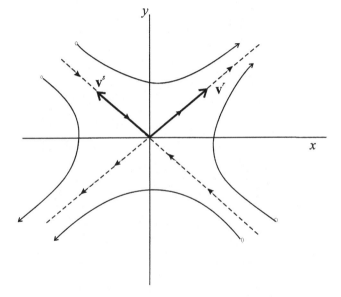

Figure 4.18.

through $\mathbf{v}^r$ then $c_2 = 0$. The solution will therefore remain on $\mathbf{v}^r$. Since r is positive, then over time the solution moves away from the origin, away from the fixed point. On the other hand, if the system starts on the line through $\mathbf{v}^s$, then $c_1 = 0$, and since $s < 0$, then as $t \to \infty$ the system tends towards the fixed point.

For initial points off the lines through the eigenvectors, then the positive root will dominate the system. Hence for points above $\mathbf{v}^r$ and $\mathbf{v}^s$, the solution path will veer towards the line through $\mathbf{v}^r$. The same is true for any initial point below $\mathbf{v}^r$ and above $\mathbf{v}^s$. On the other hand, an initial point below the line through $\mathbf{v}^s$ will be dominated by the larger root and the system will veer towards minus infinity. In this case the node is called a **saddle point**. The line through $\mathbf{v}^r$ is called the *unstable arm*, while the line through $\mathbf{v}^s$ is called the *stable arm*.

Saddle path equilibria are common in economics and one should look out for them in terms of real distinct roots of opposite sign and the fact that $\det(\mathbf{A})$ is negative. It will also be important to establish the stable and unstable arms of the saddle point, which are derived from the eigenvectors associated with the characteristic roots.

Because of the importance of saddle points in economics, we shall consider two examples here.

Example 4.13

Let

$$\dot{x} = x + y$$
$$\dot{y} = 4x + y$$

then

$$\begin{bmatrix} \dot{x} \\ \dot{y} \end{bmatrix} = \begin{bmatrix} 1 & 1 \\ 4 & 1 \end{bmatrix} \begin{bmatrix} x \\ y \end{bmatrix}$$

with

$$\mathbf{A} = \begin{bmatrix} 1 & 1 \\ 4 & 1 \end{bmatrix}, \qquad \det(\mathbf{A}) = -3, \qquad \mathbf{A} - \lambda\mathbf{I} = \begin{bmatrix} 1 - \lambda & 1 \\ 4 & 1 - \lambda \end{bmatrix}$$

giving $\det(\mathbf{A} - \lambda\mathbf{I}) = \lambda^2 - 2\lambda - 3 = (\lambda - 3)(\lambda + 1) = 0$. Hence, $\lambda = r = 3$ and $\lambda = s = -1$. For $\lambda = r = 3$ then

$$(\mathbf{A} - \lambda\mathbf{I})\mathbf{v}^r = \begin{bmatrix} -2 & 1 \\ 4 & -2 \end{bmatrix} \mathbf{v}^r = \mathbf{0}$$

i.e.

$$-2v_1^r + v_2^r = 0$$
$$4v_1^r - 2v_2^r = 0$$

Let $v_1^r = 1$, then $v_2^r = 2$. Hence, one solution is

$$\mathbf{u}^1 = e^{rt} \begin{bmatrix} 1 \\ 2 \end{bmatrix} \qquad \text{and} \qquad \mathbf{v}^r = \begin{bmatrix} 1 \\ 2 \end{bmatrix}$$

For $\lambda = s = -1$, then

$$(\mathbf{A} - \lambda\mathbf{I})\mathbf{v}^s = \begin{bmatrix} 2 & 1 \\ 4 & 2 \end{bmatrix} \mathbf{v}^s = \mathbf{0}$$

i.e.

$$2v_1^s + v_2^s = 0$$
$$4v_1^s + 2v_2^s = 0$$

Let $v_1^s = 1$, then $v_2^s = -2$. Hence, a second solution is

$$\mathbf{u}^2 = e^{st} \begin{bmatrix} 1 \\ -2 \end{bmatrix} \qquad \text{and} \qquad \mathbf{v}^s = \begin{bmatrix} 1 \\ -2 \end{bmatrix}$$

The situation is illustrated in figure 4.19. The solution paths are revealed by the direction field. The figure quite clearly shows that the unstable arm of the saddle is the line through the eigenvector $\mathbf{v}^r$, while the stable arm of the saddle is the line through the eigenvector $\mathbf{v}^s$.

Figure 4.19.

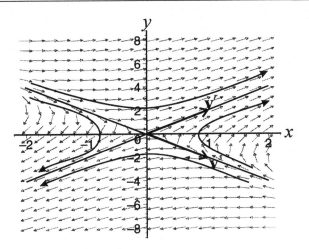

Example 4.14

Let

$$\dot{x} = 3x - 2y$$
$$\dot{y} = 2x - 2y$$

then

$$\begin{bmatrix} \dot{x} \\ \dot{y} \end{bmatrix} = \begin{bmatrix} 3 & -2 \\ 2 & -2 \end{bmatrix} \begin{bmatrix} x \\ y \end{bmatrix}$$

with

$$\mathbf{A} = \begin{bmatrix} 3 & -2 \\ 2 & -2 \end{bmatrix}, \qquad \det(\mathbf{A}) = -2, \qquad \mathbf{A} - \lambda\mathbf{I} = \begin{bmatrix} 3 - \lambda & -2 \\ 2 & -2 - \lambda \end{bmatrix}$$

giving $\det(\mathbf{A} - \lambda\mathbf{I}) = \lambda^2 - \lambda - 2 = (\lambda - 2)(\lambda + 1) = 0$. Hence, $\lambda = r = 2$ and $\lambda = s = -1$. For $\lambda = r = 2$ then

$$(\mathbf{A} - \lambda\mathbf{I})\mathbf{v}^r = \begin{bmatrix} 1 & -2 \\ 2 & -4 \end{bmatrix} \mathbf{v}^r = \mathbf{0}$$

i.e.

$$v_1^r - 2v_2^r = 0$$
$$2v_1^r - 4v_2^r = 0$$

Let $v_1^r = 2$, then $v_2^r = 1$. Hence, one solution is

$$\mathbf{u}^1 = e^{rt} \begin{bmatrix} 2 \\ 1 \end{bmatrix} \qquad \text{and} \qquad \mathbf{v}^r = \begin{bmatrix} 2 \\ 1 \end{bmatrix}$$

For $\lambda = s = -1$, then

$$(\mathbf{A} - \lambda\mathbf{I})\mathbf{v}^s = \begin{bmatrix} 4 & -2 \\ 2 & -1 \end{bmatrix} \mathbf{v}^s = \mathbf{0}$$

Figure 4.20.

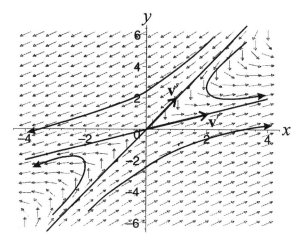

i.e.

$$4v_1^s - 2v_2^s = 0$$
$$2v_1^s - v_2^s = 0$$

Let $v_1^s = 1$, then $v_2^s = 2$. Hence, a second solution is

$$\mathbf{u}^2 = e^{st}\begin{bmatrix}1\\2\end{bmatrix} \qquad \text{and} \qquad \mathbf{v}^s = \begin{bmatrix}1\\2\end{bmatrix}$$

The situation is illustrated in figure 4.20. The solution paths are revealed by the direction field. The unstable arm of the saddle is the line through the eigenvector $\mathbf{v}^r$, while the stable arm of the saddle is the line through the eigenvector $\mathbf{v}^s$.

Case 3 (Real equal roots)

In this case $\lambda = r = s$. Throughout assume the repeated root is negative. (If it is positive then the argument is identical but the movement of the system is reversed.) There are two sub-cases to consider in line with our earlier analysis: (a) independent eigenvectors, and (b) one independent eigenvector. The two situations were found to be:

(a) $\mathbf{x} = c_1 e^{rt}\mathbf{v}^1 + c_2 e^{rt}\mathbf{v}^2$
(b) $\mathbf{x} = c_1 e^{rt}\mathbf{v} + c_2[e^{rt}t\mathbf{v} + e^{rt}\mathbf{v}^2]$

Consider each case in turn. In example 4.9 we found for two independent eigenvectors

$$x(t) = c_1 e^{rt}$$
$$y(t) = c_2 e^{rt}$$

Hence, $x/y = c_1/c_2$ is independent of t and depends only on the components of $\mathbf{v}^r$ and $\mathbf{v}^s$ and the arbitrary constants c_1 and c_2. This is a general result and so all solutions lie on straight lines through the origin, as shown in figure 4.21. In this case the origin is a *proper node* that is stable. Had the repeated root been positive, then we would have an unstable proper node. It is this situation we gave an example

Figure 4.21.

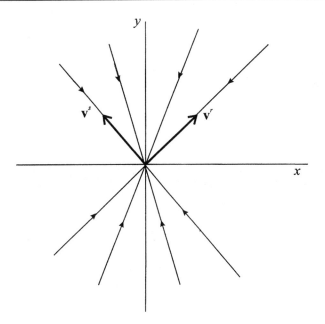

Figure 4.22.

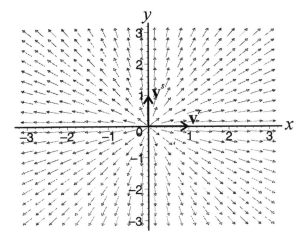

of at the beginning of section 4.6. The direction field, along with the independent vectors is shown in figure 4.22 for this example.

For the second sub-case, where again $r < 0$, for large t the dominant term must be $c_2 e^{rt} t \mathbf{v}$, and hence as $t \to \infty$ every trajectory must approach the origin and in such a manner that it is tangent to the line through the eigenvector $\mathbf{v}$. Certainly, if $c_2 = 0$ then the solution must lie on the line through the eigenvector $\mathbf{v}$, and approaches the origin along this line, as shown in figure 4.23. (Had $r > 0$, then every trajectory would have moved away from the origin.)

The approach of the trajectories to the origin depends on the eigenvectors $\mathbf{v}$ and $\mathbf{v}^2$. One possibility is illustrated in figure 4.23. To see what is happening, express

Figure 4.23.

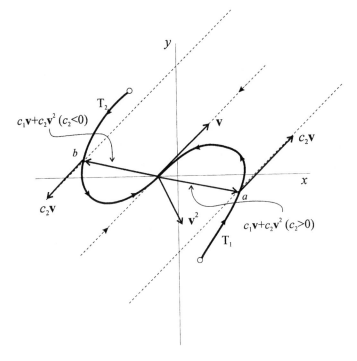

the general solution as

$$\mathbf{x} = [c_1 e^{rt}\mathbf{v} + c_2 e^{rt}\mathbf{v}^2 + c_2 e^{rt}t\mathbf{v}] = [(c_1\mathbf{v} + c_2\mathbf{v}^2) + c_2 t\mathbf{v}]e^{rt} = \mathbf{u}e^{rt}$$

Then

$$\mathbf{u} = (c_1\mathbf{v} + c_2\mathbf{v}^2) + c_2 t\mathbf{v}$$

which is a vector equation of a straight line which passes through the point $c_1\mathbf{v} + c_2\mathbf{v}^2$ and is parallel to $\mathbf{v}$. Two such points are illustrated in figure 4.23, one at point $a\,(c_2 > 0)$ and one at point $b\,(c_2 < 0)$.

We shall not go further into the mathematics of such a node here. What we can do, however, is highlight the variety of solution paths by means of two numerical examples. The first, in figure 4.24, has the orientation of the trajectories as illustrated in figure 4.23, while figure 4.25 has the reverse orientation. Whatever the orientation, the critical point is again an improper node that is stable. Had $r > 0$, then the critical point would be an improper node that is unstable.

Case 4 (Complex roots, $\alpha \neq 0$ and $\beta > 0$)

In this case we assume the roots $\lambda = r$ and $\lambda = s$ are complex conjugate and with $r = \alpha + \beta i$ and $s = \alpha - \beta i$, and $\alpha \neq 0$ and $\beta > 0$. Systems having such complex roots can be expressed

$$\dot{x} = \alpha x + \beta y$$
$$\dot{y} = -\beta x + \alpha y$$

Figure 4.24.

$$\dot{x} = -4x - y$$
$$\dot{y} = x - 2y$$

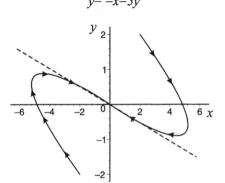

$$\dot{x} = x + 9y$$
$$\dot{y} = -x - 5y$$

Figure 4.25.

or

$$\begin{bmatrix} \dot{x} \\ \dot{y} \end{bmatrix} = \begin{bmatrix} \alpha & \beta \\ -\beta & \alpha \end{bmatrix} \begin{bmatrix} x \\ y \end{bmatrix}$$

Now express the system in terms of polar coordinates with R and θ, where

$$R^2 = x^2 + y^2 \qquad \text{and} \qquad \tan\theta = \frac{y}{x}$$

and $\dot{R} = \alpha R$ which results in

$$R = ce^{\alpha t} \qquad \text{where } c \text{ is a constant}$$

Similarly

$$\dot{\theta} = -\beta$$

giving

$$\theta = -\beta t + \theta_0 \qquad \text{where } \theta(0) = \theta_0$$

What we have here are parametric equations

$$R = ce^{\alpha t}$$
$$\theta = -\beta t + \theta_0$$

Figure 4.26.   (a)

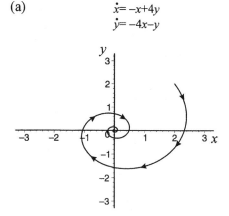

$$\dot{x} = -x + 4y$$
$$\dot{y} = -4x - y$$

(b)

$$\dot{x} = x + 4y$$
$$\dot{y} = -4x + y$$

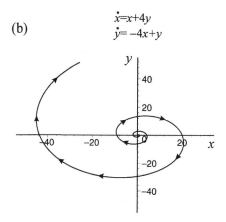

in polar coordinates of the original system. Since $\beta > 0$ then θ decreases over time, and so the motion is *clockwise*. Furthermore, as $t \to \infty$ then either $R \to 0$ if $\alpha < 0$ or $R \to \infty$ if $\alpha > 0$. Consequently, the trajectories spiral either towards the origin or away from the origin depending on the value of α. The two possibilities are illustrated in figure 4.26. The critical point in such situations is called a **spiral point**.

Case 5 (Complex roots, $\alpha = 0$ and $\beta > 0$)

In this case we assume the roots $\lambda = r$ and $\lambda = s$ are complex conjugate with $r = \beta i$ and $s = -\beta i$ (i.e. $\alpha = 0$). In line with the analysis in case 4, this means

$$\begin{bmatrix} \dot{x} \\ \dot{y} \end{bmatrix} = \begin{bmatrix} 0 & \beta \\ -\beta & 0 \end{bmatrix} \begin{bmatrix} x \\ y \end{bmatrix}$$

resulting in $\dot{R} = 0$ and $\dot{\theta} = -\beta$, giving $R = c$ and $\theta = -\beta t + \theta_0$, where c and θ_0 are constants. This means that the trajectories are closed curves (circles or ellipses) with centre at the origin. If $\beta > 0$ the movement is clockwise while if $\beta < 0$ the movement is anticlockwise. A complete circuit around the origin denotes the phase

(a)

$$\dot{x} = 3y$$
$$\dot{y} = -3x$$

Figure 4.27.

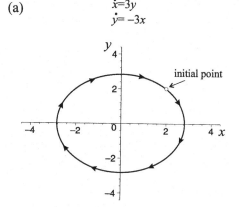

(b)

$$\dot{x} = -3y$$
$$\dot{y} = 3x$$

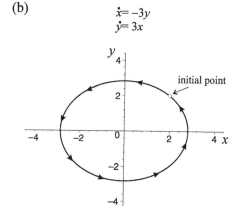

of the cycle, which is $2\pi/\beta$. The critical point is called the **centre**. These situations are illustrated in figure 4.27.

Summary

From the five cases discussed we arrive at a number of observations.

1.   After a sufficient time interval, the trajectory of the system tends towards three types of behaviour:
      (i) the trajectory approaches infinity
      (ii) the trajectory approaches the critical point
      (iii) the trajectory traverses a closed curve surrounding the critical point.
2.   Through each point (x_0, y_0) in the phase plane there is only one trajectory.
3.   Considering the set of all trajectories, then three possibilities arise:
      (i) All trajectories approach the critical point. This occurs when
         (a) $\text{tr}(\mathbf{A})^2 > 4\det(\mathbf{A})$, $r < s < 0$
         (b) $\text{tr}(\mathbf{A})^2 < 4\det(\mathbf{A})$, $r = \alpha + \beta i$, $s = \alpha - \beta i$ and $\alpha < 0$.

(ii) All trajectories remain bounded but do not approach the critical point as $t \to \infty$. This occurs when $\text{tr}(\mathbf{A})^2 < 4\det(\mathbf{A})$ and $r = \beta i$ and $s = -\beta i (\alpha = 0)$.

(iii) At least one of the trajectories tends to infinity as $t \to \infty$. This occurs when

  (a) $\text{tr}(\mathbf{A})^2 > 4\det(\mathbf{A})$, $r > 0$ and $s > 0$ or $r < 0$ and $s > 0$
  (b) $\text{tr}(\mathbf{A})^2 < 4\det(\mathbf{A})$, $r = \alpha + \beta i$, $s = \alpha - \beta i$ and $\alpha > 0$.

4.9   Stability/instability and its matrix specification

Having outlined the methods of solution for linear systems of homogeneous autonomous equations, it is quite clear that the characteristic roots play an important part in these. Here we shall continue to pursue just the two-variable cases.

For the system

$$\dot{x} = ax + by$$
$$\dot{y} = cx + dy$$

where

$$\mathbf{A} = \begin{bmatrix} a & b \\ c & d \end{bmatrix} \qquad \text{and} \qquad \mathbf{A} - \lambda\mathbf{I} = \begin{bmatrix} a - \lambda & b \\ c & d - \lambda \end{bmatrix}$$

we have already shown that a unique critical point exists if $\mathbf{A}$ is nonsingular, i.e., $\det(\mathbf{A}) \neq 0$ and that

(4.26)
$$r, s = \frac{\text{tr}(\mathbf{A}) \pm \sqrt{\text{tr}(\mathbf{A})^2 - 4\det(\mathbf{A})}}{2}$$

Furthermore, if:

  (i) $\text{tr}(\mathbf{A})^2 > 4\det(\mathbf{A})$ the roots are real and distinct
  (ii) $\text{tr}(\mathbf{A})^2 = 4\det(\mathbf{A})$ the roots are real and equal
  (iii) $\text{tr}(\mathbf{A})^2 < 4\det(\mathbf{A})$ the roots are complex conjugate.

This leads to our first distinction.

To illustrate the variety of solutions we plot the $\text{tr}(\mathbf{A})$ on the horizontal axis and the $\det(\mathbf{A})$ on the vertical, which is valid because these are scalars. The plane is then divided by plotting the curve $\text{tr}(\mathbf{A})^2 = 4\det(\mathbf{A})$ (i.e. $x^2 = 4y$), which is a parabola with minimum at the origin, as shown in figure 4.28.

Below the curve $\text{tr}(\mathbf{A})^2 > 4\det(\mathbf{A})$ and so the roots are real and distinct; above the curve the roots are complex conjugate; while along the curve the roots are real and equal.

We can further sub-divide the situations according to the sign/value of the two roots. Take first real distinct roots that lie strictly below the curve. If both roots are negative then the $\text{tr}(\mathbf{A})$ must be negative, and since $\det(\mathbf{A})$ is positive, then we are in the region below the curve and above the x-axis, labelled region I in figure 4.28. In this region the critical point is asymptotically stable.

In region II, which is also below the curve and above the x-axis, both roots are positive and the system is unstable.

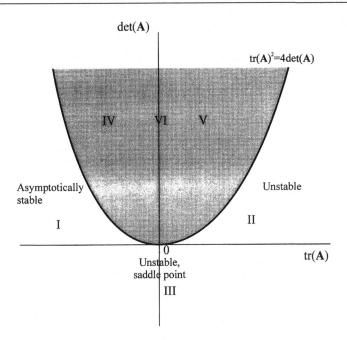

Figure 4.28.

If both roots are opposite in sign, we have found that the $\det(\mathbf{A})$ is negative and the critical point is a saddle. Hence, below the x-axis, marked region III, the critical point is an unstable saddle point. Notice that this applies whether the trace is positive or negative.

The complex region is sub-divided into three categories. In region IV the sign of α in the complex conjugate roots $\alpha \pm \beta i$ is strictly negative and the spiral trajectory tends towards the critical point in the limit. In region V α is strictly positive and the critical point is an unstable one with the trajectory spiralling away from it. Finally in region VI, which is the y-axis above zero, $\alpha = 0$ and the critical point has a centre with a closed curve as a trajectory.

It is apparent that the variety of possibilities can be described according to the $\text{tr}(\mathbf{A})$ and $\det(\mathbf{A})$ along with the characteristic roots of $\mathbf{A}$. The list with various nomenclature is given in table 4.1.

4.10 Limit cycles[9]

A limit cycle is an isolated closed integral curve, which is also called an *orbit*. A limit cycle is asymptotically stable if all the nearby cycles tend to the closed orbit from both sides. It is unstable if the nearby cycles move away from the closed orbit on either side. It is semi-stable if the nearby cycles move towards the closed orbit on one side and away from it on the other. Since the limiting trajectory is a periodic orbit rather than a fixed point, then the stability or instability is called an *orbital stability* or *instability*. There is yet another case, common

---

[9] This section utilises the **VisualDSolve** package provided by Schwalbe and Wagon (1996). It can be loaded into *Mathematica* with the **Needs** command. This package provides considerable visual control over the display of phase portraits.

Table 4.1 Stability properties of linear systems

Matrix and eigenvalues	Type of point	Type of stability
$\text{tr}(\mathbf{A}) < 0, \det(\mathbf{A}) > 0, \text{tr}(\mathbf{A})^2 > 4\det(\mathbf{A})$ $r < s < 0$	Improper node	Asymptotically stable
$\text{tr}(\mathbf{A}) > 0, \det(\mathbf{A}) > 0, \text{tr}(\mathbf{A})^2 > 4\det(\mathbf{A})$ $r > s > 0$	Improper node	Unstable
$\det(\mathbf{A}) < 0$ $r > 0, s < 0$ or $r < 0, s > 0$	Saddle point	Unstable saddle
$\text{tr}(\mathbf{A}) < 0, \det(\mathbf{A}) > 0, \text{tr}(\mathbf{A})^2 = 4\det(\mathbf{A})$ $r = s < 0$	Star node or proper node	Stable
$\text{tr}(\mathbf{A}) > 0, \det(\mathbf{A}) > 0, \text{tr}(\mathbf{A})^2 = 4\det(\mathbf{A})$ $r = s > 0$	Star node or proper node	Unstable
$\text{tr}(\mathbf{A}) < 0, \det(\mathbf{A}) > 0, \text{tr}(\mathbf{A})^2 < 4\det(\mathbf{A})$ $r = \alpha + \beta i, s = \alpha - \beta i, \alpha < 0$	Spiral node	Asymptotically stable
$\text{tr}(\mathbf{A}) > 0, \det(\mathbf{A}) > 0, \text{tr}(\mathbf{A})^2 < 4\det(\mathbf{A})$ $r = \alpha + \beta i, s = \alpha - \beta i, \alpha > 0$	Spiral node	Unstable
$\text{tr}(\mathbf{A}) = 0, \det(\mathbf{A}) > 0$ $r = \beta i, s = -\beta i$	Centre	Stable

in predatory–prey population models. If a system has closed orbits that other trajectories neither approach nor diverge from, then the closed orbits are said to be stable. Geometrically, we have a series of concentric orbits, each one denoting a closed trajectory.

In answering the question: 'When do limit cycles occur?' we draw on the **Poincaré–Bendixson theorem**. This theorem is concerned with a bounded region, which we shall call R, in which the long-term motion of a two-dimensional system is limited to it. If for region R, any trajectory starting within R stays within R for all time, then two possibilities arise:

(1)   the trajectory approaches a fixed point of the system as $t \to \infty$; or
(2)   the trajectory approaches a limit cycle as $t \to \infty$.

When trajectories that start in R remain in R for all time, then the region R is said to be the *invariant set* for the system. Trajectories cannot escape such a set.

The following points about limit cycles are worth noting.

(1)   Limit cycles are periodic motions and so the system must involve complex roots.
(2)   For a stable limit cycle, the *interior* nearby paths must diverge from the singular point (the fixed point). This occurs if the trace of the Jacobian of the system is positive.
(3)   For a stable limit cycle, the *outer* nearby paths must converge on the closed orbit, which requires a negative trace.
(4)   Points (2) and (3) mean that for a stable limit cycle the trace must change sign in the region where the limit cycle occurs.
(5)   The Poincaré–Bendixson theorem holds only for two-dimensional spaces.
(6)   If the Poincaré–Bendixson theorem is satisfied, then it can be shown that if there is more than one limit cycle they alternate between being stable and unstable. Furthermore, the outermost one and the innermost one must

be stable. This means that if there is only one limit cycle satisfying the theorem, it must be stable.

Example 4.15

The following well-known example has a limit cycle composed of the unit circle (see Boyce and DiPrima 1997, pp. 523–7):

$$x' = y + x - x(x^2 + y^2)$$
$$y' = -x + y - y(x^2 + y^2)$$

Utilising the **VisualDSolve** package within *Mathematica*, we can show the limit cycle and two trajectories: one starting at point (0.5,0.5) and the other at point (1.5,1.5). The input instructions are:

```
In[2]:= PhasePlot [{x' [t] == y[t] + x[t] - x[t] (x[t]^2 + y[t]^2),
        y' [t] == -x[t] + y[t] - y[t] (x[t]^2 + y[t]^2)},
        {x[t], y[t]}, {t, 0, 10}, {x, -2, 2}, {y, -2, 2},
        InitialValues ->
          {{0.5, 0.5}, {1.5, 1.5}}, ShowInitialValues -> True,
        FlowField -> False, FieldLength -> 1.5,
        FieldMeshSize -> 25, WindowShade -> White,
        FieldColor -> Black, Nullclines -> True,
         PlotStyle -> AbsoluteThickness [1.2],
        InitialPointStyle -> AbsolutePointSize [3],
        ShowEquilibria -> True, DirectionArrow -> True,
        AspectRatio -> 1, AxesLabel -> {x, y},
        PlotLabel -> "Unit Limit Cycle"];
```

which produces figure 4.29 showing a unit limit cycle.

Example 4.16 (Van der Pol equation)

The Van der Pol equation is a good example illustrating an asymptotically stable limit cycle. It also illustrates that a second-order differential equation can be reduced to a system of first-order differential equations that are more convenient for

Unit limit cycle

Figure 4.29.

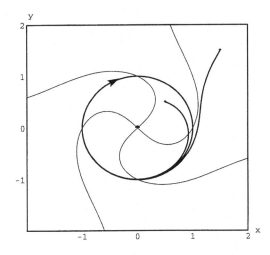

Figure 4.30.

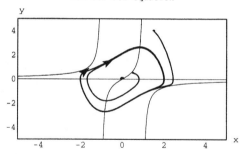

Van der Pol equation

solving. The Van der Pol equation takes the form:

(4.27)
$$\ddot{x} - \mu(1 - x^2)\dot{x} + x = 0$$

Let $y = \dot{x}$, then $\dot{y} = \ddot{x}$, so we have the two equations,

(4.28)
$$\dot{x} = y$$
$$\dot{y} = \mu(1 - x^2)y - x$$

To illustrate the limit cycle, let $\mu = 1$. The phase portrait that results is shown in figure 4.30. Here we take two initial points: (a) point (0.5,0.5), which starts inside the limit cycle; and (b) point (1.5,4), which begins outside the limit cycle.

Example 4.17 Walrasian price and quantity adjustment and limit cycles

The presence of limit cycles is illustrated by a Walrasian model which includes both price and quantity adjustments (see Flaschel *et al.* 1997 and Mas-Colell 1986). Let Y denote output of a one good economy and L labour input. $Y = f(L)$ is a production function which is twice differentiable and invertible with $L = f^{-1}(Y) = \phi(Y)$ and $\phi'(Y) > 0$. In equilibrium the price, p, is equal to marginal wage cost, where marginal wage cost is also given by $\phi'(Y)$. Thus, $p^* = \phi'(Y)$. For simplicity we assume that the marginal wage cost is a linear function of Y, with $\phi'(Y) = c_1 + c_2 Y$. Aggregate demand takes the form $D(p, L)$ and in equilibrium is equal to supply, i.e., $D[p^*, \phi(Y^*)] = Y^*$. Finally, we have both a price and a quantity adjustment:

(4.29)
$$\dot{p} = \alpha[D(p, \phi(Y)) - Y] \qquad \alpha > 0$$
$$\dot{Y} = \beta[p - \phi'(Y)] \qquad \beta > 0$$

These establish two differential equations in p and Y.

Consider the following numerical example. Let

$$\phi'(Y) = 0.87 + 0.5Y$$
$$D(p) = -0.02p^3 + 0.8p^2 - 9p + 50$$

then $(p^*, Y^*) = (13, 24.26)$ with isoclines:

$$\dot{p} = 0 \qquad Y = -0.02p^3 + 0.8p^2 - 9p + 50$$
$$\dot{Y} = 0 \qquad p = 0.87 + 0.5Y \qquad \text{or} \qquad Y = 1.74 + 2p$$

Figure 4.31 reproduces the figures derived in Flaschel *et al.* 1997 using *Mathematica*, for $\alpha = 1$ and different values of the parameter β. Not only do the figures

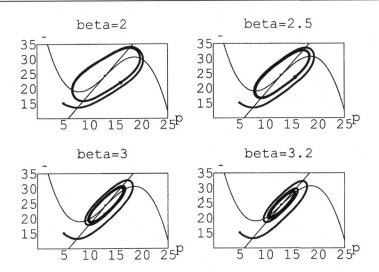

Figure 4.31.

illustrate a stable limit cycle, but they also illustrate that the limit cycle shrinks as β increases.

4.11 Euler's approximation and differential equations on a spreadsheet[10]

Although differential equations are for continuous time, if our main interest is the trajectory of a system over time, sometimes it is convenient to use a spreadsheet to do this. To accomplish this task we employ *Euler's approximation*. For a single variable the situation is shown in figure 4.32. We have the differential equation

$$\frac{dx}{dt} = f(x, t) \qquad x(t_0) = x_0 \tag{4.30}$$

Let $x = \phi(t)$ denote the unknown solution curve. At time t_0 we know $x_0 = \phi(t_0)$. We also know dx/dt at t_0, which is simply $f(x_0, t_0)$. If we knew $x = \phi(t)$, then the value at time t_1 would be $\phi(t_1)$. But if we do not have an explicit form for $x = \phi(t)$, we can still plot $\phi(t)$ by noting that at time t_0 the slope at point P is $f(x_0, t_0)$, which is given by the differential equation. The value of x_1 at time t_1 (point R) is given by

$$x_1 = x_0 + f(x_0, t_0)\Delta t \qquad \Delta t = t_1 - t_0$$

This process can be repeated for as many steps as one wishes. If f is autonomous, so $dx/dt = f(x)$, then

$$x_n = x_{n-1} + f(x_{n-1})\Delta t \tag{4.31}$$

It is clear from figure 4.32 that point R will deviate from its 'true' value at point Q, the larger the step size, given by Δt. If the step size is reduced, then the approximation is better.

---

[10] See Shone (2001) for a treatment of differential equations with spreadsheets.

Figure 4.32.

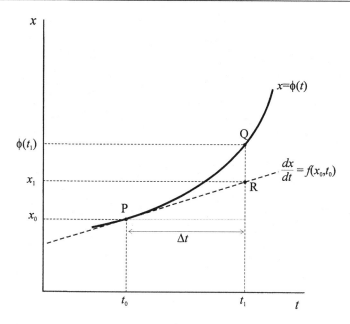

The procedure generalises quite readily to systems of equations. Let

$$\frac{dx}{dt} = f(x, y)$$

(4.32)

$$\frac{dy}{dt} = g(x, y)$$

denote a system of autonomous differential equations and let the initial value of the system be $x(t_0) = x_0$ and $y(t_0) = y_0$. Then

$$x_1 = x_0 + f(x_0, y_0)\Delta t$$

(4.33)

$$y_1 = y_0 + g(x_0, y_0)\Delta t$$

which can be repeated for further (approximate) values on the solution curve. For an autonomous system in which $y = \phi(x)$, then such a procedure allows us to plot the trajectory in the phase plane.

Example 4.18

Consider example 4.6 given by the differential equations:

$$\frac{dx}{dt} = f(x, y) = -2x - y + 9$$

$$\frac{dy}{dt} = g(x, y) = -y + x + 3$$

with $x(t_0) = 2$ and $y(t_0) = 2$. Given these values, and letting $\Delta t = 0.01$, then

$$f(x_0, y_0) = -2(2) - 2 + 9 = 3$$

$$g(x_0, y_0) = -2 + 2 + 3 = 3$$

Hence,

$$x_1 = x_0 + f(x_0, y_0)\Delta t = 2 + 3(0.01) = 2.03$$
$$y_1 = y_0 + g(x_0, y_0)\Delta t = 2 + 3(0.01) = 2.03$$

and

$$f(x_1, y_1) = -2(2.03) - 2.03 + 9 = 2.91$$
$$g(x_1, y_1) = -2.03 + 2.03 + 3 = 3$$

giving

$$x_2 = x_1 + f(x_1, y_1)\Delta t = 2.03 + 2.91(0.01) = 2.0591$$
$$y_2 = y_1 + g(x_1, y_1)\Delta t = 2.03 + 3(0.01) = 2.06$$

This process is repeated. But all this can readily be set out on a spreadsheet, as shown in figure 4.33.

The first two columns are simply the differential equations. Columns (3) and (4) employ the Euler approximation using relative addresses and the absolute address for Δt. The x-y plot gives the trajectory of the system in the phase plane, with initial value $(x_0, y_0) = (2, 2)$. As can be seen from the embedded graph in the spreadsheet, this trajectory is the same as that shown in figure 4.11 (p. 155)

The advantage of using Euler's approximation, along with a spreadsheet, is that no explicit solution need be obtained – assuming that one exists. By reducing the step size a smoother trajectory results. It is also easy to increase the number of steps.

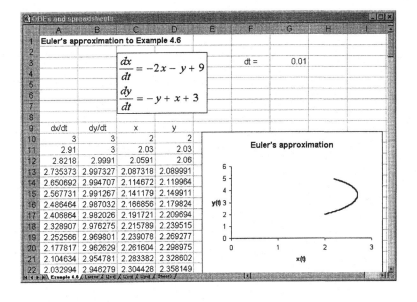

Figure 4.33.

Figure 4.34.

ODEs and spreadsheets

Lorenz curve

$$\frac{dx}{dt} = \sigma(y - x)$$
$$\frac{dy}{dt} = rx - y - xz$$
$$\frac{dz}{dt} = xy - bz$$

σ =	10
r =	28
b =	2.666667
dt =	0.01

t	dx/dt	dy/dt	dz/dt	x	y	z
0	-50	140	0	5	0	0
1	-31	124.6	6.3	4.5	1.4	0
2	-15.44	114.41	10.91874	4.19	2.646	0.063
3	-2.455	108.5118	14.83616	4.0356	3.7901	0.172187
4	8.641685	106.1484	18.69995	4.01105	4.875219	0.320549
5	18.39236	106.7127	22.97198	4.097467	5.936703	0.507549
6	27.2244	109.7186	28.02008	4.28139	7.00383	0.737268
7	35.47381	114.7676	34.17581	4.553634	8.101016	1.017469
8	43.40319	121.5141	41.77142	4.908373	9.248691	1.359227
9	51.21428	129.6304	51.16352	5.342404	10.46383	1.776941
10	59.05589	138.7686	62.7474	5.854547	11.76014	2.288577
11	67.02716	148.5209	76.96298	6.445106	13.14782	2.916051

Example 4.19 (The Lorenz curve)

The Lorenz equations are given by:

(4.34)
$$\frac{dx}{dt} = \sigma(y - x)$$
$$\frac{dy}{dt} = rx - y - xz$$
$$\frac{dz}{dt} = xy - bz$$

with parameter values $\sigma = 10$, $r = 28$, $b = 8/3$ and we take a step size of $\Delta t = 0.01$. In this example we take 2,000 steps, however figure 4.34 only shows the first few steps.

In figure 4.35 we have three generated plots, (i) (x, y), (ii) (x, z) and (iii) (y, z). These diagrams illustrate what is referred to as *strange attractors*, a topic we shall return to when we discuss chaos theory.

4.12 Solving systems of differential equations with *Mathematica* and *Maple*

Chapter 2 sections 2.11 and 2.12 outlined how to utilise *Mathematica* and *Maple* to solve single differential equations. The method for solving systems of such equations is fundamentally the same. Consider the system,

(4.35)
$$\frac{dx}{dt} = f(x, y, t)$$
$$\frac{dy}{dt} = g(x, y, t)$$

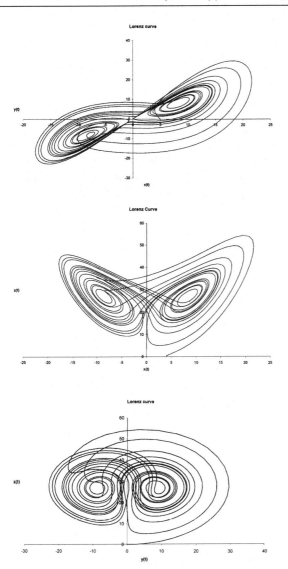

Figure 4.35.

Then the solution method in each case is:

Mathematica
```
DSolve[{x'[t]==f[x[t],y[t],t],y'[t]==g[x[t],
    y[t],t]}, {x[t],y[t]},t]
```
Maple
```
dsolve({diff(x(t),t)=f(x(t),y(t),t),diff(y(t),t)=g(x(t),
    y(t),t)}, {x(t),y(t)});
```

If initial conditions $x(0) = x0$ and $y(0) = y0$ are provided, then the input instructions are:

Mathematica

```
DSolve[{x'[t]==f[x[t],y[t],t],y'[t]==g[x[t],y[t],t],
    x(0)==x0,y(0)==y0},{x[t],y[t]},t]
```

Maple

```
dsolve(({diff(x(t),t)=f(x(t),y(t),t),diff(y(t),t)
    =g(x(t),y(t),t), x(0)=x0,y(0)=y0},{x(t),y(t)});
```

It is often easier to define the equations, variables and initial conditions first. Not only is it easier to see, but much easier in correcting any mistakes. For instance in *Mathematica* define

```
eq:={x'[t]==f[x[t],y[t],t],y'[t]==g[x[t],y[t],t],
    x[0]==x0,y[0]==y0}
var:={x[t],y[t]}
```

and then solve using

```
DSolve[eq,var,t]
```

In *Maple* define:

```
eq:=diff(x(t),t)=f(x(t),y(t),t),diff(y(t),t)=
    g(x(t),y(t),t);
init:=x(0)=x0,y(0)=y0;
var:={x(t),y(t)};
```

and then solve using

```
dsolve({eq,init},var);
```

Example 4.4 in the text can then be solved in each package as follows

Mathematica

```
eq:={x'[t]==x[t]-3y[t], y'[t]==-2x[t]+y[t],
    x[0]==4,y[0]==5}
var:={x[t],y[t]}
DSolve[eq,var,t]
```

Maple

```
eq:=diff(x(t),t)=x(t)-3*y(t), diff(y(t),t)=
    -2*x(t)+y(t);
init:=x(0)=4,y(0)=5;
var:={x(t),y(t)};
dsolve({eq,init},var);
```

Although the output looks different in the two cases, they are equivalent and identical to that provided in the text.

So long as solutions exist, then the packages will solve the system of equations. Thus, the system of three equations with initial values:

$$x'(t) = x(t)$$
$$y'(t) = x(t) + 3y(t) - z(t)$$
$$z'(t) = 2y(t) + 3x(t)$$
$$x(0) = 1, y(0) = 1, z(0) = 2$$

(4.36)

can be solved in a similar manner with no difficulty.

In the case of nonlinear systems of differential equations, or where no explicit solution can be found, then it is possible to use the **NDSolve** command in *Mathematica* and the **dsolve(..., numeric)** command in *Maple* to obtain numerical approximations to the solutions. These can then be plotted. But often more information can be obtained from direction field diagrams and phase portraits. A direction field shows a series of small arrows that are tangent vectors to solutions of the system of differential equations. These highlight possible fixed points and most especially the flow of the system over the plane. A phase portrait, on the other hand, is a sample of trajectories (solution curves) for a given system. Figure 4.36(a) shows a direction field and figure 4.36(b) a phase portrait.

In many instances direction fields and phase portraits are combined on the one diagram – as we have done in many diagrams in this chapter. The phase portrait can be derived by solving a system of differential equations, if a solution exists. Where no known solution exists, trajectories can be obtained by using numerical

Figure 4.36.

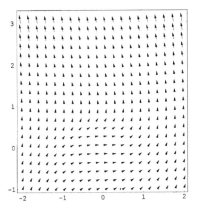

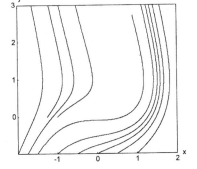

solutions. These are invariably employed for systems of nonlinear differential equation systems.

4.12.1   *Direction fields and phase portraits with* **Mathematica**

Direction fields in *Mathematica* are obtained using the **PlotVectorField** command. In order to use this command it is first necessary to load the PlotField package. There is some skill required in getting the best display of direction fields using the PlotVectorField command, and the reader should consult the references supplied on using *Mathematica* in chapter 1.

Given the system of differential equations (4.35), then a direction field can be obtained with the instructions

```
Needs["Graphics`PlotField`"]
dfield=PlotVectorField[{f(x,y,t),g(x,y,t)},
        {x,xmin,xmax}, {y,ymin,ymax},
        DisplayFunction->Identity]
Show[dfield, DisplayFunction->$DisplayFunction]
```

To obtain a 'good' display it is often necessary to adjust scaling, change the arrow lengths and change the aspect ratio. All these, and other refinements, are accomplished by optional instructions. Thus, figure 4.36(a) can be obtained from the following input

```
Needs["Graphics`PlotField`"]
dfield=PlotVectorField[{1-y,x^2+y^2}, {x,-2,2},{y,-1,3},
        Frame->True, PlotPoints->20,
        DisplayFunction->Identity]
Show[dfield, DisplayFunction->$DisplayFunction]
```

The phase portrait is not straightforward in *Mathematica* and requires solving the differential equations, either with DSolve command, if an explicit solution can be found, or the NDSolve command for a numerical approximation. If an explicit solution can be found with the DSolve command, then phase portraits can be obtained with the ParametricPlot command on supplying different values for the constants of integration. On the other hand, if a numerical approximation is required, as is often the case with nonlinear systems, then it is necessary to obtain a series of solution curves for different initial conditions. In doing this quite a few other commands of *Mathematica* are needed.

Consider the Van der Pol model, equation (4.28), a simple set of instructions to produce a diagram similar to that of figure 4.30 is

```
eq1:= {x'[t]==y[t],y'[t]==(1-x[t]^2)y[t]-x[t],
        x[0]==0.5,y[0]==0.5}
eq2:= {x'[t]==y[t],y'[t]==(1-x[t]^2)y[t]-x[t],
        x[0]==0.5,y[0]==4}
var:={x,y}
trange:={t,0,20}
```

```
sol1=NDSolve[eq1,var,trange]
sol2=NDSolve[eq2,var,trange]
graph1=ParametricPlot[Evaluate[{x[t],y[t]} /.sol1],
      {t,0,20},PlotPoints->500,
         DisplayFunction->Identity];
graph2=ParametricPlot[Evaluate[{x[t],y[t]} /.sol2],
      {t,0,20},PlotPoints->500,
         DisplayFunction->Identity];
Show[{graph1,graph2},AxesLabel->{``x'',``y''},
      DisplayFunction->$DisplayFunction];
```

The more trajectories that are required the more cumbersome these instructions become. It is then that available packages, such as the one provided by Schwalbe and Wagon (1996), become useful. For instance, figure 4.36(b) can be produced using the programme provided by Schwalbe and Wagon with the following set of instructions:

```
PhasePlot[{x'[t]==1-y[t],y'[t]==x[t]^2+y[t],^2},
      {x[t],y[t]},{t,0,3},{x,-2,2},{y,-1,3},
      InitialValues->{{-2,-1},{-1.75,-1},{-1.5,-1},
         {-1,0},{-1,-1},{-0.5,-1},{0,-1},{-1.25,0},
         {0.5,-1},{1,-1}},
      PlotPoints->500,
      ShowInitialValues->False,
      DirectionArrows->False,
      AspectRatio->1,
      AxesLabel->{x,y}]
```

When considering just one trajectory in the phase plane, the simple instructions given above can suffice. For instance, consider the Lorenz curve, given in equation (4.34), with parametric values $\sigma = 10$, $r = 28$, and $b = 8/3$. We can construct a three-dimensional trajectory from the initial point $(x0, y0, z0) = (5, 0, 0)$ using the following input instructions:

```
eqs:={x'[t]==10(y[t]-x[t]),y'[t]==28x[t]-y[t]-x[t]z[t],
      z'[t]==x[t]y[t]-(8/3)z[t],
         x[0]==5,y[0]==0,z[0]==0}
var:={x,y,z}
lorenzsol=NDSolve[eqs,var,{t,0,30},MaxSteps->3000]
lorenzgraph=ParametricPlot3D[
      Evaluate[x[t],y[t],z[t]} /.lorenzsol],
      {t,0,30},PlotPoints->2000,PlotRange->All];
```

The resulting phase line is shown in figure 4.37. This goes beyond the possibilities of a spreadsheet, and figure 4.37 should be compared with the three two-dimensional plots given in figure 4.35.

Figure 4.37.

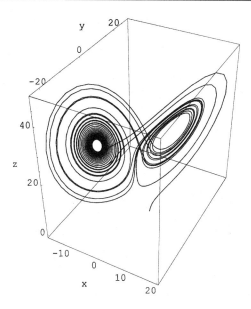

4.12.2   *Direction fields and phase portraits with* **Maple**

Direction fields and phase portraits are more straightforward in *Maple* and use the same basic input commands. Given the system of differential equations (4.35), then a direction field can be obtained with the instructions

```
with(DEtools):
with(plots):
Dfield:=dfieldplot(
       [diff(f(x(t),t)=f(x(t),y(t),t),
             diff(y(t),t)=g(x(t),y(t),t)],
             [x(t),y(t)], t=tmin..tmax,
             x=xmin..xmax, y=ymin..ymax);
display(Dfield);
```

Notice that the instruction 'with(plots):' is required for use of the **display** command. To obtain a 'good' display it is often necessary to add options with respect to arrows. For example, a *Maple* version of figure 4.36(a) can be achieved with the following input

```
with(DEtools):
with(plots):
Dfield:=dfieldplot(
       [diff(x(t),t)=1-y(t),diff(y(t),t)=x(t)^2
             +y(t)^2],
       [x(t),y(t)], t=0..1, x=-2..2, y=-1..3,
       arrows=SLIM):
display(Dfield);
```

The phase portrait, not surprisingly, uses the **phaseportrait** command of *Maple*. This particular command plots solution curves by means of numerical methods.

In a two-equation system, the programme will produce a direction field plot by default if the system is a set of autonomous equations. Since we require only the solution curves, then we include an option that indicates no arrows.

To illustrate the points just made, consider the Van der Pol model, equation (4.28), a simple set of instructions to produce a *Maple* plot similar to figure 4.30 is

```
phaseportrait(
    [D(x)(t)=y(t), D(y)(t)=(1-x(t)^2)*y(t)-x(t)],
    [x(t),y(t)], t=0..10,
    [ [x(0)=0.5,y(0)=0.5],[x(0)=0.5,y(0)=4] ],
    stepsize=.05
    linecolour=blue,
    arrows=none,
    thickness=1);
```

Producing more solution curves in *Maple* is just a simple case of specifying more initial conditions. For instance, a *Maple* version of figure 4.36(b) can be produced with the following instructions:

```
with(DEtools):
phaseportrait(
    [D(x)(t)=1-y(t),D(y)(t)=x(t)^2+y(t)^2],
    [x(t),y(t)], t=0..3,
    [[x(0)=-2,y(0)=-1],[x(0)=-1.75,y(0)=-1],
    [x(0)=1.5,y(0)=-1],[x(0)=-1,y(0)=0],
    [x(0)=-1,y(0)=-1], [x(0)=-0.5,y(0)=-1],
    [x(0)=0,y(0)=-1], [x(0)=-1.25,y(0)=0],
    [x(0)=0.5,y(0)=-1, [x(0)=1,y(0)=-1]],
    x=-2..2, y=-1..3,
    stepsize=.05,
    linecolour=blue,
    arrows=none,
    thickness=1);
```

Trajectories for three-dimensional plots are also possible with *Maple*. Consider once again the Lorenz curve, given in equation (4.34), with parameter values $\sigma = 10$, $r = 28$ and $b = 8/3$. We can construct a three-dimensional trajectory from the initial point $(x0, y0, z0) = (5, 0, 0)$ using the following input instructions:

```
with(DEtools):
DEplot3d(
    [diff(x(t),t)=10*(y(t)-x(t)),
    diff(y(t),t)=28*x(t)-y(t)-x(t)*z(t),
    diff(z(t),t)=x(t)*y(t)-(8/3)*z(t)],
    [x(t),y(t),z(t)], t=0..30,
    [[x(0)=5,y(0)=0,z(0)=0]],
    stepsize=.01,
    linecolour=BLACK,
    thickness=1);
```

Figure 4.38.

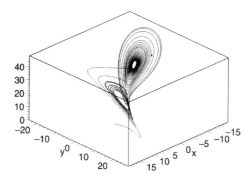

The resulting phase line is shown in figure 4.38. This goes beyond the possibilities of a spreadsheet, and figure 4.38 should be compared with the three two-dimensional plots given in figure 4.35. It is worth noting that figure 4.38 is the default plot and the orientation can readily be changed by clicking on the figure and revolving.

Appendix 4.1 Parametric plots in the phase plane: continuous variables

A trajectory or orbit is the path of points $\{x(t), y(t)\}$ in 2-dimensional space and $\{x(t), y(t), z(t)\}$ in 3-dimensional space as t varies. Such plots are simply parametric plots as far as computer programmes are concerned. There are two methods for deriving the points $(x(t), y(t))$ or $(x(t), y(t), z(t))$:

(1)   Solve for these values
(2)   Derive numerical values by numerical means:
        (a) by solving numerically, or
        (b) deriving by recursion.

Method 2(a) is used particularly in the case of differential equations, while method 2(b) is used for difference (or recursive) equations. In each of these cases initial conditions must be supplied.

4A.1 Two-variable case

Consider the solution values for x and y in example 4.1, which are

$$x(t) = 2e^{2t} \quad \text{and} \quad y(t) = 3e^{t}$$

Both x and y are expressed in terms of a common parameter, t, so that when t varies we can establish how x and y vary. More specifically, if t denotes time, then $(x(t), y(t))$ denotes a point at time t in the (x, y)-plane, i.e., a Cartesian representation of the parametric point at time t. If the differential equation system which generated $x(t)$ and $y(t)$ is autonomous, then there is only one solution curve, and we can express this in the form $y = \phi(x)$, where $y_0 = \phi(x_0)$ and (x_0, y_0) is some initial point, i.e., $x(0) = x_0$ and $y(0) = y_0$ at $t = 0$. In the present example this is readily found since

$$\frac{x}{y^2} = \frac{2e^{2t}}{(3e^t)^2} = \frac{2e^{2t}}{9e^{2t}} = \frac{2}{9}$$

Hence

$$y = \sqrt{\frac{9x}{2}}$$

Whether or not it is possible to readily find a Cartesian representation of the parametric curve, it is a simple matter to plot the parametric curve itself using software packages.

Example 4.1 with Mathematica

The two commands used in this set of instructions, **DSolve** and **ParametricPlot** are now both contained in the main package:[11]

```
Clear[x,y]
sol=DSolve[{x'[t]==2x[t],y'[t]==y[t],x[0]==2,y[0]==3},
        {x[t],y[t]},t]
solx=sol[[1,1,2]]
soly=sol[[1,2,2]]
x[t_]:=solx
y[t_]:=soly
traj=ParametricPlot[{x[t],y[t]},{t,0,1}]
```

If the equations for $x(t)$ and $y(t)$ are already known, then only the last instruction need be given. For example, if it is known that $x(t) = 2e^{2t}$ and $y(t) = 3e^t$ then all that is required is

```
traj=ParametricPlot[{2e^{2t},3e^t},{t,0,1}]
```

Example 4.1 with Maple

To use *Maple*'s routine for plotting parametric equations that are solutions to differential equations it is necessary to load the plots package first. The following input instructions will produce the trajectory for example 4.1:

```
restart;
with(plots):
sys:={diff(x(t),t)=2*x(t),diff(y(t),t)=y(t),
        x(0)=2,y(0)=3}
vars:={x(t),y(t)}:
sol:=dsolve(sys,vars,numeric);
odeplot(sol,[x(t),y(t)],0..1,labels=[x,y]);
```

---

[11] In earlier versions, **DSolve** and **ParametricPlot** needed to be loaded first since these were contained in the additional packages. This is no longer necessary, since both are contained in the basic built in functions.

Notice that we have placed a semi-colon after the 'sol' instruction so that you can observe that *Maple* produces a procedural output, which is then used in the odeplot.

If the equations for $x(t)$ and $y(t)$ are already known, then the **plot** command can be used. For example, if it is known that $x(t) = 2e^{2t}$ and $y(t) = 3e^t$ then all that is required is

```
plot([2*exp(2*t),3*exp(t),t=0..1],labels=[x,y]);
```

4A.2 Three-variable case

Plotting trajectories in 3-dimensional phase space is fundamentally the same, with just a few changes to the commands used.

Equation (4.36) with Mathematica

The input instructions are

```
Clear[x,y,z]
sol=DSolve[{x'[t]==x[t],y'[t]==x[t]+3y[t]-z[t],
    z[t]==2y[t]+3x[t],x[0]==1,y[0]==1,z[0]==2},
    {x[t],y[t],z[t]},t]
solx=sol[[1,1,2]]
soly=sol[[1,2,2]]
solz=sol[[1,3,2]]
x[t_]:=solx
y[t_]:=soly
z[t_]:=solz
traj=ParametricPlot3D[{x[t],y[t],z[t]},{t,0,5}]
```

If the equations for $x(t)$, $y(t)$ and $z(t)$ are already known, then only the last instruction need be given. For example, if it is known that $x(t) = e^t$, $y(t) = 2e^t - e^{2t} + 2te^t$ and $z(t) = 4te^t - e^{2t} + 3e^t$ then all that is required is

```
traj=ParametricPlot3D[{e^t,2e^t-e^2t+2te^t,4te^t-e^2t+3e^t},
    {t,0,5}]
```

Equation (4.36) with Maple

The input instructions are

```
restart;
with(plots):
sys:={diff(x(t),t)=x(t),diff(y(t),t)=x(t)+3*y(t)-z(t),
    diff(z(t),t)=2*y(t)+3*x(t),x(0)=1,y(0)=1,z(0)=2};
vars:={x(t),y(t),z(t)}:
sol:=dsolve(sys,vars,numeric);
odeplot(sol,[x(t),y(t),z(t)],0..5,labels=[x,y,z]);
```

If the equations for $x(t)$, $y(t)$ and $z(t)$ are already known, then we use the **spacecurve** command, as illustrated in the following instructions:

```
traj=spacecurve([exp(t),2*exp(t)-exp(2*t)+2*t*exp(t),
      4*t*exp(t)-exp(2*t)+3*exp(t)],
      t=0..5,labels=[x,y,z]);
```

Exercises

1. (i) Show that
    $$y'(x) = \frac{y}{2x}$$
    is a separable function, and solve assuming $x(0) = 2$ and $y(0) = 3$.
    (ii) Verify your result using either *Mathematica* or *Maple*.

2. For the system
    $$\dot{x} = x - 3y$$
    $$\dot{y} = -2x + y$$
    use a software package to derive the trajectories of the system for the following initial values:
    (a) $(x_0, y_0) = (4, 2)$
    (b) $(x_0, y_0) = (4, 5)$
    (c) $(x_0, y_0) = (-4, -2)$
    (d) $(x_0, y_0) = (-4, 5)$

3. For the system
    $$\dot{x} = -3x + y$$
    $$\dot{y} = x - 3y$$
    (i) Show that points $(x_0, y_0) = (4, 8)$ and $(x_0, y_0) = (4, 2)$ remain in quadrant I, as in figure 4.9.
    (ii) Show that points $(x_0, y_0) = (-4, -8)$ and $(x_0, y_0) = (-4, -2)$ remain in quadrant III, as in figure 4.9.
    (iii) Show that points $(x_0, y_0) = (2, 10)$ and $(x_0, y_0) = (-2, -10)$ pass from one quadrant into another before converging on equilibrium.
    (iv) Does the initial point $(x_0, y_0) = (2, -5)$ have a trajectory which converges on the fixed point without passing into another quadrant?

4. For the system
    $$\dot{x} = -2x - y + 9$$
    $$\dot{y} = -y + x + 3$$
    establish the trajectories for each of the following initial points (i) $(x_0, y_0) = (1, 3)$, (ii) $(x_0, y_0) = (2, 8)$, and (iii) $(x_0, y_0) = (3, 1)$, showing that all trajectories follow a counter-clockwise spiral towards the fixed point.

5. Given the dynamic system
    $$\dot{x} = 2x + 3y$$
    $$\dot{y} = 3x + 2y$$

(i) Show that the characteristic roots of the system are $r = 5$ and $s = -1$.

(ii) Derive the eigenvectors associated with the eigenvalues obtained in (i).

(iii) Show that the solution values are:

$$x(t) = c_1 e^{5t} + c_2 e^{-t}$$
$$y(t) = c_1 e^{5t} - c_2 e^{-t}$$

and verify that

$$c_1 e^{5t} \begin{bmatrix} 1 \\ 1 \end{bmatrix}, \qquad c_2 e^{-t} \begin{bmatrix} 1 \\ -1 \end{bmatrix}$$

are linearly independent.

(iv) Given $x(0) = 1$ and $y(0) = 0$, show that

$$x(t) = \tfrac{1}{2} e^{5t} + \tfrac{1}{2} e^{-t}$$
$$y(t) = \tfrac{1}{2} e^{5t} - \tfrac{1}{2} e^{-t}$$

6.   For the dynamic system

$$\dot{x} = x + 3y$$
$$\dot{y} = 5x + 3y$$

Show:

(i) that the two eigenvalues are $r = 6$ and $s = -2$

(ii) that the two eigenvectors are

$$\mathbf{v}^r = \begin{bmatrix} 1 \\ 5/3 \end{bmatrix} \quad \text{and} \quad \mathbf{v}^s = \begin{bmatrix} 1 \\ -1 \end{bmatrix}$$

(iii) and that the general solution satisfying $x(0) = 1$ and $y(0) = 3$ is

$$x(t) = \tfrac{3}{2} e^{6t} - \tfrac{1}{2} e^{-2t}$$
$$y(t) = \tfrac{5}{2} e^{6t} + \tfrac{1}{2} e^{-2t}$$

7.   Let $\mathbf{V} = \begin{bmatrix} \mathbf{v}^1 & \mathbf{v}^2 \end{bmatrix}$ denote a matrix formed from the eigenvectors. Thus, if

$$\mathbf{v}^1 = \begin{bmatrix} 1 \\ -2 \end{bmatrix} \quad \text{and} \quad \mathbf{v}^2 = \begin{bmatrix} 1 \\ 2 \end{bmatrix}$$

then

$$\mathbf{V} = \begin{bmatrix} 1 & 1 \\ -2 & 2 \end{bmatrix}$$

The determinant of this matrix is called the *Wronksian*, i.e., $\mathbf{W}(\mathbf{v}^1, \mathbf{v}^2) = \det(\mathbf{V})$. Then $\mathbf{v}^1$ and $\mathbf{v}^2$ are linearly independent if and only if $\mathbf{W}(\mathbf{v}^1, \mathbf{v}^2)$ is nonzero.

Show that for the system

$$\dot{x} = x + y$$
$$\dot{y} = -2x + 4y$$

the *Wronksian* is nonzero.

8.   Given

$$\dot{x} = x$$
$$\dot{y} = 2x + 3y + z$$
$$\dot{z} = 2y + 4z$$

(i) Find the eigenvalues and eigenvectors.
(ii) Provide the general solution.
(iii) Show that the *Wronksian* is nonzero.

9.   For each of the following systems
(a) find the eigenvalues and eigenvectors;
(b) solve the system by finding the general solution;
(c) obtain the trajectories for the specified initial points; and
(d) classify the fixed points.

(i) $$\dot{x} = -3x + y$$
       $$\dot{y} = x - 3y$$

initial points $= (1, 1), (-1, 1), (-1, -1), (1, -1), (2, 0),$
$(3, 1), (1, 3)$

(ii) $$\dot{x} = 2x - 4y$$
       $$\dot{y} = x - 3y$$

initial points $= (1, 1), (-1, 1), (4, 1), (-4, -1), (0, 1),$
$(0, -1), (3, 2), (-3, -2)$

(iii) $$\dot{x} = y$$
       $$\dot{y} = -4x$$

initial points $= (0, 1), (0, 2), (0, 3)$

(iv) $$\dot{x} = -x + y$$
       $$\dot{y} = -x - y$$

initial points $= (1, 0), (2, 0), (3, 0), (-1, 0), (-2, 0), (-3, 0).$

10.   For the following Holling–Tanner predatory–prey model

$$\dot{x} = x\left(1 - \frac{x}{6}\right) - \frac{6xy}{(8 + 8x)}$$

$$\dot{y} = 0.2y\left(1 - \frac{0.4y}{x}\right)$$

(i) Find the fixed points.
(ii) Do any of the fixed points exhibit a stable limit cycle?

11.   Consider the Rössler attractor

$$\dot{x} = -y - z$$
$$\dot{y} = x + 0.2y$$
$$\dot{z} = 0.2 + z(x - 2.5)$$

(i) Show that this system has a period-one limit cycle.
(ii) Plot $x(t)$ against $t = 200$ to 300, and hence show that the system
settles down with x having two distinct amplitudes.

12. Consider the following Walrasian price and quantity adjustment model

$$\phi'(Y) = 0.5 + 0.25Y$$
$$D(p) = -0.025p^3 + 0.75p^2 - 6p + 40$$
$$\dot{p} = 0.75[D(p, \phi(Y)) - Y]$$
$$\dot{Y} = 2[p - \phi'(Y)]$$

(i) What is the economically meaningful fixed point of this system?
(ii) Does this system have a stable limit cycle?

13. Reconsider the system in question 12, but let the quantity adjustment equation be given by

$$\dot{Y} = \beta[p - \phi'(Y)]$$

Let $\beta = 2, 2.5, 3$ and 3.2. What do you conclude about the long-run behaviour of this system?

14. Consider the following system

$$\phi'(Y) = 0.5 + 0.25Y$$
$$D(p) = -0.025p^3 + 0.75p^2 - 6p + 40$$
$$\dot{p} = \alpha[D(p, \phi(Y)) - Y]$$
$$\dot{Y} = 2[p - \phi'(Y)]$$

Let $\alpha = 0.5, 0.75$ and 1. What do you conclude about the long-run behaviour of this system?

15. Set up the Rössler attractor

$$\dot{x} = -y - z$$
$$\dot{y} = x + ay$$
$$\dot{z} = b + z(x - c)$$

on a spreadsheet with step size $\Delta t = 0.01$ and $a = 0.4, b = 2$ and $c = 4$. Plot the system for initial point $(x, y, z) = (0.1, 0.1, 0.1)$ in

(i) (x,y)-plane
(ii) (x,z)-plane
(iii) (y,z)-plane

Additional reading

Additional material on the contents of this chapter can be obtained from Arrowsmith and Place (1992), Beavis and Dobbs (1990), Borrelli *et al.* (1992), Boyce and DiPrima (1997), Braun (1983), Chiang (1984), Flaschel *et al.* (1997), Giordano and Weir (1991), Jeffrey (1990), Lynch (2001), Mas-Colell (1986), Percival and Richards (1982), Schwalbe and Wagon (1996), Shone (2001) and Tu (1994).

CHAPTER 5

Discrete systems of equations

5.1 Introduction

In chapter 3 we considered linear difference equations for a single variable, such as

$$x_t = 2x_{t-1}, \qquad x_t = 4x_{t-1} + 4x_{t-2}, \qquad x_t = ax_{t-1} + b$$

Each of these equations is linear and autonomous. But suppose we are interested in such systems as the following:

(i) $\quad x_t = ax_{t-1} + by_{t-1}$
$\qquad y_t = cx_{t-1} + dy_{t-1}$

(ii) $\quad x_t = 4x_{t-1} + 2$
$\qquad y_t = -2y_{t-1} - 3x_{t-1} + 3$

(iii) $\quad x_t = 2x_{t-1} + 3y_{t-1} + 4z_{t-1}$
$\qquad y_t = 0.5x_{t-1}$
$\qquad z_t = 0.7y_{t-1}$

All these are examples of *systems* of linear autonomous equations of the first order.

As in previous chapters, we shall here consider only autonomous equations (i.e. independent of the variable t), but we shall also largely restrict ourselves to linear systems. If all the equations in the system are linear and homogeneous, then we have a linear homogeneous system. If the system is a set of linear equations and at least one equation is nonhomogeneous, then we have a linear nonhomogeneous system. If the equations are homogeneous but at least one equation in the system is nonlinear, then we have a nonlinear homogeneous system. If at least one equation is nonlinear and at least one equation in the system is nonhomogeneous, then we have a nonlinear nonhomogeneous system. In this chapter we shall concentrate on linear homogeneous equation systems. In terms of the classification just given, systems (i) and (iii) are linear homogeneous systems, while (ii) is a linear nonhomogeneous system.

A more convenient way to express linear systems is in matrix form. Hence the three systems can equally be written in the form:

(i) $\quad \begin{bmatrix} x_t \\ y_t \end{bmatrix} = \begin{bmatrix} a & b \\ c & d \end{bmatrix} \begin{bmatrix} x_{t-1} \\ y_{t-1} \end{bmatrix} \qquad$ (or $\mathbf{u}_t = \mathbf{A}\mathbf{u}_{t-1}$)

(ii) $\quad \begin{bmatrix} x_t \\ y_t \end{bmatrix} = \begin{bmatrix} 4 & 0 \\ -3 & -2 \end{bmatrix} \begin{bmatrix} x_{t-1} \\ y_{t-1} \end{bmatrix} + \begin{bmatrix} 0 \\ 3 \end{bmatrix}$ (or $\mathbf{u}_t = \mathbf{A}\mathbf{u}_{t-1} + \mathbf{b}$)

(iii) $\quad \begin{bmatrix} x_t \\ y_t \\ z_t \end{bmatrix} = \begin{bmatrix} 2 & 3 & 4 \\ 0.5 & 0 & 0 \\ 0 & 0.7 & 0 \end{bmatrix} \begin{bmatrix} x_{t-1} \\ y_{t-1} \\ z_{t-1} \end{bmatrix}$ (or $\mathbf{u}_t = \mathbf{A}\mathbf{u}_{t-1}$)

In general, therefore, we can write first-order linear homogeneous systems as

(5.1) $\qquad \mathbf{u}_t = \mathbf{A}\mathbf{u}_{t-1}$

and a first-order linear nonhomogeneous system as

(5.2) $\qquad \mathbf{u}_t = \mathbf{A}\mathbf{u}_{t-1} + \mathbf{b}$

where $\mathbf{u}$ is a $n \times 1$ vector, $\mathbf{A}$ a $n \times n$ square matrix and $\mathbf{b}$ a $n \times 1$ vector.
Consider the system

$$\begin{bmatrix} x_t \\ y_t \end{bmatrix} = \begin{bmatrix} a & b \\ c & d \end{bmatrix} \begin{bmatrix} x_{t-1} \\ y_{t-1} \end{bmatrix}$$

Then in equilibrium $x_t = x_{t-1} = x^*$ for all t and $y_t = y_{t-1} = y^*$ for all t. Hence

$$\begin{bmatrix} x^* \\ y^* \end{bmatrix} = \begin{bmatrix} a & b \\ c & d \end{bmatrix} \begin{bmatrix} x^* \\ y^* \end{bmatrix}$$

or

$$\mathbf{u}^* = \mathbf{A}\mathbf{u}^*$$

An equilibrium solution exists, therefore, if

$$\mathbf{u}^* - \mathbf{A}\mathbf{u}^* = \mathbf{0}$$
$$\text{i.e. } (\mathbf{I} - \mathbf{A})\mathbf{u}^* = \mathbf{0}$$
$$\text{or } \mathbf{u}^* = (\mathbf{I} - \mathbf{A})^{-1}\mathbf{0} = \mathbf{0}$$

An equilibrium for a first-order linear homogeneous system is, therefore, $\mathbf{u}^* = \mathbf{0}$. This is a general result.

For a first-order linear nonhomogeneous system

$$\mathbf{u}_t = \mathbf{A}\mathbf{u}_{t-1} + \mathbf{b}$$

an equilibrium requires $\mathbf{u}_t = \mathbf{u}_{t-1} = \mathbf{u}^*$ for all t, so that

$$\mathbf{u}^* = \mathbf{A}\mathbf{u}^* + \mathbf{b}$$
$$(\mathbf{I} - \mathbf{A})\mathbf{u}^* = \mathbf{b}$$
$$\mathbf{u}^* = (\mathbf{I} - \mathbf{A})^{-1}\mathbf{b}$$

and so an equilibrium exists so long as $(\mathbf{I} - \mathbf{A})^{-1}$ exists. The solution $\mathbf{u}^* = (\mathbf{I} - \mathbf{A})^{-1}\mathbf{b}$ is the general equilibrium solution for a first-order linear nonhomogeneous system.

Example 5.1

$$x_t = 2x_{t-1} + 3y_{t-1}$$
$$y_t = -2x_{t-1} + y_{t-1}$$

or

$$\begin{bmatrix} x_t \\ y_t \end{bmatrix} = \begin{bmatrix} 2 & 3 \\ -2 & 1 \end{bmatrix} \begin{bmatrix} x_{t-1} \\ y_{t-1} \end{bmatrix}$$

i.e.

$$\mathbf{u}_t = \mathbf{A}\mathbf{u}_{t-1}$$

where

$$\mathbf{I} - \mathbf{A} = \begin{bmatrix} -1 & -3 \\ 2 & 0 \end{bmatrix}$$

$$\text{and } (\mathbf{I} - \mathbf{A})\mathbf{u}^* = \begin{bmatrix} -1 & -3 \\ 2 & 0 \end{bmatrix} \begin{bmatrix} x^* \\ y^* \end{bmatrix} = \begin{bmatrix} 0 \\ 0 \end{bmatrix}$$

the only values for x and y satisfying this system are $x^* = 0$ and $y^* = 0$.

Example 5.2

$$x_t = 4x_{t-1} + 2$$
$$y_t = -2y_{t-1} - 3x_{t-1} + 3$$

i.e.

$$\begin{bmatrix} x_t \\ y_t \end{bmatrix} = \begin{bmatrix} 4 & 0 \\ -3 & -2 \end{bmatrix} \begin{bmatrix} x_{t-1} \\ y_{t-1} \end{bmatrix} + \begin{bmatrix} 2 \\ 3 \end{bmatrix}$$

Then

$$\mathbf{u}^* = (\mathbf{I} - \mathbf{A})^{-1}\mathbf{b}$$
$$= \begin{bmatrix} -3 & 0 \\ 3 & 3 \end{bmatrix}^{-1} \begin{bmatrix} 2 \\ 3 \end{bmatrix} = \begin{bmatrix} -2/3 \\ 5/3 \end{bmatrix}$$

i.e. $x^* = -2/3$ and $y^* = 5/3$.

Having established that an equilibrium exists, however, our main interest is establishing the stability of such systems of equations. In establishing this we need to solve the system. This is fairly straightforward. For the first-order linear homogeneous equation system we have

$$\mathbf{u}_t = \mathbf{A}\mathbf{u}_{t-1}$$
$$= \mathbf{A}(\mathbf{A}\mathbf{u}_{t-2}) = \mathbf{A}^2\mathbf{u}_{t-2}$$
$$= \mathbf{A}^2(\mathbf{A}\mathbf{u}_{t-3}) = \mathbf{A}^3\mathbf{u}_{t-3}$$
$$\vdots$$

with solution

(5.3) $\mathbf{u}_t = \mathbf{A}^t \mathbf{u}_0$

where $\mathbf{u}_0$ is the initial values of the vector $\mathbf{u}$. Given $\mathbf{u}_0$ and the matrix $\mathbf{A}$, then we could compute $\mathbf{u}_{100} = \mathbf{A}^{100}\mathbf{u}_0$, or any such time period. Similarly, with the first-order nonhomogeneous linear equation system we have

$$\begin{aligned}\mathbf{u}_t &= \mathbf{A}\mathbf{u}_{t-1} + \mathbf{b} \\ &= \mathbf{A}(\mathbf{A}\mathbf{u}_{t-2} + \mathbf{b}) + \mathbf{b} = \mathbf{A}^2\mathbf{u}_{t-2} + \mathbf{A}\mathbf{b} + \mathbf{b} \\ &= \mathbf{A}^2(\mathbf{A}\mathbf{u}_{t-3} + \mathbf{b}) + \mathbf{A}\mathbf{b} + \mathbf{b} = \mathbf{A}^3\mathbf{u}_{t-3} + \mathbf{A}^2\mathbf{b} + \mathbf{A}\mathbf{b} + \mathbf{b} \\ &\vdots \end{aligned}$$

with solution

(5.4) $\mathbf{u}_t = \mathbf{A}^t\mathbf{u}_0 + (\mathbf{I} + \mathbf{A} + \mathbf{A}^2 + \ldots + \mathbf{A}^{t-1})\mathbf{b}$

Although solution (5.3) and (5.4) are possible to solve with powerful computers, it is not a useful way to proceed. We require to approach the solution from a different perspective.

It will be recalled from our analysis of differential equation systems in chapter 4 that a linear nonhomogeneous system can be reduced to a linear homogeneous system by considering deviations from equilibrium. Thus for $\mathbf{u}_t = \mathbf{A}\mathbf{u}_{t-1} + \mathbf{b}$, with equilibrium vector $\mathbf{u}^*$ we have $\mathbf{u}^* = \mathbf{A}\mathbf{u}^* + \mathbf{b}$. Subtracting we obtain

$$\mathbf{u}_t - \mathbf{u}^* = \mathbf{A}(\mathbf{u}_{t-1} - \mathbf{u}^*)$$
$$\text{or} \quad \mathbf{z}_t = \mathbf{A}\mathbf{z}_{t-1}$$

which is a linear first-order homogeneous system. In what follows, therefore, we shall concentrate more on linear homogeneous systems with no major loss.

5.2   Basic matrices with *Mathematica* and *Maple*

Both *Mathematica* and *Maple* have extensive facilities for dealing with matrices and matrix algebra. The intention in this section is to supply just the briefest introduction so that the reader can use the packages for the matrix manipulations required in this book. It is assumed that the reader is familiar with matrix algebra.

Both programmes treat matrices as a list of lists – a vector is just a single list. While most of the basic matrix manipulations are built into *Mathematica*, it is necessary to load one or even two packages in *Maple*. The two packages are (1) **linalg** and (2) **LinearAlgebra**, and are loaded with the instructions:

```
with(linalg):
with(LinearAlgebra):
```

The lists in *Mathematica* use curly braces, while those in *Maple* use straight (table 5.1).

Both programmes have palettes that speed up the entry of vectors and matrices, although *Mathematica*'s is far more extensive than that of *Maple*.

Table 5.1 Representations of matrices in *Mathematica* and *Maple*

	Mathematica	*Maple*	Conventional representation
Vector	$\{a, b, c\}$	$[a, b, c]$	$[a, b, c]$ or $\begin{bmatrix} a \\ b \\ c \end{bmatrix}$
Matrix	$\{\{a, b\}, \{c, d\}\}$	$[\,[a, b], [c, d]\,]$	$\begin{bmatrix} a & b \\ c & d \end{bmatrix}$

5.2.1   *Matrices in* **Mathematica**

To illustrate *Mathematica*'s package, let

$$mA = \begin{bmatrix} 3 & 2 & 4 \\ 1 & -2 & -3 \end{bmatrix}, \qquad mB = \begin{bmatrix} 0 & -1 & 1 \\ 2 & 3 & 0 \end{bmatrix}, \qquad mC = \begin{bmatrix} 2 & 1 \\ -1 & 0 \\ 2 & 3 \end{bmatrix}$$

then in *Mathematica* use:

```
mA={{3,2,4},{1,-2,-3}}
mB={{0,-1,1},{2,3,0}}
mC={{2,1},{-1,0},{2,3}}
mA+mB          (to add)
mA-mB          (to subtract)
mA.mC          (to multiply)
```

Notice that mA cannot be multiplied by mB. Any such attempt leads to an error message indicating that the matrices have incompatible shapes.

Square matrices have special properties. For illustrative purposes, let

$$m\mathbf{A} = \begin{bmatrix} 2 & 1 & -1 \\ 3 & 0 & 2 \\ -1 & 2 & 1 \end{bmatrix}$$

Typical properties are shown in table 5.2.

A special square matrix is the identity matrix. To specify a 3×3 identity matrix in *Mathematica* one uses Identity Matrix[3]. To construct the *characteristic polynomial* for the above square matrix, then we use[1]

```
mA-λIdentityMatrix[3]
```

and the *characteristic equation* is obtained using

```
Det[mA-λIdentityMatrix[3]]==0
```

which in turn can be solved using

```
Solve[Det[mA-λIdentityMatrix[3]]==0]
```

---

[1] The characteristic polynomial can be obtained directly with the command **CharacteristicPolynomial[mA]**.

Table 5.2 Properties of matrices and *Mathematica* input

Property	*Mathematica* input
Trace	`Tr[mA]`
Transpose	`Transpose[mA]`
Inverse	`Inverse[mA]`
Determinant	`Det[mA]`
Eigenvalues	`Eigenvalues[mA]` or `Eigenvalues[N[mA]]`
Eigenvectors	`Eigenvectors[mA]` or `Eigenvectors[N[mA]]`
Characteristic polynomial	`CharacteristicPolynomial[mA,λ]`
Matrix Power (power *n*)	`MatrixPower[mA,n]`

or

```
Solve[N[Det[mA-λIdentityMatrix[3]]]==0]
```

As one gets familiar with the package, long strings of instructions can be entered as a single instruction, as in the final solve.

To verify the results of example 4.12 in chapter 4, input the following, where we have added the instruction '// MatrixForm' to display the matrix in more familiar form

```
mA={{-2,1},{1,-2}}
Det[mA]
mA-λIdentityMatrix[2] //MatrixForm
Eigenvalues[mA]
Eigenvectors[mA]
```

All results are indeed verified.

5.2.2   *Matrices in* Maple

To illustrate *Maple*'s package, let

$$mA = \begin{bmatrix} 3 & 2 & 4 \\ 1 & -2 & -3 \end{bmatrix}, \qquad mB = \begin{bmatrix} 0 & -1 & 1 \\ 2 & 3 & 0 \end{bmatrix}, \qquad mC = \begin{bmatrix} 2 & 1 \\ -1 & 0 \\ 2 & 3 \end{bmatrix}$$

then in *Maple* use:

```
mA:=matrix([[3,2,4],[1,-2,-3]]);
mB:=matrix([[0,-1,1],[2,3,0]]);
mC:=matrix([[2,1],[-1,0],[2,3]]);
evalm(mA+mB)          (to add)
evalm(mA-mB)          (to subtract)
evalm(mA&*mC)         (to multiply)
```

Notice that mA cannot be multiplied by mB. Any such attempt leads to an error message indicating that the matrices have non-matching dimensions.

Table 5.3 Properties of matrices and *Maple* input

Property	*Maple* input
Trace	`trace(mA);`
Transpose	`transpose(mA);`
Inverse	`inverse(mA);`
Determinant	`det(mA);`
Eigenvalues	`eigenvals(mA); or evalf(eigenvals(mA));`
Eigenvectors	`eigenvects(mA); or evalf(eigenvects(mA));`
Characteristic polynomial	`charpoly(mA,'lambda');`
Matrix Power (power *n*)	`evalm(mA^n)`

Square matrices have special properties. For illustrative purposes, let

$$mA = \begin{bmatrix} 2 & 1 & -1 \\ 3 & 0 & 2 \\ -1 & 2 & 1 \end{bmatrix}$$

Typical properties are shown in table 5.3.

The *characteristic polynomial* in *Maple* simply requires the input

```
charpoly(mA,'lambda');
```

which in turn can be solved using

```
solve(charpoly(mA,'lambda')=0);
```

or

```
fsolve(charpoly(mA,'lambda')=0,lambda,complex);
```

As one gets familiar with the package, long strings of instructions can be entered as a single instruction, as in the final fsolve. Notice too that the final fsolve required the option 'complex' to list all solutions. Using

```
fsolve(charpoly(mA,'lambda')=0);
```

gives only the real solution.

To verify the results of example 4.12 in chapter 4, input the following:

```
with(linalg):
with(LinearAlgebra):
mA:=matrix([[-2,1],[1,-2]]);
det(mA);
evalm(mA-lambda*IdentityMatrix(2));
eigenvals(mA);
eigenvects(mA);
```

All results are indeed verified, when it is realised that $v^r = [1 \ -1]$ is fundamentally the same as $v^r = [-1 \ 1]$.

5.3   Eigenvalues and eigenvectors

Let us concentrate on the first-order linear homogeneous equation system

$$\begin{bmatrix} x_t \\ y_t \end{bmatrix} = \begin{bmatrix} a & b \\ c & d \end{bmatrix} \begin{bmatrix} x_{t-1} \\ y_{t-1} \end{bmatrix}$$

or $\mathbf{u}_t = \mathbf{A}\mathbf{u}_{t-1}$ with solution $\mathbf{u}_t = \mathbf{A}^t\mathbf{u}_0$. We invoke the following theorem.

THEOREM 5.1

If the eigenvalues of the matrix $\mathbf{A}$ are r and s obtained from $|\mathbf{A} - \lambda\mathbf{I}| = 0$ such that $r \neq s$, then there exists a matrix $\mathbf{V} = [\,\mathbf{v}^r \quad \mathbf{v}^s\,]$ composed of the eigenvectors associated with r and s, respectively, such that

$$\mathbf{D} = \begin{bmatrix} r & 0 \\ 0 & s \end{bmatrix} = \mathbf{V}^{-1}\mathbf{A}\mathbf{V}$$

We shall illustrate this theorem by means of an example.

Example 5.3

Let

$$\mathbf{A} = \begin{bmatrix} 2 & 1 \\ 1 & 2 \end{bmatrix}$$

The characteristic equation is $|\mathbf{A} - \lambda\mathbf{I}| = 0$, i.e.

$$\begin{vmatrix} 2 - \lambda & 1 \\ 1 & 2 - \lambda \end{vmatrix} = (2 - \lambda)^2 - 1 = \lambda^2 - 4\lambda + 3 = 0$$

Hence, $\lambda = r = 1$ and $\lambda = s = 3$.

For $\lambda = r = 1$ we have the equation

$$(\mathbf{A} - r\mathbf{I})\mathbf{v}^r = \mathbf{0}$$

or

$$\left[\begin{pmatrix} 2 & 1 \\ 1 & 2 \end{pmatrix} - \begin{pmatrix} 1 & 0 \\ 0 & 1 \end{pmatrix} \right] \begin{bmatrix} v_1^r \\ v_2^r \end{bmatrix} = \begin{bmatrix} 0 \\ 0 \end{bmatrix}$$

$$\text{i.e.} \quad \begin{bmatrix} 1 & 1 \\ 1 & 1 \end{bmatrix} \begin{bmatrix} v_1^r \\ v_2^r \end{bmatrix} = \begin{bmatrix} 0 \\ 0 \end{bmatrix}$$

Hence $v_1^r + v_2^r = 0$. Let $v_1^r = 1$ then $v_2^r = -v_1^r = -1$. Thus,

$$\mathbf{v}^r = \begin{bmatrix} 1 \\ -1 \end{bmatrix}$$

For $\lambda = s = 3$ we have

$$\left[\begin{pmatrix} 2 & 1 \\ 1 & 2 \end{pmatrix} - \begin{pmatrix} 3 & 0 \\ 0 & 3 \end{pmatrix}\right]\begin{bmatrix} v_1^s \\ v_2^s \end{bmatrix} = \begin{bmatrix} 0 \\ 0 \end{bmatrix}$$

i.e. $\begin{bmatrix} -1 & 1 \\ 1 & -1 \end{bmatrix}\begin{bmatrix} v_1^s \\ v_2^s \end{bmatrix} = \begin{bmatrix} 0 \\ 0 \end{bmatrix}$

Hence, $-v_1^s + v_2^s = 0$. Let $v_1^s = 1$, then $v_2^s = v_1^s = 1$. Thus, the second eigenvector is

$$\mathbf{v}^s = \begin{bmatrix} 1 \\ 1 \end{bmatrix}$$

Our matrix, $\mathbf{V}$, is therefore

$$\mathbf{V} = \begin{bmatrix} \mathbf{v}^r & \mathbf{v}^s \end{bmatrix} = \begin{bmatrix} 1 & 1 \\ -1 & 1 \end{bmatrix}$$

From the theorem we have $\mathbf{D} = \mathbf{V}^{-1}\mathbf{AV}$, i.e.

$$\mathbf{V}^{-1}\mathbf{AV} = \begin{bmatrix} 1 & 1 \\ -1 & 1 \end{bmatrix}^{-1}\begin{bmatrix} 2 & 1 \\ 1 & 2 \end{bmatrix}\begin{bmatrix} 1 & 1 \\ -1 & 1 \end{bmatrix} = \begin{bmatrix} 1 & 0 \\ 0 & 3 \end{bmatrix}$$

which is indeed the matrix $\mathbf{D}$ formed from the characteristic roots of $\mathbf{A}$.

Since $\mathbf{D} = \mathbf{V}^{-1}\mathbf{AV}$ then

$$\mathbf{VDV}^{-1} = \mathbf{V}(\mathbf{V}^{-1}\mathbf{AV})\mathbf{V}^{-1} = \mathbf{A}$$

Furthermore

$$\mathbf{A}^2 = (\mathbf{VDV}^{-1})(\mathbf{VDV}^{-1}) = \mathbf{VD}^2\mathbf{V}^{-1}$$

$$\mathbf{A}^3 = (\mathbf{VDV}^{-1})(\mathbf{VD}^2\mathbf{V}^{-1}) = \mathbf{VD}^3\mathbf{V}^{-1}$$

$$\vdots$$

$$\mathbf{A}^t = (\mathbf{VDV}^{-1})(\mathbf{VD}^{t-1}\mathbf{V}^{-1}) = \mathbf{VD}^t\mathbf{V}^{-1}$$

Hence

$$\mathbf{u}_t = \mathbf{A}^t\mathbf{u}_0 = \mathbf{VD}^t\mathbf{V}^{-1}\mathbf{u}_0 \tag{5.5}$$

or

$$\mathbf{u}_t = \mathbf{V}\begin{bmatrix} r^t & 0 \\ 0 & s^t \end{bmatrix}\mathbf{V}^{-1}\mathbf{u}_0$$

We can summarise the procedure as follows:

(1)   Given a first-order linear homogeneous equation system $\mathbf{u}_t = \mathbf{Au}_{t-1}$, where $\mathbf{u}$ is a 2×1 vector and $\mathbf{A}$ is a 2×2 matrix, with solution $\mathbf{u}_t = \mathbf{A}^t\mathbf{u}_0$, obtain the eigenvectors r and s (assumed to be distinct).

(2)   Derive the eigenvector $\mathbf{v}^r$ associated with the eigenvalue r and the eigenvector $\mathbf{v}^s$ associated with the eigenvalue s, and form the matrix $\mathbf{V} = [\mathbf{v}^r, \mathbf{v}^s]$.

(3)   From (2) we have the general solution

$$\mathbf{u}_t = ar^t\mathbf{v}^r + bs^t\mathbf{v}^s$$

and we can find a and b for $t = 0$ from

$$\mathbf{u}_0 = a\mathbf{v}^r + b\mathbf{v}^s$$

where $\mathbf{u}_0$ is known. This can either be done by direct substitution, or using the fact that

$$a\mathbf{v}^r + b\mathbf{v}^s = \begin{bmatrix} \mathbf{v}^r & \mathbf{v}^s \end{bmatrix} \begin{bmatrix} a \\ b \end{bmatrix} = \mathbf{u}_0$$

i.e. $\mathbf{V} \begin{bmatrix} a \\ b \end{bmatrix} = \mathbf{u}_0$

or $\begin{bmatrix} a \\ b \end{bmatrix} = \mathbf{V}^{-1}\mathbf{u}_0$

(4)   Write the solution

$$\mathbf{u}_t = ar^t\mathbf{v}^r + bs^t\mathbf{v}^s$$

But we can do this whole process in one step. First we note

$$\mathbf{u}_t = ar^t\mathbf{v}^r + bs^t\mathbf{v}^s = \begin{bmatrix} \mathbf{v}^r & \mathbf{v}^s \end{bmatrix} \begin{bmatrix} r^t & 0 \\ 0 & s^t \end{bmatrix} \begin{bmatrix} a \\ b \end{bmatrix}$$

$$= \mathbf{V}\mathbf{D}^t \begin{bmatrix} a \\ b \end{bmatrix}$$

But

$$\begin{bmatrix} a \\ b \end{bmatrix} = \mathbf{V}^{-1}\mathbf{u}_0$$

Hence

$$\mathbf{u}_t = \mathbf{V}\mathbf{D}^t\mathbf{V}^{-1}\mathbf{u}_0$$

which is the result we proved above. The gain, if there is one, in doing the four steps is the need to solve for a and b. Since this can often be done by direct substitution, then the four steps involve no inverse matrix computation.

Example 5.4

Let

$$x_{t+1} = -8 - x_t + y_t$$

$$y_{t+1} = 4 - 0.3x_t + 0.9y_t$$

setting $x_{t+1} = x_t = x^*$ and $y_{t+1} = y_t = y^*$ for all t, the fixed point is readily shown to be $(x^*, y^*) = (6.4, 20.8)$.

Now consider the system in terms of deviations from equilibrium, then

$$x_{t+1} - x^* = -(x_t - x^*) + (y_t - y^*)$$

$$y_{t+1} - y^* = -0.3(x_t - x^*) + 0.9(y_t - y^*)$$

or

$$\mathbf{u}_t = \mathbf{A}\mathbf{u}_{t-1}$$

where

$$A = \begin{bmatrix} -1 & 1 \\ -0.3 & 0.9 \end{bmatrix}$$

Solving for the eigenvalues from

$$A - \lambda I = \begin{bmatrix} -1 - \lambda & 1 \\ -0.3 & 0.9 - \lambda \end{bmatrix}$$

we have

$$|A - \lambda I| = -(1 + \lambda)(0.9 - \lambda) + 0.3 = \lambda^2 + 0.1\lambda - 0.6 = 0$$

giving $r = 0.7262$ and $s = -0.8262$.

Given $r = 0.7262$ then $(A - 0.7262I)v^r = 0$ so

$$\begin{bmatrix} -1.7262 & 1 \\ -0.3 & 0.1738 \end{bmatrix} \begin{bmatrix} v_1^r \\ v_2^r \end{bmatrix} = \begin{bmatrix} 0 \\ 0 \end{bmatrix}$$

i.e.

$$-1.7262v_1^r + v_2^r = 0$$

$$-0.3v_1^r + 0.1738v_2^r = 0$$

Let $v_2^r = 1$ then $v_1^r = 0.5793$.

For $s = -0.8262$

$$\begin{bmatrix} -0.1738 & 1 \\ -0.3 & 1.7262 \end{bmatrix} \begin{bmatrix} v_1^s \\ v_2^s \end{bmatrix} = \begin{bmatrix} 0 \\ 0 \end{bmatrix}$$

i.e.

$$-0.1738v_1^s + v_2^s = 0$$

$$-0.3v_1^s + 1.7262v_2^s = 0$$

Let $v_2^s = 1$ then $v_1^s = 5.7537$. Hence

$$V = [v^r \quad v^s] = \begin{bmatrix} 0.5793 & 5.7537 \\ 1 & 1 \end{bmatrix}$$

and

$$u_t = V \begin{bmatrix} (0.7262)^t & 0 \\ 0 & (-0.8262)^t \end{bmatrix} V^{-1} u_0$$

Suppose $x_0 = 2$ and $y_0 = 8$, i.e.

$$u_0 = \begin{bmatrix} -4.4 \\ -12.8 \end{bmatrix}$$

Then

$$\begin{bmatrix} x_{t+1} - x^* \\ y_{t+1} - y^* \end{bmatrix} = \begin{bmatrix} 0.5793 & 5.7537 \\ 1 & 1 \end{bmatrix} \begin{bmatrix} (0.7262)^t & 0 \\ 0 & (-0.8262)^t \end{bmatrix}$$

$$\begin{bmatrix} 0.5793 & 5.7537 \\ 1 & 1 \end{bmatrix}^{-1} \begin{bmatrix} -4.4 \\ -12.8 \end{bmatrix}$$

Figure 5.1.

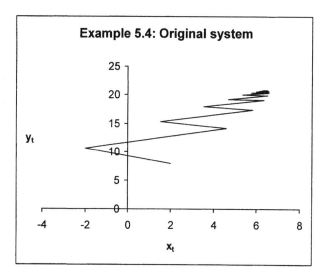

i.e.

$$x_{t+1} - x^* = -7.7526(0.7262)^t + 3.3526(-0.8262)^t$$
$$y_{t+1} - y^* = -13.3827(0.7262)^t + 5.827(-0.8262)^t$$

This procedure does give insight into the dynamics and it is possible to plot the solutions. However, if interest is purely in the dynamics of the trajectory, this can be obtained immediately using a spreadsheet. Once the equations for x_{t+1} and y_{t+1} have been entered in the first cells they are then copied down for as many periods as is necessary and the $\{x_t, y_t\}$ coordinates plotted on the *x-y* line plot, as shown in figure 5.1. This simple procedure also allows plots of $x(t)$ and $y(t)$ against time.[2]

The solution generalises to more than two equations. If **A** is a 3 × 3 matrix with distinct roots q, r and s, then the solution is

$$\mathbf{u}_t = \mathbf{V} \begin{bmatrix} q^t & 0 & 0 \\ 0 & r^t & 0 \\ 0 & 0 & s^t \end{bmatrix} \mathbf{V}^{-1} \mathbf{u}_0$$

here $\mathbf{V} = \begin{bmatrix} \mathbf{v}^q & \mathbf{v}^r & \mathbf{v}^s \end{bmatrix}$.

Example 5.5[3]

In this example we shall also illustrate how *Mathematica* or *Maple* can be employed as an aid. Let

$$\begin{bmatrix} x_t \\ y_t \\ z_t \end{bmatrix} = \begin{bmatrix} 1 & 2 & 1 \\ -1 & 1 & 0 \\ 3 & -6 & -1 \end{bmatrix} \begin{bmatrix} x_{t-1} \\ y_{t-1} \\ z_{t-1} \end{bmatrix}$$

---

[2] See Shone (2001) and section 5.5 below.
[3] Adapted from Sandefur (1990, chapter 6).

Then

$$\mathbf{A} - \lambda\mathbf{I} = \begin{bmatrix} 1-\lambda & 2 & 1 \\ -1 & 1-\lambda & 0 \\ 3 & -6 & -1-\lambda \end{bmatrix}$$

Within *Mathematica* carry out the following instructions, where we have replaced λ by a

```
m = {{1-a,2,1}, {-1,1-a,0}, {3,-6,-1-a}}
sols = Solve[ Det[m]==0, a]
```

or in *Maple*

```
m:=matrix( [ [1-a,2,1], [-1,1-a,0], [3,-6,-1-a] ] );
sols:=solve(det(m)=0,a);
```

which gives the three eigenvalues[4] $q = 0, r = -1$ and $s = 2$.

The next task is to obtain the associated eigenvectors. For $q = 0$, then

$$(\mathbf{A} - 0\mathbf{I})\mathbf{v}^r = \begin{bmatrix} 1 & 2 & 1 \\ -1 & 1 & 0 \\ 3 & -6 & -1 \end{bmatrix}\begin{bmatrix} v_1^q \\ v_2^q \\ v_3^q \end{bmatrix} = \begin{bmatrix} 0 \\ 0 \\ 0 \end{bmatrix}$$

which leads to the equations

$$v_1^q + 2v_2^q + v_3^q = 0$$
$$-v_1^q + v_2^q = 0$$
$$3v_1^q - 6v_2^q - v_3^q = 0$$

We can solve this system within *Mathematica* with the instruction

```
Solve[ {x+2y+z==0, -x+y==0, 3x-6y-z==0}, {x,y,z}]
```

or in *Maple* with the instruction

```
solve( {x+2*y+z=0, -x+y=0, 3*x-6*y-z=0}, {x,y,z});
```

which provides solutions $x = 1, y = 1$ and $z = -3$, where x is set arbitrarily at unity.

Carrying out exactly the procedure for $r = -1$ and $s = 2$ we obtain the results

$r = -1$ implies $x = 2, y = 1$ and $z = -6$

$s = 2$ implies $x = 1, y = -1$ and $z = 3$

Hence our three eigenvectors and the matrix $\mathbf{V}$ are:

$$\mathbf{v}^q = \begin{bmatrix} 1 \\ 1 \\ -3 \end{bmatrix}, \quad \mathbf{v}^r = \begin{bmatrix} 2 \\ 1 \\ -6 \end{bmatrix}, \quad \mathbf{v}^s = \begin{bmatrix} 1 \\ -1 \\ 3 \end{bmatrix}, \quad \mathbf{V} = \begin{bmatrix} 1 & 2 & 1 \\ 1 & 1 & -1 \\ -3 & -6 & 3 \end{bmatrix}$$

---

[4] This could be obtained directly using the command Eigenvalues[m] in *Mathematica* or eigenvals(m) in *Maple*.

Hence our solution is

$$\mathbf{u}_t = \mathbf{V} \begin{bmatrix} (0)^t & 0 & 0 \\ 0 & (-1)^t & 0 \\ 0 & 0 & (2)^t \end{bmatrix} \mathbf{V}^{-1} \mathbf{u}_0$$

Suppose

$$\mathbf{u}_0 = \begin{bmatrix} 3 \\ -4 \\ 3 \end{bmatrix}$$

Then

$$\begin{bmatrix} x_t \\ y_t \\ z_t \end{bmatrix} = \begin{bmatrix} 1 & 2 & 1 \\ 1 & 1 & -1 \\ -3 & -6 & 3 \end{bmatrix} \begin{bmatrix} 0^t & 0 & 0 \\ 0 & (-1)^t & 0 \\ 0 & 0 & 2^t \end{bmatrix} \begin{bmatrix} 1 & 2 & 1 \\ 1 & 1 & -1 \\ -3 & -6 & 3 \end{bmatrix}^{-1} \begin{bmatrix} 3 \\ -4 \\ 3 \end{bmatrix}$$

i.e.

$$x_t = 6(-1)^t + 2(2^t)$$
$$y_t = 3(-1)^t - 2(2^t)$$
$$z_t = -18(-1)^t + 6(2^t)$$

or

$$\begin{bmatrix} x_t \\ y_t \\ z_t \end{bmatrix} = 3(-1)^t \begin{bmatrix} 2 \\ 1 \\ -6 \end{bmatrix} + 2^{t+1} \begin{bmatrix} 1 \\ -1 \\ 3 \end{bmatrix}$$

5.4   *Mathematica* and *Maple* for solving discrete systems

Mathematica and *Maple* can be used in a variety of ways in helping to solve systems of discrete equations. Here we consider two:

(i)   Solving directly using the RSolve/rsolve command.
(ii)   Solving using the Jordan form.

5.4.1   *Solving directly*

Mathematica's **RSolve** command and *Maple*'s **rsolve** command can each handle systems of linear difference equations besides a single difference equation. In each case the procedure is similar to that outlined in chapter 3, section 3.13. Suppose we wish to solve example 5.4 with initial condition $(x_0, y_0) = (2, 8)$, i.e., the system

$$x_{t+1} = -8 - x_t + y_t$$
$$y_{t+1} = 4 - 0.3x_t + 0.9y_t$$
$$x_0 = 2, \quad y_0 = 8$$

then the instructions in each case are:

Mathematica
```
equ={x[t+1]==-8-x[t]+y[t],
      y[t+1]==4-0.3x[t]+0.9y[t],
      x[0]==2, y[0]==8}
var={x[t],y[t]}
RSolve[equ,var,t]
```
Maple
```
equ:=x(t+1)=-8-x(t)+y(t), y(t+1)=4-0.3*x(t)+0.9*y(t);
init:=x(0)=2, y(0)=8;
var:={x(t),y(t)};
rsolve({equ,init},var);
```

The output from each programme looks, on the face of it, quite different – even after using the **evalf** command in *Maple* to convert the answer to floating point arithmetic. *Maple* gives a single solution to both $x(t)$ and $y(t)$. *Mathematica*, however, gives a whole series of possible solutions depending on the value of t being greater than or equal to 1, 2 and 3, respectively, and further additional conditional statements. In economics, with t representing time, the value of t must be the same for all variables. This means we can ignore the additional conditional statements. What it does mean, however, is that only for $t \geq 3$ will the solution for $x(t)$ provided by *Mathematica* and *Maple* coincide; while $y(t)$ will coincide for $t \geq 2$. This should act as a warning to be careful in interpreting the output provided by these packages.

Turning to the three-equation system (example 5.5) with initial condition $(x_0, y_0, z_0) = (3, -4, 3)$

$$x_t = x_{t-1} + 2y_{t-1} + z_{t-1}$$
$$y_t = -x_{t-1} + y_{t-1}$$
$$z_t = 3x_{t-1} - 6y_{t-1} - z_{t-1}$$
$$x_0 = 3, \quad y_0 = -4, \quad z_0 = 3$$

then we would enter the following commands in each programme:

Mathematica
```
equ={x[t]==x[t-1]+2y[t-1]+z[t-1],
      y[t]==-x[t-1]+y[t-1],
      z[t]==3x[t-1]-6y[t-1]-z[t-1]
      x[0]==3, y[0]==-4,z[0]==3}
var={x[t],y[t],z[t]}
RSolve[equ,var,t]
```
Maple
```
equ:=x(t)=x(t-1)+2*y(t-1)+z(t-1),
      y(t)=-x(t-1)+y(t-1),
      z(t)=3*x(t-1)-6*y(t-1)-z(t-1);
init:=x(0)=3, y(0)=-4, z(0)=3;
var:={x(t),y(t),z(t)};
rsolve({equ,init},var);
```

In this instance the output in both programmes is almost identical. *Mathematica*, however, qualifies the solution for z[t] by adding 15 If[t==0,1,0]. If t is time, then this will not occur, and so this conditional statement can be ignored, in which case the two programmes give the same solution – which is also the one provided on p. 214.

5.4.2 *Solving using the Jordan form*

In section 5.3 we found the eigenvalues of the matrix **A** and used these to find the matrix **V** formed from the set of linearly independent eigenvectors of **A**. The diagonal matrix

(5.6) $$\mathbf{J} = \text{diag}(\lambda_1, \ldots, \lambda_n)$$

is the Jordan form of **A** and **V** is the transition matrix, such that

(5.7) $$\mathbf{V}^{-1}\mathbf{A}\mathbf{V} = \mathbf{J}$$

From this result we have

$$\mathbf{A}^t = \mathbf{V}\mathbf{J}^t\mathbf{V}^{-1}$$

and since the solution to the system $\mathbf{u}_t = \mathbf{A}\mathbf{u}_{t-1}$ is $\mathbf{u}_t = \mathbf{A}^t\mathbf{u}_0$, then

(5.8) $$\mathbf{u}_t = \mathbf{V}\mathbf{J}^t\mathbf{V}^{-1}\mathbf{u}_0 \quad \text{where} \quad \mathbf{J}^t = \begin{bmatrix} \lambda_1^t & 0 & \cdots & 0 \\ 0 & \lambda_2^t & \cdots & 0 \\ \vdots & \vdots & & \vdots \\ 0 & 0 & \cdots & \lambda_n^t \end{bmatrix}$$

So our only problem is to find the matrices **J** and **V**.

Both *Mathematica* and *Maple* have commands to supply these matrices directly. In *Mathematica* one uses the command **JordanDecomposition[mA]**; while in *Maple* it is necessary to first load the **linalg** package, and then to use the command **jordan(mA, 'V')**, where **mA** denotes the matrix under investigation and **V** is the transition matrix. To illustrate how to use these commands consider example 5.3, where

$$\text{mA} = \begin{bmatrix} 2 & 1 \\ 1 & 2 \end{bmatrix}$$

Mathematica
```
mA={{2,1},{1,2}}
{V,J}=JordanDecomposition[mA]
MatrixForm /@ {V,J}
MatrixForm[[Inverse[V].mA.V]]
```
Maple
```
with(linalg):
mA:=matrix( [ [2,1],[1,2] ]);
J:=jordan(mA,'V');
print(V);
evalm(V^(-1)&*mA&*V);
```

In each of these instructions the last line is a check that undertaking the matrix multiplication does indeed lead to the Jordan form of the matrix. In each package we get the Jordan form

$$\mathbf{J} = \begin{bmatrix} 1 & 0 \\ 0 & 3 \end{bmatrix}$$

However, the transition matrix in each package on the face of it looks different. More specifically,

$$\text{Mathematica} \quad \mathbf{V} = \begin{bmatrix} -1 & 1 \\ 1 & 1 \end{bmatrix}$$

$$\text{Maple} \quad \mathbf{V} = \begin{bmatrix} \frac{1}{2} & \frac{1}{2} \\ -\frac{1}{2} & \frac{1}{2} \end{bmatrix}$$

But these are fundamentally the same. We noted this when deriving the eigenvectors in the previous section. We arbitrarily chose values for v_1^r or v_2^r (along with the values associated with the eigenvalue s). In *Maple*, consider the first column, which is the first eigenvector. Setting $v_2^r = 1$, means multiplying the first term by -2, which gives a value for $v_1^r = -1$. Similarly, setting $v_1^s = 1$ in *Maple*, converts v_2^s also to the value of unity. Hence, the two matrices are identical. In each case the last instruction verifies that $\mathbf{V}^{-1}\mathbf{A}\mathbf{V} = \mathbf{J}$.

Using *Maple* verifies all the results in section 5.3. However, *Mathematica* seems to give inconsistent results for a number of the problems. In particular, it appears the transition matrices provided by *Mathematica* for examples 5.4, 5.6 and 5.7 are not correct. This shows up with the last instruction, since for these examples MatrixForm[Inverse[V].ma.V] does not give the matrix J!

It should be noted that all the examples in section 5.3 involve real and distinct roots. Even in the case of complex roots, these are distinct. A more general theorem than Theorem 5.1 is the following:

THEOREM 5.2
If $\mathbf{A}$ is a $n \times n$ square matrix with distinct eigenvalues $\lambda_1, \ldots, \lambda_n$, then the matrix $\mathbf{A}$ is diagonalisable, such that

$$\mathbf{V}^{-1}\mathbf{A}\mathbf{V} = \mathbf{J}$$

and $\mathbf{J} = \text{diag}(\lambda_1, \ldots, \lambda_n)$.

Since $\lambda_1, \ldots, \lambda_n$ are distinct eigenvalues of the matrix $\mathbf{A}$, then it is possible to find n linearly independent eigenvectors $\mathbf{v}^1, \ldots, \mathbf{v}^n$ to form the transition matrix $\mathbf{V}$.

Systems that have repeated roots involve linear dependence. Such systems involve properties of Jordan blocks, which is beyond the scope of this book. However, a complete study of the stability of discrete systems would require an understanding of Jordan blocks, see Elaydi (1996) and Simon and Blume (1994).

When the matrix $\mathbf{A}$ has repeated roots, then it is not diagonalisable. It is, however, possible to find an 'almost diagonalisable' matrix which helps in solving systems with repeated roots. As indicated in the previous paragraph, for a general system of n equations, this requires knowledge of Jordan blocks. Here we shall simply state a result for a 2×2 system.

THEOREM 5.3

If A is a 2×2 matrix, then there is a transition matrix V such that

(a) $\mathbf{V}^{-1}\mathbf{AV} = \mathbf{J}_1 = \begin{bmatrix} r & 0 \\ 0 & s \end{bmatrix}$ *for real distinct roots r and s*

(b) $\mathbf{V}^{-1}\mathbf{AV} = \mathbf{J}_2 = \begin{bmatrix} \lambda & 1 \\ 0 & \lambda \end{bmatrix}$ *for repeated root λ*

(c) $\mathbf{V}^{-1}\mathbf{AV} = \mathbf{J}_3 = \begin{bmatrix} \alpha + \beta i & 0 \\ 0 & \alpha - \beta i \end{bmatrix}$

for complex conjugate roots $\lambda = \alpha \pm \beta i$

In each case, $\mathbf{J}_i$ is the Jordan form of the particular matrix $\mathbf{A}$. We shall use theorem 5.3 when discussing the stability of discrete systems in section 5.6. Section 5.2 dealt with case (a) in detail. Here we shall consider just one example of cases (b) and (c), using both *Mathematica* and *Maple*.

Example 5.6

Consider the matrix in example 4.10, which is

$$\mathbf{A2} = \begin{bmatrix} 1 & -1 \\ 1 & 3 \end{bmatrix}$$

then the instructions in each programme are:

```
Mathematica
A2={{1,-1},{1,3}}
Eigenvalues[A2]
{V2,J2}=JordanDecomposition[A2]
MatrixForm /@ {V2,J2}
MatrixForm[Inverse[V2].A2.V2]
Maple
with(linalg):
A2:=matrix([[1,-1],[1,3]]);
eigenvals(A2);
J2:=jordan(A2,'V2');
print(V2);
evalm(V2^(-1)&*A2&*V2);
```

With each programme we get the Jordan form as

$$\mathbf{J2} = \begin{bmatrix} 2 & 1 \\ 0 & 2 \end{bmatrix}$$

Example 5.7

Next consider the matrix in example 4.11, which is

$$\mathbf{A3} = \begin{bmatrix} -3 & 4 \\ -2 & 1 \end{bmatrix}$$

then the instructions in each programme are:

Mathematica
```
A3={{-3,4},{-2,1}}
Eigenvalues[A3]
{V3,J3}=JordanDecomposition[A3]
MatrixForm /@ {V3,J3}
MatrixForm[Inverse[V3].A3.V3]
```
Maple
```
with(linalg):
A3:=matrix([[-3,4],[-2,1]]);
eigenvals(A3);
J3:=jordan(A3,'V3');
print(V3);
evalm(V3^(-1)&*A3&*V3);
```

With each programme we get the Jordan form as

$$\mathbf{J3} = \begin{bmatrix} -1 + 2i & 0 \\ 0 & -1 - 2i \end{bmatrix}$$

Verifying the results in theorem 5.3.

When considering the stability of the system

$$\mathbf{u}_t = \mathbf{A}\mathbf{u}_{t-1} \tag{5.9}$$

we can approach this from a slightly different perspective, which can provide some valuable insight into the phase portrait of discrete systems. What we intend to do is to transform the system using the matrix $\mathbf{V}$. Thus, define

$$\mathbf{z}_t = \mathbf{V}^{-1}\mathbf{u}_t \tag{5.10}$$

This implies $\mathbf{u}_t = \mathbf{V}\mathbf{z}_t$. We can therefore write system (5.9) in the form

$$\mathbf{V}\mathbf{z}_t = \mathbf{A}\mathbf{V}\mathbf{z}_{t-1}$$

premultiplying by the matrix $\mathbf{V}^{-1}$, we have

$$\mathbf{z}_t = \mathbf{V}^{-1}\mathbf{A}\mathbf{V}\mathbf{z}_{t-1} = \mathbf{J}\mathbf{z}_{t-1} \qquad \text{where } \mathbf{J} = \begin{bmatrix} r & 0 \\ 0 & s \end{bmatrix} \tag{5.11}$$

System $\mathbf{z}_t = \mathbf{J}\mathbf{z}_{t-1}$ is referred to as the **canonical form** of the system $\mathbf{u}_t = \mathbf{A}\mathbf{u}_{t-1}$. The important point is that the stability properties of (5.11) are the same as those of (5.9).

The solution to the canonical form is simply

$$\mathbf{z}_t = \mathbf{J}^t\mathbf{z}_0 = \begin{bmatrix} r^t & 0 \\ 0 & s^t \end{bmatrix}\mathbf{z}_0 \qquad \text{where } \mathbf{z}_0 = \mathbf{V}^{-1}\mathbf{u}_0$$

When considering the phase space of this canonical form it is useful to consider the following:

$$\begin{bmatrix} z_{1t} \\ z_{2t} \end{bmatrix} = \begin{bmatrix} r^t & 0 \\ 0 & s^t \end{bmatrix} \begin{bmatrix} z_{10} \\ z_{20} \end{bmatrix}$$

Now take the ratio of z_2/z_1, then

$$\frac{z_{2t}}{z_{1t}} = \frac{s^t z_{20}}{r^t z_{10}} = \left(\frac{s}{r}\right)^t \left(\frac{z_{20}}{z_{10}}\right)$$

and so the path of the system is dominated by the value/sign of s/r.

5.5 Graphing trajectories of discrete systems

The mathematics of solving simultaneous equation systems is not very straightforward and it is necessary to obtain the eigenvalues and the eigenvectors. However, it is possible to combine the qualitative nature of the phase plane discussed in the previous section and obtain trajectories using a spreadsheet or the recursive features of *Mathematica* and *Maple*.

5.5.1 Trajectories with **Excel**

Example 5.8

Consider the following system of equations

$$x_t = -5 + 0.25x_{t-1} + 0.4y_{t-1}$$
$$y_t = 10 - x_{t-1} + y_{t-1}$$
$$x_0 = 10, \quad y_0 = 5$$

In cells B8 and C8 we place the initial values for x and y, namely $x_0 = 10$ and $y_0 = 5$. In cells B9 and C9 we place the formulas. These are

```
B9 = -5 + 0.25* B8 + 0.4* C8
C8 = 10 - B8 + C8
```

These cell entries contain only relative addresses. Cells B8 and C8 are then copied to the clipboard and pasted down in cells B10:C28. Once the computations for (x_t, y_t) have been obtained, then it is a simple matter of using the x-y plot to plot the trajectory. Given the discrete nature of the system the trajectories are not the regular shapes indicated by the phase plane diagram. They constitute discrete points that are joined up. Even so, the nature of the system can readily be investigated.

Figure 5.2 shows the initial values of $x_0 = 10$ and $y_0 = 5$. Always a good check that the equations have been entered correctly is to place the equilibrium values as the initial values. The equilibrium point is $(x^*, y^*) = (10, 31.25)$. Placing these values in cells B8 and C8 leads to them being repeated in all periods. One of the advantages of this approach, besides its simplicity, is the ready investigation of the system for various initial conditions. The graphics plot can sometimes change quite dramatically!

This procedure allows quite complex discrete dynamic systems of two equations to be investigated with the minimum mathematical knowledge. Of course, to fully

Figure 5.2.

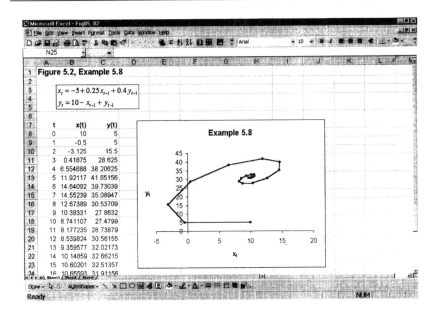

appreciate what is happening requires an understanding of the material in many of the chapters of this book. Consider the following nonlinear system, which is used to produce the Hénon map and which we shall investigate more fully in chapter 7.

Example 5.9

The system is

$$x_t = 1 - ax_{t-1}^2 + y_{t-1}$$
$$y_t = bx_{t-1}$$

Our purpose here is not to investigate the properties of this system, but rather to see how we can display trajectories belonging to it. We begin with the spreadsheet, as shown in figure 5.3. We place the values of a and b in cells E3 and E4, where $a = 1.4$ and $b = 0.3$. In cells B8 and C8 we place the initial values for x and y, which are $x_0 = 0.01$ and $y_0 = 0$. The formulas for the two equations are placed in cells B9 and C9, respectively. These take the form

    B9   1-E3*B8^2+C8

    C9 E4*B8

The cells with dollar signs indicate absolute addresses, while those without dollar signs indicate relative addresses. Cells B9 and C9 are then copied to the clipboard and pasted down. After blocking cells B8:C28 the graph wizard is then invoked and the resulting trajectory is shown in the inserted graph. The most conspicuous feature of this trajectory is that it does not have a 'pattern'. In fact, given the parameter values there are two equilibrium points: $(x_1^*, y_1^*) = (-1.1314, -0.3394)$ and $(x_2^*, y_2^*) = (0.6314, 0.1894)$, neither of which is approached within the first twenty periods. Why this is so we shall investigate in chapter 7.

Figure 5.3.

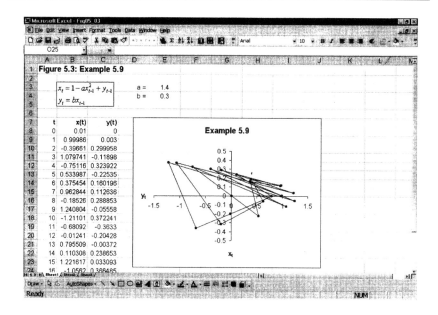

5.5.2 *Trajectories with* Mathematica *and* Maple

The spreadsheet is ideal for displaying recursive systems and the resulting trajectories. But occasionally it is useful to display these trajectories within *Mathematica* or *Maple*. In doing this care must be exercised in writing the simultaneous equations for computation so that the programmes remember earlier results and do not recompute *all* previous values on each round. This leads to more cumbersome input instructions – which is why the spreadsheet is so much easier for many problems. We shall consider once again examples 5.8 and 5.9.

Example 5.8 (cont.)

The input instructions for each programme are

Mathematica
```
Clear[x,y,t]
x[0]:=10; y[0]:=5;
x[t_]:=x[t]=-5+0.25x[t-1]+0.4y[t-1]
y[t_]:=y[t]=10-x[t-1]+y[t-1]
data:=Table[{x[t],y[t]},{t,0,20}];
ListPlot[data,PlotJoined->True,PlotRange->All]
```
Maple
```
t:='t': x:='x': y:='y':
x:=proc(t) option remember;-5+0.25*x(t-1)+0.4*y(t-1)end:
y:=proc(t) option remember; 10-x(t-1)+y(t-1) end:
x(0):=10: y(0):=5:
data:=[seq([x(t),y(t)],t=0..20)];
plot(data);
```

The *Maple* instructions join the points by default. If just a plot of points is required with *Maple*, then the last line becomes

```
plot(data, plotstyle=point);
```

The resulting trajectories are similar to that shown in the chart in figure 5.2 (p. 221). As one might expect, both *Mathematica* and *Maple* allow more control over the display of the trajectories than is available within *Excel*. Furthermore, both these programmes allow more than one trajectory to be displayed on the same diagram. This is not possible within spreadsheets. Spreadsheets can display only one (x, y)-trajectory at a time.

Example 5.9 (cont.)

The input instructions for each programme for producing discrete plot trajectories are

Mathematica
```
Clear[x,y,t,a,b]
x[0]:=0.01; y[0]:=0;
a:=1.4; b:=0.3;
x[t_]:=x[t]=1-a x[t-1]^2+y[t-1]
y[t_]:=y[t]=b x[t-1]
data=Table[{x[t],y[t]},{t,0,20}];
ListPlot[data,PlotJoined->True,PlotRange->All]
```
Maple
```
t:='t': x:='x': y:='y': a:='a': b:='b':
x:=proc(t) option remember; 1-a*x(t-1)^2+y(t-1) end:
y:=proc(t) option remember; b*x(t-1) end:
x(0):=0.01: y(0):=0:
a:=1.4: b:=0.3:
data:=[seq([x(t),y(t)],t=0..20)];
plot(data);
```

The resulting trajectories are similar to that shown in the chart in figure 5.3.

Spreadsheets do not allow three-dimensional plots, but it is very easy to adapt the instructions just presented for *Mathematica* and *Maple* to do this. The only essential difference is the final line in each programme. Assuming 'data' records the list of points $\{x(t), y(t), z(t)\}$, then a three-dimensional plot requires the instruction

Mathematica
```
ListPlot3D[data,PlotJoined->True]
```
Maple
```
plot3d(data);
```

5.6 The stability of discrete systems

5.6.1 *Real distinct roots*

For systems with real distinct roots, r and s, which therefore have linearly independent eigenvectors, we can establish the *stability* properties of such systems by considering the general solution

$$\mathbf{u}_t = ar^t\mathbf{v}^r + bs^t\mathbf{v}^s \qquad \text{where} \qquad \mathbf{u}_t = \begin{bmatrix} x_t - x^* \\ y_t - y^* \end{bmatrix}$$

If $|r| < 1$ and $|s| < 1$ then $ar^t\mathbf{v}^r \to \mathbf{0}$ and $bs^t\mathbf{v}^s \to \mathbf{0}$ as $t \to \infty$ and so $\mathbf{u}_t \to \mathbf{0}$ and consequently the system tends to the fixed point, the equilibrium point.

Return to example 5.4 where $r = 0.7262$ and $s = -0.8262$. The absolute value of both roots is less than unity, and so the system is stable. We showed this in terms of figure 5.1, where the system converges on the equilibrium, the fixed point. We pointed out above that the system can be represented in its canonical form, and the same stability properties should be apparent. To show this our first task is to compute the vector $\mathbf{z}_0$. Since $\mathbf{z}_0 = \mathbf{V}^{-1}\mathbf{u}_0$, then

$$\begin{bmatrix} z_{10} \\ z_{20} \end{bmatrix} = \begin{bmatrix} 0.5793 & 5.7537 \\ 1 & 1 \end{bmatrix}^{-1} \begin{bmatrix} -4.4 \\ -12.8 \end{bmatrix} = \begin{bmatrix} -13.3827 \\ 0.5827 \end{bmatrix}$$

and

$$z_{1t} = (0.7262)^t(-13.3827)$$

$$z_{2t} = (-0.8262)^t(0.5827)$$

Setting this up on a spreadsheet, we derive figure 5.4. The canonical form has transformed the system into the (z_1, z_2)-plane, but once again it converges on the fixed point, which is now the origin.

Now consider the situation where $|r| > 1$ and $|s| > 1$ then $\mathbf{u}_t \to \pm\infty$ depending on the sign of the characteristic roots. But this result occurs so long as at least one root is greater than unity in absolute value. This must be so. Let $|r| > 1$ and let $|s| < 1$. Then over time $bs^t\mathbf{v}^s \to \mathbf{0}$ as $t \to \infty$, while $ar^t\mathbf{v}^r \to \pm\infty$ as $t \to \infty$, which means $\mathbf{u}_t \to \pm\infty$ as $t \to \infty$. The system is unstable.

Return to example 5.3 where $r = 1$ and $s = 3$. Both roots are distinct, positive and at least one is greater than unity. It follows from our earlier argument that this system must be unstable. We have already demonstrated that the diagonal matrix

Figure 5.4.

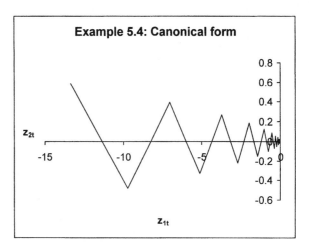

Example 5.4: Canonical form

(the Jordan form) and the transition matrix are:

$$J = \begin{bmatrix} 1 & 0 \\ 0 & 3 \end{bmatrix}, \qquad V = \begin{bmatrix} 1 & 1 \\ -1 & 1 \end{bmatrix}$$

Suppose for this system $(u_{10}, u_{20}) = (5, 2)$, then

$$\begin{bmatrix} u_{1t} \\ u_{2t} \end{bmatrix} = \begin{bmatrix} 1 & 1 \\ -1 & 1 \end{bmatrix} \begin{bmatrix} 1^t & 0 \\ 0 & 3^t \end{bmatrix} \begin{bmatrix} 1 & 1 \\ -1 & 1 \end{bmatrix}^{-1} \begin{bmatrix} 5 \\ 2 \end{bmatrix}$$

i.e.

$$u_{1t} = \frac{3}{2} + \frac{7}{2}3^t$$

$$u_{2t} = -\frac{3}{2} + \frac{7}{2}3^t$$

Therefore, as t increases $u_{1t} \to +\infty$ and $u_{2t} \to +\infty$.

Turning to the canonical form, $z_0 = V^{-1}u_0$, hence

$$\begin{bmatrix} z_{10} \\ z_{20} \end{bmatrix} = \begin{bmatrix} 3/2 \\ 7/2 \end{bmatrix}$$

and

$$z_{1t} = 1^t \left(\frac{3}{2} \right) = \frac{3}{2}$$

$$z_{2t} = 3^t \left(\frac{7}{2} \right)$$

Furthermore,

$$\frac{z_{2t}}{z_{1t}} = \left(\frac{3}{1} \right)^t \frac{7/2}{3/2} = 3^t \left(\frac{7}{3} \right)$$

and so for each point in the canonical phase space, the angle from the origin is increasing, and so the direction of the system is vertically upwards, as illustrated in figure 5.5(b). Once again, the same instability is shown in the original space, figure 5.5(a), and in its canonical form, figure 5.5(b). The fact that the trajectory in figure 5.5(b) is vertical arises from the fact that root $r = 1$.

Suppose one root is greater than unity in absolute value and the other less than unity in absolute value. Let these be $|r| > 1$ and $|s| < 1$. The system remains unstable because it will be governed by the root $|r| > 1$, and the system will be dominated by the term $ar^t v^r$. This means that for *most* initial points u_0, the system diverges from the equilibrium, from the steady state (x^*, y^*). But suppose $a = 0$, then $u_t = bs^t v^s$ and since $|s| < 1$, then the system will converge on (x^*, y^*). There exist, therefore *some* stable trajectories in the phase plane.

Example 5.10

$$x_{t+1} = -0.85078x_t - y_t$$

$$y_{t+1} = x_t + 2.35078y_t$$

Figure 5.5.

(a)

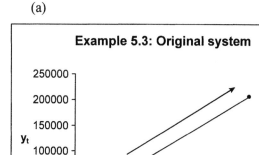

(b)

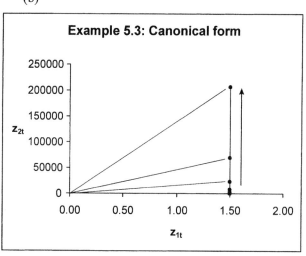

The fixed point is at the origin, i.e., $x^* = 0$ and $y^* = 0$. This system takes the matrix form

$$\begin{bmatrix} x_{t+1} \\ y_{t+1} \end{bmatrix} = \begin{bmatrix} -0.85078 & -1 \\ 1 & 2.35078 \end{bmatrix}$$

The eigenvalues of the matrix $\mathbf{A}$ of this system are readily found to be $r = 2$ and $s = -0.5$. We therefore satisfy the condition $|r| > 1$ and $|s| < 1$. Furthermore, we can obtain the eigenvectors of this system as follows

$$(\mathbf{A} - 2\mathbf{I})\mathbf{v}^r = \mathbf{0}$$

i.e. $$\begin{bmatrix} -2.85078 & -1 \\ 1 & 0.35078 \end{bmatrix} \begin{bmatrix} v_1^r \\ v_2^r \end{bmatrix} = \begin{bmatrix} 0 \\ 0 \end{bmatrix}$$

or

$$-2.85078v_1^r - v_2^r = 0$$
$$v_1^r + 0.35078v_2^r = 0$$

Let $v_1^r = 1$ then $v_2^r = -2.8508$.

The second eigenvector is found from

$$(\mathbf{A} - 0.5\mathbf{I})\mathbf{v}^s = \mathbf{0}$$

i.e. $\begin{bmatrix} -0.35078 & -1 \\ 1 & 2.85078 \end{bmatrix} \begin{bmatrix} v_1^s \\ v_2^s \end{bmatrix} = \begin{bmatrix} 0 \\ 0 \end{bmatrix}$

or

$$-0.35078v_1^s - v_2^s = 0$$
$$v_1^s + 2.85078v_2^s = 0$$

Let $v_2^s = 1$ then $v_1^s = -2.8508$. Hence

$$\mathbf{v}^r = \begin{bmatrix} 1 \\ -2.8508 \end{bmatrix}, \qquad \mathbf{v}^s = \begin{bmatrix} -2.8508 \\ 1 \end{bmatrix}$$

One eigenvector represents the stable arm while the other represents the unstable arm. But which, then, represents the stable arm? To establish this, convert the system to its canonical form, with $\mathbf{z}_{t+1} = \mathbf{V}^{-1}\mathbf{u}_{t+1}$. Now take a point on the first eigenvector, i.e., point $(1, -2.8508)$, then

$$\mathbf{z}_0 = \mathbf{V}^{-1}\mathbf{u}_0 = \begin{bmatrix} 1 & -2.8508 \\ -2.8508 & 1 \end{bmatrix}^{-1} \begin{bmatrix} 1 \\ -2.8508 \end{bmatrix} = \begin{bmatrix} 1 \\ 0 \end{bmatrix}$$

Hence,

$$z_{1t} = 2^t(1)$$
$$z_{2t} = (-0.5)^t(0) = 0$$

Therefore $z_{1t} \to +\infty$ as $t \to \infty$. So the eigenvector $\mathbf{v}^r$ must represent the unstable arm.

Now take a point on the eigenvector $\mathbf{v}^s$, i.e., the point $(-2.8508, 1)$, then

$$\mathbf{z}_0 = \mathbf{V}^{-1}\mathbf{u}_0 = \begin{bmatrix} 1 & -2.8508 \\ -2.8508 & 1 \end{bmatrix}^{-1} \begin{bmatrix} -2.8508 \\ 1 \end{bmatrix} = \begin{bmatrix} 0 \\ 1 \end{bmatrix}$$

Hence,

$$z_{1t} = 2^t(0) = 0$$
$$z_{2t} = (-0.5)^t(1)$$

Therefore $z_{2t} \to 0$ as $t \to \infty$. So the eigenvector $\mathbf{v}^s$ must represent the stable arm of the saddle point. Figure 5.6 illustrates the trajectory of the original system starting from point $(-2.8508, 1)$, and shows that it indeed converges on the point $(x^*, y^*) = (0, 0)$.[5]

Before leaving this example, notice that when we considered point $(1, -2.8508)$ on the eigenvector associated with $r = 2$, the point became $(1, 0)$ in terms of its

---

[5] The system is, however, sensitive. A plot beyond $t = 10$ has the system moving *away* from the fixed point.

Figure 5.6.

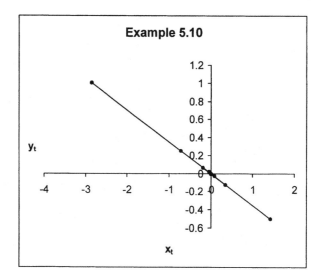

canonical representation. Similarly, point $(-2.8508, 1)$ on the eigenvector associated with $s = -0.5$ became point $(0, 1)$ in its canonical representation. In other words, the arms of the saddle point equilibrium became transformed into the two rectangular axes in z-space. This is a standard result for systems involving saddle point solutions.

So long as we have distinct characteristic roots these results hold. Here, however, we shall confine ourselves to the two-variable case. To summarise, if r and s are the characteristic roots of the matrix $\mathbf{A}$ for the system $\mathbf{u}_t = \mathbf{A}\mathbf{u}_{t-1}$ and derived from solving $|\mathbf{A} - \lambda\mathbf{I}| = 0$, then

(i)   if $|r| < 1$ and $|s| < 1$ the system is dynamically stable
(ii)   if $|r| > 1$ and $|s| > 1$ the system is dynamically unstable
(iii)   if, say, $|r| > 1$ and $|s| < 1$ the system is dynamically unstable.

In the case of (iii) the system will generally be dominated by the largest root and will tend to plus or minus infinity depending on its sign. But given the fixed point is a saddle path solution, there are some initial points that will converge on the fixed point, and these are values that lie on the stable arm of the saddle point.

As we shall see in part II, such possible solution paths are important in rational expectations theory. Under such assumed expectations behaviour, the system 'jumps' from its initial point to the stable arm and then traverses a path down the stable arm to equilibrium. Of course, if this initial 'jump' did not occur, then the trajectory would tend to plus or minus infinity and be driven away from equilibrium.

5.6.2   *Repeating roots*

When there is a repeating root, λ, the system's dynamics is dominated by the sign/value of this root. If $|\lambda| < 1$, then the system will converge on the equilibrium value: it is asymptotically stable. If $|\lambda| > 1$ then the system is asymptotically unstable. We can verify this by considering the canonical form. We have already showed that the canonical form of $\mathbf{u}_t = \mathbf{A}\mathbf{u}_{t-1}$ is

$$\mathbf{z}_t = \mathbf{J}^t\mathbf{z}_0$$

In the case of a repeated root this is

$$\mathbf{z}_t = \begin{bmatrix} \lambda^t & t\lambda^{t-1} \\ 0 & \lambda^t \end{bmatrix} \mathbf{z}_0$$

Hence

$$z_{1t} = \lambda^t z_{10} + t\lambda^{t-1} z_{20}$$

$$z_{2t} = \lambda^t z_{20}$$

Therefore if $|\lambda| < 1$, then $|\lambda^t| \rightarrow 0$ as $t \rightarrow \infty$, consequently $z_{1t} \rightarrow 0$ and $z_{2t} \rightarrow 0$ as $t \rightarrow \infty$. The system is asymptotically stable. If, on the other hand, $|\lambda| > 1$, then $|\lambda^t| \rightarrow \infty$ as $t \rightarrow \infty$, and $z_{1t} \rightarrow \pm\infty$ and $z_{2t} \rightarrow \pm\infty$ as $t \rightarrow \infty$. The system is asymptotically unstable.

We can conclude for repeated roots, therefore, that

(a)   if $|\lambda| < 1$ the system is asymptotically stable
(b)   if $|\lambda| > 1$ the system is asymptotically unstable.

Example 5.11

Consider the following system

$$x_{t+1} = 4 + x_t - y_t$$
$$y_{t+1} = -20 + x_t + 3y_t$$

Then $x^* = 12$ and $y^* = 4$. Representing the system as deviations from equilibrium, we have

$$x_{t+1} - x^* = (x_t - x^*) - (y_t - y^*)$$
$$y_{t+1} - y^* = (x_t - x^*) + 3(y_t - y^*)$$

This system can be represented in the form $\mathbf{u}_t = \mathbf{A}\mathbf{u}_{t-1}$ and the matrix of the system is

$$\mathbf{A} = \begin{bmatrix} 1 & -1 \\ 1 & 3 \end{bmatrix}$$

We have already considered this in example 5.6 with results

$$\mathbf{J} = \begin{bmatrix} 2 & 1 \\ 0 & 2 \end{bmatrix} \qquad \mathbf{V} = \begin{bmatrix} -1 & 1 \\ 1 & 0 \end{bmatrix}$$

The solution is then

$$\mathbf{u}_t = \mathbf{V}\mathbf{J}^t\mathbf{V}^{-1}\mathbf{u}_0 \qquad \text{where} \qquad \mathbf{J}^t = \begin{bmatrix} 2^t & t2^{t-1} \\ 0 & 2^t \end{bmatrix}$$

Since the stability properties of $\mathbf{u}_t = \mathbf{A}\mathbf{u}_{t-1}$ are the same as those of its canonical form, let us therefore consider

$$\mathbf{z}_t = \begin{bmatrix} 2^t & t2^{t-1} \\ 0 & 2^t \end{bmatrix} \mathbf{z}_0$$

Figure 5.7.

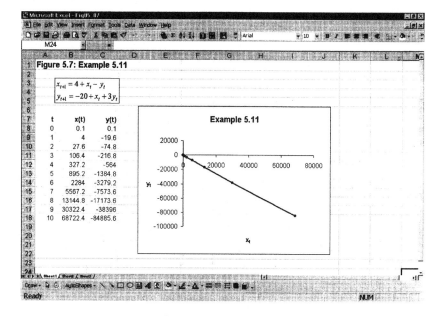

i.e.

$$z_{1t} = 2^t z_{10} + t2^{t-1} z_{20}$$
$$z_{2t} = 2^t z_{20}$$

Clearly, $z_{1t} \to \infty$ and $z_{2t} \to \infty$ as $t \to \infty$ regardless of the initial point. This is illustrated for the original system using a spreadsheet, as shown in figure 5.7 for the initial point $(0.1, 0.1)$.

Example 5.12

Consider

$$x_{t+1} = 8 + 1.5x_t - y_t$$
$$y_{t+1} = -15 + x_t - 0.5y_t$$

Then $x^* = 108$ and $y^* = 62$. Taking deviations from equilibrium

$$x_{t+1} - x^* = 1.5(x_t - x^*) - (y_t - y^*)$$
$$y_{t+1} - y^* = (x_t - x^*) - 0.5(y_t - y^*)$$

and so the matrix of this system is

$$\mathbf{A} = \begin{bmatrix} 1.5 & -1 \\ 1 & -0.5 \end{bmatrix}$$

Using either *Mathematica* or *Maple* we can establish that the eigenvalues are $\lambda = 0.5$ (repeated twice) and the Jordan form and transition matrices are

$$\mathbf{J} = \begin{bmatrix} 0.5 & 1 \\ 0 & 0.5 \end{bmatrix} \qquad \mathbf{V} = \begin{bmatrix} 1 & 1 \\ 1 & 0 \end{bmatrix}$$

Figure 5.8.

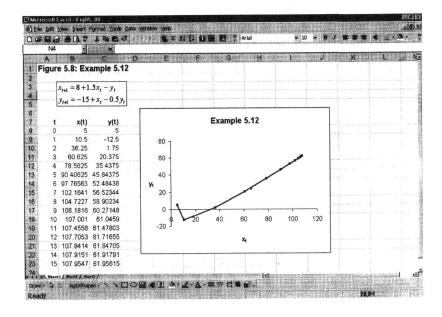

Hence,

$$\mathbf{J}^t = \begin{bmatrix} 0.5^t & t0.5^{t-1} \\ 0 & 0.5^t \end{bmatrix}$$

and the canonical form of the system is

$$\mathbf{z}_t = \begin{bmatrix} 0.5^t & t0.5^{t-1} \\ 0 & 0.5^t \end{bmatrix} \mathbf{z}_0$$

Hence

$$z_{1t} = 0.5^t z_{10} + t(0.5^{t-1})z_{20}$$

$$z_{2t} = 0.5^t z_{20}$$

Therefore, $z_{1t} \to 0$ and $z_{2t} \to 0$ as $t \to \infty$ regardless of the initial point. This is illustrated for the original system using a spreadsheet, as shown in figure 5.8 for the initial point $(5, 5)$.

5.6.3 Complex conjugate roots

Although complex conjugate roots involve distinct roots and independent eigenvectors, it is still necessary to establish the conditions for stability where $r = \alpha + \beta i$ and $s = \alpha - \beta i$. For the system $\mathbf{u}_t = \mathbf{A}\mathbf{u}_{t-1}$ where $\mathbf{A}$ is a 2×2 matrix with conjugate roots $\alpha \pm \beta i$, then the Jordan form is

$$\mathbf{J} = \begin{bmatrix} \alpha + \beta i & 0 \\ 0 & \alpha - \beta i \end{bmatrix} \quad \text{and} \quad \mathbf{J}^t = \begin{bmatrix} (\alpha + \beta i)^t & 0 \\ 0 & (\alpha - \beta i)^t \end{bmatrix}$$

Considering the canonical form $\mathbf{z}_t = \mathbf{V}\mathbf{z}_{t-1}$, then

$$\mathbf{z}_t = \mathbf{J}^t\mathbf{z}_0 = \begin{bmatrix} (\alpha + \beta i)^t & 0 \\ 0 & (\alpha - \beta i)^t \end{bmatrix} \mathbf{z}_0$$

To investigate the stability properties of systems with complex conjugate roots, we employ two results (see Simon and Blume 1994, appendix A3):

(i) $\alpha \pm i\beta = R(\cos\theta \pm i\sin\theta)$
(ii) $(\alpha \pm i\beta)^n = R^n[\cos(n\theta) \pm i\sin(n\theta)]$ (De Moivre's formula)

where

$$R = \sqrt{\alpha^2 + \beta^2} \qquad \text{and} \qquad \tan\theta = \frac{\beta}{\alpha}$$

From the canonical form, and using these two results, we have

$$z_{1t} = (\alpha + \beta i)^t\, z_{10} = R^t[\cos(t\theta) + i\sin(t\theta)]$$
$$z_{2t} = (\alpha - \beta i)^t\, z_{20} = R^t[\cos(t\theta) - i\sin(t\theta)]$$

It follows that such a system must oscillate because as t increases, $\sin(t\theta)$ and $\cos(t\theta)$ range between $+1$ and -1. Furthermore, the limit of z_{1t} and z_{2t} as $t \to \infty$ is governed by the term $|R^t| = |R|^t$. If $|R| < 1$, then the system is an *asymptotically stable focus*; if $|R| > 1$, then the system is an *unstable focus*; while if $|R| = 1$, then we have a *centre*.[6] We now illustrate each of these cases.

Example 5.13 |R| < 1

Consider the system

$$x_t = 0.5x_{t-1} + 0.3y_{t-1}$$
$$y_t = -x_{t-1} + y_{t-1}$$

Then the matrix of the system is

$$\mathbf{A} = \begin{bmatrix} 0.5 & 0.3 \\ -1 & 1 \end{bmatrix}$$

with characteristic roots $r = 0.75 + 0.48734i$ and $s = 0.75 - 0.48734i$. Hence

$$R = \sqrt{(0.75)^2 + (0.48734)^2} = 0.8944$$

Such a system should therefore have an asymptotically stable focus. We illustrate this in figure 5.9, where the original system is set up on a spreadsheet and the initial point is given by $(x_0, y_0) = (10, 5)$. As can be seen from the inserted graph, the system tends in the limit to the origin.

---

[6] See section 3.8 for the properties of R in the complex plane, especially figure 3.15.

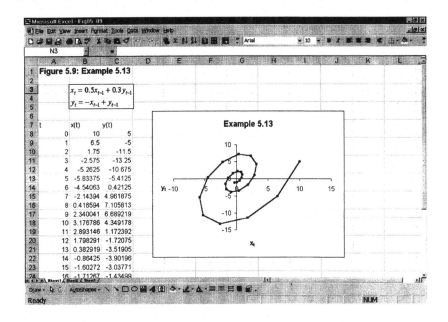

Figure 5.9.

Example 5.14 |R| > 1

Consider the system

$$x_t = x_{t-1} + 2y_{t-1}$$
$$y_t = -x_{t-1} + y_{t-1}$$

Then the matrix of the system is

$$\mathbf{A} = \begin{bmatrix} 1 & 2 \\ -1 & 1 \end{bmatrix}$$

with characteristic roots $r = 1 + i\sqrt{2}$ and $s = 1 - i\sqrt{2}$. Hence

$$R = \sqrt{(1)^2 + (\sqrt{2})^2} = \sqrt{3} = 1.73205$$

Such a system should therefore have an unstable focus. We illustrate this in figure 5.10, where the original system is set up on a spreadsheet and the initial point is given by $(x_0, y_0) = (0.5, 0.5)$. As can be seen from the inserted graph, the system is an unstable focus, spiralling away from the origin.

Example 5.15 |R| = 1

Consider the system

$$x_t = 0.5x_{t-1} + 0.5y_{t-1}$$
$$y_t = -x_{t-1} + y_{t-1}$$

Then the matrix of the system is

$$\mathbf{A} = \begin{bmatrix} 0.5 & 0.5 \\ -1 & 1 \end{bmatrix}$$

Figure 5.10.

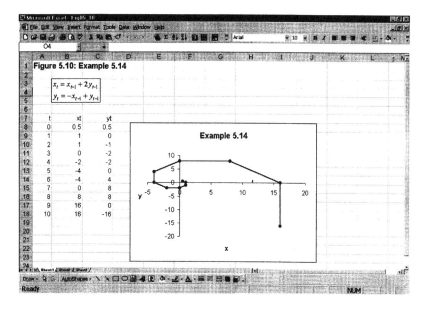

Figure 5.11.

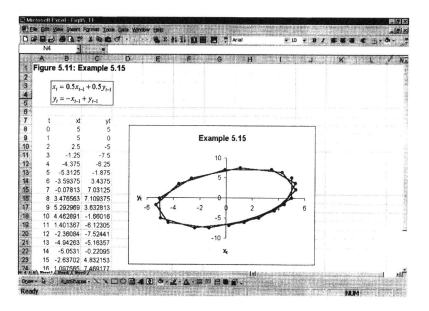

with characteristic roots $r = 0.75 + 0.661438i$ and $s = 0.75 - 0.661438i$. Hence

$$R = \sqrt{(0.75)^2 + (0.661438)^2} = 1$$

Such a system should oscillate around a centre, where the centre is the origin. We illustrate this in figure 5.11, where the original system is set up on a spreadsheet and the initial point is given by $(x_0, y_0) = (5, 5)$. As can be seen from the inserted graph the system does indeed oscillate around the origin.

5.7 The phase plane analysis of discrete systems

Consider the following system outlining discrete changes in x and y.

$$\Delta x_{t+1} = a_0 + a_1 x_t + a_2 y_t$$
$$\Delta y_{t+1} = b_0 + b_1 x_t + b_2 y_t$$

where $\Delta x_{t+1} = x_{t+1} - x_t$ and $\Delta y_{t+1} = y_{t+1} - y_t$. In equilibrium, assuming it exists, at $x = x^*$ and $y = y^*$, we have

$$0 = a_0 + a_1 x^* + a_2 y^*$$
$$0 = b_0 + b_1 x^* + b_2 y^*$$

Hence, the system in terms of deviations from equilibrium can be expressed

$$\Delta x_{t+1} = a_1(x_t - x^*) + a_2(y_t - y^*)$$
$$\Delta y_{t+1} = b_1(x_t - x^*) + b_2(y_t - y^*)$$

We can approach the problem in terms of the phase plane. As with the continuous model we first obtain the equilibrium lines $\Delta x_{t+1} = 0$ and $\Delta y_{t+1} = 0$. Consider the following system with assumed signs on some of the parameters

$$\Delta x_{t+1} = a_0 + a_1 x_t + a_2 y_t \qquad a_1, a_2 > 0$$
$$\Delta y_{t+1} = b_0 + b_1 x_t + b_2 y_t \qquad b_1 > 0, b_2 < 0$$

Then

If $\Delta x_{t+1} = 0$ then $y_t = \left(\dfrac{-a_0}{a_2}\right) - \left(\dfrac{a_1}{a_2}\right) x_t$

If $\Delta y_{t+1} = 0$ then $y_t = \left(\dfrac{-b_0}{b_2}\right) - \left(\dfrac{b_1}{b_2}\right) x_t$

Consider now points either side of $\Delta x_{t+1} = 0$.

If $\Delta x_{t+1} > 0$ then $y_t > \left(\dfrac{-a_0}{a_2}\right) - \left(\dfrac{a_1}{a_2}\right) x_t \qquad a_2 > 0$

If $\Delta x_{t+1} < 0$ then $y_t < \left(\dfrac{-a_0}{a_2}\right) - \left(\dfrac{a_1}{a_2}\right) x_t \qquad a_2 > 0$

Similarly for points either side of $\Delta y_{t+1} = 0$

If $\Delta y_{t+1} > 0$ then $y_t < \left(\dfrac{-b_0}{b_2}\right) - \left(\dfrac{b_1}{b_2}\right) x_t \qquad b_2 < 0$

If $\Delta y_{t+1} < 0$ then $y_t > \left(\dfrac{-b_0}{b_2}\right) - \left(\dfrac{b_1}{b_2}\right) x_t \qquad b_2 < 0$

The vector forces are illustrated in figures 5.12(a) and (b).

Combining the information we have the phase plane diagram for a discrete system, illustrated in figure 5.13. The combined vector forces suggest that the equilibrium is a saddle point.

Figure 5.12.

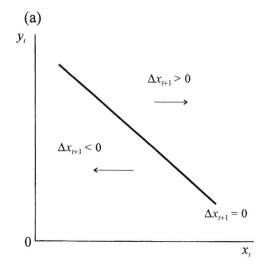

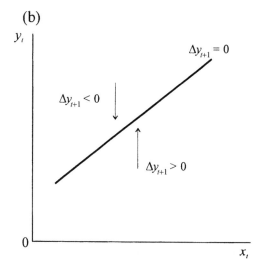

Example 5.16

Given

$$\Delta x_{t+1} = -12 + 0.3x_t + 3y_t$$
$$\Delta y_{t+1} = 4 + 0.25x_t - 1.5y_t$$

Then

$$\Delta x_{t+1} = 0 \text{ implies } y_t = 4 - 0.1x_t$$
$$\Delta y_{t+1} = 0 \text{ implies } y_t = 2.6667 + 0.1667x_t$$

and we obtain the equilibrium values

$$x^* = 5 \qquad y^* = 3.5$$

Figure 5.13.

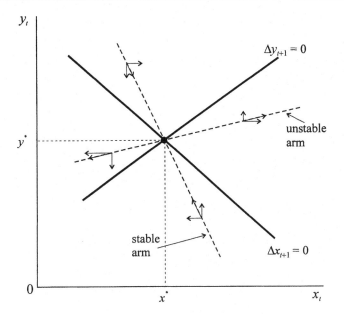

In terms of deviations from the equilibrium we have for x

$$x_{t+1} = -12 + 1.3x_t + 3y_t$$
$$x^* = -12 + 1.3x^* + 3y^*$$
$$(x_{t+1} - x^*) = 1.3(x_t - x^*) + 3(y_t - y^*)$$

and for y we have

$$y_{t+1} = 4 + 0.25x_t - 0.5y_t$$
$$y^* = 4 + 0.25x^* - 0.5y^*$$
$$(y_{t+1} - y^*) = 0.25(x_t - x^*) - 0.5(y_t - y^*)$$

Therefore the system expressed as deviations from equilibrium is

$$x_{t+1} - x^* = 1.3(x_t - x^*) + 3(y_t - y^*)$$
$$y_{t+1} - y^* = 0.25(x_t - x^*) - 0.5(y_t - y^*)$$

The dynamics of the system in the neighbourhood of (x^*, y^*) is therefore determined by the properties of

$$\mathbf{A} = \begin{bmatrix} 1.3 & 3 \\ 0.25 & -0.5 \end{bmatrix}$$

First we require to obtain the eigenvalues of the matrix $\mathbf{A}$:

$$|\mathbf{A} - \lambda \mathbf{I}| = \begin{vmatrix} 1.3 - \lambda & 3 \\ 0.25 & -(0.5 + \lambda) \end{vmatrix} = \lambda^2 - 0.8\lambda - 1.4 = 0$$

with distinct eigenvalues $r = 1.649$ and $s = -0.849$.

Next we need to obtain the associated eigenvectors, $\mathbf{v}^r$ and $\mathbf{v}^s$, respectively. Consider $r = 1.649$, then

$$\mathbf{A} - r\mathbf{I} = \begin{bmatrix} -0.349 & 3 \\ 0.25 & -2.149 \end{bmatrix}$$

Then $(\mathbf{A} - r\mathbf{I})\mathbf{v}^r = \mathbf{0}$ and

$$\begin{bmatrix} -0.349 & 3 \\ 0.25 & -2.149 \end{bmatrix} \begin{bmatrix} v_1^r \\ v_2^r \end{bmatrix} = \begin{bmatrix} 0 \\ 0 \end{bmatrix}$$

then

$$-0.349 v_1^r + 3 v_2^r = 0$$
$$0.25 v_1^r - 2.149 v_2^r = 0$$

Let $v_2^r = 1$, then $v_1^r = 8.596$, which arises from either equation.
   Similarly, for $s = -0.849$ then

$$\mathbf{A} - s\mathbf{I} = \begin{bmatrix} 2.149 & 3 \\ 0.25 & 0.349 \end{bmatrix}$$

and

$$(\mathbf{A} - s\mathbf{I})\mathbf{v}^s = \begin{bmatrix} 2.149 & 3 \\ 0.25 & 0.349 \end{bmatrix} \begin{bmatrix} v_1^s \\ v_2^s \end{bmatrix}$$

giving

$$2.149 v_1^s + 3 v_2^s = 0$$
$$0.25 v_1^s + 0.349 v_2^s = 0$$

Let $v_2^s = 1$, then $v_1^s = -1.396$. Hence the two eigenvectors are

$$\mathbf{v}^r = \begin{bmatrix} 8.596 \\ 1 \end{bmatrix}, \qquad \mathbf{v}^s = \begin{bmatrix} -1.396 \\ 1 \end{bmatrix}$$

with associated matrix

$$\mathbf{V} = \begin{bmatrix} 8.596 & -1.396 \\ 1 & 1 \end{bmatrix}$$

Hence, our solution is

$$\mathbf{u}_t = \mathbf{V} \begin{bmatrix} (1.649)^t & 0 \\ 0 & (-0.849)^t \end{bmatrix} \mathbf{V}^{-1} \mathbf{u}_0$$

Given some initial values (x_0, y_0) we could solve explicitly for $\mathbf{u}_t$.
   But we can gain insight into the dynamics of this system by looking closely at the phase plane. We have already established that for

$$\Delta x_{t+1} = 0 \text{ then } y_t = 4 - 0.1 x_t$$
$$\Delta y_{t+1} = 0 \text{ then } y_t = 2.6667 + 0.1667 x_t$$

These are drawn in figure 5.14.

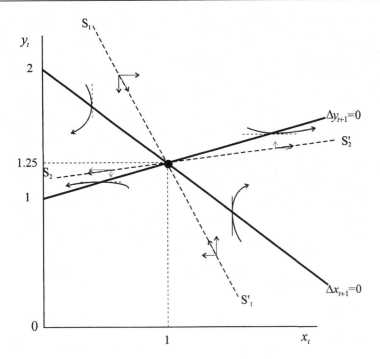

Figure 5.14.

We can also readily establish that

if $\Delta x_{t+1} > 0$ then $y_t > 4 - 0.1x_t$ and x is rising

if $\Delta x_{t+1} < 0$ then $y_t < 4 - 0.1x_t$ and x is falling

and

if $\Delta y_{t+1} > 0$ then $y_t > 2.6667 + 0.1667x_t$ and y is rising

if $\Delta y_{t+1} < 0$ then $y_t < 2.6667 + 0.1667x_t$ and y is falling

These vector forces are also illustrated in figure 5.14. The figure also illustrates that a saddle point equilibrium is present with a stable arm $S_1 S_1'$ and an unstable arm $S_2 S_2'$. In general, the system will move away from the equilibrium point, except for initial values lying on the stable arm $S_1 S_1'$.

Although the vector force diagram of discrete systems can provide much information on the dynamics of the system, the *stability* properties usually can be obtained only from its mathematical properties.

5.8 Internal and external balance

We can illustrate the use of the phase plane by considering an important policy issue that has been discussed in the literature, namely internal and external balance.[7] Having set up a macroeconomic model, a fixed target policy is then imposed on it. Two fixed targets are chosen: the level of real income and the balance on the balance of payments. Real income is considered set at the full employment level,

---

[7] See Shone (1989, chapter 11) and the seminal article by Mundell (1962).

which denotes the condition of internal balance.[8] External balance represents a zero balance on the combined current and capital account of the balance of payments. Following Tinbergen's analysis (1956), there are two policy instruments necessary for achieving the two policy objectives. These are government spending, which is used to achieve internal balance, and the interest rate, which is used to achieve external balance (by influencing explicitly net capital flows).

Suppose we set up an adjustment on the part of the two instruments that assumes that the change in the policy variable is proportional to the discrepancy between its present level and the level to achieve its target. More formally we have

$$\Delta g_{t+1} = g_{t+1} - g_t = k_1(g_t - g_t^*) \quad k_1 < 0$$
$$\Delta r_{t+1} = r_{t+1} - r_t = k_2(r_t - r_t^*) \quad k_2 < 0$$

where g_t^* is the target level of government spending in period t, and r_t^* is the target interest rate in period t.

Example 5.17

Following Shone (1989) we have the following two equations relating g_t and r_t derived from a macroeconomic model,

$$\text{IB} \quad r_t = -3.925 + 0.5g_t$$
$$\text{XB} \quad r_t = 7.958 + 0.186g_t$$

where IB denotes internal balance and XB denotes external balance. In the case of internal balance we require g_t^* which is equal to $g_t^* = 7.85 + 2r_t$, while for external balance we require r_t^* which is equal to $r_t^* = 7.958 + 0.186g_t$. Then

$$\Delta g_{t+1} = k_1(g_t - 7.85 - 2r_t) \quad k_1 < 0$$
$$\Delta r_{t+1} = k_2(r_t - 7.958 - 0.186g_t) \quad k_2 < 0$$

The isoclines are where $\Delta g_{t+1} = 0$ and $\Delta r_{t+1} = 0$ and the equations of which no more than represent the internal balance and external balance lines, respectively. The stationary values of g and r are where the two isoclines intersect, giving $g^* = 37.84$ and $r^* = 15$. The situation is illustrated in figure 5.15.

The vectors of force are readily established (noting k_1 and k_2 are negative):

if $\Delta g_{t+1} > 0$ then $r_t > -3.925 + 0.5g_t$ and g_t is rising

if $\Delta g_{t+1} < 0$ then $r_t < -3.925 + 0.5g_t$ and g_t is falling

Also

if $\Delta r_{t+1} > 0$ then $r_t < 7.958 + 0.186g_t$ and r_t is rising

if $\Delta r_{t+1} < 0$ then $r_t > 7.958 + 0.186g_t$ and r_t is falling

which are also illustrated in figure 5.15.

The use of the spreadsheet is convenient in considering this problem. To do this we need to express g_{t+1} and r_{t+1} in terms of g_t and r_t. We assume that $k_1 = -0.5$

---

[8] Internal balance can also be considered as a suitable income–inflation combination. See Shone (1979).

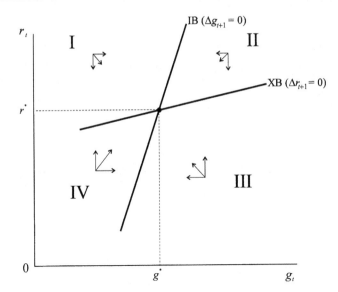

Figure 5.15.

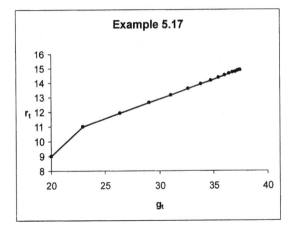

Figure 5.16.

and $k_2 = -0.75$. We then have

$$g_{t+1} = 3.925 + 0.5g_t + r_t$$

$$r_{t+1} = 5.9685 + 0.1395g_t + 0.25r_t$$

The quadrant that typified the UK economy for periods in the 1960s is quadrant IV (figure 5.15), which has the economy with a balance of payments deficit (below the XB curve) and unemployment (above the IB curve). Suppose, then, that the economy begins at point $(g_0, r_0) = (20, 9)$. The trajectory the economy follows is shown in figure 5.16.

It is very easy to use this spreadsheet to investigate the path of the economy in any of the four quadrants, and we leave this as an exercise. What can readily be established is that, regardless of the initial point, the economy moves towards the equilibrium point where the two isoclines intersect.

Example 5.18

But we have presupposed that government spending is used to achieve internal balance and the rate of interest is used to achieve external balance. Suppose we assume the opposite assignment: set interest rates to achieve internal balance and government spending to achieve external balance. Then

$$r_t^* = -3.925 + 0.5g_t$$

and

$$g_t^* = -42.785 + 5.376r_t$$

Then

$$\Delta r_{t+1} = k_3(r_t - r_t^*) = k_3(r_t + 3.925 - 0.5g_t) \qquad k_3 < 0$$
$$\Delta g_{t+1} = k_4(g_t - g_t^*) = k_3(g_t + 42.785 - 5.376r_t) \quad k_4 < 0$$

Setting $\Delta r_{t+1} = 0$ and $\Delta g_{t+1} = 0$ gives rise to the internal balance isocline and the external balance isocline, respectively, leading to the same equilibrium point $(g^*, r^*) = (37.85, 15)$, as shown in figure 5.17. However, the vector forces are now different:

if $\Delta r_{t+1} > 0$ then $r_t < -3.925 + 0.5g_t$ and r_t is rising

if $\Delta r_{t+1} < 0$ then $r_t > -3.925 + 0.5g_t$ and r_t is falling

Similarly

if $\Delta g_{t+1} > 0$ then $r_t > 7.958 + 0.186g_t$ and g_t is rising

if $\Delta g_{t+1} < 0$ then $r_t < 7.958 + 0.186g_t$ and g_t is falling

From figure 5.17 it is apparent that the equilibrium point E is a saddle point. Under this assignment economies finding themselves in sectors I and III will converge on the equilibrium only so long as they remain in these sectors, although this is

Figure 5.17.

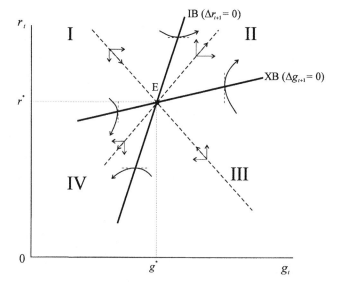

Figure 5.18.

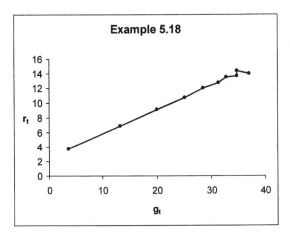

not guaranteed (see exercise 9). Any point in sectors II and IV, other than the equilibrium point, however, will move away from equilibrium (figure 5.17).

Given this alternative assignment, and assuming $k_3 = -0.75$ and $k_4 = -0.5$ we obtain the two equations

$$g_{t+1} = -21.3925 + 0.5g_t + 2.688r_t$$
$$r_{t+1} = -2.94375 + 0.375g_t + 0.25r_t$$

Taking a point once again in quadrant IV, but now close to the equilibrium, point $(37, 14)$, the spreadsheet calculations quite readily show the economy diverging from the equilibrium, as illustrated in figure 5.18, where we plot only up to period 9.[9]

Again it is very easy to use this spreadsheet to investigate the path of the economy for any initial point in any of the four quadrants. This we leave as an exercise.

Comparing figures 5.15 and 5.17 leads to an important policy conclusion. It is not the slopes of the internal and external balance lines *per se* which governs the dynamics, but rather the **policy assignment**. This was Mundell's conclusion (1962). He put it differently and claimed that stability requires pairing the instrument with the target over which it has the greatest relative impact: *the principle of effective market classification*. Government spending has the greatest relative impact on income and hence on achieving internal balance. This immediately implies that the interest rate has the greatest relative impact on the balance of payments, and hence on achieving external balance. Consequently, the assignment represented in figure 5.15 is stable while that in figure 5.17 is unstable.

This approach to dynamics is readily generalised. Consider again internal and external balance, but now using the two instruments government spending, g, and the exchange rate, S. The situation is shown in figure 5.19 (Shone 1989, chapter 11).

We can capture this situation with the two linear equations

$$\text{IB} \quad S_t = a_0 - a_1 g_t \quad a_1 > 0$$
$$\text{XB} \quad S_t = b_0 + b_1 g_t \quad b_1 > 0$$

---

[9] Note how sensitive discrete systems can be to initial conditions. Placing the 'equilibrium' values $(37.847, 14.9985)$ as the initial conditions, still has the system diverging!

Figure 5.19.

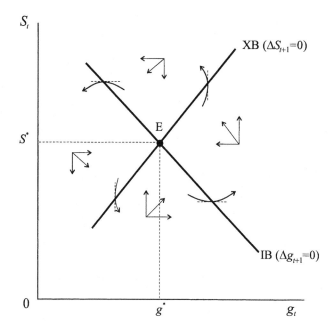

where $a_0 > b_0$. Equilibrium is readily found to be

$$g^* = \frac{a_0 - b_0}{a_1 + b_1} \qquad S^* = \frac{a_0 b_1 + a_1 b_0}{a_1 + b_1}$$

However, in order to consider the dynamics of this point we need to specify some assignment. Suppose we assign government spending to internal balance and the exchange rate to external balance, satisfying

$$\Delta g_{t+1} = g_{t+1} - g_t = k_1(g_t - g_t^*) \quad k_1 < 0$$
$$\Delta S_{t+1} = S_{t+1} - S_t = k_2(S_t - S_t^*) \quad k_2 < 0$$

The equations for g_t^* and S_t^* are

$$g_t^* = (a_0/a_1) - (1/a_1)S_t$$
$$S_t^* = b_0 + b_1 g_t$$

Hence

IB $\Delta g_{t+1} = k_1[g_t - (a_0/a_1) + (1/a_1)S_t]$

XB $\Delta S_{t+1} = k_2[S_t - b_0 - b_1 g_t]$

It is readily established (noting k_1 and k_2 are negative) that:

if $\Delta g_{t+1} > 0$ then $S_t < a_0 + a_1 g_t$ and g_t is rising

if $\Delta g_{t+1} < 0$ then $S_t > a_0 + a_1 g_t$ and g_t is falling

if $\Delta S_{t+1} > 0$ then $S_t < b_0 + b_1 g_t$ and S_t is rising

if $\Delta S_{t+1} < 0$ then $S_t > b_0 + b_1 g_t$ and S_t is falling

Figure 5.20.

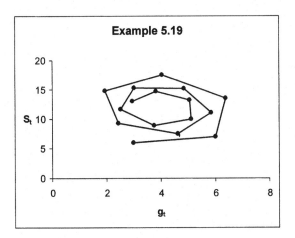

Example 5.19

with resulting forces illustrated in figure 5.19. This quite clearly illustrates an anticlockwise motion. What we cannot establish is whether the system converges on the equilibrium or moves away from it.

Example 5.19

To illustrate this suppose we have for internal and external balance the equations

IB $\quad S_t = 20 - 2g_t$

XB $\quad S_t = -4 + 4g_t$

with equilibrium $g^* = 2.5$ and $S^* = 10$. Further, suppose adjustment is of the form

$$\Delta g_{t+1} = -0.75(g_t - g_t^*)$$
$$\Delta S_{t+1} = -0.5(S_t - S_t^*)$$

where

$$g_t^* = -2.5 + 0.5S_t$$
$$S_t^* = 20 - 4g_t$$

then

$$g_{t+1} = -1.875 + 0.25g_t + 0.375S_t$$
$$S_{t+1} = 10 - 2g_t + 0.5S_t$$

Given an initial point $(g_0, S_0) = (4, 12)$, figure 5.20 shows the typical anticlockwise spiral trajectory that is tending towards the equilibrium.

5.9   Nonlinear discrete systems

Just as we can encounter nonlinear equations of the form $x_t = f(x_{t-1})$, so we can have nonlinear systems of equations of the form

$$x_t = f(x_{t-1}, y_{t-1})$$
$$y_t = g(x_{t-1}, y_{t-1})$$

where we assume just a one-period lag. A steady state (x^*, y^*) exists for this system if it satisfies

$$x^* = f(x^*, y^*)$$
$$y^* = g(x^*, y^*)$$

It is possible to investigate the stability properties of this nonlinear system in the neighbourhood of the steady state so long as f and g are continuous and differentiable. Under such conditions we can expand the system in a Taylor expansion about (x^*, y^*), i.e.

$$x_t - x^* = \frac{\partial f(x^*, y^*)}{\partial x_{t-1}}(x_{t-1} - x^*) + \frac{\partial f(x^*, y^*)}{\partial y_{t-1}}(y_{t-1} - y^*)$$

$$y_t - y^* = \frac{\partial g(x^*, y^*)}{\partial x_{t-1}}(x_{t-1} - x^*) + \frac{\partial g(x^*, y^*)}{\partial y_{t-1}}(y_{t-1} - y^*)$$

Let

$$a_{11} = \frac{\partial f(x^*, y^*)}{\partial x_{t-1}}, \qquad a_{12} = \frac{\partial f(x^*, y^*)}{\partial y_{t-1}}$$

$$a_{21} = \frac{\partial g(x^*, y^*)}{\partial x_{t-1}}, \qquad a_{22} = \frac{\partial g(x^*, y^*)}{\partial y_{t-1}}$$

then

$$x_t - x^* = a_{11}(x_{t-1} - x^*) + a_{12}(y_{t-1} - y^*)$$
$$y_t - y^* = a_{21}(x_{t-1} - x^*) + a_{22}(y_{t-1} - y^*)$$

or

$$\begin{bmatrix} x_t - x^* \\ y_t - y^* \end{bmatrix} = \begin{bmatrix} a_{11} & a_{12} \\ a_{21} & a_{22} \end{bmatrix} \begin{bmatrix} x_{t-1} - x^* \\ y_{t-1} - y^* \end{bmatrix}$$

i.e.

$$\mathbf{u}_t = \mathbf{A}\mathbf{u}_{t-1}$$

which is no more than a first-order linear system with solution

$$\mathbf{u}_t = \mathbf{V}\mathbf{D}'\mathbf{V}^{-1}\mathbf{u}_0$$

and where $\mathbf{D}$ is the diagonal matrix with distinct eigenvalues r and s on the main diagonal, $\mathbf{V} = [\,\mathbf{v}^r \quad \mathbf{v}^s\,]$ is the matrix of eigenvectors associated with r and s, and $\mathbf{u}_0$ is a vector of initial values.

It should be noted that the matrix $\mathbf{A}$ is simply the Jacobian matrix, $\mathbf{J}$, of the nonlinear system evaluated at a fixed point (x^*, y^*). Under certain restrictions on $\mathbf{A}$ (or $\mathbf{J}$), the linear system 'behaves like' the nonlinear system. The situation can be illustrated by means of figure 5.21. The nonlinear system, N, can be mapped into an equivalent linear system, L, by the mapping F, such that the qualitative properties of the linear system in the neighbourhood of $\mathbf{0}$ are the same as that of the nonlinear system in the neighbourhood of $\mathbf{0}$.[10] In other words, the two systems are topologically equivalent.

---

[10] F is then said to be a diffeomorphism.

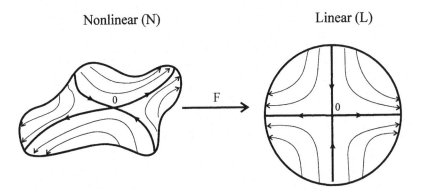

Nonlinear (N)   Linear (L)   Figure 5.21.

What are these restrictions? We require $\text{tr}(\mathbf{J}) \neq 0$ and $\det(\mathbf{J}) \neq 0$.[11] Since the two systems are topologically equivalent, then the dynamics of N in the neighbourhood of **0** can be investigated by means of the linear system in the neighbourhood of **0**. We do this by establishing the eigenvalues and eigenvectors of **J**. More specifically, we require conditions to be imposed on the eigenvalues. If r and s are the two eigenvalues then the systems are topologically equivalent if:

(1) r and s are distinct real roots and $|r| < 1$ and $|s| < 1$.
(2) r and s are distinct but complex and lie strictly inside the unit circle.[12]

If r and s in the neighbourhood of (x^*, y^*) satisfy this second condition, then (x^*, y^*) is said to be a **hyperbolic** fixed point.

Exercises

1.   Convert example 5.4 into a system of difference equations and establish the qualitative properties of the system in terms of the isoclines and vector forces. Does this confirm the stability established in section 5.2?

2.   Convert example 5.6 into a system of difference equations and establish the qualitative properties of the system in terms of the isoclines and vector forces. Does this illustrate that the equilibrium point is a saddle path solution?

3.   For example 5.4 use a spreadsheet to verify that the system converges on the fixed point $(x^*, y^*) = (6.4, 20.8)$ for each of the following initial points: (3,10), (3,30), (10,10), (10,30).

4.   Set up example 5.5 on a spreadsheet and investigate its characteristics. In particular, consider:
        (a) different initial values
        (b) plot $x(t)$, $y(t)$, and $z(t)$ against t
        (c) plot $y(t)$ against $x(t)$
        (d) plot $z(t)$ against $x(t)$
        (e) plot $x(t)$ against $z(t)$.

[11] An alternative way to state the condition is that **J** must be invertible.
[12] See sub-section 3.8.1, p. 110.

5. Use either *Mathematica* or *Maple* and do a 3D plot of the solution to example 5.5 for the initial point $\mathbf{u}^0 = (3, -4.3)$.

6. Use either *Mathematica* or *Maple* and derive a 3D directional field for example 5.5. Does this give you any more insight into the dynamics of the system over what you gained from question 4?

7. For each of the following systems:
    (a) find the eigenvalues of the system
    (b) find the eigenvectors of the system
    (c) establish the diagonal matrix of the system.

    (i) $x_{t+1} = y_t$
          $y_{t+1} = -x_t$

    (ii) $x_{t+1} = -2x_t + y_t$
          $y_{t+1} = x_t + 2y_t$

    (iii) $x_{t+1} = 3x_t - 4y_t$
          $y_{t+1} = x_t - 2y_t$

8. For the model

    IB: $r_t = -3.925 + 0.5g_t$
    XB: $r_t = 7.958 + 0.186g_t$

    where

    $$\Delta g_{t+1} = -0.5(g_t - g_t^*)$$
    $$\Delta r_{t+1} = -0.75(r_t - r_t^*)$$

    use a spreadsheet to plot the trajectories for the following initial values:
    (a) $(g_0, r_0) = (20, 12)$
    (b) $(g_0, r_0) = (20, 20)$
    (c) $(g_0, r_0) = (50, 10)$
    (d) $(g_0, r_0) = (50, 20)$

9. For the assignment of interest rates to achieve internal balance and government spending to achieve external balance, we have the set of equations

    $$g_{t+1} = -21.3925 + 0.5g_t + 2.688r_t$$
    $$r_{t+1} = -2.94375 + 0.375g_t + 0.25r_t$$

    (a) Take four initial points, one in each of the sectors represented in figure 5.17, and use a spreadsheet to investigate the economy's trajectory.
    (b) Take a variety of points in sectors I and III and establish whether the trajectories remain in these sectors.
    (c) Take a point on the stable arm and, using a spreadsheet, establish that the trajectory tends to the equilibrium point.

10. For the system

    IB: $S_t = 5 + 2g_t$
    XB: $S_t = 20 - 4g_t$

where

$$\Delta g_{t+1} = -0.75(g_t - g_t^*)$$
$$\Delta S_{t+1} = -0.5(S_t - S_t^*)$$

and

$$g_t^* = -2.5 + 0.5S_t$$
$$S_t^* = 20 - 4g_t$$

for the target equations, using a spreadsheet establish the trajectories for the following initial conditions:
(a) $(g_0, S_0) = (2.5, 12)$
(b) $(g_0, S_0) = (3, 10)$
(c) $(g_0, S_0) = (1, 5)$
(d) $(g_0, S_0) = (1, 12)$

11.   Let

$$mA = \begin{bmatrix} 2 & 3 \\ 1 & -2 \end{bmatrix}, \qquad mB = \begin{bmatrix} 4 & -2 \\ 1 & -1 \end{bmatrix}, \qquad mC = \begin{bmatrix} 3 & 2 & 1 \\ -1 & 0 & 3 \end{bmatrix}$$

Using any software package, perform the following operations
   (i) Trace and determinant of $mA \times mB$
  (ii) Transpose of $mA \times mC$
 (iii) Inverse of mB
  (iv) Eigenvalues and eigenvectors of mA and mB
   (v) Characteristic polynomial of mA.

12.   Solve the following system using a software package

$$x_{t+1} = -5 + x_t - 2y_t$$
$$y_{t+1} = 4 + x_t - y_t$$
$$x_0 = 1, \qquad y_0 = 2$$

13.   What is the Jordan form, **J**, and the transition matrix, **V**, of the following matrix?

$$mA = \begin{bmatrix} 1 & -2 \\ 1 & -1 \end{bmatrix}$$

Hence show that $\mathbf{V}^{-1}.\mathbf{mA}.\mathbf{V} = \mathbf{J}$.

14.   For the system in question 12, set this up on a spreadsheet.
   (i) What is the fixed point of the system?
  (ii) Plot the trajectory from the initial point. Does this trajectory converge on the fixed point?

15.   For the following system, establish the Jordan form and the transition matrix. Represent the original system and its canonical form on a spreadsheet, and hence show whether the system is asymptotically stable.

$$x_t = 5.6 - 0.4x_{t-1}$$
$$y_t = 3.5 + 0.4x_{t-1} - 0.5y_{t-1}$$
$$x_0 = 2, \qquad y_0 = 1$$

Additional reading

Discrete systems of equations are discussed less frequently than continuous systems of equations, but additional material on the mathematical contents of this chapter can be found in Azariades (1993), Chiang (1984), Elaydi (1996), Goldberg (1961), Griffiths and Oldknow (1993), Holmgren (1994), Kelley and Peterson (2001), Lynch (2001), Sandefur (1990), Shone (2001), Simon and Blume (1994) and Tu (1994). On internal and external balance, references will be found in the main body of the chapter in section 5.8.

CHAPTER 6

Optimal control theory

6.1 The optimal control problem

Consider a fish stock which has some natural rate of growth and which is harvested. Too much harvesting could endanger the survival of the fish, too little and profits are forgone. Of course, harvesting takes place over time. The obvious question is: 'what is the best harvesting rate, i.e., what is the optimal harvesting?' The answer to this question requires an *optimal path or trajectory* to be identified. 'Best' itself requires us to specify a criterion by which to choose between alternative paths. Some policy implies there is a means to influence (control) the situation. If we take it that $x(t)$ represents the *state* of the situation at time t and $u(t)$ represents the *control* at time t, then the **optimal control problem** is to find a trajectory $\{x(t)\}$ by choosing a set $\{u(t)\}$ of controls so as to maximise or minimise some objective that has been set. There are a number of ways to solve such a control problem, of which the literature considers three:

(1)   Calculus of variations
(2)   Dynamic programming
(3)   Maximum principle.

In this chapter we shall deal only with the third, which now is the dominant approach, especially in economics. This approach is based on the work of Pontryagin *et al.* (1962), and is therefore sometimes called the **Pontryagin maximum principle**.

Since minimising some objective function is the same as maximising its negative value, then we shall refer in this chapter only to maximising some objective function. Second, our control problem can either be in *continuous time* or in *discrete time*. To see the difference and to present a formal statement of the optimal control problem from the maximum principle point of view, consider table 6.1. In each case, the objective is to maximise J and so find a trajectory $\{x(t)\}$ by choosing a suitable value $\{u(t)\}$. What table 6.1 presents is the most general situation possible for both the continuous and discrete formulations of the optimal control problem under the maximisation principle. There are some special cases, the most important being the distinction between finite and infinite horizon models. In the latter case the terminal time period is at infinity. All the problems we shall discuss in this chapter involve autonomous systems, and so t does not enter explicitly into V, f or F. An important aspect of control problems is that of time preference. The

Table 6.1 The control problem

Continuous	Discrete
$\max\limits_{\{u(t)\}} J = \displaystyle\int_{t_0}^{t_1} V(\mathbf{x}, \mathbf{u}, t)dt + F(\mathbf{x}^1, t)$	$\max\limits_{\{\mathbf{u}_t\}} J = \displaystyle\sum_{t=0}^{T-1} V(\mathbf{x}_t, \mathbf{u}_t, t) + F(\mathbf{x}^T, t)$
$\dot{\mathbf{x}} = f(\mathbf{x}, \mathbf{u}, t)$	$\mathbf{x}_{t+1} - \mathbf{x}_t = f(\mathbf{x}_t, \mathbf{u}_t, t)$
$\mathbf{x}(t_0) = \mathbf{x}^0$	$\mathbf{x}_t = \mathbf{x}^0 \quad$ when $t = 0$
$\mathbf{x}(t_1) = \mathbf{x}^1$	$\mathbf{x}_t = \mathbf{x}^T \quad$ when $t = T$
$\{\mathbf{u}(t)\} \in U$	$\mathbf{u}_t \in U$

t_0 (or $t = 0$) is initial time
t_1 (or T) is terminal time
$\mathbf{x}(t) = \{x_1(t), \ldots, x_n(t)\}$ or $\mathbf{x}_t = \{x_{1t}, \ldots, x_{nt}\}$ n-state variables
$\mathbf{x}(t_0) = \mathbf{x}^0$ or $\mathbf{x}_t = \mathbf{x}^0$ for $t = 0$ is the initial state
$\mathbf{x}(t_1) = \mathbf{x}^1$ or $\mathbf{x}_t = \mathbf{x}^T$ for $t = T$ is the final state (or terminal state)
$\mathbf{u}(t) = \{u_1(t), \ldots, u_m(t)\}$ or $\mathbf{u}_t = \{u_{1t}, \ldots, u_{mt}\}$ m-control variables
$\{\mathbf{u}(t)\}$ is a continuous control trajectory $t_0 \le t \le t_1$
$\{\mathbf{u}_t\}$ is a discrete control trajectory $0 \le t \le T$
U is the set of all admissible control trajectories
$\dot{\mathbf{x}}(t) = f(\mathbf{x}, \mathbf{u}, t)$ or $\mathbf{x}_{t+1} - \mathbf{x}_t = f(\mathbf{x}_t, \mathbf{u}_t, t)$ denote the equations of motion
J is the objective function
$V(\mathbf{x}(t), \mathbf{u}(t), t)$ or $V(\mathbf{x}_t, \mathbf{u}_t, t)$ is the intermediate function
$F(\mathbf{x}^1, t)$ or $F(\mathbf{x}^T, t)$ is the final function

simplest models involve no discounting. It is sometimes easier to consider a model with no discounting, and then to consider the more realistic case of the same model with discounting. In many models the terminal value $F(x^T)$ is zero, but this need not always be so.

A typical continuous optimal control problem incorporating the assumptions of (1) a finite time horizon, T, (2) only autonomous equations, (3) a zero function in the terminal state and, (4) only one state variable and one control variable is

(6.1)
$$\max_{\{u(t)\}} J = \int_0^T V(x, u)dt$$
$$\dot{x} = f(x, u)$$
$$x(0) = x^0$$
$$x(T) = x^T$$

where the state variable, x and the control variable, u, are both functions of time t.

The situation is illustrated in figure 6.1. The paths u^* and u^{**} both constitute solutions to the differential equation $\dot{x} = f(x, u)$. The problem, however, is to choose one path that maximises the relation J and that satisfies the terminal condition $x(t^*) = x^T$ and $x(t^{**}) = x^T$.

6.2　The Pontryagin maximum principle: continuous model

As just pointed out, the objective is to find a control trajectory $\{u(t)\}$ that maximises J and takes the system from its present state x^0 to its terminal state x^T. What is required, therefore, is a 'set of weights' that allows a comparison of the different trajectories of alternative controls. Also note that the emphasis of this formulation

Figure 6.1.

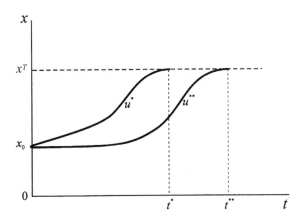

of the control problem is to find the optimal control trajectory $\{u(t)\}$. Once this is known the optimal state trajectory $\{x(t)\}$ can be computed. The 'weights' are achieved by defining a **Hamiltonian** for the control problem (6.1).

As with Lagrangian multipliers, let $\lambda(t)$ denote the Lagrangian multiplier for the constraint $\dot{x} = f(x, u)$. This is referred to as the *costate variable* or *adjoint variable*. Then

$$L = \int_0^T V(x, u)dt + \int_0^T \lambda[f(x, u) - \dot{x}]dt$$

$$= \int_0^T [V(x, u) + \lambda f(x, u) - \lambda \dot{x}]dt$$

The **Hamiltonian function** is defined as

$$H(x, u) = V(x, u) + \lambda f(x, u) \tag{6.2}$$

Hence

$$L = \int_0^T [H(x, u) - \lambda \dot{x}]dt \tag{6.3}$$

Equation (6.3) can be further transformed by noting that (see exercise 2)

$$-\int_0^T \lambda dt = \int_0^T x\dot{\lambda}dt - [\lambda(T)x(T) - \lambda(0)x(0)] \tag{6.4}$$

which allows us to express L as

$$L = \int_0^T [H(x, u) + \dot{\lambda}x]dt - [\lambda(T)x(T) - \lambda(0)x(0)] \tag{6.5}$$

Consider what happens to the state variable when the control variable changes, i.e., let $\{u(t)\}$ change to $\{u(t) + \Delta u(t)\}$ with the result on the state trajectory from $\{x(t)\}$ to $\{x(t) + \Delta x(t)\}$. Then the change in the Lagrangian, ΔL, is

$$\Delta L = \int_0^T \left[\frac{\partial H}{\partial x}dx + \frac{\partial H}{\partial u}du + \dot{\lambda}dx\right]dt - \lambda(T)dx^T$$

$$= \int_0^T \left[\frac{\partial H}{\partial u}du + \left(\frac{\partial H}{\partial x} + \dot{\lambda}\right)dx\right]dt - \lambda(T)dx^T$$

For a maximum $\Delta L = 0$. This implies the necessary conditions:

(i) $\qquad \dfrac{\partial H}{\partial u} = 0 \qquad 0 \le t \le T$

(ii) $\qquad \dot{\lambda} = -\dfrac{\partial H}{\partial x} \qquad 0 \le t \le T$

(iii) $\qquad \lambda(T) = 0$ (or $x(T) = x^T$ if x^T is known)

Condition (i) states that the Hamiltonian function is maximised by the choice of the control variable at each point along the optimum trajectory – where we are assuming an interior solution and no constraint on the control variable. Condition (ii) is concerned with the rate of change of the costate variable, λ. It states that the rate of change of the costate variable is equal to the negative of the Hamiltonian function with respect to the corresponding state variable.[1] Condition (iii) refers to the costate variable in the terminal state, and indicates that it is zero; or if the terminal value $x(T) = x^T$ is given then $dx^T = 0$.

From the definition of the Hamiltonian function, the differential equation for the state variable can be expressed in terms of it as follows

$$\dot{x} = f(x, u) = \frac{\partial H}{\partial \lambda}$$

We therefore arrive at the following procedure. Add a costate variable λ to the problem and define a Hamiltonian function $H(x, u) = V(x, u) + \lambda f(x, u)$ and solve for trajectories $\{u(t)\}$, $\{\lambda(t)\}$, and $\{x(t)\}$ satisfying:

(6.6)

(i) $\qquad \dfrac{\partial H}{\partial u} = 0 \qquad 0 \le t \le T$

(ii) $\qquad \dot{\lambda} = -\dfrac{\partial H}{\partial x} \qquad 0 \le t \le T$

(iii) $\qquad \dot{x} = \dfrac{\partial H}{\partial \lambda} = f(x, u)$

(iv) $\qquad x(0) = x^0$

(v) $\qquad \lambda(T) = 0 \qquad$ (or $x(T) = x^T$)

These results can be generalised for $x_1(t), \ldots, x_n(t)$ state variables, $\lambda_1(t), \ldots, \lambda_n(t)$ costate variables and $u_1(t), \ldots, u_m(t)$ control variables:

(6.7)

(i) $\qquad \dfrac{\partial H}{\partial u_i} = 0 \qquad i = 1, \ldots, m \qquad 0 \le t \le T$

(ii) $\qquad \dot{\lambda} = -\dfrac{\partial H}{\partial x_i} \qquad i = 1, \ldots, n \qquad 0 \le t \le T$

(iii) $\qquad \dot{x} = \dfrac{\partial H}{\partial \lambda_i} = f(x, u) \qquad i = 1, \ldots, n$

---

[1] If there were, for example, two state variables x_1 and x_2 and two corresponding costate variables λ_1 and λ_2, then

$$\dot{\lambda}_1 = -\partial H/\partial x_1 \qquad 0 \le t \le T$$
$$\dot{\lambda}_2 = -\partial H/\partial x_2 \qquad 0 \le t \le T$$

(iv) $x_i(0) = x_i^0$ $i = 1, \ldots, n$

(v) $\lambda_i(T) = 0$ $i = 1, \ldots, n$ (or $x_i(T) = x_i^T$ $i = 1, \ldots n$)

We shall now illustrate the continuous control problem by considering three examples. In each case we have the initial value and the terminal value for the state variable, i.e., $x(0) = x^0$ and $x(T) = x^T$ are given, as of course is T.

Example 6.1

In this first example we consider a boundary solution. The control problem is:

$$\max_{\{u\}} \int_0^1 5x \, dx$$
$$\dot{x} = x + u$$
$$x(0) = 2, \qquad x(1) \text{ free}$$
$$u(t) \in [0, 3]$$

The Hamiltonian for this problem is

$$H(x, u) = V(x, u) + \lambda f(x, u)$$
$$= 5x + \lambda(x + u)$$
$$= (5 + \lambda)x + \lambda u$$

With first-order conditions:

(i) $\dfrac{\partial H}{\partial u} = \lambda$

(ii) $\dot{\lambda} = -\dfrac{\partial H}{\partial x} = -(5 + \lambda)$

(iii) $\dot{x} = x + u$

(iv) $x(0) = 2$

(v) $\lambda(1) = 0$

Condition (i) is no help in determining u^*. If $\lambda > 0$ then H is a maximum at $u = 3$ the boundary, hence $u^*(t) = 3$, as shown in Figure 6.2(a).
From (ii) we have

$$\dot{\lambda} = -\lambda - 5$$
$$\lambda^*(t) = ke^{-t} - 5$$
$$\lambda^*(1) = ke^{-1} - 5 = 0$$
$$k = 5e^1$$
$$\therefore \quad \lambda^*(t) = 5e^{1-t} - 5$$

Since $u^*(t) = 3$

$$\dot{x}^* = x^* + 3$$
$$x^*(t) = -3 + ke^t$$
$$x(0) = -3 + ke^0 = 2$$
$$\therefore \quad k = 5$$

Figure 6.2.

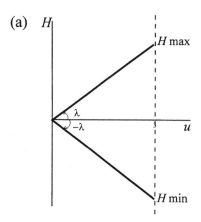

(a) H

H max

λ

$-\lambda$

u

H min

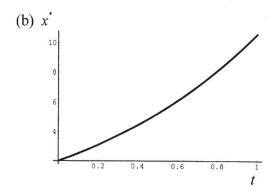

(b) x^*

Hence

$$x^*(t) = -3 + 5e^t$$

Although the control variable remains constant throughout, the state variable increases from $x(0) = 2$, as shown in figure 6.2(b).

Example 6.2

The control problem is

$$\max_{\{u\}} \int_0^1 u^2 \, dt$$

$$\dot{x} = -u$$

$$x(0) = 1$$

$$x(1) = 0$$

The Hamiltonian for this problem is

$$H(x, u) = V(x, u) + \lambda f(x, u)$$
$$= u^2 + \lambda(-u)$$

with first-order conditions:

(i) $\dfrac{\partial H}{\partial u} = 2u - \lambda = 0$

(ii) $\dot{\lambda} = -\dfrac{\partial H}{\partial x} = 0$

(iii) $\dot{x} = -u$

(iv) $x(0) = 1$

(v) $x(1) = 0$

From (i)

$$2u = \lambda$$
$$u = \tfrac{1}{2}\lambda$$

Thus

$$\dot{x} = -\dfrac{\lambda}{2}$$
$$\dot{\lambda} = 0$$

Solving these with a software package we obtain

$$x(t) = c_1 - \dfrac{\lambda t}{2}$$
$$\lambda(t) = c_2$$

But $x(0) = 1$ so

$$1 = c_1 - \dfrac{0}{2} \qquad \text{or} \qquad c_1 = 1$$

Similarly $x(1) = 0$

$$x(1) = 1 - \dfrac{\lambda}{2} = 0$$

$$\therefore \quad \lambda = 2 \qquad \text{or} \qquad c_2 = 2$$

$$x^* = 1 - \dfrac{2t}{2} = 1 - t$$

$$u^* = \tfrac{1}{2}\lambda = 1$$

These optimal paths are illustrated in figure 6.3.

Example 6.3

The control problem is

$$\max_{\{u\}} - \int_0^1 \tfrac{1}{4}(x^2 + u^2)dt$$

$$\dot{x} = x + u$$

$$x(0) = 2, \quad x(1) = 0$$

Figure 6.3.

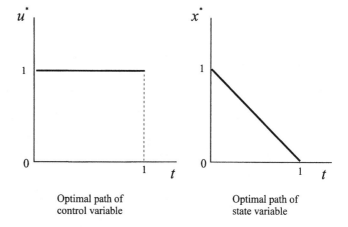

Optimal path of
control variable

Optimal path of
state variable

The Hamiltonian for this problem is

$$H(x, u) = V(x, u) + \lambda f(x, u)$$

$$= \frac{-(x^2 + u^2)}{4} + \lambda(x + u)$$

With first-order conditions

(i) $\dfrac{\partial H}{\partial u} = -\dfrac{u}{2} + \lambda = 0$ implying $u = 2\lambda$

(ii) $\dot{\lambda} = -\dfrac{\partial H}{\partial x} = -\left(\dfrac{-x}{2} + \lambda\right) = \tfrac{1}{2}x - \lambda$

(iii) $\dot{x} = x + u$ implying $\dot{x} = x + 2\lambda$

Substituting (i) into (iii) and eliminating u, we arrive at two differential equations in terms of x and λ

$$\dot{x} = x + 2\lambda$$
$$\dot{\lambda} = \tfrac{1}{2}x - \lambda$$

Although a simple set of differential equations, the solution values are rather involved, especially when solving for the constants of integration. The general solution is[2]

$$x(t) = c_1 e^{\sqrt{2}t} + c_2 e^{-\sqrt{2}t}$$

$$\lambda(t) = \frac{c_1}{2}(\sqrt{2} - 1)e^{\sqrt{2}t} - \frac{c_2}{2}(\sqrt{2} + 1)e^{-\sqrt{2}t}$$

However we can solve for c_1 and c_2 by using the conditions $x(0) = 2$ and $x(1) = 0$ as follows

$$x(0) = c_1 + c_2 = 2$$

$$x(1) = c_1 e^{\sqrt{2}t} + c_2 e^{-\sqrt{2}t} = 0$$

---

[2] The software packages give, on the face of it, quite different solutions. They are, however, identical. The results provided here are a re-arrangement of those provided by *Maple*.

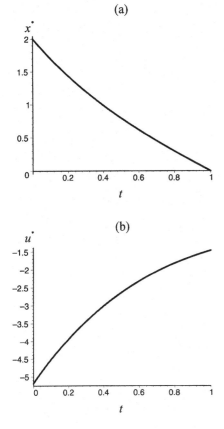

Figure 6.4.

Solving we get $c_1 = -0.1256$ and $c_2 = 2.1256$. All this can be done with the help of computer software programs, with the resulting trajectories for x^* and u^* shown in figure 6.4(a) and (b).

What these examples show is a pattern emerging for solving the control problem. The steps are:

(1)   Specify the Hamiltonian and obtain the maximisation conditions
(2)   Use the equation $\partial H/\partial u$ to solve for u in terms of the costate variable λ
(3)   Obtain two differential equations: one for the state variable, x, and one for the costate variable, λ
(4)   Solve the differential equations deriving general solutions
(5)   Use the conditions on $x(0)$ and $x(T)$ to obtain values for the coefficients of integration
(6)   Substitute the optimal path for λ^* into the equation for u to obtain the optimal path u^* for the control variable.

6.3   The Pontryagin maximum principle: discrete model

The discrete time control model based on the maximum principle of Pontryagin takes a similar approach to the continuous time formulation so we can be brief, although some care must be exercised in the use of time periods. Again we let x denote the only state variable, u the only control variable and λ the costate variable. Our problem amounts to:

(6.8)

$$\max_{\{u_t\}} J = \sum_{t=0}^{T-1} V(x_t, u_t)$$

$$x_{t+1} - x_t = f(x_t, u_t)$$

$$x_0 = a$$

The Lagrangian is then

(6.9)

$$L = \sum_{t=0}^{T-1} \{V(x_t, u_t) + \lambda_{t+1}[f(x_t, u_t) - (x_{t+1} - x_t)]\}$$

Define the discrete form Hamiltonian function

(6.10)

$$H(x_t, u_t) = V(x_t, u_t) + \lambda_{t+1}f(x_t, u_t)$$

then

$$L = \sum_{t=0}^{T-1} [H(x_t, u_t) - \lambda_{t+1}(x_{t+1} - x_t)]$$

which can be maximised by satisfying the conditions

$$\frac{\partial L}{\partial u_t} = \frac{\partial H}{\partial u_t} = 0 \qquad t = 0, \dots, T-1$$

$$\frac{\partial L}{\partial x_t} = \frac{\partial H}{\partial x_t} + \lambda_{t+1} - \lambda_t = 0 \qquad t = 1, \dots, T-1$$

$$\frac{\partial L}{\partial \lambda_{t+1}} = \frac{\partial H}{\partial \lambda_{t+1}} - (x_{t+1} - x_t) \qquad t = 0, \dots, T-1$$

$$\frac{\partial L}{\partial x_T} = -\lambda_T = 0$$

More succinctly:

(i) $$\frac{\partial H}{\partial u_t} = 0 \qquad t = 0, \dots, T-1$$

(ii) $$\lambda_{t+1} - \lambda_t = -\frac{\partial H}{\partial x_t} \qquad t = 1, \dots, T-1$$

(6.11)

(iii) $$x_{t-1} - x_t = \frac{\partial H}{\partial \lambda_{t+1}} = f(x_t, u_t) \qquad t = 0, \dots, T-1$$

(iv) $$\lambda_T = 0$$

(v) $$x_0 = a$$

It is useful to verify these conditions for, say, $T = 3$, most especially noting the range for t for condition (ii).

But how do we go about solving such a model? Unlike the continuous time model it is not simply solving two differential equations. It is true that in each time period we have two difference equations for the state and costate variables that require solving simultaneously. One solution method is to program the problem, as in Conrad and Clark (1987). A simpler method in the case of numerical examples is to use a spreadsheet. To illustrate the solution method by means of a spreadsheet, consider the following example.

Example 6.4[3]

Iron ore sells on the market at a constant price p per period but costs $c_t = by_t^2/x_t$, where x_t denotes the remaining reserves at the beginning of period t and y_t is the production in period t. The mine is to be shut down in period 10. What is the optimal production schedule $\{y_t^*\}$ for $t = 0, \ldots, 9$ given $p = 3$, $b = 2$ and the initial reserves $x_0 = R = 600$ tons? (Assume no discounting over the period.)

Let us first set up the model in general terms, replacing u_t by y_t. The objective function $V(x_t, y_t)$ is no more than the (undiscounted) profit, namely

$$V(x_t, y_t) = py_t - \frac{by_t^2}{x_t} = \left(p - \frac{by_t}{x_t}\right)y_t$$

Next we note that if x_t denotes the remaining reserves at the beginning of period t, then $x_{t+1} = x_t - y_t$ or $x_{t+1} - x_t = -y_t$. Thus, our Hamiltonian function is

$$H(x_t, y_t) = \left(p - \frac{by_t}{x_t}\right)y_t - \lambda_{t+1}y_t$$

Our optimality conditions are therefore:

(i) $\quad \dfrac{\partial H}{\partial y_t} = p - \dfrac{2by_t}{x_t} - \lambda_{t+1} = 0 \qquad t = 0, \ldots, 9$

(ii) $\quad \lambda_{t+1} - \lambda_t = -\dfrac{\partial H}{\partial x_t} = -\left(\dfrac{by_t^2}{x_t^2}\right) \qquad t = 1, \ldots, 9$

(iii) $\quad x_{t-1} - x_t = -y_t \qquad t = 0, \ldots, 9$

(iv) $\quad x_0 = R$

(v) $\quad \lambda_T = 0$

To solve this problem for a particular numerical example, let $p = 3$, $b = 2$ and $R = 600$. The computations are set out in detail in figure 6.5. In doing these computations we begin in period 10 and work backwards (see exercise 1 on backward solving).

Since $\lambda_{10} = 0$ then from (i) we know

$$3 - 4\left(\frac{y_9}{x_9}\right) = 0$$

which allows us to compute y_9/x_9. Having solved for y_9/x_9 we can then use condition (ii) to solve for λ_9. We do this repeatedly back to period 0. This gives us columns 2 and 3 of the spreadsheet. Since $x_0 = R = 600$, we have the first entry in the $x(t)$ column. Then y_0 is equal to $x_0(y_0/x_0)$ and finally $x_1 = x_0 - y_0$. This allows us to complete the final two columns.

The optimal production path $\{y_t^*\}$ is therefore given by the final column in figure 6.5 and its path, along with that of the reserves, is shown in figure 6.6(a).

---

[3] This is adapted from Conrad and Clark (1987, p. 20).

Figure 6.5.

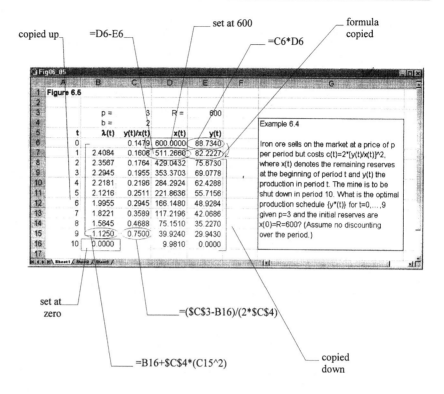

Given the computations the trajectory for (λ_t^*, x_t^*) can also be plotted, which is shown in figure 6.6(b), which are direct plottings from a spreadsheet.

In this example we solved the discrete optimisation problem by taking account of the first-order conditions and the constraints. We employed the spreadsheet merely as a means of carrying out some of the computations. However, spreadsheets come with nonlinear programming algorithms built in. To see this in operation, let us re-do the present example using *Excel*'s nonlinear programming algorithm, which is contained in the *Solver* add-on package.[4] The initial layout of the spreadsheet is illustrated in figure 6.7.

It is important to note that when setting out this initial spreadsheet we place in cells B7 to B16 some 'reasonable' numbers for extraction. Here we simply assume a constant rate of extraction of 60 throughout the 10 periods $t = 0$ to $t = 9$. Doing this allows us to compute columns D and E. Column D sets $\lambda_{10} = 0$ and then copies *backwards* the formula

$$\lambda_t = \lambda_{t+1} + \left(\frac{by_t^2}{x_t^2}\right)$$

for cells D16 to D8 (no value is placed in cell D7). The values in column E are the values for the objective function $V(x_t, y_t)$. The value for L, which is the sum of the values in column E for periods $t = 0$ to $t = 9$, is placed in cell E19. At the moment this stands at the value 1448.524.

---

[4] On using *Excel*'s Solver see Whigham (1998), Conrad (1999) and Judge (2000).

(a)

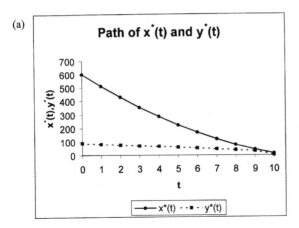

Figure 6.6.

(b)

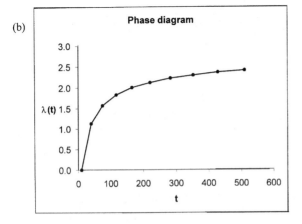

Figure 6.7.

Fig06_07							
	A	B	C	D	E	F	G
1	**Figure 6.7**						
2							
3		p =	3	R =	600		
4		b =	2				
5							
6	t	y(t)	x(t)	λ(t)	V(x,y)		
7	0	60.0000	600		168.0000		
8	1	60.0000	540.0000	3.0795	166.6667		
9	2	60.0000	480.0000	3.0548	165.0000		
10	3	60.0000	420.0000	3.0236	162.8571		
11	4	60.0000	360.0000	2.9828	160.0000		
12	5	60.0000	300.0000	2.9272	156.0000		
13	6	60.0000	240.0000	2.8472	150.0000		
14	7	60.0000	180.0000	2.7222	140.0000		
15	8	60.0000	120.0000	2.5000	120.0000		
16	9	60.0000	60.0000	2.0000	60.0000		
17	10	0	0.0000	0			
18							
19			L = Sum V =		1448.524		
20							

Sheet1 / Sheet2 / Sheet3 /

Figure 6.8.

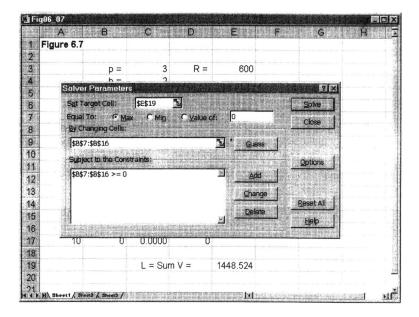

Of course it would be most unlikely if L were at a maximum with such arbitrary numbers for extraction. The maximum control problem is to maximise the value in cell E19, i.e., maximise L, subject to any constraints and production flows. The constraints are already set in the spreadsheet, although we do require others on the sign of variables. First move the cursor to cell E19 and then invoke the solver. By default this is set to maximise a cell value, namely cell E19. We next need to inform the programme which is the control variable and hence which values can be changed, i.e., what cells it can change in searching for a maximum. These are cells B7 to B16. In specifying the above problem we implicitly assumed x_t and y_t were both positive. In particular, we assumed the level of production, the control variable, was positive. We need to include this additional constraint in the Solver so that any negative values are excluded from the search process. The Solver window is shown in figure 6.8.

Once all this information has been included the Solver can do its work. The result is shown in the spreadsheet in figure 6.9. As can be observed this gives more or less the same results as figure 6.5, as it should. The value of the objective function has also increased from 1448.52 to 1471.31.

It should be noted in figure 6.9 that in period 10 we have $\lambda(10) = 0$ and at this value $x(10) = 9.9811$. We have to assume that the reserves in period 10 are therefore 9.9811 and that these are simply left in the ground. In other words, $x(T)$ is free. The shadow price of a free product is zero, hence $\lambda(10) = 0$, and this implies it is not optimal to mine the remaining reserves. Hence $F(x^T) = 0$ or x^T is free.

We have spent some time on this problem because it illustrates the use of spreadsheets without having to handle algebraically the first-order conditions. It also has the advantage that it can handle corner solutions.[5] Most important of all, it provides a way of solving real-life problems.

---

[5] Corner solutions would require setting out the Kuhn–Tucker conditions for optimisation. See Chiang (1984), Simon and Blume (1994) and Huang and Crooke (1997).

Figure 6.9.

Figure 6.9

	p =	3	R =	600
	b =	2		
t	y(t)	x(t)	λ(t)	V(x,y)
0	88.7247	600		239.9339
1	82.2427	511.2753	2.4084	220.2694
2	75.6645	429.0325	2.3567	200.3051
3	69.0667	353.3680	2,2945	180.2015
4	62.4424	284.3013	2.2181	159.8982
5	55.7095	221.8589	2.1216	139.1509
6	48.9298	166.1493	1.9955	117.9704
7	42.0684	117.2196	1.8220	96.0097
8	35.2272	75.1512	1.5644	72.6560
9	29.9429	39.9240	1.1250	44.9145
10	0	9.9811	0	
			L = Sum V =	1471.31

6.4 Optimal control with discounting

We have noted that a major feature of the control problem is to maximise the objective function $V(x, u)$. However, for many economic problems $V(x, u)$ would represent such things as profits or net benefits. The economist would not simply maximise such an income stream without first discounting it to the present. Thus, if δ were the rate of discount then the aim of the control would be to

$$\max_{\{u(t)\}} J = \int_0^T e^{-\delta t} V(x, u) dt \tag{6.12}$$

subject to various conditions which are unaffected by the discounting. Thus, the typical continuous time maximisation principle problem with discounting is the control problem

$$\begin{aligned} &\max_{\{u(t)\}} J = \int_0^T e^{-\delta t} V(x, u) dt \\ &\dot{x} = f(x, u) \\ &x(0) = x^0 \\ &x(T) = x^T \end{aligned} \tag{6.13}$$

while the discrete form is

$$\begin{aligned} &\max_{\{u_t\}} J = \sum_{t=0}^{T-1} \rho^t V(x_t, u_t) \\ &x_{t+1} - x_t = f(x_t, u_t) \\ &x_0 = a \end{aligned} \tag{6.14}$$

where $\rho = 1/(1 + \delta)$ and ρ is the discount *factor* while δ is the discount *rate*.

Let us first consider the discrete form. The Lagrangian is

(6.15)
$$L = \sum_{t=0}^{T-1} \rho^t \{ V(x_t, u_t) + \rho \lambda_{t+1} [f(x_t, u_t) - (x_{t+1} - x_t)] \}$$

Notice in this expression that λ_{t+1} is discounted to period t by multiplying it by the discount factor ρ. But then the *whole* expression {.} is discounted to the present by multiplying by the term ρ^t.

We now introduce a new concept: the *current value Hamiltonian function*, denoted $H_c(x, u)$. This is defined, for the discrete case, as

(6.16)
$$H_c(x_t, u_t) = V(x_t, u_t) + \rho \lambda_{t+1} f(x_t, u_t)$$

and in all other respects the optimisation conditions are similar, i.e.

(i) $\dfrac{\partial H_c}{\partial u_t} = 0 \qquad t = 0, \ldots, T-1$

(ii) $\rho \lambda_{t+1} - \lambda_t = -\dfrac{\partial H_c}{\partial x_t} \qquad t = 1, \ldots, T-1$

(6.17)
(iii) $x_{t-1} - x_t = \dfrac{\partial H_c}{\partial \rho \lambda_{t+1}} = f(x_t, u_t) \qquad t = 0, \ldots, T-1$

(iv) $\lambda_T = 0$

(v) $x_0 = a$

We can illustrate this with the mine example (example 6.4), but now assume a discount rate of 10%. With a discount rate of 10% the discount factor $\rho = 1/(1 + 0.1) = 0.909091$.

Example 6.5

Given $p = 3$, $R = 600$ and $\rho = 0.909091$

$$\max_{\{y_t\}} J = \sum \rho^t \left(p - \frac{by_t}{x_t} \right) y_t$$

$$x_{t+1} - x_t = -y_t$$

$$x_0 = R$$

The current value Hamiltonian is

$$H_c(x_t, y_t) = \left(p - \frac{by_t}{x_t} \right) y_t - \rho \lambda_{t+1} y_t$$

with optimality conditions:

(i) $\dfrac{\partial H_c}{\partial y_t} = p - \dfrac{2by_t}{x_t} - \rho \lambda_{t+1} = 0 \qquad t = 0, \ldots, 9$

(ii) $\rho \lambda_{t+1} - \lambda_t = -\dfrac{\partial H_c}{\partial x_t} = -\left(\dfrac{by_t^2}{x_t^2} \right) \qquad t = 1, \ldots, 9$

(iii) $x_{t-1} - x_t = \dfrac{\partial H_c}{\partial \rho \lambda_{t+1}} = -y_t \qquad t = 0, \ldots, 9$

Figure 6.10.

Figure 6.10 spreadsheet contents:

| | p = 3 | | ρ = 0.909091 | |
| | b = 2 | | δ = 0.1 | Example 6.5 |

t	y(t)	x(t)	λ(t)	V(x,y)
0	182.2140	600		435.9689
1	127.8322	417.7860	1.7854	277.5179
2	89.6113	289.9537	1.7767	176.4004
3	63.0999	200.3424	1.7634	112.3604
4	44.3863	137.2426	1.7413	71.3397
5	31.3973	92.8563	1.7062	45.3020
6	22.2845	61.4589	1.6482	28.6150
7	15.9201	39.1745	1.5501	17.8686
8	11.4942	23.2543	1.3748	10.7856
9	8.8238	11.7601	1.0236	5.6109
10	0	2.9362	0	

L = Sum V = 1181.769

Example 6.5 text box:

Iron ore sells on the market at a price of p per period but costs c(t) = 2*y(t)^2/x(t), where x(t) denotes the remaining reserves at the beginning of period t and y(t) the production in period t. The mine is to be shut down in period 10. What is the optimal production schedule, y*(t), for t=0..9 given p = 3, the initial reserves are R=600 and the discount rate is 10%?

(iv) $\lambda_T = 0$

(v) $x_0 = R = 600$

It should be noted that the only difference between this and the undiscounted conditions is in terms of condition (i), where λ_{t+1} is multiplied by the discount factor. Once again we use *Excel*'s *Solver* to handle the computations of this problem, with the results shown in figure 6.10, which should be compared with figure 6.9.

Notice once again that in period 10 we have $\lambda(10) = 0$ and that at this value $x(10) = 2.9362$. This level of reserves in period 10 is simply left in the ground, $x(T)$ is free. The shadow price of a free good is zero, hence $\lambda(10) = 0$, and this implies it is not optimal to mine the remaining reserves. Put another way, it is cheaper to leave the remaining reserves unmined than incur the costs of mining them.

What these computations show is a similar trajectory for optimal production but starting from a much higher level of production. This is understandable. The future in a discounting model is weighted less significantly than the present. The comparison is shown in figure 6.11.

Consider now discounting under a continuous time model. Consider the control problem

$$\max_{\{u(t)\}} J = \int_0^T e^{-\delta t} V(x, u) dt$$
$$\dot{x} = f(x, u)$$
$$x(0) = 0$$
$$x(T) = x^T$$

(6.18)

The Lagrangian is

$$L = \int_0^T \{e^{-\delta t} V(x, u) + \lambda [f(x, u) - \dot{x}]\} dt$$

Figure 6.11.

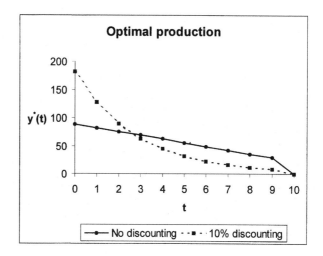

and the Hamiltonian is

$$H(x, u) = e^{-\delta t}V(x, u) + \lambda f(x, u)$$

Define the *current value Hamiltonian function*, H_c, by

$$H_c(x, u) = V(x, u) + \mu f(x, u)$$

then

$$H_c = He^{\delta t} \qquad \text{or} \qquad H = H_c e^{-\delta t}$$
$$\mu = \lambda e^{\delta t} \qquad \text{or} \qquad \lambda = \mu e^{-\delta t}$$

Now reconsider our five optimality conditions. Since $e^{\delta t}$ is a constant for a change in the control variable, then condition (i) is simply $\partial H_c / \partial u = 0$. The second condition is less straightforward. We have

$$\dot{\lambda} = -\frac{\partial H}{\partial x} = -\frac{\partial H_c}{\partial x} e^{-\delta t}$$

From $\lambda = \mu e^{-\delta t}$

$$\dot{\lambda} = \dot{\mu} e^{-\delta t} - \delta \mu e^{-\delta t}$$

Equating these we have

$$-\frac{\partial H_c}{\partial x} e^{-\delta t} = \dot{\mu} e^{-\delta t} - \delta \mu e^{-\delta t}$$

$$\text{or} \quad \dot{\mu} = -\frac{\partial H_c}{\partial x} + \delta \mu$$

Condition (iii) is

$$\dot{x} = \frac{\partial H}{\partial \lambda} = \frac{\partial H_c}{\partial \lambda} e^{-\delta t} = \frac{\partial H_c}{\partial \mu} = f(x, u)$$

while condition (iv) becomes

$$\lambda(T) = \mu(T)e^{-\delta t} = 0$$

and condition (v) remains unchanged.

To summarise, define the current value Hamiltonian and current value Lagrangian multiplier, i.e.

$$H_c(x, u) = H(x, u)e^{\delta t} = V(x, u) + \mu f(x, u)$$

where $\lambda = \mu e^{-\delta t}$. Then the optimality conditions are:

(i) $\dfrac{\partial H_c}{\partial u} = 0$ $0 \le t \le T$

(ii) $\dot{\mu} = -\dfrac{\partial H_c}{\partial x} + \delta \mu$ $0 \le t \le T$

(iii) $\dot{x} = \dfrac{\partial H_c}{\partial \mu} = f(x, u)$

(iv) $x(0) = x^0$

(v) $\mu(T)e^{-\delta t} = 0$ (or $x(T) = x^T$)

(6.19)

These optimality conditions allow us to eliminate the control variable u using condition (i) and to obtain two differential equations: one for the state variable, x, and the other for the current value costate variable, μ.

Example 6.6

$$\max_{\{u\}} J = -\int_0^{10} u^2 e^{-0.1t} dt$$

$$\dot{x} = u$$
$$x(0) = 0$$
$$x(10) = 1000$$

and find the optimal path $x^*(t)$.

The current value Hamiltonian is

$$H_c = -u^2 + \mu u$$

with optimality conditions

(i) $\dfrac{\partial H_c}{\partial u} = -2u + \mu = 0$

(ii) $\dot{\mu} = 0 + 0.1\mu$

(iii) $\dot{x} = u$

From (i) we have $u = 0.5\mu$, which when substituted into (iii) gives $\dot{x} = 0.5\mu$. Thus we have two differential equations

$$\dot{x} = 0.5\mu$$
$$\dot{\mu} = 0.1\mu$$

Solving we obtain

$$x(t) = c_1 + c_2 e^{0.1t}$$

$$\mu(t) = 0.2c_2 e^{0.1t}$$

Given $x(0) = 0$ and $x(10) = 1000$ then we can solve for c_1 and c_2 by solving

$$c_1 + c_2 = 0$$
$$0.2c_2e = 1000$$

which gives $c_1 = -581.9767$ and $c_2 = 581.9767$. Hence

$$x^*(t) = -581.9767 + 581.9767e^{0.1t}$$
$$= 581.9767(e^{0.1t} - 1)$$

6.5   The phase diagram approach to continuous time control models

First let us reconsider examples 6.1–6.3.

Example 6.1 (cont.)

In example 6.1 we derived the two differential equations

$$\dot{x} = x + u$$
$$\dot{\lambda} = -(5 + \lambda)$$

In this instance, $\partial H/\partial u = \lambda$ which is of no help in eliminating u. We did, however, establish that H is a maximum when $u = 3$ and that this variable remains constant throughout. Therefore,

$$\dot{x} = x + 3$$
$$\dot{\lambda} = -5 - \lambda$$

and so we have two isoclines. The x-isocline at $x = -3$ and the λ-isocline at $\lambda = -5$. Furthermore,

$$\dot{x} > 0 \qquad \text{implies} \qquad x > -3$$
$$\dot{\lambda} < 0 \qquad \text{implies} \qquad \lambda > -5$$

so we know that the optimal trajectory starting from $x(0) = 2$ will lead to a rise in the state variable x and a fall in the costate variable λ. This is verified in figure 6.12. The system begins from point $(x(0), \lambda(0)) = (2, 8.5914)$, satisfying the initial condition on the state variable x; and has a terminal point $(x(1), \lambda(1)) = (10.5914, 0)$, which satisfies the terminal condition on the costate variable, λ. Of all possible trajectories in the phase plane, this is the optimal trajectory.

Example 6.2 (cont.)

In example 6.2 we derived the following two differential equations

$$\dot{x} = -\tfrac{1}{2}\lambda$$
$$\dot{\lambda} = 0$$

There is only one isocline for this problem. When $\dot{x} = 0$ then $\lambda = 0$ and so the x-isocline coincides with the x-axis. Our initial point is $(x(0), \lambda(0)) = (1, 2)$ and

Figure 6.12.

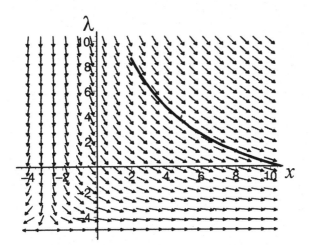

Figure 6.13.

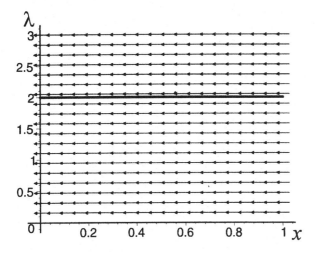

for $\lambda > 0$ we have $\dot{x} < 0$ and so the trajectory is moving to the left. Earlier we demonstrated that λ remains at the value of 2 throughout the trajectory. When $t = 1$ then $x(1) = 0$, which satisfies the condition on the terminal point, which in the phase plane is the point $(x(1), \lambda(1)) = (0, 2)$. As can be seen in terms of figure 6.13, the optimal trajectory in the phase plane is the horizontal line pointing to the left.

Example 6.3 (cont.)

The two differential equations we derived for example 6.3 were

$$\dot{x} = x + 2\lambda$$
$$\dot{\lambda} = \tfrac{1}{2}x - \lambda$$

When $\dot{x} = 0$ then $\lambda = -\frac{1}{2}x$ and when $\dot{\lambda} = 0$ then $\lambda = \frac{1}{2}x$. We have therefore two distinct isoclines in this example. Furthermore,

$$\text{if } \dot{x} > 0 \text{ then } x + 2\lambda > 0 \text{ implying } \lambda > -\tfrac{1}{2}x$$

Hence, above the x-isocline, x is rising while below it is falling. Similarly,

$$\text{if } \dot{\lambda} > 0 \text{ then } \tfrac{1}{2}x - \lambda > 0 \text{ implying } \lambda < \tfrac{1}{2}x$$

Hence, below the λ-isocline, λ is rising while above it is falling. This suggests that we have a saddle-point solution.

This is also readily verified by considering the eigenvalues of the system. The matrix of the system is

$$\mathbf{A} = \begin{bmatrix} 1 & 2 \\ \frac{1}{2} & -1 \end{bmatrix}$$

with eigenvalues $r = \sqrt{2}$ and $s = -\sqrt{2}$. Since these are real and of opposite sign, then we have a saddle point solution.

When $t = 0$ we already have $x(0) = 2$ but we need to solve for $\lambda(0)$. But

$$\lambda(0) = \frac{c_1}{2}(\sqrt{2} - 1) - \frac{c_2}{2}(\sqrt{2} + 1)$$

and we know that $c_1 = -0.1256$ and $c_2 = 2.1256$. Substituting these values we get $\lambda(0) = -2.6$. The initial point $(x(0), \lambda(0)) = (2, -2.6)$ therefore begins below the x-isocline, and so the vector forces are directing the system up and to the left. The optimal trajectory is shown in figure 6.14.

It is apparent from example 6.3 and 6.6 that the maximisation approach of Pontryagin gives us first-order conditions in terms of the Hamiltonian which, in the present simple models, leads to two differential equations in terms of the state variable x and the costate variable λ (or μ). Control problems, however, pose two difficulties:

(1)   the differential equations are often nonlinear
(2)   in economics functional forms are often unspecified.[6]

Even the most simple control problem can lead to nonlinear differential equations, and although we have developed techniques elsewhere for dealing with these,[7] until the advent of the computer they were largely left to the mathematician. When the functional forms are not even specified then there are no explicit differential equations to solve. However, the qualitative properties of the fixed points can still be investigated by considering the system's qualitative properties in the phase plane.

First consider a simple example for which we have an explicit solution.

---

[6] What we often know are certain properties. Thus we may have a production function $y = f(k)$ where $f(k)$ is unspecified other than being continuous, differentiable and where $f'(k) > 0$ and $f''(k) < 0$.
[7] See sections 2.7 and 3.9.

Figure 6.14.

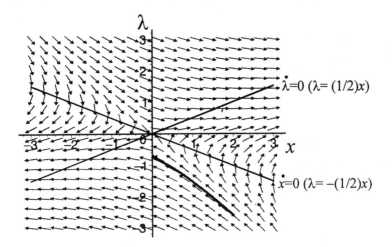

Example 6.7[8]

Our problem is

$$\max_{\{u\}} J = \int_0^\infty (20 \ln x - 0.1u^2)dt$$

$$\dot{x} = u - 0.1x$$

$$x(0) = 80$$

The Hamiltonian for this problem is

$$H = 20 \ln x - 0.1u^2 + \lambda(u - 0.1x)$$

with first-order conditions

$$\frac{\partial H}{\partial u} = -0.2u + \lambda = 0$$

$$\dot{\lambda} = -\frac{\partial H}{\partial x} = -\left(\frac{20}{x} - 0.1\lambda\right)$$

$$\dot{x} = u - 0.1x$$

which can be reduced to two differential equations in terms of x and λ

$$\dot{x} = -0.1x + 5\lambda$$

$$\dot{\lambda} = \frac{-20}{x} + 0.1\lambda$$

The fixed point of this system is readily found by setting $\dot{x} = 0$ and $\dot{\lambda} = 0$, giving $x^* = 100$ and $\lambda^* = 2$. Furthermore, the two isoclines are readily found to be

$$\lambda = 0.02x \qquad (\dot{x} = 0)$$

$$\lambda = \frac{200}{x} \qquad (\dot{\lambda} = 0)$$

and illustrated in figure 6.15.

[8] Adapted from Conrad and Clark (1987, pp. 46–8).

Figure 6.15 also shows the vector of forces in the four quadrants, which readily indicate a saddle point solution. This can be verified by considering a linearisation about the fixed point $(x^*, \lambda^*) = (100, 2)$. This gives the linear equations

$$\dot{x} = -0.1(x - x^*) + 5(\lambda - \lambda^*)$$
$$\dot{\lambda} = 0.002(x - x^*) + 0.1(\lambda - \lambda^*)$$

The resulting matrix of the linear system is

$$\mathbf{A} = \begin{bmatrix} -0.1 & 5 \\ 0.002 & 0.1 \end{bmatrix}$$

with eigenvalues $r = 0.14142$ and $s = -0.14142$, confirming a saddle point solution.

To establish the equations of the arms of the saddle point solution, take first the eigenvalue $r = 0.14142$. Then

$$(\mathbf{A} - r\mathbf{I})\mathbf{v}^r = \mathbf{0}$$

i.e.

$$\left(\begin{bmatrix} -0.1 & 5 \\ 0.002 & 0.1 \end{bmatrix} - 0.14142 \begin{bmatrix} 1 & 0 \\ 0 & 1 \end{bmatrix} \right) \begin{bmatrix} v_1^r \\ v_2^r \end{bmatrix} = \begin{bmatrix} 0 \\ 0 \end{bmatrix}$$

or

$$\begin{bmatrix} -0.24142 & 5 \\ 0.002 & -0.04142 \end{bmatrix} \begin{bmatrix} v_1^r \\ v_2^r \end{bmatrix} = \begin{bmatrix} 0 \\ 0 \end{bmatrix}$$

Using the first equation,

$$-0.24142 v_1^r + 5 v_2^r = 0$$

Figure 6.15.

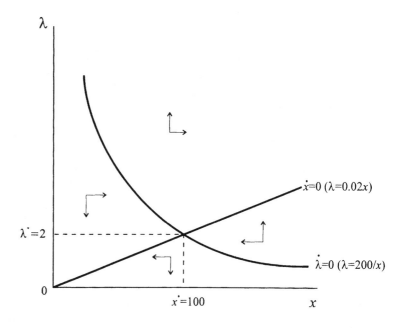

Let $v_1^r = 1$, then

$$5v_2^r = 0.24142$$

$$v_2^r = 0.048284$$

Therefore,

$$(\lambda - \lambda^*) = 0.048284(x - x^*)$$

$$(\lambda - 2) = 0.048284(x - 100)$$

i.e.

$$\lambda = -2.8284 + 0.48284x$$

and since this is positively sloped it represents the equation of the unstable arm.

Now consider the second eigenvalue, $s = -0.14142$

$$(\mathbf{A} - r\mathbf{I})\mathbf{v}^s = \left(\begin{bmatrix} -0.1 & 5 \\ 0.002 & 0.1 \end{bmatrix} + 0.14142 \begin{bmatrix} 1 & 0 \\ 0 & 1 \end{bmatrix} \right) \begin{bmatrix} v_1^s \\ v_2^s \end{bmatrix} = \begin{bmatrix} 0 \\ 0 \end{bmatrix}$$

i.e.

$$\begin{bmatrix} 0.04142 & 5 \\ 0.002 & 0.24142 \end{bmatrix} \begin{bmatrix} v_1^s \\ v_2^s \end{bmatrix} = \begin{bmatrix} 0 \\ 0 \end{bmatrix}$$

Using again the first equation, then

$$0.04142v_1^s + 5v_2^s = 0$$

Let $v_1^s = 1$, then

$$5v_2^s = -0.04142$$

$$v_2^s = -0.008284$$

Therefore,

$$(\lambda - \lambda^*) = -0.008284(x - x^*)$$

$$(\lambda - 2) = -0.008284(x - 100)$$

i.e.

$$\lambda = 2.8284 - 0.00828284x$$

and since this is negatively sloped it represents the equation of the stable arm.

If $x(0) = 80$ then the value of λ on the stable arm is $\lambda(0) = 2.16568$. The trajectory, along with isoclines and the stable arm, are shown in figure 6.16. Although the point begins on the stable arm, it gets pulled away before it reaches the equilibrium! What this diagram reveals is that this system is *very sensitive to initial conditions*. But the direction field does show a clear saddle point equilibrium.

Example 6.8 (Ramsey growth model)

In this example we shall consider the Ramsey growth model,[9] which is the basis of much of the optimal growth theory literature. We shall consider the model in terms

[9] Ramsey (1928). See also Burmeister and Dobell (1970), Barro and Sala-i-Martin (1995) and Romer (2001).

Figure 6.16.

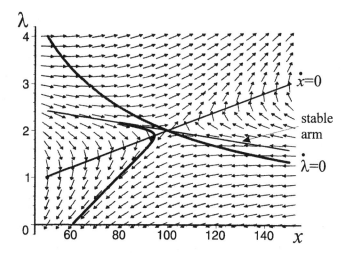

of continuous time. We begin with simple definitions of income and investment, namely

(6.20)

$$Y(t) = C(t) + I(t)$$
$$I(t) = \dot{K}(t) + \delta K(t)$$

Hence

$$\frac{Y(t)}{L(t)} = \frac{C(t)}{L(t)} + \frac{\dot{K}(t)}{L(t)} + \frac{\delta K(t)}{L(t)}$$

i.e. $$y(t) = c(t) + \frac{\dot{K}(t)}{L(t)} + \delta k(t)$$

But

$$k = \frac{d}{dt}\left(\frac{K}{L}\right) = \frac{L\dot{K} - K\dot{L}}{L^2} = \frac{\dot{K}}{L} - \left(\frac{K}{L}\right)\frac{\dot{L}}{L}$$

$$= \frac{\dot{K}}{L} - k\frac{\dot{L}}{L}$$

We assume population grows at a constant rate n, so that $\dot{L}/L = n$ hence

$$\frac{\dot{K}}{L} = \dot{k} + kn$$

and

$$y(t) = c(t) + \dot{k}(t) + (n + \delta)k(t)$$

If we have a homogeneous of degree one production function then we can express output, y, as a function of k. Thus, $y = f(k)$. Dropping the time variable for convenience, we therefore have the condition

(6.21)

$$\dot{k} = f(k) - (n + \delta)k - c$$

In order to consider the optimal growth path we require to specify an objective. Suppose $U(c)$ denotes utility as a function of consumption per head. The aim is to maximise the discounted value of utility subject to the equation we have just derived, i.e.

$$\max_{\{c\}} J = \int_0^\infty e^{-\beta t} U(c) dt$$

$$\dot{k} = f(k) - (n + \delta)k - c$$

$$k(0) = k_0$$

$$0 \le c \le f(k)$$

The current value Hamiltonian function is

$$H_c = U(c) + \mu[f(k) - (n + \delta)k - c]$$

with first-order conditions:

(i) $\dfrac{\partial H_c}{\partial c} = U'(c) - \mu = 0$

(ii) $\dot{\mu} = -\mu f'(k) + \mu(n + \delta) + \beta \mu$

(iii) $\dot{k} = f(k) - (n + \delta)k - c$

or

(i) $U'(c) = \mu$

(ii) $\dot{\mu} = -\mu f'(k) + (n + \delta + \beta)\mu$

(iii) $\dot{k} = f(k) - (n + \delta)k - c$

As they stand these equations are not easy to interpret or solve. We can, however, with some rearrangement, derive two differential equations in terms of the state variable k and the control variable c.

From (i) differentiate with respect to time. Then

$$\frac{d[U'(c)]}{dt} = \dot{\mu}$$

$$U''(c)\frac{dc}{dt} = \dot{\mu} = -\mu f'(k) + (n + \delta + \beta)\mu$$

i.e. $U''(c)\dot{c} = -\mu[f'(k) - (n + \delta + \beta)]$

or

$$-\frac{U''(c)}{U'(c)}\dot{c} = f'(k) - (n + \delta + \beta) \quad \text{(since } \mu = U'(c)\text{)}$$

Now define Pratt's measure of relative risk aversion[10]

$$\sigma(c) = -\frac{cU''(c)}{U'(c)}$$

then

$$\frac{\sigma(c)}{c}\dot{c} = f'(k) - (n + \delta + \beta)$$

---

[10] Pratt (1964), see also Shone (1981, application 2, section A2.4).

or

$$\dot{c} = \frac{1}{\sigma(c)}[f'(k) - (n + \delta + \beta)]c$$

We therefore have two differential equations

$$\dot{c} = \frac{1}{\sigma(c)}[f'(k) - (n + \delta + \beta)]c$$

$$\dot{k} = f(k) - (n + \delta)k - c$$

If $\dot{c} = 0$ then $f'(k^*) = n + \delta + \beta$. On the other hand, if $\dot{k} = 0$ then $c^* = f(k^*) - (n + \delta)k^*$. Furthermore, if $\dot{c} > 0$ then $f(k^*) > (n + \delta + \beta)$ which implies $k < k^*$ as seen in terms of the upper diagram of figure 6.17. Hence, to the left of the $\dot{c} = 0$ isocline, c is rising; to the right of $\dot{c} = 0$, then c is falling. Similarly, if $\dot{k} > 0$ then $f(k^*) - (n + \delta)k^* > c$. Thus below the $\dot{k} = 0$ isocline k is rising, while above the $\dot{k} = 0$ isocline k is falling. The vector forces clearly indicate that (k^*, c^*) is a saddle point solution. The only optimal trajectory is that on the stable arm. For any k_0 the only viable level of consumption is that represented by the associated point on the stable arm. Given the initial point on the stable arm, the system is directed towards the equilibrium. Notice that in equilibrium k is constant and so capital is growing at the same rate as the labour force. Furthermore, since k is constant in equilibrium then so is y, and hence Y is also growing at the same rate as the labour force. We have, therefore, a balanced-growth equilibrium.

Example 6.9 (Ramsey growth model: a numerical example)

Consider the optimal growth problem

$$\max_{\{c\}} J = \int_0^\infty e^{-\beta t} U(c) dt$$

$$\dot{k} = f(k) - (n + \delta)k - c$$

$$k(0) = k_0$$

$$0 \le c \le f(k)$$

where

$$\beta = 0.02, f(k) = k^{0.25}, n = 0.01, \delta = 0.05, k(0) = 2$$

and

$$U(c) = \frac{c^{1-\theta}}{1-\theta}$$

If $\theta = \frac{1}{2}$, then $U(c) = 2\sqrt{c}$.[11] Then our maximisation problem is

$$\max_{\{c\}} J = \int_0^\infty e^{-0.02t} 2\sqrt{c}\, dt$$

$$\dot{k} = k^{0.25} - 0.06k - c$$

$$k(0) = 2$$

---

[11] Notice that this utility function has a relative measure of risk aversion equal to θ.

Figure 6.17.

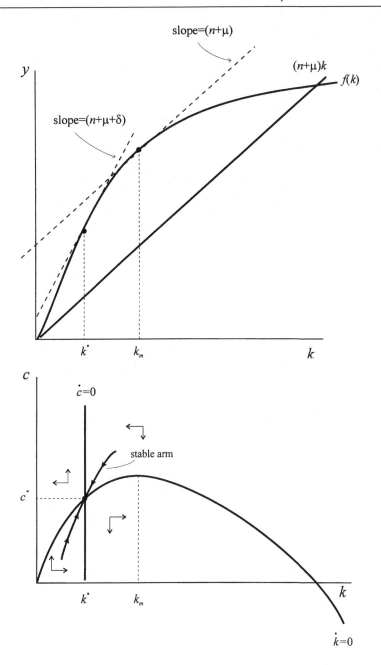

The current value Hamiltonian is

$$H_c = 2\sqrt{c} + \mu(k^{0.25} - 0.06k - c)$$

with first-order conditions

(i) $\dfrac{\partial H_c}{\partial c} = 2\left(\tfrac{1}{2}\right)c^{-1/2} - \mu = 0$

(ii) $\dot{\mu} = -\mu(0.25)k^{-0.75} + 0.08\mu$

(iii) $\dot{k} = k^{0.25} - 0.06k - c$

From the first condition we have $c^{-1/2} = \mu$. Differentiating this with respect to time, then

$$-\tfrac{1}{2}c^{-3/2}\dot{c} = \dot{\mu}$$

Using condition (ii) we have

$$-\tfrac{1}{2}c^{-3/2}\dot{c} = -\mu(0.25)k^{-0.75} + 0.08c^{-1/2}$$

But $\mu = c^{-1/2}$ hence

$$-\tfrac{1}{2}c^{-3/2}\dot{c} = -c^{-1/2}(0.25)k^{-0.75} + 0.08c^{-1/2}$$

Dividing throughout by $c^{-1/2}$ we obtain

$$-\tfrac{1}{2}c^{-1}\dot{c} = -(0.25)k^{-0.75} + 0.08$$

i.e.

$$\dot{c} = 2c(0.25)k^{-0.75} - 2(0.08)c$$
$$= (0.5k^{-0.75} - 0.16)c$$

We now have two differential equations for the state variables c and k, which are

$$\dot{c} = (0.5k^{-0.75} - 0.16)c$$
$$\dot{k} = k^{0.25} - 0.06k - c$$

The first thing to note about these equations is that they are nonlinear and therefore not easy to solve without some software.[12] Using either *Mathematica* or *Maple* (or *Excel* as indicated in n. 12), the following equilibrium values are obtained

$$k^* = 4.5688, \quad c^* = 1.1879$$

Second we note that the consumption-isocline is given by the formula $c = k^{0.75} - 0.06k$. Differentiating this with respect to k and setting this equal to zero allows us to solve for the value of k at which consumption is at a maximum

$$c = k^{0.25} - 0.06k$$
$$\frac{dc}{dk} = 0.25k^{-0.75} - 0.06 = 0$$
$$k_{max} = 6.7048$$

At this value of k then consumption takes the value $c_{max} = 1.2069$.[13]

---

[12] If you do not have a software package like *Mathematica* or *Maple*, you can use *Excel's Solver* to solve for the equilibrium values. Place an arbitrary value of k in one cell; say, our starting value of 2. Suppose this is cell C3. Now place the formula

$$= (0.5*\$C\$3\hat{}(-0.75) - 0.16)*(\$C\$3\hat{}0.25 - 0.06*\$C\$3)$$

in the target cell. In the Solver window declare the cell where the formula is located as the target cell and set this to have a value of zero; allow cell C3 to be the cell whose values are changed. In order to avoid the problem of a zero solution, place a constraint on C3 that it should be greater than or equal to unity. Having calculated the equilibrium value of k in this manner, it is a simple matter then to solve for the equilibrium value of consumption, c.

[13] Note that the c-isocline cuts the k-axis at 0 and the value 42.5727.

To establish the properties of the equilibrium, we can linearise the system around the point $(k^*, c^*) = (4.5688, 1.1879)$. Let

$$\dot{c} = f(c, k) = (0.5k^{-0.75} - 0.16)c$$
$$\dot{k} = g(c, k) = k^{0.25} - 0.06k - c$$

The system can then be written in the linearised form

$$\dot{c} = f_c(c^*, k^*)(c - c^*) + f_k(c^*, k^*)(k - k^*)$$
$$\dot{k} = g_c(c^*, k^*)(c - c^*) + g_k(c^*, k^*)(k - k^*)$$

with

$$f_c(c^*, k^*) = 0, \qquad f_k(c^*, k^*) = -0.0312$$
$$g_c(c^*, k^*) = -1, \qquad g_k(c^*, k^*) = 0.02$$

and so the matrix of the system is

$$\mathbf{A} = \begin{bmatrix} 0 & -0.0312 \\ -1 & 0.02 \end{bmatrix}$$

with eigenvalues $r = 0.1869$ and $s = -0.1669$. Since these are opposite in sign, then the equilibrium is a saddle point solution.

Given that we are dealing with a numerical example then we can approximate the saddle path equations utilising the linear approximation to the system. First take the eigenvalue $r = 0.1869$

$$(\mathbf{A} - r\mathbf{I})\mathbf{v}^r = \mathbf{0}$$

i.e.

$$\begin{bmatrix} -0.1869 & -0.0312 \\ -1 & -0.1669 \end{bmatrix} \begin{bmatrix} v_1^r \\ v_2^r \end{bmatrix} = \begin{bmatrix} 0 \\ 0 \end{bmatrix}$$

then

$$-v_1^r - 0.1669v_2^r = 0$$
$$v_1^r = -0.1669v_2^r$$

Let $v_2^r = 1$ then $v_1^r = -0.1669$. This saddle path is therefore negatively sloped and denotes the unstable arm. Turn next to the eigenvalue $s = -0.1669$ then

$$\begin{bmatrix} 0.1669 & -0.0312 \\ -1 & 0.1869 \end{bmatrix} \begin{bmatrix} v_1^s \\ v_2^s \end{bmatrix} = \begin{bmatrix} 0 \\ 0 \end{bmatrix}$$

and

$$-v_1^s + 0.1869v_2^s = 0$$
$$v_1^s = 0.1869v_2^s$$

Let $v_2^s = 1$ then $v_1^s = 0.1869$. This saddle path is positively sloped and represents the stable arm. The equation of the stable arm can be found from

$$c - c^* = 0.1869(k - k^*)$$
$$c - 1.1879 = 0.1869(k - 4.5688)$$
$$c = -0.33399 + 0.1869k$$

Figure 6.18.

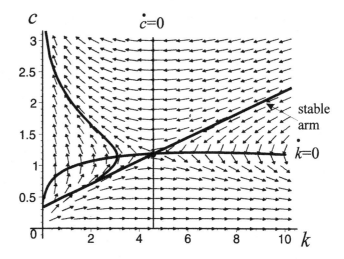

All these results are illustrated in figure 6.18 in the neighbourhood of the fixed point. As can be seen from figure 6.18, however, although the trajectory does begin on the saddle path, the system is extremely sensitive to initial conditions, and given the initial point $(k(0), c(0)) = (2, 0.70779)$, the trajectory begins to move away from the saddle path before it reaches the equilibrium! The direction field shown in figure 6.18 does, however, illustrate the existence of the stable arm with trajectories tending to the balanced-growth path equilibrium.

What these examples show is that we can eliminate the control variable using the first-order conditions and derive two differential equations, one for the state variable and another for the costate variable. These can more generally be expressed

$$\dot{x} = R(x, \lambda)$$
$$\dot{\lambda} = S(x, \lambda)$$

We can then define two isoclines, one for $\dot{x} = 0$ (or $R = 0$), and another for $\dot{\lambda} = 0$ (or $S = 0$). As these examples illustrate, however, such isoclines do not always exist. When they both exist, the state space is separated into four quadrants. Each quadrant exerts different dynamic forces on any trajectory beginning in it. In most of these examples we know the initial point and terminal point. The derived dynamic equations maximise the objective function, satisfy the equation of motion and satisfy initial and terminal states. So we know the optimal trajectory.

When we have two state variables, as in example 6.8 (and its numerical version, example 6.9), then we sketch the state-space only and the optimal trajectory $\{\mathbf{x}(t)\}$.

If we have a discrete system then

$$x_{t+1} - x_t = R(x_t, \lambda_t)$$
$$\lambda_{t+1} - \lambda_t = S(x_t, \lambda_t)$$

and the isoclines remain $R = 0$ ($\Delta x_{t+1} = 0$) and $S = 0$ ($\Delta \lambda_{t+1} = 0$).

For many problems we do not have specific functional forms either for the objective function or for the equations of motion. This was the situation in the general Ramsey growth model (example 6.8). It is in such circumstances that deriving isoclines and establishing properties of the state space provides *qualitative insight into the optimal path*. For instance, example 6.8 illustrates that the trajectory of the economy is along the stable arm eventually resulting in a balanced-growth equilibrium. Such a path will maximise discounted consumption over the infinite time horizon.

Exercises

1. Given the following stages of production labelled I, II, III and IV, a variety of possible processes can be followed, as shown in the accompanying figure, where the cost of transforming from one stage into another is indicated in the circle while the two states are labelled A, B, C, etc.

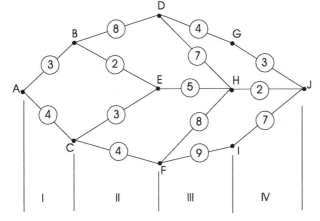

(i) Compute all possible solution paths and show which is the minimum.
(ii) 'Back solve' by starting at the terminal state J and minimise at each node arrived at. Is this the same solution path you derived in (i) when then looked at forward?
(iii) Why is it sensible to 'back solve' but not to 'forward solve'?

2. Prove that

$$-\int_{t_0}^{t_1} \lambda \dot{x}\, dt = \int_{t_0}^{t_1} x\dot{\lambda}\, dt - [\lambda(t_1)x(t_1) - \lambda(t_0)x(t_0)]$$

3. (i) For the model in section 6.2 derive the optimal path for production under both no discounting and discounting at 10% under the following alternative assumptions:
    (a) $p = 5$
    (b) $b = 3$
    (c) $R = 800$
   (ii) What conclusions do you draw?

4.   Consider the model in example 6.5. Suppose the manager is unsure of the discount rate. He decides to choose three rates: 5%, 10% and 15%. Compare the optimal production schedules under each assumption.

5.   Consider examples 6.4 and 6.5 under the assumption that price is expected to rise at 5% per period (i.e. inflation is 5%), but costs are not subject to any rise; derive the optimal production schedule in each case assuming $p_0 = 3$.

6.   Consider example 6.4 under the assumption that price is expected to rise at 10% per period and costs are expected to rise at 15% per period. Derive the optimal production schedule assuming $p_0 = 3$ and $b_0 = 2$.

7.   Set up the following problem as a control problem.

A government has an objective function that indicates it wants to maximise votes, v, by pursing policies towards unemployment, u, and inflation π. The party is constrained in its behaviour by the existence of an augmented Phillips curve of the form

$$\pi = -\alpha(u - u_n) + \pi^e \quad \alpha > 0$$

and expectations take the form of adaptive expectations, i.e.

$$\dot{\pi}^e = \beta(\pi - \pi^e) \qquad \beta > 0$$

The government has just won the election at $t = 0$ and the next election is in 5 years' time. It assumes that voters have poor memories, and weight more heavily the economic situation the closer it is to the election. It accordingly assumes a weighting factor of $e^{0.05t}$.

8.   Solve the following control problem

$$\max_{\{u\}} - \int_0^1 \left(\frac{x^2}{4} - \frac{u^2}{9}\right) dt$$

$$\dot{x} = -x + u$$

$$x(0) = 5, \quad x(1) = 10$$

Plot the trajectory in (x, λ)-space.

9.   Solve the following control problem

$$\max_{\{u\}} \int_0^1 (3x^2 - u^2) dt$$

$$\dot{x} = 2x + u$$

$$x(0) = 10, \quad x(1) = 15$$

Plot the trajectory in (x, λ)-space

10.   Solve the equilibrium for the following Ramsey model. Linearise the system about the equilibrium and establish its stability properties

$$\max_{\{c\}} J = \int_0^\infty e^{-0.03} U(c) dt$$

$\dot{k} = k^{0.3} - (n + \delta)k - c$

$k(0) = 1$

where $U(c) = 4c^{1/4}$, $n = 0.02$, $\delta = 0.03$

Additional reading

Beavis and Dobbs (1990), Blackburn (1987), Bryson, Jr. and Ho (1975), Burmeister and Dobell (1970), Chiang (1992), Conrad (1999), Conrad and Clark (1987), Fryer and Greenman (1987), Intriligator (1971), Kirk (1970), Léonard and Long (1992), Pontryagin *et al.* (1962), Ramsey (1928), Romer (2001) and Takayama (1994).

CHAPTER 7

Chaos theory

7.1 Introduction

The interest and emphasis in deterministic systems was a product of nineteenth-century classical determinism, most particularly expressed in the laws of Isaac Newton and the work of Laplace. As we pointed out in chapter 1, if a set of equations with specified initial conditions prescribes the evolution of a system uniquely with no external disturbances, then its behaviour is deterministic and it can describe a system for the indefinite future. In other words, it is fully predictable. This view has dominated economic thinking, with its full embodiment in neoclassical economics. Furthermore, such systems were believed to be ahistoretic. In other words, such systems were quite reversible and would return to their initial state if the variables were returned to their initial values. In such systems, history is irrelevant. More importantly from the point of view of economics, it means that the equilibrium of an economic system is not time-dependent.

Although the physical sciences could in large part undertake controlled experiments and so eliminate any random disturbances, this was far from true in economics. This led to the view that economic systems were subject to random shocks, which led to indeterminism. Economic systems were much less predictable. The random nature of time-series data led to the subject of econometrics. The subject matter of econometrics still adheres to the view that economic systems can be captured by deterministic components, which are then augmented by either additive or multiplicative error components. These error components pick up the stochastic nature of the data series, most especially time-series data. For instance, the classical linear model takes the form

$$(7.1) \qquad \mathbf{y} = \mathbf{X}\beta + \varepsilon \quad \varepsilon \sim N(\mathbf{0}, \sigma^2 \mathbf{I})$$

Not only is $\mathbf{X}\beta$ assumed linear but, more significantly from the point of view of our present discussion, it is assumed to be deterministic. All randomness is attributed to the error term. Even where the error term has distributions that are not normally distributed, the econometric approach effectively partitions the problem into a deterministic component and a random component. Randomness cannot and does not arise from the deterministic component in this approach. Such a view of the world is a 'shotgun wedding of deterministic theory with "random shocks"' (Mirowski 1986, p. 298). Mandelbrot (1987), in particular, was an ardent critic of the way econometrics simply borrowed classical determinism and added a random component. The emphasis of econometrics on the Central Limit Theorem was, in Mandelbrot's view, flawed. It is not our intention here, however, to expand on these views. Suffice it to say that the dichotomy between deterministic economic elements of a system and additive random components is still the mainstay of the econometric approach.

Three important considerations came out of these early discussions that are relevant for this chapter.

1. *Linearity, far from being the norm, is the exception.* Linear economic models lead to unique equilibrium points, which are either globally stable or globally unstable. On the other hand, nonlinear systems can lead to multiple equilibria and hence, local stability and instability. However, nonlinear systems also tend to lead to complexity. Until the development of chaos theory, there was little formal way of handling complex systems. On a more practical note, the study of complex systems could not have occurred without the development of computers and computer software.

2. *Many economic time series are generated by discrete processes.* The second consideration, once again highlighted by Mandelbrot, is that many economic time series are generated by discrete processes, and therefore should not be modelled as continuous processes. The emphasis of continuous processes comes, once again, from the physical sciences. We already noted in earlier chapters that a discrete equivalent of a continuous system could exhibit instability while its continuous version is stable! Although this is not always the case, it does highlight the importance of modelling systems with discrete models if discrete processes generate the time series.

3. *The occurrence of bifurcations.* A third strand was consideration of a system's equilibrium to changes in the value of important parameters. It became clear that for some systems, their behaviour could suddenly change dramatically at certain parameter values. This led to the study of bifurcation.

This chapter is concerned with how deterministic systems can exhibit chaos, and to all intents and purposes have the characteristics of randomness: a randomness, however, which does not occur from random shocks to the system. We find that such behaviour occurs when parameters of the system take certain values. The parameter value at which the system's behaviour changes is called a *bifurcation value*. We therefore begin our discussion with bifurcation theory.

7.2 Bifurcations: single-variable case

In this and the next section we shall confine ourselves to studying some of the properties of first-order systems that depend on just one parameter. We shall represent this with

$$x_{t+1} = f(x_t, \lambda) \tag{7.2}$$

in which f is nonlinear. Two examples are[1]:

(i) $x_{t+1} = 1.5x_t(1 - x_t) - \lambda$

(ii) $x_{t+1} = \lambda x_t(1 - x_t)$

and we shall make great use of these two equations to illustrate bifurcation theory and chaos.

But what do we mean by the terms 'bifurcation' and 'chaos'? *Bifurcation theory* is the study of points in a system at which the qualitative behaviour of the system changes. In terms of our general representation, $f(x^*, \lambda)$ denotes an equilibrium point, a stationary point, whose value depends on the precise value of the parameter λ. Furthermore, the stability properties of the equilibrium point will also depend on the value of λ. At certain values of λ the characteristics of the system change, sometimes quite dramatically. In other words, the qualitative behaviour of the system either side of such values is quite different. These points are called **bifurcation points**. The types of bifurcations encountered in dynamic systems are often named according to the type of graph they exhibit, e.g., cusp bifurcation and pitchfork bifurcation, to name just two. But such classifications will become clearer once we have described how to construct a bifurcation diagram. As we shall note in a moment when we consider the two examples in detail, for certain values of the parameter λ a system may settle down to a periodic cycle: cycles of 2, 4, 8, etc. or cycles of odd-numbered periods, like 3. However, there comes a point, a value of λ beyond which there is no regular cycle of any period. When this happens the system becomes irregular or **chaotic**. As we shall see, the bifurcation diagram is most useful in showing the occurrence of chaotic behaviour of dynamic systems.

Example 7.1

We shall now consider the first example in detail to highlight some points about bifurcation theory, and consider the logistic equation in detail in the next section. First, we need to establish the fixed points of the system. These are found by solving

$$x^* = 1.5x^*(1 - x^*) - \lambda$$

or solving

$$15x^{*2} - 5x^* + 10\lambda = 0$$

i.e.

$$x^* = \frac{1 \pm \sqrt{1 - 24\lambda}}{6}$$

If $1 - 24\lambda < 0$, i.e., $\lambda > 1/24$, then no equilibrium exists. If $1 - 24\lambda > 0$, i.e., $\lambda < 1/24$, then two equilibria exist

$$x_1^* = \frac{1 - \sqrt{1 - 24\lambda}}{6} \quad \text{and} \quad x_2^* = \frac{1 + \sqrt{1 - 24\lambda}}{6}$$

---

[1] The first example is adapted from Sandefur (1990), while the second example has been widely investigated by mathematicians. A good starting point, however, is May (1976).

In order to investigate the stability of these equilibria, we need to consider $f'(x^*)$. This is $f'(x^*) = 1.5 - 3x^*$. Substituting the lower value we have

$$f'(x_1^*) = 1 + 0.5\sqrt{1 - 24\lambda} > 1 \qquad \text{for all } \lambda < 1/24$$

Hence, x_1^* is unstable or repelling.

Next consider the stability of x_2^*

$$f'(x_2^*) = 1 - 0.5\sqrt{1 - 24\lambda} < 1 \qquad \text{for all } \lambda < 1/24$$

The system is stable or attracting if $-1 < f'(x_2^*) < 1$, i.e., if $-0.625 < \lambda < 1/24$ or $-0.625 < \lambda < 0.041667$.

The third and final situation is where $\lambda = 1/24$. In this case the two fixed points are the same with value $1/6$. Furthermore, $f'(1/6) = 1$, and so the stability of this fixed point is inconclusive or semistable. The value $\lambda = 1/24$ is a *bifurcation value*.

We can combine all this information about the equilibrium points and their attraction or repelling on a diagram which has the parameter λ on the horizontal axis, and the equilibrium point x^* on the vertical axis. Such a diagram is called a **bifurcation diagram**, and such a diagram is shown in figure 7.1 for the present problem. It is to be noted that the heavy (continuous and dotted) line denoting the equilibrium values for various values of the parameter λ is a parabola, which satisfies the equation

$$(6x^* - 1)^2 = 1 - 24\lambda$$

Figure 7.1.

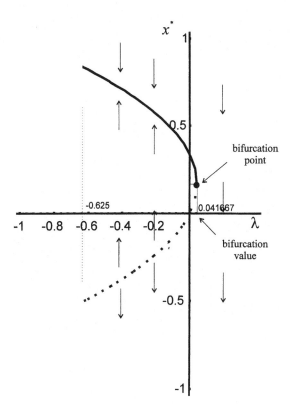

with vertex $(\lambda, x^*) = (1/24, 1/6)$ occurring at the bifurcation value $\lambda = 1/24$ with corresponding equilibrium value $x^* = 1/6$. The vertical arrows show the stability properties of the equilibria. Notice that inside the parabola the arrows point up while outside of the parabola the arrows point down. In particular, for $\lambda > 1/24$ the system will tend to minus infinity; if $\lambda = 1/24$ then there is only one equilibrium value $(x^* = 1/6)$ which is semistable *from above*; and if $-0.625 < \lambda < 0.041667$ then there are two equilibrium values, the greater one of which is stable and the lower one unstable.

We can be more precise. Let N_λ denote the number of equilibrium values of the system when the parameter is equal to λ, then for any interval $(\lambda_0 - \varepsilon, \lambda_0 + \varepsilon)$ if N_λ is not constant, λ_0 is called a **bifurcation value**, and the system is said to undergo a **bifurcation** as λ passes through λ_0. For the example we have been discussing

(7.3)
$$N_\lambda = \begin{cases} 2, & \text{for } \lambda < 1/24 \\ 1, & \text{for } \lambda = 1/24 \\ 0, & \text{for } \lambda > 1/24 \end{cases}$$

and so $\lambda = 1/24$ is a bifurcation. Furthermore, this is the only value of λ for which N_λ is not a constant, and so the system has just this one bifurcation value.

Figure 7.1 also illustrates what is called a **saddle node bifurcation**. It is called this because at the value λ_0 the fixed points of the system form a U-shaped curve that is opened (in this instance opened to the left).

Example 7.2 (saddle-node bifurcation)

In this example we shall take a similar case, but consider a continuous model. Let

(7.4)
$$x'(t) = \lambda - x(t)^2$$

For equilibrium we have

$$0 = \lambda - x^{*2}$$
$$x^* = \sqrt{\lambda}$$

If $\lambda < 0$ then no equilibrium exists. For $\lambda > 0$ there are two fixed points one for $+\sqrt{\lambda}$ and another for $-\sqrt{\lambda}$. In order to consider the stability conditions for continuous systems we need to consider $f'(x^*)$ in the neighbourhood of the fixed point. If $f'(x^*) < 0$, then x^* is locally stable; and if $f'(x^*) > 0$, then x^* is locally unstable. Since $f'(x^*) = -2x^*$, then $f'(x_1^*) = f'(+\sqrt{\lambda}) = -2\sqrt{\lambda} < 0$ for $\lambda > 0$, and so $x_1^* = +\sqrt{\lambda}$ is stable. On the other hand, $f'(x_2^*) = f'(-\sqrt{\lambda}) = +2\sqrt{\lambda} > 0$ for $\lambda > 0$, and so $x_2^* = -\sqrt{\lambda}$ is unstable. At $\lambda = 0$ the two fixed points coincide and the fixed point is stable from above. The situation is shown in figure 7.2.

Summarising in the neighbourhood of the point $\lambda = 0$,

(7.5)
$$N_\lambda = \begin{cases} 2, & \text{for } \lambda > 0 \\ 1, & \text{for } \lambda = 0 \\ 0, & \text{for } \lambda < 0 \end{cases}$$

and once again we have a saddle node bifurcation occurring this time at $\lambda = 0$.

Figure 7.2.

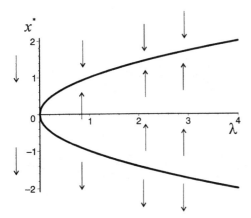

Example 7.3 (transcritical bifurcation)

Consider another example of a continuous nonlinear dynamical system

$$x'(t) = \lambda x - x^2 = x(\lambda - x) \tag{7.6}$$

with fixed points

$$x_1^* = 0 \qquad \text{and} \qquad x_2^* = \lambda$$

Obviously, the two fixed points become identical if $\lambda = 0$. Summarising in the neighbourhood of $\lambda = 0$, we have

$$N_\lambda = \begin{cases} 2, & \text{for } \lambda < 0 \\ 1, & \text{for } \lambda = 0 \\ 2, & \text{for } \lambda > 0 \end{cases} \tag{7.7}$$

and so $\lambda = 0$ is a bifurcation value.

Turning to the stability properties, we have $f'(x^*) = \lambda - 2x^*$ and

$$f'(0) = \lambda \begin{cases} > 0 \text{ for } \lambda > 0 \text{ hence unstable} \\ < 0 \text{ for } \lambda < 0 \text{ hence stable} \end{cases}$$

For the second fixed point we have

$$f'(\lambda) = -\lambda \begin{cases} < 0 \text{ for } \lambda > 0 \text{ hence stable} \\ > 0 \text{ for } \lambda < 0 \text{ hence unstable} \end{cases}$$

Another way to view this is to consider $x_1^* = 0$ being represented by the horizontal axis in figure 7.3, and $x_2^* = \lambda$ being represented by the 45°-line. The two branches intersect at the origin and there takes place an *exchange of stability*. This is called a **transcritical bifurcation**. The characteristic feature of this bifurcation point is that the fixed points of the system lie on two intersecting curves, neither of which bends back on themselves (unlike the saddle-node bifurcation).

Figure 7.3.

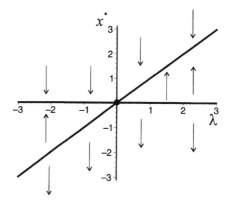

Example 7.4 (pitchfork bifurcation)

Consider the following continuous nonlinear dynamical system

(7.8) $$x'(t) = \lambda x(t) - x(t)^3 = x(t)(\lambda - x(t)^2)$$

This system has three critical points:

$$x_1^* = 0, \qquad x_2^* = +\sqrt{\lambda} \qquad x_3^* = -\sqrt{\lambda}$$

where the second and third fixed points are defined only for positive λ. Summarising in the neighbourhood of $\lambda = 0$ we have

(7.9) $$N_\lambda = \begin{cases} 1 \text{ for } \lambda \leq 0 \\ 3 \text{ for } \lambda > 0 \end{cases}$$

and so $\lambda = 0$ is a bifurcation value.

Since $f'(x^*) = \lambda - 3x^{*2}$, then at each fixed point we have

$$f'(0) = \lambda \begin{cases} < 0 \text{ for } \lambda < 0 \text{ hence stable} \\ > 0 \text{ for } \lambda > 0 \text{ hence unstable} \end{cases}$$

$$f'(+\sqrt{\lambda}) = -2\lambda < 0 \text{ for } \lambda > 0 \text{ hence stable}$$

$$f'(-\sqrt{\lambda}) = -2\lambda < 0 \text{ for } \lambda > 0 \text{ hence stable}$$

The characteristic feature of this bifurcation is that at the origin we have a U-shaped curve, which here is open to the right, and another along the horizontal axis that crosses the vertex of the U. It forms the shape of a pitchfork, as shown in figure 7.4. It is therefore called a **pitchfork bifurcation**.[2]

It is important to recall in all this discussion of bifurcation points that the properties, especially the stability/instability properties, are defined only for neighbourhoods of the bifurcation point. There may be other bifurcation points belonging to the system with different properties.

---

[2] Example 7.4 illustrates what is sometimes referred to as a 'supercritical pitchfork'. If we have the same continuous nonlinear system but with $-x^3$ replaced with $+x^3$, then we have a 'subcritical pitchfork'.

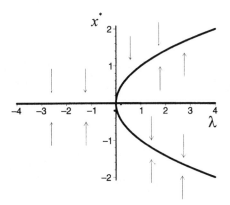

Figure 7.4.

7.3 The logistic equation, periodic-doubling bifurcations and chaos

Chaos theory is a new and growing branch of mathematics that has some important implications for economic systems. As an introduction to this subject return to the generic form of the logistic difference equation

$$x_{t+1} = f(x_t, \lambda) = \lambda x_t(1 - x_t) \quad 0 \le \lambda \le 4 \tag{7.10}$$

For this generic form of the logistic equation x must lie in the closed interval $[0,1]$. But this places an upper limit on the value of λ. To see this, first establish the value of x at which f is a maximum. This is

$$f'(x) = \lambda - 2\lambda x = 0$$
$$x = \frac{1}{2}$$

At this value of x, $f(\frac{1}{2}) = \lambda/4$ and since x cannot exceed 1, then λ cannot exceed 4. Therefore the generic logistic equation is defined for $0 \le \lambda \le 4$.

It would appear that this simple nonlinear equation would show an orbit, a time path $\{x_t\}$, which would be quite simple. As figure 7.5 shows, however, this is far from true. In this figure we have drawn the orbit for 100 periods for three different values of λ, (a) $\lambda = 3.2$, (b) $\lambda = 3.85$ and (c) $\lambda = 4$. In each case the initial value is $x_0 = 0.1$. In figure 7.5(a) the time path settles down to a two-cycle very quickly. When $\lambda = 3.85$ there is some initial chaotic behaviour, but then the series settles down to a three-cycle. This is an example of *transient chaos* (Hommes 1991). In figure 7.5(c) there is no periodic behaviour shown at all. The series is **aperiodic** or **chaotic**. It is apparent, therefore, that this simple equation can exhibit very different time paths depending on the value of λ. The question is can we identify when the system changes from one type of orbit into another? Put another way, can we identify any bifurcation points for the logistic equation?

In order to do this, first establish the equilibrium points where $x_{t+1} = x_t = x^*$ for all t. This is where

$$x^* = \lambda x^*(1 - x^*)$$
$$\lambda x^{*2} + (1 - \lambda)x^* = 0$$
$$x^*[\lambda x^* + (1 - \lambda)] = 0$$

Figure 7.5.

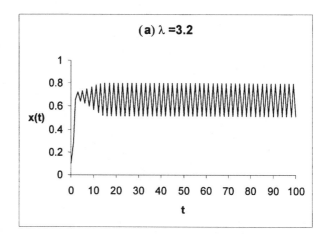

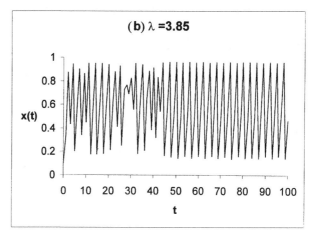

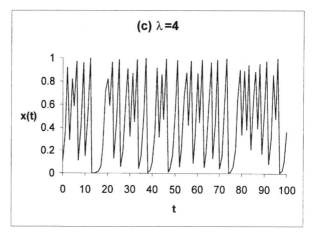

i.e.

$$x^* = 0 \quad \text{or} \quad x^* = \frac{\lambda - 1}{\lambda} \tag{7.11}$$

To investigate the stability of these solutions we shall employ the linear approximation discussed in chapters 2 and 3, namely

$$x_{t+1} = f(x^*, \lambda) + f'(x^*, \lambda)(x_t - x^*)$$

But $f(x^*, \lambda) = 0$ or $f(x^*, \lambda) = (\lambda - 1)/\lambda$, and $f'(x^*, \lambda) = \lambda - 2\lambda x^*$. Thus,

$$f'(x^*, \lambda) = \begin{cases} \lambda \text{ for } x^* = 0 \\ 2 - \lambda \text{ for } x^* = \dfrac{\lambda - 1}{\lambda} \end{cases}$$

Consider $x^* = 0$. Then we have

$$x_{t+1} = \lambda x_t$$

with solution

$$x_t = \lambda^t x_0$$

which is stable if $0 < \lambda < 1$. Next consider $x^* = (\lambda - 1)/\lambda$, then

$$x_{t+1} = x^* + (2 - \lambda)(x_t - x^*)$$
$$\text{or} \quad u_{t+1} = (2 - \lambda)u_t$$

where $u_{t+1} = x_{t+1} - x^*$ and $u_t = x_t - x^*$. This has the solution

$$u_t = (2 - \lambda)^t u_0$$

which is stable so long as $|2 - \lambda| < 1$ or $-1 < 2 - \lambda < 1$, giving a range for λ of $1 < \lambda < 3$.

What we observe is that for $0 \le \lambda < 1$ the only solution is $x^* = 0$ and this is locally stable. For $1 < \lambda < 3$ we have an equilibrium solution $x^* = (\lambda - 1)/\lambda$, which varies with λ. The situation is shown in figure 7.6. At $\lambda = 1$, where the two solution curves intersect, there is an *exchange of stability* from one equilibrium solution to the other.

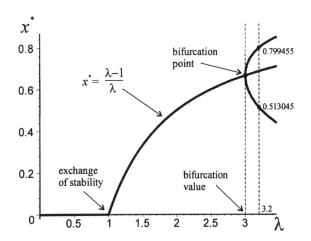

Figure 7.6.

Figure 7.7.

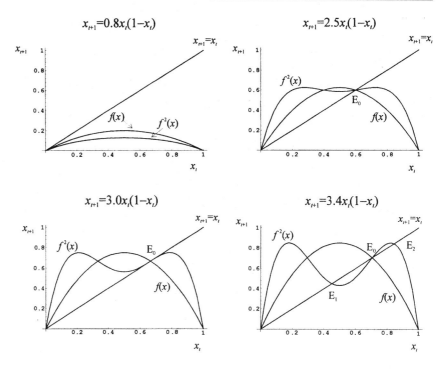

Of course, λ is not necessarily restricted to a range below 3. The question is: What happens to the solution values as λ is allowed to increase? We began to answer this question in chapter 3. In section 3.9 we investigated the range for λ that led to a two-cycle result. This range we established as $3 < \lambda < 3.449$. In other words, at $\lambda = 3$ the solution becomes unstable but gives rise to a stable two-cycle result, as shown in figure 7.6. Consequently, the value $\lambda = 3$ is a dividing value between a unique solution (other than zero) and a two-cycle solution. The value $\lambda = 3$ is a pitchfork bifurcation.[3] Again, the actual values of the two limit points depend on the precise value of λ. For example, in section 3.9 we established the two limit values of 0.799455 and 0.513045 for $\lambda = 3.2$ (see also appendices 3.1 and 3.2).

The reason for this apparent instability of one solution and the occurrence of a stable two-cycle is illustrated in figure 7.7(a)–(d), where $f(x) = \lambda x(1 - x)$ and $f^2(x) = f(f(x))$. In figure 7.7(a) $\lambda = 0.8$ and so the only solution is $x^* = 0$. Any (positive) value x_0 'close to' zero will be attracted to $x^* = 0$. Also note that the two-cycle curve $f^2(x)$ lies wholly below the 45°-line and so no two-cycles occur. For this solution, $f'(x^* = 0, \lambda = 0.8) = 0.8 < 1$, and so $x^* = 0$ is stable. In figure 7.7(b) $\lambda = 2.5$ and we have solution $x^* = (\lambda - 1)/\lambda = 0.6$ and $f'(x^* = 0.6, \lambda = 2.5) = 2 - 2.5 = -0.5$, with $|f'(x^* = 0.6, \lambda = 2.5)| < 1$ and so $x^* = 0.6$ is stable. Also note that $f^2(x)$ cuts the 45°-line just once, at E_0 and so no two-cycles occur. The situation begins to change in figure 7.7(c) where $\lambda = 3$. Here $x^* = (\lambda - 1)/\lambda = 2/3$ and $f'(x^* = 2/3, \lambda = 3) = 2 - 3 = -1$, and so $x^* = 2/3$ is semistable. The fact that $f'(x^* = 2/3, \lambda = 3) = -1$ is semistable is shown in figure 7.7(c) by the feature that the two-cycle $f^2(x)$ is *tangent* to the 45°-line at point E_0. Because

---

[3] It is sometimes called a **period-doubling bifurcation**, since it denotes the value of λ at which a stable two-period cycle occurs.

Figure 7.8.

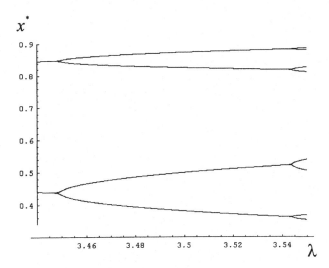

$x^* = 2/3$ lies on $f(x)$ where this intersects the 45°-line, then it is stable for $\lambda < 3$. However if $\lambda > 3$ then $f^2(x)$ begins to intersect the 45°-line in three places. The instability of the single solution and the stability of the two-cycle is more clearly shown in figure 7.7(d), where $\lambda = 3.4$. A number of features should be noted about this figure. First, $f(x)$ and $f^2(x)$ intersect at the common point $E_0 = 0.70588$. This is unstable. We can establish this by computing $f^{2'}(x_0^*)$, which has a value of 1.96, and since $f^{2'}(x_0^*) > 1$, $x_0^* = 0.70588$ is unstable. Second, there are two stable equilibrium points E_1 and E_2 with the following characteristics

$$E_1: \quad x_1^* = 0.451963 \quad f'(x^*, \lambda) = -0.76$$
$$E_2: \quad x_2^* = 0.842154 \quad f'(x^*, \lambda) = -0.76$$

since $f^{2'}(x_1^*) = f^{2'}(x_2^*) = -0.76$, then both E_1 and E_2 are stable. However, at $\lambda = 3.449$ the two-cycle becomes unstable.

But what occurs at and beyond the point where $\lambda = 3.449$? What occurs is two period-doubling bifurcation points, i.e., each of the two solutions themselves become unstable but divide into two stable solutions, leading to a total of four solutions. In other words, we have a four-cycle solution. The range for a four-cycle result can be found in a similar manner to the range for a two-cycle result, i.e., by finding the values of a which satisfy the equation

$$a = f(f(f(f(a)))) \qquad \text{or} \qquad a = f^4(a) \tag{7.12}$$

and whose stability is established by solving[4]

$$-1 < f'(a_1)f'(a_2)f'(a_3)f'(a_4) < 1 \tag{7.13}$$

This is even more tedious than the two-cycle result, and can only sensibly be solved with the help of a computer. However, we illustrate the result over the range $3.44 < \lambda < 3.55$ in figure 7.8.

Figure 7.8 shows that the four-cycle itself becomes unstable and bifurcates into an eight-cycle. What is more surprising, however, is that the value of λ at which

---

[4] See theorem 3.2, p. 93 and appendices 3.1 and 3.2.

Figure 7.9.

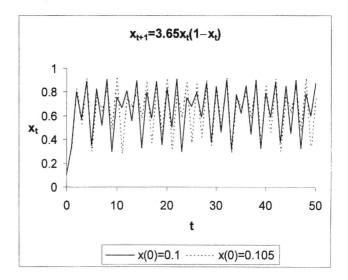

further bifurcations occur approaches a limit of approximately $\lambda = 3.57$. After this value, the system exhibits **chaotic behaviour**, i.e., behaviour that, although generated by a deterministic system, has all the characteristics of random behaviour. There are no regular cycles. A typical situation is illustrated in figure 7.9 for $\lambda = 3.65$. In this figure we plot the series

(7.14) $$x_{t+1} = 3.65x_t(1 - x_t)$$

for two different starting values: $x_0 = 0.1$ and $x_0 = 0.105$. These starting values are very close to one another, however, the two systems diverge from one another after about ten periods. This is because of the chaotic nature of the system. With chaotic systems we have *sensitive dependence to initial conditions*.

But another characteristic arises in the case of a series entering the chaotic region for its parameter value. Consider the following example provided by Baumol and Benhabib (1989):

(7.15) $$x_{t+1} = 3.94x_t(1 - x_t) \qquad x_0 = 0.99$$

whose graph is derived using a spreadsheet, and shown in figure 7.10. Although the series is chaotic, it is not purely random, and in particular exhibits sudden changes. In figure 7.10 the series suddenly changes from showing an oscillatory behaviour to one that is almost horizontal (which it does for about ten periods) and then just as suddenly, and for no obvious reason, begins to oscillate once again.

For the logistic curve the characteristics listed in table 7.1 have been established. It should be noted that a three-period cycle is also present, and first shows itself at the point $\lambda = 3.8284$. In fact, we derived a three-period cycle in chapter 3 (p. 97). Just as there are repeating even-numbered cycles, so there are repeated odd-numbered cycles. Two- and three-period cycles (and even a four-period cycle) can be shown quite clearly using the cobweb diagram we will develop in chapter 8. On the vertical axis we have x_{t+1} and on the horizontal axis x_t. The 45°-line represents the equilibrium condition with $x_{t+1} = x_t$. The curve is $f(x_t) = \lambda x_t(1 - x_t)$. If $\lambda = 3.2$ and $x_0 = 0.513045$ a two-cycle results, as shown in figure 7.11(a). On the other hand, if $\lambda = 3.839$ and $x_0 = 0.48912$ then a stable three-cycle results, as shown in

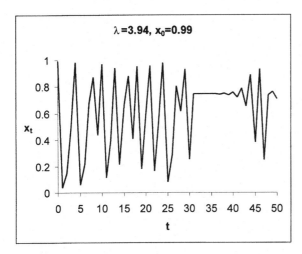

$\lambda=3.94, x_0=0.99$

Table 7.1 Properties of the logistic curve

Description	Value of λ	Comments
Exchange of stability	1	First bifurcation point
Fixed point becomes unstable (2-cycles appear)	3	Second bifurcation point e.g. $\lambda = 3.2$, section 3.9, p. 118
2-cycle becomes unstable (4-cycles appear)	3.44949	Established in section 3.9
4-cycle becomes unstable (8-cycles appear)	3.54409	
Upper limit value on 2-cycles (chaos begins)	3.57	
First odd-cycle appears	3.6786	
Cycles with period 3 appear	3.8284	e.g. $\lambda = 3.84$, section 3.9, p. 118
Chaotic regions ends	4	

figure 7.11(b). When $\lambda = 3.59$ and $x_0 = 0.4$ many periods occur (figure 7.11(c)), but the values that x takes are bounded. When $\lambda = 4$ and $x_0 = 0.2$ then the series is chaotic. This is revealed in figure 7.11(d) by the fact that all values of x in the closed interval [0,1] occur, i.e., the web covers the whole possible graph.

What we observe, then, is that from a very simple deterministic equation a whole spectrum of patterns emerge, and in particular an apparent random series arises for a parameter value of $\lambda > 3.57$.

With such a diversity of equilibrium solutions depending on the value of λ, it would be interesting to know what the bifurcation diagram for the logistic equation would look like over the range $0 \leq \lambda \leq 4$. We need to plot the relationship between x^* and λ between the values of 0 and 4. Before the advent of computers, this would be virtually impossible, but now it is relatively easy. The result is shown in figure 7.12,[5] while a closer look at the range $3 \leq \lambda \leq 4$ is shown in figure 7.13. Notice in figure 7.13 the 'windows' occurring. Three are marked on the diagram. The first window marked is for the occurrence of a six-period cycle; the second is the occurrence of a five-period cycle, while the third is for a three-period cycle.

---

[5] The bifurcation diagram plots only stable equilibrium points, so in the range $3 < \lambda < 3.449$ only two curves are plotted. The bifurcation point $\lambda = 3$ is not a saddle node bifurcation but rather a pitchfork bifurcation, as shown in figure 7.6. It is therefore more useful to think of this point as a *period-doubling bifurcation*.

Figure 7.11.

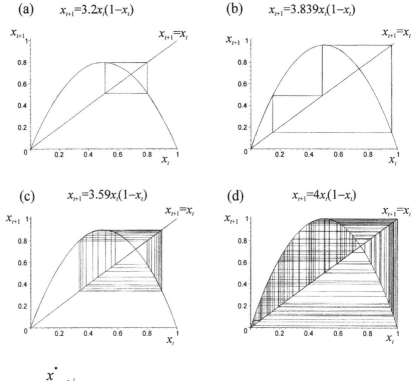

(a) $x_{t+1}=3.2x_t(1-x_t)$

(b) $x_{t+1}=3.839x_t(1-x_t)$

(c) $x_{t+1}=3.59x_t(1-x_t)$

(d) $x_{t+1}=4x_t(1-x_t)$

Figure 7.12.

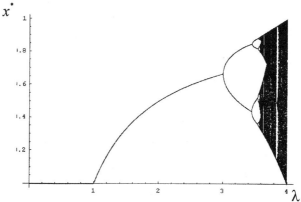

Such windows represent stable periodic orbits that are surrounded by chaotic behaviour (the dark regions).

These two diagrams show an amazing diversity of equilibria for such a simple deterministic equation. Such results direct attention to three observations:

(1)   the presence of nonlinearity can give rise to deterministic chaos,
(2)   in the presence of chaos there exists the sensitive dependence to initial conditions, and
(3)   in the presence of chaos prediction, even for a simple deterministic system, is virtually impossible.

Bifurcation diagrams require a considerable amount of routine computations and there are now a growing supply of such routines written by mathematicians

Figure 7.13.

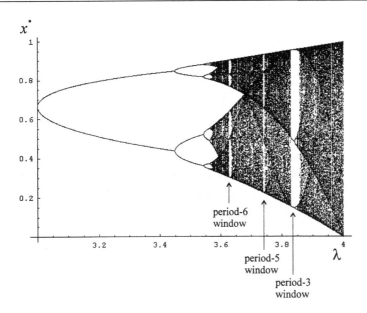

and computer programmers, both in *Mathematica* and *Maple*. This is also true of strange attractors, such as the Hénon map and the Lorenz strange attractor, which we discuss in section 7.7. The interested reader should consult the various sources at the end of this chapter. In general for the present text, the bifurcation diagrams in *Mathematica* utilise the routine provided by Gray and Glynn (1991), while a number of the chaos diagrams in *Maple* utilise the routines provided by Lynch (2001).[6]

7.4 Feigenbaum's universal constant

In discussing the logistic equation we noted that the first bifurcation occurred at value 3, the second at value $1 + \sqrt{6} = 3.44949$, while a third occurs at value 3.54409. We can think of these values as representing the point at which a 2^k-cycle first appears. Thus

$$\text{for } k = 0 \text{ a } 2^0\text{-cycle occurs at } \lambda_0 = 3$$
$$\text{for } k = 1 \text{ a } 2^1\text{-cycle occurs at } \lambda_1 = 1 + \sqrt{6} = 3.44949$$
$$\text{for } k = 2 \text{ a } 2^2\text{-cycle occurs at } \lambda_2 = 3.54409$$

and so on. If λ_k denotes such occurrences of a 2^k-cycle, then three results have been shown to hold for large k:

(i) $\lambda_{k+1} \approx 1 + \sqrt{3 + \lambda_k} \quad k = 2, 3, \dots$

(ii) $\lim_{k \to \infty} \lambda_k = 3.57$

(iii)   If $d_k = \dfrac{\lambda_k - \lambda_{k-1}}{\lambda_{k+1} - \lambda_k} \quad k = 2, 3, 4, \dots$

      then $\lim_{k \to \infty} d_k = \delta = 4.669202$

---

[6] The printing of such diagrams can be problematic and will certainly depend on the internal RAM of the printer.

Table 7.2 Approximations for the occurrence of the 2*k*-cycle

k	0	1	2	3	4	5	6
λ_k	3	3.44949	3.54409	3.56441	3.56876	3.56969	3.56989
d_k		4.75148	4.655512	4.671264	4.677419	4.65	

δ is called the Feigenbaum constant after its discoverer, and is important because it is a universal constant.

The first result is only approximate, and there are a number of ways of approximating the value of λ_{k+1} (see exercise 2). Although these approximations are supposed to hold only for large k, they are reasonable even for small k. Using a procedure provided by Gray and Glynn (1991, p. 125) we derive a more accurate estimate of the two-cycle bifurcation points. In particular, table 7.2 provides the first seven points and computes λ_k and d_k. As can be seen, λ_k is rapidly approaching the limit of 3.57, while d_k approaches the limit of 4.6692, although not so rapidly and not uniformly.

7.5 Sarkovskii theorem

In this section we have a very limited objective. Our intention is to present the background concepts necessary to understand the significance of the Sarkovskii theorem, which is central to periodic orbits of nonlinear systems. The ideas and concepts are explained by means of the logistic equation, most of the properties of which we have already outlined.

In table 7.3 we list the first 30 positive integers, where we have expressed some of the numbers in a way useful for interpreting a Sarkovskii ordering.

Using the numbers in table 7.3 as a guide, we can identify the following series, where $a \succ b$ means a precedes b in the order and 'odd number' means the odd numbers except unity (table 7.4).

Every possibly positive integer is accounted for only once by all series taken together.

A Sarkovskii ordering is then

$$S_0 \succ S_1 \succ S_2 \succ \ldots \succ S_k \succ \ldots \succ 2^4 \succ 2^3 \succ 2^2 \succ 2 \succ 1$$

We are now in a position to state the theorem.

THEOREM 7.1 (Sarkovskii)
Let f be a continuous function defined over a closed interval $[a,b]$ which has a periodic point with prime period n. If $n \succ m$ in a Sarkovskii ordering, then f also has a periodic point with prime period m.

Another theorem occurring just over a decade later is the following.[7]

---

[7] Sarkovskii's paper of 1964 was not known to Western mathematicians until the publication of Li and Yorke's paper in 1975.

Table 7.3 Expressing the first 30 integers for a Sarkovskii ordering

1			11		21	
2			12	$2^2.3$	22	2.11
3			13		23	
4	2^2		14	2.7	24	$2^3.3$
5			15		25	
6	2.3		16	2^4	26	2.13
7			17		27	
8	2^3		18	2.9	28	$2^2.7$
9			19		29	
10	2.5		20	$2^2.5$	30	2.15

Table 7.4 The series of a Sarkovskii ordering

Series	Numbers in the series	Description of the series
S_0	$3 \succ 5 \succ 7 \succ \ldots$	odd numbers
S_1	$2.3 \succ 2.5 \succ 2.7 \succ \ldots$	2.(odd numbers)
S_2	$2^2.3 \succ 2^2.5 \succ 2^2.7 \succ \ldots$	2^2.(odd numbers)
$\vdots$	$\vdots$	$\vdots$
S_k	$2^k.3 \succ 2^k.5 \succ 2^k.7 \succ \ldots$	2^k.(odd numbers)
–	$\succ 2^4 \succ 2^3 \succ 2^2 \succ 2 \succ 1$	Powers of 2 in descending order*

Note: *Recall $2^1 = 2$ and $2^0 = 1$.

THEOREM 7.2 (Li–Yorke)

If a one-dimensional system can generate a three-cycle then it can generate cycles of every length along with chaotic behaviour.

The Li–Yorke theorem is a corollary of the Sarkovskii theorem. If $m = 3$ in the Sarkovskii theorem, then $n = 5$, say ($n \succ m$) also has a periodic point. Therefore for all $n \succ m$ f will have a periodic point. Hence, if a one-dimensional system can generate a three-cycle, it must be capable of generating a cycle of any length.

The windows in figure 7.13 represent period-6, period-5 and period-3 cycles, respectively. The period-5 lies to the left of period-3, with period-3 being the highest ordering. But why is period-6 to the left of period-5? Period-6 is equivalent to period-2.3 in the Sarkovskii ordering and so belongs to the series S_1. All periods in S_1 are to the left of all periods in S_0. Hence, period-6 is to the left of period-5, which in turn is to the left of period-3.

Suppose a continuous function f over the closed interval $[a,b]$ has a period-5 cycle, then according to the Sarkovskii theorem it has cycles of all periods with the possible exception of period-3. Notice that the possibility of a period-3 is not ruled out. Similarly, if f has no point of period-2, then there do not exist higher-order periodicities, including chaos.

The Sarkovskii theorem, and to some extent the Li–Yorke theorem, demonstrates that even systems that exhibit chaotic behaviour still have a *structure*. The word 'chaos' conjures up purely unsystematic patterns and unpredictability. Although the movement of an individual series may be aperiodic, chaotic systems themselves have structural characteristics that can be identified.

7.6   Van der Pol equation and Hopf bifurcations

We met the Van der Pol equation in chapter 4 when we considered limit points. In this section our interest is in the Van der Pol equation and its bifurcation features. The nonlinear equation is a second-order differential equation of the form

(7.16)
$$\ddot{x} = \mu(1 - x^2)\dot{x} - x$$

Second-order differential equations can be expressed in the form of a system of first-order differential equations with suitable transformations. Let $\dot{x} = y$ then $\dot{y} = \ddot{x}$, hence we have the system of first-order equations:

(7.17)
$$\dot{x} = y$$
$$\dot{y} = \mu(1 - x^2)y - x$$

and the only unknown parameter is μ. The fixed points of the system are established by setting $\dot{x} = 0$ and $\dot{y} = 0$, which is the singular point $P = (0, 0)$. Furthermore, the linearisation of the system can be expressed as

$$\begin{bmatrix} \dot{x} \\ \dot{y} \end{bmatrix} = \begin{bmatrix} 1 & 0 \\ -(1 + 2\mu xy) & \mu(1 - x^2) \end{bmatrix} \begin{bmatrix} x \\ y \end{bmatrix}$$

Expanding the system around the fixed-point, $P = (0, 0)$, we have

$$\begin{bmatrix} \dot{x} \\ \dot{y} \end{bmatrix} = \begin{bmatrix} 1 & 0 \\ -1 & \mu \end{bmatrix} \begin{bmatrix} x \\ y \end{bmatrix}$$

Hence the matrix of the linearised system is

$$\mathbf{A} = \begin{bmatrix} 1 & 0 \\ -1 & \mu \end{bmatrix}$$

whose eigenvalues are

(7.18)
$$\lambda_1 = \frac{\mu - \sqrt{\mu^2 - 4}}{2} \quad \text{and} \quad \lambda_2 = \frac{\mu + \sqrt{\mu^2 - 4}}{2}$$

Using these eigenvalues we can identify five cases, as shown in table 7.5. Figure 7.14 illustrates each of these cases.

If we concentrate on the equilibrium values for x and y, say x^* and y^*, then for $\mu < 0, x^* = 0$ and $y^* = 0$ and the system moves along the μ-axis. At $\mu = 0$ the system changes dramatically taking on the shape of a circle at this value. Then, as μ continues in the positive direction the system takes on a limit cycle in the x-y plane for any particular positive value of μ, the shape of which is no longer a circle. All of these are schematically illustrated in figure 7.15, which also shows the movement of the system by means of arrows. Clearly the system exhibits a bifurcation at the value $\mu = 0$. This is an example of a **Hopf bifurcation**.

Table 7.5 Properties of the Van der Pol equation

Cases	Parameter values	Properties
I	$\mu \leq -2$	both eigenvalues are real and negative, P is a *stable node*
II	$-2 < \mu < 0$	eigenvalues are complex with negative real parts, P is a *stable focus*
III	$\mu = 0$	eigenvalues are purely imaginary, P is a *centre*
IV	$0 < \mu < 2$	eigenvalues are complex, with positive real parts, P is an *unstable focus*
V	$\mu \geq 2$	both eigenvalues are real and positive, P is an *unstable node*

Figure 7.14.

(a) Stable node ($\mu = -2.5$)

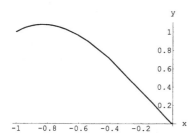

(b) Stable focus ($\mu = -0.5$)

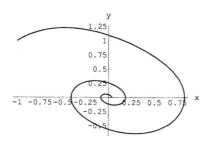

(c) Centre ($\mu = 0$)

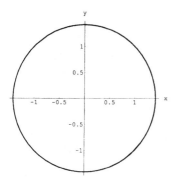

(d) Unstable focus ($\mu = 0.5$)

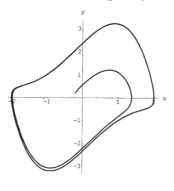

(e) Stable node ($\mu = 2.5$)

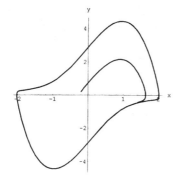

Figure 7.15.

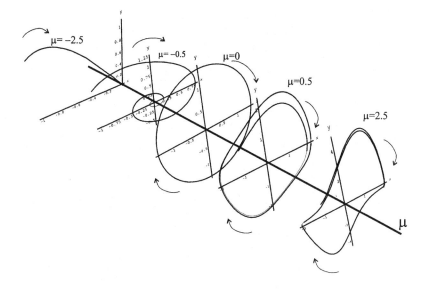

More generally, a Hopf bifurcation occurs when there is a change in the stability of a fixed point into a limit cycle. Clearly a limit cycle can occur only if the system is defined for two variables and at least one parameter. All these conditions are satisfied by the Van der Pol equation. As μ passes through $\mu = 0$, the system changes from a stable equilibrium at the origin for $\mu < 0$ into a limit cycle for $\mu \geq 0$. Hence $\mu = 0$ gives rise to a Hopf bifurcation that occurs at the origin in the (x,y)-plane.

There are in fact two types of Hopf bifurcations, one in which the limit cycles are created about a stable point (a *subcritical Hopf bifurcation*) and one in which the limit cycles are created around an unstable critical point (a *supercritical Hopf bifurcation*).

Limit cycles of finite amplitude may also suddenly appear as the parameter of the system is varied. In the physical sciences such *large-amplitude limit cycles* are more common than supercritical Hopf bifurcations (Lynch 2001). More importantly for economics, these systems exhibit multiple stable equilibria for which the system may jump from one stable equilibrium to another as the parameter of the system is varied. Equally significant for economics is that the existence of multistable solutions allows for the possibility of **hysteresis**.

Example 7.5 (Large-amplitude limit cycle bifurcation)[8]

Consider the system

$$\dot{x} = x(\lambda + x^2 - x^4)$$
$$\dot{y} = -1$$

(7.19)

For system (7.19) the only critical point is $x^* = 0$. Let $f(x) = x(\lambda + x^2 - x^4)$ then $f'(x) = \lambda + 3x^2 - 5x^4$ and $f'(x^* = 0) = \lambda$. Therefore the critical point $x^* = 0$ is

[8] Lynch (2001).

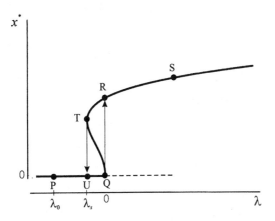

Figure 7.16.

stable for $\lambda < 0$ and unstable for $\lambda > 0$. The system undergoes a subcritical Hopf bifurcation at $\lambda = 0$. However, for a certain range of λ, say $\lambda > \lambda_s$, the system also has a stable large-amplitude limit cycle. The bifurcation diagram for this system is illustrated in figure 7.16.[9]

As can be seen in figure 7.16, over the range $\lambda_s < \lambda < 0$, there exist two steady-state solutions. A number of important implications follow from this feature. First, which steady state is approached depends on the initial conditions. If the equations represented some economic system, then in all probability the welfare attached to one of the stable equilibrium would be quite different from that of the other. Policy-makers may, therefore, attempt to push the system in the direction of one particular stable equilibrium by changing the initial conditions. Second, the system exhibits hysteresis. Suppose the value of λ started at $\lambda_0 < \lambda_s$, figure 7.16. As λ is increased then x remains at $x^* = 0$ until $\lambda = 0$. At $\lambda = 0$, however, there is a sudden jump to the large-amplitude limit cycle. This is so because $\lambda = 0$ is a subcritical Hopf bifurcation. As λ continues to increase, the value of x^* follows the upper path, along RS. The path traversed is then PQRS. Now suppose the value of λ is decreased to its former level λ_0. The system moves down along the upper path SRT. Once $\lambda = \lambda_s$, the system jumps down to $x^* = 0$ (point U) and then remains there as λ is decreased further. The 'return trip' is therefore SRTUP, which is quite different from its outward journey. The system is hysteretic.

7.7 Strange attractors

We noted in the last section how with a two-dimensional system a Hopf bifurcation could arise. In the Van der Pol equation, once $\mu \geq 0$ then the system gets attracted to a limit cycle. But other two- or higher-dimensional systems can have 'strange' attractors. We shall discuss the concept of strange attractors by way of examples. The examples we consider are the Hénon map and the Lorenz attractor.[10]

---

[9] Part of the bifurcation diagram can be constructed using the implicit plot routines in either *Mathematica* or *Maple*. Just do the implicit plot of $\lambda + x^2 - x^4 = 0$ for $-1 < \lambda < 2$ and $0 < x < 2$, and the result is as portrayed in figure 7.16.

[10] See also the Rössler attractor in exercises 9 and 10.

7.7.1   *The Hénon map*

The Hénon map arises from a set of two equations involving two parameters, which are real numbers

(7.20)
$$x_{t+1} = 1 - ax_t^2 + y_t \quad a > 0$$
$$y_{t+1} = bx_t \qquad\qquad |b| < 1$$

We can think of this as the function

(7.21)
$$H_{a,b}(x_t, y_t) = \begin{bmatrix} 1 - ax_t^2 + y_t \\ bx_t \end{bmatrix}$$

or simply H. To establish some of the properties of the Hénon map, let

$$f(x, y) = 1 - ax^2 + y$$
$$g(x, y) = bx$$

Then the Jacobian, **J**, is

$$\mathbf{J} = \begin{bmatrix} f_x & f_y \\ g_x & g_y \end{bmatrix} = \begin{bmatrix} -2ax & 1 \\ b & 0 \end{bmatrix}$$

whose determinant is $-b$ and eigenvalues

$$\lambda = -ax \pm \sqrt{a^2x^2 + b}$$

which is readily obtained using either *Mathematica* or *Maple* – in fact all the mathematical properties we are about to discuss are obtained using either of these software programmes. Hence, the eigenvalues are real only if $\sqrt{a^2x^2 + b} \geq 0$. Furthermore, the fixed points of the Hénon map are found to be

(7.22)
$$P_1 = \begin{cases} x = \dfrac{1}{2a}\left(b - 1 + \sqrt{(1 - b)^2 + 4a}\right) \\[2mm] y = \dfrac{b}{2a}\left(b - 1 + \sqrt{(1 - b)^2 + 4a}\right) \end{cases},$$

$$P_2 = \begin{cases} x = \dfrac{1}{2a}\left(b - 1 - \sqrt{(1 - b)^2 + 4a}\right) \\[2mm] y = \dfrac{b}{2a}\left(b - 1 - \sqrt{(1 - b)^2 + 4a}\right) \end{cases}$$

which exist if $a \geq -\frac{1}{4}(1 - b)^2$.

Turning now to the stability properties of the fixed points, we recall that the fixed point is attracting if the eigenvalue is less than unity in absolute value. It can be established (Gulick 1992, pp. 171–2) that

(1)   If $a < -\frac{1}{4}(1 - b)^2$, then H has no fixed points
(2)   If $-\frac{1}{4}(1 - b)^2 < a < \frac{3}{4}(1 - b)^2$ and $a \neq 0$, then H has two fixed points, P_1 and P_2, of which P_1 is attracting and P_2 is a saddle point

If the parameter b is set fixed over the interval $[0,1]$ and a is allowed to vary, then there will be two bifurcation values for a: one at $-(1 - b)^2/4$ and another at $3(1 - b)^2/4$, with the system changing from an attracting fixed point to one of a saddle point.

Figure 7.17 shows the Hénon map with parameters $a = 1.4$ and $b = 0.3$ and with initial point $(x_0, y_0) = (0.1, 0)$. The two fixed points are $P_1 = (0.6314, 0.1894)$

Figure 7.17.

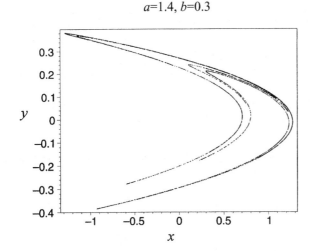

a=1.4, b=0.3

Figure 7.18.

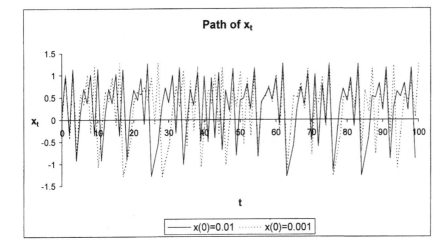

and $P_2 = (-1.1314, -0.3394)$, and the figure illustrates the existence of a strange attractor.

Why then is it called a strange attractor? For $b = 0.3$ the Feigenbaum constant of a for the Hénon map is 1.0580459 (Gulick 1992, p. 173). One would assume that for $a > 1.06$ with chaos present that the iterates would virtually fill the whole map. But this is not the case. For example, given the parameter values $a = 1.4$ and $b = 0.3$, then no matter what the starting values for x and y, the sequence of points $\{x(t), y(t)\}$ is attracted to the orbit shown in figure 7.17, and such an orbit seems rather a 'strange' shape. At the same time, however, the trajectory $\{x(t), y(t)\}$ is very sensitive to initial conditions. This is illustrated in figure 7.18 in the case of variable x, for the same parameter values and $(x_0, y_0) = (0.001, 0)$, where we plot the first 100 observations.[11] So although the two sequences converge on the attractor illustrated in figure 7.17, they approach it quite differently. Because

---

[11] This plot is derived using *Excel* rather than *Mathematica* or *Maple*, since spreadsheets are good for plotting time-series or discrete trajectories quickly and easily. See section 5.5.

this attractor is sensitive to initial conditions, then it is called a *chaotic attractor*. The word 'strange' refers to the geometrical shape of the attractor, while the word 'chaotic' indicates sensitivity to initial conditions and therefore refers to the dynamics of the attractor (Hommes 1991).

We have already noted that when a series is chaotic then it is very sensitive to initial conditions. We have also noted in terms of the Hénon map, that regardless of the initial value, the orbit will settle down to that indicated in figure 7.17 if $a = 1.4$ and $b = 0.3$. Now if two series are chaotic then they will diverge from one another, and such a divergence will increase exponentially, as illustrated in figure 7.18. If it is possible to measure the divergence between two series then we can obtain some measure of chaos. Furthermore, looking at the Hénon map, if we divide the rectangular box into very tiny rectangles then, by means of a computer, it is possible to establish how many times points in the attractor are visited by trajectories of various points. The **Lyapunov dimension** or Lyapunov number does just this. For instance, the Lyapunov number for the Hénon map is 1.26. The following theorem has been demonstrated (Gulick 1992).

THEOREM 7.3

(1)   If an attractor has a non-integer Lyapunov number then it is a strange attractor.

(2)   If an attractor has sensitive dependence on initial conditions then it has a Lyapunov number greater than unity.

The Hénon map satisfies (1), so it is a strange attractor; but it also satisfies (2), so it is also called a **chaotic attractor**. It is possible to have a strange attractor that is not chaotic and a chaotic attractor that is not strange. However, most strange attractors are also chaotic. The Lyapunov dimension is important in the area of empirical chaos, and is used in the economics literature to detect chaos.[12]

7.7.2   The Lorenz attractor

The Lorenz attractor was probably the first strange attractor to be discussed in the literature, and was certainly the origin of the term 'butterfly effect'.[13] The Lorenz system is composed of three differential equations

$$\dot{x} = -\sigma(x - y)$$

(7.23) $$\dot{y} = rx - y - xz$$

$$\dot{z} = xy - bz$$

Solving for the steady state, we obtain three fixed points

$$P_1 = (0, 0, 0)$$

(7.24) $$P_2 = (\sqrt{b(r - 1)}, \sqrt{b(1 - r)}, r - 1)$$

$$P_3 = (-\sqrt{b(r - 1)}, -\sqrt{b(1 - r)}, r - 1)$$

---

[12] There are other measures of chaos, such as Brock's residual test (Brock 1986).

[13] The title of Lorenz's address to the American Association for the Advancement of Sciences in 1979 was: 'Predictability: Does the flap of the butterfly's wings in Brazil set off a tornado in Texas.'

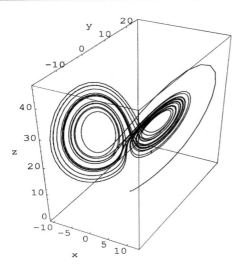

Figure 7.19.

The critical point P_0 holds for all values of r, while critical points P_1 and P_2 only hold for $r \geq 1$, where $P_0 = P_1 = P_2$ for $r = 1$. There is therefore a bifurcation at $r = 1$. As r passes through this value the critical point P_0 bifurcates and the critical points P_1 and P_2 come into existence. A typical plot of the Lorenz system is shown in figure 7.19 for $\sigma = 3$, $r = 26.5$ and $b = 1$. Starting at the value $(x_0, y_0, z_0) = (0, 1, 0)$ the system first gets drawn to point P_2 then after moving around and away from this point it gets drawn to point P_1. This process keeps repeating itself.

In order to consider the stability properties of the Lorenz system we need to consider the linear approximation. The coefficient matrix of the linearised system is

$$\mathbf{A} = \begin{bmatrix} -\sigma & \sigma & 0 \\ r - z & -1 & -x \\ y & x & -b \end{bmatrix}$$

This leads to a set of cubic characteristic equations, one for each of the three critical points. There has been much investigation into the properties of these for various values of the parameters, which is beyond the scope of this book. Asymptotic stability is assured, however, if the real parts of the eigenvalues are negative. It can be shown that if $1 < r < r_H$ where

$$r_H = \frac{\sigma(\sigma + b + 3)}{\sigma - b - 1}$$

then the real parts of the eigenvalues are negative and so the three critical points are asymptotically stable. Furthermore, if $r = r_H$ then two of the roots are imaginary and there occurs a Hopf bifurcation. When $r > r_H$ there is one negative real eigenvalue and two complex eigenvalues with positive real parts and the three critical points are unstable.

Figure 7.20 shows the paths of two Lorenz systems. Both are drawn for $\sigma = 10$ and $b = 8/3$. With these values then $r_H = 24.7368$. In figure 7.20(a) we have $r = 22.4$ with initial point $(7,7,20)$, which is 'close to' the strange attractor; and in figure 7.20(b) we have $r = 28$. The first shows what an asymptotically stable

Figure 7.20.

(a) σ = 10, b = 8/3, r = 22.4

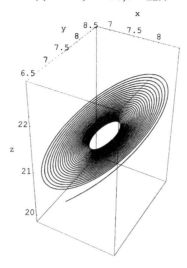

(b) σ = 10, b = 8/3, r = 28

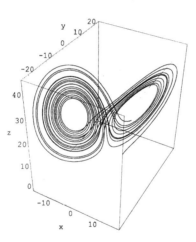

system looks like, with the system being attracted to one of the fixed points. What is not so clear is what an unstable Lorenz system would look like. Figure 7.20(b) shows one such possibility, with the system starting from point (5,5,5) constantly being first attracted to one fixed point and then the other repeatedly.

The Lyapunov dimension for the Lorenz system is 2.07. Then by theorem 7.3 it is a strange attractor (the Lyapunov number is noninteger) and it is also chaotic (the Lyapunov number exceeds unity).

7.8   Rational choice and erratic behaviour

In this first economic application of chaos theory we consider the situation where preferences depend on experience, and is based on the paper by Benhabib and

Day (1981). In such a situation choices can show cyclical patterns or even erratic (chaotic) patterns. The type of situations envisaged in which preferences depend on experience is where an individual reads a novel, then sees the movie rather than read the book a second time, but as a consequence of seeing the movie is stimulated to re-read the novel. This consumption pattern is intertemporal. Furthermore, although habit is a strong pattern of human behaviour, so is novelty. So from time to time we do something quite different. For example, the person who holidays each year in Majorca, but then suddenly decides a holiday in the Alps is what is required. Or the individual who alternates between a beach holiday and one in the mountains or the country. The feature here is a shift in consumption pattern that then shifts back. Such choice behaviour is ruled out in neoclassical consumer theory. Neoclassical consumer theory cannot handle novelty in choice behaviour.

The analysis begins with the typical Cobb–Douglas utility function that is maximised subject to the budget constraint. Here x and y denote the consumption of the two goods, p and q their prices, respectively, and m is the individual's level of income

$$\max U = x^a y^{1-a}$$
$$\text{s.t.} \quad px + qy = m \tag{7.25}$$

Setting up the Lagrangian

$$L = x^a y^{1-a} - \lambda(m - px - qy)$$

leads to the first-order conditions

$$\partial L/\partial x = aU/x - \lambda p = 0$$
$$\partial L/\partial y = (1 - a)U/y - \lambda q = 0$$
$$\partial L/\partial \lambda = m - px - qy = 0$$

From these conditions we readily establish the demand curves

$$x = \frac{m}{p} a, \qquad y = \frac{m}{q}(1 - a) \tag{7.26}$$

Now assume that the parameter a in the utility function, which represents a property of preferences, depends *endogenously* on past choices. More specifically, assume

$$a_{t+1} = bx_t y_t \tag{7.27}$$

The parameter b in equation (7.27) denotes an 'experience-dependent' parameter. The greater the value of b the greater the value of the parameter a in the next period and so the more preferences swing in favour of good x.

Substituting (7.27) into the demand equations (7.26), then

$$x_{t+1} = \frac{m}{p} bx_t y_t, \qquad y_{t+1} = \frac{m}{q}(1 - bx_t y_t) \tag{7.28}$$

Concentrating on x_{t+1}, then from the budget equation we have

$$y_t = \frac{m - px_t}{q}$$

so

$$x_{t+1} = \frac{mbx_t(1 - px_t)}{q}$$

Taking the short run and normalising prices at unity, so that $p = q = 1$, then

(7.29) $$x_{t+1} = bmx_t(m - x_t)$$

The fixed point of equation (7.29) is found by solving

$$x^* = bmx^*(m - x^*)$$

which is

$$x^* = \frac{bm^2 - 1}{bm}$$

So such consumption will only be positive if $bm^2 > 1$. Furthermore, since

$$x_{t+1} = f(x_t) = bmx_t(m - x_t)$$

represents consumption of good x, then this is at a maximum when $f'(x) = 0$, i.e.

$$f'(x) = bm^2 - 2bmx = 0$$
$$x = \frac{m}{2}$$

and maximum consumption is $f(m/2) = bm^3/4$. Since maximum consumption cannot exceed total income (recall $p = 1$), then $f(m/2) \leq m$, or

$$\frac{bm^3}{4} \leq m \qquad \text{implying} \qquad bm^2 \leq 4$$

To summarise, we have established two sets of constraints $bm^2 > 1$ and $bm^2 \leq 4$. Putting these together, then

(7.30) $$1 < bm^2 \leq 4$$

Benhabib and Day (1981) in considering equation (7.29) and the constraints (7.30), establish the following results:

(1)   A three-period cycle exists and so by the Li–Yorke theorem, period cycles of every order exist, including chaos.

(2)   Chaos begins at a critical value $c = 2.57$ over the interval $x \in [0, m]$ where $c < bm^2 \leq 4$.

Benhabib and Day also make the following observation. The smaller the experience parameter b, the greater the income endowment m must be in order to generate chaotic behaviour. What this suggests is that for individuals with low income, long-run patterns of consumption tend to be stable. However, as income grows, so does the possibility of instability, and erratic (chaotic) behaviour becomes more likely at very high levels of income.[14]

---

[14]   Does this explain the erratic consumption patterns of individuals like the DJ Chris Evans, Sir Elton John or that of Victoria and David Beckham?

Figure 7.21.

(a) Labour market

$$L_t = min\{L^d_t, L^s_t\}$$

(b) Goods market

$$y_t = min\{y^d_t, y^s_t\}$$
$$I_t = max\{0, y^s_t - y^d_t\}$$

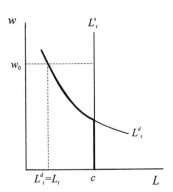

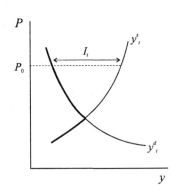

7.9 Inventory dynamics under rational expectations

This section discusses a disequilibrium inventory model by Hommes (1991), where a full discussion can be found (1991, chapter 28). In this model the short side of the market determines market values. We discuss this concept in chapter 8, but the situation is illustrated in figure 7.21 for both the labour market and the product market. Labour supply, L^s_t, is assumed constant at the value of c. Labour demand, L^d_t, is less straightforward and we shall approach a discussion of this by considering first aggregate supply. For the moment, we assume it is a downward sloping curve, as shown in figure 7.21.[15] Actual labour employed, L_t, is then given by the short side of the market, so $L_t = min\{L^d_t, L^s_t\}$, and is shown by the heavy line in figure 7.21(a). Figure 7.21(b) shows aggregate demand, y^d_t, and aggregate supply, y^s_t. I_t denotes the level of inventories, and is positive when there is excess demand, otherwise it is zero, i.e., $I_t = max\{0, y^s_t - y^d_t\}$.

We denote expected aggregate demand by $E(y^d_t)$ and the desired level of inventories by I^d_t. It is assumed that desired inventories are proportional to expected aggregate demand, $I^d_t = \beta E(y^d_t)$. Production is assumed proportional to labour employed, δL_t, and so δ denotes labour productivity. Aggregate supply, therefore, is inventories over from the last period plus current production, i.e., $y^s_t = I_{t-1} + \delta L_t$. On the other hand, aggregate supply is based on expected aggregate demand plus desired inventories. Thus

$$y^s_t = I_{t-1} + \delta L_t$$
$$y^d_t = E\left(y^d_t\right) + I^d_t = E\left(y^d_t\right) + \beta E\left(y^d_t\right)$$
$$= (1+\beta)E\left(y^d_t\right)$$

Setting these equal to each other gives

$$L_t = \frac{(1+\beta)E\left(y^d_t\right) - I_{t-1}}{\delta} \tag{7.31}$$

---

[15] Figure 7.21 presents the terms in a more familiar setting, but wages and prices do not enter this modelling framework.

Hence labour demand is given by

(7.32)
$$L_t^d = \max \left\{ 0, \frac{(1+\beta)E\left(y_t^d\right) - I_{t-1}}{\delta} \right\}$$

Aggregate demand in the economy is assumed to be a linear function of labour employed, $y_t^d = a + bL_t$, where b can be thought of as the marginal propensity to consume, and we assume labour productivity is greater than the marginal propensity to consume, $\delta > b$. The final element of the model is our rational expectations assumption. We assume $E(y_t^d) = y_t^d$, i.e., perfect foresight.

The model can therefore be summarised by six equations

(1)
$$L_t^d = \max \left\{ 0, \frac{(1+\beta)E\left(y_t^d\right) - I_{t-1}}{\delta} \right\}$$

(2) $L_t^s = c$ where c is a constant

(7.33) (3) $y_t^d = a + bL_t$

(4) $y_t^s = I_{t-1} + \delta L_t$

(5) $I_t = \max \left\{ 0, y_t^s - y_t^d \right\}$

(6) $E\left(y_t^d\right) = y_t^d$

Consider now the labour market in terms of figure 7.21(a). At a wage rate, w_0, say, actual labour employed, L_t, must be positive and equal to labour demand. Therefore

(7.34)
$$L_t = \frac{(1+\beta)E\left(y_t^d\right) - I_{t-1}}{\delta} = \frac{(1+\beta)(a+bL_t) - I_{t-1}}{\delta}$$

Solving (7.34) for L_t gives

(7.35)
$$L_t = \frac{(1+\beta)a - I_{t-1}}{\delta - b(1+\beta)}$$

This value must lie between 0 and c. Assume $\delta - b(1+\beta) > 0$, then

$$\frac{(1+\beta)a - I_{t-1}}{\delta - b(1+\beta)} < c$$

which implies

$$(1+\beta)a - c[\delta - b(1+\beta)] < I_{t-1}$$

Let $\gamma_1 = (1+\beta)a - c[\delta - b(1+\beta)]$ then $I_{t-1} > \gamma_1$. Similarly, if $L_t > 0$ then $I_{t-1} < a(1+\beta)$. Let $\gamma_2 = a(1+\beta)$, then putting these together, we have that if L_t lies between 0 and c, then $\gamma_1 < I_{t-1} < \gamma_2$.

We need, however, to consider three situations: (i) $I_{t-1} \leq \gamma_1$, (ii) $\gamma_1 < I_{t-1} < \gamma_2$, and (iii) $I_{t-1} \geq \gamma_2$.

(i) $I_{t-1} \leq \gamma_1$

If $I_{t-1} \leq \gamma_1$ then $L_t = c$ since this is the short side of the market in these circumstances. Then

$$I_t = y_t^s - y_t^d$$
$$= I_{t-1} + \delta c - a - bc$$

i.e.

$$I_t = I_{t-1} + (\delta - b)c - a \tag{7.36}$$

(ii) $\gamma_1 < I_{t-1} < \gamma_2$

Then

$$I_t = y_t^s - y_t^d$$

$$= I_{t-1} + \delta L_t - a - bL_t$$

$$= I_{t-1} + \delta - b \left[\frac{(1+\beta)a - I_{t-1}}{\delta - b(1+\beta)} \right] - a$$

On expanding and simplifying

$$I_t = \frac{-b\beta I_{t-1}}{\delta - b(1+\beta)} + \frac{a\delta\beta}{\delta - b(1+\beta)} \tag{7.37}$$

(iii) $I_{t-1} \geq \gamma_2$

Under these circumstances L_t given by equation (7.35) is negative and so $L_t = L_t^d = 0$. Hence

$$I_t = y_t^s - y_t^d = I_{t-1} - a \tag{7.38}$$

Combining all three cases, then $I_t = f(I_{t-1})$ is a piecewise function of the form

$$I_t = \begin{cases} I_{t-1} + (\delta - b)c - a & I_{t-1} \leq \gamma_1 \\ \dfrac{-b\beta I_{t-1}}{\delta - b(1+\beta)} + \dfrac{a\delta\beta}{\delta - b(1+\beta)} & \gamma_1 < I_{t-1} < \gamma_2 \\ I_{t-1} - a & I_{t-1} \geq \gamma_2 \end{cases} \tag{7.39}$$

and describes the inventory dynamics of the present model.

Equilibrium investment is defined only for the range $\gamma_1 < I_{t-1} < \gamma_2$. In this instance

$$I^* = \frac{-b\beta I^*}{\delta - b(1+\beta)} + \frac{a\delta\beta}{\delta - b(1+\beta)}$$

i.e. $I^* = \dfrac{a\delta\beta}{\delta - b}$

and since we have assumed $\delta > b$, then this is positive.

We shall now pursue this model in terms of a numerical example.

Example 7.6

Let

$$a = 0.2, \quad b = 0.75, \quad c = 1, \quad \delta = 1$$

and for the moment we shall leave β unspecified. If $\beta = 0.2$, then $\gamma_1 = 0.14$ and $\gamma_2 = 0.24$. Equilibrium investment is given by $I^* = 0.16$, which lies between the two parameter values. The piecewise difference equation is then given

Figure 7.22.

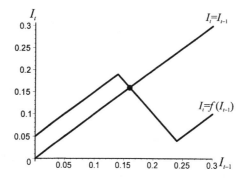

Figure 7.23.

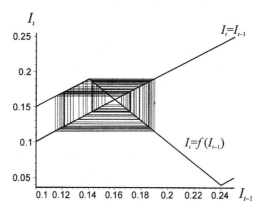

by

$$I_t = \begin{cases} I_{t-1} + 0.05 & I_{t-1} \le 0.14 \\ -1.5I_{t-1} + 0.4 & 0.14 < I_{t-1} < 0.24 \\ I_{t-1} - 0.2 & I_{t-1} \ge 0.24 \end{cases}$$

The situation is shown in figure 7.22.

The equation $I_t = f(I_{t-1})$ is clearly nonlinear, even though it is made up of linear segments. Although the equilibrium level of investment, $I^* = 0.16$, exists and is identified in terms of figure 7.22 where the diagonal cuts the function $f(I_{t-1})$, it is not at all obvious that this fixed point will be approached in the present case. In fact, as figure 7.23 illustrates, the system is chaotic, as shown by the cobweb not settling down at the fixed point from a starting value of $I_0 = 0.14$.[16]

In constructing figure 7.23 we assumed that $\beta = 0.2$. If, as we just indicated, this results in chaotic behaviour, then it would be useful to see the bifurcation diagram for I^* against β. In doing this we allow β to range over the interval 0 to 1/3, this

---

[16] The procedure for constructing cobwebs for piecewise functions is covered in chapter 8. However, *Mathematica* can be used to produce this function with the **Which** command as follows

```
f[x_]:=Which[x<=0.14,x+0.05,x>0.14 && x<0.24,0.4-1.5x,
    x>=0.24,x-0.2]
```

Maple's definition for the piecewise function is

```
f:=x->piecewise(x<=0.14,x+0.05,x>0.14 and x<0.24,0.4-1.5*x,
    x>=0.24,x-0.2);
```

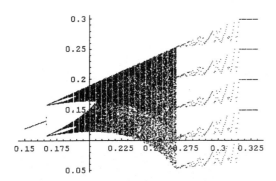

Figure 7.24.

latter value comes from setting $\delta - b(1 + \beta) = 0$ for the values given above. In constructing the bifurcation diagram it is important to realise that the intervals for the piecewise function vary with the change in β. Given the values above, we have the piecewise difference equation

$$I_t = \begin{cases} I_{t-1}+0.05 & I_{t-1} \le 0.2(1+\beta)-[1-0.75(1+\beta)] \\ \dfrac{-0.75\beta I_{t-1}}{1-0.75(1+\beta)}+\dfrac{0.2\beta}{1-0.75(1+\beta)} & 0.2(1+\beta)-[1-0.75(1+\beta)]<I_{t-1} < 0.2(1+\beta) \\ I_{t-1}-0.2 & I_{t-1} \ge 0.2(1+\beta) \end{cases}$$

which we use to construct the bifurcation diagram shown in figure 7.24. It is apparent from this figure that although the system exhibits chaos over certain ranges for β, there is regular alternating behaviour. For $\beta = 0.25$ the system is chaotic.

The model offers much more possibilities depending on the values of the parameters. All we have done here is illustrate the presence of chaos in such a dynamic inventory model.

Exercises

1. The logistic equation $x_{t+1} = \lambda x_t(1 - x_t)$ has $\lambda_0 = 3$ and $\lambda_1 = 3.4495$. Given the Feigenbaum constant of $\delta = 4.669$ use this to predict the value of λ at which $k = 2$ doubling takes place. Compare it with the value derived by the computer programme provided in Gray and Glynn (1991, p. 125).

2. Given λ_0, λ_1 and the universal Feigenbaum constant $\delta = 4.669$, establish that

$$\lambda_2 = \frac{\lambda_1 - \lambda_0}{\delta} + \lambda_1$$

$$\lambda_3 = \frac{\lambda_2 - \lambda_1}{\delta} + \lambda_2 = (\lambda_1 - \lambda_0)\left(\frac{1}{\delta^2} + \frac{1}{\delta}\right) + \lambda_1$$

and find the value for λ_k. Show that

$$\lim_{k \to \infty} \lambda_k = \frac{\lambda_1 - \lambda_0}{\delta - 1} + \lambda_1$$

and hence show that if $\lambda_0 = 3$ and $\lambda_1 = 3.4495$ then the approximate value at which chaos begins for the logistic equation is 3.572.

3.   (i) Show that

$$x_{n+1} = \lambda x_n(1 - x_n)$$

has the same properties as

$$y_{n+1} = y_n^2 + c$$

if

$$c = \frac{\lambda(2 - \lambda)}{4} \qquad \text{and} \qquad y_n = \frac{\lambda}{2} - \lambda x_n$$

(ii) Verify by constructing bifurcation diagrams for each function.

4.   Obtain the bifurcation diagram for the following **tent function**.

$$T(x) = \begin{cases} 2x & 0 \le x \le \frac{1}{2} \\ 2(1 - x) & \frac{1}{2} < x \le 1 \end{cases}$$

5.   Construct a bifurcation diagram for the following equation

$$\dot{x} = 4x - \frac{\lambda x}{1 + 4x^2}$$

What type of bifurcation results?

6.   Consider the equation discussed by Baumol and Benhabib (1989)

$$x_{t+1} = 3.94x_t(1 - x_t)$$

Establish the series for $x_0 = 0.99$ and $x_0 = 0.9901$ for $t = 0, \ldots, 100$, and hence establish that the series is sensitive to initial conditions.

7.   Set up the Hénon map

$$x_{t+1} = 1 - ax_t^2 + y_t$$
$$y_{t+1} = bx_t$$

on a spreadsheet. Let $a = 1.4$ and $b = 0.3$. Plot the series x_t for initial conditions $x_0 = 0.1$ and $x_0 = 0.101$ for $t = 0, \ldots, 100$ and $y_0 = 0.1$. Does the series show sensitivity to initial conditions?

8.   Consider the Hénon map

$$x_{t+1} = 1 - ax_t^2 + y_t$$
$$y_{t+1} = 0.3x_t$$

Let $a = 0.3675$ $x_0 = 0.1$ and $y_0 = 0.1$. Plot the series x_t for $t = 200, \ldots, 300$ and hence show that a two-cycle results. Is the two-cycle still present when $a = 0.9125$?

9.   The Rössler equations take the form

$$\dot{x} = -y - z$$
$$\dot{y} = x + ay$$
$$\dot{z} = b + z(x - c)$$

Let $a = 0.398$, $b = 2$ and $c = 4$.

(i) Plot the trajectory for initial point $(x(0), y(0), z(0)) = (0.1, 0.1, 0.1)$, and hence show this results in a chaotic folded band.

(ii) Does the same chaotic attractor appear for the following parameter values?

$a = 0.2, b = 0.2$ and $c = 5.7$
where $(x(0), y(0), z(0)) = (5, 5, 5)$

10.   Consider the Rössler equations of the form

$$\dot{x} = -y - z$$
$$\dot{y} = x + 0.2y$$
$$\dot{z} = 0.2 + z(x - c)$$

Show that
  (i) a period-one limit cycle occurs when $c = 2.3$
  (ii) a period-two limit cycle occurs when $c = 3.3$
  (iii) a period-three limit cycle occurs when $c = 5.3$
  (iv) chaos occurs when $c = 6.3$.
In each case assume the initial point is $(1, 1, 1)$ and consider $t = 50$ to 100

Additional reading

Further material on chaos theory can be found in Baker and Gollub (1990), Baumol and Benhabib (1989), Benhabib and Day (1981), Brock (1986), Gleick (1988), Gray and Glynn (1991), Gulick (1992), Hilborn (1994), Holmgren (1994), Hommes (1991), Kesley (1988), Lynch (2001), May (1976), Mandelbrot (1987), Medio (1992), Mirowski (1986), Sandefur (1990) and Tu (1994).

PART II

Applied economic dynamics

CHAPTER 8

Demand and supply models

8.1 Introduction

Every student of economics is introduced to demand and supply and from then it becomes a major tool of analysis, both at the microeconomic and macroeconomic level. But the treatment is largely static, with the possible exception of the cobweb model. But even when teaching this subject to first-year students, there is something unsatisfactory about the textbook analysis. Consider the situation shown in figure 8.1, where D denotes the demand curve and S the supply curve. We have a single market and the analysis is partial, i.e., this is the only market under investigation. For simplicity we also assume that the demand and supply curves have conventional slopes and are linear.

Suppose the price is presently P_0. What happens? The typical textbook argument is that there is excess demand at this price and so suppliers, noting they can sell all they wish, will raise the price. This process will continue until the market is in equilibrium and there is no longer excess demand. But what is going on during this process? At the price P_0 do we assume that demand is not satisfied and that the quantity actually transacted is Q_0, but that in the *next period* the price is higher? Or do we assume that these curves indicate market wishes on the part of demanders and suppliers and that such excess demand is a signal to the market that a better deal can be struck? Under this assumption *no* transactions take place until point E is reached where there is no excess demand, and so no pressure for suppliers to put up the price. This too presupposes adjustment in price is done by suppliers. A similar story underlies the tâtonnement process, whereby demands and supplies are matched by some fictitious auctioneer, and once matched then, and only then, do trades take place. With excess demand, if transactions did take place then some demand would go unsatisfied. Such individuals would be willing to offer a higher price in order for their demands to be met. This may be true in some markets. But do you find yourself going into a shop and offering a higher price? No! In a typical market economy price is *set* by producers and *adjusted* by producers in the light of circumstances.

You may argue that at price P_0 suppliers see their stocks falling. Of course, this presupposes they satisfy some of the excess demand out of stocks. This means that the quantity traded is *not* the same as the quantity supplied – it is not the same as Q_0. The quantity supplied refers to new production. The amount traded is now argued to be current production plus some stocks. Whether the quantity traded

Figure 8.1.

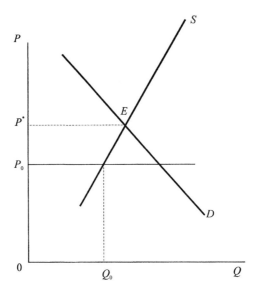

is the same as the quantity supplied depends on current production, the level of stocks, and the quantity supplied from stocks. The suppliers (or more typically the retailers!) drop in stocks signal to suppliers to raise the price and raise the *next period*'s level of production. This will continue until point E is reached and there is no further adjustment in stock levels. Although a plausible story, it cannot occur in a market where there are no stocks.

Of course, what we are attempting to describe here is a *dynamic adjustment process*: an explanation of how and why the price will move from P_0 to P^*. What these different stories indicate is that there is more than one explanation for the adjustment process. Often no explanation is given. Elementary textbooks are prone to say that when there is excess demand price will rise and when there is excess supply price will fall. This is not an explanation of *why* the price is adjusting; it is simply a statement that this is what happens. As such it is consistent with the different explanations provided above, which are by no means exhaustive. Put another way, the dynamic process is left implicit rather than explicit.

Given the widespread use of demand and supply by economists then there is need to consider *explicitly* the economic dynamics underlying such markets. It is fitting, therefore, that we begin our application of dynamics with the topic of demand and supply.

8.2   A simple demand and supply model in continuous time

Consider a simple continuous price-adjustment demand and supply model of the form

(8.1)
$$q^d = a - bp \qquad b > 0$$
$$q^s = c + dp \qquad d > 0$$
$$\frac{dp}{dt} = \alpha(q^d - q^s) \qquad \alpha > 0$$

where quantities demanded and supplied, q^d and q^s, and price, p, are assumed to be continuous functions of time.

The fixed point, the equilibrium point, of this system is readily found by setting $dp/dt = 0$, which gives

$$p^* = \frac{a - c}{b + d} \tag{8.2}$$

and equilibrium quantity

$$q^* = \frac{ad + bc}{b + d} \tag{8.3}$$

For a solution (a fixed point, an equilibrium point) to exist in the positive quadrant, then $a > c$ and $ad + bc > 0$.

We can solve for the price path by substituting the demand and supply equations into the price adjustment equation giving the following first-order linear nonhomogeneous differential equation

$$\frac{dp}{dt} + \alpha(b + d)p = \alpha(a - c) \tag{8.4}$$

with solution

$$p(t) = \frac{a - c}{b + d} + \left[p_0 - \left(\frac{a - c}{b + d} \right) \right] e^{-\alpha(b+d)t} \tag{8.5}$$

which satisfies the initial condition $p(0) = p_0$.

It may be thought that the dynamics of this model are quite explicit, but this is not in fact the case. To see this consider the movement of the quantity over time. The first thing we must note is that there are two different quantities $q^d(t)$ and $q^s(t)$. So long as the price is not the equilibrium price, then these quantities will differ, and it is this difference that forces the price to alter. Thus

$$q^d(t) = \frac{ad + bc}{b + d} + b \left[p_0 - \left(\frac{a - c}{b + d} \right) \right] e^{-\alpha(b+d)t} \tag{8.6}$$

and

$$q^s(t) = \frac{ad + bc}{b + d} + d \left[p_0 - \left(\frac{a - c}{b + d} \right) \right] e^{-\alpha(b+d)t} \tag{8.7}$$

The situation is illustrated in figure 8.2 for an initial price below the equilibrium price.

What this model lacks is a statement about the quantity transacted or traded on the market. To make a statement about the quantity traded we must make an additional assumption. Suppose we make the following assumption:

ASSUMPTION 1
In disequilibrium, the short side of the market is transacted.

Let $q(t)$ denote the quantity traded, then this assumption amounts to

$$q(t) = q^s(t) \quad \text{for} \quad p_0 \leq p^*$$
$$q(t) = q^d(t) \quad \text{for} \quad p_0 \geq p^*$$

Figure 8.2.

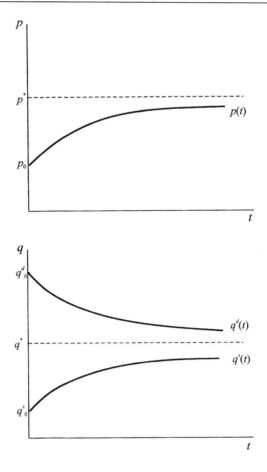

or, more succinctly

$$q(t) = \min(q^d(t), q^s(t))$$

The logic behind assumption 1 is that the model contains no stocks, and when the price is below the equilibrium price, the current production is all that can be supplied onto the market. Some demand will go unsatisfied. If, on the other hand, the price is above the equilibrium price, and current production is in excess of demand, suppliers cannot force people to purchase the goods, and so will sell only what is currently demanded. Although when price is below the equilibrium price and the quantity traded is what is currently produced, the excess demand gives a signal to suppliers to increase future production and to raise the price. The model is less satisfactory when interpreting what is happening when the price is above the equilibrium price. In this instance there will be unsold goods from current production. The model has nothing to say about what happens to these goods. All we can say is that in the future suppliers will decrease their current production and lower the price.

If stocks were included in the model and the stocks, which accumulated when the price was above the equilibrium price, could be sold off when there is excess demand, then we move away from assumption 1 to a different assumption. By way of example suppose we make the following assumption:

ASSUMPTION 2
Stocks are sufficiently plentiful to allow all demands to be met at any price, and price adjusts in proportion to the change in stock levels.

Thus, if $i(t)$ denotes the inventory holding of stocks at time t, then

$$\frac{di}{dt} = q^s - q^d$$

$$i = i_0 + \int_0^t (q^s - q^d)dt$$

and price adjusts according to

$$\frac{dp}{dt} = -\alpha \frac{di}{dt} = -\alpha(q^s - q^d) = \alpha(q^d - q^s) \quad \alpha > 0$$

On the face of it this appears to be the same model, resulting as it does in the same first-order linear nonhomogeneous differential equation. It is true that the solution for the price gives exactly the same solution path. The difference in the model arises in terms of the quantity *traded*. The time path of the quantity demanded, and the time path of the quantity supplied, are as before. For a price above the equilibrium price it is still the case that the quantity traded is equal to the quantity demanded (the short side of the market), and the unsold production goes into stock holdings. It is this rise in stocks that gives the impetus for suppliers to drop the price. On the other hand, when the price is below the equilibrium price, the quantity traded is equal to the quantity demanded (the long side of the market!). The excess demand over current production is met out of stocks. The fall in stock holdings is the signal to producers to raise the price and raise the level of production. Under this second assumption, therefore, we have

$$q(t) = q^d(t) \text{ for all } p$$

What is invariably missing from elementary discussions of demand and supply is the *dynamics* of the quantity traded. At any point in time there can be only one quantity traded, and whether this is equal to the quantity demanded, the quantity supplied or some other quantity depends on what is assumed about the market process when in a disequilibrium state.

To illustrate the significance of the arguments just presented let us consider the labour market. Here we are not concerned with the derivation of the demand for labour and the supply of labour, we shall simply assume that labour demand, *LD*, is negatively related to the real wage rate, *w*, and labour supply, *LS*, is positively related to the real wage rate. Since we are concerned here only with the dynamic process of market adjustment, we shall assume labour demand and labour supply are linear functions of the real wage rate, and we set up the model in continuous time. Thus

$$LD(t) = a - bw(t) \qquad b > 0$$
$$LS(t) = c + dw(t) \qquad d > 0 \tag{8.8}$$
$$LD(t) = LS(t)$$

Figure 8.3.

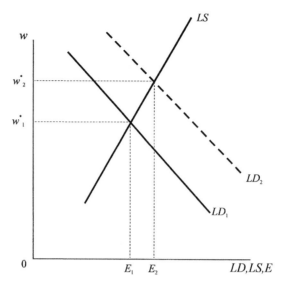

The **flexible wage theory** asserts that wages are highly flexible and will always alter to achieve equilibrium in the labour market, i.e., the wage rate will adjust to establish $LD(t) = LS(t)$. Let us be a little more specific. A typical textbook version (Parkin and King 1995, chapter 29) is that if the real wage is below the equilibrium wage $(w < w^*)$, then the demand for labour is above the supply of labour. Employers will raise the wage rate in order to attract labour, and that this will continue until a wage rate of w^* is established. On the other hand, if the wage rate is above the equilibrium wage rate, then households will not be able to find jobs and employers will have many applicants for their vacancies. There will be an incentive for employers to lower the wage rate, and for labour to accept the lower wage in order to get employed. This will continue until the wage rate of w^* is established.

The dynamic adjustment just mentioned is *assumed* to take place very quickly, almost instantaneously. For this reason the model is often referred to as a **market clearing model**.[1] At any point in time the wage rate is equal to the equilibrium wage rate, and the quantity of employment is equal to labour demand that is equal to labour supply. Let employment at time t be denoted $E(t)$, then in the flexible wage theory, the wage will adjust until $LD(t) = LS(t) = E(t)$. A shift in either the demand curve for labour or the supply curve of labour will alter the equilibrium wage rate and the level of employment. Thus a rise in the capital stock will increase the marginal product of labour and shift the labour demand curve to the right. This will lead to a rise in the real wage rate and a rise in the level of employment, as illustrated in figure 8.3.

A different wage theory, however, is also prevalent in the literature, called the **sticky wage theory**. This asserts that money wage rates are fixed by wage contracts and adjust only slowly. If this assumption is correct, then it does not follow that the real wage will adjust to maintain equality between labour demand and labour

---

[1]   This is the basic assumption underlying the approach by Barro and Grilli (1994) in their elementary textbook, *European Macroeconomics*.

Figure 8.4.

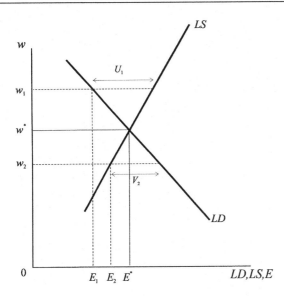

supply. Suppose at the ruling money wage and price level the real wage is above the market clearing wage, as shown in figure 8.4 at the real wage rate w_1. The labour market is in disequilibrium and there is no presumption in this theory that the real wage will fall, at least in the short and (possibly) medium term. At this real wage rate there is an excess supply of labour. But *employment* will be determined by the demand for labour, and the excess supply will simply increase the level of unemployment. Employment will be at the level E_1 and unemployment will be increased by U_1. It is just like our earlier model of stock accumulation. However, in this model it is not so easy for employers to reduce the wage on offer.

At a real wage rate of w_2, which is below the market clearing wage rate of w^*, there is an excess demand for labour. Employment, however, is no longer determined by the demand curve of labour. If individuals are not willing to put themselves on to the labour market at that real wage, then employers will simply be faced with vacancies. Employment will be at the level E_2 and vacancies will rise by V_2. Of course, if such a situation prevails there will be pressure on the part of firms to increase the nominal wage, and hence increase the real wage, in order to attract individuals into the labour market. There will be dynamic forces present which will push up the nominal, and hence the real, wage rate. What we observe, then, is that the short side of the market determines the level of employment.

But the labour market illustrates another implicit dynamic assumption. When the real wage is below the market clearing wage then there will be pressure on firms to raise the nominal wage in order to fill their vacancies. When the real wage is above the market clearing wage employers may wish to reduce their nominal, and hence their real, wage but may be prevented from doing so because of contractual arrangements. In other words, there is an *asymmetric* market adjustment: real wages may rise quicker when there is excess demand for labour than they will fall when there is an equivalent excess supply of labour. Such asymmetric market adjustment takes us yet further into realms of additional assumptions specific to the labour market. What appeared to be a straightforward demand and supply model takes on a rather complex pattern depending on the assumptions of dynamic adjustment.

8.3   The cobweb model

In the previous section we referred to the possibility that price would be altered *in the next period* in the light of what happened in this period. Whenever decisions in one period are based on variables in another period we inherently have a dynamic model. The simplest of such models is the cobweb model of demand and supply. This model is also set out most usually in a discrete form. This is understandable. The model was originally outlined for agriculture (Ezekiel 1938), and concentrated on the decision-making of the farmer. First we shall consider a simple linear version of the model.

Demand at time t is related to the price ruling at time t. Letting q_t^d denote the quantity demanded at time t and p_t the actual price at time t, then we have

$$q_t^d = a - bp_t \quad b > 0$$

However, the farmer when making a decision of what to grow or what to produce will need to make a decision much earlier, and he will make a decision of what quantity to supply, q_t^s, based on what price he expects to receive at time t, i.e., p_t^e. Accordingly, the supply equation takes the form

$$q_t^s = c + dp_t^e \quad d > 0$$

At any point in time, the market is considered to be in equilibrium and so the quantity traded, q_t, is equal to the quantity demanded, which is equal to the quantity supplied. The model is, then

(8.9)
$$q_t^d = a - bp_t$$
$$q_t^s = c + dp_t^e$$
$$q_t^d = q_t^s = q_t$$

As the model stands it cannot be solved because of the unobservable variable p_t^e. We therefore have to make a further assumption about how the supplier forms his or her expectation or makes a decision about the expected price. The simplest assumption of all is that he or she expects the price at time t to be what it was in the previous period. This assumption, of course, amounts to assuming $p_t^e = p_{t-1}$. The model now becomes

(8.10)
$$q_t^d = a - bp_t$$
$$q_t^s = c + dp_{t-1}$$
$$q_t^d = q_t^s = q_t$$

Substituting the demand and supply equations into the equilibrium condition we obtain

$$a - bp_t = c + dp_{t-1}$$

(8.11)
$$p_t = \left(\frac{a-c}{b}\right) - \left(\frac{d}{b}\right)p_{t-1}$$

which is a first-order nonhomogeneous dynamic system. Notice that it is also an autonomous dynamic system because it does not depend explicitly on the variable t.

The system is in equilibrium when the price remains constant for all time periods, i.e., $p_t = p_{t-1} = \ldots = p^*$. Thus

$$p^* = \frac{a - c}{b + d} \qquad \text{where} \quad p^* \geq 0 \quad \text{if} \quad a \geq c \qquad (8.12)$$

With linear demand and supply curves, therefore, there is only one fixed point, one equilibrium point. However, such a fixed point makes economic sense (i.e. for price to be nonnegative) only if the additional condition $a \geq c$ is also satisfied.

To solve this model, as we indicated in part I, we can reduce the nonhomogeneous difference equation to a homogeneous difference equation by taking deviations from the equilibrium. Thus

$$p_t = \left(\frac{a - c}{b} \right) - \left(\frac{d}{b} \right) p_{t-1}$$

$$p^* = \left(\frac{a - c}{b} \right) - \left(\frac{d}{b} \right) p^*$$

$$p_t - p^* = - \left(\frac{d}{b} \right) (p_{t-1} - p^*)$$

with solution

$$p_t - p^* = \left(-\frac{d}{b} \right)^t (p_0 - p^*)$$

which satisfies the initial condition $p_t = p_0$ when $t = 0$. More fully

$$p_t = \left(\frac{a - c}{b + d} \right) + \left(-\frac{d}{b} \right)^t \left[p_0 - \left(\frac{a - c}{b + d} \right) \right] \qquad (8.13)$$

With the usual shaped demand and supply curves, i.e., $b > 0$ and $d > 0$, then $d/b > 0$, hence $(-d/b)^t$ will alternate in sign, being positive for even numbers of t and negative for odd numbers of t. Furthermore, if $0 < |-d/b| < 1$ then the series will become damped, and in the limit will tend towards the equilibrium price. On the other hand, if $|-d/b| > 1$ then the system will diverge from the equilibrium price. Finally, if $|b| = |d|$ (or $|-d/b| = 1$), then the system will neither converge nor diverge and will exhibit a two-period cycle. These results were verified by means of a simple numerical example and solved by means of a spreadsheet in chapter 3, figure 3.11.

Example 8.1

By way of variation, here we shall solve a numerical version of the system using *Mathematica* and *Maple* (see Eckalbar 1993). The input instructions for each package are

    Mathematica

```
{a,b,c,d}={20,4,2,2.5}
A=-b/d
pt1[pt_]:=A*pt
price[t_,p0_]:=ListPlot[NestList[pt1,p0,t],
    PlotJoined->True, PlotRange->All,
        AxesOrigin->{0,0}]
price[20,1]
```

    Maple

```
A:=20: b:=4: c:=2: d:=2.5:
A:=-d/b;
sol:=rsolve(p(t)=A*p(t-1),p):
equ:=subs(p(0)=1,sol):
f:=t->equ:
points:=[seq([t,f(t)],t=0..20):
plot(points);
```

In *Mathematica*, we first set values for the parameters a, b, c and d, namely $\{a, b, c, d\} = \{20, 4, 2, 2.5\}$. We then define the ratio $(-d/b) = A$, resulting in $A = -0.625$, and define the recursive function pt1[pt_] := A*pt. It now remains to generate the series of values for the price using the **NestList** command, and to plot the resulting series using the **ListPlot** command. The result is figure 8.5.

Notice that this version of the cobweb allows different periods to be specified and a different initial price. Thus, price[50,2] would indicate a plot of 50 periods with an initial price of 2.

Figure 8.5 can also be generated using the *Maple* commands given above. Again, we input the values for the four parameters and define A. In *Maple* we approach the next part slightly differently. We solve the difference equation, using the **rsolve** command. Then define the equation for the initial price being unity, and use this to define the mapping f. Next we create a series of points using the sequence command and plot these to create figure 8.5.

It is readily observed from figure 8.5 that this system is dynamically stable, with the price converging on the equilibrium price – since deviations from equilibrium converge on zero. Using a software package such as *Mathematica* or *Maple* different values for the parameters can readily be investigated. For instance, parameter

Figure 8.5.

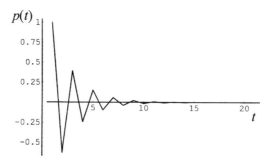

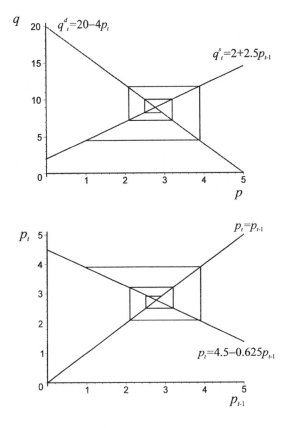

Figure 8.6.

values {20, 4, 2, 6} and price [20,1] will readily be shown to exhibit an unstable system with price diverging from its equilibrium. This stability and instability is purely dependent on the value of A. In figure 8.5 the system is stable and $A = -0.625$ while the alternative parameter values gives $A = -1.5$ leading to an unstable system. All this we investigated in chapter 3.

Nothing in the analysis so far would indicate why it is referred to as the 'cobweb' model. This is because we have concentrated solely on the time path of price in the system. There are two ways to exhibit the cobweb. One is to show the sequence of points on a demand and supply diagram (figure 8.6(a))[2] and the other is to plot the differential equation for price in relation to the 45°-line (figure 8.6(b)). In many ways figure 8.6(a) is more revealing because it shows the behaviour of both price and quantity. Here we have a convergent cobweb. The same convergence pattern is shown in figure 8.6(b), but here concentration is on the price sequence. The second approach, however, is more useful for mathematical investigation (especially of nonlinear systems).

So far we have concentrated on the very simple linear model. A number of avenues can be explored. Within the confines of the linear model, it is possible to specify a different behaviour for the expected price. It may be argued that expecting the price in the current period to be what it was in the previous period is very naïve and takes no account of the trend in prices. It is possible, therefore, to specify an

---

[2] Notice that quantity is on the vertical axis and price on the horizontal axis.

adaptive expectation in which the expected price is an adjustment of the forecast error in the previous guess. More specifically, we can write

(8.14)
$$p_t^e = p_{t-1}^e - \lambda(p_{t-1}^e - p_{t-1})$$

If $\lambda = 1$ then this amounts to our previous model. In other words, the previous model can be considered as a special case of the present model in which $\lambda = 1$. The model in full is

(8.15)
$$q_t^d = a - bp_t \quad b > 0$$
$$q_t^s = c + dp_{t-1} \quad d > 0$$
$$p_t^e = p_{t-1}^e - \lambda\left(p_{t-1}^e - p_{t-1}\right) \quad 0 \le \lambda \le 1$$
$$q_t^d = q_t^s = q_t$$

We can solve this model by noting

$$p_t^e = (1 - \lambda)p_{t-1}^e + \lambda p_{t-1}$$

$$p_t^e = \frac{q_t^s - c}{d} = \frac{q_t^d - c}{d} = \frac{a - bp_t - c}{d}$$

$$\therefore \quad p_{t-1}^e = \left(\frac{a - c}{d}\right) - \left(\frac{b}{d}\right)p_{t-1}$$

Hence

(8.16)
$$a - bp_t = c + d(1 - \lambda)\left[\left(\frac{a - c}{d}\right) - \left(\frac{b}{d}\right)p_{t-1}\right] + d\lambda p_{t-1}$$

i.e. $\quad p_t = \lambda\left(\frac{a - c}{d}\right) + \left[1 - \lambda - \left(\frac{\lambda d}{b}\right)\right]p_{t-1}$

Setting $p_t = p_{t-1} = \ldots = p^*$ for all t readily gives the same equilibrium price, namely $p^* = (a - c)/(b + d)$. As in our earlier and simpler model, taking deviations from equilibrium readily gives the solution

(8.17)
$$p_t - p^* = \left[1 - \lambda - \left(\frac{\lambda d}{b}\right)\right]^t (p_0 - p^*)$$

Let the term in square brackets be denoted B, then for this model to exhibit a convergent oscillatory solution it is necessary for $-1 < B < 0$, in other words it is necessary to satisfy the condition

(8.18)
$$\frac{1}{\lambda} - 1 < \frac{d}{b} < \frac{2}{\lambda} - 1$$

Of course, there can be many other specifications for price expectation, each giving rise to a different model. For instance, we can postulate the following (Goodwin 1947)

(8.19)
$$p_t^e = p_{t-1} + \eta(p_{t-1} - p_{t-2})$$

where η is the coefficient of expectations. If $\eta = 0$ then $p_t^e = p_{t-1}$, which is our original formulation. If $\eta > 0$ then price is expected to move in the same direction as in the past; while if $\eta < 0$, then price is expected to reverse itself. The extent of these price movements is very dependent on the magnitude of η. The full model is

$$q_t^d = a - bp_t \quad b > 0$$
$$q_t^s = c + dp_{t-1} \quad d > 0$$
$$p_t^e = p_{t-1} + \eta(p_{t-1} - p_{t-2})$$
$$q_t^d = q_t^s = q_t$$

(8.20)

The model can be solved algebraically, but it can also be easily investigated by means of a spreadsheet. To do this we first do some algebraic manipulation. Substituting the expectations equation into the supply equation, and then equating this with demand, we find

$$a - bp_t = c + d[p_{t-1} + \eta(p_{t-1} - p_{t-2})]$$

$$\text{i.e.} \quad p_t = \left(\frac{a-c}{b}\right) - \left(\frac{d}{b}\right)(1+\eta)p_{t-1} + \left(\frac{d\eta}{b}\right)p_{t-2}$$

(8.21)

which is a second-order difference equation.

Example 8.2

Suppose we set up the initial spreadsheet with the following parameter values, and the necessary *two* initial prices

$$\begin{array}{lll} a = 100 & c = -20 & \eta = -1.2 \\ b = 2 & d = 1.25 & \\ p_0 = 20 & p_1 = 24 & \end{array}$$

The model is illustrated in figure 8.7. Having set up the model, it is quite easy to change the value of the parameters, but most especially η, and see the result on the price series. In most spreadsheets the price plot will change interactively as the parameter values are changed. It is of course possible to solve the model algebraically and investigate the restrictions on the parameter values (see Gandolfo 1971, pp. 91–6), but any student of economics can investigate the properties of this model by means of a spreadsheet.

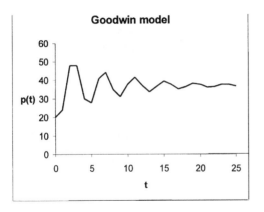

Figure 8.7.

8.4   Cobwebs with *Mathematica* and *Maple*

The intention of this section is to provide routines for creating cobwebs using *Mathematica* and *Maple*. There are many ways to do this and here we shall provide only one for each package. *Mathematica*'s routine is based on Gray and Glynn (1991, chapter 7), while *Maple*'s routine is an adaptation of this. The *Maple* routine is written as a procedure, a mini-programme. The reason for this is so many cobwebs can be then created with the minimum of input instructions. A different *Maple* routine can be found in Lynch (2001).[3] Both the routines below can handle linear and nonlinear equations and can also be adapted to deal with stepwise functions. Since the *Mathematica* routine is the basis for the two instructions, a detailed explanation of this is provided in appendix 8.1. This appendix also provides the *Maple* routine just as a set of input instructions rather than as a procedure.

We consider only the recursive form of the cobweb, as illustrated in figure 8.6(b) and begin with the linear recursive equation

(8.22)
$$x_t = f(x_{t-1}) = a + bx_{t-1}$$

The instructions for each programme are as follows, where we use the recursive equation in figure 8.6(b) as an illustration:

Mathematica[4]
```
f[x_]:=a+b*x
{a=4.5,b=-0.625}
x0=1
points=Rest[Partition[Flatten[Transpose[
     {NestList[f,x0,20],NestList[f,x0,20]}] ],2,1]];
web=ListPlot[points,PlotJoined->True]
lines=Plot[{f[x],x},{x,0,5}]
cobweb=Show[web,lines]
```
Maple
```
restart;
with(linalg):
with(plots):
cobweb:=proc(f,x0,n,xmin,xmax)
     local fk,list1,list2,list3,list4,web,lines;
     fk:=(x,k)->simplify((f@@k)(x));
     list1:=transpose(array([[seq(fk(x0,k),k=0..n)],
          [seq(fk(x0,k),k=0..n)]])):
     list2:=convert(convert(list1,vector),list):
     list3:=convert(transpose(array(
          [list2[1..nops(list2)-1],
          list2[2..nops(list2)]])),listlist):
     list4:=[list3[2..nops(list3)]]:
```

---

[3] See Lynch (2001, pp. 249–50). Here Lynch provides a routine for the tent function, which is a stepwise function, but this is readily adapted for any linear or nonlinear function.

[4] Intermediate displays in *Mathematica* can be suppressed by including the instruction: DisplayFunction->Identity, then in the final display using the Show command, include DisplayFunction->$DisplayFunction. See figure 8.8(a) and appendix 8.1.

```
web:=plot(list4):
lines:=plot({f(x),x},x=xmin..xmax,colour=blue):
display({web,lines});
```
```
end:
f:=x->4.5-0.625*x;
cobweb(f,1,20,0,5);
```

The cobweb procedure for *Maple* requires you to first define the function f and then to supply the values for *x0*, *n*, *xmin* and *xmax*. The penultimate line therefore defines the function and then the input instruction cobweb(f,1,20,0,5) indicates to use the procedure for the defined function, give *x0* a value of unity, *n* a value of 20, and *xmin* and *xmax* values of 0 and 5, respectively. These instructions produce a similar plot to the *Mathematica* instructions given above.

Nonlinear equations too are readily handled. If we are considering, for example, the nonlinear logistic equation

$$x_t = f(x_{t-1}) = rx_{t-1}(1 - x_{t-1}) \qquad x_0 = 0.1$$

with $r = 3.85$, then in *Mathematica* we replace the first three lines with

```
f[x_]:=r*x*(1-x)
{r=3.85}
x0=0.1
```

and we also need to change the range for x in the 'lines' input to $\{x,0,1\}$. In *Maple*, on the other hand, we simply replace the last two lines with

```
f:=x->3.85*x*(1-x);
cobweb(f,0.1,20,0,1);
```

Figure 8.8 shows screen shots of the final output for each programme. As can be seen from the figure, the results are virtually the same. It is, of course, possible to include instructions for labelling the axes and provide headings, but we have not done that here.

It is also fairly straightforward to deal with piecewise functions, and we shall illustrate exactly how in the next section.

8.5   Cobwebs in the phase plane

Return to our linear cobweb model in which supply is based on last period's price. The resulting difference equation is

$$p_t = \left(\frac{a-c}{b}\right) - \left(\frac{d}{b}\right)p_{t-1}$$

or

$$p_t = A - Bp_{t-1}$$
$$\text{where} \quad A = \frac{a-c}{b} \quad \text{and} \quad B = \frac{d}{b}$$

Hence, the function $p_t = f(p_{t-1}) = A - Bp_{t-1}$ is linear in the phase space in which p_{t-1} is on the horizontal axis and p_t is on the vertical axis. Figure 8.9 illustrates

Figure 8.8.   *(a) Mathematica*

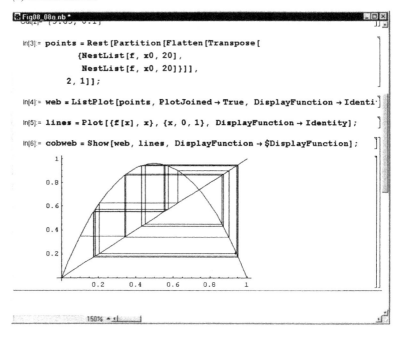

(b) Maple

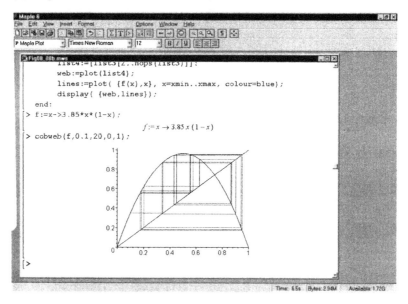

two possibilities in which demand and supply have conventional slopes. The linear mapping is shown by the line denoted L. The 45°-line, denoted E, satisfies the condition

$$p_t = p_{t-1} \qquad \text{for all } t$$

and p^* denotes a fixed point, an equilibrium point.

Figure 8.9.

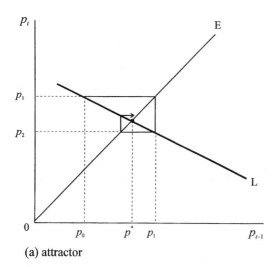

(a) attractor

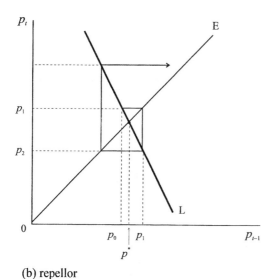

(b) repellor

Whether such a fixed point is stable, unstable or periodic can be established from the slope of L. If $0 < |-B| < 1$, as in figure 8.9(a), then p^* is an **attractor**, and the price sequence $\{p_t\}$, starting at p_0, converges on p^*. Starting at p_0, then, $p_1 = A - Bp_0$, which is read off the line L. This is the same as p_1 on the E-line. At p_1, then $p_2 = A - Bp_1$, which again is read off the line L. The sequence will continue until p^* is reached. On the other hand, the sequence $\{p_t\}$ starting at p_0 in figure 8.9(b), diverges from p^*. This is because $|-B| > 1$, and so p^* is a **repellor**.

What happens when $|-B| = 1$, where the slope of the demand curve in absolute value is equal to the slope of the supply curve? We then have

$$p_t = A - p_{t-1}$$

The situation is illustrated in figure 8.10. In chapter 3, section 3.4, we defined a solution y_n as *periodic* if $y_{n+m} = y_n$, and the smallest integer for m is the period

Figure 8.10.

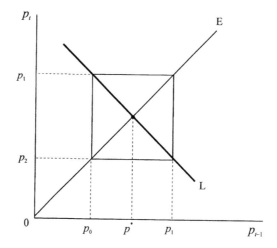

of the solution. In the present example, beginning at p_0, we have

$$p_1 = A - p_0$$
$$p_2 = A - p_1 = A - (A - p_0) = p_0$$
$$p_3 = A - p_2 = A - p_0$$
$$p_4 = A - p_3 = A - (A - p_0) = p_0$$

If follows, therefore, that

$$p_0 = p_2 = p_4 = \ldots \qquad \text{and} \qquad p_1 = p_3 = p_5 = \ldots$$

We have a two-period cycle solution. In fact, with linear demand and supply, with equal slopes in absolute value, there can only be a two-period cycle and no higher one is possible.

Discrete systems have come under increasing investigation in recent years because of the possibility of chaotic behaviour to which they can give rise (see chapter 7). By way of introduction to this analysis we shall continue with our simple linear example and consider how *Mathematica* can be used to investigate cobweb models. It will be found that the phase plane plays an important part in this approach. Although a little repetitive, we shall provide both *Mathematica* and *Maple* instructions for deriving the cobwebs. However, since the *Maple* procedure never changes, we shall simply write 'cobweb procedure'.

Example 8.3

We shall illustrate the technique by means of the following simple cobweb model

$$q_t^d = 24 - 5p_t$$
$$q_t^s = -4 + 2p_{t-1}$$
$$q_t^d = q_t^s = q_t$$

which has equilibrium values $p^* = 4$ and $q^* = 4$. The resulting difference equation is

$$p_t = 5.6 - 0.4p_{t-1}$$

The objective is to plot a sequence of points in the phase plane. Joining up these points forms the web of the cobweb. Superimposed on this web is the line $f(p) = 5.6 - 0.4p$ and the 45°-line. A full explanation of the instructions for *Mathematica* and *Maple* are given in appendix 8.1.

Mathematica
```
f[p_]:=5.6-0.4p
p0=1
points=Rest[Partition[Flatten[Transpose[
        {NestList[f,p0,20],NestList[f,p0,20]}
            ] ], 2, 1 ] ];
web=ListPlot[points,PlotJoined->True]
lines=Plot[ {f[p],p}, {p,0,10} ]
cobweb=Show[web,lines,
        AxesLabel->{"pt-1","pt"} ]
```
Maple
```
`cobweb procedure'
f:p->5.6-0.4*p
cobweb(f,1,20,0,10)
```

Notice in the *Maple* instructions that although the procedure defines the function in terms of the variable x, we define f in terms of p. We can do this, and we do it repeatedly throughout this chapter, because the variables within the procedure are defined *locally*. The result is shown in figure 8.11.

To illustrate the generality of this approach, and to highlight a nonlinear cobweb, consider the following model.

Example 8.4

$$q_t^d = 4 - 3p_t$$
$$q_t^s = p_{t-1}^2$$
$$q_t^d = q_t^s = q_t$$

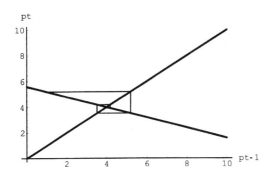

Figure 8.11.

Figure 8.12.

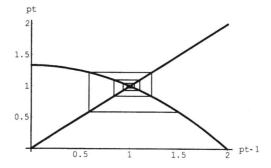

The equilibrium, assuming a positive price, is given by $p^* = 1$ and $q^* = 1$, and the difference equation is given by

$$p_t = (4/3) - (1/3)p_{t-1}^2$$

The question now arises as to whether the solution $p^* = 1$ is stable or not. Using *Mathematica* we can input the following instructions (where we have included solving for equilibrium price):

> *Mathematica*
> ```
> f[p_]:=(4/3)-(1/3)p^2
> EquPrice=Solve[p==f[p],p]
> p0=1.5
> points=Rest[Partition[Flatten[Transpose[
>     {NestList[f,p0,20],NestList[f,p0,20]}
>         ] ], 2, 1 ] ];
> web=ListPlot[points,PlotJoined->True]
> lines=Plot[ {f[p],p}, {p,0,2} ]
> cobweb=Show[web,lines,
>     AxesLabel->{"pt-1","pt"} ]
> ```

Maple's instructions are

> *Maple*
> ```
> `cobweb procedure'
> f:=p->(4/3)-(1/3)*p^2
> EquPrice:=solve(p=f(p),p);
> cobweb(f,1.5,20,0,2);
> ```

The resulting cobweb is illustrated in figure 8.12. The model, therefore, has a locally stable solution for a positive price equilibrium.

It should be noted[5] that at the equilibrium point we have

$$f'(p^*) = 2(-1/3)p^* = -2/3$$
$$\text{i.e.} \quad |f'(p^*)| < 1$$

---

[5] See chapter 3, section 3.4.

which verifies the local stability of $p^* = 1$. Although this particular nonlinearity leads to a stable solution, some authors (e.g. Waugh 1964) have argued that other types will lead to a two-period cycle and may well be the norm.

One especially important nonlinearity can arise where there is a price ceiling set (Waugh, 1964). Consider the following linear demand and supply model.

Example 8.5

$$q_t^d = 42 - 4p_t$$
$$q_t^s = 2 + 6p_{t-1}$$
$$q_t^d = q_t^s = q_t$$

The difference equation from this model is

$$p_t = 10 - 1.5p_{t-1}$$

with equilibrium values $p^* = 4$ and $q^* = 26$. Since the slope of the function $f(p) = 10 - 1.5p$ is greater than unity in absolute terms, then the cobweb is unstable. This is readily verified starting with a price of $p_0 = 3.5$.

Suppose a price ceiling $p_c = 6$ is set, then the price in any period cannot exceed this ceiling. What we have, then, is a function which is kinked at $p = 8/3$, the value where $p_c = f(p)$. This can be expressed as

$$f(p) = \begin{cases} 6 & p < 8/3 \\ 10 - 1.5p & p \geq 8/3 \end{cases}$$

Within *Mathematica* there is only a slight difference in defining the function. We define it using the **If** command, i.e.

```
f[p_]:=If[ p<8/3,6,10-1.5p]
```

i.e. if $p < 8/3$ then $f(p)$ takes the value 6, otherwise it takes the value $10 - 1.5p$. The remaining instructions for creating the cobweb remain unaffected, although we have added the price ceiling to the lines, i.e.

```
lines=Plot[ {f[p], p, 6}, {p,0,6}]
```

In *Maple* we use a similar instruction using the piecewise function, i.e.

```
f:p->piecewise(p<8/3,6,10-1.5*p);
```

which says for p less than 8/3 take the value 6, else take the value 10–1.5p for $p \geq 8/3$. All other instructions remain the same.

The full instructions for both packages, including a plot of $f(p)$, are:

Mathematica
```
f[p_]:=If[p<8/3,6,10-1.5p]
Plot[f[p],{p,0,6}]
p0=3.5
points=Rest[Partition[Flatten[Transpose[
      {NestList[f,p0,10],NestList[f,p0,10]}
          ] ], 2, 1 ] ];
web=ListPlot[points,PlotJoined->True]
```

Figure 8.13.

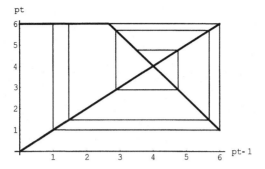

```
lines=Plot[ {f[p],p,6}, {p,0,6} ]
cobweb=Show[web,lines,
    AxesLabel->{"pt-1","pt"} ]
```
Maple
```
`cobweb procedure'
f:p->piecewise(p<8/3,6,10-1.5*p);
cobweb(f,3.5,10,0,6);
```

which results in the cobweb shown in figure 8.13.

What figure 8.13 shows is that initially, starting from a price of $p_0 = 3.5$, the market is unstable, moving away from the equilibrium price $p^* = 4$. However, once the price ceiling is reached, the system settles down to a two-period cycle, oscillating between $p = 1$ and $p = 6$. Although the equilibrium is not attained, the ceiling does limit the price variation.

8.6   Cobwebs in two interrelated markets[6]

Interrelated markets with time lags illustrate the application of discrete dynamic systems. An early example was the corn–hog cycle mentioned by Ezekiel (1938) and Waugh (1964). The model amounts to two markets:

Corn market

$$d_t^c = a_1 - b_1 p_t^c \qquad b_1 > 0$$
(8.23)
$$s_t^c = c_1 + d_1 p_{t-1}^c \qquad d_1 > 0$$
$$d_t^c = s_t^c$$

Hog market

$$d_t^h = a_2 - b_2 p_t^h \qquad\qquad b_2 > 0$$
(8.24)
$$s_t^h = c_2 + d_2 p_{t-1}^h + e p_{t-1}^c \qquad d_1 > 0, \quad e < 0$$
$$d_t^h = s_t^h$$

where

$$d^c = \text{demand for corn} \qquad d^h = \text{demand for hogs}$$
$$s^c = \text{supply of corn} \qquad s^h = \text{supply of hogs}$$
$$p^c = \text{price of corn} \qquad p^h = \text{price of hogs}$$

---

[6] This section requires knowledge of chapter 5.

The corn market is our typical cobweb with a one-period lag on supply, i.e., farmers base the supply in period t on the expected price of corn, which they assume is the same as it was last period. The corn market is independent of the hog market. However, the hog market besides having a similar time lag on the supply also depends on what farmers expect the corn price to be – since this is food for the hogs. It is assumed that farmers expect the price of corn to be what it was last period. *This model can apply to any animal–feed interaction.*

The model can be handled by deriving a system of difference equations, which is accomplished by substituting the respective demand and supply equations into the equilibrium conditions and suitably re-arranging the results. The results are

$$p_t^c = \left(\frac{a_1 - c_1}{b_1}\right) - \left(\frac{d_1}{b_1}\right) p_{t-1}^c$$

$$p_t^h = \left(\frac{a_2 - c_2}{b_2}\right) - \left(\frac{d_2}{b_2}\right) p_{t-1}^h - \left(\frac{e}{b_2}\right) p_{t-1}^c$$

(8.25)

Let p_c^* and p_h^* denote the equilibrium prices in the corn and hog markets, respectively. Then taking deviations from equilibria, we have

$$p_t^c - p_c^* = -\left(\frac{d_1}{b_1}\right)(p_{t-1}^c - p_c^*)$$

$$p_t^h - p_h^* = -\left(\frac{d_2}{b_2}\right)(p_{t-1}^h - p_h^*) - \left(\frac{e}{b_2}\right)(p_{t-1}^c - p_c^*)$$

Let

$$A_1 = -d_1/b_1 \qquad A_2 = -d_2/b_2 \qquad B = -e/b_2$$
$$x_t = p_t^c - p_c^* \qquad \text{implies} \qquad x_{t-1} = p_{t-1}^c - p_c^*$$
$$y_t = p_t^h - p_h^* \qquad \text{implies} \qquad y_{t-1} = p_{t-1}^h - p_h^*$$

Then the system can be written more succinctly as

$$x_t = A_1 x_{t-1}$$
$$y_t = A_2 y_{t-1} + B x_{t-1}$$

or in matrix notation

$$\begin{bmatrix} x_t \\ y_t \end{bmatrix} = \begin{bmatrix} A_1 & 0 \\ B & A_2 \end{bmatrix} \begin{bmatrix} x_{t-1} \\ y_{t-1} \end{bmatrix}$$

Equilibria in the two markets require $x_t = x_{t-1} = x^*$ for all t, and $y_t = y_{t-1} = y^*$ for all t. Using these conditions, the equilibria are readily found to be

$$p_c^* = \frac{a_1 - c_1}{b_1 + d_1}$$

$$p_h^* = \left(\frac{a_2 - c_2}{b_2 + d_2}\right) - \frac{e}{b_2 + d_2}\left(\frac{a_1 - c_1}{b_1 + d_1}\right)$$

(8.26)

We investigated the properties of such systems in chapter 5.

Let **A** denote the matrix of the system, where

$$\mathbf{A} = \begin{bmatrix} A_1 & 0 \\ B & A_2 \end{bmatrix}$$

with characteristic equation $|\mathbf{A} - \lambda\mathbf{I}| = (A_1 - \lambda)(A_2 - \lambda) = 0$, then the characteristic roots are $r = A_1$ and $s = A_2$. Stability in the corn and hog market is assured if $|r| < 1$ and $|s| < 1$, i.e., $|-d_1/b_1| < 1$ and $|-d_2/b_2| < 1$. It should be noted that $|-d_1/b_1| < 1$ is the condition for stability in the corn market, while $|-d_2/b_2| < 1$ is the condition for stability in the hog market, assuming constant corn prices.

Example 8.6

To pursue the analysis further we shall consider the following numerical example. For corn we have

$$d_t^c = 24 - 5p_t^c$$
$$s_t^c = -4 + 2p_{t-1}^c$$
$$d_t^c = s_t^c$$

while for the hog market we have

$$d_t^h = 20 - 5p_t^h$$
$$s_t^h = 2.5 + 2.5p_{t-1}^h - 2p_{t-1}^c$$
$$d_t^h = s_t^h$$

Substituting and solving for p_t^c and p_t^h, respectively, we obtain

$$p_t^c = 5.6 - 0.4p_{t-1}^c$$
$$p_t^h = 3.5 + 0.4p_{t-1}^c - 0.5p_{t-1}^h$$

The equilibrium price in each market is readily found to be $p_c^* = 4$ and $p_h^* = 3.4$. The question now arises as to whether this combined equilibrium is stable.

Taking deviations from equilibrium, the system reduces down to

$$\begin{bmatrix} x_t \\ y_t \end{bmatrix} = \begin{bmatrix} -0.4 & 0 \\ 0.4 & -0.5 \end{bmatrix} \begin{bmatrix} x_{t-1} \\ y_{t-1} \end{bmatrix}$$

with characteristic equation

$$|\mathbf{A} - \lambda\mathbf{I}| = (-0.4 - \lambda)(-0.5 - \lambda) = 0$$

and characteristic roots $r = -0.4$ and $s = -0.5$.

For $r = -0.4$ we have

$$(\mathbf{A} - r\mathbf{I})\mathbf{v}^r = \mathbf{0}$$

so that

$$\begin{bmatrix} -0.4 + 0.4 & 0 \\ 0.4 & -0.5 + 0.4 \end{bmatrix} \begin{bmatrix} v_1^r \\ v_2^r \end{bmatrix} = \begin{bmatrix} 0 \\ 0 \end{bmatrix}$$

or

$$\begin{bmatrix} 0 & 0 \\ 0.4 & -0.1 \end{bmatrix} \begin{bmatrix} v_1^r \\ v_2^r \end{bmatrix} = \begin{bmatrix} 0 \\ 0 \end{bmatrix}$$

then

$$0.4v_1^r - 0.1v_2^r = 0$$

Let $v_1^r = 1$ then $v_2^r = 0.4v_1^r/0.1 = 4$. Hence the eigenvector associated with $r = -0.4$ is

$$\mathbf{v}^r = \begin{bmatrix} 1 \\ 4 \end{bmatrix}$$

For $s = -0.5$ we have

$$(\mathbf{A} - s\mathbf{I})\mathbf{v}^s = \mathbf{0}$$

giving

$$\begin{bmatrix} -0.4+0.5 & 0 \\ 0.4 & -0.5+0.5 \end{bmatrix}\begin{bmatrix} v_1^s \\ v_2^s \end{bmatrix} = \begin{bmatrix} 0 \\ 0 \end{bmatrix}$$

or

$$\begin{bmatrix} 0.1 & 0 \\ 0.4 & 0 \end{bmatrix}\begin{bmatrix} v_1^s \\ v_2^s \end{bmatrix} = \begin{bmatrix} 0 \\ 0 \end{bmatrix}$$

Hence, $0.1v_1^s = 0$ giving $v_1^s = 0$. v_2^s can be anything, so let it be unity. Then

$$\mathbf{v}^s = \begin{bmatrix} 0 \\ 1 \end{bmatrix}$$

Hence, the matrix composed of both eigenvectors, denoted $\mathbf{V}$, is given by

$$\mathbf{V} = [\mathbf{v}^r \quad \mathbf{v}^s] = \begin{bmatrix} 1 & 0 \\ 4 & 1 \end{bmatrix}$$

Hence

$$\mathbf{u}_t = \mathbf{V}\mathbf{D}^t\mathbf{V}^{-1}\mathbf{u}_0$$

or

$$\begin{bmatrix} x_t \\ y_t \end{bmatrix} = \begin{bmatrix} 1 & 0 \\ 4 & 1 \end{bmatrix}\begin{bmatrix} (-0.4)^t & 0 \\ 0 & (-0.5)^t \end{bmatrix}\begin{bmatrix} 1 & 0 \\ 4 & 1 \end{bmatrix}^{-1}\begin{bmatrix} x_0 \\ y_0 \end{bmatrix}$$

As $t \to \infty$ then each of the terms $(-0.4)^t$ and $(-0.5)^t$ tends to zero, and so $x_t \to 0$ and $y_t \to 0$, which in turn means $p_t^c \to p_c^*$ and $p_t^h \to p_h^*$. The interrelated market is, therefore, dynamically stable.

8.7 Demand and supply with stocks

In section 8.1 we indicated that suppliers often change prices in response to their level of stocks. This, of course, applies only to non-perishable goods. It is surprising, therefore, that there are so few demand and supply models with stock behaviour built in. Here we shall consider just a few simple stock models.

Stocks can be built up only when there is excess supply. Furthermore, stocks are specified for a point in time. Let Q_t denote the level of stocks at the *end* of period t. Then the change in stocks *over period t* is $Q_t - Q_{t-1}$ and this arises from the excess supply over period t, i.e.

$$\Delta Q_t = Q_t - Q_{t-1} = q_t^s - q_t^d$$

We continue to assume a linear demand and supply model. What happens in such a model depends on how suppliers alter prices in response to stock changes. We consider two alternative assumptions

ASSUMPTION 1
Suppliers raise the price if stocks in the previous period fall, and the rise in price is set proportional to the fall in stocks

$$p_t - p_{t-1} = -\gamma_1 \Delta Q_{t-1} \quad \gamma_1 > 0$$

ASSUMPTION 2
Suppliers raise the price if stocks in the previous period fall below a given level, $\overline{Q}$, and the rise in price is set proportional to the deviation of stocks from the specified level

$$p_t - p_{t-1} = -\gamma_2 (Q_{t-1} - \overline{Q}) \quad \gamma_2 > 0$$

Under assumption 1 we have the model

(8.27)
$$q_t^d = a - bp_t$$
$$q_t^s = c + dp_t$$
$$p_t - p_{t-1} = -\gamma_1 \Delta Q_{t-1}$$

where $\Delta Q_t = q_t^s - q_t^d$ for any period t. Therefore,

$$p_t - p_{t-1} = -\gamma_1 (q_{t-1}^s - q_{t-1}^d)$$
$$p_t = p_{t-1} - \gamma_1 (c + dp_{t-1} - a + bp_{t-1})$$
$$= p_{t-1} + \gamma_1 (a - c) - \gamma_1 (b + d)p_{t-1}$$

i.e.

(8.28)
$$p_t = \gamma_1 (a - c) + [1 - \gamma_1 (b + d)]p_{t-1}$$

The fixed point of this system, the equilibrium point, is found by setting $p_t = p^*$ for all t. With result

$$p^* = \frac{a - c}{b + d}$$

the same equilibrium we found in earlier models.

Although the behaviour of suppliers in response to stock changes does not affect the equilibrium price (and hence also the equilibrium quantity), it does have an impact on the path to equilibrium. The solution to the difference equation (8.28) is

(8.29)
$$p_t = \frac{a - c}{b + d} + [1 - \gamma_1 (b + d)]^t \left(p_0 - \frac{a - c}{b + d} \right)$$

where p_0 is the price at time $t = 0$.

There are three possible time paths for price:

(i)   If $0 < 1 - \gamma_1 (b + d) < 1$ then the system converges steadily on the equilibrium value. This occurs if $0 < \gamma_1 < 1/(b + d)$.

(ii) If $-1 < 1 - \gamma_1(b+d) < 0$ then the system converges on the equilibrium in terms of damped oscillations. This occurs if $1/(b+d) < \gamma_1 < 2/(b+d)$.

(iii) If $1 - \gamma_1(b+d) < -1$ then the system has explosive oscillations. This occurs if $\gamma_1 > 2/(b+d)$.

Example 8.7

Consider the following model

$$q_t^d = 20 - 4p_t$$
$$q_t^s = 2 + 2.5p_t$$
$$p_t - p_{t-1} = -0.2\Delta Q_t$$

then

$$p_t = 3.6 - 0.3p_{t-1}$$

with fixed point $p^* = 2.769$ and solution

$$p_t = 2.769 + (-0.3)^t(p_0 - 2.769)$$

and the system converges on the equilibrium in terms of damped oscillations.

Turn now to assumption 2. Our model is

$$q_t^d = a - bp_t$$
$$q_t^s = c + dp_t \qquad\qquad (8.30)$$
$$p_t - p_{t-1} = -\gamma_2(Q_{t-1} - \overline{Q})$$

Substituting, we have

$$p_t = p_{t-1} - \gamma_2(Q_{t-1} - \overline{Q})$$

However, we need to establish $Q_{t-1} - \overline{Q}$. Lag this equation by one period, then

$$p_{t-1} = p_{t-2} - \gamma_2(Q_{t-2} - \overline{Q})$$

Hence,

$$p_t - p_{t-1} = p_{t-1} - p_{t-2} - \gamma_2(Q_{t-1} - Q_{t-2})$$
$$p_t = 2p_{t-1} - p_{t-2} - \gamma_2\left(q_{t-1}^s - q_{t-1}^d\right)$$
$$= 2p_{t-1} - p_{t-2} - \gamma_2(c + dp_{t-1} - a + bp_{t-1})$$

i.e.

$$p_t = \gamma_2(a - c) + [2 - \gamma_2(b+d)]p_{t-1} - p_{t-2} \qquad\qquad (8.31)$$

which is a second-order difference equation.

First establish the equilibrium, which is obtained by setting $p_t = p^*$ for all t. This is readily found to be the same, namely $p^* = (a - c)/(b + d)$. Of course, the time path to equilibrium is quite different from that under assumption 1. As we demonstrated in chapter 3, section 3.8, the solution to such a second-order difference equation is

(8.32)
$$p_t = \frac{a-c}{b+d} + c_1 r^t + c_2 s^t$$

where r and s are the characteristic roots of

(8.33)
$$x^2 - [2 - \gamma_2(b+d)]x + 1 = 0$$

The time path of prices, then, is very dependent on the sign/value of the roots r and s.

Example 8.8

Consider the same basic model as in example 8.7, with $\gamma_2 = \gamma_1 = 0.2$, then our model is

$$q_t^d = 20 - 4p_t$$
$$q_t^s = 2 + 2.5p_t$$
$$p_t - p_{t-1} = -0.2(Q_{t-1} - \overline{Q})$$

resulting in a difference equation

$$p_t = 3.6 + 0.7p_{t-1} - p_{t-2}$$

This has the characteristic equation

$$x^2 - 0.7x + 1 = 0$$

with characteristic roots $r = 0.35 + 0.9367i$ and $s = 0.35 - 0.9367i$, with $R = \sqrt{\alpha^2 + \beta^2} = 1$ (see chapter 3, section 3.8). This means that price oscillates with constant amplitude.

So far we have assumed that supply is a function of the current price. What difference do we have if supply is determined by expected price? Here we shall consider just the simplest cobweb model that includes stock behaviour under assumption 1. Our model is

(8.34)
$$q_t^d = a - bp_t$$
$$q_t^s = c + dp_t^e$$
$$p_t - p_{t-1} = -\gamma_1 \Delta Q_{t-1}$$
$$p_t^e = p_{t-1}$$

Then

$$p_t = p_{t-1} - \gamma_1\left(q_{t-1}^s - q_{t-1}^d\right)$$
$$= p_{t-1} - \gamma_1(c + dp_{t-2} - a + bp_{t-1})$$

i.e.

(8.35)
$$p_t = \gamma_1(a-c) + (1 - \gamma_1 b)p_{t-1} - \gamma_1 dp_{t-2}$$

This too is a second-order difference equation that is neither the same as equation (8.28) nor equation (8.31). It does, however, have the same equilibrium of

$p^* = (a-c)/(b+d)$. The general solution to equation (8.35) is

$$p_t = \frac{a-c}{b+d} + c_1 r^t + c_2 s^t$$

where r and s are the characteristic roots of

$$x^2 - (1 - \gamma_1 b)x + \gamma_1 d = 0 \tag{8.36}$$

Example 8.9

Again we consider the same basic model in example 8.7 with $\gamma_1 = 0.2$ and $p_t^e = p_{t-1}$. Our model is then

$$q_t^d = 20 - 4p_t$$
$$q_t^s = 2 + 2.5p_t^e$$
$$p_t - p_{t-1} = -0.2\Delta Q_{t-1}$$
$$p_t^e = p_{t-1}$$

resulting in a difference equation

$$p_t = 3.6 + 0.2p_{t-1} - 0.5p_{t-2}$$

This has characteristic equation

$$x^2 - 0.7x + 0.5 = 0$$

with characteristic roots $r = 0.1 + 0.7i$ and $s = 0.1 - 0.7i$, with $R = \sqrt{\alpha^2 + \beta^2} = 0.707$. Since $R < 1$ this system oscillates, with the oscillations becoming smaller over time.

The results of examples 8.7–8.9 can readily be verified by means of a spreadsheet. In example 8.7 we set the initial price at unity, $p(0) = p0 = 1$. The price in period 1 for this series is $p(1) = 3.3$, and we use this price in examples 8.8 and 8.9 for the price in period 1. Doing this allows all three examples to start with the same two prices. The only difference between the series, then, is the assumption about stock behaviour and the assumption about expected prices. The resulting three price series are illustrated in figure 8.14. This figure shows that the price path under assumption 1 oscillates with damped oscillations; that the price path under assumption 2 oscillates with constant amplitude, while the price path under assumption 1 with a lag on the supply side oscillates with damped oscillations.

What all these examples illustrate is the point we made at the very beginning, in section 8.1. Namely, the behaviour of the system depends very much on how suppliers change prices in response to stock levels. The last example illustrates too that the behaviour of the system also depends on how expectations are modelled.

8.8   Stability of the competitive equilibrium

Consider a competitive market composed of three commodities X_0, X_1 and X_2, with prices P_0, P_1 and P_2, respectively. If D_i and S_i denote the demand and supply functions for each commodity ($i = 0, 1, 2$), then define $E_i = D_i - S_i$ as the excess demand functions. Each excess demand is assumed to be a function of all three

Figure 8.14.

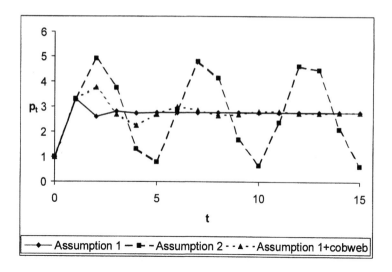

prices, hence

(8.37) $E_i = E_i(P_0, P_1, P_2) \quad i = 0, 1, 2$

We assume E_i is homogeneous of degree zero and the market satisfies Walras' law. The first assumption allows us to choose a commodity as numeraire, say commodity X_0. Then

(8.38) $E_i = E_i\left(1, \frac{P_1}{P_0}, \frac{P_2}{P_0}\right) = E_i(1, p_1, p_2) \quad i = 0, 1, 2$

where $p_i = P_i/P_0 (i = 1, 2)$. The assumption that Walras' law holds means

$$P_0 E_0 + P_1 E_1 + P_2 E_2 \equiv 0$$

or

(8.39) $E_0 + p_1 E_1 + p_2 E_2 \equiv 0$

When markets 1 and 2 are in equilibrium so that $E_1 = E_2 = 0$, then it automatically follows from Walras' law that $E_0 = 0$, which means that this market too is in equilibrium. This means market equilibrium and its stability can be considered purely in terms of commodities 1 and 2.

Now describe the dynamic adjustment process as prices changing in proportion to their excess demand. More formally

(8.40) $\dot{p}_i = k_i E_i \qquad k_i > 0, \quad i = 1, 2$

Equilibrium requires $\dot{p}_1 = 0$ and $\dot{p}_2 = 0$ (which automatically implies $\dot{p}_0 = 0$) and this will lead to equilibrium prices p_1^* and p_2^*, i.e., $E_1(1, p_1^*, p_2^*) = 0$ and $E_2(1, p_1^*, p_2^*) = 0$. Define the vector $\mathbf{p}^* = (p_1^*, p_2^*)$. Assume such an equilibrium exists. Here we are not concerned with existence but rather with the stability of the competitive equilibrium.

Stability can be considered in terms of the phase plane (p_1, p_2), obtaining the two equilibrium lines $\dot{p}_1 = 0$ and $\dot{p}_2 = 0$, which divide the phase plane into regions, and then considering the vector forces in the various regions. This we now do.

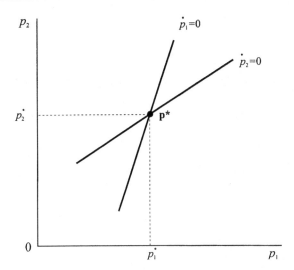

Figure 8.15.

Consider $\dot{p}_1 = 0$ first. Differentiate E_1 with respect to p_1 and p_2, i.e.

$$E_{11}dp_1 + E_{12}dp_2 = 0$$

Then

$$\left.\frac{dp_2}{dp_1}\right|_{\dot{p}_1=0} = \frac{-E_{11}}{E_{12}}$$

Similarly, for $\dot{p}_2 = 0$ we have

$$E_{21}dp_1 + E_{22}dp_2 = 0$$

$$\text{and} \quad \left.\frac{dp_2}{dp_1}\right|_{\dot{p}_2=0} = \frac{-E_{21}}{E_{22}}$$

These results give the slopes of the isoclines in the (p_1,p_2)-plane, as illustrated in figure 8.15. However, we have yet to establish the sign of the slopes or the relative slopes.

We make the assumption that commodities 1 and 2 are gross substitutes.[7] This means

(a) $E_{11} < 0$ and $E_{12} > 0$
(b) $E_{22} < 0$ and $E_{21} > 0$

It follows from condition (a) that the slope of the $\dot{p}_1 = 0$ isocline is positive, and it follows from condition (b) that the slope of the $\dot{p}_2 = 0$ isocline is positive. We further assume that commodities 0 and 1 and 0 and 2 are gross substitutes. This means $E_{01} > 0$ and $E_{02} > 0$. But how does this help us? Since E_i are homogeneous of degree zero, then from Euler's theorem[8] we have

(a) $E_{10} + p_1E_{11} + p_2E_{12} = 0$
(b) $E_{20} + p_1E_{21} + p_2E_{22} = 0$

[7] Gross substitutability refers to the uncompensated demand curve while net substitutability refers to the compensated demand curve. See Shone (1975, section 4.4).
[8] See Chiang (1984, p. 418).

From condition (a), and taking account of $E_{10} > 0$, we have

$$p_1 E_{11} + p_2 E_{12} < 0 \qquad \text{implying} \qquad \frac{p_2}{p_1} < \frac{-E_{11}}{E_{12}}$$

Similarly, from condition (b), and taking account of $E_{20} > 0$, we have

$$p_1 E_{21} + p_2 E_{22} < 0 \qquad \text{implying} \qquad \frac{p_2}{p_1} > \frac{-E_{21}}{E_{22}} \quad (\text{since } E_{22} < 0)$$

From these results it follows

$$\frac{-E_{21}}{E_{22}} < \frac{p_2}{p_1} < \frac{-E_{11}}{E_{12}}$$

i.e.

$$\left. \frac{dp_2}{dp_1} \right|_{\dot{p}_2 = 0} < \left. \frac{dp_2}{dp_1} \right|_{\dot{p}_1 = 0}$$

as illustrated in figure 8.16.

Now consider the situation each side of the isocline $\dot{p}_1 = 0$. In figure 8.16(a) we move from point a to point b. The only price changing is p_1, hence we have $E_{11} < 0$ and $E_{21} > 0$. Differentiating $\dot{p}_1 = k_1 E_1$ with respect to p_1, we obtain

$$\frac{d\dot{p}_1}{dp_1} = k_1 E_{11} < 0$$

or

$$\text{sign}(d\dot{p}_1) = \text{sign}(k_1 E_{11} dp_1)$$

Hence, to the right of $\dot{p}_1 = 0$, $\dot{p}_1 < 0$ and p_1 is falling. To the left of $\dot{p}_1 = 0$, where $dp_1 < 0$, then $\text{sign}(d\dot{p}_1) > 0$ and so $\dot{p}_1 > 0$. Carrying out the same logic for figure 8.16(b) we have $\dot{p}_2 = k_2 E_2$

$$\frac{d\dot{p}_2}{dp_1} = k_2 E_{21} > 0$$

$$\text{sign}(d\dot{p}_2) = \text{sign}(k_2 E_{21} dp_1)$$

Hence, to the right of $\dot{p}_2 = 0$ we have $\dot{p}_2 > 0$ and p_2 is rising; to the left of $\dot{p}_2 = 0$, p_2 is falling. Combining all these vector forces, we have the situation shown in figure 8.17.

A system which begins in region I will either directly converge on $\mathbf{p}^*$, or will move into either quadrants II and IV and then converge on $\mathbf{p}^*$. Similarly, any initial point lying in quadrant III will either converge directly on $\mathbf{p}^*$ or will move into either quadrant II and IV and then converge on $\mathbf{p}^*$. Points of the system beginning in region II will remain in that region with a trajectory converging on $\mathbf{p}^*$. Similarly, an initial point in region IV will have a trajectory remaining in this region and converging on $\mathbf{p}^*$.

Example 8.10

The market can be illustrated by means of the following numerical example, where we postulate only the excess demand curves for commodities 1 and 2. Suppose,

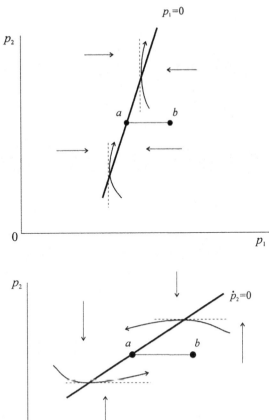

Figure 8.16.

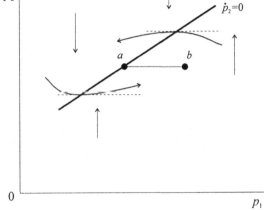

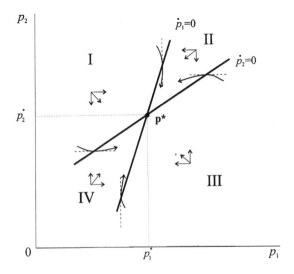

Figure 8.17.

Figure 8.18.

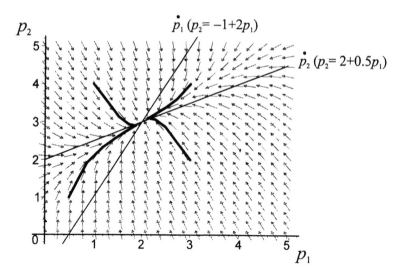

then

$$E_1 = 3 - 6p_1 + 3p_2$$
$$E_2 = 16 + 4p_1 - 8p_2$$

with dynamic adjustments

$$\dot{p}_1 = 2E_1$$
$$\dot{p}_2 = 3E_2$$

We first must establish whether an equilibrium exists (and with meaningful prices). In equilibrium $\dot{p}_1 = 0$ and $\dot{p}_2 = 0$ implying $E_1 = 0$ and $E_2 = 0$. Solving the two linear equations readily reveals $\mathbf{p}^* = (p_1^*, p_2^*) = (2, 3)$. Furthermore, the two iso-clines are readily shown to be

$$\dot{p}_1 = 0 \qquad \text{implying} \qquad p_2 = -1 + 2p_1$$
$$\dot{p}_2 = 0 \qquad \text{implying} \qquad p_2 = 2 + 0.5p_1$$

The trajectories can be derived by solving the two dynamic equations

$$\dot{p}_1 = 2(3 - 6p_1 + 3p_2) = 6 - 12p_1 + 6p_2$$
$$\dot{p}_2 = 3(16 + 4p_1 - 8p_2) = 48 + 12p_1 - 24p_2$$

as outlined in part I. In figure 8.18, derived using *Maple* and annotated, we have four trajectories with starting values

$$(0.5, 1), (3, 2), (3, 4), (1, 4)$$

along with the direction field. This figure shows quite clearly the stability of the competitive equilibrium.

8.9 The housing market and demographic changes

In this section we shall consider a model of Mankiw and Weil (1989) which deals with the impact of the 'baby boom' of earlier years and its impact on the housing market and later the 'baby bust' and its impact on the housing market. The model is captured by the following set of equations:

(i) $H_d = f(R)N$

(ii) $R = R(h)$ $R' > 0$ (8.41)

(iii) $R(h) = rP - \dot{p}$

(iv) $\dot{H} + dH = g(P)N$ $g' > 0$

where

> H = stock of housing
> H_d = demand for housing
> R = real rental price
> N = adult population
> $h = H/N$ = housing per adult
> P = real price of a standardised housing unit
> rP = operating cost of owning a home (r assumed constant)
> d = rate of depreciation
> $\dot{H}$ = net investment in housing
> $\dot{H} + dH$ = gross investment in housing
> $n = \dot{N}/N$ = growth in population

The first equation denotes the demand for housing in which the variable N acts as a shift parameter, and here attempts to capture demographic changes in the population. From this equation it follows that the demand for housing per adult is given by $H_d/H = f(R)$. Consequently the rental associated with such demand is given by the inverse of f, i.e., $R_d = f^{-1}(h) = R(h)$. The market clearing condition is that $R = R_d$, hence $R = R(h)$, which is the second equation in the model. In interpreting the third equation we note that rP is defined as the operating cost of owning a home (where r is assumed constant), i.e., the user cost, and this needs to be adjusted for the change in the price of the house – invariably the capital gain. In a perfectly functioning housing market, this should be equal to the real rental price. If this was not the case then there would be a movement out of home ownership into rented accommodation if $R < rP - \dot{p}$ and into home ownership if the reverse inequality was true. Gross investment (net investment, $\dot{H}$, plus depreciation, dH) is assumed to be an increasing function of the price of housing, $g(P)$ and $g' > 0$, and proportional to the adult population.

Rather than deal with the model in terms of H it is easier to manage by considering $h = H/N$. Differentiating h with respect to time, then

$$\dot{h} = \frac{N\dot{H} - H\dot{N}}{N^2} = \frac{\dot{H}}{N} - \left(\frac{H}{N}\right)\frac{\dot{N}}{N}$$

$$= \frac{\dot{H}}{N} - nh$$

$$= \frac{g(P)N - dH}{N} - nh$$

i.e.

$$\dot{h} = g(P) - (d + n)h$$

The model can therefore be expressed in terms of two differential equations

(8.42)

$$\dot{P} = rP - R(h)$$
$$\dot{h} = g(P) - (d+n)h$$

which allows a solution for P and h.

Suppose there exists a fixed point (h^*, P^*) such that $\dot{P} = 0$ and $\dot{h} = 0$. Such a fixed point denotes an equilibrium combination of P and h. In order to see what is happening in this model we need to investigate it in terms of the phase plane. Consider the price equation first. In a steady state we have $\dot{P} = 0$, which implies

$$rP = R(h)$$
$$P = \frac{R(h)}{r}$$
$$\frac{dP}{dh} = \frac{R'(h)}{r} < 0 \qquad \text{since } R'(h) < 0$$

Hence the price stability condition gives rise to a downward sloping line in the phase plane where P is on the vertical axis and h on the horizontal axis, as shown in figure 8.19.

To the right (and above) this line we have the condition that $P > R(h)/r$, which implies $\dot{P} > 0$, and so house prices are rising. Similarly, to the left (and below) the line shown in figure 8.19 we have $P < R(h)/r$, which implies $\dot{P} < 0$ and house prices are falling.

Now consider the second equation. In equilibrium there is no change in the number of houses per adult of the population, i.e., $\dot{h} = 0$. Hence

$$g(P) = (d+n)h$$
$$g'(P)\frac{dP}{dh} = d+n$$

i.e.

$$\frac{dP}{dh} = \frac{d+n}{g'(P)} > 0 \qquad \text{since } g'(P) > 0$$

Figure 8.19.

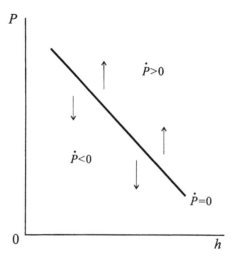

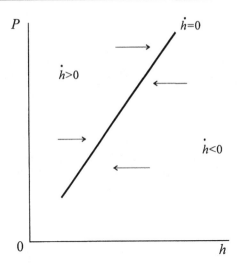

Figure 8.20.

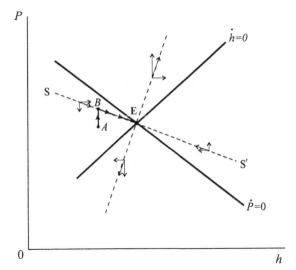

Figure 8.21.

This stability condition gives rise to an upward sloping line in the phase plane, as shown in figure 8.20. Above and to the left of the stability condition $\dot{h} > 0$ and so h is rising, while below and to the right of $\dot{h} = 0$, h is falling.

We are now in a position to put the information together, as illustrated in figure 8.21. The phase diagram illustrates the vector of forces in the various quadrants. It also illustrates the presence of a saddle point, point E, with SS' denoting the *stable* arm of the saddle point. A market which starts out of equilibrium, such as point A in figure 8.21, will initially exhibit a rapid rise in house prices, pushing the system from point A to point B on the saddle path SS', and then over time the system will move down the stable arm of the saddle path to the equilibrium point E.

Consider the market in equilibrium and a 'baby boom' occurs, resulting in a rise in the shift parameter n. For the moment let us concentrate solely on the equilibrium lines. The price equation is independent of n and so this has no effect on this line. However, the change in n will raise the absolute value of the slope

Figure 8.22.

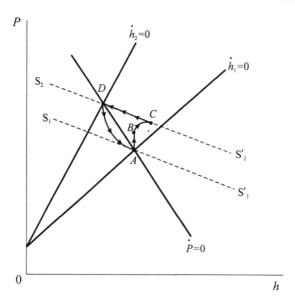

(d + n). Consequently there will be a new housing line to the left of the original. In figure 8.22 we have labelled this h_2. There is a saddle path $S_1 S_1'$ associated with the saddle point A, and there is another saddle path associated with the saddle point D, each denoting stable arms of their respective saddle points.

Suppose it is *announced* that there is a 'baby boom' and that the population is now growing at 1 per cent higher than previously, but it is also indicated that this will last for only a short period, say ten years, and then the growth will return to its previous level. What will be the movement of house prices, P, and housing per adult, h? The market, having perfect foresight, will know that there will be a rise in house prices, and so the system will move vertically up from point A to point B, this movement being purely the announcement effect. At this stage there is no increase in housing demand (since the babies have not yet become adults), and so the system is still governed by the dynamic forces associated with point A. Accordingly, the system will move in the north easterly direction, along a path like BC. Once the 'baby boom' takes place and the increase in population takes place and becomes part of the housing market, then the market will be governed by the new saddle path $S_2 S_2'$. Accordingly the system will move along this stable arm of the saddle point towards point D. However, if there is then a reduction in population growth, which returns to its former level, then the system will move along the path indicated by the arrows and towards point A. (Notice that point D, although governing the movement after point C is reached, will not necessarily be achieved.) This analysis is based on perfect foresight and movements are dominated by the stable arms of the saddle points.

In comparison the authors consider a naïve model in which house prices are assumed to remain constant at any moment of time – a very naïve version indeed! In this instance there are no capital gains (since $\dot{P} = 0$) and so $P = R(h)/r$. Since prices cannot be changing at any level of h, then the market is always positioned along the line $\dot{P} = 0$. In terms of figure 8.22, there would be no movements of

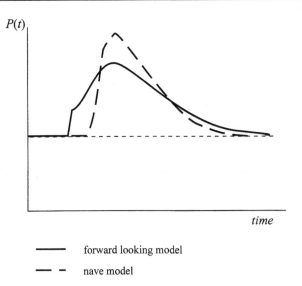

Figure 8.23.

——— forward looking model

— — nave model

the system when the announcement was made, it would simply remain at point *A*. Once the baby boom became of adult age and entered the housing market, there would be a shift left in the $\dot{h}_1 = 0$ line, moving the system towards point *D*. The system would move up the $\dot{P} = 0$ line towards point *D*, reaching point *D* at the height of the growth, and then returning down the $\dot{P} = 0$ line towards point *A*. The difference in price movement of this naïve version in comparison with the perfect foresight version is illustrated in figure 8.23.

Two observations can be made in the light of figure 8.23:

(1) A model of perfect foresight would always indicate a rise in house prices prior to the 'baby boom' becoming of adult age. This is a testable hypothesis.

(2) The range of price movement in the perfect foresight model is less than it would be in the naïve model. This is not so readily testable since it depends on a counterfactual question.

8.10 Chaotic demand and supply[9]

We have pointed out that chaotic behaviour can arise only in the presence of nonlinearity. Although it is possible to have both nonlinear demand *and* supply, the most significant nonlinearity is in supply, most especially when supply involves a time lag. Take a typical case that at low prices supply increases slowly, say because of start-up costs and fixed costs of production. Furthermore, suppose at high prices then again supply increases only slowly, say because of capacity constraints. This suggests a S-shaped supply curve. The logistic equation exhibits such a S-shape. An alternative specification, which is frequently employed in modelling, is the **arctan function**. One such specification of supply in terms of expected prices is

$$q_t^s = \arctan\left(\mu p_t^e\right) \tag{8.43}$$

---

[9] This section draws heavily on Hommes (1991, section 1.5).

Figure 8.24.

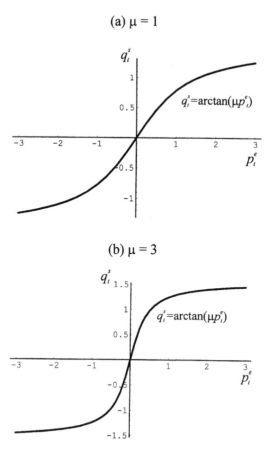

(a) $\mu = 1$

(b) $\mu = 3$

This specification sets the origin at the inflection point, which is unique, and so prices and quantities can be negative as well as positive. The parameter μ determines the steepness of the S-shape. For instance, figure 8.24(a) has $\mu = 1$ while figure 8.24(b) has $\mu = 3$. The higher the value of μ the steeper the S-shape. Note in figure 8.24 that price is on the horizontal axis and quantity is on the vertical axis – the reverse of conventional economics texts.

For simplicity we assume demand is linear and a function of actual prices, i.e.

(8.44)
$$q_t^d = a - bp_t \qquad b > 0$$

A typical nonlinear cobweb is then

(8.45)
$$q_t^d = a - bp_t$$
$$q_t^s = \arctan\left(\mu p_t^e\right)$$
$$p_t^e = p_{t-1}^e + \lambda\left(p_{t-1} - p_{t-1}^e\right)$$
$$q_t^d = q_t^s$$

The expression for expected prices is a typical *adaptive expectations* assumption, which can be written

(8.46)
$$p_t^e = \lambda p_{t-1} + (1 - \lambda)p_{t-1}^e$$

From the first, second and fourth equation of (8.45) we have

$$p_t = \frac{a - q_t^d}{b} = \frac{a - q_t^s}{b} = \frac{a - \arctan\left(\mu p_t^e\right)}{b}$$

From (8.46) we have $p_{t+1}^e = \lambda p_t + (1 - \lambda)p_t^e$ which on re-arrangement gives

$$p_t = \frac{p_{t+1}^e - (1 - \lambda)p_t^e}{\lambda}$$

Hence

$$\frac{p_{t+1}^e - (1 - \lambda)p_t^e}{\lambda} = \frac{a - \arctan\left(\mu p_t^e\right)}{b}$$

i.e.

$$p_{t+1}^e = (1 - \lambda)p_t^e + \frac{\lambda a}{b} - \frac{\lambda \arctan\left(\mu p_t^e\right)}{b} \tag{8.47}$$

or $p_{t+1}^e = f(p_t^e)$. Notice that (8.47) is a recursive equation for *expected* prices.

For given values of the parameters a, b, λ and μ we can establish the fixed point(s) of equation (8.47). But is this value unique? More specifically, what happens to the fixed point of expected prices, p^{e*}, when the demand curve shifts? A shift in the demand curve is captured by a variation in the parameter a. If we allow the parameter a to vary between -1.25 and $+1.25$ we can establish the equilibrium points for p^e by plotting the bifurcation diagram of p^{e*} against a.

Example 8.11

Let

$$\lambda = 0.3, \qquad b = 0.25, \qquad \mu = 3$$

then

$$p_{t+1}^e = 0.7p_t^e + \frac{0.3a}{0.25} - \frac{0.3 \arctan\left(3p_t^e\right)}{0.25}$$

The resulting bifurcation diagram is shown in figure 8.25.

μ = 3

Figure 8.25.

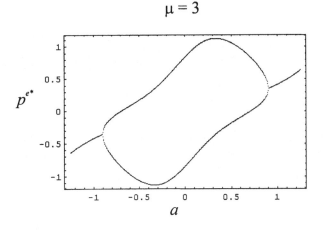

Figure 8.26.

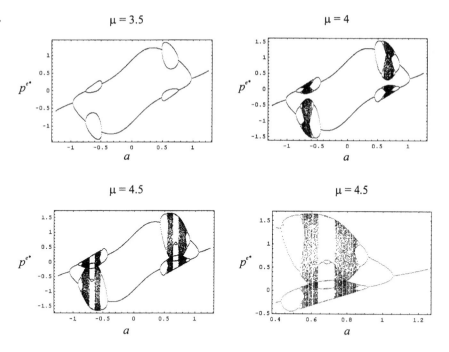

For low values of a, there is a unique equilibrium for expected price. Around the value $a = -0.9$ a period-doubling bifurcation occurs. The stable two orbit remains until a reaches about 0.9, and then a period-halving occurs. Thereafter the system settles down again to a unique stable equilibrium. An important observation to make about this diagram is that it is symmetrical about the origin.[10] This is a characteristic feature of arctan.

The question now arises: What happens when μ takes on different values? A most complex set of results can occur. For instance, figure 8.26 sets out three possibilities: $\mu = 3.5$, $\mu = 4$ and $\mu = 4.5$. In figure 8.26(a)–(c) we have a ranging over the interval -1.25 to $+1.25$. In figure 8.26(d) we have $\mu = 4.5$ and a ranging over a smaller interval, namely 0.4 to 1.25.

Figure 8.26(a) ($\mu = 3.5$) shows a doubling bifurcation turning into a period-four orbit, which then turns into a period-two orbit and finally to a stable equilibrium. In Figure 8.26(b) ($\mu = 4$) there is this same basic pattern, but within the period-four orbit there occurs periods of chaos. Such periods of chaos within the period-four orbit become larger as μ rises. A closer look at the chaotic region on the right of figure 8.26(c) ($\mu = 4.5$) shows some unusual patterns within the chaotic region, as shown in figure 8.26(d).

What is clearly illustrated by this example is that in the presence of nonlinearity markets can exhibit a variety of price behaviour, including a chaotic one. It is important, therefore, to have some clear estimation of a system's parameter values (including their margin of error!) and to establish the likely equilibria of the system for such values. If chaos is present, then the system is sensitive to initial conditions.

[10] This applies also to the diagrams in figure 8.26.

In such circumstances regression results, which are often employed in empirical work, may not be very meaningful.

Appendix 8.1 Obtaining cobwebs using *Mathematica* and *Maple*

8A.1 Mathematica[11]

To employ *Mathematica* to derive linear and nonlinear cobwebs, the main problem is deriving the sequence of points that make up the web. Here we derive the method for the linear case, since it is easier to represent and follow through. But once it has been obtained, it can be used for *both* linear and nonlinear cases. The example is from section 8.4.

First we define the price function:

```
f[p_]:= 5.6-0.4p
```

It is, of course, possible to be general and input this in the form f[p_]:=a − b p and then define $a = 5.6$ and $b = 0.4$. However, we shall continue with the numerical example. The next step is to generate a series of prices starting from the initial price, p0 (in this appendix we shall not subscript the t indicators since this will not be done within *Mathematica*). This can be accomplished quite easily with the **NestList** command and using the instruction

```
NestList[f,p0,3]
```

This will generate a sequence {pt} beginning at p0 and supplying a further three observations, i.e., it will generate the series {p0,p1,p2,p3}.

For any price p we know that the value on the line is $f(p)$. For instance at p0 the point on the line is p1 $= f$(p0). Thus, point A in figure 8A.1 is (p0,f(p0)) or (p0,p1). Point B is the associated point on the 45°-line, and is therefore represented by point (p1,p1). Point C, once again, is read off the line and is (p1,f(p1)) = (p1,p2). Point D is (p2,p2) since it is on the 45°-line; while point E is (p2,p3). The points emerging, therefore, are:

(p0,p1), (p1,p1), (p1,p2), (p2,p2), (p2,p3), . . .

Since these points consist solely of prices from the series {pt}, then it must be possible to generate these sequences of points with a suitable transformation of {pt}. This indeed can be done, but it requires a little manipulation. Consider the sequence derived using NestList[f,p0,3]. The sequence would be {p0,p1,p2,p3}. Now form the series

```
{NestList[f,p0,3], NestList[f,p0,3]}
```

The result would be:

{{p0,p1,p2,p3}, {p0,p1,p2,p3}}

---

[11] A neater more efficient version is provided in Gray and Glynn (1991, chapter 7). The less efficient version provided here is more intuitive.

Figure 8A.1

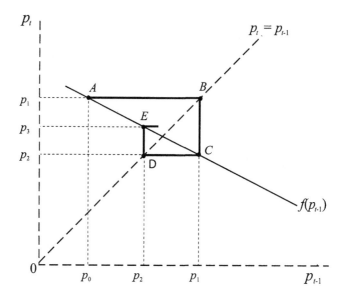

This can be considered as a matrix of dimension 2×4. Now transpose this matrix using

```
Transpose[ {NestList[f,p0,3], NestList[f,p0,3]} ]
```

which will give the list

$\{\{p0,p0\}, \{p1,p1\}, \{p2,p2\}, \{p3,p3\}\}$

which is a 4×2 matrix. Now we need to collapse this list by getting rid of the inner brackets. We do this using the **Flatten** command. Thus

```
Flatten[Transpose[{NestList[f,p0,3],
        NestList[f,p0,3]} ]]
```

gives the series $\{p0, p0, p1, p1, p2, p2, p3, p3\}$. The next step is to take groups of 2 and move along the sequence one element at a time, i.e., we wish to form the sequence

$\{\{p0,p0\}, \{p0,p1\}, \{p1,p1\}, \{p1,p2\}, \{p2,p2\}, \{p2,p3\}, \{p3,p3\}\}$

We accomplish this using the **Partition** command. Thus Partition[list,2,1] will take a 'list' and convert it into another list each element composed of two elements, and moving along 'list' one element at a time. Consequently, the sequence just given would be generated from the instruction

```
Partition[Flatten[Transpose[
        {NestList[f,p0,3], NestList[f,p0,3]} ] ], 2,1 ]
```

where we have written this over two lines for ease of viewing. The final step is to remove the first element $\{p0,p0\}$, since this is not part of the cobweb. This is accomplished using the **Rest** command. Thus, Rest[*s*] deletes the first element of the series denoted '*s*'. Our list of points, therefore, is achieved with the rather involved instruction

```
points=Rest[Partition[Flatten[Transpose[
    {NestList[f,p0,3], NestList[f,p0,3]}
        ] ], 2,1 ] ];
```

where the semicolon at the end of the instruction suppresses the points being listed.

Having obtained the list of points, we need to join them up. Let us refer to this as 'web'. Then the web is the plotting of the list of points just derived and joined together. We do this with the **ListPlot** command, and qualifying it with the instruction PlotJoined->True, which instructs the programme to join up the points. Thus

```
web=ListPlot[points, PlotJoined->True ]
```

To complete the picture we need to draw the line $f(p) = 5.6 - 4.0p$ and the 45°-line. These can be done together with the instruction

```
lines=Plot[ {f[p],p}, {p,0,10} ]
```

Our cobweb is then achieved with the final instruction

```
Show[web,lines,
    AxesLabel->{"pt-1","pt"} ]
```

which also includes an instruction to label the respective axes.

To summarise, where we have specified p0 to have a value of unity and increased the run to twenty:

```
f[p_]:=5.6-0.4p
p0=1
points=Rest[Partition[Flatten[Transpose[
    {NestList[f,p0,20],NestList[f,p0,20]}
        ] ], 2, 1 ] ];
web=ListPlot[points,PlotJoined->True,
    DisplayFunction->Identity]
lines=Plot[ {f[p],p}, {p,0,10},
    DisplayFunction->Identity ]
cobweb=Show[web,lines,
    AxesLabel->{"pt-1","pt"},
    DisplayFunction->$DisplayFunction ]
```

In these final set of instructions we have suppressed the list of points by using the semicolon and we have suppressed intermediate displays by using the instruction: DisplayFunction->Identity. The display is turned on again in the final line by adding, DisplayFunction->$DisplayFunction. The result is shown in figure 8A.2.

This set of instructions can be used for any cobweb, whether linear or nonlinear. In fact, with only a slight modification, it can be used to investigate any first-order difference equation model. For instance, we used a variant of it in chapter 7 when we investigated the properties of the logistic equation.

Figure 8A.2

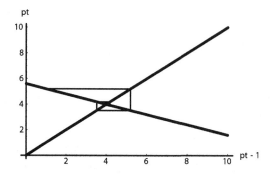

8A.2 Maple

The logic and development here is similar to the previous outline but there are
some differences. Since we shall be using linear algebra and plotting routines then
these two libraries need to be called. The first few lines of the programme are
then

```
with(linalg):
with(plots):
f:=p->5.6-0.4*p;
fn:=(p,n)->simplify( (f@@n)(p) );
```

where the last line allows us to specify the initial values of *p* and the number *n*.
In what follows we take these to be 1 and 20, respectively. Our next task is to
repeat the sequence twice and to transpose it into a 21 × 2 matrix. In the following
instructions this is called *list1*. Next we convert to an array by converting *list1* into
a vector and converting this in turn into a list. This we call *list2*. The next stage is
to make up two lists from *list2*, one in which the first element is dropped and the
second in which the last element is dropped. These two lists are combined, made
into an array, then transposed, and finally converted to a list of lists. This we label
list3. The final list, *list4*, is derived by dropping the first element. The four lists
are

```
list1:=transpose(array([[seq(fn(1,n),n=0..20)],
     [seq(fn(1,n), n=0..20) ] ] ) );
list2:=convert(convert(list1,vector),list);
list3:=convert(transpose(array(
     [ list2[1..nops(list2)-1],
       list2[2..nops(list2)] ]
           ) ), listlist);
list4:=[list3[2..nops(list3)] ];
```

In these instructions the term 'nops' denotes the number of elements in the specified
list. Thus, nops(list2) denotes the number of elements in *list2*.

The web is simply the plot of *list4*, since by default the points are joined. We
add finally the line $f(p) = 5.6 - 4.0p$ and the 45°-lines with the instruction

```
lines:=plot( {f(p),p}, p=0..10):
```

(Notice that we suppress the output by using the colon – which we also do with the web). The full instructions are:

```
with(linalg):
with(plots):
f:=p->5.6-0.4*p
fn:=(p,n)->simplify( (f@@n)(p) );
list1:=transpose(array([[seq(fn(1,n),n=0..20)],
    [seq(fn(1,n), n=0..20) ] ] ) ):
list2:=convert(convert(list1,vector),list):
list3:=convert(transpose(array(
    [ list2[1..nops(list2)-1],
    list2[2..nops(list2)] ]
    ) ), listlist):
list4:=[list3[2..nops(list3)] ]:
web:=plot(list4):
lines:=plot( {f(p),p}, p=0..10):
display( {web,lines} );
```

In these instructions we have suppressed all lists by placing a colon at the end of the instructions that generate them. In section 8.4 we present these instructions as a procedural mini-programme. An alternative derivation of a cobweb with *Maple* can be found in Lynch (2001, chapter 14).

As with *Mathematica* this routine can be used to derive a cobweb for *any* function $f(p)$, whether it is linear or nonlinear (including the possibility that $f(p)$ is kinked – as in the case of a price ceiling).

Exercises

1.　(i)　Show that if $b < 0$ in $q_t^d = a - bp_t$ and $d > 0$ in $q_t^s = c + dp_{t-1}$ then the cobweb is still convergent if $0 < d/(-b) < 1$ and divergent if $d/(-b) > 1$.

　　(ii)　Is the behaviour oscillatory?

2.　Establish the convergence, divergence, or oscillation of the following systems.

(i)　$q_t^d = 100 - 2p_t$　　　　(ii)　$q_t^d = 5 + 2p_t$

　　$q_t^s = -20 + 3p_{t-1}$　　　　　$q_t^s = 35 + p_{t-1}$

　　$p_0 = 10$　　　　　　　　　$p_0 = 10$

(iii)　$q_t^d = 100 - 2p_t$　　　(iv)　$q_t^d = 18 - 3p_t$

　　$q_t^s = -20 + 3p_{t-1}$　　　　　$q_t^s = -10 + 4p_{t-1}$

　　$p_0 = 24$　　　　　　　　　$p_0 = 1$

3.　Establish the time path of p_t for the following models.

(i)　$q_t^d = 100 - 2p_t$　　　　　　(ii)　$q_t^d = 5 + 2p_t$

　　$q_t^s = -20 + 3p_t^e$　　　　　　　$q_t^s = 35 + p_t^e$

　　$p_t^e = p_{t-1}^e - 0.5\left(p_{t-1}^e - p_{t-1}\right)$　　　$p_t^e = p_{t-1}^e - 0.2\left(p_{t-1}^e - p_{t-1}\right)$

　　$p_0 = 10$　　　　　　　　　　　$p_0 = 10$

4. Determine the stability of the following systems.

(i) $q_t^d = 250 - 50p_t$ 　　　(ii) $q_t^d = 100 - 0.5p_t$
   $q_t^s = 25 + 25p_{t-1}$ 　　　　　　$q_t^s = 50 - 0.1p_{t-1}$
   $q_t^d = q_t^s = q_t$ 　　　　　　　$q_t^d = q_t^s = q_t$

5. Determine whether an equilibrium exists for the following models, and whether they are stable.

(i) $q_t^d = 50 - 4p_t$ 　　　　(ii) $q_t^d = 50 - 4p_t$
   $q_t^s = 10 + 10p_{t-1} - p_{t-1}^2$ 　　　$q_t^s = 2 + 10p_{t-1} - p_{t-1}^2$
   $q_t^d = q_t^s = q_t$ 　　　　　　　$q_t^d = q_t^s = q_t$

6. Consider the following market:

$$q_t^d = 52 - 9p_t$$
$$q_t^s = 3 + 5p_{t-1}$$
$$q_t^d = q_t^s = q_t$$

(i) Find the equilibrium price and quantity.
(ii) Assume p_0 is 10% below the equilibrium price. Use a spreadsheet to establish how long it takes for the price to be within 1% of the equilibrium price.

7. Consider the following model

$$q_t^d = 52 - 9p_t$$
$$q_t^s = 3 + 5p_t^e$$
$$p_t^e = p_{t-1}^e - \lambda\left(p_{t-1}^e - p_{t-1}\right)$$
$$q_t^d = q_t^s = q_t$$

Assuming p_0 is 10% below the equilibrium price, how long does it take for the price to be within 1% of the equilibrium when:

(i) $\lambda = 1$
(ii) $\lambda = 0.75$
(iii) $\lambda = 0.5$
(iv) $\lambda = 0.25$

8. Given the system

$$q^d(t) = 250 - 50p(t) - 2p'(t)$$
$$q^s(t) = 25 + 25p(t)$$
$$q^d(t) = q^s(t) = q(t)$$

(i) Solve for $p(t)$.
(ii) Is this market stable?

9. The labour market is characterised by the following demand and supply equations

$$LD_t = 42 - 4w_t$$
$$LS_t = 2 + 6w_{t-1}$$
$$LD_t = LS_t$$

(i) Establish the equilibrium real wage.

(ii) Suppose a minimum wage is imposed of $w_m = 3$. Investigate the result on the dynamic outcome.

10. In the linear cobweb model of demand and supply, demonstrate that the steeper the demand curve relative to the supply curve, the more damped the oscillations and the more rapidly equilibrium is reached.

11. Given the following system

$$q_t^d = 10 - 2p_t$$
$$q_t^s = 4 + 2p_{t-1}$$
$$q_t^d = q_t^s$$

Show that this leads to a difference equation with solution

$$p_t = 1.5 + (-1)^t (p_0 - 1.5)$$

which has periodicity of 2 with values p_0 and $3 - p_0$.

12. Use *Mathematica* or *Maple* to investigate the stability of $p^* = 1$ for the nonlinear model

$$q_t^d = 4 - 3p_t$$
$$q_t^s = p_{t-1}^2$$
$$q_t^d = q_t^s = q_t$$

by trying initial values for p_0 from $p_0 = 0$ to $p_0 = 2$.

13. For the cobweb model

$$q_t^d = 24 - 5p_t$$
$$q_t^s = -4 + 2p_t^e$$
$$p_t^e = p_{t-1}^e - \lambda \left(p_{t-1}^e - p_{t-1} \right) \qquad 0 \le \lambda \le 1$$
$$q_t^d = q_t^s = q_t$$

using *Mathematical* or *Maple* investigate the stability or otherwise of the equilibrium for different values of λ.

14. Given the nonlinear system

$$\dot{P} = rP - R(h)$$
$$\dot{h} = g(P) - (d + n)h$$

(i) Derive the linear approximation about (P^*, h^*).

(ii) Assume

$$R'(h^*) = -0.5 \qquad r = 0.05 \qquad n = 0.01$$
$$g'(P^*) = 1 \qquad d = 0.02$$

and that the system is initially in equilibrium at $P^* = 1$ and $h^* = 1$. Show that the two isoclines through this equilibrium are

$$\dot{P} = 0 \qquad \text{implying} \qquad P = 11 - 10h$$
$$\dot{h} = 0 \qquad \text{implying} \qquad P = 0.97 + 0.03h$$

(iii) Show that the characteristic values of the system are $r = 0.7182$ and $s = -0.6982$ and hence verify that $(P^*, h^*) = (1, 1)$ is a saddle path equilibrium.

15.   Consider the recursive equation (8.47)

$$p_{t+1}^e = (1 - \lambda)p_t^e + \frac{\lambda a}{b} - \frac{\lambda \arctan(\mu p_t^e)}{b}$$

Let $a = 0.8$, $b = 0.25$ and $\mu = 4$. Construct a bifurcation diagram for p^e against λ for the interval $0.15 \leq \lambda \leq 0.75$. Comment on your results.

Additional reading

Further material on the contents of this chapter can be found in Allen (1965), Barro and Grilli (1994), Baumol (1959), Buchanan (1939), Chiang (1984), Eckalbar (1993), Ezekiel (1938), Gandolfo (1971), Goodwin (1947), Hommes (1991), Mankiw and Weil (1989), Nerlov (1958), Parkin and King (1995), Shone (1975) and Waugh (1964).

CHAPTER 9

Dynamic theory of oligopoly

Very few topics in the theory of the firm have been considered from a dynamic point of view. There has been some work on the dynamics of advertising and the topic of diffusion (see Shone 2001). One topic that has been considered is the stability of the Cournot solution in oligopoly. Even this topic, however, is rarely treated in intermediate microeconomics textbooks. We shall try to redress this balance in this chapter and consider in some detail the dynamics of oligopoly, both discrete and continuous versions.

To highlight a number of the issues discussed in the literature, we concentrate on a single simple example. We outline first the static result that is found in most intermediate textbooks. Here, however, we utilise the mathematical packages in order to derive the results and especially the graphical output. We then turn to the dynamics. From the very outset it is important to be clear on the dynamic assumptions made. In the spirit of Cournot (see Friedman 1983, Gandolfo 1997) in each time period each firm recalls the choices made by itself and other firms in the industry. Furthermore, each firm assumes that in time period t its rivals will choose the same output level they chose in time period $t - 1$, and chooses its own output so as to maximise its profits at time t. This is by no means the only dynamic specification. It assumes that output adjusts completely and instantaneously. Other models assume that output does not adjust completely and instantaneously. We shall consider all these in turn. Given the assumption of instantaneous adjustment just outlined, a number of propositions can be found in the literature that we need to discuss. These are:

(1)   with linear demand and constant marginal costs, for the discrete model
       (a) if $n = 2$ (duopoly) the situation is stable
       (b) if $n = 3$ the system gives rise to constant oscillations
       (c) if $n > 3$ the system is unstable.
(2)   Increasing marginal costs are a stabilising influence.

9.1   Static model of duopoly

The model we shall consider in this chapter has a very simple linear demand curve and, at this stage, constant marginal costs. The model is as follows.

(9.1)

$$p = 9 - Q$$
$$Q = q_1 + q_2$$
$$TC_1 = 3q_1$$
$$TC_2 = 3q_2$$

Since our interest is with stability and the impact of increasing the number of firms in the industry, or changing the specification of marginal cost, we assume for simplicity that all firms are identical for any size n, where n represents the number of firms in the industry. Since this model of duopoly is dealt with in most intermediate microeconomic textbooks, we shall be brief.

Total revenue and profits for each firm are:

Firm 1 $TR_1 = pq_1 = (9 - q_1 - q_2)q_1$ $\pi_1 = (9 - q_1 - q_2)q_1 - 3q_1$

Firm 2 $TR_2 = pq_2 = (9 - q_1 - q_2)q_2$ $\pi_2 = (9 - q_1 - q_2)q_2 - 3q_2$

Since the **conjectural variation** is that firm 1 will maximise its profits under the assumption that firm 2 holds its output constant, then we can differentiate the profit function of firm 1 with respect to q_1, holding q_2 constant. The same conjectural variation holds for firm 2, so it will maximise its profits under the assumption that firm 1 will hold its output level constant, so here we differentiate the profit function of firm 2 with respect to q_2, holding q_1 constant. Doing this we obtain

$$\frac{\partial \pi_1}{\partial q_1} = 6 - 2q_1 - q_2 = 0$$

$$\frac{\partial \pi_2}{\partial q_2} = 6 - q_1 - 2q_2 = 0$$

Solving we obtain the two reaction functions

(9.2)

Firm 1 R_1 $q_1 = 3 - \frac{1}{2}q_2$

Firm 2 R_2 $q_2 = 3 - \frac{1}{2}q_1$

The Cournot solution, then, is where the two reaction curves intersect, i.e., where $(q_1^*, q_2^*) = (2, 2)$. The situation is shown in figure 9.1.

Notice that the isoprofit curves for firm 1 are at a maximum, for any given level of output for firm 2, at the point on the reaction curve for firm 1. Furthermore, the preference direction is in the direction of the arrow on the reaction curve. The highest level of profits for firm 1 is at point A, where it is a monopolist. Similarly, the isoprofit curves for firm 2 are at a maximum, for any given level of output for firm 1, at the point on the reaction curve for firm 2. Firm 2's preference direction is in the direction of the arrow on its reaction curve, and the highest level of profits it can reach is indicated by point B, where firm 2 is a monopolist.

The reaction functions play an important role in our dynamic analysis. In this static duopoly model, they have also been interpreted as Nash solutions for each firm, respectively, and so the Nash solution to the game is where they are consistent: where they geometrically intersect. Hence, the solution is often called a Cournot–Nash solution. What figure 9.1 also shows is that the Cournot–Nash solution is not optimal. This is illustrated by the fact that the isoprofit curves through the Cournot–Nash solution reveal that higher profits can be achieved, as shown by the

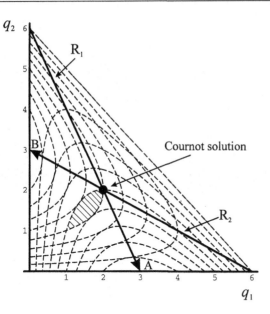

Figure 9.1.

shaded area, but that this would require some form of cooperation (collusion!) on the part of the two firms.

But how do we know whether from some arbitrary starting position the Cournot–Nash solution will be achieved? In other words, is the Cournot–Nash solution dynamically stable? In order to answer this question we must set up the model in dynamic terms. Only then can we answer this question. Whatever the answer happens to be, the same question applies when we increase the number of firms in the industry. As we do so, we must move away from the diagrammatic formulation of the model and concentrate on its mathematical specification.

In the next section we consider a discrete model with output adjusting completely and instantaneously. Our main concern is with the dynamic stability of oligopoly as the number of firms in the industry increases.

9.2 Discrete oligopoly models with output adjusting completely and instantaneously

9.2.1 Constant marginal costs

Two-firm case (n = 2)

In the static model the assumption was that firm 1 would maximise its profits under the assumption that firm 2 would hold its output level constant. A similar condition applies also to firm 2. Here we assume that in time period t its rivals will choose the same output level they chose in time period $t - 1$, and chooses its own output at time t so as to maximise its profits at time t. More specifically, $q_{1,t}$ is chosen so as to maximise firm 1's profits in time period t, under the assumption that firm 2 has output in time period t the same level it was in time period $t - 1$, so that $q_{2,t} = q_{2,t-1}$. While for firm 2, $q_{2,t}$ is chosen so as to maximise firm 2's profits in time period t, under the assumption that firm 1 has output in time period t the same level it was in time period $t - 1$, so that $q_{1,t} = q_{1,t-1}$.

These dynamic specifications for each firm change the form of the total revenue function, and hence the profit functions. Total costs are unaffected. The profit function for each firm is

Firm 1 $\pi_{1,t} = (9 - q_{1,t} - q_{2,t-1})q_{1,t} - 3q_{1,t}$

Firm 2 $\pi_{2,t} = (9 - q_{1,t-1} - q_{2,t})q_{2,t} - 3q_{2,t}$

Again, in the spirit of Cournot, each firm is maximising its profits under the conjectural variation that the other firm is holding its output level constant. Therefore,

$$\frac{\partial \pi_{1,t}}{\partial q_{1,t}} = 6 - 2q_{1,t} - q_{2,t-1} = 0$$

$$\frac{\partial \pi_{2,t}}{\partial q_{2,t}} = 6 - q_{1,t-1} - 2q_{2,t} = 0$$

which results in the following dynamic adjustments

(9.3)
$$q_{1,t} = 3 - \tfrac{1}{2}q_{2,t-1}$$
$$q_{2,t} = 3 - \tfrac{1}{2}q_{1,t-1}$$

What we have here is a simultaneous set of difference equations, which can be solved in *Mathematica* using the **RSolve** command; and, in *Maple*, using the **rsolve** command. We do this for arbitrary initial values q_{10} and q_{20} respectively. With the instructions,

```
RSolve[{q1[t]==3-(1/2)q2[t-1],q2[t]==3-(1/2) q1[t-1],
     q1[0]==q10, q2[0]==q20},{q1[t],q2[t]},t] //
          FullSimplify
```

for *Mathematica* we obtain the result

```
{{q1[t]->2+2^-1-t(q10-q20+(-1)^t(-4+q10+q20)),
     q2[t]->2+2^-1-t(-q10+q20+(-1)^t(-4+q10+q20))}}
```

It is useful to do this generalisation first because the result can then readily be set up on a spreadsheet, which often allows plots of the trajectories much easier than either *Mathematica* or *Maple*. The following instructions using *Maple*

```
rsolve({q1(t)=3-(1/2)*q2(t-1),q2(t)=3-(1/2)*q1(t-1),
     q1(0)=q10,q2(0)=q20},{q1(t),q2(t)});
```

gives the result

$$\left\{ q2(t) = -2\left(\frac{-1}{2}\right)^t + 2 + \frac{1}{2}\left(\frac{1}{2}\right)^t q20 - \frac{1}{2}\left(\frac{1}{2}\right)^t q10 \right.$$

$$+ \frac{1}{2}\left(\frac{-1}{2}\right)^t q20 + \frac{1}{2}\left(\frac{-1}{2}\right)^t q10,$$

$$q1(t) = -2\left(\frac{-1}{2}\right)^t + 2 - \frac{1}{2}\left(\frac{1}{2}\right)^t q20 + \frac{1}{2}\left(\frac{1}{2}\right)^t q10$$

$$\left. + \frac{1}{2}\left(\frac{-1}{2}\right)^t q20 + \frac{1}{2}\left(\frac{-1}{2}\right)^t q10 \right\}$$

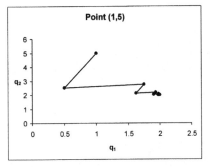

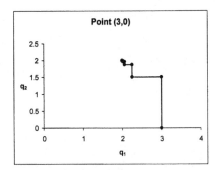

Figure 9.2.

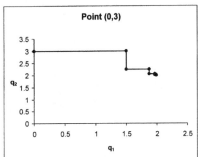

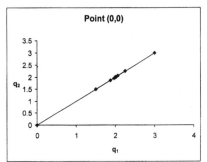

This second result allows us to see more clearly that we can express it in the form

$$q_{1,t} = 2 - 2\left(\frac{-1}{2}\right)^t + \frac{1}{2}\left(\frac{-1}{2}\right)^t (q_{10} + q_{20}) + \frac{1}{2}\left(\frac{1}{2}\right)^t (q_{10} - q_{20})$$

$$q_{2,t} = 2 - 2\left(\frac{-1}{2}\right)^t + \frac{1}{2}\left(\frac{-1}{2}\right)^t (q_{10} + q_{20}) + \frac{1}{2}\left(\frac{1}{2}\right)^t (-q_{10} + q_{20})$$

(9.4)

Since these solutions involve the terms $(1/2)^t$ and $(-1/2)^t$, then as t tends to infinity these terms tend to zero, and so the system converges on the equilibrium point $(q_1^*, q_2^*) = (2, 2)$ regardless of the initial values.

Figure 9.2 shows this convergence for four different initial values:

$(q_{10}, q_{20}) = (1, 5)$, i.e., an arbitrary point
$(q_{10}, q_{20}) = (3, 0)$, i.e., where firm 1 begins from a monopoly position
$(q_{10}, q_{20}) = (0, 3)$, i.e., where firm 2 begins from a monopoly position
$(q_{10}, q_{20}) = (0, 0)$, which can be thought of as the position where both firms are deciding to enter the industry

What is illustrated here is the general result that for linear demand and constant marginal costs, Cournot duopoly is dynamically stable.

Before leaving this duopoly example, it is useful to consider how the situation can be investigated by means of a spreadsheet. In setting the problem up on a spreadsheet, it is useful to include the initial values separately and then write the formulas in the row for time period 0, using relative and absolute addresses. This has the advantage of checking the formulas, since at time $t = 0$ the result should be

Figure 9.3.

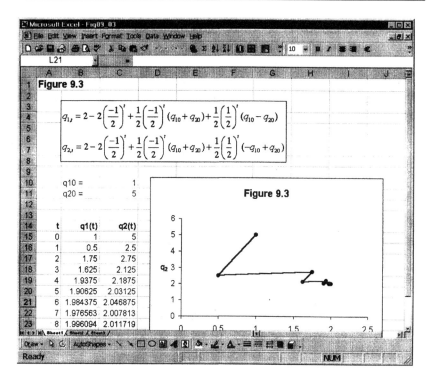

the initial values. Once the formulas have been entered for q_1 and q_2, respectively, for time period 0, taking note of absolute and relative addresses, then the results can be copied down for as many periods as desired. The trajectories are then derived by plotting $(q_1(t), q_2(t))$ using the spreadsheet's *x-y* plot. The situation is illustrated in figure 9.3 for the initial point $(q_{10}, q_{20}) = (1, 5)$.

Of course, it is even simpler to place the initial values in the row for $t = 0$ and specify

$$q_{1,t} = 3 - \tfrac{1}{2}q_{2,0}$$
$$q_{2,t} = 3 - \tfrac{1}{2}q_{1,0}$$

with relative addresses, and then copy down for as many periods as one wishes.[1] This is the way figure 9.2 and later figures are constructed. In this procedure there is no need to solve the difference equations. This simple approach is especially useful for $n \geq 3$.

What we now need to investigate is whether this stability holds for $n \geq 3$.

Three-firm case (n = 3)

We continue with our example, which assumes linear demand and constant marginal costs. Our model is now

---

[1] Recall, a quick check on the correct entry of the formulas is to place the equilibrium value as the initial value, and then all entries for output of a given firm should be the same.

$$p = 9 - Q$$
$$Q = q_1 + q_2 + q_3$$
$$TC_1 = 3q_1$$
$$TC_2 = 3q_2 \qquad (9.5)$$
$$TC_3 = 3q_3$$

Profits are readily found to be

$$\pi_1 = (9 - q_1 - q_2 - q_3)q_1 - 3q_1$$
$$\pi_2 = (9 - q_1 - q_2 - q_3)q_2 - 3q_2$$
$$\pi_3 = (9 - q_1 - q_2 - q_3)q_3 - 3q_3$$

resulting in three reaction *planes*

$$R_1 \qquad q_1 = 3 - \tfrac{1}{2}(q_2 + q_3)$$
$$R_2 \qquad q_2 = 3 - \tfrac{1}{2}(q_1 + q_3) \qquad (9.6)$$
$$R_3 \qquad q_3 = 3 - \tfrac{1}{2}(q_1 + q_2)$$

These three planes intersect at the unique value $(q_1^*, q_2^*, q_3^*) = (\tfrac{3}{2}, \tfrac{3}{2}, \tfrac{3}{2})$, the static Cournot–Nash solution for a three-firm oligopoly, given the present model. This is shown in figure 9.4.

Given exactly the same assumptions about dynamic behaviour as we outlined above in equation (9.3), then the profit for each firm is

Firm 1 $\qquad \pi_{1,t} = (9 - q_{1,t} - q_{2,t-1} - q_{3,t-1})q_{1,t} - 3q_{1,t}$

Firm 2 $\qquad \pi_{2,t} = (9 - q_{1,t-1} - q_{2,t} - q_{3,t-1})q_{2,t} - 3q_{2,t}$

Firm 3 $\qquad \pi_{3,t} = (9 - q_{1,t-1} - q_{2,t-1} - q_{3,t})q_{3,t} - 3q_{3,t}$

Again, in the spirit of Cournot, each firm is maximising its profits under the conjectural variation that the other firms are holding their output levels constant.

Figure 9.4.

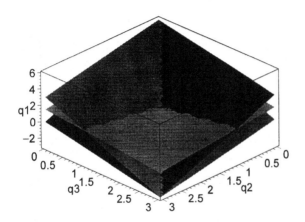

Therefore

$$\frac{\partial \pi_{1,t}}{\partial q_{1,t}} = 6 - 2q_{1,t} - q_{2,t-1} - q_{3,t-1} = 0$$

$$\frac{\partial \pi_{2,t}}{\partial q_{2,t}} = 6 - q_{1,t-1} - 2q_{2,t} - q_{3,t-1} = 0$$

$$\frac{\partial \pi_{3,t}}{\partial q_{3,t}} = 6 - q_{1,t-1} - q_{2,t-1} - 2q_{3,t} = 0$$

which results in the following dynamic adjustments

(9.7)
$$q_{1,t} = 3 - \tfrac{1}{2}q_{2,t-1} - \tfrac{1}{2}q_{3,t-1}$$

$$q_{2,t} = 3 - \tfrac{1}{2}q_{1,t-1} - \tfrac{1}{2}q_{3,t-1}$$

$$q_{3,t} = 3 - \tfrac{1}{2}q_{1,t-1} - \tfrac{1}{2}q_{2,t-1}$$

What we have here is a simultaneous set of three difference equations, which can be solved in *Mathematica* using the **RSolve** command; and, in *Maple*, using the **rsolve** command for some initial values q_{10}, q_{20} and q_{30}. The instructions are identical to those given above, so we shall not reproduce them here. The results, however, are quite revealing. With some re-arrangement of the results provided by the packages, we can express the solutions in the form

(9.8)
$$q_{1,t} = \frac{3}{2} - \frac{3}{2}(-1)^t + \frac{1}{3}(-1)^t(q_{10} + q_{20} + q_{30}) + \frac{1}{3}\left(\frac{1}{2}\right)^t (2q_{10} - q_{20} - q_{30})$$

$$q_{2,t} = \frac{3}{2} - \frac{3}{2}(-1)^t + \frac{1}{3}(-1)^t(q_{10} + q_{20} + q_{30}) + \frac{1}{3}\left(\frac{1}{2}\right)^t (-q_{10} + 2q_{20} - q_{30})$$

$$q_{3,t} = \frac{3}{2} - \frac{3}{2}(-1)^t + \frac{1}{3}(-1)^t(q_{10} + q_{20} + q_{30}) + \frac{1}{3}\left(\frac{1}{2}\right)^t (-q_{10} - q_{20} + 2q_{30})$$

It is no longer the case that as t tends to infinity the system will converge on the Cournot–Nash solution. In fact, because of the terms $(-1)^t$, the system will begin to oscillate between two values. Figure 9.5 shows the trajectory $\{q_{1t}, q_{2t}, q_{3t}\}$ for two initial values: (a) point (1,2,3) and (b) point (3,0,0). The figures readily reveal the general result that for linear demand with constant marginal costs, with three firms in the industry, the path of output for each firm will eventually give rise to a constant oscillation over time. In this example output for each firm oscillates between 1 and 2.

The plot in figure 9.5(a) can be generated by the two programmes by means of the following instructions. Figure 9.5(b) is generated by a similar set of instructions:

Mathematica
```
Needs["Graphics`Graphics3D`"]
q1[t_]:=(3/2)-(3/2)(-1)^t+(1/3)(-1)^t(6)+(1/3)(1/2)^t(-3)
q2[t_]:=(3/2)-(3/2)(-1)^t+(1/3)(-1)^t(6)+(1/3)(1/2)^t(0)
q3[t_]:=(3/2)-(3/2)(-1)^t+(1/3)(-1)^t(6)+(1/3)(1/2)^t(3)
```

(a) Initial point = (1,2,3)

Figure 9.5.

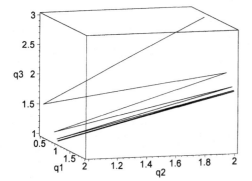

(b) Initial point = (3,0,0)

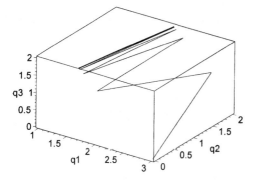

```
points=Evaluate[Table[{q1[t],q2[t],q3[t]},{t,0,10}]
ScatterPlot3D[points,PlotJoined->True,
       AxesLabel={``q1'',''q2'',''q3''},
       PlotStyle->Thickness[0.01]];
```

Maple

```
with(plots):
q1:=t->(3/2)-(3/2)*(-1)^t+(1/3)*((-1)^t)*6+(1/3)*((1/2)^t)*(-3);
q2:=t->(3/2)-(3/2)*(-1)^t+(1/3)*((-1)^t)*6+(1/3)*((1/2)^t)*(0);
q3:=t->(3/2)-(3/2)*(-1)^t+(1/3)*((-1)^t)*6+(1/3)*((1/2)^t)*3;
points:=[seq([q1(t),q2(t),q3(t)],t=0..10)];
pointplot3d(points,
       axes=BOXED, connect=true,thickness=2,
       labels=[``q1'',''q2'',''q3''],
       colour=black,
       orientation=[-17,79]);
```

Figure 9.5 was in fact generated by the *Maple* instructions.[2]

---

[2] Orientation in either programme requires some trial and error to get a perspective that is the most revealing of the 3-dimensional plot. Figure 9.5(b) has orientation =[−56,50]. It is usually necessary to join up the points because this gives a better view of the discrete trajectory.

Four-firm case (n = 4)

Our model is now

(9.9)

$$p = 9 - Q$$
$$Q = q_1 + q_2 + q_3 + q_4$$
$$TC_1 = 3q_1$$
$$TC_2 = 3q_2$$
$$TC_3 = 3q_3$$
$$TC_4 = 3q_4$$

Profits are readily found to be

$$\pi_1 = (9 - q_1 - q_2 - q_3 - q_4)q_1 - 3q_1$$
$$\pi_2 = (9 - q_1 - q_2 - q_3 - q_4)q_2 - 3q_2$$
$$\pi_3 = (9 - q_1 - q_2 - q_3 - q_4)q_3 - 3q_3$$
$$\pi_4 = (9 - q_1 - q_2 - q_3 - q_4)q_4 - 3q_4$$

resulting in four reaction **planes**

$$R_1 \qquad q_1 = 3 - \tfrac{1}{2}(q_2 + q_3 + q_4)$$
$$R_2 \qquad q_2 = 3 - \tfrac{1}{2}(q_1 + q_3 + q_4)$$
$$R_3 \qquad q_3 = 3 - \tfrac{1}{2}(q_1 + q_2 + q_4)$$
$$R_4 \qquad q_4 = 3 - \tfrac{1}{2}(q_1 + q_2 + q_3)$$

These four reaction functions can be solved for the unique value $(q_1^*, q_2^*, q_3^*, q_4^*) = (\tfrac{6}{5}, \tfrac{6}{5}, \tfrac{6}{5}, \tfrac{6}{5})$, the static Cournot–Nash solution for a four-firm oligopoly, given the present model.

Given exactly the same assumptions about dynamic behaviour as we outlined above, then the profit for each firm is

Firm 1 $\qquad \pi_{1,t} = (9 - q_{1,t} - q_{2,t-1} - q_{3,t-1} - q_{4,t-1})q_{1,t} - 3q_{1,t}$

Firm 2 $\qquad \pi_{2,t} = (9 - q_{1,t-1} - q_{2,t} - q_{3,t-1} - q_{4,t-1})q_{2,t} - 3q_{2,t}$

Firm 3 $\qquad \pi_{3,t} = (9 - q_{1,t-1} - q_{2,t-1} - q_{3,t} - q_{4,t-1})q_{3,t} - 3q_{3,t}$

Firm 4 $\qquad \pi_{4,t} = (9 - q_{1,t-1} - q_{2,t-1} - q_{3,t-1} - q_{4,t})q_{4,t} - 3q_{4,t}$

Differentiating, we obtain

$$\frac{\partial \pi_{1,t}}{\partial q_{1,t}} = 6 - 2q_{1,t} - q_{2,t-1} - q_{3,t-1} - q_{4,t-1} = 0$$

$$\frac{\partial \pi_{2,t}}{\partial q_{2,t}} = 6 - q_{1,t-1} - 2q_{2,t} - q_{3,t-1} - q_{4,t-1} = 0$$

$$\frac{\partial \pi_{3,t}}{\partial q_{3,t}} = 6 - q_{1,t-1} - q_{2,t-1} - 2q_{3,t} - q_{4,t-1} = 0$$

$$\frac{\partial \pi_{4,t}}{\partial q_{4,t}} = 6 - q_{1,t-1} - q_{2,t-1} - q_{3,t-1} - 2q_{4,t} = 0$$

which results in the following dynamic adjustments

$$q_{1,t} = 3 - \tfrac{1}{2}q_{2,t-1} - \tfrac{1}{2}q_{3,t-1} - \tfrac{1}{2}q_{4,t-1}$$

$$q_{2,t} = 3 - \tfrac{1}{2}q_{1,t-1} - \tfrac{1}{2}q_{3,t-1} - \tfrac{1}{2}q_{4,t-1}$$

$$q_{3,t} = 3 - \tfrac{1}{2}q_{1,t-1} - \tfrac{1}{2}q_{2,t-1} - \tfrac{1}{2}q_{4,t-1}$$

$$q_{4,t} = 3 - \tfrac{1}{2}q_{1,t-1} - \tfrac{1}{2}q_{2,t-1} - \tfrac{1}{2}q_{3,t-1}$$

We can, once again, express the solutions in the form

$$q_{1,t} = \frac{6}{5} - \frac{6}{5}\left(\frac{-3}{2}\right)^t + \frac{1}{4}\left(\frac{-3}{2}\right)^t (q_{10} + q_{20} + q_{30} + q_{40})$$

$$+ \frac{1}{4}\left(\frac{1}{2}\right)^t (3q_{10} - q_{20} - q_{30} - q_{40})$$

$$q_{2,t} = \frac{6}{5} - \frac{6}{5}\left(\frac{-3}{2}\right)^t + \frac{1}{4}\left(\frac{-3}{2}\right)^t (q_{10} + q_{20} + q_{30} + q_{40})$$

$$+ \frac{1}{4}\left(\frac{1}{2}\right)^t (-q_{10} + 3q_{20} - q_{30} - q_{40})$$

$$q_{3,t} = \frac{6}{5} - \frac{6}{5}\left(\frac{-3}{2}\right)^t + \frac{1}{4}\left(\frac{-3}{2}\right)^t (q_{10} + q_{20} + q_{30} + q_{40})$$

$$+ \frac{1}{4}\left(\frac{1}{2}\right)^t (-q_{10} - q_{20} + 3q_{30} - q_{40})$$

$$q_{4,t} = \frac{6}{5} - \frac{6}{5}\left(\frac{-3}{2}\right)^t + \frac{1}{4}\left(\frac{-3}{2}\right)^t (q_{10} + q_{20} + q_{30} + q_{40})$$

$$+ \frac{1}{4}\left(\frac{1}{2}\right)^t (-q_{10} - q_{20} - q_{30} + 3q_{40})$$

(9.10)

Because of the presence of $(-3/2)^t$, then as t approaches infinity, these terms become larger, and so the system is unstable. Figure 9.6 shows the path output for firms 1 and 2 for the initial point $(q_{10}, q_{20}, q_{30}, q_{40}) = (3, 0, 0, 0)$, i.e., where firm 1 begins from a monopoly position. Firms 3 and 4 have identical time paths for output as firm 2. Of course, output cannot become negative. But what figure 9.6 illustrates is the inherent instability with four firms. In fact we have illustrated here the general result that for a linear demand curve and constant marginal costs, for $n > 3$, the system is unstable.

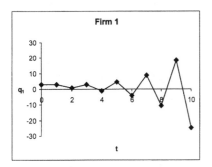

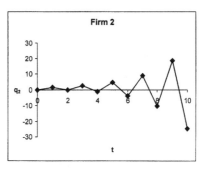

Figure 9.6.

Figure 9.7.

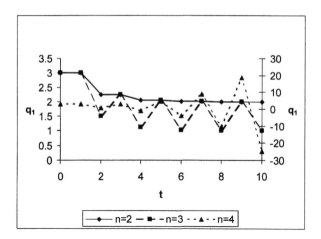

Concentrating on firm 1 for the moment, we can plot the time path of output for $n = 2, 3$ and 4 starting at the initial same monopoly value, i.e., $q_1 = 3$, while all other output levels are zero no matter how many firms there are in the industry. This is illustrated in figure 9.7, where we have the situation for $n = 2$ and 3 in relation to the left axis and $n = 4$ refers to the right axis. It quite readily reveals that the stability exhibited for $n = 2$ is the exception rather than the rule!

9.2.2   *Increasing marginal costs*

Two-firm case (n = 2)

We retain the basic model, with the exception that each firm has rising marginal cost. In particular, we assume

(9.11)

$$p = 9 - Q$$
$$Q = q_1 + q_2$$
$$TC_1 = 3q_1^2$$
$$TC_2 = 3q_2^2$$

Profits are then

Firm 1 $\quad \pi_{1,t} = (9 - q_{1,t} - q_{2,t-1})q_{1,t} - 3q_{1,t}^2$

Firm 2 $\quad \pi_{2,t} = (9 - q_{1,t-1} - q_{2,t})q_{2,t} - 3q_{2,t}^2$

Differentiating

$$\frac{\partial \pi_{1,t}}{\partial q_{1,t}} = 9 - 8q_{1,t} - q_{2,t-1} = 0$$

$$\frac{\partial \pi_{2,t}}{\partial q_{2,t}} = 9 - q_{1,t-1} - 8q_{2,t} = 0$$

which results in the following dynamic adjustments

$$q_{1,t} = \frac{9}{8} - \frac{1}{8}q_{2,t-1}$$

$$q_{2,t} = \frac{9}{8} - \frac{1}{8}q_{1,t-1}$$

Setting $q_{1,t} = q_1$ and $q_{2,t} = q_2$ for all t, we can readily solve for the Cournot–Nash solution, which is $(q_1^*, q_2^*) = (1, 1)$. Solving the difference equations for initial values $(q_{1,0}, q_{2,0}) = (q_{10}, q_{20})$, we obtain the solutions

$$q_{1,t} = 1 - \left(\frac{-1}{8}\right)^t + \frac{1}{2}\left(\frac{-1}{8}\right)^t (q_{10} + q_{20}) + \frac{1}{2}\left(\frac{1}{8}\right)^t (q_{10} - q_{20})$$

$$q_{2,t} = 1 - \left(\frac{-1}{8}\right)^t + \frac{1}{2}\left(\frac{-1}{8}\right)^t (q_{10} + q_{20}) + \frac{1}{2}\left(\frac{1}{8}\right)^t (-q_{10} + q_{20})$$

(9.12)

Since these solutions involve $(1/8)^t$ and $(-1/8)^t$, then as t tends to infinity these terms tend to zero, and so the system converges on the equilibrium point $(q_1^*, q_2^*) = (1, 1)$, regardless of the initial values. Since the terms in brackets involve $(1/8)$ in absolute value, rather than our earlier $(1/2)$ in absolute value, then the system will converge on the equilibrium much quicker.

We conclude, then, for the case of two firms with increasing marginal costs, that the system remains stable and approaches equilibrium much more rapidly.

Three-firm case $(n = 3)$

The profit for each firm is

Firm 1 $\pi_{1,t} = (9 - q_{1,t} - q_{2,t-1} - q_{3,t-1})q_{1,t} - 3q_{1,t}^2$

Firm 2 $\pi_{2,t} = (9 - q_{1,t-1} - q_{2,t} - q_{3,t-1})q_{2,t} - 3q_{2,t}^2$

Firm 3 $\pi_{3,t} = (9 - q_{1,t-1} - q_{2,t-1} - q_{3,t})q_{3,t} - 3q_{3,t}^2$

Differentiating

$$\frac{\partial \pi_{1,t}}{\partial q_{1,t}} = 9 - 8q_{1,t} - q_{2,t-1} - q_{3,t-1} = 0$$

$$\frac{\partial \pi_{2,t}}{\partial q_{2,t}} = 9 - q_{1,t-1} - 8q_{2,t} - q_{3,t-1} = 0$$

$$\frac{\partial \pi_{3,t}}{\partial q_{3,t}} = 9 - q_{1,t-1} - q_{2,t-1} - 8q_{3,t} = 0$$

which results in the following dynamic adjustments

$$q_{1,t} = \frac{9}{8} - \frac{1}{8}q_{2,t-1} - \frac{1}{8}q_{3,t-1}$$

$$q_{2,t} = \frac{9}{8} - \frac{1}{8}q_{1,t-1} - \frac{1}{8}q_{3,t-1}$$

$$q_{3,t} = \frac{9}{8} - \frac{1}{8}q_{1,t-1} - \frac{1}{8}q_{2,t-1}$$

Setting $q_{1,t} = q_1$, $q_{2,t} = q_2$ and $q_{3,t} = q_3$ for all t, we can readily solve for the Cournot–Nash solution, which is $(q_1^*, q_2^*, q_3^*) = (\frac{9}{10}, \frac{9}{10}, \frac{9}{10})$. Solving the difference equations for initial values $(q_{1,0}, q_{2,0}, q_{3,0}) = (q_{10}, q_{20}, q_{30})$, we obtain the solutions

(9.13)

$$q_{1,t} = \frac{9}{10} - \frac{9}{10}\left(\frac{-1}{4}\right)^t + \frac{1}{3}\left(\frac{-1}{4}\right)^t(q_{10} + q_{20} + q_{30})$$

$$+ \frac{1}{3}\left(\frac{1}{8}\right)^t(2q_{10} - q_{20} - q_{30})$$

$$q_{2,t} = \frac{9}{10} - \frac{9}{10}\left(\frac{-1}{4}\right)^t + \frac{1}{3}\left(\frac{-1}{4}\right)^t(q_{10} + q_{20} + q_{30})$$

$$+ \frac{1}{3}\left(\frac{1}{8}\right)^t(-q_{10} + 2q_{20} - q_{30})$$

$$q_{3,t} = \frac{9}{10} - \frac{9}{10}\left(\frac{-1}{4}\right)^t + \frac{1}{3}\left(\frac{-1}{4}\right)^t(q_{10} + q_{20} + q_{30})$$

$$+ \frac{1}{3}\left(\frac{1}{8}\right)^t(-q_{10} - q_{20} + 2q_{30})$$

Unlike the constant marginal cost, with increasing marginal cost the three-firm dynamic oligopoly model becomes stable. This is because the terms involving $(-1/4)^t$ and $(1/8)^t$ will tend to zero as t tends to infinity, and so the system converges on the equilibrium point $(q_1^*, q_2^*, q_3^*) = (\frac{9}{10}, \frac{9}{10}, \frac{9}{10})$. This can readily be verified using the 3-dimensional plot instructions given earlier.

Four-firm case (n = 4)

The profit for each firm is

Firm 1 $\pi_{1,t} = (9 - q_{1,t} - q_{2,t-1} - q_{3,t-1} - q_{4,t-1})q_{1,t} - 3q_{1,t}^2$

Firm 2 $\pi_{2,t} = (9 - q_{1,t-1} - q_{2,t} - q_{3,t-1} - q_{4,t-1})q_{2,t} - 3q_{2,t}^2$

Firm 3 $\pi_{3,t} = (9 - q_{1,t-1} - q_{2,t-1} - q_{3,t} - q_{4,t-1})q_{3,t} - 3q_{3,t}^2$

Firm 4 $\pi_{4,t} = (9 - q_{1,t-1} - q_{2,t-1} - q_{3,t-1} - q_{4,t})q_{4,t} - 3q_{4,t}^2$

Differentiating

$$\frac{\partial \pi_{1,t}}{\partial q_{1,t}} = 9 - 8q_{1,t} - q_{2,t-1} - q_{3,t-1} - q_{4,t-1} = 0$$

$$\frac{\partial \pi_{2,t}}{\partial q_{2,t}} = 9 - q_{1,t-1} - 8q_{2,t} - q_{3,t-1} - q_{4,t-1} = 0$$

$$\frac{\partial \pi_{3,t}}{\partial q_{3,t}} = 9 - q_{1,t-1} - q_{2,t-1} - 8q_{3,t} - q_{4,t-1} = 0$$

$$\frac{\partial \pi_{4,t}}{\partial q_{4,t}} = 9 - q_{1,t-1} - q_{2,t-1} - q_{3,t-1} - 8q_{4,t} = 0$$

which results in the following dynamic adjustments

$$q_{1,t} = \frac{9}{8} - \frac{1}{8}q_{2,t-1} - \frac{1}{8}q_{3,t-1} - \frac{1}{8}q_{4,t-1}$$

$$q_{2,t} = \frac{9}{8} - \frac{1}{8}q_{1,t-1} - \frac{1}{8}q_{3,t-1} - \frac{1}{8}q_{4,t-1}$$

$$q_{3,t} = \frac{9}{8} - \frac{1}{8}q_{1,t-1} - \frac{1}{8}q_{2,t-1} - \frac{1}{8}q_{4,t-1}$$

$$q_{4,t} = \frac{9}{8} - \frac{1}{8}q_{1,t-1} - \frac{1}{8}q_{2,t-1} - \frac{1}{8}q_{3,t-1}$$

(9.14)

Setting $q_{1,t} = q_1, q_{2,t} = q_2, q_{3,t} = q_3$ and $q_{4,t} = q_4$ for all t, we can readily solve for the Cournot–Nash solution, which is $(q_1^*, q_2^*, q_3^*, q_4^*) = (\frac{9}{11}, \frac{9}{11}, \frac{9}{11}, \frac{9}{11})$. Solving the difference equations for initial values $(q_{1,0}, q_{2,0}, q_{3,0}, q_{4,0}) = (q_{10}, q_{20}, q_{30}, q_{40})$, we obtain the solution

$$q_{1,t} = \frac{9}{11} - \frac{9}{11}\left(\frac{-3}{8}\right)^t + \frac{1}{4}\left(\frac{-3}{8}\right)^t (q_{10} + q_{20} + q_{30} + q_{40})$$
$$+ \frac{1}{4}\left(\frac{1}{8}\right)^t (3q_{10} - q_{20} - q_{30} - q_{40})$$

$$q_{2,t} = \frac{9}{11} - \frac{9}{11}\left(\frac{-3}{8}\right)^t + \frac{1}{4}\left(\frac{-3}{8}\right)^t (q_{10} + q_{20} + q_{30} + q_{40})$$
$$+ \frac{1}{4}\left(\frac{1}{8}\right)^t (-q_{10} + 3q_{20} - q_{30} - q_{40})$$

(9.15)

$$q_{3,t} = \frac{9}{11} - \frac{9}{11}\left(\frac{-3}{8}\right)^t + \frac{1}{4}\left(\frac{-3}{8}\right)^t (q_{10} + q_{20} + q_{30} + q_{40})$$
$$+ \frac{1}{4}\left(\frac{1}{8}\right)^t (-q_{10} - q_{20} + 3q_{30} - q_{40})$$

$$q_{4,t} = \frac{9}{11} - \frac{9}{11}\left(\frac{-3}{8}\right)^t + \frac{1}{4}\left(\frac{-3}{8}\right)^t (q_{10} + q_{20} + q_{30} + q_{40})$$
$$+ \frac{1}{4}\left(\frac{1}{8}\right)^t (-q_{10} - q_{20} - q_{30} + 3q_{40})$$

Once again, the unstable system with constant marginal cost becomes a stable system when marginal cost is rising.

Figure 9.8 compares the time path of output q_1 for $n = 2$, 3 and 4, for both constant marginal costs and increasing marginal costs. This figure readily shows the special case of stability for constant marginal costs, and the stabilising influence that arises when marginal costs are rising.

9.3 Discrete oligopoly models with output not adjusting completely and instantaneously

9.3.1 *Constant marginal costs*

Two-firm case (n = 2)

Still in keeping with the Cournot spirit of dynamic adjustment, we now turn to incomplete and noninstantaneous adjustment. In particular, we assume that for

Figure 9.8.

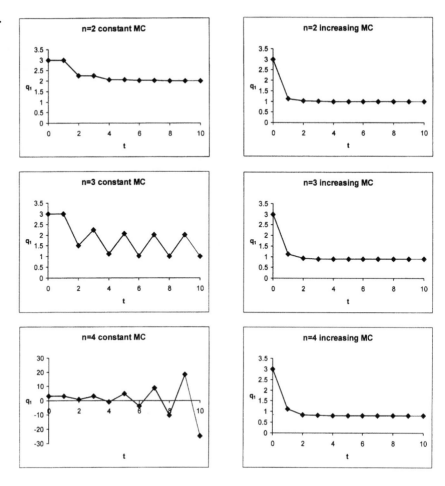

each firm

(9.16)

$$q_{1,t} - q_{1,t-1} = k_1(x_{1,t} - q_{1,t-1}) \quad k_1 > 0$$
$$q_{2,t} - q_{2,t-1} = k_2(x_{2,t} - q_{2,t-1}) \quad k_2 > 0$$

where $x_{1,t}$ and $x_{2,t}$ are the desired output levels for each firm. What these adjustment equations indicate is that each firm adjusts its previous period's output by a proportion of the discrepancy between its desired output level at time t and its output level in the previous period. Note also, however, that the optimal value at time t is adjusted according to the information at time $t - 1$. Output at time t can therefore be considered a two-step procedure. The adjustment is illustrated in figure 9.9. The system at time $t - 1$ is at point A. Given the adjustment equations (9.16) the system moves in the next period to point B, and so on. What is not obvious is whether it will converge on the Cournot solution, point C. Nor is it obvious what shape the trajectory will take. These two issues we need to investigate.

The desired output levels on the part of each firm are given by their reaction function, so that

Figure 9.9.

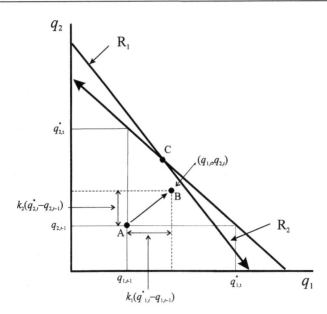

$$x_{1,t} = 3 - \tfrac{1}{2}q_{2,t-1}$$
$$x_{2,t} = 3 - \tfrac{1}{2}q_{1,t-1}$$

(9.17)

Substituting and simplifying we have

$$q_{1,t} = 3k_1 + (1 - k_1)q_{1,t-1} - \tfrac{1}{2}k_1 q_{2,t-1}$$
$$q_{2,t} = 3k_2 - \tfrac{1}{2}k_2 q_{1,t-1} + (1 - k_2)q_{2,t-1}$$

(9.18)

Although these difference equations can be solved, the output is long and unwieldy. We can however, obtain some additional insight if we assume that $k_1 = k_2 = k$ and solve for initial values $q_{1,0} = q_{10}$ and $q_{2,0} = q_{20}$. The solutions are

$$q_{1,t} = 2 - 2\left(\frac{-3k}{2} + 1\right)^t + \frac{1}{2}\left(\frac{-3k}{2} + 1\right)^t (q_{10} + q_{20})$$
$$+ \frac{1}{2}\left(\frac{-k}{2} + 1\right)^t (q_{10} - q_{20})$$

(9.19)

$$q_{2,t} = 2 - 2\left(\frac{-3k}{2} + 1\right)^t + \frac{1}{2}\left(\frac{-3k}{2} + 1\right)^t (q_{10} + q_{20})$$
$$+ \frac{1}{2}\left(\frac{-k}{2} + 1\right)^t (-q_{10} + q_{20})$$

Since $k > 0$, then both roots are less than $+1$. Accordingly, stability will be assured if the roots are greater than -1. Furthermore, $\left(\frac{-3k}{2} + 1\right)$ is less than $\left(\frac{-k}{2} + 1\right)$ and so the root $\left(\frac{-3k}{2} + 1\right)$ dominates the system. Stability requires that $\left(\frac{-3k}{2} + 1\right) > -1$ or

Figure 9.10.

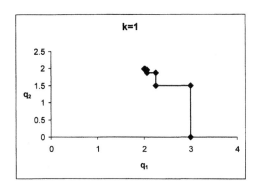

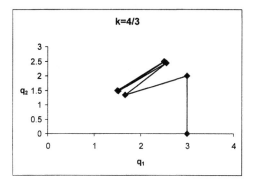

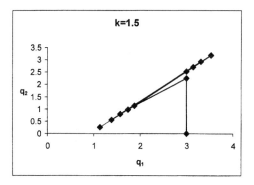

$k < 4/3$. If $k = 4/3$ then the root is -1, and the system oscillates, after a certain time period. If $k > 4/3$ then the system is explosive.

Although the duopoly model with complete and instantaneous adjustment is stable, the same cannot be said of partial adjustment. In this instance, duopoly can exhibit stable, oscillatory and explosive adjustment paths depending on the size of the adjustment coefficient k. One example of each is illustrated in figure 9.10. When $k = 1$ the system converges on the fixed point. For $k = 4/3$ the system soon converges on the two values which the system oscillates between, namely 1.5 and 2.5. However, when $k = 1.5$ the system is explosive, oscillating with greater amplitude either side of the fixed point.

Three-firm case (n = 3)

Retaining our assumption of identical adjustment coefficients, then $(k > 0)$

$$q_{1,t} - q_{1,t-1} = k(x_{1,t} - q_{1,t-1})$$
$$q_{2,t} - q_{2,t-1} = k(x_{2,t} - q_{2,t-1})$$
$$q_{3,t} - q_{3,t-1} = k(x_{3,t} - q_{3,t-1})$$

with optimal outputs given by

$$x_{1,t} = 3 - \tfrac{1}{2}q_{2,t-1} - \tfrac{1}{2}q_{3,t-1}$$
$$x_{2,t} = 3 - \tfrac{1}{2}q_{1,t-1} - \tfrac{1}{2}q_{3,t-1} \tag{9.20}$$
$$x_{3,t} = 3 - \tfrac{1}{2}q_{1,t-1} - \tfrac{1}{2}q_{2,t-1}$$

Substituting and simplifying we obtain the following difference equations

$$q_{1,t} = 3k + (1-k)q_{1,t-1} - \tfrac{1}{2}kq_{2,t-1} - \tfrac{1}{2}kq_{3,t-1}$$
$$q_{2,t} = 3k - \tfrac{1}{2}kq_{1,t-1} + (1-k)q_{2,t-1} - \tfrac{1}{2}kq_{3,t-1} \tag{9.21}$$
$$q_{3,t} = 3k - \tfrac{1}{2}kq_{1,t-1} - \tfrac{1}{2}kq_{2,t-1} + (1-k)q_{3,t-1}$$

Solving for initial values $q_{1,0} = q_{10}, q_{2,0} = q_{20}$ and $q_{3,0} = q_{30}$ we have

$$
\begin{aligned}
q_{1,t} = {} & \frac{3}{2} - \frac{3}{2}(-2k+1)^t + \frac{1}{3}(-2k+1)^t(q_{10} + q_{20} + q_{30}) \\
& + \frac{1}{3}\left(\frac{-k}{2}+1\right)^t(2q_{10} - q_{20} - q_{30}) \\
q_{2,t} = {} & \frac{3}{2} - \frac{3}{2}(-2k+1)^t + \frac{1}{3}(-2k+1)^t(q_{10} + q_{20} + q_{30}) \\
& + \frac{1}{3}\left(\frac{-k}{2}+1\right)^t(-q_{10} + 2q_{20} - q_{30}) \\
q_{3,t} = {} & \frac{3}{2} - \frac{3}{2}(-2k+1)^t + \frac{1}{3}(-2k+1)^t(q_{10} + q_{20} + q_{30}) \\
& + \frac{1}{3}\left(\frac{-k}{2}+1\right)^t(-q_{10} - q_{20} + 2q_{30})
\end{aligned}
\tag{9.22}
$$

Since $k > 0$, then each root is less than $+1$. In addition, $(-2k + 1)$ is less than $(\frac{-k}{2} + 1)$ and so the root $(-2k + 1)$ dominates the system. Stability requires that $-2k + 1 > -1$ or $k < 1$. If $k = 1$ then the system oscillates; and if $k > 1$ the equilibrium values is never attained. One example of each is illustrated in figure 9.11. These three-dimensional plots were produced as discussed earlier. In figure 9.11(a) $k = 0.8$ and the system which has firm 1 as a monopolist converges on the equilibrium. In figure 9.11(b), with $k = 1$, the system soon begins to os-cillate between two values. When $k = 1.2$, however, the system oscillates with

Figure 9.11.

(a) $k = 0.8$

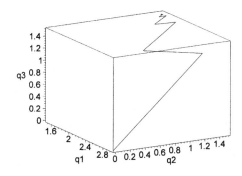

(b) $k = 1$

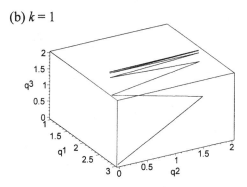

(c) $k = 1.2$

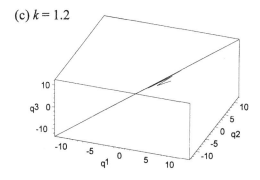

ever-increasing amplitude. Although output cannot be negative, once again what
we are attempting to illustrate is the inherent instability when $k > 1$.

Four-firm case (n = 4)

Following exactly the same analysis as for $n = 3$, we obtain solutions

$$q_{1,t} = \frac{6}{5} - \frac{6}{5}\left(\frac{-5k}{2} + 1\right)^t + \frac{1}{4}\left(\frac{-5k}{2} + 1\right)^t (q_{10} + q_{20} + q_{30} + q_{40})$$

$$+ \frac{1}{4}\left(\frac{-k}{2} + 1\right)^t (3q_{10} - q_{20} - q_{30} - q_{40})$$

$$q_{2,t} = \frac{6}{5} - \frac{6}{5}\left(\frac{-5k}{2} + 1\right)^t + \frac{1}{4}\left(\frac{-5k}{2} + 1\right)^t (q_{10} + q_{20} + q_{30} + q_{40})$$

$$+ \frac{1}{4}\left(\frac{-k}{2} + 1\right)^t (-q_{10} + 3q_{20} - q_{30} - q_{40})$$

$$q_{3,t} = \frac{6}{5} - \frac{6}{5}\left(\frac{-5k}{2} + 1\right)^t + \frac{1}{4}\left(\frac{-5k}{2} + 1\right)^t (q_{10} + q_{20} + q_{30} + q_{40})$$

$$+ \frac{1}{4}\left(\frac{-k}{2} + 1\right)^t (-q_{10} - q_{20} + 3q_{30} - q_{40})$$

(9.23)

$$q_{4,t} = \frac{6}{5} - \frac{6}{5}\left(\frac{-5k}{2} + 1\right)^t + \frac{1}{4}\left(\frac{-5k}{2} + 1\right)^t (q_{10} + q_{20} + q_{30} + q_{40})$$

$$+ \frac{1}{4}\left(\frac{-k}{2} + 1\right)^t (-q_{10} - q_{20} - q_{30} + 3q_{40})$$

With $k > 0$, stability requires $(\frac{-5k}{2} + 1) > -1$ or $k < 4/5$. If $k = 4/5$ then the system oscillates; while if $k > 4/5$ it is explosive. Figure 9.12 illustrates each of these, where we show only the results for output q_1.

9.3.2   *Increasing marginal costs*

Two-firm case ($n - 2$)

Returning to the model

$$p = 9 - Q$$
$$Q = q_1 + q_2$$
$$TC_1 = 3q_1^2$$
$$TC_2 = 3q_2^2$$

(9.24)

Figure 9.12.

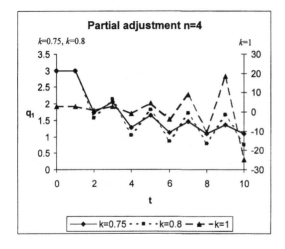

with reaction functions

(9.25)
$$x_{1,t} = \frac{9}{8} - \frac{1}{8}q_{2,t-1}$$
$$x_{2,t} = \frac{9}{8} - \frac{1}{8}q_{1,t-1}$$

and once again assume for $k > 0$ that

$$q_{1,t} - q_{1,t-1} = k(x_{1,t} - q_{1,t-1})$$
$$q_{2,t} - q_{2,t-1} = k(x_{2,t} - q_{2,t-1})$$

Substituting the reaction functions, we obtain the following difference equations

(9.26)
$$q_{1,t} = \frac{9k}{8} + (1-k)q_{1,t-1} - \frac{k}{8}q_{2,t-1}$$
$$q_{2,t} = \frac{9k}{8} - \frac{k}{8}q_{1,t-1} + (1-k)q_{2,t-1}$$

Given the initial conditions $q_{1,0} = q_{10}$ and $q_{2,0} = q_{20}$ we have solutions

(9.27)
$$q_{1,t} = 1 - \left(\frac{-9k}{8}+1\right)^t + \frac{1}{2}\left(\frac{-9k}{8}+1\right)^t(q_{10}+q_{20})$$
$$+ \frac{1}{2}\left(\frac{-7k}{8}+1\right)^t(q_{10}-q_{20})$$
$$q_{2,t} = 1 - \left(\frac{-9k}{8}+1\right)^t + \frac{1}{2}\left(\frac{-9k}{8}+1\right)^t(q_{10}+q_{20})$$
$$+ \frac{1}{2}\left(\frac{-7k}{8}+1\right)^t(-q_{10}+q_{20})$$

Since $k > 0$, then stability requires $\frac{-9k}{8}+1 > -1$, or $k < 16/9$. The system exhibits oscillations and explosive behaviour if $k = 16/9$ and $k > 16/9$, respectively.

Three-firm case (n = 3)

Following the same procedure as in sub-section 9.3.1 we derive the results

(9.28)
$$q_{1,t} = \frac{9}{10} - \frac{9}{10}\left(\frac{-5k}{4}+1\right)^t + \frac{1}{3}\left(\frac{-5k}{4}+1\right)^t(q_{10}+q_{20}+q_{30})$$
$$+ \frac{1}{3}\left(\frac{-7k}{8}+1\right)^t(2q_{10}-q_{20}-q_{30})$$
$$q_{2,t} = \frac{9}{10} - \frac{9}{10}\left(\frac{-5k}{4}+1\right)^t + \frac{1}{3}\left(\frac{-5k}{4}+1\right)^t(q_{10}+q_{20}+q_{30})$$
$$+ \frac{1}{3}\left(\frac{-7k}{8}+1\right)^t(-q_{10}+2q_{20}-q_{30})$$
$$q_{3,t} = \frac{9}{10} - \frac{9}{10}\left(\frac{-5k}{4}+1\right)^t + \frac{1}{3}\left(\frac{-5k}{4}+1\right)^t(q_{10}+q_{20}+q_{30})$$
$$+ \frac{1}{3}\left(\frac{-7k}{8}+1\right)^t(-q_{10}-q_{20}+2q_{30})$$

Since $k > 0$, then the smallest root is $(\frac{-5k}{4} + 1)$, which must be larger than -1 for stability, i.e., $k < 8/5$.

Four-firm case ($n = 4$)

Following the same procedure as we did to derive equations (9.23) we obtain the results

$$
\begin{aligned}
q_{1,t} ={}& \frac{9}{11} - \frac{9}{11}\left(\frac{-11k}{8} + 1\right)^t + \frac{1}{4}\left(\frac{-11k}{8} + 1\right)^t (q_{10} + q_{20} + q_{30} + q_{40}) \\
&+ \frac{1}{4}\left(\frac{-7k}{8} + 1\right)^t (3q_{10} - q_{20} - q_{30} - q_{40}) \\
q_{2,t} ={}& \frac{9}{11} - \frac{9}{11}\left(\frac{-11k}{8} + 1\right)^t + \frac{1}{4}\left(\frac{-11k}{8} + 1\right)^t (q_{10} + q_{20} + q_{30} + q_{40}) \\
&+ \frac{1}{4}\left(\frac{-7k}{8} + 1\right)^t (-q_{10} + 3q_{20} - q_{30} - q_{40}) \\
q_{3,t} ={}& \frac{9}{11} - \frac{9}{11}\left(\frac{-11k}{8} + 1\right)^t + \frac{1}{4}\left(\frac{-11k}{8} + 1\right)^t (q_{10} + q_{20} + q_{30} + q_{40}) \\
&+ \frac{1}{4}\left(\frac{-7k}{8} + 1\right)^t (-q_{10} - q_{20} + 3q_{30} - q_{40}) \\
q_{4,t} ={}& \frac{9}{11} - \frac{9}{11}\left(\frac{11k}{8} + 1\right)^t + \frac{1}{4}\left(\frac{-11k}{8} + 1\right)^t (q_{10} + q_{20} + q_{30} + q_{40}) \\
&+ \frac{1}{4}\left(\frac{-7k}{8} + 1\right)^t (-q_{10} - q_{20} - q_{30} + 3q_{40})
\end{aligned}
\tag{9.29}
$$

Since $k > 0$ and the smallest root is $(\frac{-11k}{8} + 1)$, then for stability we require $k < 16/11$.

Table 9.1 sets out the value of k for stability for $n = 2, 3$ and 4 and under constant and increasing marginal costs.

What this table reveals is the following:

(1) As the number of firms in the industry increases, the size of k falls, so the likelihood of instability is increased with the number of firms in the industry.

(2) The presence of increasing marginal costs acts as a stabilising influence, raising the critical value of k, and so increasing the range over which the systems exhibit stability.

Table 9.1 Stability values for k

	Constant MC	Increasing MC
$n = 2$	$k < 4/3$	$k < 16/9$
$n = 3$	$k < 1$	$k < 16/10$
$n = 4$	$k < 4/5$	$k < 16/11$

(3)   The presence of increasing marginal costs does not rule out oscillations or instability. Oscillations and instability can occur for any number of firms in the industry if k is sufficiently large enough.

9.4   Continuous modelling of oligopoly

So far the discrete form of the oligopoly model has been investigated. We now turn to its continuous representation. It cannot be guaranteed that the results which hold for $n = 2, 3$ and 4 for the discrete model hold for its continuous counterpart. As with the discrete model, consideration will be given to the case of both constant and increasing marginal costs.

9.4.1   Constant marginal costs

Two-firm case $(n = 2)$

The same example is used; paying particular attention to what happens when there is an increase in the number of firms and what happens when the assumption of constant marginal costs is changed to one of increasing marginal costs. For the two-firm case our model is

(9.30)
$$p(t) = 9 - Q(t)$$
$$Q(t) = q_1(t) + q_2(t)$$
$$TC_1(t) = 3q_1(t)$$
$$TC_2(t) = 3q_2(t)$$

This leads to total revenue and profits for each firm of

Firm 1 $TR_1(t) = (9 - q_1(t) - q_2(t))q_1(t)$
$\pi_1(t) = (9 - q_1(t) - q_2(t))q_1(t) - 3q_1(t)$
Firm 2 $TR_2(t) = (9 - q_1(t) - q_2(t))q_2(t)$
$\pi_2(t) = (9 - q_1(t) - q_2(t))q_1(t) - 3q_2(t)$

We now specify the dynamics. We assume that for firm 1 output is adjusted continuously in proportion to the discrepancy between the desired level and the actual level. The same applies to firm 2. Hence

Firm 1 $\dfrac{dq_1(t)}{dt} = k_1(x_1(t) - q_1(t)) \quad k_1 > 0$

Firm 2 $\dfrac{dq_2(t)}{dt} = k_2(x_2(t) - q_2(t)) \quad k_2 > 0$

The desired level of output for each firm is the output level that maximises profits under the assumption that the other firm does not alter its output level. Differentiating each profit function under the assumed conjectural variation, and setting equal to zero

$$\frac{\partial \pi_1(t)}{\partial q_1(t)} = 6 - 2q_1(t) - q_2(t) = 0$$

$$\frac{\partial \pi_2(t)}{\partial q_2(t)} = 6 - q_1(t) - 2q_2(t) = 0$$

Then

$$x_1(t) = 3 - \tfrac{1}{2}q_2(t)$$

$$x_2(t) = 3 - \tfrac{1}{2}q_1(t)$$

(9.31)

Substituting these into the dynamic adjustment equations, we obtain

$$\frac{\partial q_1(t)}{\partial t} = 3k_1 - k_1 q_1(t) - \frac{k_1}{2} q_2(t)$$

$$\frac{\partial q_2(t)}{\partial t} = 3k_2 - \frac{k_2}{2} q_1(t) - k_2 q_2(t)$$

First consider the fixed point of the system. This is where output levels do not change. These represent two isoclines, which are given by

$$q_1(t) = 3 - \tfrac{1}{2}q_2(t)$$

$$q_2(t) = 3 - \tfrac{1}{2}q_1(t)$$

which are no more than the same reaction functions we have above and in the previous models, and which intersect at $(q_1^*, q_2^*) = (2, 2)$. The equilibrium is therefore unaffected.

Consider now the model in matrix form. We have

$$\begin{bmatrix} \dot{q}_1(t) \\ \dot{q}_2(t) \end{bmatrix} = \begin{bmatrix} 3k_1 \\ 3k_2 \end{bmatrix} + \begin{bmatrix} -k_1 & -\frac{k_1}{2} \\ -\frac{k_2}{2} & -k_2 \end{bmatrix} \begin{bmatrix} q_1(t) \\ q_2(t) \end{bmatrix}$$

and the matrix of the system is

$$\mathbf{A} = \begin{bmatrix} -k_1 & -\frac{k_1}{2} \\ -\frac{k_2}{2} & -k_2 \end{bmatrix}$$

with $\text{tr}(\mathbf{A}) = -(k_1 + k_2) < 0$ and $\det(\mathbf{A}) = k_1 k_2 - \frac{k_1 k_2}{4} = \frac{3k_1 k_2}{4} > 0$, which hold regardless of the values that k_1 and k_2 take, so long as they are both positive. Furthermore,

$$\text{tr}(\mathbf{A})^2 - 4 \det(\mathbf{A}) = (k_1 + k_2)^2 - 3k_1 k_2$$

$$= (k_1 - k_2)^2 + k_1 k_2$$

which is positive since $k_1 > 0$ and $k_2 > 0$. These results indicate that the equilibrium is stable, and that any cyclical behaviour is ruled out.

Although both *Mathematica* and *Maple* can solve the linear differential equation system, the solution is once again unwieldy. Letting $k_1 = k_2 = k$, however, we obtain the following more insightful solutions

$$q_1(t) = 2 - 2e^{\left(-\frac{3k}{2}\right)t} + \frac{1}{2}e^{\left(-\frac{3k}{2}\right)t}(q_{10} + q_{20}) + \frac{1}{2}e^{\left(-\frac{k}{2}\right)t}(q_{10} - q_{20})$$

$$q_2(t) = 2 - 2e^{\left(-\frac{3k}{2}\right)t} + \frac{1}{2}e^{\left(-\frac{3k}{2}\right)t}(q_{10} + q_{20}) + \frac{1}{2}e^{\left(-\frac{k}{2}\right)t}(-q_{10} + q_{20})$$

(9.32)

Figure 9.13.

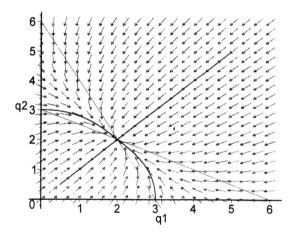

which tend to the equilibrium point $(q_1^*, q_2^*) = (2, 2)$ as t tends to infinity. We illustrate this for $k = 0.5$ in figure 9.13, which shows the phase diagram for this two-firm model under continuous adjustment.

As can be seen from figure 9.13, all paths converge on the equilibrium regardless of the initial values. It should be noted that this is in marked contrast to the discrete model, in which stable, unstable and oscillatory behaviour is feasible depending on the size of the adjustment coefficient. In the present formulation, the size of the adjustment coefficient has no bearing on the stability/instability of the system, all it does is change the speed of convergence.

Three-firm case (n = 3)

Performing the same analysis as in the previous case, the model reduces down to the following

(9.33)
$$
\begin{bmatrix} \dot{q}_1(t) \\ \dot{q}_2(t) \\ \dot{q}_3(t) \end{bmatrix} = \begin{bmatrix} 3k_1 \\ 3k_2 \\ 3k_3 \end{bmatrix} + \begin{bmatrix} -k_1 & -\frac{k_1}{2} & -\frac{k_1}{2} \\ -\frac{k_2}{2} & -k_2 & -\frac{k_2}{2} \\ -\frac{k_3}{2} & -\frac{k_3}{2} & -k_3 \end{bmatrix} \begin{bmatrix} q_1(t) \\ q_2(t) \\ q_3(t) \end{bmatrix}
$$

and the matrix of the system is

$$
\mathbf{A3} = \begin{bmatrix} -k_1 & -\frac{k_1}{2} & -\frac{k_1}{2} \\ -\frac{k_2}{2} & -k_2 & -\frac{k_2}{2} \\ -\frac{k_3}{2} & -\frac{k_3}{2} & -k_3 \end{bmatrix}
$$

with $\text{tr}(\mathbf{A3}) = -(k_1 + k_2 + k_3) < 0$ and $\det(\mathbf{A3}) = -\frac{1}{2} k_1 k_2 k_3 < 0$, which holds regardless of the values of the adjustment coefficients. Since $\det(\mathbf{A3}) < 0$ a saddle-point solution results.

If we assume that $k_1 = k_2 = k_3 = k$, then the solutions are

$$q_1(t) = \frac{3}{2} - \frac{3}{2}e^{-2kt} + \frac{1}{3}e^{-2kt}(q_{10} + q_{20} + q_{30}) + \frac{1}{3}e^{-(k/2)t}(2q_{10} - q_{20} - q_{30})$$

$$q_2(t) = \frac{3}{2} - \frac{3}{2}e^{-2kt} + \frac{1}{3}e^{-2kt}(q_{10} + q_{20} + q_{30}) + \frac{1}{3}e^{-(k/2)t}(-q_{10} + 2q_{20} - q_{30}) \qquad (9.34)$$

$$q_3(t) = \frac{3}{2} - \frac{3}{2}e^{-2kt} + \frac{1}{3}e^{-2kt}(q_{10} + q_{20} + q_{30}) + \frac{1}{3}e^{-(k/2)t}(-q_{10} - q_{20} + 2q_{30})$$

Since tr($\mathbf{A3}$) is now $-3k < 0$ and the det($\mathbf{A3}$) is now $-\frac{1}{2}k^3 < 0$, then the system has a saddle point solution at $(q_1^*, q_2^*, q_3^*) = (\frac{3}{2}, \frac{3}{2}, \frac{3}{2})$.

Four-firm case ($n = 4$)

This model reduces to

$$\begin{bmatrix} \dot{q}_1(t) \\ \dot{q}_2(t) \\ \dot{q}_3(t) \\ \dot{q}_4(t) \end{bmatrix} = \begin{bmatrix} 3k_1 \\ 3k_2 \\ 3k_3 \\ 3k_4 \end{bmatrix} + \begin{bmatrix} -k_1 & -\frac{k_1}{2} & -\frac{k_1}{2} & -\frac{k_1}{2} \\ -\frac{k_2}{2} & -k_2 & -\frac{k_2}{2} & -\frac{k_2}{2} \\ -\frac{k_3}{2} & -\frac{k_3}{2} & -k_3 & -\frac{k_3}{2} \\ -\frac{k_4}{2} & -\frac{k_4}{2} & -\frac{k_4}{2} & -k_4 \end{bmatrix} \begin{bmatrix} q_1(t) \\ q_2(t) \\ q_3(t) \\ q_4(t) \end{bmatrix} \qquad (9.35)$$

and the matrix of the system is

$$\mathbf{A4} - \begin{bmatrix} -k_1 & -\frac{k_1}{2} & -\frac{k_1}{2} & -\frac{k_1}{2} \\ -\frac{k_2}{2} & -k_2 & -\frac{k_2}{2} & -\frac{k_2}{2} \\ -\frac{k_3}{2} & -\frac{k_3}{2} & -k_3 & -\frac{k_3}{2} \\ -\frac{k_4}{2} & -\frac{k_4}{2} & -\frac{k_4}{2} & -k_4 \end{bmatrix}$$

With tr($\mathbf{A4}$) $= -(k_1 + k_2 + k_3 + k_4) < 0$ and det($\mathbf{A4}$) $= \frac{5}{16}k_1k_2k_3k_4 > 0$, which holds regardless of the values of the adjustment coefficients. We now see the saddle point solution does not hold for $n = 4$.

If we assume $k_1 = k_2 = k_3 = k_4 = k$ then we can express the solutions in the form

$$q_1(t) = \frac{6}{5} - \frac{6}{5}e^{-(5k/2)t} + \frac{1}{4}e^{-(5k/2)t}(q_{10} + q_{20} + q_{30} + q_{40})$$
$$+ \frac{1}{4}e^{-(k/2)t}(3q_{10} - q_{20} - q_{30} - q_{40})$$

$$q_2(t) = \frac{6}{5} - \frac{6}{5}e^{-(5k/2)t} + \frac{1}{4}e^{-(5k/2)t}(q_{10} + q_{20} + q_{30} + q_{40})$$
$$+ \frac{1}{4}e^{-(k/2)t}(-q_{10} + 3q_{20} - q_{30} - q_{40})$$

$$\qquad (9.36)$$

$$q_3(t) = \frac{6}{5} - \frac{6}{5}e^{-(5k/2)t} + \frac{1}{4}e^{-(5k/2)t}(q_{10} + q_{20} + q_{30} + q_{40})$$
$$+ \frac{1}{4}e^{-(k/2)t}(-q_{10} - q_{20} + 3q_{30} - q_{40})$$

$$q_4(t) = \frac{6}{5} - \frac{6}{5}e^{-(5k/2)t} + \frac{1}{4}e^{-(5k/2)t}(q_{10} + q_{20} + q_{30} + q_{40})$$
$$+ \frac{1}{4}e^{-(k/2)t}(-q_{10} - q_{20} - q_{30} + 3q_{40})$$

Table 9.2 Stability properties on trace and determinant

n	Trace	Determinant
2	$-(k_1 + k_2) < 0$	$(3/4)k_1 k_2 > 0$
3	$-(k_1 + k_2 + k_3) < 0$	$-(1/2)k_1 k_2 k_3 < 0$
4	$-(k_1 + k_2 + k_3 + k_4) < 0$	$(5/16)k_1 k_2 k_3 k_4 > 0$
5	$-(k_1 + k_2 + k_3 + k_4 + k_5) < 0$	$-(3/16)k_1 k_2 k_3 k_4 k_5 < 0$
6	$-(k_1 + k_2 + k_3 + k_4 + k_5 + k_6) < 0$	$(7/64)k_1 k_2 k_3 k_4 k_5 k_6 > 0$

Since $\text{tr}(\mathbf{A}4)$ is now $-4k < 0$, $\det(\mathbf{A}4)$ is now $\frac{5}{16}k^4 > 0$ and

$$tr(\mathbf{A}4)^2 - 4\det(\mathbf{A}4) = 16k^2 - \tfrac{5}{4}k^4 = \tfrac{1}{4}k^2(64 - 5k^2)$$

then the system has an improper node if $k < \sqrt{\frac{64}{5}}$ and a spiral node if $k > \sqrt{\frac{64}{5}}$, where the node is at point $(q_1^*, q_2^*, q_3^*, q_4^*) = (\frac{6}{5}, \frac{6}{5}, \frac{6}{5}, \frac{6}{5})$.

The pattern emerging for the continuous model with constant marginal costs appears complex. The pattern emerging can be seen in terms of table 9.2.

Although the trace remains negative, the determinant alternates in sign – positive for even numbers and negative for odd numbers. Nor is cyclical behaviour ruled out, as we noted in the case of four firms. What appears to emerge is saddle point solutions whenever n is odd, and either an improper node or a spiral node whenever n is even.

What can be concluded with some confidence from this fairly exhaustive example is that the asymptotic stability exhibited for duopoly is a rather special case.

9.4.2   *Increasing marginal costs*

Two-firm case (n = 2)

Returning to the model

(9.37)

$$p(t) = 9 - Q(t)$$
$$Q(t) = q_1(t) + q_2(t)$$
$$TC_1(t) = 3q_1^2(t)$$
$$TC_2(t) = 3q_2^2(t)$$

the desired output levels are

$$x_1(t) = \frac{9}{8} - \frac{1}{8}q_2(t)$$
$$x_2(t) = \frac{9}{8} - \frac{1}{8}q_1(t)$$

while the dynamics are the same as in the situation of constant marginal costs. The adjustment equations become

$$\frac{\partial q_1(t)}{\partial t} = \frac{9k_1}{8} - k_1 q_1(t) - \frac{k_1}{8} q_2(t)$$

$$\frac{\partial q_2(t)}{\partial t} = \frac{9k_2}{8} - \frac{k_2}{8} q_1(t) - k_2 q_2(t)$$

Equilibrium is at $(q_1^*, q_2^*) = (1, 1)$.

The system can be expressed,

$$\begin{bmatrix} \dot{q}_1(t) \\ \dot{q}_2(t) \end{bmatrix} = \begin{bmatrix} \frac{9k_1}{8} \\ \frac{9k_2}{8} \end{bmatrix} + \begin{bmatrix} -k_1 & -\frac{k_1}{8} \\ -\frac{k_2}{8} & -k_2 \end{bmatrix} \begin{bmatrix} q_1(t) \\ q_2(t) \end{bmatrix}$$

and the matrix of the system is

$$\mathbf{B2} = \begin{bmatrix} -k_1 & -\frac{k_1}{8} \\ -\frac{k_2}{8} & -k_2 \end{bmatrix}$$

with $tr(\mathbf{B2}) = -(k_1 + k_2) < 0$ and $det(\mathbf{B2}) = \frac{63}{64} k_1 k_2 > 0$. Furthermore,

$$tr(\mathbf{B2})^2 - 4 \det(\mathbf{B2}) = (k_1 + k_2)^2 - \frac{63 k_1 k_2}{16}$$

$$= (k_1 - k_2)^2 + \frac{k_1 k_2}{16}$$

which is positive. Once again for duopoly in the presence of increasing marginal costs, the equilibrium is stable and any cyclical behaviour is ruled out.

Under the simplifying assumption that $k_1 = k_2 = k$, we obtain the solutions

$$q_1(t) = 1 - e^{-\left(\frac{9k}{8}\right)t} + \frac{1}{2} e^{-\left(\frac{9k}{8}\right)t} (q_{10} + q_{20}) + \frac{1}{2} e^{-\left(\frac{7k}{8}\right)t} (q_{10} - q_{20})$$

$$q_2(t) = 1 - e^{-\left(\frac{9k}{8}\right)t} + \frac{1}{2} e^{-\left(\frac{9k}{8}\right)t} (q_{10} + q_{20}) + \frac{1}{2} e^{-\left(\frac{7k}{8}\right)t} (-q_{10} + q_{20})$$

(9.38)

which tends to the equilibrium point $(q_1^*, q_2^*) = (1, 1)$ as t tends to infinity. The stability of duopoly under increasing marginal costs is illustrated in figure 9.14. Once again, all paths converge on the equilibrium regardless of the initial values.

Figure 9.14.

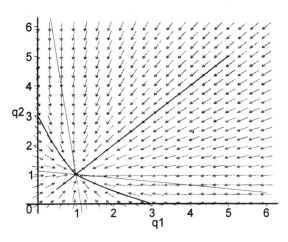

Three-firm case (n = 3)

Following a similar procedure, the system for three firms can be expressed

$$
(9.39) \qquad
\begin{bmatrix} \dot{q}_1(t) \\ \dot{q}_2(t) \\ \dot{q}_3(t) \end{bmatrix}
=
\begin{bmatrix} \frac{9k_1}{8} \\ \frac{9k_2}{8} \\ \frac{9k_3}{8} \end{bmatrix}
+
\begin{bmatrix}
-k_1 & -\frac{k_1}{8} & -\frac{k_1}{8} \\
-\frac{k_2}{8} & -k_2 & -\frac{k_2}{8} \\
-\frac{k_3}{8} & -\frac{k_3}{8} & -k_3
\end{bmatrix}
\begin{bmatrix} q_1(t) \\ q_2(t) \\ q_3(t) \end{bmatrix}
$$

and the matrix of the system is

$$
\mathbf{B3} =
\begin{bmatrix}
-k_1 & -\frac{k_1}{8} & -\frac{k_1}{8} \\
-\frac{k_2}{8} & -k_2 & -\frac{k_2}{8} \\
-\frac{k_3}{8} & -\frac{k_3}{8} & -k_3
\end{bmatrix}
$$

with $\mathrm{tr}(\mathbf{B3}) = -(k_1 + k_2 + k_3) < 0$ and $\det(\mathbf{B3}) = -\frac{245}{256} k_1 k_2 k_3 < 0$. Since the determinant is negative we have a saddle point solution, with node at $(q_1^*, q_2^*, q_3^*) = (\frac{9}{10}, \frac{9}{10}, \frac{9}{10})$.

Assuming $k_1 = k_2 = k_3 = k$ then we have the solutions

$$
q_1(t) = \frac{9}{10} - \frac{9}{10} e^{-(\frac{5k}{4})t} - e^{-(\frac{5k}{4})t}(q_{10} + q_{20} + q_{30}) + \frac{1}{3} e^{-(\frac{7k}{8})t}(2q_{10} - q_{20} - q_{30})
$$

$$
(9.40) \quad q_2(t) = \frac{9}{10} - \frac{9}{10} e^{-(\frac{5k}{4})t} - e^{-(\frac{5k}{4})t}(q_{10} + q_{20} + q_{30}) + \frac{1}{3} e^{-(\frac{7k}{8})t}(-q_{10} + 2q_{20} - q_{30})
$$

$$
q_3(t) = \frac{9}{10} - \frac{9}{10} e^{-(\frac{5k}{4})t} - e^{-(\frac{5k}{4})t}(q_{10} + q_{20} + q_{30}) + \frac{1}{3} e^{-(\frac{7k}{8})t}(-q_{10} - q_{20} + 2q_{30})
$$

Four-firm case (n = 4)

Repeating the same analysis, the system for four firms can be expressed

$$
(9.41) \qquad
\begin{bmatrix} \dot{q}_1(t) \\ \dot{q}_2(t) \\ \dot{q}_3(t) \\ \dot{q}_4(t) \end{bmatrix}
=
\begin{bmatrix} \frac{9k_1}{8} \\ \frac{9k_2}{8} \\ \frac{9k_3}{8} \\ \frac{9k_4}{8} \end{bmatrix}
+
\begin{bmatrix}
-k_1 & -\frac{k_1}{8} & -\frac{k_1}{8} & -\frac{k_1}{8} \\
-\frac{k_2}{8} & -k_2 & -\frac{k_2}{8} & -\frac{k_2}{8} \\
-\frac{k_3}{8} & -\frac{k_3}{8} & -k_3 & -\frac{k_3}{8} \\
-\frac{k_4}{8} & -\frac{k_4}{8} & -\frac{k_4}{8} & -k_4
\end{bmatrix}
\begin{bmatrix} q_1(t) \\ q_2(t) \\ q_3(t) \\ q_4(t) \end{bmatrix}
$$

and the matrix of the system is

$$
\mathbf{B4} =
\begin{bmatrix}
-k_1 & -\frac{k_1}{8} & -\frac{k_1}{8} & -\frac{k_1}{8} \\
-\frac{k_2}{8} & -k_2 & -\frac{k_2}{8} & -\frac{k_2}{8} \\
-\frac{k_3}{8} & -\frac{k_3}{8} & -k_3 & -\frac{k_3}{8} \\
-\frac{k_4}{8} & -\frac{k_4}{8} & -\frac{k_4}{8} & -k_4
\end{bmatrix}
$$

with $\mathrm{tr}(\mathbf{B4}) = -(k_1 + k_2 + k_3 + k_4) < 0$ and $\det(\mathbf{B4}) = \frac{3773}{4096} k_1 k_2 k_3 k_4 > 0$. The saddle point solution disappears once again, and we have either an improper node or a spiral node, with the node at point $(q_1^*, q_2^*, q_3^*, q_4^*) = (\frac{9}{11}, \frac{9}{11}, \frac{9}{11}, \frac{9}{11})$.

Table 9.3 Roots for firm sizes 2, 3 and 4

n	Constant marginal costs		Increasing marginal costs	
2	$\dfrac{-3k}{2}$,	$\dfrac{-k}{2}$	$\dfrac{-9k}{8}$,	$\dfrac{-7k}{8}$
3	$-2k$,	$\dfrac{-k}{2}$	$\dfrac{-5k}{4}$,	$\dfrac{-7k}{8}$
4	$\dfrac{-5k}{2}$,	$\dfrac{-k}{2}$	$\dfrac{-11k}{8}$,	$\dfrac{-7k}{8}$

Assuming $k_1 = k_2 = k_3 = k_4 = k$ then we have the solution

$$q_1(t) = \frac{9}{11} - \frac{9}{11}e^{-\left(\frac{11k}{8}\right)t} + \frac{1}{4}e^{-\left(\frac{11k}{8}\right)t}(q_{10} + q_{20} + q_{30} + q_{40})$$

$$+ \frac{1}{4}e^{-\left(\frac{7k}{8}\right)t}(3q_{10} - q_{20} - q_{30} - q_{40})$$

$$q_2(t) = \frac{9}{11} - \frac{9}{11}e^{-\left(\frac{11k}{8}\right)t} + \frac{1}{4}e^{-\left(\frac{11k}{8}\right)t}(q_{10} + q_{20} + q_{30} + q_{40})$$

$$+ \frac{1}{4}e^{-\left(\frac{7k}{8}\right)t}(-q_{10} + 3q_{20} - q_{30} - q_{40})$$

$$q_3(t) = \frac{9}{11} - \frac{9}{11}e^{-\left(\frac{11k}{8}\right)t} + \frac{1}{4}e^{-\left(\frac{11k}{8}\right)t}(q_{10} + q_{20} + q_{30} + q_{40})$$

$$+ \frac{1}{4}e^{-\left(\frac{7k}{8}\right)t}(-q_{10} - q_{20} + 3q_{30} - q_{40})$$

$$q_4(t) = \frac{9}{11} - \frac{9}{11}e^{-\left(\frac{11k}{8}\right)t} + \frac{1}{4}e^{-\left(\frac{11k}{8}\right)t}(q_{10} + q_{20} + q_{30} + q_{40})$$

$$+ \frac{1}{4}e^{-\left(\frac{7k}{8}\right)t}(-q_{10} - q_{20} - q_{30} + 3q_{40})$$

(9.42)

We can compare the constant and increasing marginal cost situations by identifying the *distinct* roots in each case. These are shown in table 9.3 for $n = 2$, 3 and 4 and for constant k.

For $n = 2$, the dominant root is $-3k/2$ for constant marginal costs and $-9k/8$ for increasing marginal costs. In fact, in each case the dominant root is shown in the left-hand column. The dominant root is always smaller for increasing marginal costs than for constant marginal costs, showing that increasing marginal costs has a stabilising influence. Also notice, however, that as n increases so does the dominant root, and so the more probable that the industry exhibits instability.

9.5   A nonlinear model of duopolistic competition (R&D)

A quite different dynamic duopoly model is that discussed by Parker, Whitby and Tobias (2000).[3] The model consists of two firms, which we shall call A and B, producing a similar technological product. Rather than competing on price,

---

[3] I am grateful to Simon Whitby for supplying some additional information on the parameters used in this model and for clarifying a number of points.

Table 9.4 Nonlinear model of duopolistic competition

Firm A	where
$R^A_{t+1} = \max[0, R^A_t + a(S^A_t - S^B_t)]$	R^A = resource allocations to R&D by firm A
	a = policy parameter for firm A
$S^A_t = \left(\dfrac{2m^A}{\pi}\right)\arctan(R^A_t) - n^A$	S^A = product quality standard for firm A
	S^B = product quality standard for firm B
	n^A, n^B = shift parameters
$\Delta k^A_{t+1} = \gamma(S^A_t - \bar{S})$	Δk^A = change in market share for firm A
	γ = market share adjustment parameter
	$\bar{S}$ = average product standard of the industry
Firm B	R^B = resource allocations to R&D by firm B
$R^B_{t+1} = \max[0, R^B_t + b(S^B_t - S^A_t)]$	b = policy parameter for firm B
	k^A = market share of firm A
$S^B_t = \left(\dfrac{2m^B}{\pi}\right)\arctan(R^B_t) - n^B$	k^B = market share of firm B
$\Delta k^B_{t+1} = \gamma(S^B_t - \bar{S})$	Δk^B = change in market share for firm B

Figure 9.15.

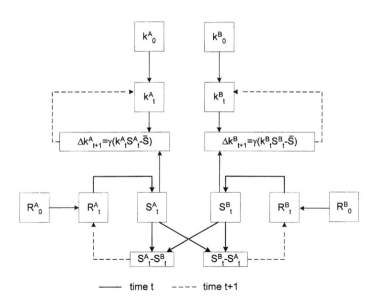

— time t   - - - - time t+1

however, competition is through product innovation. It is assumed that the more resources are allocated to research and development (R&D) the greater the standard or quality that results. A higher quality leads to a competitive advantage in the market, leading in turn to a greater market share. It is assumed that each firm can monitor the product standard of its competitor at zero cost. The authors do not explicitly consider market share, and here we extend the model by introducing a simple dynamic adjustment to market share which responds to the firm's quality standard relative to the average quality standard of the industry.

The model is captured in terms of the set of relationships in table 9.4.

The model's basic structure is shown in figure 9.15. The resources each firm devotes to R&D in time period *t* determine the product quality standard in that period. A competitive advantage occurs at time t if the quality standard achieved in time t is greater than for their competitor. This in turn alters the market share for time $t + 1$. Given just two firms, only one firm can have a competitive advantage (say firm A if $S^A > S^B$).

9.5.1   No learning

Each firm is assumed to adjust the resource allocation to R&D according to their competitive advantage. Parker *et al.* consider two possible policy alternatives:

Reinforcing policy ($a > 0, b > 0$)

Research funds are increased when performance is good and reduced when performance is bad. The change is set proportional to the differential in performance, i.e.

$$R^A_{t+1} - R^A_t = a(S^A_t - S^B_t) \qquad a > 0$$
$$R^B_{t+1} - R^B_t = b(S^B_t - S^A_t) \qquad b > 0$$

Counteracting policy ($a < 0, b < 0$)

Research funds are increased when performance is bad and decreased when performance is good. The change is set proportional to the differential in performance, i.e.

$$R^A_{t+1} - R^A_t = a(S^A_t - S^B_t) \qquad a < 0$$
$$R^B_{t+1} - R^B_t = b(S^B_t - S^A_t) \qquad b < 0$$

Of course, one firm could be reinforcing while the other is pursuing a counteracting policy, which results in four basic interactions.

The critical relationship is that between product quality standard and R&D allocations. A typical relationship is S-shaped indicating low improvements in standard for low levels of R&D, much greater improvements for higher levels, but a tailing off in improvements in standard once diminishing returns set in, which occurs at high levels of R&D. Such an S-shaped curve can be captured by arctan.[4] Thus

$$S^A_t = \left(\frac{2m^A}{\pi}\right) \arctan\left(R^A_t\right) - n^A \qquad \text{for firm A}$$

$$S^B_t = \left(\frac{2m^B}{\pi}\right) \arctan\left(R^B_t\right) - n^B \qquad \text{for firm B}$$

(9.43)

are the functions employed to represent quality standard by each firm. The higher the value of m the steeper the S-function, while a positive n shifts it down. The inflexion point occurs on the y-axis at the value of n.

---

[4] We employed a similar relationship in the previous chapter, section 8.10.

Substituting the quality standard into the resource function we have

$$R_{t+1}^A = \max\left[0, R_t^A + \left\{a\left(\frac{2m^A}{\pi}\right)\arctan\left(R_t^A\right)\right.\right.$$

$$\left.\left. - a\left(\frac{2m^B}{\pi}\right)\arctan\left(R_t^B\right) - a(n^A - n^B)\right\}\right]$$

(9.44)

$$R_{t+1}^B = \max\left[0, R_t^B + \left\{b\left(\frac{2m^B}{\pi}\right)\arctan\left(R_t^B\right)\right.\right.$$

$$\left.\left. - b\left(\frac{2m^A}{\pi}\right)\arctan\left(R_t^A\right) - b(n^B - n^A)\right\}\right]$$

for firms A and B, respectively. Given the parameters m^A, m^B, n^A and n^B, then we have the recursive equations

(9.45)
$$R_{t+1}^A = f^A\left(R_t^A, R_t^B\right)$$
$$R_{t+1}^B = f^B\left(R_t^A, R_t^B\right)$$

which allows us to plot the trajectories $\{R_t^A, R_t^B\}$ for alternative policy options given $\{R_0^A, R_0^B\}$. Given the values for R_t^A and R_t^B, we can compute the product quality standard for firm A and B, respectively. Given some initial market share $\{k_0^A, k_0^B\}$ it is possible to compute the market shares for the next period. To do this, however, we need to define the average product quality standard for the industry, $\overline{S}$. This is defined as the weighted sum of the product quality standard for each firm, where the weight is the respective market share. We therefore have

(9.46)
$$\overline{S}_t = k_t^A S_t^A + k_t^B S_t^B \qquad k_t^A + k_t^B = 1$$

and

(9.47)
$$k_{t+1}^A = k_t^A + \gamma\left(S_t^A - \overline{S}_t\right)$$
$$k_{t+1}^B = k_t^B + \gamma\left(S_t^B - \overline{S}_t\right)$$

Although there are no known methods for solving equations (9.44), we can readily employ a spreadsheet to carry out simulations.

For simplicity the authors treat the functions (9.43) as identical for each firm and give values to the parameters m and n of 100 and 40, respectively. If both firms engage in a reinforcing policy, then whichever firm starts with the greater resources devoted to R&D will have the greater product quality standard and hence the competitive advantage. The market share for the firm with the competitive advantage will rise while that for the other firm will fall until it goes out of business. Given the symmetrical nature of the firms, if the same resources are devoted to R&D, then the market share will remain unaffected regardless of the values of a and b.

Example 9.1 (Reinforcing policy by both firms)

To see the model in operation, consider the following values

$$m^A = m^B = 100 \qquad R_0^A = 10 \qquad R_0^B = 8$$
$$n^A = n^B = 40 \qquad k_0^A = 0.5 \qquad k_0^B = 0.5$$
$$\gamma = 0.01$$

Figure 9.16.

	A	B	C	D	E	F	G	H
1								
2								
3	a =	0.1	mA =	100	nA =	40	γ =	0.01
4	b =	0.2	mB =	100	nB =	40		
5								
6	t	RA(t)	RB(t)	SA(t)	SB(t)	kA(t)	kB(t)	Sbar
7	0	10	8	53.6549	52.08332	0.5	0.5	52.86911
8	1	10.15716	7.685684	53.75244	51.76308	0.507858	0.492142	52.77339
9	2	10.15917	7.287813	53.75367	51.31881	0.517648	0.482352	52.57921
10	3	10.16164	6.800841	53.75518	50.7057	0.529393	0.470607	52.32007
11	4	10.16474	6.190946	53.75707	49.80498	0.543744	0.456256	51.9539
12	5	10.16876	5.400529	53.75952	48.34392	0.561776	0.438224	51.38627
13	6	10.17429	4.317409	53.76289	45.5101	0.585508	0.414492	50.34217
14	7	10.18277	2.66685	53.76805	37.16139	0.619715	0.380285	47.45279
15	8	10.20039	0	53.77875	0	0.682868	0.317132	36.72378
16	9	20.19415	0	56.85008	0	0.853418	0.146582	48.51685
17	10	30.191	0	57.89213	0	0.93675	0.06325	54.23044
18	11	40.18889	0	58.41626	0	0.973367	0.026633	56.86044
19	12	50.18731	0	58.73168	0	0.988925	0.011075	58.08122
20	13	60.18604	0	58.94234	0	0.995429	0.004571	58.67295
21	14	70.18498	0	59.093	0	0.998123	0.001877	58.98211
22	15	80.18407	0	59.20609	0	0.999232	0.000768	59.16064

The model is illustrated in the spreadsheet in figure 9.16. The parameter values are set out at the top of the spreadsheet. The initial conditions R_0^A and R_0^B allow for columns R_t^A and R_t^B to be computed recursively. Once these values have been obtained, then the columns for S_t^A and S_t^B are computed. We have added one additional constraint, however, in computing columns D and E of the spreadsheet. Since quality standard cannot be negative, we have for columns D and E the formulas

$$= \max\left[\left(\frac{2m^A}{\pi}\right)\arctan\left(R_t^A\right) - n^A, 0\right]$$

$$= \max\left[\left(\frac{2m^B}{\pi}\right)\arctan\left(R_t^B\right) - n^B, 0\right]$$

for firms A and B, respectively. Given the values for the product quality standard, we compute the market shares and the average product quality standard for the industry using the formulas in equations (9.46) and (9.47). Once again, however, in constructing columns F and G of the spreadsheet, we add the constraint that the market share cannot be negative and must sum to unity, i.e., columns F and G have the formulas

$$= \max\left[k_t^A + \gamma\left(S_t^A - \overline{S}_t\right), 0\right] \qquad \text{for column F}$$

$$= 1 - k_t^A \qquad \text{for column G}$$

for k_t^A and k_t^B, respectively. It is now easy to plot resource allocations, product quality standard and market shares.

For example, given firm A has more resources devoted initially to improving product quality standard, firm A will soon dominate the market. Figure 9.17(b) shows that by period 10 firm A has a virtual monopoly.

Figure 9.17.

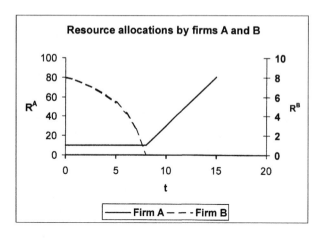

(a)

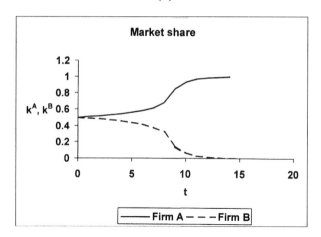

(b)

If one firm engages in a reinforcing policy while the other engages in a counter-acting policy, then the system will oscillate – oscillations occurring in particular with the amount of resources devoted to R&D and in terms of market share. Such oscillations depend not only on the value and sign of a and b but also on the initial resources devoted to R&D. Various possibilities are readily investigated once the model is set up on a spreadsheet or in mathematical software packages. The authors plot the path of R_t^A and R_t^B against t after the system settles down, i.e., they plot the paths for $t = 200 \ldots 250$. Since the equations are symmetrical, then oscillations of one period will show up in the phase plane (once the system has settled down) as simply two points; two-period oscillations as four points, and so on. Choosing the same four paired combinations (a, b) and initial resource allocations $R_0^A = 10$ and $R_0^B = 15$ as Parker *et al.* with $m = 100$ and $n = 40$ for both firms, period 1, 2 and 4 along with chaotic behaviour can be observed in figure 9.18, where the trajectories are plotted for t from 200 to 250.

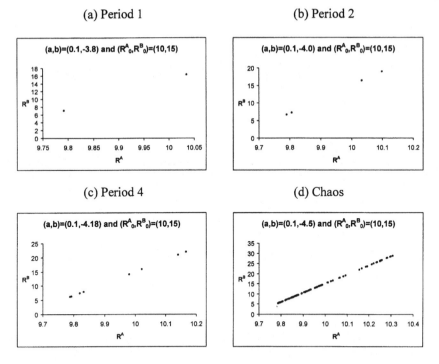

Figure 9.18.

Figure 9.18 was produced with *Excel*. If *Mathematica* or *Maple* is used for constructing this and other figures, then the following instructions can be used. In these instructions we provide a plot of R_t^A for $t = 200$ to 250 and a plot of the trajectory $\{R_t^A, R_t^B\}$ for the same time period:

Mathematica
```
Clear[RA,RB,t,a,b,mA,mB,nA,nB]
RA[0]:=10; RB[0]:=15;
a:=0.1; b:=-3.8; mA:=100; mB:=100; nA:=40; nB:=40;
RA[t_]:=RA[t]=
    Max[0,RA[t-1]+(2 a mA/π)(ArcTan[RA[t-1]])-
    (2 a mB/π)(ArcTan[RB[t-1]])-a(nA-nB)]
RB[t_]:=RB[t]=
    Max[0,RB[t-1]+(2 b mB/π)(ArcTan[RB[t-1]])-
    (2 b mA/π)(ArcTan[RA[t-1]])-b(nB-nA)]
dataRA=Table[{t,RA[t]},{t,200,250}];
dataRARB=Table[{RA[t],RB[t]},{t,200,250}];
ListPlot[dataRA, PlotJoined->True]
ListPlot[dataRARB,PlotStyle->PointSize[0.02]];
```

Maple
```
RA:='RA': RB:='RB': t:='t': a:='a': b:='b':
mA:='mA': mB:='mB': nA:='nA': nB:='nB':
a:=0.1: b:=-3.8: mA:=100: mB:=100: nA:=40: nB:=40:
```

```
RA:=proc(t) option remember;
    max(0,evalf(RA(t-1)+(2*a*mA/Pi)*(arctan (RA(t-1)))-
    (2*a*mB/Pi)*(arctan(RB(t-1)))-a*(nA-nB))) end;
RB:=proc(t) option remember;
    max(0,evalf(RB(t-1)+(2*b*mB/Pi)*(arctan (RB(t-1)))-
    (2*b*mA/Pi)*(arctan(RA(t-1)))-b*(nB-nA))) end;
RA(0):=10: RB(0):=15:
dataRA:=[seq([t,RA(t)],t=200..250)]:
dataRARB:=[seq([RA(t),RB(t)],t=200..250)]:
plot(dataRA);
plot(dataRARB,style=point);
```

The only item in these instructions that needs to be changed in producing figure 9.18 is the value of the parameter b, which takes on the four values $b = -3.8, -4.0, -4.18$ and -4.5.

9.5.2   *Learning*

The model is further extended by the authors to take account of learning. The possibility of adaptation is taken into account by allowing the policy parameters a and b to change. In establishing when to change the policy a simple rule is chosen. Let f denote the frequency of choosing when to change policy (assumed constant), e.g., every year or every quarter. Then define M, the sum of the difference in product quality standard between the last decision point and the present one, assumed to be at time t, i.e.

$$M = \sum_{t-f+1}^{t} \left(S_t^A - S_t^B \right)$$

If $M > 0$ then the current policy is assumed satisfactory and no change in policy is made. If, however, $M < 0$, then a change is considered necessary. Since a positive value of M for firm A implies a negative value of M for firm B and vice versa, then at any decision point one firm will always be altering its policy.

The authors consider two policy adaptations.

Proportional policy adaptation

A change amounting to a proportion of the existing policy, i.e.

$$a_s = \alpha a_{s-1} \quad 0 < \alpha < 1$$
$$b_s = \beta b_{s-1} \quad 0 < \beta < 1$$

Absolute policy adaptation

A change amounting to a fixed amount is applied to the existing policy; this amount can be either positive or negative, i.e.

$$a_s = a_{s-1} + \alpha \quad \alpha \neq 0$$
$$b_s = b_{s-1} + \beta \quad \beta \neq 0$$

In each policy adaptation s describes a particular stretch of f time periods. With the proportional policy adaptation there is no change in policy stance, only the extent of reinforcing or counteracting is diminished. However, absolute policy adaptation allows for a reversal of policy stance, with reinforcing becoming counteracting or vice versa. It also allows for the intensifying or constraining of an existing policy stance.

The resource allocation computations now become

$$R_{t+1}^A = \max\left[0, R_t^A + \left\{a_s\left(\frac{2m^A}{\pi}\right)\arctan\left(R_t^A\right)\right.\right.$$
$$\left.\left. - a_s\left(\frac{2m^B}{\pi}\right)\arctan\left(R_t^B\right) - a_s(n^A - n^B)\right\}\right]$$

$$R_{t+1}^B = \max\left[0, R_t^B + \left\{b_s\left(\frac{2m^B}{\pi}\right)\arctan\left(R_t^B\right)\right.\right.$$
$$\left.\left. - b_s\left(\frac{2m^A}{\pi}\right)\arctan\left(R_t^A\right) - b_s(n^B - n^A)\right\}\right]$$

For instance, if f is 10 then the first policy choice is when $t = 9$ (since period 0 is considered as part of the decision period) and the policy is implemented at time $t = 10$. The next decision is at time $t = 19$ and implemented at time $t = 20$, and so on. The policy parameters a and b remain constant between one decision period and the next.

Example 9.2 (Proportional adaptation)

Consider the following example of proportional adaptation given by the authors. Let

$$m^A = m^B = 100 \qquad n^A = n^B = 40$$
$$\alpha = 0.8 \qquad \beta = 0.9$$
$$a_0 = 0.1 \qquad b_0 = -5.0$$
$$f = 10$$

Figure 9.19 illustrates that with proportional adaptation, after an early period of erratic behaviour, the system settles down to periodic behaviour, the amplitude of which is reduced in stages by the change in policy and that this applies to both firms in the industry.

Example 9.3 (Absolute adaptation)

In the example of absolute adaptation given by the authors with values

$$m^A = m^B = 100 \qquad n^A = n^B = 40$$
$$\alpha = -0.05 \qquad \beta = 0.2$$
$$a_0 = 0.13 \qquad b_0 = -5.0$$
$$f = 10$$

the system exhibits some initial dampening, but then oscillations become more pronounced and the time path of resource allocations to R&D more erratic, as

Figure 9.19.

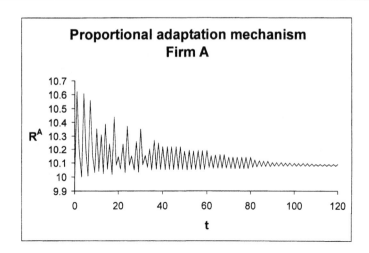

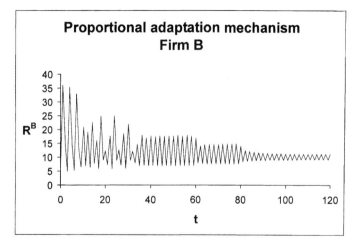

illustrated in figure 9.20. This arises because of the change in policy stance that
can occur with absolute adaptation.

The model allows for some interesting simulations concerning policy adaptation
beyond those considered here where decision-makers can engage in complex 'what
if' scenarios. In such considerations, however, it is most important to bear in mind
exactly when the decision is made and when the policy is implemented.

9.6   Schumpeterian dynamics

The model in the previous section was a type of model that partly explained the
difference between firms by emphasising that sometimes firms with the higher-
quality product survived. Survival, however, was dependent on adaptive behaviour.
The model is in the spirit of a Schumpeterian evolution theory. In this section
we shall consider a similar model that allows for two types of evolutionary processes. The first is in terms of 'survival of the fittest'. In other words, we consider a firm's 'fitness' relative to that of the industry. We shall refer to this as

Table 9.5 Evolutionary model of oligopoly

$\pi_t^i = p_t^i - c_t^i$	π_t^i = profit margin of firm i at time t
$\bar{\pi}_t = \sum_{i=1}^{n} k_t^i \pi_t^i$	p_t^i = product price of firm i at time t
$\bar{c}_t = \sum_{i=1}^{n} k_t^i c_t^i$	c_t^i = unit cost of firm i at time t
$\hat{k}_{t+1}^i = \alpha(\pi_t^i - \bar{\pi}_t) \quad \alpha \geq 0$	c_t^m = minimum unit cost at time t
$\Delta c_{t+1}^i = -\beta(c_t^i - c_t^m) \quad \beta \geq 0$	k_t^i = market share of firm i at time t
	$\hat{k}_{t+1}^i = \dfrac{k_{t+1}^i - k_t^i}{k_t^i}$ = percentage change in market share
	$\bar{\pi}_t$ = average industry profit at time t
	α = speed of selection parameter
	β = speed of imitation parameter

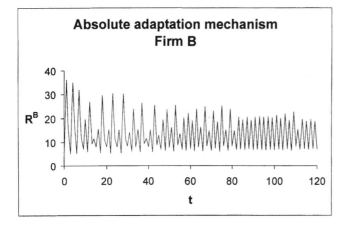

Figure 9.20.

the *selection process*. The second element is imitation, i.e., firms with inferior technology can imitate firms with superior technology. Put another way, a firm can reduce the efficiency gap through imitation. We shall refer to this as the *imitation process*. The model is captured in terms of the relationships set out in table 9.5.

Consider first the selection process. We assume that the percentage change in market share of the ith firm is dependent on its relative fitness compared with the industry average. We measure fitness in terms of profit margins. Hence

(9.48)
$$\hat{k}_{t+1}^i = \alpha \left(\pi_t^i - \overline{\pi}_t \right) \quad i = 1, \ldots, n \quad \alpha \geq 0$$

We assume the speed of selection parameter, α, is the same for all firms. As in the previous section, we measure the average profit as a weighted sum of the profits of all firms in the industry, where the weights are the respective market shares, i.e.

(9.49)
$$\overline{\pi}_t = \sum_{i=1}^n k_t^i \pi_t^i \quad \sum_{i=1}^n k_t^i = 1 \quad \text{for all } t$$

where $\pi_t^i = p_t^i - c_t^i$ is the profit margin for the ith firm at time t. Notice that if $\alpha = 0$ market shares remain unaffected and so what equation (9.48) is attempting to capture is the extent to which firms with above average profits increase their market share while those with below average profits lose some of their market share.

Next we allow for imitation. We assume this is captured by a reduction in a firm's unit costs. A firm's unit costs can be reduced if it imitates the 'best' firm in the industry. We assume that the 'best' firm is that with the lowest unit cost at time t. We further assume that firms have full information on the technology of their competitors and that imitation is costless. Imitation, then, is captured by the relationship

(9.50)
$$\Delta c_{t+1}^i = -\beta \left(c_t^i - c_t^m \right) \quad \beta \geq 0$$

where c_t^m is the minimum unit cost at time t and β measures the speed of imitation. Of course, if $\beta = 0$ no imitation takes place.

Example 9.4 (Constant price, selection, no imitation)

The basic workings of the model are illustrated in the spreadsheet in figure 9.21. Price for all three firms is set at 18; unit costs are initially set at 8, 10 and 12 for firms 1, 2 and 3, respectively, which in this example remain constant for all time periods. This leads to profit margins of 10 for firm 1, 8 for firm 2 and 6 for firm 3. These too remain constant for all time periods. Firm 1 is the firm with the lowest unit costs. Market shares are initially set at $1/3$ for each firm. Subsequent market shares are calculated using

(9.51)
$$k_{t+1}^i = k_t^i \left(1 + \hat{k}_t^i \right)$$

where $\hat{k}_{t+1}^i$ is given by formula (9.48). The final two columns compute average profits and average unit costs for the industry.

Figure 9.22(a) shows the profile of market shares. Given no imitation, the process is governed purely by selection. What we readily observe is 'survival of the fittest'. By about period 8, firms 2 and 3 have virtually zero market share and firm 1 is a virtual monopolist. As can be seen in terms of figure 9.22(b), in this example

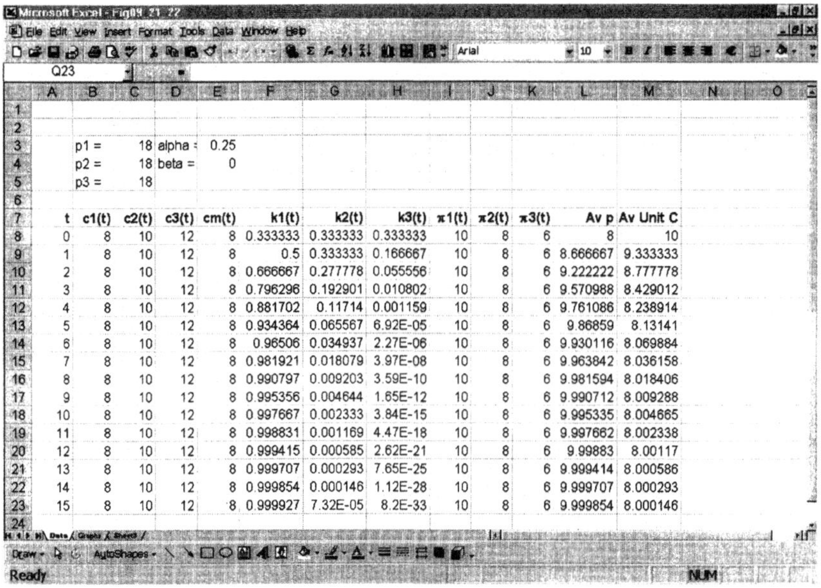

Figure 9.21.

t	c1(t)	c2(t)	c3(t)	cm(t)	k1(t)	k2(t)	k3(t)	π1(t)	π2(t)	π3(t)	Av p	Av Unit C
0	8	10	12	8	0.333333	0.333333	0.333333	10	8	6	8	10
1	8	10	12	8	0.5	0.333333	0.166667	10	8	6	8.666667	9.333333
2	8	10	12	8	0.666667	0.277778	0.055556	10	8	6	9.222222	8.777778
3	8	10	12	8	0.796296	0.192901	0.010802	10	8	6	9.570988	8.429012
4	8	10	12	8	0.881702	0.11714	0.001159	10	8	6	9.761086	8.238914
5	8	10	12	8	0.934364	0.065567	6.92E-05	10	8	6	9.86859	8.13141
6	8	10	12	8	0.96506	0.034937	2.27E-06	10	8	6	9.930116	8.069884
7	8	10	12	8	0.981921	0.018079	3.97E-08	10	8	6	9.963842	8.036158
8	8	10	12	8	0.990797	0.009203	3.59E-10	10	8	6	9.981594	8.018406
9	8	10	12	8	0.995356	0.004644	1.65E-12	10	8	6	9.990712	8.009288
10	8	10	12	8	0.997667	0.002333	3.84E-15	10	8	6	9.995335	8.004665
11	8	10	12	8	0.998831	0.001169	4.47E-18	10	8	6	9.997662	8.002338
12	8	10	12	8	0.999415	0.000585	2.62E-21	10	8	6	9.99883	8.00117
13	8	10	12	8	0.999707	0.000293	7.65E-25	10	8	6	9.999414	8.000586
14	8	10	12	8	0.999854	0.000146	1.12E-28	10	8	6	9.999707	8.000293
15	8	10	12	8	0.999927	7.32E-05	8.2E-33	10	8	6	9.999854	8.000146

average unit costs for the industry tend to unit costs of the most efficient firm and profits also tend to the level of profits of the most efficient firm.

Example 9.5 (Constant price, selection, imitation)

A different pattern emerges when imitation is allowed $\beta > 0$. Consider the following values

$$c_0^1 = 8 \qquad k_0^1 = 1/3 \qquad p = 18$$
$$c_0^2 = 10 \qquad k_0^2 = 1/3 \qquad \alpha = 0.25$$
$$c_0^3 = 12 \qquad k_0^3 = 1/3 \qquad \beta = 0.5$$

Now firms 2 and 3 can prevent themselves being pushed out of the market by imitating firm 1, the most efficient firm. Over time, the industry emerges with a more-or-less identical product produced by each firm. All firms' unit costs converge on the unit costs of the most efficient firm, which implies that the average does also, as shown in figure 9.23(b). Since price is constant, then it also follows that profits of each firm converge to the same level, namely that of firm 1. This must also be the case for average industry profits. As figure 9.23(a) illustrates, in the early period firm 1, the most efficient firm, gains in market share at the expense of firms 2 and 3. But as firms 2 and 3 begin to imitate the most efficient firm, and so achieve a lowering of unit costs, market shares stabilise. After about period 8, firm 1 has 66% of the market, firm 2 has 27% while firm 3 has 7%. The initial cost advantage of firm 1 leads to an increase in market share and a permanent market advantage. However, the process of imitation prevents firms 2 and 3 from being

Figure 9.22.

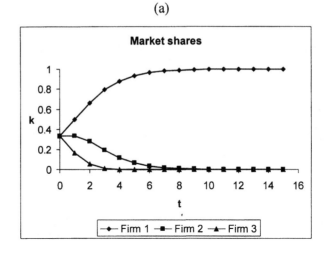

(a)

(b)

driven out of the market, and eventual market shares reflect the initial differences in cost advantage.

The model allows for other considerations, such as product differentiation. In this instance brand loyalty may allow a firm to charge a higher price. The spreadsheet shown in figure 9.21 readily allows for such a consideration. Models incorporating any combinations of the following are possible.

Selection	$\alpha > 0$
Imitation	$\beta > 0$
Product differentiation	Product prices different

However, none of these models exhibits oscillatory behaviour, the type of behaviour we encountered in the previous section involving R&D. This follows from the fact that both speed parameters α and β are positive. The selection parameter reinforces the advantage of the firm with higher than average profits and diminishes consistently the market share of firms with below average profits. Where imitation

Figure 9.23.

(a)

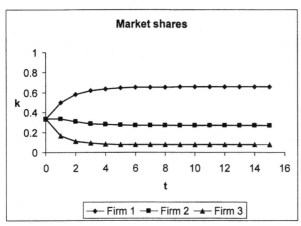

(b)

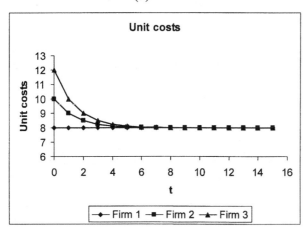

takes place, it is always leading to a lowering of unit costs as the firm imitates the most efficient firm. Although to some extent offsetting the selection process, it cannot lead to oscillatory behaviour.

Exercises

1. For the general linear demand model with constant marginal costs

$$p = A - BQ$$
$$Q = q_1 + q_2$$
$$TC_1 = a_1 q_1$$
$$TC_2 = a_2 q_2$$

Show that if $a_1 = a_2$ then $q_1^* = q_2^*$ for the Cournot solution.

2.   For the n-firm oligopoly model with constant and equal marginal costs

$$p = A - BQ$$

$$Q = \sum_{i=1}^{n} q_i$$

$$TC_i = aq_i \quad i = 1 \dots n$$

Show
  (i) q_i^* is the same for all i.
  (ii) the reaction curves can be expressed

$$q_i = \frac{(A - a) - B \sum_{j \neq i} q_j}{2B}$$

3.   The text states that for linear demand and constant marginal costs the duopoly model is dynamically stable. Set up a spreadsheet which allows for the following parameter values: A, B, a_1, and a_2 for the model

$$p = A - BQ \qquad B > 0$$
$$Q = q_1 + q_2$$
$$TC_1 = a_1 q_1$$
$$TC_2 = a_2 q_2$$

Hence show
  (i)   equilibrium q_1^* and q_2^* are

$$q_1^* = \frac{A - 2a_1 + a_2}{3B}$$

$$q_2^* = \frac{A + a_1 - 2a_2}{3B}$$

  (ii) that no matter what the initial value for (q_{10}, q_{20}), the system always converges on the equilibrium.

4.   For the duopoly model

$$p = 9 - Q$$
$$Q = q_1 + q_2$$
$$TC_1 = a_1 q_1$$
$$TC_2 = a_2 q_2$$

  (i)   Establish the equilibrium for q_1 and q_2 in terms of a_1 and a_2. Show that if $a_1 < a_2$ then $q_1^* > q_2^*$.
  (ii) Let $a_1 = 3$ and $a_2 = 5$ and consider initial points
        (a) firm 1 the monopolist
        (b) firm 2 the monopolist
        From which initial point does the system reach equilibrium sooner?

5.   Consider the model set out in equation (9.5). Let the costs, however, be $TC_i = 5q_i$, $i = 1, 2, 3$.
  (i)   Is the equilibrium point (q_1^*, q_2^*, q_3^*) closer to the origin?
  (ii) Establish the reaction curves for this model.
  (iii) Does this system also oscillate with constant amplitude?

6.   Consider the model

$$p = 9 - Q$$
$$Q = q_1 + q_2 + q_3$$
$$TC_1 = 3q_1$$
$$TC_2 = 2q_2$$
$$TC_3 = q_3$$

   (i) Establish the Cournot equilibrium.
   (ii) Plot trajectories from initial points where each firm is a monopolist.
   (iii) Under the assumption that each firm maximises its profits under the conjectural variation that the other firms are holding their output levels constant, solve the system's difference equations.

7.   Consider the model

$$p = 15 - 2Q$$
$$Q = q_1 + q_2 + q_3$$
$$TC_1 = 5q_1$$
$$TC_2 = 3q_2$$
$$TC_3 = 2q_3$$

   (i) Establish the Cournot solution.
   (ii) Plot trajectories from initial points where each firm is a monopolist.
   (iii) Under the assumption that each firm maximises its profits under the conjectural variation that the other firms are holding their output levels constant, solve the system's difference equations.
   (iv) Is the system dynamically stable?

8.   Consider the following four models

   (a) $p = 20 - 3Q$ (b) $p = 20 - 3Q$
        $Q = q_1 + q_2$ $Q = q_1 + q_2 + q_3$
        $TC_1 = 4q_1$ $TC_1 = 4q_1$
        $TC_2 = 4q_2$ $TC_2 = 4q_2$
                                  $TC_3 = 4q_3$

   (c) $p = 20 - 3Q$ (d) $p = 20 - 3Q$
        $Q = q_1 + q_2$ $Q = q_1 + q_2 + q_3$
        $TC_1 = 4q_1^2$ $TC_1 = 4q_1^2$
        $TC_2 = 4q_2^2$ $TC_2 = 4q_2^2$
                                  $TC_3 = 4q_3^2$

   (i) Establish the Cournot solution for each.
   (ii) What, if anything do you observe about the dynamic behaviour in comparing $n = 2$ as against $n = 3$ for constant MC? (Take initial points from the monopoly position in each case.)
   (iii) What, if anything, do you observe about the dynamic behaviour in comparing model (a) with model (b) and model (c) with model (d)? (Take initial points from the monopoly position in each case.)

9.   Consider the continuous model

$$p(t) = 20 - 3Q(t)$$
$$Q(t) = q_1(t) + q_2(t)$$
$$TC_1(t) = 4q_1(t)$$
$$TC_2(t) = 4q_2(t)$$
$$\dot{q}_1(t) = 0.2(x_1(t) - q_1(t))$$
$$\dot{q}_2(t) = 0.2(x_2(t) - q_2(t))$$

where $x_i(t)$ $i = 1, 2$ is the desired output level that maximises profits under the assumption that the other firm does not alter its output level.
   (i) Find the Cournot solution.
   (ii) Is the system dynamically stable?
   (iii) Construct a phase diagram which includes the direction field and trajectories for initial conditions:
      (a) firm 1 a monopolist
      (b) firm 2 a monopolist
      (c) (0,0)

10.   Construct a phase diagram with direction field for the continuous model

$$p(t) = 20 - 5Q(t)$$
$$Q(t) = q_1(t) + q_2(t)$$
$$TC_1(t) = 4q_1^2(t)$$
$$TC_2(t) = 4q_2^2(t)$$
$$\dot{q}_1(t) = 0.2(x_1(t) - q_1(t))$$
$$\dot{q}_2(t) = 0.2(x_2(t) - q_2(t))$$

along the lines of sub-section 9.4.2. Is it true for this model that all paths converge on the equilibrium regardless of the initial value?

11.   Re-do figure 9.18 but plotting the trajectories $\{k_t^A, k_t^B\}$ and show that the same pattern emerges.

12.   Show the path R_t^A for $t = 200 \ldots 250$ for the same values given in figure 9.18(d). Show that the series is sensitive to initial conditions by setting $R_0^A = 10.1$ and show this series for $t = 200 \ldots 250$ on the same graph.

13.   Re-do figure 9.18 under the following alternative assumptions. Treat each one separately
      (a) $m^A = 100$ $m^B = 110$
      (b) $n^A = 40$ $n^B = 50$
      What do you conclude?

14.   Consider the example of the proportional adaptation model in sub-section 9.5.2 but with $f = 20$. What do you conclude about increasing the length of the decision span?

15.   Show that the two adaptation policies in sub-section 9.5.2 are special cases of the following more general adaptation policy

$$a_s = \alpha_0 + \alpha_1 a_{s-1}$$
$$b_s = \beta_0 + \beta_1 b_{s-1}$$

Derive the paths for R_t^A and R_t^B given the following adaptive policies on the part of firms A and B

$$a_s = -0.05 + 0.8a_{s-1}$$
$$b_s = +0.2 + 0.9b_{s-1}$$

given $(a_0, b_0) = (0.13, -5.0)$, $\left(R_0^A, R_0^B\right) = (10, 5)$ and $f = 10$.

Additional reading

Friedman (1983), Gandolfo (1997), Gehrig (1981), Henderson and Quandt (1971), McMannus (1962), Okuguchi (1970, 1976), Okuguchi and Szidarovsky (1988, 1990), Parker, Whitby and Tobias (2000) and Theocharis (1960).

CHAPTER 10

Closed economy dynamics

The IS-LM model is still one of the main models with which to introduce macroeconomics.[1] In its static form it comprises an IS curve, which denotes real income and interest rate combinations which lead to equilibrium in the goods market, and an LM curve, which denotes real income and interest rate combinations which lead to equilibrium in the money market. Overall equilibrium is established where the IS curve cuts the LM curve. It is then common to consider comparative statics, which involves changing one or more exogenous variables or changing some parameter of the model. Very rarely do we observe any detailed analysis of what happens *out of equilibrium*, and yet this is what we are more likely to be observing around us. In this chapter we will reconsider this model from a dynamic point of view, beginning with a simple linear version and extending the analysis to more complex formulations and nonlinear specifications.

In the first two sections we consider the goods market and then the goods market along with the money market using simple discrete dynamic models of the macroeconomy. In these formulations we introduce dynamics through the goods market equilibrium condition. Rather than assume aggregate income equals aggregate expenditure *in the same period*, we make the assumption that income in period t is equal to total expenditure *in the previous period*. On the other hand, we assume that the money market clears in the *same* time period, i.e., the demand and supply of real money balances in any time period t are equal.

Next we consider continuous versions of the IS-LM model introducing differential speeds of adjustment in the goods market and the money market. Similar to the discrete models, we assume that the goods market is slower to adjust to equilibrium than the money market. In the case of the money market we consider instantaneous adjustment and noninstantaneous adjustment. In section 10.3 we specifically assume real investment is negatively related to the rate of interest only. However, in section 10.4 we allow investment to be positively related to the level of real income. This is found to be significant for the issue of stability, and it is this topic that we pay attention to in section 10.4.

All the models in sections 10.1–10.4 are linear. In section 10.5 we turn to a nonlinear IS-LM model. Even here, however, we consider the dynamics of the model only after using a linear approximation. Finally, in section 10.6, we outline the Tobin–Blanchard model. The IS-LM model determines income and interest rates and has nothing to say about the impact the behaviour of the stock market has

---

[1] We consider a dynamic IS-LM-BP model in chapter 12.

on these. Using the q-theory of investment, the Tobin–Blanchard model provides some alternative dynamic behaviour.

10.1   Goods market dynamics

By way of introduction to lags in the IS-LM model, consider the simplest of goods market models in discrete form, with investment constant, i.e., $I_t = I$ for all t

$$C_t = a + bY_t$$
$$E_t = C_t + I_t \qquad\qquad (10.1)$$
$$Y_t = E_t$$

where

$$C = \text{consumption}$$
$$Y = \text{income}$$
$$E = \text{total expenditure}$$
$$I = \text{investment}$$

This is a *static* model with equilibrium

$$Y^* = \frac{a+I}{1-b} \qquad\qquad (10.2)$$

Two generalisations are possible which give this model some dynamic character. One is to assume consumption is related to lagged income. The model is, then

$$C_t = a + bY_{t-1}$$
$$E_t = C_t + I \qquad\qquad (10.3)$$
$$Y_t = E_t$$

which immediately gives the difference equation

$$Y_t = (a+I) + bY_{t-1} \qquad\qquad (10.4)$$

An alternative formulation is to assume a lag between production, Y_t, and expenditure E_t. Suppose that production in time t is related to overall expenditure in time $t-1$. Then we have the model

$$C_t = a + bY_t$$
$$E_t = C_t + I \qquad\qquad (10.5)$$
$$Y_t = E_{t-1}$$

This also gives rise to the *same* difference equation, namely

$$Y_t = (a+I) + bY_{t-1} \qquad\qquad (10.6)$$

The equilibrium level of income remains what it was in the static model. Since $Y_t = Y_{t-1} = Y^*$ for all t in equilibrium, then $Y^* = (a+I) + bY^*$ or

$$Y^* = \frac{a+I}{1-b} \qquad\qquad (10.7)$$

However, given some initial level of income we can plot the path of income. More explicitly, we can solve this model as follows

$$Y_t = (a + I) + bY_{t-1}$$
$$Y^* = (a + I) + bY^*$$
$$Y_t - Y^* = b(Y_{t-1} - Y^*)$$

Defining $y_t = Y_t - Y^*$, then

$$y_t = by_{t-1}$$

with solution

$$y_t = b^t y_0$$

or

(10.8)
$$Y_t = \frac{a + I}{1 - b} + b^t \left(Y_0 - \frac{a + I}{1 - b} \right)$$

So long as $0 < b < 1$, then income will converge on the equilibrium value.

If we begin in equilibrium and shock demand, say with a rise in investment to $I_1 = I_0 + \Delta I$, then

(10.9)
$$Y_t = \frac{a + I_1}{1 - b} + b^t \left(Y_0 - \frac{a + I_1}{1 - b} \right)$$

and income converges on the new equilibrium level, $Y_1^* = (a + I_1)/(1 - b)$. Given this path of income we immediately have the path for consumption, namely

(10.10)
$$C_t = \frac{a + bI_1}{1 - b} + b^{t+1} \left(Y_0 - \frac{a + I_1}{1 - b} \right)$$

Example 10.1

The situation is illustrated in table 10.1. The table is based on the relationships

$$C_t = 110 + 0.75Y_t$$
$$I = 300$$
$$E_t = C_t + I$$
$$Y_t = E_{t-1}$$

Equilibrium income is initially £1640 million. Investment rises by £20 million, resulting in a new equilibrium level of income of £1720 million. However, income takes time to converge on this level of income, as shown in table 10.1.

The model is illustrative of the influence of lags. It also shows the **dynamic multiplier** in operation. The income multiplier with respect to a change in investment is

(10.11)
$$k = \frac{\Delta Y}{\Delta I}$$

which in the present example is 4. This is the multiplier from one equilibrium to the next. But with income changing we define $\Delta Y_t = Y_t - Y_0^*$, the deviation

Table 10.1 Dynamic multiplier

t	Y_t	k_t
0	1640	
1	1660	1
2	1675	1.75
3	1686.25	2.31
4	1694.69	2.73
5	1701.02	3.05
6	1705.76	3.29
7	1709.32	3.47
8	1711.99	3.60
9	1713.99	3.70
10	1715.50	3.77
11	1716.62	3.83
12	1717.47	3.87
13	1718.10	3.90
14	1718.58	3.93
15	1718.93	3.95
16	1719.20	3.96
17	1719.40	3.97
18	1719.55	3.98
19	1719.66	3.98
20	1719.75	3.99
⋮	⋮	⋮
∞	1720	4

of income from the *initial equilibrium level*, and so we have a **period** multiplier defined by:

$$k_t = \frac{\Delta Y_t}{\Delta I}$$

What is clearly revealed from table 10.1 is that $k_t \to k$ as $t \to \infty$. This is understandable since $Y_t \to Y_1^*$ as $t \to \infty$.

In this naïve model income converges steadily on the new equilibrium level of income. So long as $0 < b < 1$ this must be so. Furthermore, income cannot oscillate. In section 3.10, however, we considered the multiplier–accelerator model. In its discrete form this is

$$C_t = a + bY_{t-1}$$
$$I_t = I_0 + v(Y_{t-1} - Y_{t-2})$$
$$E_t = C_t + I_t \tag{10.12}$$
$$Y_t = E_t$$

Then

$$Y_t = a + bY_{t-1} + I_0 + vY_{t-1} - vY_{t-2}$$

i.e.

$$Y_t - (b+v)Y_{t-1} + vY_{t-2} = a + I_0 \tag{10.13}$$

with equilibrium income of

$$Y^* = \frac{a + I_0}{1 - b}$$

while the solution to (10.13) is

$$Y_t = Y^* + c_1 r^t + c_2 s^t$$

where

$$r = \frac{(b + v) + \sqrt{(b + v)^2 - 4v}}{2}, \qquad s = \frac{(b + v) - \sqrt{(b + v)^2 - 4v}}{2}$$

Example 10.2

$$C_t = 110 + 0.75Y_{t-1}$$
$$I_t = 300 + 1.5(Y_{t-1} - Y_{t-2})$$
$$E_t = C_t + I_t$$
$$Y_t = E_t$$

then

(10.14)
$$Y_t - 2.25Y_{t-1} + 1.5Y_{t-2} = 410$$

and $Y^* = 1640$. The roots to

$$x^2 - 2.25x + 1.5 = 0$$

are complex conjugate, with $r = 1.125 + 0.484123i$ and $s = 1.125 - 0.484123i$, and so income will oscillate. Furthermore, $R = \sqrt{\alpha^2 + \beta^2} = 1.22474 > 1$ and so income will diverge from the new equilibrium. This is shown in figure 10.1. The initial level of income is the original equilibrium level of £1,640. In period 1 autonomous investment is raised by £20, which is maintained for all periods thereafter, so income in period 1 is £1,660. Income in period 3 and beyond is then specified according to the recursive equation (10.14). However, as figure 10.1 reveals, income never reaches the new equilibrium of £1,720. Of course, this is not the only possibility and the resulting path of income depends very much on whether $\sqrt{(b + v)^2 - 4v}$ is real or complex.

Figure 10.1.

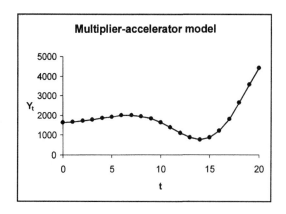

10.2   Goods and money market dynamics[2]

The previous section considered only the goods market, and even then only in simple terms. The essence of the IS-LM model is the *interaction* between the goods market and the money market. This interaction is even more significant when there are lags in the system. Again we illustrate this by introducing a lag into the goods market of the form $Y_t = E_{t-1}$. On the other hand, we assume the money market adjusts in the same time period t, so that the demand for real money balances in time t is equal to the supply of real money balances in time t. This is a reasonable assumption. Algebraically, our model is

Goods market

$c_t = a + b y_t^d$ $0 < b < 1$

$y_t^d = y_t - tax_t$

$tax_t = t_0 + t_1 y_t$ $0 < t_1 < 1$

$i_t = i_0 - h r_t$ $h > 0$

$g_t = g$

$e_t = c_t + i_t + g_t$

Money market

$m_t^d = m_0 + k y_t - u r_t$ $k > 0, u > 0$

$m_t^s = m$

$m_t^d = m_t^s$

where

c = real consumption

y = real income

y^d = real disposable income

tax = real taxes

i = real investment

r = the nominal rate of interest   (10.15)

g = real government spending

e = real total expenditure

m^d = the demand for real money
        balances

m^s = the supply of real money
        balances

On substitution, we arrive at the difference equation

$$y_t = (a - bt_0 + i_0 + g) - b\left(\frac{m_0 - m}{u}\right) + \left[b(1 - t_1) - \left(\frac{kh}{u}\right)\right] y_{t-1} \qquad (10.16)$$

Or more simply

$$y_t = A + B y_{t-1}$$

where

$$A = a - bt_0 + i_0 + g - h\left(\frac{m_0 - m}{u}\right)$$

$$B = b(1 - t_1) - \left(\frac{kh}{u}\right)$$

setting $y_t = y_{t-1} = y^*$ the equilibrium level of income is found to be

$$y^* = \frac{(a - bt_0 + i_0 + g) - h\left(\dfrac{m_0 - m}{u}\right)}{1 - b(1 - t_1) + \left(\dfrac{kh}{u}\right)} \qquad (10.17)$$

---

[2] The model in this section is based on Teigen (1978, introduction to chapter 1).

Define $x_t = y_t - y^*$, then

$$x_t = Bx_{t-1}$$

with solution

$$x_t = B^t x_0$$

or

$$y_t = y^* + B^t(y_0 - y^*)$$

The stability of the equilibrium now depends on whether $B < 1$ or $B > 1$. If $B < 1$ then this amounts to

$$-\left[\frac{1 - b(1 - t_1)}{h}\right] < \frac{k}{u}$$

But why express the condition in this way? The equation for the IS curve is the solution for goods market equilibrium. This takes the form

$$y_t = a - bt_0 + i_0 + g + b(1 - t_1)y_t - hr_t$$

or

$$r_t = \frac{a - bt_0 + i_0 + g}{h} - \frac{[1 - b(1 - t_1)]y_t}{h}$$

The LM curve is the solution for the money market. This takes the form

$$r_t = \frac{m_0 - m}{u} + \left(\frac{k}{u}\right)y_t$$

Hence, the stability condition

$$B < 1 \quad \text{or} \quad -\frac{[1 - b(1 - t_1)]}{h} < \frac{k}{u}$$

amounts to the slope of the IS curve being less steep than the slope of the LM curve. This is definitely satisfied for the usual case where the IS curve is negatively sloped and the LM curve is positively sloped. With $0 < b < 1$ and $0 < t_1 < 1$, then $0 < 1 - b(1 - t_1) < 1$. With $h > 0$ then $-[1 - b(1 - t_1)]/h < 0$ while $k/u > 0$. A shift, say, in the IS curve to the right will lead to a rise in income over time, converging on the new equilibrium level.

Example 10.3

This is illustrated in table 10.2, which is based on the following numerical model.

$$c_t = 110 + 0.75y_t^d$$
$$y_t^d = y_t - tax_t$$
$$tax_t = -80 + 0.2y_t$$
$$i_t = 320 - 4r_t$$
$$g_t = 330 \text{ for all } t$$
$$e_t = c_t + i_t + g_t$$
$$y_t = e_{t-1}$$
$$m_t^d = 20 + 0.25y_t - 10r_t$$

Table 10.2 Dynamic impact of a rise in government spending by 20 million

t	y_t	tax_t	y_t^d	c_t	r_t	i_t	m_t^s	bd_t	s_t	k_t
0	2000.00	320.00	1680.00	1370.00	5.00	300.00	470.00	10.00	310.00	0.00
1	2020.00	324.00	1696.00	1382.00	5.50	298.00	470.00	26.00	314.00	1.00
2	2030.00	326.00	1704.00	1388.00	5.75	297.00	470.00	24.00	316.00	1.50
3	2035.00	327.00	1708.00	1391.00	5.88	296.50	470.00	23.00	317.00	1.75
4	2037.50	327.50	1710.00	1392.50	5.94	296.25	470.00	22.50	317.50	1.88
5	2039.75	327.75	1711.00	1393.25	5.97	296.13	470.00	22.25	317.75	1.94
6	2039.38	327.88	1711.50	1393.63	5.98	296.06	470.00	22.13	317.88	1.97
7	2039.69	327.94	1711.75	1393.81	5.99	296.03	470.00	22.06	317.94	1.98
8	2039.84	327.97	1711.88	1393.91	6.00	296.02	470.00	22.03	317.97	1.99
9	2039.92	327.98	1711.94	1393.95	6.00	296.01	470.00	22.02	317.98	2.00
10	2039.96	327.99	1711.97	1393.98	6.00	296.00	470.00	22.01	317.99	2.00
11	2039.98	328.00	1711.98	1393.99	6.00	296.00	470.00	22.00	318.00	2.00
12	2039.99	328.00	1711.99	1393.99	6.00	296.00	470.00	22.00	318.00	2.00
13	2040.00	328.00	1712.00	1394.00	6.00	296.00	470.00	22.00	318.00	2.00
14	2040.00	328.00	1712.00	1394.00	6.00	296.00	470.00	22.00	318.00	2.00
15	2040.00	328.00	1712.00	1394.00	6.00	296.00	470.00	22.00	318.00	2.00

$$m_t^s = 470$$
$$m_t^d = m_t^s$$

Table 10.2 shows income gradually rising from the initial equilibrium level £2,000 million to the new equilibrium level of £2,040 million arising from a sustained increase in government spending of £20 million, occurring in period 1. As income rises the demand for real money balances increases, leading to a rise in the rate of interest. The rate of interest gradually rises from 5% to 6%. The rise in the rate of interest leads to a gradual fall in investment. Table 10.2 also shows the path of other endogenous variables – such as taxes, disposable income, consumption, etc. It also illustrates the path of the budget deficit, denoted $bd_t = g_t - tax_t$, along with the dynamic multiplier in the final column.

10.3 IS-LM continuous model: version 1

We shall begin with the simplest formulation of the model. Real expenditure is the sum of consumer expenditure, investment expenditure and government expenditure (where we assume the economy is closed). Consumers' expenditure is related to real disposable income, investment expenditure is negatively related to the rate of interest, and government expenditure is assumed to be exogenous. We therefore postulate a very simple linear expenditure function

$$e(t) = a + b(1 - t_1)y(t) - hr(t)$$
$$a > 0, \quad 0 < b < 1, \quad 0 < t_1 < 1, \quad h > 0$$

(10.18)

where

e = real expenditure

a = autonomous expenditure

b = marginal propensity to consume

t_1 = marginal rate of tax

y = real income

h = coefficient of investment in response to r

r = nominal interest rate

The demand for real money balances is assumed to be positively related to real income and negatively related to the nominal interest rate

(10.19) $$m^d(t) = ky(t) - ur(t) \qquad k, u > 0$$

The nominal money supply is assumed exogenous at $M_s = M_0$ and the price level is assumed constant. Hence, real money balances are exogenous at $m_0 = M_0/P$.

It is now necessary to be more precise on the adjustment assumptions in each of the markets. We assume that in the goods market, income adjusts according to the excess demand in that market and that interest rates adjust according to the excess demand in the money market, i.e.

(10.20)
$$\dot{y} = y'(t) = \alpha(e(t) - y(t)) \qquad \alpha > 0$$
$$\dot{r} = r'(t) = \beta(m^d(t) - m_0) \qquad \beta > 0$$

These differential equations can be expressed explicitly in terms of y and r, where we now assume these variables are continuous functions of time, and that we drop the time variable for convenience

(10.21)
$$\dot{y} = \alpha[b(1 - t_1) - 1]y - \alpha hr + \alpha a$$
$$\dot{r} = \beta ky - \beta ur - \beta m_0$$

The equilibrium lines in the (y,r)-phase plane are established simply by setting $\dot{y} = 0$ and $\dot{r} = 0$ respectively. For $\dot{y} = 0$ we derive the equilibrium line

$$-\alpha[1 - b(1 - t_1)]\, y - \alpha hr + \alpha a = 0$$

i.e. $$r = \frac{a - [1 - b(1 - t_1)]y}{h}$$

which is no more than the IS curve. This equilibrium line has a positive intercept (a/h) and a negative slope $(-(1 - b(1 - t_1))/h)$. Similarly, for $\dot{r} = 0$ we derive the equilibrium line which is no more than the LM curve. This equilibrium line has a negative intercept $-m_0/u$ and a positive slope k/u.

The model has just one fixed point for which $\dot{y} = 0$ and $\dot{r} = 0$. This is the point

(10.22) $$(y^*, r^*) = \left(\frac{a + (h/u)m_0}{1 - b(1 - t_1) + (kh/u)}, \frac{-(m_0/u)(1 - b(1 - t_1)) + (k/u)a}{1 - b(1 - t_1) + (kh/u)} \right)$$

and is shown by point E_0 in figure 10.1.

More importantly, we need to consider the dynamic forces in operation when each of the markets are not in equilibrium. First consider the goods market. For points to the right of the IS curve, as drawn in figure 10.2, we have

$$r > \frac{a - [1 - b(1 - t_1)]y}{h}$$
$$0 > a + b(1 - t_1)y - hr - y$$

implying $\dot{y} < 0$. Hence, to the right of the IS curve income is falling. By the same reasoning it is readily established that for points to the left of the IS curve income

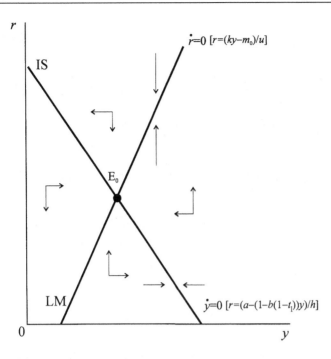

Figure 10.2.

is rising. Considering next the money market, for points to the right of the LM curve

$$r > \frac{ky - m_0}{u}$$

$$0 > ky - ur - m_0$$

implying $\dot{r} > 0$, and so interest rates are rising. Similarly, to the left of the LM curve it is readily established that interest rates are falling. The implied vectors of force in the four quadrants are illustrated in figure 10.2, which clearly indicate a counter-clockwise movement.

Suppose the economy is in all-round equilibrium, shown by point E_0 in figure 10.3. Now consider the result of a fall in the nominal money supply. This will shift the money market equilibrium line to the left. The new equilibrium will be at point E_1. But what trajectory will the economy take in getting from E_0 to E_1? Four possible paths are drawn, labelled T_1, T_2, T_3 and T_4, respectively.

Trajectory T_1 makes a very extreme assumption on the part of adjustment in the money market and the goods market. It assumes that the money market adjusts instantaneously, with interest rates adjusting immediately to preserve equilibrium in the money market. With such immediate adjustment, then in the first instance the economy must move from E_0 vertically up to point A. This is because income has not yet had a chance to change, and is still at the level y_0. With the sharp rise in interest rates, investment will fall, and through the multiplier impact on income, income will fall. As income falls, the demand for money declines, and so too does the rate of interest. The interest rate will fall always in such a manner that equilibrium is preserved in the money market. This means that the adjustment must take place *along* the new LM curve, as shown by trajectory T_1. Under this assumption of instantaneous adjustment in the money market, the interest rate

Figure 10.3.
A monetary
contraction
Note: Vector forces
are with respect to
E₁ and *not* E₀

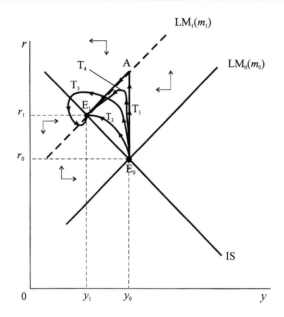

**Figure 10.3.
A monetary
contraction**
Note: Vector forces
are with respect to
E_1 and *not* E_0

overshoots its new equilibrium value and then settles down at the new equilibrium rate. Real income, on the other hand, falls continually until the new equilibrium level is reached.

Trajectory T_2, on the other hand, indicates that both markets adjust imperfectly in such a manner that the economy gradually moves from E_0 to E_1, with interest rates rising gradually until they reach the new level of r_1, and income falling gradually until it reaches its new level of y_1. If the economy conforms to this trajectory, then no overshooting occurs. But our analysis in part I indicates that there is no reason to assume that this is the only possible trajectory – given the vector of forces present. For instance, trajectory T_3 shows a sharper rise in interest rates than in trajectory T_2, and overshooting of interest rates *and* income, with a resulting counter-clockwise spiral towards the new equilibrium E_1. If we assume that the money market, although not adjusting instantaneously, is very quick to adjust, and that the goods market is also adjusting quickly, then trajectory T_3 is more likely. This is an important observation. A spiralling trajectory to the new equilibrium (trajectory T_3) is more likely if *both* markets have quick adjustment speeds, and consequently the more likely overshooting will be observed in *both* endogenous variables y and r. Even so, a counter-clockwise *spiral* is not the most likely outcome; it is more likely to be trajectory T_4. This is because, in general, the money market is relatively much quicker to adjust than the goods market and the adjustment path will be contained within the triangle E_0AE_1, being drawn *towards* trajectory T_1.

A similar analysis holds for a monetary expansion, shown in figure 10.4, where the economy is initially at equilibrium point E_0. Under instantaneous adjustment in the money market, the trajectory is T_1. Interest rates fall to point A on the new LM curve. The sharp fall in interest rates stimulates investment, which, through the multiplier, stimulates the level of income. As income rises the demand for money rises and so too do interest rates, but in such a manner that the money market clears

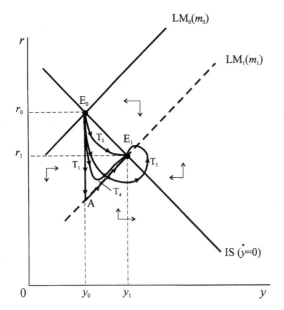

Figure 10.4.
A monetary
expansion
Note: Vector forces
are with respect to
E_1 and *not* E_0

continually. Hence the economy moves along the new LM curve until equilibrium E_1 is reached. Once again, interest rates overshoot their new equilibrium level, but the level of income adjusts gradually until its new equilibrium level is achieved. If both markets show a fair degree of adjustment, then path T_2 will be followed. However, this would require the goods market to adjust quite quickly. In this instance, interest rates fall gradually until the new level of r_1 is reached, and income rises gradually until the new level of y_1 is reached. There is no overshooting either of the interest rate or of income. If both the money market and the goods market are quick to adjust, then the economy is more likely to follow the trajectory illustrated by T_3 in figure 10.4. In other words, a spiral path to the new equilibrium, moving in a counter-clockwise direction, and such that both the rate of interest and the level of income overshoot their equilibrium values. However, with the dominance of adjustment in the money market, a counter-clockwise movement will be observed but *it is not likely to be a spiral path*. The most likely trajectory is T_4.

It is apparent from this discussion that the speed of adjustment is very much to do with the values of the *reaction coefficients* α and β in the dynamic system. The higher the value of the coefficient, the quicker the market responds to a disequilibrium. To some extent, it is the *relative* values of these coefficients that will determine which trajectory the economy will take. To clarify this point, let us consider a numerical example.

Example 10.4

Since throughout the price level is constant, we shall assume that this has a value of unity. The assumed parameter values and the initial level of the money stock are

$$a = 50 \qquad k = 0.25$$
$$b = 0.75 \qquad m_0 = 8$$

Figure 10.5.

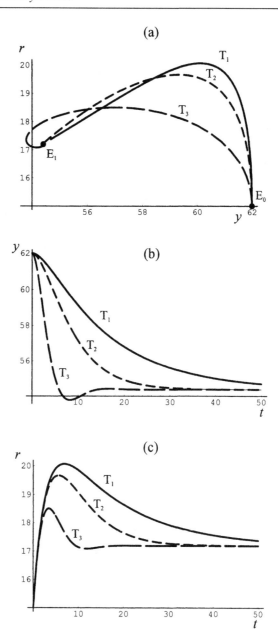

$$t_1 = 0.25 \qquad u = 0.5$$
$$h = 1.525$$

The economy's equilibrium is $(y_0, r_0) = (62, 15)$, shown by point E_0 in figure 10.5(a). A fall in the real money stock to $m_1 = 5$ leads to the new equilibrium point[3] $(y_1, r_1) = (54, 17)$ and shown by point E_1. The resulting differential

---

[3] More exactly $(y_1, r_1) = (54.375, 17.1875)$.

equation system, with unspecified values for α and β, is

$$\dot{y} = -0.4375\alpha y - 1.525\alpha r + 50\alpha$$
$$\dot{r} = 0.25\beta y - 0.5\beta r - 5\beta$$

The trajectory the economy takes to the new equilibrium will depend very much on the values of α and β. Consider three possible combinations, leading to three possible trajectories

$$T_1: \quad \alpha = 0.05 \quad T_2: \quad \alpha = 0.1 \quad T_3: \quad \alpha = 0.5$$
$$\beta = 0.8 \qquad\qquad \beta = 0.8 \qquad\qquad \beta = 0.8$$

If the money market is quicker to adjust than the goods market, as is the most likely situation, then typical trajectories are T_1 and T_2 in figure 10.5(a). In these cases the economy will exhibit overshooting of the interest rate, first rising above the equilibrium level and then falling, with the new equilibrium interest rate higher than initially, as shown in figure 10.5(a). On the other hand, there will be a gradual decrease in the level of income to the new lower equilibrium level. A counter-clockwise spiral pattern, as shown by trajectory T_3, will occur only if *both* the money market and the goods market are quick to adjust, as illustrated in figure 10.5(c). Although a counter-clockwise spiral is possible, therefore, it is not the most likely outcome of this dynamic system because the goods market is not likely to be quick to adjust.

10.4 Trajectories with *Mathematica, Maple* and *Excel*

Figure 10.5(a) set out three trajectories employed in example 10.4. In this and later chapters we shall be producing a number of trajectories for both continuous and discrete systems of equations. We shall therefore take a digression and out-line exactly how to do this with three different software packages: *Mathematica*, *Maple* and (for discrete systems) *Excel*.[4] Figure 10.5 will be used throughout as an example.

10.4.1 Mathematica

To produce trajectories and other plots with *Mathematica*, two commands of impor-tance are used, namely the **NDSolve** command and the **ParametricPlot** command. The first command is used to obtain a numerical solution to the differential equa-tion system, which it does by producing an **InterpolatingFunction**. The second command is then used to plot the values of the InterpolatingFunction.

The input instructions are as follows:

```
sol1=NDSolve[ y'[t]==2.5-0.07625r[t]-0.021875y[t],
   r'[t]==-4.0-0.4r[t]+0.2y[t],
   y[0]==62,r[0]==15}, {y,r},{t,0,50}]
tr1=ParametricPlot[ {y[t],r[t]} /. sol1, {t,0,50},
   PlotPoints->200];
```

---

[4] See Shone (2001) for a demonstration of how to produce trajectories on a spreadsheet for continuous systems of two equations employing Euler's approximation.

```
sol2=NDSolve[ y'[t]==5-0.1525r[t]-0.04375y[t],
  r'[t]==-4.0-0.4r[t]+0.2y[t],
  y[0]==62,r[0]==15}, {y,r},{t,0,50}]
tr2=ParametricPlot[ {y[t],r[t]} /. sol2, {t,0,50},
  PlotPoints->200];
sol3=NDSolve[ y'[t]==25-0.7625r[t]-0.21875y[t],
  r'[t]==-4.0-0.4r[t]+0.2y[t],
  y[0]==62,r[0]==15}, {y,r},{t,0,50}]
tr3=ParametricPlot[ {y[t],r[t]} /. sol3, {t,0,50},
  PlotPoints->200];
trajectories=Show[tr1,tr2,tr3];
pathy1=Plot[ y[t] /.sol1, {t,0,50}, PlotPoints->200];
pathy2=Plot[ y[t] /.sol2, {t,0,50}, PlotPoints->200];
pathy3=Plot[ y[t] /.sol3, {t,0,50}, PlotPoints->200];
pathy=Show[pathy1,pathy2,pathy3];
pathr1=Plot[ r[t] /.sol1, {t,0,50}, PlotPoints->200];
pathr2=Plot[ r[t] /.sol2, {t,0,50}, PlotPoints->200];
pathy3=Plot[ r[t] /.sol3, {t,0,50}, PlotPoints->200];
pathr=Show[pathr1,pathr2,pathr3];
```

***Note*:**

1. We use the **NDSolve** rather than **DSolve** because we are deriving a numerical solution.

2. The simultaneous equations include the two initial values for y and r, which in the present example denotes the initial equilibrium before a disturbance.

3. The parameter values include the fall in the money supply to $m_0 = 5$ and we are deriving trajectory T_1, so $\alpha = 0.05$ and $\beta = 0.8$.

4. **ParametricPlot** is a built in command in *Mathematica* v2.0 and higher, and so can be employed without recourse to other subroutines.

5. There is no comma after $\{y[t],r[t]\}$ because these coordinates are specified for the solution values derived earlier. Thus, the qualifier '/. sol1' instructs the programme to plot the coordinates using each value derived from the output of sol1.

6. Interim displays can be suppressed by including the option Display Function->Identity in each and then in the Show command include the option DisplayFunction-> $DisplayFunction. For instance trajectory 1 can be written

```
tr1=ParametricPlot[ {y[t],r[t]} /. sol1, {t,0,50},
  PlotPoints->200, DisplayFunction->Identity]
```

and trajectories can be written

```
trajectories=Show[tr1,tr2,tr3,
  DisplayFunction->$DisplayFunction];
```

10.4.2   Maple

In some respects it is easier to produce trajectories in *Maple*, but more involved to produce the values for plotting $y(t)$ and $r(t)$. The reason for this is because we can use *Maple*'s **phaseportrait** command to produce the trajectories. This implicitly uses the numerical solution for the differential equations. Thus, the three trajectories and their combined display for figure 10.5 is as follows:

```
with(DEtools):
with(plots):
tr1:=phaseportrait(
   [D(y)(t)=2.5-0.07625*r(t)-0.021875*y(t),
   D(r)(t)=-4-0.4*r(t)+0.2*y(t)],
   [y(t),r(t)], t=0..50,
   [[y(0)=62,r(0)=15]],
   stepsize=.05,
   linecolour=black,
   arrows=none,
   thickness=2):
tr2:=phaseportrait(
   [D(y)(t)=5-0.1525*r(t)-0.04375*y(t),
   D(r)(t)=-4-0.4*r(t)+0.2*y(t)],
   [y(t),r(t)], t=0..50,
   [[y(0)=62,r(0)=15]],
   stepsize=.05,
   linecolour=red,
   arrows=none,
   thickness=2):
tr3:=phaseportrait(
   [D(y)(t)=25-0.7625*r(t)-0.21875*y(t),
   D(r)(t)=-4-0.4*r(t)+0.2*y(t)],
   [y(t),r(t)], t=0..50,
   [[y(0)=62,r(0)=15]],
   stepsize=.05,
   linecolour=blue,
   arrows=none,
   thickness=2):
display(tr1,tr2,tr3);
```

Notes:

1.   It is necessary to load the **DEtools** and **plots** subroutines first.
2.   Using **phaseportrait** implicitly uses a numerical solution to the differential equations.
3.   A small stepsize, here 0.05, produces a smoother plot.
4.   Having arrows set at none means the direction field is not included.

Figures 10.5(b) and 10.5(c) can be produced with a similar set of instructions, except now we use DEplot with the option 'scene'. The instructions are:

```
pathy1=DEplot(
  [D(y)(t)=2.5-0.07625*r(t)-0.021875*y(t),
  D(r)(t)=-4-0.4*r(t)+0.2*y(t)],
  [y(t),r(t)], t=0..50,
  [[y(0)=62,r(0)=15]],
  stepsize=.05,
  linecolour=black,
  arrows=none,
  thickness=2,
  scene=[t,y]):
pathy2=DEplot(
  [D(y)(t)=5-0.1525*r(t)-0.04375*y(t),
  D(r)(t)=-4-0.4*r(t)+0.2*y(t)],
  [y(t),r(t)], t=0..50,
  [[y(0)=62,r(0)=15]],
  stepsize=.05,
  linecolour=black,
  arrows=none,
  thickness=2,
  scene=[y,t]):
pathy3=DEplot(
  [D(y)(t)=25-0.7625*r(t)-0.21875*y(t),
  D(r)(t)=-4-0.4*r(t)+0.2*y(t)],
  [y(t),r(t)], t=0..50,
  [[y(0)=62,r(0)=15]],
  stepsize=.05,
  linecolour=blue,
  arrows=none,
  thickness=2,
  scene=[t,y]):
  display(pathy1,pathy2,pathy3);
pathr1=DEplot(
  [D(y)(t)=2.5-0.07625*r(t)-0.021875*y(t),
  D(r)(t)=-4-0.4*r(t)+0.2*y(t)],
  [y(t),r(t)], t=0..50,
  [[y(0)=62,r(0)=15]],
  stepsize=.05,
  linecolour=black,
  arrows=none,
  thickness=2,
  scene=[t,r]):
pathr2=DEplot(
  [D(y)(t)=5-0.1525*r(t)-0.04375*y(t),
  D(r)(t)=-4-0.4*r(t)+0.2*y(t)],
  [y(t),r(t)], t=0..50,
```

```
        [[y(0)=62,r(0)=15]],
        stepsize=.05,
        linecolour=black,
        arrows=none,
        thickness=2,
        scene=[r,t]):
    pathr3=DEplot(
        [D(y)(t)=25-0.7625*r(t)-0.21875*y(t),
        D(r)(t)=-4-0.4*r(t)+0.2*y(t)],
        [y(t),r(t)], t=0..50,
        [[y(0)=62,r(0)=15]],
        stepsize=.05,
        linecolour=blue,
        arrows=none,
        thickness=2,
        scene=[t,r]):
    display(pathr1,pathr2,pathr3);
```

10.4.3 Excel

Discrete trajectories can also be derived using *Excel*, although there are some limitations. Consider a discrete variant of example 10.4.

$$y_{t+1} - y_t = -0.4375\alpha y_t - 1.525\alpha r_t + 50\alpha$$
$$r_{t+1} - r_t = 0.25\beta y_t - 0.5\beta r_t - 5\beta$$

or the recursive form

$$y_{t+1} = (1 - 0.4375\alpha)y_t - 1.525\alpha r_t + 50\alpha$$
$$r_{t+1} = 0.25\beta y_t + (1 - 0.5\beta)r_t - 5\beta$$

This numerical example is set out in the spreadsheet shown in figure 10.6. The spreadsheet shows the data computations which can be used to produce a given trajectory or a multiple time plot of $y(t)$ or $r(t)$.

The initial values are the equilibrium values $y^* = 62$ and $r^* = 15$. Cells B13 and C13 write out the formulas using both absolute addresses for the parameters α and β and relative addresses for $y(0)$ and $r(0)$. These cells are then copied to the clipboard and pasted down up to $t = 50$. A similar procedure is done for columns F and G along with columns J and K. Unfortunately spreadsheets cannot plot more than one trajectory on the same graph. Selecting cells B12 : C62 and invoking the chart wizard and selecting the *x-y* plot option produces a plot of trajectory T_1. Similarly, selecting cells F12 : G62 produces trajectory T_2 and selecting J12 : K62 produces trajectory T_3.

To produce the discrete equivalent of figure 10.5(b) first select cells A12 : B62 and while holding down the Ctrl-key, select cells F12 : F62 and, while continuing to hold down the Ctrl-key, select cells J12 : J62. Invoking the chart wizard and selecting the *x-y* plot option produces figure 10.5(b). In the same manner figure 10.5(c) can be produced for a multiple plot of $r(t)$ against t.

Figure 10.6.

Figure 10.6 - discrete version of figure 10.5

$$y_{t+1} = (1-0.4375\alpha)y_t - 1.525\alpha r_t + 50\alpha$$

$$r_{t+1} = 0.25\beta y_t + (1-0.5\beta)r_t - 5\beta$$

T1	alpha =	0.05	T2	alpha =	0.1	T3	alpha =	0.5
	beta =	0.8		beta =	0.8		beta =	0.8
t	y(t)	r(t)	t	y(t)	r(t)	t	y(t)	r(t)
0	62.00	15.00	0	62.00	15.00	0	62.00	15.00
1	62.00	17.40	1	62.00	17.40	1	62.00	17.40
2	61.82	18.84	2	61.63	18.84	2	60.17	18.84
3	61.53	19.67	3	61.06	19.63	3	57.64	19.34
4	61.18	20.11	4	60.40	19.99	4	55.29	19.13
5	60.81	20.30	5	59.71	20.07	5	53.61	18.54
6	60.43	20.34	6	59.03	19.99	6	52.75	17.84
7	60.06	20.29	7	58.40	19.80	7	52.60	17.25
8	59.70	20.19	8	57.83	19.56	8	52.94	16.87

The instructions provided in this section allow the reproduction of all two-dimensional trajectories provided in this book. They can be used to produce trajectories for any similar set of differential or difference equations.

10.5   Some important propositions

Similar results can be derived for an increase in the money supply (see exercise 7). The most likely trajectory to the new equilibrium point is for the economy to exhibit an overshoot with regard to its interest rate response (falling sharply and then rising somewhat), while income will gradually rise to its new higher equilibrium level.

Does the economy exhibit the same type of dynamic behaviour for a shock to the goods market, i.e., a shift in the IS curve? The situation is shown in figures 10.7 and 10.8. Consider first a fiscal expansion (*a* rising from 50 to 55) which shifts the IS curve from IS_0 to IS_1, as illustrated in figure 10.7. The economy moves from equilibrium point E_0 to equilibrium point E_1. But what dynamic path does it take to the new equilibrium? If we again assume that the money market adjusts instantaneously, then there will be a gradual rise in income as the multiplier impact of the expansion moves through the economy. The increase in income will raise the demand for money and hence raise the rate of interest. This rise in interest rate will be such as to maintain equilibrium in the money market. Hence, the economy will move along the LM curve until the new equilibrium is reached. There is no overshooting either of income or of interest rates. With less than instantaneous adjustment in the money market ($\beta = 0.8$), and a sluggish adjustment in the goods market ($\alpha = 0.1$), then the economy will follow trajectory T_2, with interest rates rising gradually until the new level r_1 is reached, and income adjusting gradually until the new level of y_1 is reached. Again the economy exhibits no overshooting. Only in the *unlikely* event that the goods market adjusts very rapidly (e.g. $\alpha = 0.5$) along with the money market will the economy exhibit a spiral path following a counter-clockwise movement to the new equilibrium, trajectory T_3, and with the economy exhibiting overshooting behaviour (see exercise 9).

In the case of a fiscal contraction (*a* falling from 50 to 45), illustrated in figure 10.8, the economy will follow trajectory T_1 with instantaneous adjustment

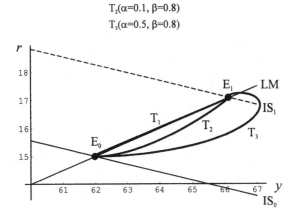

Figure 10.7.

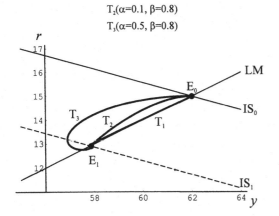

Figure 10.8.

in the money market, with interest rates and income declining steadily until the new equilibrium is reached. Similarly, if the money market is quick to adjust (but not instantaneous, e.g., $\beta = 0.8$) and the goods market is sluggish in its adjustment ($\alpha = 0.1$), then path T_2 will be followed. Only in the *unlikely* event that the goods market is very quick to adjust (e.g. $\alpha = 0.5$) as well as the money market (e.g. $\beta = 0.8$) will a spiral path like T_3 be followed (see exercise 10).

We can make a number of important propositions about the dynamic behaviour of (closed) economies concerning money market shocks and goods market shocks.

PROPOSITION 1
If the money market is quick to adjust and the goods market is sluggish in its adjustment, then a monetary shock will most likely lead to a counter-clockwise movement with the interest rate overshooting its equilibrium value and income gradually changing to its new equilibrium level.

COROLLARY 1 *A counter-clockwise* spiral *to a new equilibrium arising from a monetary shock is only likely to occur in the event that both the money market and goods market are quick to adjust to disequilibrium states.*

PROPOSITION 2

If the money market is quick to adjust and the goods market is sluggish in its adjustment, then a goods market shock will most likely lead to a gradual movement of the economy to its new equilibrium, with the economy exhibiting no overshooting of either interest rates or income.

COROLLARY 2   *A counter-clockwise* spiral *to a new equilibrium aris-ing from a fiscal shock is only likely to occur in the event that both the* money market *and* goods market *are quick to adjust to disequilibrium states.*

Can we make any observations about the dynamic behaviour of this economy when there is a *combined* fiscal and monetary shock? In carrying out this particular analysis we shall simply assume that the money market is quick to adjust, but not instantaneous, and that the goods market is sluggish in its adjustment. In figure 10.9 we illustrate a fiscal and monetary expansion, a rising from 50 to 55 and m rising from 8 to 12. In figure 10.10 we illustrate a fiscal and monetary contraction, a falling from 50 to 45 and m falling from 8 to 5. Under the assumption made about relative adjustment, it is very likely that the trajectory of the economy in each case is a counter-clockwise movement to the new equilibrium, with major overshooting of interest rates and a gradual change in income to the new equilibrium level. Overshooting of income will, once again, occur only if the goods market adjusts

Figure 10.9.

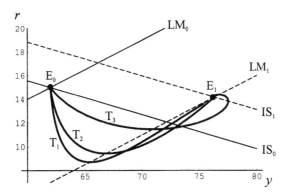

Figure 10.10.

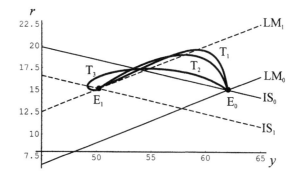

quickly to a disequilibrium along with the money market, trajectory T_3. Similarly, a combined fiscal and monetary contraction, which is illustrated in figure 10.10, leads to a sharp rise in interest rates in the short period, and as income begins to fall, interest rates too are brought down. There is unlikely to be any overshooting of income. Only in the unlikely event that the goods market adjusts quickly to a disequilibrium along with the money market will this occur, trajectory T_3. These results should not be surprising. The initial impact on interest rates comes about because of the shift in the LM curve. Only when income begins to adjust will this effect be reversed.

In the case of fiscal and monetary shocks opposing each other, and under the same assumption about relative adjustment behaviour, the dynamic path to the new equilibrium can have various possibilities depending on which shock is the greater. Figure 10.11 illustrates a fiscal expansion and a monetary contraction, with equilibrium points E_0 and E_1, respectively. If the fiscal expansion is the more

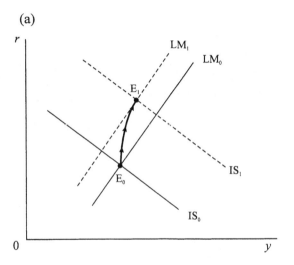

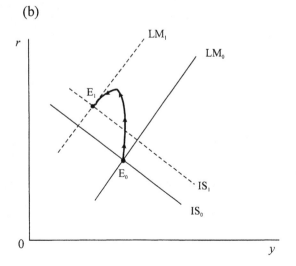

Figure 10.11.
Monetary
contraction and
fiscal expansion

Figure 10.12.
Monetary
expansion and
fiscal contraction

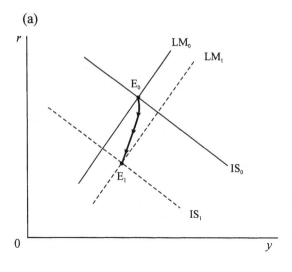

(a)

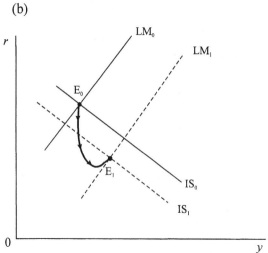

(b)

dominant of the two shocks (figure 10.11(a)), then the economy will traverse a smooth path from E_0 to E_1 with a rise in interest rates and a rise in income. On the other hand, if the monetary contraction dominates (figure 10.11(b)), then the economy will move counter-clockwise, with interest rates overshooting their new equilibrium level and income gradually falling. Similarly, in figure 10.12 we show a fiscal contraction and a monetary expansion. If the fiscal contraction dominates (figure 10.12(a)), then the economy will decline gradually from equilibrium point E_0 to E_1. On the other hand, if the monetary expansion dominates, the decline in the interest rate may very well overshoot its equilibrium level, although income will gradually rise.

We arrive, then, at two further propositions:

PROPOSITION 3
If the money market is quick to adjust and the goods market is sluggish in its adjustment, then a fiscal expansion (contraction) combined with

a monetary expansion (contraction) will more likely lead to a counter-clockwise movement, with interest rates rising (falling) initially and then falling (rising) into the medium and long term; while income will gradually rise (fall) until its new equilibrium position is reached.

PROPOSITION 4

If the money market is quick to adjust and the goods market is sluggish in its adjustment, then a fiscal expansion (contraction) combined with a monetary contraction (expansion) will give rise to a gradual change in interest rates and income if the fiscal shock dominates, but will exhibit interest rate overshooting if the monetary shock dominates.

There is one important observation we can draw from this analysis about the dynamic behaviour of the economy. Given the assumption about relative speeds of adjustment, then interest rate volatility is far more likely to be observed than income volatility.

10.6 IS-LM continuous model: version 2

In this section we shall extend the investment function to include real income. In other words, business will alter the level of investment according to the level of income; the higher the level of income the more business undertakes new investment. We shall continue with a simple linear model, but this simple extension will lead to the possibility that the IS curve is positively sloped. In considering the implications of this we shall consider some explicit numerical examples in order to see the variety of solution trajectories. In one case we shall derive an explicit saddle path solution. Since the formal derivation is similar to the previous section we can be brief.

The model is[5]

$$
\begin{aligned}
e &= a + b(1 - t)y - hr + jy \\
m^d &= ky - ur \\
\dot{y} &= \alpha(e - y) \\
\dot{r} &= \beta(m^d - m_0)
\end{aligned}
\qquad (10.23)
$$

where

$$
\begin{aligned}
&a > 0, 0 < b < 1, 0 < t < 1, h > 0, j > 0, \\
&k > 0, u > 0, \alpha > 0, \beta > 0
\end{aligned}
$$

which gives the two differential equations

$$
\begin{aligned}
\dot{y} &= \alpha[b(1 - t) + j - 1]y - \alpha hr + \alpha a \\
\dot{r} &= \beta ky - \beta ur - \beta m_0
\end{aligned}
\qquad (10.24)
$$

with the IS curve obtained from setting $\dot{y} = 0$ as

$$
r = \frac{a - [1 - b(1 - t) - j]y}{h}
$$

---

[5] Although we use t for the marginal rate of tax, there should be no confusion with the same letter standing for time.

and an LM curve obtained from setting $\dot{r} = 0$ as

$$r = \frac{ky - m_0}{u}$$

The major difference between this version and the one in the previous section is that now the IS curve can have either a negative slope (if $b(1 - t) + j < 1$) or a positive slope (if $b(1 - t) + j > 1$), and that the positive slope is more likely the larger the value of the coefficient j. Since we dealt with a negatively sloped IS curve in the previous section, let us consider here the implications of a positively sloped IS curve, i.e., we assume $b(1 - t) + j > 1$.

For a *positively* sloped IS curve, points to the *left* of this line represent

$$r > \frac{a - [1 - b(1 - t) - j]y}{h}$$

$$0 > a + [b(1 - t) + j]y - hr - y$$

implying $\dot{y} < 0$. Hence, to the *left* of the IS curve income is falling. Similarly, by the same reasoning, for points to the *right* of the IS curve income is rising.

There is no change for the LM curve, and we have already established that for points to the *right* of the LM curve interest rates are rising while to the *left* of the LM curve interest rates are falling.

With a positively sloped IS curve, there are two possibilities:

(i)   the IS curve is less steep than the LM curve
(ii) the IS curve is steeper than the LM curve.

The two possibilities, along with the vector of forces outlined above, are illustrated in figure 10.13(a) and (b).

Figure 10.13(a) reveals a counter-clockwise trajectory while figure 10.13(b) reveals an unstable situation, although it does indicate that a trajectory *might* approach the equilibrium point. Neither situation is straightforward. Although figure 10.13(a) indicates a counter-clockwise trajectory, is the trajectory tending *towards* the equilibrium or *away* from it? There is nothing within the model as laid down so far to indicate which is the case.

In order to see what the difficulty is, consider the following two numerical examples.

Example 10.5			*Example 10.6*		
$a = 2$	$k = 0.25$	$\alpha = 0.05$	$a = 2$	$k = 0.25$	$\alpha = 0.2$
$b = 0.75$	$u = 0.5$	$\beta = 0.8$	$b = 0.8$	$u = 0.25$	$\beta = 0.3$
$t = 0.25$	$m_0 = 8$		$t = 0.2$	$m_0 = 8$	
$h = 1.525$			$h = 1.525$		
$j = 0.8$			$j = 0.95$		

Solution   *Solution*

$y^* = 66$ $y^* = 55.3$
$r^* = 17$ $r^* = 22.3$

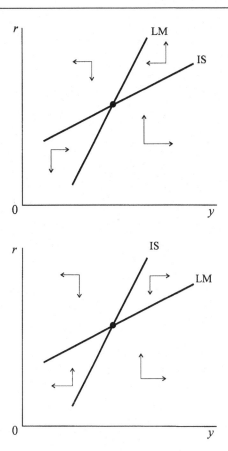

Figure 10.13.

Intercepts and slopes

IS intercept $= 1.3$
IS slope $= 0.238$
LM intercept $= -16$
LM slope $= 0.5$

Intercepts and slopes

IS intercept $= 1.3$
IS slope $= 0.387$
LM intercept $= -32$
LM slope $= 1$

Both examples typify the situation in figure 10.13(a), with a positive IS curve, and the IS curve less steep than the LM curve. However, the dynamics of both these examples is different. Both lead to a counter-clockwise path. However, example 10.5 leads to a stable path which appears to traverse a straight line path after a certain time period, while example 10.6 leads to an unstable spiral, as illustrated in figure 10.14(a) and 10.14(b) (see exercise 11). But, then, what is it that is different between these two examples? To answer this question we need to consider the differential equation system in terms of deviations from equilibrium, and then to consider the trace and determinant of the dynamic system.[6]

Return to the general specification of the differential equations

$$\dot{y} = \alpha[b(1-t)+j-1]y - \alpha hr + \alpha a$$
$$\dot{r} = \beta ky - \beta ur - \beta m_0$$

---

[6] See chapter 4.

Figure 10.14.

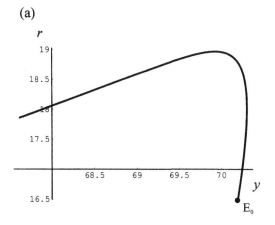

(a)

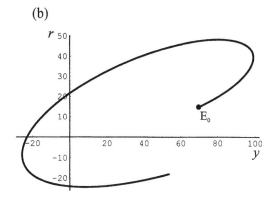

(b)

and consider the equilibrium values of the variables, i.e.

$$0 = \alpha[b(1-t)+j-1]y^* - \alpha hr^* + \alpha a$$
$$0 = \beta ky^* - \beta ur^* - \beta m_0$$

Subtracting the second set from the first we have

(10.25)
$$\dot{y} = \alpha[b(1-t)+j-1](y-y^*) - \alpha h(r-r^*)$$
$$\dot{r} = \beta k(y-y^*) - \beta u(r-r^*)$$

and the matrix of this system is

(10.26)
$$\mathbf{A} = \begin{bmatrix} \alpha[b(1-t)+j-1] & -\alpha h \\ \beta k & -\beta u \end{bmatrix}$$

whose trace and determinant are

(10.27)
$$\text{tr}(\mathbf{A}) = \alpha[b(1-t)+j-1] - \beta u$$
$$\det(\mathbf{A}) = -\alpha\beta u[b(1-t)+j-1] + \alpha\beta kh$$

Using these results we can summarise the properties of the systems in examples 10.5 and 10.6 in terms of the values for their trace and determinant. These are

Example 10.5

$\text{tr}(\mathbf{A}) = -0.382$

$\det(\mathbf{A}) = 0.008$ where $\text{tr}(\mathbf{A})^2 > 4 \det(\mathbf{A})$

Example 10.6

$\text{tr}(\mathbf{A}) = 0.043$

$\det(\mathbf{A}) = 0.014$ where $\text{tr}(\mathbf{A})^2 < 4 \det(\mathbf{A})$

In terms of table 4.1 in part I (p. 180), it is clear that example 10.5 satisfies the conditions for an asymptotically stable node while example 10.6 satisfies the condition of an unstable spiral, verifying what is shown in figure 10.13(a). Notice that in both examples the determinant of the system is positive. Although this is necessary for a spiral path, it is not sufficient to determine whether the path is stable or unstable. This requires information on the sign of the trace. A stable spiral requires the trace to be negative; while an unstable spiral arises if the trace is positive – and in both cases the condition that $\text{tr}(\mathbf{A})^2 < 4 \det(\mathbf{A})$ needs to be satisfied. Unfortunately, there is no geometric representation of the trace requirement. It can be ascertained only from the system itself. Even so, a comparison of the two examples indicates quite clearly that for an unstable spiral to be more likely, it is necessary for the coefficient of induced spending $(b(1-t)+j)$ to be high and for there to be quick adjustment in both markets (large values for the reaction coefficients α and β). If the IS curve is positively sloped, and is less steep than the LM curve, the most likely result is a counter-clockwise stable spiral.

Let us now consider a third example for which the IS curve is positively sloped but is steeper than the LM curve.

Example 10.7

Parameter values			*Solution*	*Intercepts and slopes*
$a = -25$	$k = 0.22$	$\alpha = 0.05$	$y^* = 65.4$	IS intercept $= -25$
$b = 0.75$	$u = 0.75$	$\beta = 0.8$	$r^* = 10.5$	IS slope $= 0.5125$
$t_1 = 0.25$	$m_0 = 8$			
$h = 1$				LM intercept $= -10.7$
$j = 0.95$				LM slope $= 0.293$

$\text{tr}(\mathbf{A}) = -0.574375$

$\det(\mathbf{A}) = -0.006575$ where $\text{tr}(\mathbf{A})^2 > 4 \det(\mathbf{A})$

This example typifies the situation in figure 10.13(b). But in order to see what is happening, we need to derive the characteristic equations of the system. In terms of deviations from the equilibrium we have the general results indicated already in terms of the equation system given above. Substituting the numerical values given in example 10.7, we obtain the following differential equation system

$$\dot{y} = 0.025625(y - y^*) - 0.05(r - r^*)$$
$$\dot{r} = 0.176(y - y^*) - 0.6(r - r^*)$$

whose characteristic roots can be obtained from

$$|A - \lambda I| = 0$$

i.e.

$$\begin{vmatrix} 0.025625 - \lambda & -0.05 \\ 0.176 & -0.6 - \lambda \end{vmatrix} = 0$$

Which leads to the quadratic equation

$$\lambda^2 + 0.574375\lambda - 0.006575 = 0$$

with solutions

$$r = 0.0112277 \qquad s = -0.585603$$

Using the first solution, we have

$$\begin{bmatrix} 0.025625 & -0.05 \\ 0.176 & -0.6 \end{bmatrix} \begin{bmatrix} y - y^* \\ r - r^* \end{bmatrix} = 0.0112277 \begin{bmatrix} y - y^* \\ r - r^* \end{bmatrix}$$

which leads to the relationship

$$r - r^* = 0.287945(y - y^*)$$

On the other hand, using the second characteristic root, and following through the same procedure, we find

$$r - r^* = 12.224555(y - y^*)$$

These two results indicate two saddle paths; one of which is stable and the other is unstable. To verify this, we use *Mathematica* to plot ten trajectories of example 10.7, which are illustrated in figure 10.15. Given the vectors of force already established for figure 10.13(b), which typifies example 10.7, it is clear that the first characteristic root leads to an unstable saddle path, while the second characteristic root leads to a stable saddle path. The dynamics of this system, then, is *schematically* illustrated in figure 10.16, showing the saddle paths (denoted $S_1 S'_1$ and $S_2 S'_2$ associated with r and s, respectively) in relation to the IS and LM curves. The equilibrium of this system, then, is unstable except for the unlikely event that the initial point lies on the stable saddle path denoted $S_2 S'_2$ in figure 10.16. Also notice

Figure 10.15.

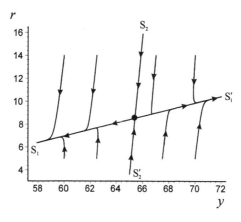

Figure 10.16.

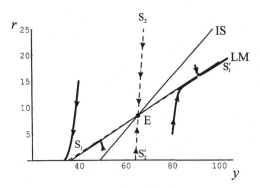

from figure 10.16 that one of the saddle paths is almost identical to the LM curve. This is a result of the assumption of rapid adjustment in the money market relative to the goods market. With perfect adjustment in the money market, then one saddle path would be *identical* with the LM curve, and this would be the *unstable* saddle path in the present context.

10.7   Nonlinear IS-LM model

In this section we shall consider a nonlinear version of the IS-LM model. We can be brief because much of the analysis has already been carried out. In this version consumption spending in real terms is related to real income (where we assume disposable income has been eliminated); investment is inversely related to the nominal rate of interest (we assume expected inflation is zero) and positively to the level of real income; government spending is assumed exogenous. Our expenditure function, in real terms, is then

$$e = c(y) + i(r, y) + g \qquad 0 < c_y < 1, i_r < 0, i_y > 0 \tag{10.28}$$

The demand for real money balances, m^d, is assumed to be positively related to real income (the transactions demand for money) and inversely related to the rate of interest (the speculative demand for money). Thus

$$m^d = l(y, r) \quad l_y > 0, l_r < 0 \tag{10.29}$$

The dynamics are in terms of excess demand in the goods market and excess demand for real money balances, i.e.

$$\dot{y} = \alpha(e - y) \qquad \alpha > 0$$
$$\dot{r} = \beta(l(y, r) - m_0) \quad \beta > 0 \tag{10.30}$$

where m_0 is the supply of real money balances, and m_0 is assumed exogenous.

Equilibrium in the goods market requires $\dot{y} = 0$ or $e = y$, while equilibrium in the money market requires $\dot{r} = 0$ or $l(y, r) = m_0$. Suppose such a fixed point exists and is denoted (y^*, r^*). The question arises is whether such an equilibrium is dynamically stable. Given the nonlinear nature of the system, and the fact that no explicit functional forms are specified, then it is not possible to establish this in any absolute sense. We can, however, use the linearisation technique discussed in part I to establish the stability *in the neighbourhood of the equilibrium point.*[7] As we mentioned in part I, when employing such a linearisation, only *local* stability can be established. But even this is better than having nothing to say on the matter.

Expanding the above system around the fixed point (y^*, r^*) gives

$$\dot{y} = \alpha \left[\frac{\partial(e-y)}{\partial y}(y-y^*) + \frac{\partial(e-y)}{\partial r}(r-r^*) \right]$$

$$\dot{r} = \beta \left[\frac{\partial(l-m_0)}{\partial y}(y-y^*) + \frac{\partial(l-m_0)}{\partial r}(r-r^*) \right]$$

But

$$\frac{\partial(e-y)}{\partial y} = c_y + i_y - 1, \qquad \frac{\partial(e-y)}{\partial r} = i_r$$

$$\frac{\partial(l-m_0)}{\partial y} = l_y, \qquad \frac{\partial(l-m_0)}{\partial r} = l_r$$

Hence

(10.31)
$$\dot{y} = \alpha(c_y + i_y - 1)(y - y^*) + \alpha i_r(r - r^*)$$
$$\dot{r} = \beta l_y(y - y^*) + \beta l_r(r - r^*)$$

which can be written as a matrix dynamic system in the form

(10.32)
$$\begin{bmatrix} \dot{y} \\ \dot{r} \end{bmatrix} = \begin{bmatrix} \alpha(c_y + i_y - 1) & \alpha i_r \\ \beta l_y & \beta l_r \end{bmatrix} \begin{bmatrix} y - y^* \\ r - r^* \end{bmatrix}$$

and where the matrix of the system is

(10.33)
$$\mathbf{A} = \begin{bmatrix} \alpha(c_y + i_y - 1) & \alpha i_r \\ \beta l_y & \beta l_r \end{bmatrix}$$

The dynamics of the system can now be determined from the properties of $\mathbf{A}$. These are

(10.34)
$$\text{tr}(\mathbf{A}) = \alpha(c_y + i_y - 1) + \beta l_r$$
$$\det(\mathbf{A}) = \alpha\beta(c_y + i_y - 1)l_r - \alpha\beta i_r l_y$$
$$= -\alpha\beta[l_r(1 - c_y - i_y) + i_r l_y]$$

Can we interpret any *economic* meaning to the $\text{tr}(\mathbf{A})$ and the $\det(\mathbf{A})$? To see if we can, let us consider the slopes of the IS and LM curves. For the IS curve we have $y = e$, hence

$$y = c(y) + i(y, r) + g$$

Totally differentiating this expression with respect to y and r we obtain

$$dy = c_y dy + i_y dy + i_r dr$$

and so the slope of the IS curve, denoted dr/dy, is given by

$$(1 - c_y - i_y)dy = i_r dr$$

$$\text{or} \quad \frac{dr}{dy} = \frac{1 - c_y - i_y}{i_r}$$

[7] See section 2.7.

The slope of the LM curve is established in the same manner (and noting that m_0 is exogenous)

$$0 = l_y dy + l_r dr$$

$$\frac{dr}{dy} = \frac{-l_y}{l_r}$$

If the IS curve is less steep than the LM curve, then

$$\frac{1 - c_y - i_y}{i_r} < \frac{-l_y}{l_r}$$

i.e.

$$l_r(1 - c_y - i_y) + i_r l_y < 0$$

$$-\alpha\beta[l_r(1 - c_y - i_y) + i_r l_y] > 0$$

Hence, $\det(\mathbf{A}) > 0$. This is certainly satisfied in the usual case of a negatively sloped IS curve and a positively sloped LM curve. But we have already established in the previous section that a stable solution will occur if both the IS and the LM curves are positively sloped but that the IS curve is less steep than the LM curve *and* that the trace of the system is negative in sign.

10.8 Tobin–Blanchard model

10.8.1   *The model in outline*[8]

There has been some interest by economists as to whether stock market behaviour can influence income and interest rates – at least in the short run. The IS-LM model so far outlined does not allow for any such link. It is plausible to think that investment will, in some way, be influenced by stock market behaviour. Such a link was considered by Blanchard (1981) following on the approach to investment suggested by Tobin (1969), and what is referred to as the *q-theory of investment*.

The variable q represents the market value of equities as a ratio of the replacement cost. It can be understood as follows.[9] If all future returns are equal, and denoted R, and are discounted at the interest rate r, then the present value of equities, V say, is equal to R/r. On the other hand, firms will invest until the replacement cost of any outstanding capital stock, RC, is equal to the return on investment, R/ρ, where ρ is the marginal efficiency of capital. Then

$$q = \frac{V}{RC} = \frac{R/r}{R/\rho} = \frac{\rho}{r} \tag{10.35}$$

Consequently, net investment is a positive function of q, which still means that it is inversely related to r. In the long run $r = \rho$ and so $q = 1$, and there is no net investment. The upshot of this approach is that investment, rather than being inversely related to r is positively related to q. This in turn means aggregate expenditure (and hence aggregate demand) is positively related to q.

---

[8] A different treatment than the one presented here, also utilising phase diagrams, is provided in Romer (2001, chapter 8). See also Obstfeld and Rogoff (1999, section 2.5.2).

[9] See Stevenson, Muscatelli and Gregory (1988, pp. 156–9) for a fuller discussion.

We can accordingly express aggregate expenditure, e, as

$$a(t) = a_1 y(t) + a_2 q(t) + g \qquad 0 < a_1 < 1, a_2 > 0$$

where g is real government spending. The goods market is assumed to adjust with a lag, with reaction coefficient $\sigma > 0$, thus

$$\dot{y}(t) = \sigma(e(t) - y(t)) \qquad \sigma > 0$$

The money market, on the other hand, is assumed to adjust instantaneously, and so the demand for real money balances is equal to the supply of real money balances, i.e.

$$ky(t) - ur(t) = m_0 \qquad k > 0, u > 0$$

The next equation relates the rate of interest (on bonds) to the yield on equities, which are equal because it is assumed that bonds and equities are perfect substitutes, i.e.

$$r(t) = \frac{b_1 y(t) + \dot{q}^e(t)}{q(t)}$$

where $b_1 y$ constitutes the firms' profits, which are assumed proportional to output, and $\dot{q}^e$ constitutes expected capital gains. Finally, we assume rational expectations, which in the present model is equivalent to perfect foresight, and so $\dot{q}^e = \dot{q}$. Suppressing the time variable, then the model can be stated in terms of five equations

$$
\begin{aligned}
e &= a_1 y + a_2 q + g \\
m_0 &= ky - ur \\
\dot{y} &= \sigma(e - y) \\
r &= \frac{b_1 y + \dot{q}^e}{q} \\
\dot{q}^e &= \dot{q}
\end{aligned}
$$

(10.36)

which can be reduced to two nonlinear nonhomogeneous differential equations, namely

$$
\begin{aligned}
\dot{y} &= \sigma(a_1 - 1)y + \sigma a_2 q + \sigma g \\
\dot{q} &= \left(\frac{kq}{u} - b_1\right) y - \frac{q m_0}{u}
\end{aligned}
$$

(10.37)

First we need to establish the existence of a fixed point, an equilibrium point. We do this by setting $\dot{y} = 0$ and $\dot{q} = 0$, and solving for y and q. This is no more than where the two isoclines intersect. So let us first look at these separately. First consider the $\dot{y} = 0$ isocline, which we shall refer to as the IS curve since it implies goods market equilibrium. We have

$$
\begin{aligned}
\dot{y} &= \sigma(a_1 y + a_2 q + g - y) = 0 \\
&-(1 - a_1)y + a_2 q + g = 0
\end{aligned}
$$

i.e. $\quad q = \dfrac{(1 - a_1)y - g}{a_2}$

which is linear with intercept on the q-axis of $-g/a_2$ and slope of $(1 - a_1)/a_2$. Since we have assumed that a_1 lies between zero and unity, then the slope of this line is positive.

Next consider the $\dot{q} = 0$ isocline, which we shall refer to as the LM curve since it implies money market equilibrium. We have

$$\dot{q} = \left(\frac{kq}{u} - b_1\right) y - \frac{qm_0}{u} = 0$$

$$q\left(\frac{ky}{u} - \frac{m_0}{u}\right) = b_1 y$$

i.e. $$q = \frac{ub_1 y}{(ky - m_0)}$$

which is nonlinear, and has an asymptote at $y = m_0/k$, which means that q is positive only if $y > m_0/k$. This we shall assume to be the case. Also, as $y \to \infty$, then $q \to ub_1/k$. Although it is possible to solve for y and q, the solution involves a quadratic and does not reveal anything new.

What we have here, however, is a nonlinear nonhomogeneous differential equation system. To establish the nature of the equilibrium we need to consider the vectors of forces in the four quadrants. We have already established that the $\dot{y} = 0$ isocline is positively sloped. Furthermore, if $\dot{y} > 0$ then

$$q > \frac{(1 - a_1)y - g}{a_2}$$

Hence, above the $\dot{y} = 0$ isocline, y is rising while below it y is falling, as illustrated in figure 10.17.

In establishing the nature of the forces either side of the $\dot{q} = 0$ isocline we first need to establish its slope. We find this with a little manipulation as follows

$$q = \frac{ub_1 y}{(ky - m_0)}$$

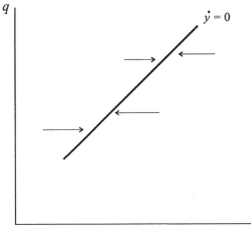

Figure 10.17.

$$\frac{dq}{dy} = \frac{(ky - m_0)ub_1 - ub_1yk}{(ky - m_0)^2} = \frac{b_1}{(ky - m_0)/u} - \frac{u_2b_1y\left(\dfrac{k}{u}\right)}{(ky - m_0)^2}$$

$$= \frac{b_1 - q\left(\dfrac{k}{u}\right)}{r}$$

The slope of the LM curve in (q, y)-space is therefore ambiguous. The slope is positive if $b_1 > qk/u$ and negative if $b_1 < qk/u$. To interpret these two situations, consider a rise in income, shown by the movement from point A to point B in figures 10.18(a) and (b). From the money market equation this will raise the rate of interest, r; from the yield on equities equation, this will raise profits and hence the equity yield. If the rise in income raises the yield on equities by less than it raises r then q must fall in order to re-establish equilibrium between r and the yield on equities $((b_1y + \dot{q})/q)$, as shown in figure 10.18(a) by the movement from point B to point C. This Blanchard called the 'bad news' case because the rise in

Figure 10.18.

(a) 'bad news'

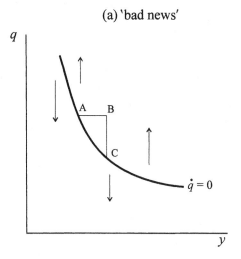

(b) 'good news'

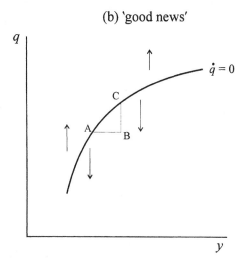

income led to a fall in stock market prices. On the other hand, if the increase in income increases r by less than the yield on equities $((b_1 y + \dot{q})/q)$, then q must rise, as shown in figure 10.18(b) by the movement from point B to point C. This Blanchard called the 'good news' case, since the rise in income leads to a rise in stock market prices.

Whether the $\dot{q} = 0$ isocline is negatively sloped ('bad news') or positively sloped ('good news'), if $\dot{q} > 0$ then

$$q > \frac{u b_1 y}{(ky - m_0)}$$

and so above the $\dot{q} = 0$ isocline q is rising while below it q is falling, as shown by the arrows in figure 10.18.

The combined vector forces in both the 'bad news' case and the 'good news' case are illustrated in figures 10.18(a) and (b). In each case, the vector forces indicate

(a) 'bad news'

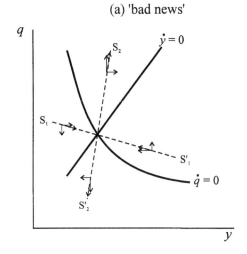

Figure 10.19.

(b) 'good news'

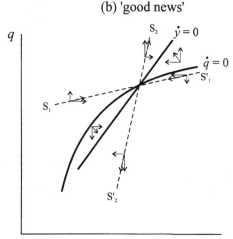

Figure 10.20.

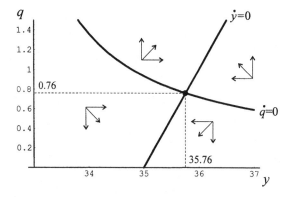

a saddle path solution. Given the assumption of rational expectations, and given that for any value of y there is a unique point, (a unique value of q) on the saddle path, then the economy will be at this value of q and will, over time, converge on the equilibrium.[10]

Example 10.8

Let us illustrate the model with a numerical example. In this example we consider only the 'bad news' case. The model is

$$e = 0.8y + 0.2q + 7$$
$$8 = 0.25y - 0.2r$$
$$\dot{y} = 2(e - y)$$
$$r = \frac{0.1y + \dot{q}}{q}$$

leading to the two nonlinear nonhomogeneous differential equations

$$\dot{y} = 14 - 0.4y + 0.4q$$
$$\dot{q} = 1.25qy - 0.1y - 40q$$

with equilibrium values $y^* = 35.76$ and $q^* = 0.76$ (and $r^* = 4.7$). The solution with vector forces is shown in figure 10.20.

Let us take this numerical example further and consider the linear approximation. Taking a Taylor expansion around the equilibrium, we have

$$\dot{y} = -0.4(y - y^*) + 0.4(q - q^*)$$
$$\dot{q} = 1.25q^*(y - y^*) - 0.1(y - y^*) - 40(q - q^*) + 1.25y^*(q - q^*)$$

i.e.

$$\dot{y} = -0.4(y - y^*) + 0.4(q - q^*)$$
$$\dot{q} = 0.85(y - y^*) + 4.7(q - q^*)$$

---

[10] There is a problem if the LM curve is everywhere steeper than the IS curve (see Scarth 1996).

Figure 10.21.

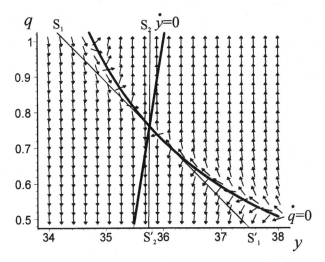

The matrix of the system is

$$\mathbf{A} = \begin{bmatrix} -0.4 & 0.4 \\ 0.85 & 4.7 \end{bmatrix}$$

with characteristic equation $\lambda^2 - 4.43\lambda - 2.22 = 0$ and characteristic roots $r = 4.7658$ and $s = -0.4658$. The fact that the characteristic roots have opposite signs verifies the saddle point equilibrium (as does the fact that $\det(\mathbf{A})$ is negative, i.e., $\det(\mathbf{A}) = -2.22$). The general solution is

$$y(t) = y^* + c_1 e^{4.7658t} + c_2 e^{-0.4658t}$$
$$q(t) = q^* + c_3 e^{4.7658t} + c_4 e^{-0.4658t}$$

The saddle paths are readily found by solving

$$(\mathbf{A} - r\mathbf{I})\mathbf{v}^r = \mathbf{0}$$

and

$$(\mathbf{A} - s\mathbf{I})\mathbf{v}^s = \mathbf{0}$$

giving the two respective eigenvectors

$$\mathbf{v}^r = \begin{bmatrix} 1 \\ 12.9145 \end{bmatrix}, \qquad \mathbf{v}^s = \begin{bmatrix} 1 \\ -0.1645 \end{bmatrix}$$

where $\mathbf{v}^s$ is the stable arm of the saddle point.

These results, using the above linearisation, are shown in figure 10.21, which includes the direction field for the linearisation.[11]

---

[11] In this example, the stable arm is almost identical with the linear approximation to $\dot{q} = 0$ at (y^*, q^*), see exercise 13.

10.8.2   *Unanticipated fiscal and monetary expansion*

We are now in a position to consider the effects of fiscal and monetary policy. In this sub-section we shall concentrate on unanticipated changes in policy, leaving anticipated changes to sub-section 10.8.3.

Fiscal expansion

Consider first a fiscal expansion, a rise in g. This has no impact on the $\dot{q} = 0$ isocline but decreases the intercept of the $\dot{y} = 0$ isocline, i.e., it shifts this isocline right (down). The situation for both the 'bad news' case and the 'good news' case is illustrated in figure 10.22 (where we assume that the $\dot{q} = 0$ isocline is less steep than the $\dot{y} = 0$ isocline). In each case the initial equilibrium is at point E_1 where $\dot{y}_1 = 0$ intersects $\dot{q} = 0$. The associated stable arm of the saddle point is $S_1 S_1'$. A rise in g shifts the IS curve down to $\dot{y}_2 = 0$. Initially income does not alter, and the system 'jumps' to the new saddle path at point A, and then over time

Figure 10.22.

(a) Bad news

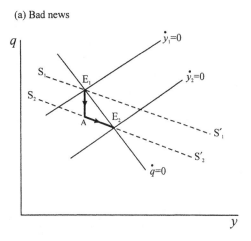

(b) Good news

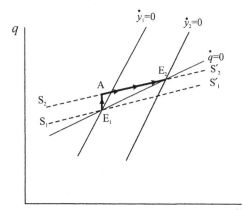

moves along S_2S_2' to the new equilibrium point E_2. Although income rises in both situations, in the 'bad news' case asset prices decline, while in the 'good news' case they rise.

Monetary expansion

Consider next monetary expansion, a rise in m_0. This has no impact on the IS curve, but shifts the $\dot{q} = 0$ isocline up, since

$$\left.\frac{dq}{dm_0}\right|_{\dot{q}=0} = \left(\frac{b_1 y}{u}\right)(ky - m_0)^2 > 0$$

The system 'jumps' from E_1 to point A on the new saddle path S_2S_2' and then moves along this until the new equilibrium point E_2 is reached, as shown in figure 10.23. In each case income rises and asset prices rise from one equilibrium point

(a) Bad news

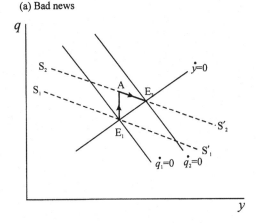

Figure 10.23.

(b) Good news

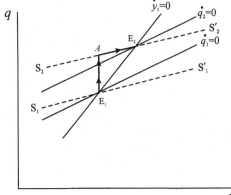

to the next but the path of asset prices is different between the 'bad news' case and the 'good news' case.[12]

Even though the fiscal and monetary changes were unanticipated, it is assumed that the moment they are implemented the economy 'jumps' from the initial equilibrium to a point on the saddle path, and then adjusts over time along the stable arm of the saddle point. But what happens if the changes are announced in advance?

10.8.3 Anticipated fiscal and monetary policy

Suppose some policy change is announced at time t_0 and to be implemented in some future time t_1. In this instance the policy change is anticipated, and some response can occur now in anticipation of what is known to occur once the policy is actually implemented. However, what occurs now is governed by the dynamics of the original equilibrium, since the new equilibrium has yet to come about.

Fiscal expansion

Consider first a fiscal expansion. We have already established that this will not shift the $\dot{q} = 0$ isocline but will shift the IS curve down. In anticipation of what will happen to stock market prices, the system will move from point E_1 to point A' (where A' falls short of point A on the saddle path), as shown in figure 10.24. In the 'bad news' case, stock market prices fall while in the 'good news' case they rise. This movement, of course, is simply anticipating the final implication of the policy change. But from the time the policy is announced until the time the policy is implemented, the economy is driven by the dynamic forces associated with the initial equilibrium point E_1. Hence, the system moves from point A' to point B' (on the saddle path S_2S_2'). The policy is now carried out, and the system moves along S_2S_2' from point B' to point E_2. The impact on income in the two cases is now different. In the 'bad news' case income falls and then rises, while in the 'good news' case it continually rises over time. On the other hand, asset prices gradually fall (if rather irregularly) in the 'bad news' case, and gradually rise (if rather irregularly) in the 'good news' case.

Monetary expansion

Finally consider the case of monetary expansion, which is announced in advance, and shown in figure 10.25. As in the previous situation, in the first instance the asset price will move part way towards its new equilibrium value, shown by point A'. It will then be governed by forces associated with the initial equilibrium point E_1, and so will move along the trajectory with points $A'B'$. Point B' is associated with the time the policy is implemented. Thereafter, the system will move along the stable arm of the saddle point, i.e., along S_2S_2', until point E_2 is reached.

---

[12] For a fuller discussion of what is taking place over the adjustment path, see Blanchard (1981).

(a) Bad news

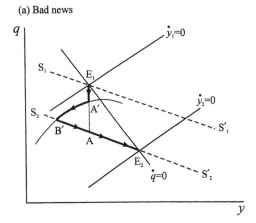

(b) Good news

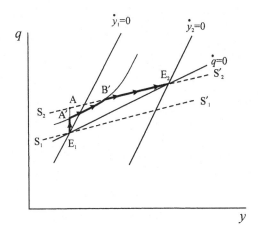

Comparing figure 10.24 with 10.22 and figure 10.25 with 10.23 shows quite a different behaviour and that it makes quite a difference to the dynamic path of the economy whether policies are announced (anticipated) or not. This is important. There has been a growing tendency on the part of policy-makers to announce in advance their policy intentions – and, at least in the UK, this applies to both monetary and fiscal policy.

10.9   Conclusion

Although the IS-LM model is considered in some detail in intermediate macroeconomics, little attention has been paid to its dynamic characteristics. In this chapter we have concentrated on discussing the dynamics of the IS-LM model – both in discrete terms and by means of continuous time variables. Such a treatment has allowed us to consider possible trajectories for income and the rate of interest. Although we have not dealt with other endogenous variables, it is quite clear

Figure 10.25.

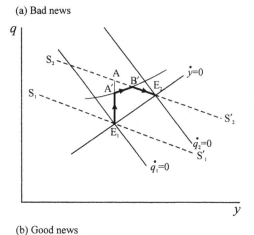

(a) Bad news

(b) Good news

that we can obtain their paths from a knowledge of $y(t)$ and $r(t)$. For instance, given $y(t)$ we can compute $tax(t) = t_0 + t_1 y(t)$, which in turn allows us to compute disposable income, $y^d(t) = y(t) - tax(t)$. This in turn allows us to compute consumption, $c(t) = a + by^d(t)$, and so on. However, this is possible only when we have explicit functional forms for all relationships in the model.

What we observe from this chapter is the importance of different adjustment speeds in the goods market relative to the money market, where the latter adjusts more quickly than the former. Although a number of trajectories exhibit a counter-clockwise movement towards equilibrium, a counter-clockwise *spiral*, although possible, is not so likely given a quick adjustment in the money market. *Overshooting, however, especially of the rate of interest, is likely to be a common occurrence, as is interest rate volatility.*

With investment related to both the rate of interest and the level of income, it is possible to have a positively sloped IS curve. If the IS curve is steeper than the LM curve then the most likely outcome is an unstable saddle path. This result not only depends on investment being significantly and positively related to income, but also on the (realistic) assumption that the money market is quicker to adjust than the goods market. Although we have considered this possibility in the confines of a simple (linear) model, it does beg the question of whether it will occur in a more complex linear model or even in a nonlinear model. We do not, however, investigate these questions in this text.

Finally, we extended the IS-LM analysis to allow for stock market behaviour employing the Tobin–Blanchard model. Once again the differential speeds of adjustment in the goods market relative to the asset market was shown to be important for dynamic trajectories. This model also highlighted the importance of unanticipated against anticipated policy changes.

Exercises

1. Consider the model

   $$C_t = 110 + 0.75Y_t$$

   $$I_t = 300$$

   $$E_t = C_t + I_t$$

   $$Y_t = E_{t-1}$$

   Plot the solution path for income and consumption for three different adjustment lags, j=1,2,3 for a permanent increase in investment of £10 million beginning in period 1.

2. Consider the numerical model in example 10.2, but assume that

   $$i_t = 320 - 4r_{t-1}$$

   Show that this leads to a second-order difference equation for income. Either solve this second-order equation for $y_0 = 2000$, $y_1 = 2010$ and $y_2 = 2010$. Hence plot the path of $y(t)$ and $r(t)$; or else set the problem up on a spreadsheet and plot $y(t)$ and $r(t)$.

3. Reconsider the model in exercise 1 and establish the dynamic multiplier for each of the three time lags in response to a rise in investment of £20 million. What can you conclude from these results?

4. Consider the model

   $$C_t = 110 + 0.75Y_t$$

   $$I_t = 4(Y_t - Y_{t-1})$$

   $$E_t = C_t + I_t$$

   $$Y_t = E_{t-1}$$

   (i) Show that this results in a second-order difference equation for income. Solve this equation.

   (ii) Suppose

   $$I_t = 4(C_t - C_{t-1})$$

   Does this lead to a different time path for income?

5. For the numerical model in example 10.2 set up a spreadsheet and derive the solution path for *all* endogenous variables resulting from a rise in

real money balances of £20 million. Compare your results with those provided in table 10.2.

6. Set up a spreadsheet to derive trajectories for the discrete model

$$y_{t+1} - y_t = \alpha[b(1-t) - 1]y_t - \alpha hr_t + \alpha a$$
$$r_{t+1} - r_t = \beta ky_t - \beta ur_t - \beta m_0$$

Derive the equilibrium income and interest rate, by setting $y_{t+1} = y_t = \ldots$ and $r_{t+1} = r_t = \ldots$ and place cells on the spreadsheet to compute such equilibria. Use the parameter values in the text to derive the three trajectories T_1 ($\alpha = 0.05$, $\beta = 0.8$), T_2 ($\alpha = 0.1$, $\beta = 0.8$) and T_3 ($\alpha = 0.5$, $\beta = 0.8$).

How would you use this specification to:
(i) show a goods market shock?
(ii) show a money market shock?

7. Show that for the same system outlined for figure 10.4 that a monetary expansion from $m_0 = 8$ to $m_1 = 12$ leads to a new equilibrium point $(y, r) = (72.2, 12.1)$. Using either *Mathematica* or *Maple*, establish three trajectories for the same combinations of α and β as in exercise 6. Or, using the discrete form of the model outlined in exercise 6, set up the model on a spreadsheet and obtain the three trajectories.

8. Use the spreadsheet model of exercise 6 to investigate the implications for the three trajectories T_1, T_2 and T_3 of
(i) a higher marginal propensity to consume
(ii) a lower marginal rate of tax
(iii) investment being more interest-sensitive (higher h)
(iv) a higher income velocity of circulation of money (lower k)
(v) a more interest-sensitive demand for money (higher u).

9. Use your model in exercise 6 and verify that if the parameter a rises from 50 to 55 the adjustment path exhibits overshooting of both y and r if $\alpha = 0.5$ and $\beta = 0.8$.

10. Use your model in exercise 6 and verify that if the parameter a falls from 50 to 45 the adjustment path exhibits overshooting of both y and r if $\alpha = 0.5$ and $\beta = 0.8$.

11. Use *Mathematica* or *Maple* to derive the trajectory $\{y(t), r(t)\}$ for examples 10.5 and 10.6 in section 10.6. Verify the statements in the text, namely
(i) Example 10.5 leads to a stable path which appears to traverse a straight line path after a certain time period.
(ii) Example 10.6 leads to an unstable spiral.

12. Reconsider example 10.6 in section 10.6. Does the same saddle path result if $\alpha = 0.1$ and $\beta = 0.8$?

13. (i) Show that the linear approximation to the $\dot{q} = 0$ isocline in the Tobin–Blanchard model is

$$q = q^* - \left[\frac{b_1 m_0 u}{(ky^* - m_0)^2}\right](y - y^*)$$

(ii)   In example 10.8 show that the equation for the linear approximation
to $\dot{q} = 0$ at (y^*, q^*) is

$q = 7.23352 - 0.181008y$

while the equation for the saddle path is

$q = 6.64988 - 0.164683y$

14.   Consider the following IS-LM model

$$e = a + b(1 - t)y - hr + jy \qquad a = 5 \qquad k = 0.5$$
$$m^d = ky - ur \qquad\qquad\qquad b = 0.75 \qquad u = 0.3$$
$$\dot{y} = \alpha(e - y)$$
$$\dot{r} = \beta(m^d - m_0) \qquad\qquad\quad t = 0.25 \qquad \alpha = 0.25$$
$$\qquad\qquad\qquad\qquad\qquad\quad h = 0.3 \qquad \beta = 0.4$$
$$\qquad\qquad\qquad\qquad\qquad\quad j = 0.4 \qquad m_0 = 10$$

(i)   Find y^* and r^*.
(ii)   What are the equations for the IS curve and the LM curve?
(iii)   Obtain the trace and determinant of the system, and hence establish
whether a stable or unstable spiral is present.

15.   Given the Tobin–Blanchard model

$e = 0.8y + 0.2q + 7$

$16 = 0.5y - 0.25r$

$\dot{y} = 2(e - y)$

$r = \dfrac{0.15y + \dot{q}}{q}$

(i)   Find y^* and q^*.
(ii)   Show that the fixed point (y^*, q^*) is a saddle point equilibrium.
(iii)   Derive the equation of the stable arm of the saddle point.

Additional reading

Additional material on the contents of this chapter can be obtained from
Blanchard (1981), McCafferty (1990), Obstfeld and Rogoff (1999), Romer (2001),
Scarth (1996), Shone (1989, 2001), Stevenson, Muscatelli and Gregory (1988),
Teigen (1978) and Tobin (1969).

CHAPTER 11

The dynamics of inflation and unemployment

11.1 The Phillips curve

At the heart of most discussions of inflation is the Phillips curve which, in its modern formulation, stipulates a relationship between price inflation, π, and unemployment, u, augmented for inflationary expectations, π^e. Thus

(11.1) $$\pi = f(u) + \xi\pi^e \quad 0 < \xi \le 1$$

This relationship is the *expectations-augmented Phillips curve*. The only slight difference from standard textbook treatments is the presence of ξ lying between zero and unity. The reason for introducing this will become clear.

Next we make a simple assumption about expected inflation, namely

(11.2) $$\dot{\pi}^e = \beta(\pi - \pi^e) \quad \beta > 0$$

This is no more than a continuous version of adaptive expectations. When the actual rate of inflation exceeds the expected rate, expectations are revised upwards and when the actual rate is below the expected rate, then expectations are revised downwards.

Suppose the government attempts to maintain unemployment at some constant level, u^*.[1] We further suppose that they are successful and so $f(u^*)$ is a constant and known. To establish the implications of such a policy, differentiate the Phillips curve relationship (11.1) with respect to time under the assumption that $u = u^*$ and substitute in equation (11.2). Then

$$\dot{\pi} = \xi\dot{\pi}^e = \xi\beta(\pi - \pi^e) = \beta(\xi\pi - \xi\pi^e)$$

But $\xi\pi^e = \pi - f(u^*)$, and so

$$\dot{\pi} = \beta[\xi\pi - \pi + f(u^*)]$$

i.e.

(11.3) $$\dot{\pi} = \beta f(u^*) - \beta(1 - \xi)\pi$$

which is linear with intercept $\beta f(u^*)$ and slope $-\beta(1 - \xi)$. Relationship (11.3) is illustrated in figure 11.1.

---

[1] u^* is often assumed to be the level of unemployment associated with full employment. This was the type of policy pursued in the UK between 1945 and 1979.

Figure 11.1.

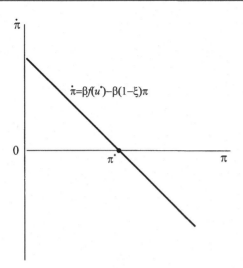

$$\dot{\pi} = \beta f(u^*) - \beta(1-\xi)\pi$$

First we need to establish whether a fixed point exists. For such a point $\dot{\pi} = 0$, i.e.

$$\beta f(u^*) - \beta(1-\xi)\pi^* = 0$$

or

$$\pi^* = \frac{f(u^*)}{1-\xi} \tag{11.4}$$

Only if $0 < \xi < 1$, however, will π^* exist. In particular, if $\xi = 1$ then π^* is un-defined. Second, if $0 < \xi < 1$, then π^* is asymptotically globally stable since the relationship between $\dot{\pi}$ and π is negatively sloped. Third, if $\xi = 1$ inflation is always correctly anticipated and $\pi = \pi^e$ and $\dot{\pi}^e = 0$. In this instance the rate of unemployment is constant regardless of the rate of inflation. This unemployment rate, following the work of Friedman and Phelps, is referred to as the *natural rate of unemployment* (or the *non-accelerating inflation rate of unemployment*, NAIRU), and denoted u_n. This rate satisfies $f(u_n) = 0$.

The situation is illustrated in the more conventional diagram, figure 11.2. How-ever, we can go further. Since $\dot{\pi} = \beta f(u)$ and $f'(u) < 0$, if $u = u^* < u_n$ then it follows that $\dot{\pi} > 0$; while if $u = u^* > u_n$, then $\dot{\pi} < 0$. This implies that if the government maintains the level of unemployment below the natural level (here we ignore $u^* > u_n$) then permanent inflation will be the result. This is because expected inflation always lags behind actual inflation and the economy is forever trying to catch up with what it observes.

It is common in a number of studies to assume a relationship between inflation, π, and real income, y, and expected inflation, π^e. In particular it is common to express this relationship in the form

$$\pi = \alpha(y - y_n) + \pi^e \quad \alpha > 0 \tag{11.5}$$

where y and y_n are in natural logarithms and y_n is the natural level of income (the income level associated with u_n), and where the relationship is referred to as 'the

Figure 11.2.

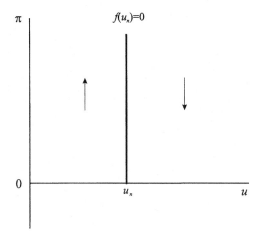

Phillips curve'. This is not the relationship between inflation and unemployment and in fact embodies *two* reaction functions.[2] It is worth spelling these out in detail because of the common occurrence of this equation.

Following the original formulation of the Phillips curve, we postulate a relationship of the form

$$\pi = -\gamma_1(u - u_n) + \pi^e \quad \gamma_1 > 0$$

This is the first reaction function indicating the response of price inflation to the unemployment gap. It implies a specific functional form for $f(u)$. The second reaction function is a formulation of *Okun's law*[3] and is given by

$$u - u_n = -\gamma_2(y - y_n) \quad \gamma_2 > 0$$

Substituting this into the previous equation we obtain

$$\pi = \gamma_1\gamma_2(y - y_n) + \pi^e$$

or

(11.6) $$\pi = \alpha(y - y_n) + \pi^e \quad \alpha > 0$$

Although both π, in terms of the unemployment gap, and π, in terms of the output gap, are both referred to as 'the Phillips curve', the second is more suspect because it involves an additional behavioural relationship, namely *Okun's law* – which is far from being a law. We shall, however, conform to common usage and refer to both as the Phillips curve.

11.2 Two simple models of inflation

Macroeconomic modelling has generally incorporated the Phillips curve within an IS-LM framework. In this section we shall consider the simplest of these models to

---

[2] See Shone (1989, chapter 3) for a more detailed discussion on this.
[3] See Shone (1989, appendix 3.2).

highlight the dynamics. Basically, the goods market and money market combine to give the aggregate demand curve (see Shone (1989, chapter 2). To see this, consider the following simple linear model, where variables (other than inflation and rates of interest) are in logarithms.

Goods market

$$c = a + b(1 - t)y$$
$$i = i_0 - h(r - \pi^e) \tag{11.7}$$
$$y = c + i + g$$

Money market

$$m_d = ky - ur$$
$$m_s = m - p \tag{11.8}$$
$$m_d = m_s$$

where

$c =$ real consumption
$y =$ real GDP
$i =$ real investment
$r =$ nominal rate of interest
$\pi^e =$ expected inflation
$g =$ real government spending
$m_d =$ real money demand
$m_s =$ real money supply
$m =$ nominal money stock
$p =$ price level

Solving for y and r we obtain

$$y^* = \frac{(a + i_0 + g) + (h/u)(m - p) + h\pi^e}{1 - b(1 - t) + (hk/u)}$$
$$r^* = \frac{ky^* - (m - p)}{u} \tag{11.9}$$

The main focus of attention is on y^*, the equilibrium level of real income. It should be noted that this is a linear equation in terms of $m - p$ and π^e, i.e.

$$y = a_0 + a_1(m - p) + a_2\pi^e \quad a_1 > 0, \ a_2 > 0 \tag{11.10}$$

and this represents the aggregate demand curve, the AD curve. Why? Because it denotes equilibrium in *both* the goods market and the money market. In other words, all points along the AD curve denote equilibrium in both the goods market and the money market.

We can express the aggregate demand curve in the usual way as a relationship between p and equilibrium y, with p on the vertical axis and y on the horizontal axis. Then

$$p = \left(\frac{a_0 + a_1 m}{a_1}\right) - \left(\frac{1}{a_1}\right)y + \left(\frac{a_2}{a_1}\right)\pi^e$$

i.e. $p = c_0 - c_1 y + c_2 \pi^e$

Figure 11.3.

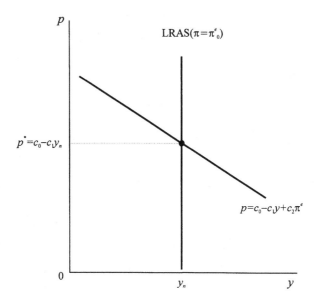

where

$$c_0 = \frac{a_0 + a_1 m}{a_1}, \qquad c_1 = \frac{1}{a_1}, \qquad c_2 = \frac{a_2}{a_1}$$

which clearly indicates an inverse relationship between the price level, p, and the level of real income, y.

It is at this point we introduce inflation, π. We assume that the rate of inflation is proportional to the output gap and adjusted for expected inflation, as outlined in the previous section, i.e.

$$\pi = \alpha(y - y_n) + \pi^e \quad \alpha > 0$$

y_n is the output level for which $\pi = \pi^e = 0$. It represents the long-run situation where prices are completely flexible. Under this condition the equilibrium price level is p^* and $y = y_n$ regardless of p and so the *long-run* aggregate supply curve is vertical at y_n. The situation is illustrated in figure 11.3.

Although figure 11.3 expresses p as a function of y, the more interesting and revealing relationship is that between y and real money balances, $m - p$, i.e., $y = a_0 + a_1(m - p) + a_2\pi^e$. Only when there is a change in real money balances (a change in $m - p$) will there be a shift in AD.

This is important. In elementary courses in economics it is quite usual to say something like 'a decrease in the money supply shifts LM left, raising r and reducing y'. But money supply has hardly *ever* decreased! What has decreased is the *growth* in the money supply. This leads to a fall in p. So long as m falls *more* than p, then real money balances will fall, i.e., $m - p < 0$. It is this which shifts the LM curve to the left.[4] In other words, only when $m - p \neq 0$ will the aggregate demand curve shift.

---

[4] See chapter 10 on the IS-LM model.

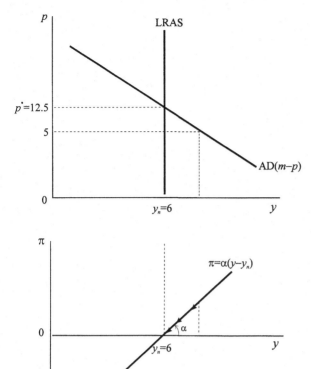

Figure 11.4.

Example 11.1

To illustrate this model, let $\pi^e = 0$ and let

$$y = 9 + 0.4(m - p) \qquad m = 5$$
$$\pi = 0.2(y - y_n) \qquad y_n = 6$$

then

$$p = 27.5 - 2.5y$$

In equilibrium $y = y_n$ hence $\pi = 0$, i.e., $y^* = 6$ and $p^* = 12.5$. The situation is illustrated in figure 11.4.

At a price level below (or above) $p^* = 12.5$, forces will come into play to move the economy towards equilibrium. To illustrate these dynamic forces, consider the following discrete version of the model. We have (noting we have the natural logarithm of prices)

$$y_{t-1} = 9 + 0.4(m_{t-1} - p_{t-1})$$
$$\pi_t = p_t - p_{t-1} = 0.2(y_{t-1} - y_n)$$

i.e.

$$\pi_t = 0.2[9 + 0.4(m_{t-1} - p_{t-1}) - 6]$$
$$= 0.6 + 0.08(m_{t-1} - p_{t-1})$$

Figure 11.5.

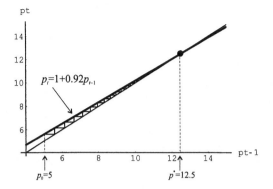

But $m_{t-1} = m_t = 5$ for all t and so

$$\pi_t = 1 - 0.08p_{t-1}$$

Since prices are in natural logarithms, then $\pi_t = p_t - p_{t-1}$, hence

$$p_t - p_{t-1} = 1 - 0.08p_{t-1}$$
$$\text{i.e.} \quad p_t = 1 + 0.92p_{t-1}$$

We can either use the original formulation of the model in a spreadsheet, or this linear relationship[5] $p_t = f(p_{t-1}) = 1 + 0.92p_{t-1}$, as shown in figure 11.5. Either way, we can first solve for the fixed point $p_t = p^*$ for all t so that

$$p^* = 1 + 0.92p^*$$
$$p^* = 12.5$$

The spreadsheet representation is illustrated in figure 11.6, which shows the system converging on equilibrium for an initial price of $p_0 = 5$. Convergence to equilibrium in the neighbourhood of $p^* = 12.5$ is assured because $|f'(p^*)| < 1$ (see n. 5).

The model just discussed has a major weakness and that is that in the long run the only acceptable level of inflation is zero, since only this is consistent with the (assumed) zero expectations value of inflation. But can a situation arise in which $\pi = \pi^e$ at some positive value and the economy is in long-run equilibrium with income at the natural level?

To answer this question, first return to our aggregate demand relation

$$y = a_0 + a_1(m - p) + a_2\pi^e$$

If we take the time derivative of this relationship[6] we obtain the *demand pressure curve*, with formula

$$\dot{y} = a_1(\dot{m} - \pi) + a_2\dot{\pi}^e$$

---

[5] Given $p_t = f(p_{t-1}) = 1 + 0.92p_{t-1}$ then $f'(p) = 0.92 < 1$, which is the requirement for stability as indicated in part I.

[6] We assume that the variables are in logarithms and so $dp/dt = d\ln P/dt = \pi$.

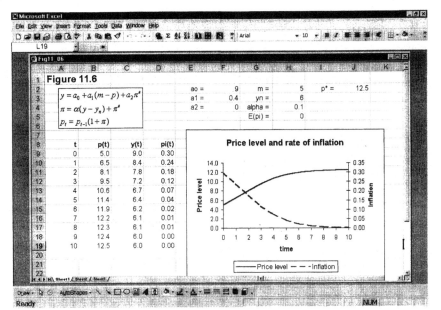

Figure 11.6.

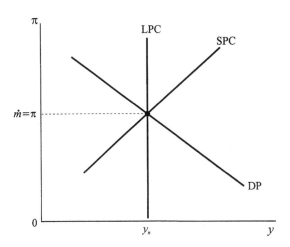

Figure 11.7.

where monetary growth, $\dot{m}$, is exogenously given. We can now combine this with the Phillips curve and a dynamic adjustment for inflationary expectations, giving the model

$$\dot{y} = a_1(\dot{m} - \pi) + a_2\dot{\pi}^e \quad a_1 > 0, \; a_2 > 0$$
$$\pi = \alpha(y - y_n) + \pi^e \quad \alpha > 0 \quad (11.11)$$
$$\dot{\pi}^e = \beta(\pi - \pi^e) \quad \beta > 0$$

The model is captured in terms of figure 11.7 in its more traditional form. The demand pressure curve intersects the short-run Phillips curve on the long-run Phillips curve. Since in this situation $\pi = \pi^e$, then it follows $y = y_n$ and $\dot{\pi}^e = 0$, which implies $\dot{m} = \pi$.

To consider the dynamics of the model, it can be reduced to two differential equations.[7] From the Phillips curve and the dynamic adjustment equations we immediately obtain

$$\dot{\pi}^e = \alpha\beta(y - y_n)$$

For the demand pressure curve we substitute the short-run Phillips curve for π and the result just obtained for $\dot{\pi}^e$ i.e.

$$
\begin{aligned}
\dot{y} &= a_1(\dot{m} - \pi) + a_2\dot{\pi}^e \\
&= a_1\dot{m} - a_1[\alpha(y - y_n) + \pi^e] + a_2\alpha\beta(y - y_n) \\
&= a_1\dot{m} - \alpha(a_1 - a_2\beta)(y - y_n) - a_1\pi^e
\end{aligned}
$$

Thus, we have the two differential equations

(11.12)

$$\dot{\pi}^e = \alpha\beta(y - y_n)$$
$$\dot{y} = a_1\dot{m} - \alpha(a_1 - a_2\beta)(y - y_n) - a_1\pi^e$$

which can be solved for y^* and π^{e*}. Notice that the model solves for the time path of *expected* inflation, but the time path of *actual* inflation is readily obtained from the short-run Phillips relationship, i.e.

$$\pi(t) = \alpha(y(t) - y_n) + \pi^e(t)$$

To solve for equilibrium, a steady state, we set $\dot{\pi}^e = 0$ and $\dot{y} = 0$. From the first condition it immediately follows that $y = y_n$. Combining this result with $\dot{\pi}^e = 0$ and $\dot{y} = 0$ immediately gives the result $\pi^{e*} = \dot{m}$. (In what follows we shall suppress the asterisk.)

First consider the $\dot{\pi}^e = 0$ isocline. In this instance it readily follows that $y = y_n$ and so the isocline is vertical at the natural level of income. If $y > y_n$ then $\dot{\pi}^e > 0$ and hence π^e is rising, and so to the right of the vertical isocline we have vector forces pushing up expected inflation. Similarly, when $y < y_n$ then $\dot{\pi}^e < 0$ and there are forces pushing down the rate of expected inflation. These forces are illustrated in figure 11.8(a). Consider next the $\dot{y} = 0$ isocline. In this case

$$a_1\dot{m} - \alpha(a_1 - a_2\beta)(y - y_n) = a_1\pi^e$$

$$\therefore \quad \pi^e = \dot{m} - \alpha\left(1 - \frac{a_2\beta}{a_1}\right)(y - y_n)$$

which is negatively sloped if $1 - (a_2\beta/a_1) > 0$, which we assume to be the case. If $\dot{y} > 0$ then

$$\pi^e < \dot{m} - \alpha\left(1 - \frac{a_2\beta}{a_1}\right)(y - y_n)$$

---

[7] This is a simpler version of a similar model discussed in McCafferty (1990, chapter 7).

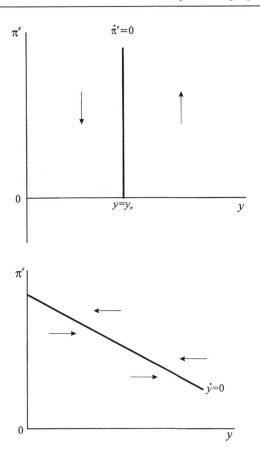

Figure 11.8.

and so to the left (below) the $\dot{y} = 0$ isocline there are forces present increasing y. Similarly, to the right (above) this isocline there are forces decreasing y. These forces are illustrated in figure 11.8(b).

Combining the two isoclines leads to four quadrants with vector forces as shown in figure 11.9. What this shows is a counter-clockwise movement of the system. Hence, starting at any point such as point A, the system will move in an anticlockwise direction either converging directly on the equilibrium point, as shown by trajectory T_1, or converging on the equilibrium point with a counter-clockwise spiral, as shown by trajectory T_2. Which of these two trajectories materialises depends on the values of the exogenous variables and parameters of the dynamic system. Of course, there is nothing in the qualitative dynamics preventing the counter-clockwise spiral *diverging* from the equilibrium. All we know from figure 11.9 is that the equilibrium is a spiral node.

We can illustrate the model with a numerical example. We shall present this model first in continuous time and then in discrete time. The discrete time version has the merit that the system's dynamics can readily be investigated on a spreadsheet.

Figure 11.9.

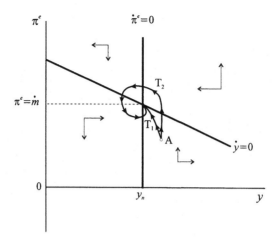

Example 11.2

Consider the numerical model

$$\dot{y} = 10(15 - \pi) + 0.5\dot{\pi}^e$$
$$\pi = 0.2(y - 15) + \pi^e$$
$$\dot{\pi}^e = 1.5(\pi - \pi^e)$$

Equilibrium income and expected inflation is readily found to be $y^* = 15$ and $\pi^{e*} = 15$, which is equal to the actual rate of inflation and to the growth of the money supply. We have already established that the $\dot{\pi}^e = 0$ isocline is vertical at the natural level of income, namely $y^* = y_n = 15$. On the other hand, the demand pressure curve $\dot{y} = 0$ is given by

$$\pi^e = \dot{m} - \alpha \left(1 - \frac{a_2 \beta}{a_1} \right)(y - y_n)$$

i.e. $\pi^e = 17.775 - 0.185y$

and it is readily verified that $\pi^{e*} = 15$ when $y^* = 15$. Furthermore, the two differential equations take the form

$$\dot{y} = 177.75 - 1.85y - 10\pi^e$$
$$\dot{\pi}^e = -4.5 + 0.3y$$

which in terms of deviations from equilibrium are

$$\dot{y} = -1.85(y - y^*) - 10(\pi^e - \pi^{e*})$$
$$\dot{\pi}^e = 0.3(y - y^*)$$

Hence, the matrix of this system is

$$A = \begin{bmatrix} -1.85 & -10 \\ 0.3 & 0 \end{bmatrix}$$

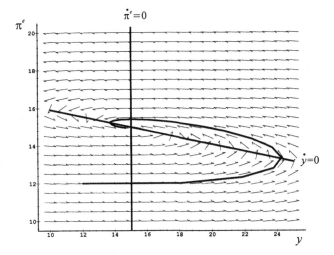

Figure 11.10.

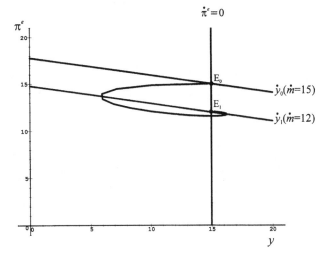

Figure 11.11.

with $\text{tr}(\mathbf{A}) = -1.85$ and $\det(\mathbf{A}) = 3$. From chapter 4, table 4.1 (p. 180), since $\text{tr}(\mathbf{A}) < 0, \det(\mathbf{A}) > 0$ and $\text{tr}(\mathbf{A})^2 < 4\det(\mathbf{A})$ then we have a spiral node. Furthermore, the characteristic roots of $\mathbf{A}$ are $r, s = -0.925 \pm 1.4644i$ and since α in the characteristic roots $r, s = \alpha \pm \beta i$ is negative, then the system is asymptotically stable. We verify this by using a software package to derive the direction field of this system along with a trajectory beginning at point $(y_0, \pi_0^e) = (12, 12)$, as shown in figure 11.10.

Consider the system in equilibrium at $\pi^* = \pi^e = 15$ and $y = y_n = 15$. Now let monetary growth decline from $\dot{m}_0 = 15$ to $\dot{m}_1 = 12$. The result is shown in figure 11.11. In line with our previous analysis, we have an anticlockwise spiral that converges on the new equilibrium point E_1.

We noted above that although the model solves for $\pi^e(t)$ we can derive $\pi(t)$ from the short-run Phillips curve. What is the difference between the path of $\pi^e(t)$ and the path of $\pi(t)$? These paths for a reduction in monetary growth just analysed

Figure 11.12.

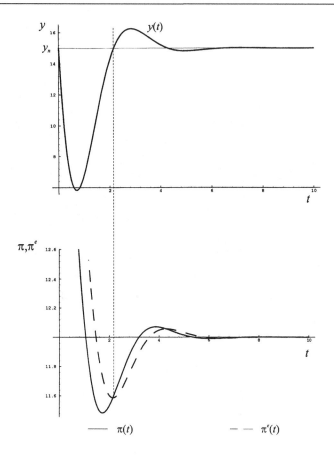

$$\quad\quad\quad\quad \text{———} \ \pi(t) \quad\quad\quad\quad\quad \text{– –} \ \pi^e(t)$$

are shown in figure 11.12, which also shows the path of $y(t)$ over part of the adjustment period. What the lower diagram illustrates is not only the cycle nature of actual and expected inflation, but that actual inflation is initially below expected inflation. This is because actual income initially falls short of the natural level and so dampens inflation. When, however, income is above the natural level then actual inflation is above expected inflation and so pushes up actual inflation.

Example 11.3

Next consider a discrete version of the model with the same parameter values. The model is

$$y_t - y_{t-1} = 10(\dot{m}_{t-1} - \pi_{t-1}) + 0.5(\pi_t^e - \pi_{t-1}^e)$$
$$\pi_t = 0.2(y_t - y_n) + \pi_t^e$$
$$\pi_t^e - \pi_{t-1}^e = 1.5(\pi_{t-1} - \pi_{t-1}^e)$$

which leads to the two difference equations

$$y_t = 177.75 - 0.85y_{t-1} - 10\pi_{t-1}^e$$
$$\pi_t^e = -4.5 + 0.3y_{t-1} + \pi_{t-1}^e$$

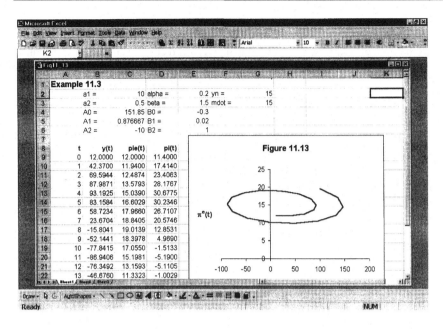

Figure 11.13.

These are readily set out on a spreadsheet as shown in figure 11.13, which includes the dynamic path of the system from a starting value of $(y_0, \pi_0^e) = (12, 12)$.

The system, however, now *diverges* from the fixed point in a counter-clockwise direction! Why is this? The matrix of the system is

$$
\mathbf{A} = \begin{bmatrix} -0.85 & -10 \\ 0.3 & 1 \end{bmatrix}
$$

with characteristic equation $\lambda^2 - 0.15\lambda + 2.15 = 0$ and complex roots, $r, s = \alpha \pm \beta i$, i.e.

$$
r = 0.075 + 1.4644i
$$
$$
s = 0.075 - 1.4644i
$$

For discrete systems, stability requires[8]

$$
\left| \sqrt{\alpha^2 + \beta^2} \right| < 1
$$

However, in this example $\left| \sqrt{\alpha^2 + \beta^2} \right| = 1.4663$ and so the system, illustrated in figure 11.13, is explosive.

This example should act as a warning. It is not possible to attribute the same properties to discrete systems as occur in continuous systems. The more complex the system the more likely the discrete system will exhibit different properties from its continuous counterpart.

---

[8] See section 3.8 and Azariadis (1993, pp. 36–8).

11.3   Deflationary 'death spirals'[9]

At the time of writing (mid-2001), Japan was in a recession and the USA began to experience a serious downturn – enough for some economists to wonder whether a major deflation worldwide was likely. In explaining such a possibility, interest has returned to the concept of the liquidity trap. Not in the sense of the early literature that considered a low positive nominal interest rate so that the demand for real money balances became infinitely elastic at this value, but because the nominal interest rate cannot be negative. These two types of liquidity trap are conceptually different. The floor of zero on the nominal interest rate leads to what Groth (1993) has called a *dynamic liquidity trap*. Here we shall present a simplified version of the model outlined in Groth (1993) and similar to the one utilised by Krugman (1999).

The model is in natural logarithms, except for all inflation rates and the nominal interest rate.

(1)	$c = a + b(1 - t)y$	$c = $ consumption
(2)	$i = i_0 - h(r - \pi^e)$	$y = $ income
(3)	$y = c + i + g$	$i = $ investment
(4)	$m_d = ky - ur$	$r = $ nominal interest rate
(5)	$m_s = m - p$	$\pi^e = $ expected inflation
(6)	$m_d = m_s$	$m_d = $ demand for real money balances
(7)	$\pi = \alpha(y - y_n) + \pi^e$	$m_s = $ supply of real money balances
(8)	$\dot{\pi}^e = \beta(\pi - \pi^e)$	$m = $ nominal money supply
		$p = $ price level
		$y_n = $ natural level of income
		$\pi = $ inflation
		$\dot{\pi}^e = d\pi^e/dt$

g, y_n and m are assumed constant, as are all autonomous expenditures (a and i_0) and all parameters (b, t, h, k, u, α and β). The first six equations are the familiar IS-LM model, equation (7) is the expectations augmented Phillips curve and equation (8) specifies adaptive expectations.

The dynamics of the model is analysed in terms of (m_s, π^e)-phase space, i.e., we need to derive two equations of the form

$$\dot{m}_s = f(m_s, \pi^e)$$
$$\dot{\pi}^e = g(m_s, \pi^e)$$

Although the algebra is a little tedious, it does allow us to investigate various numerical versions of the model. From equation (5), and noting m is constant, we have $\dot{m}_s = -\pi$ and substituting equation (7) into this we have

(11.13) $$\dot{m}_s = -[\alpha(y - y_n) + \pi^e]$$

---

[9]   I am grateful to Christian Groth, University of Copenhagen, for drawing my attention to the literature on which this section is based.

From equation (7) we immediately have $\pi - \pi^e = \alpha(y - y_n)$, which on substitution into equation (8), gives

$$\dot{\pi}^e = \alpha\beta(y - y_n) \tag{11.14}$$

In order to eliminate income, y, in each dynamic equation, we require to solve the IS-LM component of the model embedded in equations (1)–(6). Combining (1), (2) and (3) we derive the IS-curve in exactly the same way we did in chapter 10. This is

$$r = \left(\frac{a + i_0 + g}{h}\right) + \pi^e - \frac{[1 - b(1 - t)]y}{h} \tag{11.15}$$

From equations (4), (5) and (6) we obtain the LM-curve

$$r = \frac{-m_s}{u} + \frac{ky}{u} \tag{11.16}$$

Substituting equation (11.16) into equation (11.15) we derive an expression for equilibrium income

$$y^* = \frac{(a + i_0 + g) + h\pi^e + (h/u)m_s}{1 - b(1 - t) + (kh/u)} \tag{11.17}$$

Substituting equation (11.17) into equation (11.13) we obtain

$$\dot{m}_s = \left\{\frac{-\alpha(a + i_0 + g)}{1 - b(1 - t) + (kh/u)} + \alpha y_n\right\} - \frac{\alpha(h/u)m_s}{1 - b(1 - t) + (kh/u)}$$
$$- \left\{\frac{\alpha h}{1 - b(1 - t) + (kh/u)} + 1\right\}\pi^e \tag{11.18}$$

which is a linear function of m_s and π^e. Substituting equation (11.17) into equation (11.14) we obtain

$$\dot{\pi}^e = \left\{\frac{\alpha\beta(a + i_0 + g)}{1 - b(1 - t) + (kh/u)} - \alpha\beta y_n\right\} + \frac{\alpha\beta(h/u)m_s}{1 - b(1 - t) + (kh/u)}$$
$$+ \frac{\alpha\beta h\pi^e}{1 - b(1 - t) + (kh/u)} \tag{11.19}$$

which is also linear in m_s and π^e.

We shall simplify these linear equations by writing them in the form

$$\dot{m}_s = A + Bm_s + C\pi^e$$
$$\dot{\pi}^e = D + Em_s + F\pi^e$$

Using these equations we can define the (m_s, π^e)-phase plane with isoclines $\dot{m}_s = 0$ and $\dot{\pi}^e = 0$. We shall now pursue this model by means of a numerical example.

Example 11.4

Consider the model

$$c = 60 + 0.75(1 - 0.2)y \qquad a = 60$$
$$i = 430 - 4(r - \pi^e) \qquad b = 0.75 \quad t = 0.2$$
$$y = c + i + g \qquad i_0 = 430 \quad h = 4$$
$$m_d = 0.25y - 10r \qquad g = 330$$
$$m_s = 450 - p \qquad k = 0.25 \quad u = 10$$
$$m_d = m_s \qquad m = 450 \quad p = 0$$
$$\pi = 0.1(y - 2000) + \pi^e \qquad y_n = 2000$$
$$\dot{\pi}^e = 0.08(\pi - \pi^e) \qquad \alpha = 0.1$$
$$\qquad \beta = 0.08$$

Then

$$\dot{m}_s = 36 - 0.08m_s - 1.8\pi^e$$
$$\dot{\pi}^e = -2.88 + 0.0064m_s + 0.064\pi^e$$

Setting $\dot{m}_s = 0$ and $\dot{\pi}^e = 0$ we derive the two isoclines

(11.20)
$$\dot{m}_s = 0 \qquad \pi^e = 20 - 0.0444m_s$$
$$\dot{\pi}^e = 0 \qquad \pi^e = 45 - 0.1m_s$$

with fixed point $(m_s^*, \pi^{e*}) = (450, 0)$. The two isoclines identify four quadrants, as shown in figure 11.14.

To derive the vector forces in each quadrant, we note that

$$\dot{m}_s > 0 \text{ implies } \pi^e < 20 - 0.0444m_s$$

therefore below $\dot{m}_s = 0$ and m_s is rising while above it it is falling. Similarly,

$$\dot{\pi}^e > 0 \text{ implies } \pi^e > 45 - 0.1m_s$$

therefore above $\dot{\pi}^e = 0$ and π^e is rising while below it it is falling. The vector forces, therefore, indicate a counter-clockwise movement around the fixed point.

To consider (local) stability, consider the linear system in terms of deviations from equilibrium, then

$$\dot{m}_s = -0.08(m_s - m_s^*) - 1.8(\pi^e - \pi^{e*})$$
$$\dot{\pi}^e = 0.0064(m_s - m_s^*) + 0.064(\pi^e - \pi^{e*})$$

Figure 11.14.

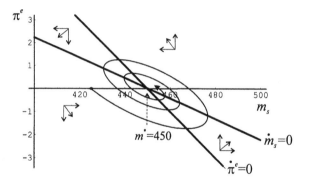

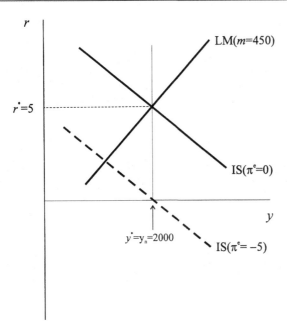

whose matrix is

$$\mathbf{A} = \begin{bmatrix} -0.08 & -1.8 \\ 0.0064 & 0.064 \end{bmatrix}$$

with

$$\text{tr}(\mathbf{A}) = -0.016$$
$$\det(\mathbf{A}) = 0.0064$$

which indicates local stability.[10] In fact, as Groth (1993) indicates, stability is guaranteed if $\beta u / m_s^* < 1$, and in the present example $\beta u / m_s^* = 0.00178$ and so stability is assured.

Before continuing with this example, it is useful to display the results in the more familiar IS-LM model. The equations for the IS-curve and the LM-curve are

$$\text{IS}: \quad r = 205 - 0.1y$$
$$\text{LM}: \quad r = -45 + 0.025y$$

which intersect at the point $(y^*, r^*) = (2000, 5)$ with $\pi = \pi^e = 0$, as shown in figure 11.15.

So far, however, we have not taken account of the nominal interest rate floor of zero. If the equilibrium interest rate is $r = 0$, then $m_d = k y_n = 500$, which is equal to the money supply, m_s. But if $r = 0$, then π^e must be equal to minus the real rate of interest, where $rreal = r - \pi^e$. Therefore in our numerical example it follows that $\pi^e = -5$. This is illustrated by the dotted line in figure 11.15, which passes through point $y = y_n = 2000$ for $r = 0$.

---

[10] The eigenvectors are $-0.008 \pm 0.0796i$ and since the real part is negative, the system is asymptotically stable. See chapter 4.

The resulting kink in the money demand curve at $r = 0$ results in a kink in *both* isoclines $\dot{m}_s = 0$ and $\dot{\pi}^e = 0$. To establish exactly where these kinks occur we note that the equilibrium interest rate for the general model is

$$r^* = \frac{(k/u)(a + i_0 + g)}{1 - b(1 - t) + (kh/u)} + \left\{ \frac{(h/u)(k/u)}{1 - b(1 - t) + (kh/u)} - \frac{1}{u} \right\} m_s$$

(11.21)

$$+ \frac{(kh/u)\pi^e}{1 - b(1 - t) + (kh/u)}$$

i.e.

$$r^* = G + H m_s + J \pi^e$$

For our numerical example, this expression is

$$r^* = 41 - 0.08 m_s + 0.2\pi^e$$

and so the relationship between π^e and m_s when $r^* = 0$ is given by

(11.22)

$$\pi^e = -205 + 0.4 m_s$$

Equating equation (11.22) with each equation in (11.20) gives the kinks at the following values

$$\dot{m}_s = 0 \qquad (m_s, \pi^e) = (506.3, -2.48)$$
$$\dot{\pi}^e = 0 \qquad (m_s, \pi^e) = (500, -5)$$

At these values the isoclines become horizontal, as illustrated in figure 11.16. Note in particular, that $\dot{\pi}^e$ is equal to the real rate of interest that we established above, namely -5.

Now return to equation (11.14) where $\dot{\pi}^e = \alpha\beta(y - y_n)$. It immediately follows that

$$\dot{\pi}^e = 0 \quad \text{implies} \quad y = y_n$$
$$\dot{\pi}^e > 0 \quad \text{implies} \quad y > y_n$$
$$\dot{\pi}^e < 0 \quad \text{implies} \quad y < y_n$$

Figure 11.16.

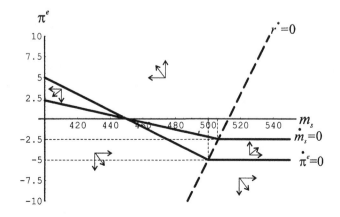

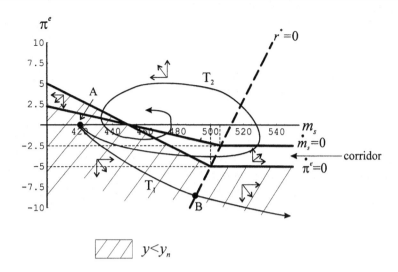

Figure 11.17.

But we established earlier that for $\dot{\pi}^e < 0$ the economy is below the $\dot{\pi}^e = 0$ iso-cline. So the recessionary region is shown by the area below this isocline, as illustrated in figure 11.17, and identified by the shaded area.

Consider a situation where the economy is in recession, and at point A in figure 11.17, where $y < y_n$ and there is excess capacity. Suppose the line marked T_1 shows the trajectory of the economy. But at point B, the economy hits the nominal interest rate floor, and thereafter moves in the southeast direction and always away from the fixed point. It cannot get out of the dynamic liquidity trap. The output gap feeds expectations of deflation, and since the nominal interest rate cannot fall any further below zero, this implies a rise in the real interest rate. This in turn worsens the output gap. The economy falls into a deflationary spiral that it cannot escape. More significantly, raising the money supply to expand the economy will not alleviate the situation.

Now consider an independent Central Bank's solution to the economy's problem at point A. Given the economy is in recession, it could expand the money supply. At point A the nominal rate of interest is positive. If it expands the money supply immediately, we may suppose the economy moves along trajectory T_2. It passes into the corridor (what Krugman calls the 'window of opportunity') and can manoeuvre the economy to equilibrium. On the other hand, if it misses the corridor and follows trajectory T_1, then deflation passes the point of no return. What Krugman argues is that if the Central Bank increases monetary growth rapidly then trajectory T_1 is more likely.

It is interesting in this regard to comment on the behaviour of the European Central Bank (ECB) in April–May 2001. The USA was concerned about a recession and the Fed (Federal Reserve) lowered interest rates in a set of steps. The independent Bank of England also lowered UK interest rates. However, the ECB kept interest rates constant, i.e., refused to expand the money supply. Europe at the time was in a situation of below full capacity ($y < y_n$), with high levels of unemployment, especially in Germany. If, then, the economy (Europe in this instance) follows path T_1 by the time the ECB decides to act, it may be too late. As Krugman (1999) says,

> conservative monetary policy may seem prudent and responsible to the European Central Bank today, just as it did to the Bank of Japan not long ago, but in retrospect that supposed prudence may look like disastrous folly.

11.4   A Lucas model with rational expectations

In line with earlier sections, our aim in this one is to introduce a simple macroeconomic model to illustrate how rational expectations are employed in macroeconomic modelling. From the outset we need to be absolutely clear about variables for which expectations are formed. In particular, we need to specify the date the expectation was formed, and second the future time period about which the expectation is being formed. To be more precise, suppose we have a variable X about which expectations are being formed. If the expectation is made at time t, then we write E_t to denote an expectation being formed at time t. But it is possible to formulate an expectation about X one period ahead, i.e., $E_t X_{t+1}$, or two periods ahead, $E_t X_{t+2}$, etc. In fact, we can formulate an expectation for any future time period. By the same reasoning, an expectation about X_{t+1} may have been made two periods ago, i.e., $E_{t-1} X_{t+1}$ is an expectation made at time $t-1$ about variable X at time $t+1$. So far we are simply specifying a notation to express expectations. No statement has been made about how such expectations are *formed*. Thus, if π denotes inflation, then $E_t \pi_{t+1}$ denotes expected inflation[11] next period having been made in period t. Since prices p_t are usually expressed in natural logarithms, as we shall be doing in this section, then

$$E_t \pi_{t+1} = E_t p_{t+1} - p_t$$

The model we shall investigate is

(11.23)

$$
\begin{aligned}
y_t^d &= a_0 + a_1(m_t - p_t) + \varepsilon_t & a_0 > 0,\ a_1 > 0 \\
y_t^s &= y_n + b_1(p_t - E_{t-1}p_t) + v_t & b_1 > 0 \\
y_t^d &= y_t^s = y_t \\
\varepsilon &\sim N\big(0, \sigma_\varepsilon^2\big), & v \sim N\big(0, \sigma_v^2\big)
\end{aligned}
$$

This model has a variety of new features that are worth commenting on. First, aggregate demand is the same as our earlier section but has a random component added to it. Second, the Phillips curve is in the Lucas form, i.e., the natural level of income is adjusted by deviations of prices from expected prices. Third, the aggregate supply also involves random shocks. Fourth, the random components are normally distributed with zero mean and constant variance. For those readers less familiar with stochastic equations, the random terms simply act like shocks to the AD and AS curves. On average, since their means are zero, the likely expected curve is the respective deterministic component.

---

[11]   Although it is common to write π_{t+1}^e, this does not make it explicit when the expectation was formed. It is implicitly assumed to be at time t.

First we solve the model under the assumption that expectations are given. Thus, we can express the equations in matrix form as follows

$$\begin{bmatrix} 1 & a_1 \\ 1 & -b_1 \end{bmatrix} \begin{bmatrix} y_t \\ p_t \end{bmatrix} = \begin{bmatrix} a_0 + a_1 m + \varepsilon_t \\ y_n - b_1 E_{t-1} p_t + v_t \end{bmatrix}$$

Using Cramer's rule we can solve for y_t and p_t

$$y_t = \frac{a_0 b_1 + a_2 y_n}{a_1 + b_1} + \frac{a_1 b_1 m_t}{a_1 + b_1} - \frac{a_1 b_1 E_{t-1} p_t}{a_1 + b_1} + \frac{b_1 \varepsilon_t + a_1 v_t}{a_1 + b_1}$$

$$p_t = \frac{a_0 - y_n}{a_1 + b_1} + \frac{a_1 m_t}{a_1 + b_1} + \frac{b_1 E_{t-1} p_t}{a_1 + b_1} + \frac{\varepsilon_t - v_t}{a_1 + b_1}$$

(11.24)

These are the reduced form equations under the assumption that expected prices are exogenous. The next step in the rational expectations procedure is to take the expected value at time $t-1$ for the variable p_t. In other words, the expectation of the variable p is derived in the same manner that determines the variable p itself. Thus

$$E_{t-1} p_t = \frac{a_0 - y_n}{a_1 + b_1} + \frac{a_1 E_{t-1} m_t}{a_1 + b_1} + \frac{b_1 E_{t-1} p_t}{a_1 + b_1} + \frac{E_{t-1} \varepsilon_t - E_{t-1} v_t}{a_1 + b_1}$$

But $E_{t-1} \varepsilon_t = E_{t-1} v_t = 0$, hence

$$E_{t-1} p_t = \frac{a_0 - y_n}{a_1 + b_1} + \frac{a_1 E_{t-1} m_t}{a_1 + b_1} + \frac{b_1 E_{t-1} p_t}{a_1 + b_1}$$

$$\therefore \quad E_{t-1} p_t = \frac{a_0 - y_n}{a_1} + E_{t-1} m_t$$

which is the rational expectations solution for $E_{t-1} p_t$. Now having solved for $E_{t-1} p_t$ we can substitute this into the reduced form equations. Doing so, and simplifying, we obtain the solutions for y_t and p_t as follows

$$y_t = y_n + \frac{a_1 b_1 (m_t - E_{t-1} m_t)}{a_1 + b_1} + \frac{b_1 \varepsilon_t + a_1 v_t}{a_1 + b_1}$$

$$p_t = \frac{a_0 - y_n}{a_1} + \frac{a_1 m_t - b_1 E_{t-1} m_t}{a_1 + b_1} + \frac{\varepsilon_t - v_t}{a_1 + b_1}$$

(11.25)

To see that this model is consistent with our earlier results, consider the following two cases:

(i)   constant money *supply* and correct expectations
(ii)   constant monetary *growth* and correct expectations.

To analyse these two cases we first need to obtain the rate of inflation $\pi_t = p_t - p_{t-1}$

$$p_t = \frac{a_0 - y_n}{a_1} + \frac{a_1 m_t - b_1 E_{t-1} m_t}{a_1 + b_1} + \frac{\varepsilon_t - v_t}{a_1 + b_1}$$

$$p_{t-1} = \frac{a_0 - y_n}{a_1} + \frac{a_1 m_{t-1} - b_1 E_{t-2} m_{t-1}}{a_1 + b_1} + \frac{\varepsilon_{t-1} - v_{t-1}}{a_1 + b_1}$$

But $\pi_t = p_t - p_{t-1}$, hence

$$\pi_t = \frac{a_1(m_t - m_{t-1})}{a_1 + b_1} + \frac{b_1(E_{t-1}m_t - E_{t-2}m_{t-1})}{a_1 + b_1}$$
$$+ \frac{(\varepsilon_t - \varepsilon_{t-1}) - (v_t - v_{t-1})}{a_1 + b_1}$$

Under the condition that $m_t = m_{t-1}$ and $E_{t-1}m_t = E_{t-2}m_{t-1}$, then

(11.26)
$$\pi_t = \frac{(\varepsilon_t - \varepsilon_{t-1}) - (v_t - v_{t-1})}{a_1 + b_1}$$

with no random shocks ($\varepsilon_t = \varepsilon_{t-1} = 0$ and $v_t = v_{t-1} = 0$) then $\pi_t = 0$, which was the first model we analysed in section 11.2.

Under the condition of constant monetary growth, λ, which is expected, then

$$m_t - m_{t-1} = \lambda$$

$$E_{t-1}m_t - E_{t-2}m_{t-1} = \lambda$$

so that

$$\pi_t = \frac{a_1\lambda}{a_1 + b_1} + \frac{b_1\lambda}{a_1 + b_1} + \frac{(\varepsilon_t - \varepsilon_{t-1}) - (v_t - v_{t-1})}{a_1 + b_1}$$

(11.27)
$$\text{i.e.} \quad \pi_t = \lambda + \frac{(\varepsilon_t - \varepsilon_{t-1}) - (v_t - v_{t-1})}{a_1 + b_1}$$

with no random shocks inflation is equal to monetary growth, λ, the result next analysed in section 11.2.

It is worth summarising a number of features of this model.

(1)   Since

$$y_t = y_n + \frac{a_1 b_1(m_t - E_{t-1}m_t)}{a_1 + b_1} + \frac{b_1\varepsilon_t + a_1 v_t}{a_1 + b_1}$$

then the correct *forecast* on the part of market participants means that income can still deviate from the natural level *in the short run*, but only due to random factors either on the demand side or on the supply side.

(2)   The deviation of y_t from y_n depends not only on the level of the random elements, but also on:
   (a) The parameters of the economic system (both AD and AS).
   (b) The correctness of forecasting government monetary policy. Assuming no shocks ($\varepsilon_t = v_t = 0$) then income can still be above/below the natural level if forecasters underestimate/overestimate the money supply.

(3)   A positive monetary surprise (i.e. $m_t > E_{t-1}m_t$) means a rise in y_t, p_t and π_t.

(4)   Although p_t includes forecast errors these are random in nature and so there are no *systematic* forecast errors. To see this, note

$$p_t - E_{t-1}p_t = \frac{a_1(m_t - E_{t-1}m_t)}{a_1 + b_1} + \frac{\varepsilon_t - v_t}{a_1 + b_1}$$

If the money stock is constant (i.e. $m_t = E_{t-1}m_t$), or if the money stock is forecasted correctly ($E_{t-1}m_t = m_t$), or if the money stock itself is subject to random shocks (which then means $m_t - E_{t-1}m_t$ is a random variable), then $p_t - E_{t-1}p_t$ is purely a random variable. Thus, the (mathematical conditional) expectation is

$$E(p_t - E_{t-1}p_t) = \frac{E(\varepsilon_t) - E(v_t)}{a_1 + b_1} = 0$$

(5) It can be shown (see exercise 5) that any systematic component of a money supply rule has no bearing on the solution value of output, i.e., systematic elements of policy which are known have no impact on real output.

(6) A systematic component of a money supply rule *can* have a bearing on the solution of p_t, and hence on π_t (see exercise 6).

(7) The procedure here adopted for deriving the rational expectations is possible only if the reduced form equations can be derived. Where this cannot be done, then other procedures are necessary. (See Holden, Peel and Thompson 1985; Leslie 1993).

(8) Most attention has been on the result derived in (1) indicating policy impotence with regard to influencing the level of real income. So long as the money supply is correctly forecasted (i.e. there are no monetary surprises), then income can deviate from the natural level only as a result of random shocks to either aggregate demand or aggregate supply.

11.5 Policy rules

In the previous section we pointed out the possibility of policy impotence. Let us make this more precise. Consider some policy rule for the money supply. A variety has been considered – some active and some passive. An *active policy rule* is one in which the policy in period t depends on the performance of the economy in the previous periods. A *passive policy rule* is completely independent of recent economic performance. For our present analysis we shall consider policy rules based only on variables in the previous period. This in no way invalidates the conclusions.

Let x denote the policy instrument used for monetary control[12] and let $\mathbf{q}$ denote a vector of economy variables. Then an active policy rule takes the form

$$m_t = f(x_{t-1}, \mathbf{q}_{t-1}) \tag{11.28}$$

where $f(x, \mathbf{q})$ is nonstochastic and can be linear or nonlinear. A passive policy rule, on the other hand, can take the form

$$m_t = g(x_{t-1}) \tag{11.29}$$

where $g(x)$ is nonstochastic which can be linear or nonlinear.

Return now to the result in the previous section for income, given in equation (11.25)

$$y_t = y_n + \frac{a_1 b_1 (m_t - E_{t-1}m_t)}{a_1 + b_1} + \frac{b_1 \varepsilon_t + a_1 v_t}{a_1 + b_1}$$

---

[12] A typical choice for x is either the money base or the rate of interest.

This result suggests that income will deviate from its natural level for two basic reasons:

(1)   deviation of m_t from $E_{t-1}m_t$
(2)   random occurrences to either aggregate demand or aggregate supply.

Here our concentration is on the first. Given either of the two rules above, so long as they are nonstochastic then

(11.30)

$$E_{t-1}m_t = E_{t-1}f(x_{t-1}, \mathbf{q}) = f(x_{t-1}, \mathbf{q})$$
$$E_{t-1}m_t = E_{t-1}g(x_{t-1}) = g(x_{t-1})$$

which implies that deviations $m_t - E_{t-1}m_t = 0$ for both the active and the passive policy rule. It does not matter therefore whether the rule is active or passive nor whether it is simple or complex, the result is still the same. Deviations will be nonnegative only when forecasters get the government's policy rule wrong. This would especially be true when the government 'changed' the rule without announcing it. Under rational expectations theory, however, market participants would soon come to know the rule as they attempted to minimise their errors.

If the policy rule involved a random component, w_t, which we again assume is normally distributed with zero mean and constant variance, then the two rules can take the form

$$m_t = f(x_{t-1}, \mathbf{q}) + w_t$$
$$m_t = g(x_{t-1}) + w_t$$

where $w_t \sim N(0, \sigma_w^2)$. Taking expectations at time $t - 1$, i.e., E_{t-1}, we immediately arrive at the nonstochastic component since $E_{t-1}w_t = 0$. Hence

$$m_t - E_{t-1}m_t = w_t$$

in both cases. The result on income is the same, namely

$$y_t = y_n + \frac{a_1 b_1 w_t + b_1 \varepsilon_t + a_1 v_t}{a_1 + b_1}$$

The only reason why income deviates from its natural level is because of random shocks, including random elements to the policy rule.

Before leaving this topic a warning is in order. The impotence of policy may appear to be solely because of the assumption of rational expectations. But this is not true. It also depends on the model chosen to illustrate the problem. In particular the result crucially depends on the assumption of completely flexible prices and a vertical long-run Phillips curve. (See Attfield, Demery and Duck 1985, chapter 4).

11.6   Money, growth and inflation

In this section we turn to yet another model where inflation takes place in a growing economy. In such models it is common to establish that along the equilibrium growth path, the expected rate of inflation equals the rate of monetary expansion minus the warranted rate of growth.[13] Furthermore, in models involving rational expectations (which amount to perfect foresight models) then expected inflation equals actual inflation.

The model we use is that given by Burmeister and Dobell (1970, chapter 6) and taken up by George and Oxley (1991). In this model agents have perfect foresight and all markets are assumed to clear continuously.[14] The model assumes a fixed money growth rule of the type advocated frequently by Milton Friedman.

The goods market is captured by the following set of equations

$$Y = F(K, L)$$
$$y = f(k)$$
$$C = cY$$
$$Y = cY + \dot{K} + \delta K$$

(11.31)

where

Y = output

K = capital stock

L = labour

$y = Y/L$

$k = K/L$

C = consumption

c = marginal propensity to consume

$\dot{K} = dK/dt$ = net investment

δ = depreciation

The final equation in (11.31) is no more than income equals consumption plus investment, and is the condition for equilibrium in the goods market. This condition is assumed to hold continuously. In line with our discussion of the Solow growth model in section 2.7, we can derive the following differential equation

$$\dot{k} = sf(k) - (n + \delta)k$$

(11.32)

where

$s = 1 - c$

$n = \dot{L}/L$ (the rate of growth of the labour force)

Turning now to the money market we assume a constant monetary growth rule

$$\frac{\dot{M}}{M} = \lambda \quad \text{or} \quad \dot{M} = \lambda M$$

(11.33)

The real demand for money *per capita*, $m = M/L$, is given by

$$m = \frac{M}{L} = PG(y, r)$$

(11.34)

---

[13] For an analysis of the production function and the resulting differential equation, see section 2.7.
[14] As we have pointed out elsewhere, these are two quite separate assumptions.

where

$$m = per\ capita\ \text{nominal money balances}$$
$$P = \text{price level}$$
$$r = \text{nominal interest rate}$$
$$G_y = \partial G/\partial y > 0$$
$$G_r = \partial G/\partial r < 0$$

The model is more easily analysed in terms of *per capita* real money balances, namely $x = m/P$, where

(11.35)
$$x = \frac{m}{P} = G(y, r)$$

Equation (11.35) is assumed to hold continuously because the money market is assumed to be always in equilibrium. From equation (11.35) we assume we can derive the implicit function

$$r = H(y, x)$$

In this model there are only two assets: money and physical capital. The real rate of interest is the nominal rate, r, minus the rate of inflation, π (where $\pi^e = \pi$). In equilibrium this will be equated with the marginal product of capital, $f'(k)$, adjusted for the rate of depreciation, δ, i.e.

(11.36)
$$r - \pi = f'(k) - \delta$$
$$\text{or}\quad r = f'(k) - \delta + \pi$$

We now require to obtain a differential equation for x. Since $x = m/P$ then $\dot{x}$ is

$$\dot{x} = \frac{\dot{m}}{P} - \left(\frac{\dot{P}}{P}\right)x \quad \text{or} \quad \dot{x} = \frac{\dot{m}}{P} - \pi x$$
$$\text{i.e.}\quad \dot{x} = \frac{\dot{m}}{P} + (f'(k) - r - \delta)x$$

But

$$\dot{m} = \frac{\dot{M}}{L} - \left(\frac{M}{L}\right)\frac{\dot{L}}{L}$$
$$= (\lambda - n)\frac{M}{L} = (\lambda - n)m = (\lambda - n)Px$$

and so

$$\dot{x} = \frac{(\lambda - n)Px}{P} + (f'(k) - r - \delta)x$$
$$= (f'(k) + \lambda - \delta - n - r)x$$

i.e.

(11.37)
$$\dot{x} = (f'(k) + \lambda - \delta - n - H(f(k), x))x$$

We can establish the first isocline quite easily. In equilibrium $k = k^*$ and $x = x^*$ with the result that $\dot{k} = 0$ and $\dot{x} = 0$. Consider $\dot{k} = 0$, then

$$sf(k^*) = (n + \delta)k^*$$

and for positive k this is unique, as illustrated in figure 11.18.

It is also independent of x. Hence, in (x, k)-space this gives rise to a vertical isocline at k^*, as shown in figure 11.19. For $k < k^*$ then k is rising while for $k > k^*$, k is falling, leading to the vector forces shown in Figure 11.19.

The isocline $\dot{x} = 0$ is less straightforward, and in general is nonlinear. We shall pursue this isocline by means of a numerical example, using the figures in George and Oxley (1991, p. 218).

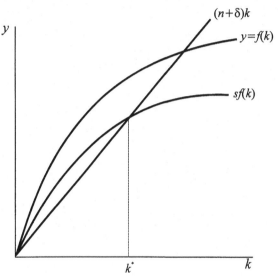

Figure 11.18.

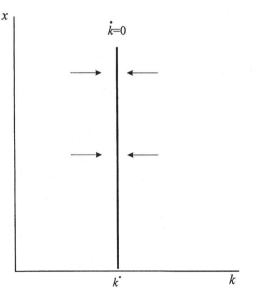

Figure 11.19.

Example 11.5

Let

$$y = 2k^{0.25}$$
$$\ln x = \ln y - 0.25 \ln r$$
$$s = 0.2, \quad \delta = 0.03, \quad \lambda = 0.05, \quad n = 0.02$$

Then

$$\dot{k} = 0.4k^{0.25} - 0.05k$$

If $\dot{k} = 0$ then

$$k(0.4k^{-0.75} - 0.05) = 0$$

i.e. $k^* = 0$ or $k^* = 16$.

Before considering $\dot{x} = 0$, we note that

$$x = yr^{-0.25}$$
$$\therefore \quad r = y^4 x^{-4} = (2k^{0.25})^4 x^{-4} = 16kx^{-4}$$
$$\text{and } f'(k) = 0.5k^{-0.75}$$

Hence

$$\dot{x} = (0.5k^{-0.75} - 16kx^{-4})x$$

If $\dot{x} = 0$ then

$$(0.5k^{-1.75} - 16x^{-4})kx = 0$$

So $\dot{x} = 0$ if

$$x = 0 \quad \text{or} \quad (0.5k^{-1.75} - 16x^{-4}) = 0$$

The second term leads to the isocline

$$x = 2.3784k^{0.4375}$$

which is nonlinear, and is shown in figure 11.20.

Figure 11.20.

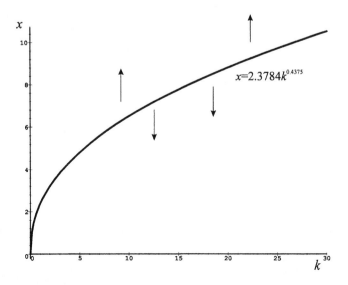

$x = 2.3784k^{0.4375}$

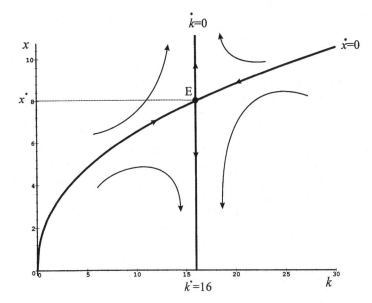

Figure 11.21.

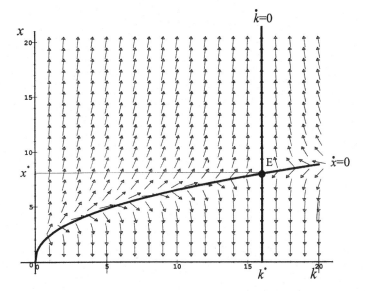

Figure 11.22.

Since $\dot{x} > 0$ when $x > 2.3784\,k^{0.4375}$ then above the isocline vector forces are pushing x up; while below the isocline they are pushing x down. These forces are also illustrated in figure 11.20.

The system's dynamics are shown in figure 11.21. The two isoclines intersect at the equilibrium point E, where $(k^*, x^*) = (16, 8)$. What figure 11.21 shows is not only a nonlinear isocline, but that the equilibrium is a saddle-point solution whose stable arm is given by the equation satisfying $\dot{x} = 0$. The full dynamics of the system are shown in figure 11.22, which uses *Maple*'s **phaseportrait** command to plot the vector forces and the $\dot{x} = 0$ isocline, and which has then been annotated to complete the figure.

11.7   Cagan model of hyperinflation

11.7.1   Original model

Cagan argued that during periods of hyperinflation the main determinant of the demand to hold money balances was the expected rate of inflation – the higher the rate of expected inflation the lower the demand to hold real money balances. Income and interest rates could be thought of as constant during periods of hyperinflation relative to the impact of expected inflation. The Cagan (1956) model consists of two equations, a demand for money equation (where nominal demand is equated with nominal supply) and an equation for adaptive expectations

(11.38)
$$m(t) - p(t) = -\alpha \pi^e(t) \qquad \alpha > 0$$
$$\dot{\pi}^e(t) = \gamma[\pi(t) - \pi^e(t)] \quad \gamma > 0$$

where

$$m = \ln M = \text{logarithm of nominal money stock}$$
$$p = \ln P = \text{logarithm of prices}$$
$$\pi^e = \text{expected inflation}$$
$$\pi = \text{inflation}$$

Also note that since $p(t)$ is a logarithm then $\dot{p}(t) = \pi(t)$. In order to appreciate the dynamics of this model, differentiate the first equation in (11.38) with respect to time, holding the money stock constant at some level, then

$$-\dot{p}(t) = -\alpha \dot{\pi}^e(t)$$
$$= -\alpha \gamma[\pi(t) - \pi^e(t)]$$

But $\dot{p}(t) = \pi(t)$ so

$$-\pi(t) = -\alpha \gamma[\pi(t) - \pi^e(t)]$$
$$\text{i.e.} \quad \pi(t) = \frac{-\alpha \gamma \pi^e(t)}{1 - \alpha \gamma} = \frac{\gamma[m(t) - p(t)]}{1 - \alpha \gamma}$$

or

(11.39)
$$\dot{p}(t) = \frac{\gamma[m(t) - p(t)]}{1 - \alpha \gamma}$$

which is a first-order differential equation.

The fixed point of equation (11.39) satisfies $\dot{p}(t) = 0$, which means $p(t) = m(t)$. Differentiating this result with respect to time t gives the typical monetarist result $\dot{p}(t) = \pi(t) = m(t)$, i.e., inflation is equal to the growth of the money supply. The

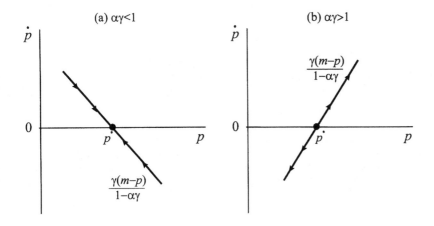

Figure 11.23.

fixed point is stable only if the coefficient of $p(t)$ is negative, which requires

$$1 - \alpha\gamma > 0 \quad \text{or} \quad \alpha\gamma < 1$$

The situation is shown in figure 11.23(a).

Cagan's stability condition emphasises that with a highly sensitive demand for money function (α high), then stability requires inflationary expectations to adapt slowly to past inflation rates ($\gamma = 1/\alpha$ small). If this is not the case, then the system is unstable, as shown in figure 11.23(b), and the economy will exhibit either accelerating inflation or accelerating deflation depending on the initial price level.

Now consider the Cagan model with rational expectations as represented by perfect foresight. Then

$$m(t) - p(t) = -\alpha\pi^e(t) \quad \alpha > 0$$
$$\dot{\pi}^e(t) = \pi(t)$$

(11.40)

Hence

$$m(t) - p(t) = -\alpha\pi(t) = -\alpha\dot{p}(t)$$

i.e.

$$\dot{p}(t) = -\frac{1}{\alpha}[m(t) - p(t)]$$

(11.41)

Since the coefficient of $p(t)$ is $1/\alpha > 0$, then this system is globally unstable. The dynamics is captured in terms of figure 11.24. Assume the system is in equilibrium with $p_0 = p^*$ with money supply m_0. Now suppose there is a rise in the money supply from m_0 to m_1. To restore equilibrium in the money market the demand for real money balances must also increase. In the present model this can occur only if expected inflation (equal to actual inflation) falls. But as the inflation rate falls the price level starts to fall ($\pi < 0$). With the money stock now fixed at m_1, real money balances rise. To re-establish equilibrium in the money market means that

Figure 11.24.

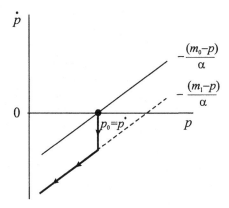

the demand for real money balances must fall, which means $\pi^e = \pi$ also falls. The result is a continuing fall in the price level.

11.7.2   Cagan model with sluggish wages[15]

This version of the model consists of the following equations, where we have suppressed the time variable

(11.42)

$$m - p = ky - \alpha\pi^e \quad \alpha > 0$$
$$y = c + (1 - \theta)n \quad 0 < \theta < 1$$
$$w - p = a - \theta n$$
$$\dot{w} = \beta(n - \bar{n}) \quad \beta > 0$$
$$\pi^e = \pi = \dot{p}$$

where all variables are in natural logarithms except for inflation rates and where

$$m = \text{stock of money}$$
$$p = \text{price level}$$
$$y = \text{income}$$
$$\pi^e = \text{expected inflation}$$
$$n = \text{labour}$$
$$w = \text{money wages}$$
$$\bar{n} = \text{natural level}$$
$$\pi = \dot{p} = \text{inflation}$$

The first equation adds an income component to the Cagan demand for money equation. The second equation arises from a Cobb–Douglas production function, while the third equation is that real wages is equal to the marginal physical product of labour. The fourth equation is the Phillips curve while the fifth equation is the assumption of perfect foresight.

[15] This draws on Turnovsky (1995, section 6.2).

From the first and last equations we have

$$m - p = ky - \alpha \dot{p}$$

$$\dot{p} = \frac{ky}{\alpha} - \frac{(m-p)}{\alpha}$$

From the second and third equations we have

$$\theta n = a - (w - p)$$

$$y = c + (1 - \theta)\left[\frac{a}{\theta} - \frac{w-p}{\theta}\right]$$

$$= c + \frac{a(1-\theta)}{\theta} - \left(\frac{1-\theta}{\theta}\right)(w - p)$$

Substituting this result into the previous one, we have

$$\dot{p} = \frac{k}{\alpha}\left[c + \frac{a(1-\theta)}{\theta}\right] - \frac{k}{\alpha}\left(\frac{1-\theta}{\theta}\right)(w-p) - \frac{m-p}{\alpha}$$

$$\dot{p} = \frac{k}{\alpha}\left[c + \frac{a(1-\theta)}{\theta}\right] - \frac{m}{\alpha} + \left[\frac{k}{\alpha}\left(\frac{1-\theta}{\theta}\right) + \frac{1}{\alpha}\right]p - \frac{k}{\alpha}\left(\frac{1-\theta}{\theta}\right)w$$

Turning to the second differential equation,

$$\dot{w} = \beta(n - \bar{n})$$

$$n = \frac{a}{\theta} - \frac{w-p}{\theta}$$

$$\therefore \quad \dot{w} = \beta\left[\frac{a}{\theta} - \frac{w-p}{\theta} - \bar{n}\right] = \beta\left(\frac{a}{\theta} - \bar{n}\right) + \frac{\beta}{\theta}p - \frac{\beta}{\theta}w$$

The model therefore comprises the following two differential equations

$$\dot{p} = \frac{k}{\alpha}\left[c + \frac{a(1-\theta)}{\theta}\right] - \frac{m}{\alpha} + \left[\frac{k}{\alpha}\left(\frac{1-\theta}{\theta}\right) + \frac{1}{\alpha}\right]p - \frac{k}{\alpha}\left(\frac{1-\theta}{\theta}\right)w$$

$$\dot{w} = \beta\left(\frac{a}{\theta} - \bar{n}\right) + \frac{\beta}{\theta}p - \frac{\beta}{\theta}w$$

(11.43)

Or in matrix form

$$\begin{bmatrix} \dot{p} \\ \dot{w} \end{bmatrix} = \begin{bmatrix} \frac{k}{\alpha}\left[c + \frac{a(1-\theta)}{\theta}\right] - \frac{m}{\alpha} \\ \beta\left(\frac{a}{\theta} - \bar{n}\right) \end{bmatrix} + \begin{bmatrix} \frac{k}{\alpha}\left(\frac{1-\theta}{\theta}\right) + \frac{1}{\alpha} & -\frac{k}{\alpha}\left(\frac{1-\theta}{\theta}\right) \\ \frac{\beta}{\theta} & -\frac{\beta}{\theta} \end{bmatrix}\begin{bmatrix} p \\ w \end{bmatrix}$$

where the matrix of the system is

$$\mathbf{A} = \begin{bmatrix} \frac{k}{\alpha}\left(\frac{1-\theta}{\theta}\right) + \frac{1}{\alpha} & -\frac{k}{\alpha}\left(\frac{1-\theta}{\theta}\right) \\ \frac{\beta}{\theta} & -\frac{\beta}{\theta} \end{bmatrix}$$

(11.44)

and where $\det(\mathbf{A}) = -\beta/\alpha\theta < 0$. Hence this system is represented by a saddle point solution. To illustrate the model consider the following numerical example.

Example 11.6

The equations are

$$m - p = 0.25y - 2\pi^e$$
$$y = 3 + 0.75n$$
$$w - p = 2 - 0.25n$$
$$\dot{w} = 0.3(n - 20)$$
$$\pi^e = \pi = \dot{p}$$

If $m = 20$ then we have

$$\dot{p} = -8.875 + 0.875p - 0.375w$$
$$\dot{w} = -3.6 + 1.2p - 1.2w$$

The fixed point of the system is found by setting $\dot{p} = 0$ and $\dot{w} = 0$ with result $(w^*, p^*) = (12.5, 15.5)$. The resulting isoclines are

$$\dot{p} = 0 \qquad p = 10.1429 + 0.4286w$$
$$\dot{w} = 0 \qquad p = 3 + w$$

In matrix form the system is

$$\begin{bmatrix} \dot{p} \\ \dot{w} \end{bmatrix} = \begin{bmatrix} -8.875 \\ -3.6 \end{bmatrix} + \begin{bmatrix} 0.875 & -0.375 \\ 1.2 & -1.2 \end{bmatrix} \begin{bmatrix} p \\ w \end{bmatrix}$$

and so the matrix of the system is

$$\mathbf{A} = \begin{bmatrix} 0.875 & -0.375 \\ 1.2 & -1.2 \end{bmatrix}$$

with $\mathrm{tr}(\mathbf{A}) = -0.325$ and $\det(\mathbf{A}) = -0.6$. Since $\det(\mathbf{A}) < 0$ then we have a saddle point equilibrium. The saddle point equilibrium is also verified by computing the eigenvalues. The eigenvalues are $r = -0.954$ and $s = 0.629$, and since these are opposite in sign we have a saddle point solution. The eigenvectors associated with the eigenvalues are

$$\mathbf{v}^r = \begin{bmatrix} 0.2009 \\ 0.9796 \end{bmatrix} = \begin{bmatrix} 1 \\ 4.8761 \end{bmatrix} \qquad \mathbf{v}^s = \begin{bmatrix} 0.8361 \\ 0.5486 \end{bmatrix} = \begin{bmatrix} 1.5241 \\ 1 \end{bmatrix}$$

To derive the saddle paths we need to consider $(\mathbf{A} - r\mathbf{I})\mathbf{v}^r = 0$ and $(\mathbf{A} - s\mathbf{I})\mathbf{v}^s = 0$. Consider $r = -0.954$ first. Then

$$(\mathbf{A} - r\mathbf{I})\mathbf{v}^r = \begin{bmatrix} 1.829 & -0.375 \\ 1.2 & -0.246 \end{bmatrix} \begin{bmatrix} p - \bar{p} \\ w - \bar{w} \end{bmatrix} = \begin{bmatrix} 0 \\ 0 \end{bmatrix}$$

Using the first equation, then

$$1.829(p - 15.5) - 0.375(w - 12.5) = 0$$
$$p = 12.9371 + 0.205w$$

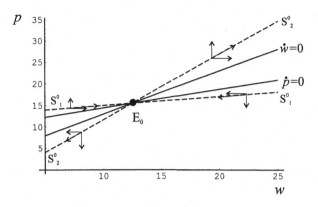

Figure 11.25.

Next consider $s = 0.629$, then

$$(\mathbf{A} - s\mathbf{I})\mathbf{v}^s = \begin{bmatrix} 0.246 & -0.375 \\ 1.2 & -1.829 \end{bmatrix} \begin{bmatrix} p - \bar{p} \\ w - \bar{w} \end{bmatrix} = \begin{bmatrix} 0 \\ 0 \end{bmatrix}$$

Again using the first equation, then

$$0.246(p - 15.5) - 0.375(w - 12.5) = 0$$
$$p = -3.5549 + 1.5244w$$

i.e.

$$S_1^0 : \qquad p = 12.9371 + 0.205w \qquad \text{stable arm}$$
$$S_2^0 : \qquad p = -3.5549 + 1.5244w \qquad \text{unstable arm}$$

The vector forces of this extended Cagan model are illustrated in figure 11.25.

When $\dot{p} > 0$ then $p > 10.1429 + 0.4286w$, so above the $\dot{p} = 0$ isocline p is rising while below p is falling. Similarly, when $\dot{w} > 0$ then $p > 3 + w$, and so above the $\dot{w} = 0$ isocline w is rising while below w is falling.

Consider now a one-off rise in the money supply, so $m = 25$. This has an impact only on the $\dot{p} = 0$ isocline, which shifts up. The equation of this new isocline is

$$p = 13 + 0.4286w$$

resulting in a new equilibrium of $(w^*, p^*) = (17.5, 20.5)$. The situation is illustrated in figure 11.26. Notice that $dp^* = dw^* = dm = 5$. This readily follows from the equation of $\dot{w} = 0$. The new stable saddle path is $S_1^1 S_1^1$ which passes through the fixed point E_1. But what trajectory does the economy follow? In this model we assume that prices are flexible and can 'jump' to the new stable arm immediately. This is an implication of the assumption of rational expectations with perfect foresight. Wages are assumed to alter continuously but sluggishly owing to wage contracts. The path the economy follows, therefore, is $E_0 \rightarrow A \rightarrow E_1$ as shown by the heavy line in figure 11.26.

Figure 11.26.

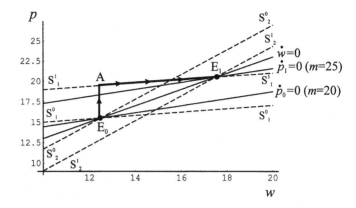

11.8   Unemployment and job turnover

In order to introduce the dynamics of unemployment (and employment) we consider in this section a very extreme model in which we assume that at the ruling wage there is full employment in the sense that the number of jobs is matched by the number of households seeking employment. The working population, N, is assumed fixed and the number of jobs available is constant. At any instant of time a fraction s of individuals become unemployed and *search* over firms to find a suitable job. Let f denote the probability of *finding* a job, i.e., the fraction finding a job. At any moment of time, if u is the fraction of the participating labour force unemployed, then

$$s(1-u)N = \text{individuals entering the unemployment pool}$$

$$fuN = \text{individuals exiting the unemployment pool.}$$

The change in the unemployment pool, uN, is therefore given by the differential equation

(11.45)
$$\frac{d(uN)}{dt} = s(1-u)N - fuN \qquad 0 < s < 1, \ 0 < f < 1$$

Since N is constant then

(11.46)
$$\dot{u} = \frac{du}{dt} = s(1-u) - fu$$
$$\text{or} \quad \dot{u} = s - (s+f)u$$

Equilibrium requires that $du/dt = 0$, or

$$s - (s+f)u^* = 0$$

(11.47)
$$\text{i.e.} \quad u^* = \frac{s}{s+f} = \frac{s/f}{1+(s/f)}$$

where

$$\frac{\partial u^*}{\partial s} = \frac{f}{(s+f)^2} > 0, \qquad \frac{\partial u^*}{\partial f} = \frac{-s}{(s+f)^2} < 0$$

In other words, the equilibrium unemployment rate – the natural rate in this model – rises the more individuals enter the unemployment pool to actively search for a

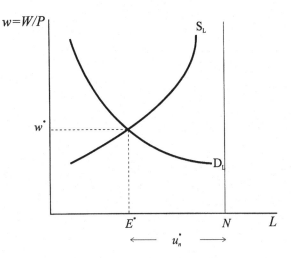

Figure 11.27.

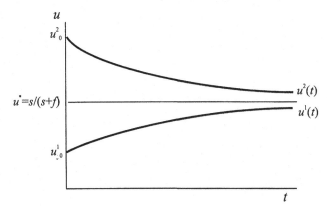

job; and falls the greater the job-finding rate. But this simple model says more than this about the equilibrium (natural) level of unemployment. It says that the level of u^* occurs because individuals need to seek alternative employment and that the search for a new job takes time.

The time path of unemployment is readily found by solving the differential equation (11.46). If $u(0) = u_0$, then

$$u(t) = u^* + (u_0 - u^*)e^{-(s+f)t} \qquad u^* = \frac{s}{s+f}$$

Since both s and f are positive then this solution implies that unemployment tends to its equilibrium value over time. The situation is illustrated in figure 11.27.

In this model concentration is on the level of *unemployment*. Of course, if N is fixed then employment, E, is simply $E = (1-u)N$ or $e = E/N = (1-u)$, where e is the employment rate. In order to lay the foundation for other dynamic theories it is worth noting that at any moment of time there will be an unemployment rate of $u = U/N$, and a vacancy rate of $v = V/N$. Since N is constant throughout we can concentrate on the rates u, v and e.

At any moment of time there will be an unemployment rate u and a vacancy rate v, where those individuals who are unemployed are attempting to match themselves with the available vacancies. Since we have assumed that the number of jobs is matched by the number seeking employment, then $u = v$. The problem is one of matching the unemployed to the vacancies. Accordingly the literature refers to the matching rate or 'exchange technology' (Mortensen 1990). In other words, the unemployed and the jobs that employers are seeking to fill are 'inputs' into the meeting process. Let this be denoted $m(u, v)$.

Given $m(u, v)$, then for such a meeting to take place there must either be some unemployment or some vacancies. More formally $m(0,v) = m(u,0) = 0$. Furthermore, the marginal contribution of each 'input' is positive, i.e., $\partial m/\partial u > 0$ and $\partial m/\partial v > 0$. Following Diamond (1982) it is further assumed that the average return to each 'input' is diminishing, i.e., m/u and m/v diminishes with u and v, respectively. Finally, and purely for mathematical convenience, we assume that $m(u, v)$ is homogeneous of degree k, so that

$$m(u, v) = u^k m(1, v/u)$$

Using this analysis we can write the change in employment as the total match $Nm(u, v)$ minus those losing a job $s(1-u)N$, i.e.

(11.48)
$$\frac{dE}{dt} = \frac{d(eN)}{dt} = Nm(u, v) - s(1 - u)N$$

$$\text{or} \quad \frac{de}{dt} = \dot{e} = m(u, v) - se$$

Although the time path of employment, $e(t)$, must mirror the time path of the unemployment rate, $u(t)$, since $e = 1 - u$, the present formulation directs attention to the matching rate $m(u, v)$.

In general (Mortensen 1990), the equilibrium hiring frequency $m(u, v)/u$ will be a function of the present value of employment per worker to the firm, q, and the employment rate, e. This can be established by noting that

(11.49)
$$\frac{m(u, v)}{u} = \frac{u^k m(1, v/u)}{u} = u^{k-1} m(1, v/u)$$
$$= (1 - e)^{k-1} m(1, v/u) = h(q, e)$$

The hiring function $h(q, e)$ is a function of q since the value of v/u in (11.49) is that determined in equilibrium. In equilibrium, the return on filling a vacancy (mq/v) is equal to the cost of filling a vacancy, c, i.e.

(11.50)
$$\left[\frac{m(u, v)}{v}\right] q = c$$

which gives

$$(1 - e)^{k-1} q = \frac{cv/u}{m(1, v/u)}$$

which means that the hiring frequency is related to both q and e. Furthermore, we can establish from this last result that $h_q > 0$ and $h_e < 0$ if $k > 1$ and $h_e > 0$ if

$k < 1$. Hence

$$\frac{m(u, v)}{u} = h(q, e) \qquad h_q > 0, \qquad \begin{cases} h_e < 0 \text{ if } k > 1 \\ h_e > 0 \text{ if } k < 1 \end{cases}$$

$$\therefore \quad m(u, v) = uh(q, e) = (1 - e)h(q, e)$$

which in turn leads to the following equilibrium adjustment equation

$$\dot{e} = (1 - e)h(q, e) - se \tag{11.51}$$

The profit to the firm of hiring an additional worker is related to q and the employment rate, e. i.e., $\pi(q, e)$, and will be different for different models of the labour market. This profit arises from the difference in the marginal revenue product per worker, MRP_L, less the wage paid, w. If we denote the MRP_L by $x(e)$, then $\pi(q, e) = x(e) - w$.[16] However, the future profit stream per worker to the firm is

$$rq = x(e) - w - s(q - k_v) + \dot{q}$$

where rq represents the opportunity interest in having a filled vacancy and k_v is the capital value of a vacant job, i.e., the present value of employment to the firm is the profit from hiring the worker less the loss from someone becoming unemployed plus any capital gain.

Since in equilibrium no vacancies exist, then $k_v = 0$ and so

$$rq = \pi(q, e) - sq + \dot{q}$$

$$\text{or} \quad \dot{q} = (r + s)q - \pi(q, e) \tag{11.52}$$

To summarise, we have two differential equations in e and q, i.e.

$$\dot{e} = (1 - e)h(q, e) - se$$

$$\dot{q} = (r + s)q - \pi(q, e) \tag{11.53}$$

Whether a unique equilibrium exists rests very much on the degree of homogeneity of the match function, i.e., the value of k in $m(u, v) = u^k m(1, v/u)$, and the productivity per worker $x(e)$.

11.9 Wage determination models and the profit function

In order to establish the properties of this differential equation system we need to have information on the partial derivatives of the profit function, i.e., π_q and π_e. But this in turn requires a statement about wage determination, and there are a variety of wage determination models. Here we shall consider just two: a market clearing model and a shirking model.[17]

---

[16] In the case of the shirking model of wage determination $MRP_L = x(e) - a\lambda$, where λ denotes the average number of times that the effort of each worker is checked and a the fixed cost required to do the checking.

[17] This analysis draws heavily on Mortensen (1990) who also considers an insider–outsider model of wage determination.

For instance, in the simplest model, Diamond (1971), all workers are identical and all have the same reservation wage and so the wage must equal the value of leisure forgone when employed, denoted b. Thus, $w = b$ and the profit function is $\pi(q, e) = x(e) - b$, with $\pi_q = 0$ and $\pi_e < 0$ if $x'(e) < 0$, i.e., if we have diminishing returns to labour employed.

In the case of the shirking model, an individual can receive a wage w and if successful at shirking can receive a value b in leisure. If, however, the employer monitors the worker with a frequency λ and fires them if they are found shirking, then the equilibrium wage must exceed b to ensure that the expected worker cost of shirking per period is no less than the benefit b. If y_e denotes the expected present value of a worker's income when employed and y_u the expected present value of a worker's future income when unemployed, then in equilibrium

$$\lambda(y_e - y_u) = b$$

Furthermore

$$ry_e = w + s(y_u - y_e) + \dot{y}_e$$
$$ry_u = b + \left[\frac{m(u, v)}{u}\right](y_e - y_u) + \dot{y}_u$$

The first equation states that the opportunity interest from holding a job must equal the wage received plus the income she receives when unemployed, which she faces with probability s, plus any capital gain. The second equation states that the opportunity interest on being unemployed must equal the return from not working (including any unemployment benefit) plus the income she receives when employed, which she faces with an average match of $m(u, v)/u$, plus any capital gain.

In equilibrium $\dot{y}_e = 0$ and

$$ry_e = w - \frac{sb}{\lambda}$$

$$ry_u = b + \left[\frac{m(u, v)}{u}\right]\left(\frac{b}{\lambda}\right)$$

Hence

$$r(y_e - y_u) = w - b - \frac{sb}{\lambda} - \left[\frac{m(u, v)}{u}\right]\left(\frac{b}{\lambda}\right)$$

$$\frac{rb}{\lambda} = w - b - \frac{sb}{\lambda} - \left[\frac{m(u, v)}{u}\right]\left(\frac{b}{\lambda}\right)$$

In other words the wage rate is

$$w = b + \left[r + s + \frac{m(u, v)}{u}\right]\left(\frac{b}{\lambda}\right)$$

(11.54)

$$= b + [r + s + h(q, e)]\left(\frac{b}{\lambda}\right)$$

Using this result we can obtain the optimal values for λ, w and $\pi(q, e)$ (see exercise 6), i.e.,

$$\lambda = (b/a)^{\frac{1}{2}}[r + s + h(q, e)]^{\frac{1}{2}}$$
$$w = b + (ab)^{\frac{1}{2}}[r + s + h(q, e)]^{\frac{1}{2}} \tag{11.55}$$
$$\pi(q, e) = x(e) - b - 2(ab)^{\frac{1}{2}}[r + s + h(q, e)]^{\frac{1}{2}}$$

Thus the optimal wage paid exceeds the market clearing wage and is an increasing function of $h(q, e)$, so long as $a > 0$.

We therefore have two alternative dynamic systems:

Model 1 Market clearing

$$\dot{e} = (1 - e)h(q, e) - se$$
$$\dot{q} = (r + s)q - x(e) + b \tag{11.56}$$

Model 2 Shirking model

$$\dot{e} = (1 - e)h(q, e) - se$$
$$\dot{q} = (r + s)q - x(e) + b + 2(ab)^{\frac{1}{2}}[r + s + h(q, e)]^{\frac{1}{2}} \tag{11.57}$$

Both systems are nonlinear and the dynamics depend on the value of k, and hence on the properties of $h(q, e)$, and on the properties of $x(e)$.

An equilibrium steady state requires $\dot{e} = 0$ and $\dot{q} = 0$. So in both models equilibrium satisfies

$$(1 - e^*)h(q^*, e^*) = se^*$$

in other words, the hire flow must equal the turnover flow. The isocline $\dot{e} = 0$ is called by Mortensen (1990) the *employment singular curve* and for $x'(e) < 0$ and $k < 1$ this curve is upward sloping. For instance, if $m(u, v) = (uv)^{\frac{1}{4}}$ so that $m(u, v) = u^{\frac{1}{2}}(v/u)^{\frac{1}{4}}$ with $k = \frac{1}{2}$ we derive the following results (see exercise 7).

$$v = \left(\frac{q}{c}\right)^{\frac{4}{3}} u^{\frac{1}{3}}$$

$$h(q, e) = (1 - e)^{-\frac{2}{3}}\left(\frac{q}{c}\right)^{\frac{1}{3}} \qquad h_q > 0, \; h_e > 0$$

For $\dot{e} = 0$ then

$$q = \frac{c(se)^3}{1 - e}$$

To pursue this analysis further, consider the following example in which we derive explicitly the isocline $\dot{q} = 0$, called the *value singular curve* by Mortensen.

Figure 11.28.

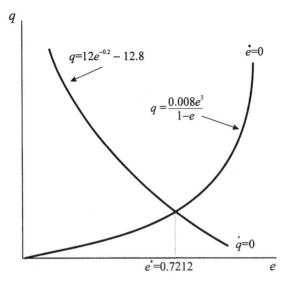

Example 11.7

Let

$$m(u, v) = (uv)^{\frac{1}{4}}$$
$$x(e) = 3e^{-0.2}$$
$$r = 0.05, \quad a = 0.1, \quad c = 1, \quad s = 0.2, \quad b = 3.2$$

then

$$h(q, e) = (1 - e)^{-\frac{2}{3}} q^{\frac{1}{3}}$$

and for $\dot{e} = 0$

$$q = \frac{0.008e^3}{1 - e}$$

Considering $\dot{q} = 0$ for each model we have
Model 1

$$\dot{q} = 0.25q - 3e^{-0.2} + 3.2 = 0$$
$$\text{i.e.} \quad q = 12e^{-0.2} - 12.8$$

Hence the equilibrium level of employment is found from solving

$$\frac{0.008e^3}{1 - e} = 12e^{-0.2} - 12.8$$

which can be done by means of a software package.[18] The solution is found to be $e^* = 0.7212$. The stylised situation is shown in figure 11.28.

---

[18] Recall that if you do not have a software package like *Mathematica* or *Maple*, you can use the *Solver* of *Excel*'s spreadsheet.

Model 2

In the case of model 2, the shirking model, the $\dot{q} = 0$ isocline is given by

$$\dot{q} = 0.25q - 3e^{-0.2} + 3.2 + 2[(0.1)(3.2)]^{\frac{1}{2}} \left[0.25 + \frac{0.008e^3}{1-e} \right]^{\frac{1}{2}}$$

i.e. $\dot{q} = 12e^{-0.2} - 12.8 - (2.56)^{\frac{1}{2}} \left[0.25 + \frac{0.008e^3}{1-e} \right]^{\frac{1}{2}}$

Qualitatively this leads to the same situation as in figure 11.28 except that the $\dot{q} = 0$ isocline is below that of model 1, so leading to a smaller level of equilibrium employment. In fact, given the parameter values this is found to be $e^* = 0.3207$.

These equilibrium values are consistent with the equilibrium wages in the two models, which are:

Model 1 $w = b = 3.2$

Model 2 $w = b + (ab)^{\frac{1}{2}} [r + s + h(q, e)]^{\frac{1}{2}} = 3.4836$

Since the two models are *qualitatively* identical, we shall pursue here only the simple market clearing model illustrated in figure 11.28.

11.10   Labour market dynamics

The situation we have developed so far for the simple market clearing model is a set of differential equations given by

$$\dot{e} = (1 - e)h(q, e) - se$$
$$\dot{q} = (r + s)q - x(e) + b$$

which reproduces equations (11.56). The isocline $\dot{e} = 0$ is upward sloping and $\dot{q} = 0$ is downward sloping. Given the parameter values in example 11.7 we have the equilibrium point $(e^*, q^*) = (0.7212, 0.0108)$ which is *unique*. The isoclines are given by

$\dot{e} = 0$ implying $q = \dfrac{0.008e^3}{1-e}$

$\dot{q} = 0$ implying $q = 12e^{-0.2} - 12.8$

furthermore

when $\dot{e} > 0$ then $q > \dfrac{0.008e^3}{1-e}$

so employment is rising above the $\dot{e} = 0$ isocline and falling below this isocline.
Similarly

when $\dot{q} > 0$ then $q > 12e^{-0.2} - 12.8$

so the present value of the future profit stream of the marginal worker is rising above the $\dot{q} = 0$ isocline and falling below this isocline. These vector forces are

Figure 11.29.

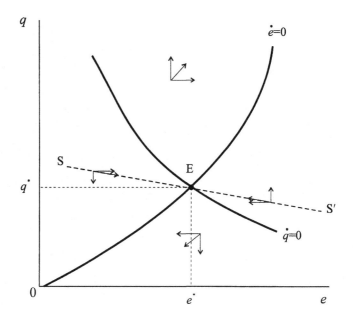

illustrated in figure 11.29 and indicate that the equilibrium point E is a saddle point solution. This property is also true for model 2 in which wages are determined within a shirking model.[19]

Given the saddle point nature of the equilibrium in all models the only solution trajectories are those which lie on the saddle path SS′. Suppose the present level of employment is e_0, as shown in figure 11.30, then the only rational expectations trajectory must be the starting point (e_0, q_0) at point A and the path along SS′ to point E. Any point below SS′, such as point B, tends the system to zero present value profit stream from the marginal worker; or, such as point C, to an ever expanding profit, i.e., an unstable speculative bubble.

The solution value so far is unique because we have assumed $k < 1$ and $x'(e) < 0$. A number of labour economists, however, have been investigating the situation of increasing returns in the production exchange process, which allows various possibilities for $x(e)$. Consider the situation shown in figure 11.31 in which the $\dot{e} = 0$ isocline is upward sloping while the isocline $\dot{q} = 0$ takes a variety of shapes.

There are now three solutions: a low (L), medium (M) and high (H) (e, q)-pair. The medium employment level is unstable. But for any level of employment such as e_0 in figure 11.31, there are two values of q consistent with the rational expectations behaviour of the system: point A on $S_1 S_1'$ and point B on $S_2 S_2'$. In the case of point A, the system will tend to solution point L; while for point B, the system will tend to solution point H. It is also possible that in the neighbourhood of point M a stable limit cycle can occur.

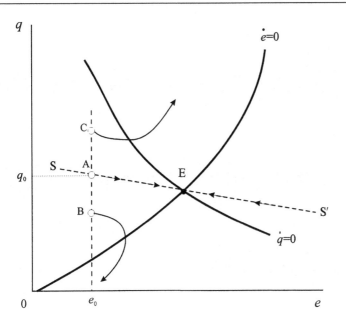

Figure 11.30.

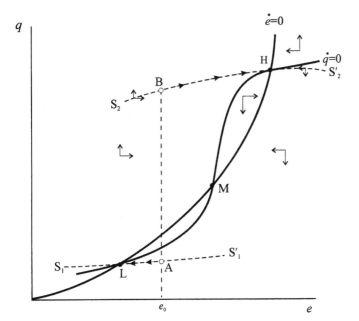

Figure 11.31.

This second version of the model, exhibiting as it does multiple equilibria arising from increasing returns, illustrates a point we made in chapter 1. Rational
expectations alone is not sufficient to determine outcomes. At e_0 points A and
B are equally likely and yet the solution points L and H, respectively, involve
quite different welfare implications. This suggests quite strongly that some policy
coordination is necessary to fix the system on one or other of the solution paths.

Exercises

1.   (i) Solve the nonhomogeneous differential equation

$$\frac{d\pi}{dt} = \beta f(u) - \beta(1 - \xi)\pi$$

for $\pi(0) = \pi_0$.

(ii) Show that for $\beta > 0$ and $0 < \xi < 1$ the equilibrium π^* is asymptotically stable.

2.   Given the model

$$y_{t-1} = 9 + 0.2(m_{t-1} - p_{t-1})$$
$$\pi_t = \alpha(y_{t-1} - y_n) \qquad\qquad \alpha > 0$$

if $m_t = 5$ and $y_n = 6$, use a spreadsheet to investigate the dynamics of the system for different values of α.

3.   For the system

$$\dot{y} = -1.85(y - y^*) - 10(\pi^e - \pi^{e*})$$
$$\dot{\pi}^e = 0.3(y - y^*)$$

establish that the characteristic roots are complex conjugate and that $r, s = \alpha \pm \beta i$ has $\alpha < 0$.

4.   Show that if

$$E_t P_{t+1} - E_{t-1} P_t = (1 - \lambda)(P_t - E_{t-1} P_t) \quad 0 \le \lambda \le 1$$

then

$$P_t = \left(\frac{M_t}{a+b}\right) + \left(\frac{b}{a+b}\right)(1 - \lambda)\sum_{k=0}^{\infty} \lambda^k P_{t-k}$$

5.   Consider the model

$$y_t^d = a_0 + a_1(m_t - p_t)$$
$$y_t^s = y_n + b_1(p_t - E_{t-1} p_t)$$
$$y_t^d = y_t^s = y_t$$

where expectations are formed rationally.

(i) Show that if money supply follows a systematic component such that $m_t = \mu_0$ which is correctly anticipated by market participants, then $y = y_n$.

(ii) Show that if $m_t = \mu_0 + z_t$ where $z_t \sim N(0, \sigma_z^2)$, then

$$y_t = y_n + \frac{a_1 b_1 z_t}{a_1 + b_1}$$

Interpret this result.

6.   In the shirking model of wage determination the firm chooses the optimal value of λ. Given

$$rq = \max_{\lambda}\{x(e) - a\lambda - w - sq + \dot{q}\}$$

(i) Show that

$$\lambda = \left(\frac{b}{a}\right)^{\frac{1}{2}} [r + s + h(q, e)]^{\frac{1}{2}}$$

(ii) Hence show that

$$w = b + (ab)^{\frac{1}{2}} [r + s + h(q, e)]^{\frac{1}{2}}$$

$$\pi(q, e) = x(e) - b - 2(ab)^{\frac{1}{2}} [r + s + h(q, e)]$$

7.   Given $m(u, v) = (uv)^{\frac{1}{4}}$ and $[m(u, v)/v]q = c$

     (i) Show that

$$v = \left(\frac{q}{c}\right)^{\frac{4}{3}} u^{\frac{1}{3}}$$

     (ii) Hence show that

$$h(q, e) = (1 - e)^{-\frac{2}{3}} \left(\frac{q}{c}\right)^{\frac{1}{3}}$$

     (iii) Verify $h_q > 0$ and $h_e > 0$.

     (iv) Show that the $\dot{e} = 0$ isocline is given by:

$$q = \frac{c(se)^3}{1 - e}$$

8.   Given $m(u, v) = \sqrt{uv}$ and $[m(u, v)/v]q = c$

     (i) Show that

$$v = (1 - e)(c/q)^2$$

     (ii) Hence show that $h(q, e)$ is independent of e.

9.   For the numerical model (11.4) establish the new steady-state equilibrium values for k and x for each of the following, and illustrate diagrammatically the trajectory the economy follows

     (i) A rise in s from 0.2 to 0.3

     (ii) A rise in n from 0.05 to 0.06

     (iii) A rise in technology such that $y = 5\,k^{0.25}$.

10.   For the numerical model (11.4) establish the new steady-state equilibrium values for k and x for a rise in monetary growth from $\lambda = 5\%$ to $\lambda = 6\%$. What trajectory does the economy traverse?

11.   Consider the model

     (1) $c = a + b(1 - t)y$ $a = 100$ $b = 0.8$ $t = 0.25$

     (2) $i = i_0 - h(r - \pi^e)$ $i_0 = 600$ $h = 2.5$

     (3) $y = c + i + g$ $g = 525$

     (4) $m_d = ky - ur$ $k = 0.25$ $u = 5$

     (5) $m_s = m - p$ $m = 700$ $p = 0$

     (6) $m_d = m_s$ $\alpha = 0.2$

     (7) $\pi = \alpha(y - y_n) + \pi^e$ $y_n = 3000$

     (8) $\dot{\pi}^e = \beta(\pi - \pi^e)$ $\beta = 0.05$

(i) What is the fixed point of the system?

(ii) Derive equations for the two isoclines

(iii) Derive an equation for $r^* = 0$ and hence establish the presence of a corridor.

12.   In the Cagan model with perfect foresight we have the model

$$m - p = -\alpha \pi^e$$

$$\pi^e = \pi$$

Given seigniorage is defined as

$$S = \frac{\Delta M}{P}$$

and money grows at a constant rate λ

(i) Express $\ln S$ in terms of λ.

(ii) Establish that the value of λ which maximises seigniorage is

$$\lambda_m = \frac{1}{\alpha}$$

Additional reading

Further material on the contents of this chapter can be found in Attfield, Demery and Duck (1985), Azariades (1993), Burmeister and Dobell (1970), Cagan (1956), Carter and Maddock (1984), Diamond (1971, 1982), Frisch (1983), George and Oxley (1991), Groth (1993), Holden, Peel and Thompson (1989), Krugman (1999), McCafferty (1990), Mortensen (1990), Pissarides (1976, 1985), Scarth (1996), Sheffrin (1983), Shone (1989) and Turnovsky (1995).

CHAPTER 12

Open economy dynamics: sticky price models

In this chapter and chapter 13 we shall consider a number of open economy models that exhibit dynamic behaviour. We shall start with the very simplest – the income–expenditure model considered at the beginning of all courses on macroeconomics. This model assumes a fixed exchange rate. Simple as it is, it will allow us to set the scene and illustrate, in the simplest possible terms, how instability may occur, *but is less likely to occur in an open economy* in comparison to a closed one. We then do the same in the context of the IS-LM model we discussed in chapter 10, extending it to the open economy, but considering the situation under both a fixed and a flexible exchange rate. This forms the basis of the Mundell–Fleming model. This model was originally concerned with the relative impact of monetary and fiscal policy under fixed and floating exchange rate regimes, but with perfect capital mobility. It has become the standard model of open economy macroeconomics, and so we shall look into its dynamic properties in some detail – for models with some (but not perfect) capital mobility and for situations of perfect capital mobility. We shall find that the assumption about the degree of capital mobility is quite important to the dynamic results. As in earlier chapters, we shall be particularly interested in what happens out of equilibrium, and hence in the dynamic forces in operation in an open economy.

12.1 The dynamics of a simple expenditure model

The simplest macroeconomic model for an open economy is the one where prices are assumed constant, and so we need not distinguish between real and nominal variables. Expenditure, E, is the sum of consumption expenditure, C, investment expenditure, I, government expenditure G, and expenditure on net exports, NX – where net exports are simply the difference between exports, X, and imports, M. We make four behavioural assumptions with respect to consumption expenditure, net taxes, investment expenditure and imports. Consumption expenditure is assumed to be a linear function of disposable income, where disposal income, Y^d, is defined as the difference between income, Y, and net taxes, T, and we make a further behavioural assumption that net taxes is linearly related to income. Investment expenditure is assumed to be positively related to the level of income (we shall consider investment and interest rates more fully in the IS-LM dynamic model). Finally, we assume that imports are linearly related to the level of income. We treat government spending and exports as exogenous. The definitions and behavioural equations of our model are, then

(12.1)

$$E = C + I + G + NX$$
$$C = a + bY^d \qquad a > 0, 0 < b < 1$$
$$Y^d = Y - T$$
$$T = T_0 - tY \qquad 0 < t < 1$$
$$I = I_0 + jY \qquad j > 0$$
$$M = M_0 + mY \qquad 0 < m < 1$$
$$NX = X - M$$

We now make a dynamic assumption about how the model adjusts over time. We assume that national income will adjust continuously over time in response to the excess demand in the goods market. More explicitly, we assume

(12.2)

$$\frac{dY}{dt} = \lambda(E - Y) \quad \lambda > 0$$

In other words, when expenditure exceeds income, then there will be pressure in the economy for income to rise. This is because firms can sell all they wish, and with stocks running down then they will expand their production, take on more labour and so raise the overall level of economic activity. On the other hand, if expenditure falls short of income, then there will be a build up of stocks. Firms will cut back on production, possibly lay off workers, and generally lead to a reduction in economic activity. Equilibrium in this model is therefore defined to be a situation where income is not changing, or where $E = Y$.

Substituting the equations in (12.1) into equation (12.2), we obtain the following differential equation

(12.3)

$$\frac{dY}{dt} = \lambda(a - bT_0 + I_0 + G + X - M_0) - \lambda[1 - b(1 - t) - j + m]Y$$
$$= \lambda A - \lambda[1 - b(1 - t) - j + m]Y$$

where A denotes all autonomous expenditures.

First consider equilibrium in this model. This requires $dY/dt = 0$, i.e.

(12.4)

$$\lambda A - \lambda[1 - b(1 - t) - j + m]Y = 0$$
$$Y^* = \frac{A}{1 - b(1 - t) - j + m}$$

But our main concern is whether this equilibrium is stable or unstable. Since there is only one equilibrium, one fixed point, in this model then the situation will either be globally stable or globally unstable. Two situations are illustrated in figures 12.1 and 12.2. In figure 12.1 the growth line is negatively sloped. Hence, for income less than the equilibrium level, income will rise; while for income above the equilibrium level, income will fall. Hence, the fixed point is a stable one. In figure 12.2, on the other hand, the growth line is positively sloped. In this case, if income is below the equilibrium level then it will decline, and decline continually. If, on the other hand, income is above the equilibrium level, then income will rise continually. In other words, the equilibrium is globally unstable.

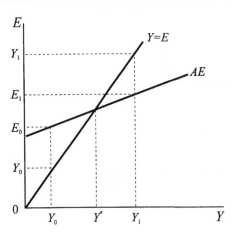

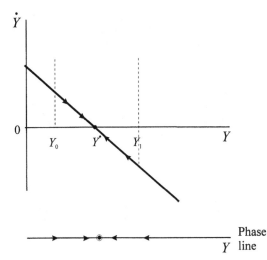

Phase
Y line

It is clear from the differential equation in (12.3) that the slope of the growth line will be negative if $b(1 - t) + j - m < 1$. This also ensures that the simple expenditure multiplier, k, is positive, i.e.

$$k = \frac{1}{1 - b(1 - t) - j + m} > 0$$

But there is no reason for $b(1 - t) + j - m < 1$. Suppose investment responds quite readily to income, with $j = 0.3$. The marginal propensity to consume can during some periods be quite high. Suppose then, that $b = 0.95$. Further assume that the marginal rate of tax is $t = 0.25$. Finally, assume the marginal propensity to import is 0.2. Then $b(1 - t) + j - m = 0.8125$, and since this is less than unity the economy exhibits stability. However, in the absence of trade (with $m = 0$), then we have $b(1 - t) + j = 1.0125$, which is greater than unity and the economy would exhibit an unstable situation. Why is there this difference?

Take the closed economy first, and assume that income begins initially below the equilibrium level. As illustrated in figure 12.2 at $Y = Y_0$, the change in

Figure 12.2.

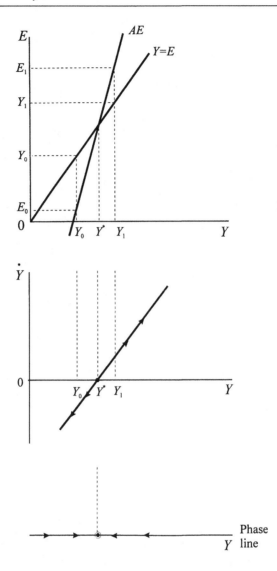

income is negative and income would decline. The reason is that at this initial level of income, income exceeds aggregate expenditure ($Y_0 > AE_0$). There is a build up of stocks and so firms lay off workers. Because h is high, they lay off quite a number of workers. But the loss in income of the workers means that they in turn have less disposable income. With a high marginal propensity to spend, this means a major cut in consumer spending. But this will itself lead to a further excess supply of goods, and so firms will respond with further cuts. Hence, the economy goes into continuous decline. If income had begun above the equilibrium level, at $Y = Y_1$, with stocks running down, then firms would expand their production, disposable income would rise and consumption expenditure would rise. The economy would expand. Of course, once it reached full employment, then this would eventually manifest itself in rising prices (which we have assumed constant so far).

Why is the open economy different? Again begin with income below the equilibrium level, as typified by the situation in figure 12.1 for $Y = Y_0$. At this level of income, if the economy were not importing then there would be a running down of stocks as expenditure is in excess of income. But with the economy open, part of this demand is directed abroad and so the run-down in stocks at home is not as great. *Hence openness tends to dampen the multiplier.* Furthermore, the greater the marginal propensity to import the more likely stability because the greater the stabilising influence.[1] We shall state this in the form of a proposition:

PROPOSITION 1
The higher the marginal propensity to import, the more likely the economy will exhibit a stable equilibrium.

We can consider this proposition in more detail by considering a simple numerical discrete model that we can investigate by means of a spreadsheet. The model is an extension of that provided in table 10.2 (but here we ignore the money market). In line with our discussion in chapter 10, we introduce dynamics into this discrete model by assuming that income in period t adjusts according to total expenditure in the previous period. Our model is

$$E_t = C_t + I_t + G_0 + NX$$
$$C_t = 100 + 0.75Y_t^d$$
$$Y_t^d = Y_t - Tax_t$$
$$Tax_t = -80 + 0.2Y_t$$
$$I_t = 320 + 0.1Y_t$$
$$M_t = 10 + 0.2Y_t$$
$$NX_t = X_0 - M_t$$
$$Y_t = E_{t-1}$$

where we assume government spending remains constant at $G_0 = £330$ million for all periods and exports remain constant at $X_0 = £440$ million for all periods – unless either is shocked. Equilibrium income is readily found to be equal to $Y^* = £2500$ million, which can be found from the resulting difference equation

$$Y_t = 1250 + 0.5Y_{t-1}$$

A rise in government spending from £330 million to £400 million results in a new equilibrium level of income of £2640 million. The movement of the economy over time in terms of the main variables is illustrated in table 12.1, which also includes the dynamic multiplier. What the table shows is that all variables gradually tend to their new levels as the multiplier impact comes closer to its final value. A marginal propensity to import of $m = 0.3$ (and with autonomous exports at £690 million) also leads to an initial equilibrium level of income of £2500 million. For the same rise in government spending from £330 million to

---

[1] Exactly the same argument holds for the tax rate. The higher the marginal rate of tax the greater the stabilising influence on the economy, and the more likely the equilibrium is stable.

Table 12.1 Impact of a rise in government spending of £70 million

t	E_t	Y_t	Tax_t	Yd_t	C_t	I_t	M_t	NX_t	k_t
0	2500.00	2500.00							
1	2570.00	2500.00	420.00	2080.00	1670.00	570.00	512.00	−70.00	0.00
2	2605.00	2570.00	434.00	2136.00	1712.00	577.00	524.00	−84.00	1.00
3	2622.50	2605.00	441.00	2164.00	1733.00	580.50	531.00	−91.00	1.50
4	2631.25	2622.50	444.50	2178.00	1743.50	582.25	534.50	−94.50	1.75
5	2635.63	2631.25	446.25	2185.00	1748.75	583.13	536.25	−96.25	1.88
6	2637.81	2635.63	447.13	2188.50	1751.38	583.56	537.13	−97.13	1.94
7	2638.91	2637.81	447.56	2190.25	1752.69	583.78	537.56	−97.56	1.97
8	2639.45	2638.91	447.78	2191.13	1753.34	583.89	537.78	−97.78	1.98
9	2639.73	2639.45	447.89	2191.56	1753.67	583.95	537.89	−97.89	1.99
10	2639.86	2639.73	447.95	2191.78	1753.84	583.97	537.95	−97.95	2.00
11	2639.93	2639.86	447.97	2191.89	1753.92	583.99	537.97	−97.97	2.00
12	2639.97	2639.93	447.99	2191.95	1753.96	583.99	537.99	−97.99	2.00
13	2639.98	2639.97	447.99	2191.97	1753.98	584.00	537.99	−97.99	2.00
14	2639.99	2639.98	448.00	2191.99	1753.99	584.00	538.00	−98.00	2.00
15	2640.00	2639.99	448.00	2191.99	1753.99	584.00	538.00	−98.00	2.00
16	2640.00	2640.00	448.00	2192.00	1754.00	584.00	538.00	−98.00	2.00
17	2640.00	2640.00	448.00	2192.00	1754.00	584.00	538.00	−98.00	2.00
18	2640.00	2640.00	448.00	2192.00	1754.00	584.00	538.00	−98.00	2.00
19	2640.00	2640.00	448.00	2192.00	1754.00	584.00	538.00	−98.00	2.00
20	2640.00	2640.00	448.00	2192.00	1754.00	584.00	538.00	−98.00	2.00

£400 million, the economy also gradually approaches its new equilibrium level of income (namely £2617 million) marginally sooner than with a lower marginal propensity to import (see exercise 4).

This can also be seen in terms of figure 12.3, which captures the movement of the economy in the first few periods. It is clear that the new level of income is lower. *The economy is inherently more stable the higher the marginal propensity to import.* Of course, the corollary of this is that government spending has less influence on the domestic economy. Or, put another way, the more open an economy the greater the change in government spending necessary to achieve a given change in national income.

12.2   The balance of payments and the money supply

We precede our discussion of open economy models under fixed and flexible exchange rates with a consideration of two interrelated variables: the balance of payments and the money supply. Both of these play a prominent role in the modelling to follow, and it is important that they are fully understood. This is quite important because we shall be setting up the models in real terms, even though we shall be assuming that prices at home and abroad are constant. This assumption of constant prices will be relaxed in chapter 13.

12.2.1   The balance of payments

We define the balance of payments in *real terms*, bp, as the sum of real net exports, nx, and real net capital flows, cf, i.e.

(12.5) $$bp = nx + cf$$

Consider first net exports.

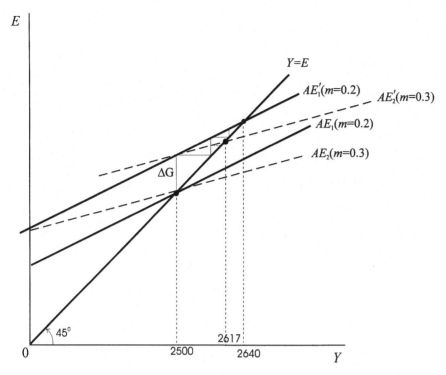

Figure 12.3.

Net exports in *nominal* terms, *NX*, is the *value* of exports minus the *value* of imports. Since we do not distinguish between goods in our modelling, then exports and imports in domestic currency are priced in terms of the domestic price level *P*. Making a clear distinction between real and nominal variables we have

$$NX = Px - Pz$$

where x is real exports and z real imports. Defining S as the spot exchange rate expressed as domestic currency per unit of foreign currency,[2] and letting P^* denote the price level abroad, then

$$NX = Px - SP^*z$$

Dividing throughout by P to bring everything into real terms

$$\frac{NX}{P} = x - \left(\frac{SP^*}{P}\right)z$$

or

$$nx = x - Rz \qquad \text{where } R = \frac{SP^*}{P} \tag{12.6}$$

and where R define the real exchange rate, a variable which features prominently in later models.[3]

---

[2] This means that a *rise* is S denotes a devaluation of the domestic currency while a *fall* in S indicates a revaluation of the domestic currency.

[3] This variable denotes the competitiveness of home goods relative to those abroad.

Real exports depend on income abroad and the real exchange rate (competitiveness). We assume a simple linear function

(12.7) $x = x_0 + fR \quad f > 0$

The constant x_0 can be considered as relating to income abroad, but we shall be holding this constant throughout. The second term captures competitiveness. Suppose the home currency depreciates, so S rises and hence so does R. Then domestic prices fall relative to those abroad and hence exports are stimulated. There is then a positive relationship between real exports and the real exchange rate.[4]

In the case of real imports we assume

(12.8) $Rz = z_0 + my - gR \quad 0 < m < 1, g > 0$

where m is the marginal propensity to import, and real imports decline with a devaluation of the domestic currency (a rise in S). Combining the results we can now express real net exports as

$$\begin{aligned} nx &= (x_0 + fR) - (z_0 + my - gR) \\ &= (x_0 - z_0) + (f + g)R - my \\ &= nx_0 + (f + g)R - my \end{aligned}$$

(12.9)

where $nx_0 = x_0 - z_0$.

Turning now to real net capital flows, *cf*, we assume that

(12.10) $cf = cf_0 + v(r - r^*) \quad v > 0$

where cf_0 is real net capital flows independent of interest rates, and r and r^* are the *nominal* interest rates at home and abroad (which are here equal to the real rates since we shall be holding prices at home and abroad constant). At this point we do not need to consider expected changes in the exchange rate.[5] The modelling is for a fixed exchange rate with no expected devaluation or revaluation, i.e., $dS^e/dt = 0$. In chapter 13 we shall relax this assumption. Under this assumption, capital flows

---

[4] We are assuming here that the Marshall–Lerner condition is satisfied. Differentiating net exports with respect to S we have

$$\begin{aligned} \frac{dNX}{dS} &= P\frac{dx}{dS} - SP^*\frac{dz}{dS} - P^*z \\ &= P\frac{x}{S}\left(\frac{S}{x}\frac{dx}{dS}\right) - SP^*\frac{z}{S}\left(\frac{S}{z}\frac{dz}{dS}\right) - P^*z \\ &= P^*xE_x - P^*zE_z - P^*z \end{aligned}$$

where E_x and E_z are the export and import price elasticities, respectively. Assuming initially $x = z$, then

$$\frac{dNX}{dS} = P^*x(E_x - E_z - 1)$$

or $\dfrac{dNX}{dS} > 0 \quad$ if $E_x + E_z > 1$

i.e. $|E_x| + |E_z| > 1$

[5] Had we done so then the net capital flow equation would become

$$cf = cf_0 + v(r - r^* - \dot{S}^e)$$

in real terms according to the uncovered interest differential, $r - r^*$, with an inflow if $r > r^*$ and vice versa.

Combining net exports and the capital flow equation, we arrive at an expression for the balance of payments

$$
\begin{aligned}
bp &= nx + cf \\
&= nx_0 + (f + g)R - my + cf_0 + v(r - r^*) \\
&= bp_0 + (f + g)R - my + v(r - r^*)
\end{aligned}
\tag{12.11}
$$

where $bp_0 = nx_0 + cf_0$. Balance of payments equilibrium occurs when $bp = 0$, a deficit when $bp < 0$ and a surplus when $bp > 0$.

Recall that in chapter 10 we discussed the IS-LM model. We can now introduce a third relationship into the framework. Under the assumption of fixed exchange rates, the BP curve denotes combinations of income and interest rates for which the balance of payments is in equilibrium. Setting $bp = 0$ and expressing the result as r a function of y, we have

$$
r = \left[r^* - \frac{bp_0 + (f + g)R}{v} \right] + \left(\frac{m}{v} \right) y
\tag{12.12}
$$

hence the BP curve is, in general, positively sloped. But also note that if $bp < 0$ then

$$
bp_0 + (f + g)R - my + v(r - r^*) < 0
$$

i.e. $\quad r < \left[r^* - \dfrac{bp_0 + (f + g)R}{v} \right] + \left(\dfrac{m}{v} \right) y$

In other words, below the BP curve the balance of payments is in deficit, while above the BP curve the balance of payments is in surplus. This information is displayed in figure 12.4.

One way to account for the situations off the BP curve is to take a point on the BP curve, such as point A in figure 12.4, and move horizontally across to point B, moving to a point below the BP curve. Since the rate of interest remains constant, then so too do net capital flows. On the other hand, the rise in the level of income raises the level of imports, and hence worsens the current account. Hence, if initially the balance of payments was zero, then it must now be negative as a result of the worsening current account balance. Note also that this helps to explain why the BP curve is positively sloped. Given the deficit at point B, then this can be eliminated by raising the rate of interest. This will increase the net capital inflow, so bringing the balance of payments back into equilibrium (at point C). A similar argument applies to points above the BP curve.

Care must be exercised in interpreting the BP curve, and points off it. The BP curve denotes combinations of income and interest rates for which $bp = 0$. In other words, we interpret **external equilibrium** as a situation where the current account is matched by the capital account but with opposite sign (i.e. $nx = - cf$ or $bp = 0$). This is not the only definition of external equilibrium, but it is the one we shall use throughout this chapter. But what about the vectors of force either side of the BP curve? It is here we must be especially careful. If the exchange rate is fixed, then although there is some force acting on the *market* exchange rate, there is no change in the *parity* rate, and it is the parity rate that determines the

Figure 12.4.

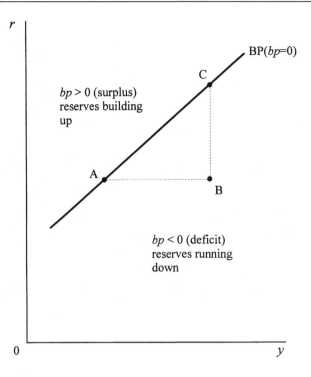

intercept of the BP curve.[6] If the economy is below the BP curve, then the balance of payments is in deficit. What is occurring in this situation is a running down of the country's reserves. Such a situation can persist in the short term, but not necessarily in the medium and long term. A similar situation arises in the case of a surplus, which occurs above the BP curve. Here the economy is adding to its reserves. The implication of the change in the reserve position of the economy depends on a number of factors. These include:

(i)   The change in the money supply resulting from a change in the reserves. (We shall take this up in the next sub-section.)

(ii)   The extent to which the authorities sterilise the impact on the money supply.
        (We shall also take this up in the next sub-section.)

(iii)   Whether a change in the parity rate is considered a possibility.

What we observe here are asset market forces that act on the economy in the medium and long term. We shall return to these where appropriate.

It is also worth noting some special cases:

(i)   If $v = 0$ then the BP curve is vertical at income level

$$y = \frac{bp_0 + (f + g)R}{m}$$

[6] The *market* exchange rate is determined by the demand and supply of foreign exchange, but the *parity* rate is set by the authorities. Under the Bretton Woods system, where exchange rates were fixed *vis-à-vis* the dollar, the market exchange rate could fluctuate either side of the parity rate by ± 1 per cent.

(ii)   If $v = \infty$ there is perfect capital mobility and the BP curve is horizontal at $r = r^*$.

(iii)   With some, but not perfect, capital mobility then the BP curve is positively sloped. However, there are two further categories which can be distinguished here, depending on the relative slopes of the BP and LM curves, which are both positively sloped:

     (a) the BP curve is steeper than the LM curve

     (b) the BP curve is less steep than the LM curve.

Situations (i) and (ii) are illustrated in figure 12.5.

   Before we consider the IS-LM-BP model we need to take note of the fact that the expenditure function has now altered, since it includes net exports, and hence

(a) Perfect capital immobility   **Figure 12.5.**

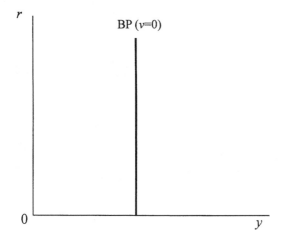

(b) Perfect capital mobility

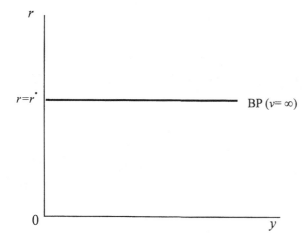

so too has the IS-curve that we developed in chapter 10. To be specific

$$e = a + [b(1-t)+j]y - hr + nx_0 + (f+g)R - my$$
$$= [a + nx_0 + (f+g)R] + [b(1-t)+j-m]y - hr$$

which leads to an IS curve of

(12.13)
$$r = \frac{a + nx_0 + (f+g)R}{h} - \frac{[1 - b(1-t) - j + m]y}{h}$$

which indicates a change in the position of the IS curve and in its slope relative to that in the closed economy.

12.2.2   *The money supply in an open economy*

In the model developed in chapter 10 the money supply was exogenous and fixed. In an open economy with a fixed exchange rate this is no longer the case. To see why this is so, we need to be clear on the definition of money for an open economy. Here we shall consider just the narrow definition of money, the money base, and denoted $M0$, and a broader definition of money supply, namely $M1$. Specifically

(12.14)
$$M0 = Cp + CBR$$
$$Ms = Cp + D$$

where

$M0 =$ money base
$Cp =$ cash held by the public
$CBR =$ commercial bank reserves at the Central Bank
$Ms =$ money supply (here $M1$)
$D =$ sight deposits

We shall further assume a simple money multiplier relationship between Ms and $M0$,[7] i.e.

(12.15)
$$Ms = qM0$$

Return to the money base $M0 = Cp + CBR$. This is the money base from the point of view of Central Bank liabilities. It is possible to consider a consolidated banking system from the point of view of the asset side.[8] The money base from the asset side denotes Central Bank Credit, CBC, and international reserves, IR.[9] Thus

(12.16)
$$M0 = Cp + CBR = CBC + IR$$

Hence

(12.17)
$$Ms = qM0 = q(CBC + IR)$$

---

[7] If $Cp = cD$ and $CBR = rD$ then $Ms = cD + D = (1+c)D$ and $M0 = cD + rD = (c+r)D$. Hence, $Ms/M0 = (1+c)/(c+r)$ or $Ms = qM0$. See Shone (1989, pp.147–51).
[8] See Copeland (2000, pp. 120–8).
[9] International reserves, IR, should not be confused with commercial bank reserves at the Central Bank, CBR.

Looking at the money base from the point of view of assets means that any change in the money base can occur from two sources:

(i)   Open market operations (including sterilisation) which operates through changes in CBC.

(ii)   Changes in the foreign exchange reserves that, under a fixed exchange rate, is equal to the balance of payments.

Open market operations, ΔCBC, can usefully be thought of in terms of two components. (a) Open market operations which have nothing to do with the balance of payments, denoted μ, and which we shall refer to as autonomous open market operations. (b) A component that is responding to the change in the reserves. Let, then

$$\Delta CBC = \mu - \lambda \Delta IR \quad 0 \le \lambda \le 1 \tag{12.18}$$

where λ denotes the sterilisation coefficient. If $\lambda = 0$ then regardless of the change in reserves, no sterilisation occurs; if $\lambda = 1$, then we have perfect sterilisation. Thus, for a surplus on the balance of payments and a rise in the money base of ΔIR, the Central Bank *reduces* the money base by an equal amount. If the country has a deficit, leading to a reduction in the money base, then the Central Bank *increases* the money base by an equal amount. Where some, but not perfect, sterilisation occurs, then $0 < \lambda < 1$.

We are now in a position to consider the money supply in more detail.

$$Ms = q(CBC + IR)$$
$$\Delta Ms = q(\Delta CBC + \Delta IR)$$
$$= q(\mu - \lambda \Delta IR + \Delta IR)$$
$$= q[\mu + (1 - \lambda)\Delta IR]$$

Hence

$$\frac{\Delta Ms}{P} = \frac{\mu q}{P} + \frac{q(1 - \lambda)\Delta IR}{P} \tag{12.19}$$

Consider the two extreme cases:

(i) $\mu = 0$ and $\lambda = 0$, no autonomous open market operations and no sterilisation

$$\frac{\Delta Ms}{P} = \frac{q \Delta IR}{P} = q.bp \qquad \text{where } bp = \frac{\Delta IR}{P}$$

i.e. real money balances change by a multiple of the balance of payments (in real terms). A deficit leads to a fall in the money supply, while a surplus leads to a rise in the money supply.

(ii) $\mu = 0$ and $\lambda = 1$ no autonomous open market operations and perfect sterilisation

$$\frac{\Delta Ms}{P} = 0$$

i.e. under no autonomous open market operations and perfect sterilisation there is no change in the money supply regardless of the balance of payments situation.

Figure 12.6.

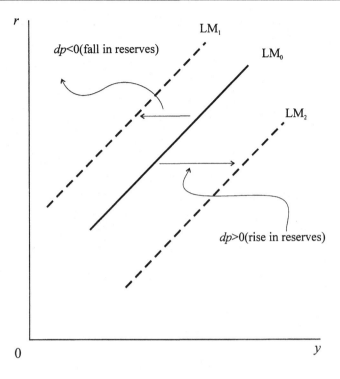

It should be noted that retaining the assumption of an exogenous and constant money supply for an open economy is equivalent to assuming no autonomous open market operations and perfect sterilisation (i.e. case (ii)). In general, this is not true, and so for an open economy the money supply should be treated as *endogenous*.

With no sterilisation, a deficit on the balance of payments under a fixed exchange rate leads to a shift left in the LM curve, while a surplus on the balance of payments leads to a shift right in the LM curve, as illustrated in figure 12.6.

We are now in a position to consider the dynamics of monetary and fiscal policy under a fixed exchange rate.

12.3   Fiscal and monetary expansion under fixed exchange rates

12.3.1   *Fiscal expansion*

In chapter 10 we have already established the vectors of force either side of the IS curve and the LM curve. Even with the IS curve re-specified for an open economy, as outlined in the previous section, the forces either side remain the same. In sub-section 12.2.1 we established the deficit/surplus situation either side of the BP curve. In a dynamic context, the BP curve is the condition for which $bp = 0$. There is *no* equivalent to the adjustment functions in the goods market or the money market. Why is this? The exchange rate, S, is assumed to be fixed. Prices at home, P, and abroad, P^*, are assumed constant. Hence the real exchange rate, $R = SP^*/P$, is constant. Once income and interest rates are determined by the dynamics of the

Table 12.2 Parameter values and equilibrium points for figure 12.8

Equations:	Parameter values:		
$e = a + (f + g)R + b(1 - t)y - hr + jy - my$	$a = 43.5$	$m = 0.2$	$S = 1.764$
$m_d = Md/P = ky - ur$	$f = 5$	$P = 1$	$P^* = 1$
$m_s = Ms/P = q(CBC_0 + IR_0) + q[\mu + (1 - \lambda)\Delta IR]$	$g = 2$	$k = 0.25$	$x_0 = 0$
$R = SP^*/P$	$R = SP^*/P = S$	$u = 0.5$	$z_0 = 24$
$nx = (x_0 - z_0) + (f + g)R - my$	$b = 0.75$	$CBC = 0$	$cf_0 = 20.5$
$cf = cf_0 + v(r - r^*)$	$t = 0.3$	$IR_0 = 3$	$v = 1$
$bp = nx + cf$	$h = 2$	$q = 1$	$r^* = 15$
$dy/dt = \dot{y} = \alpha(e - y) \qquad \alpha > 0$	$j = 0$	$\lambda = 0, \mu = 0$	$\alpha = 0.05$
$dr/dt = \dot{r} = \beta(m_d - m_s) \quad \beta > 0$			$\beta = 0.8$

Intercepts and slopes:	Solutions for point E_0:
IS intercept $= 27.924$	
IS slope $= -0.3375$	$y = 40.506$
	$r = 14.253$
LM intercept $= -6$	
LM slope $= 0.5$	$nx = -19.753$
	$cf = 19.753$
BP intercept $= 6.152$	$bp = 0$
BP slope $= 0.2$	
	Solutions for point E_1:
IS_1 intercept $= 32.924$	$y = 46.476 \quad Ms = 3$
IS_1 slope $= -0.3375$	$r = 17.238$
	$bp = 1.791$
LM_1 intercept $= -8.791$	Solutions for point E_2:
LM_1 slope $= 0.5$	$y = 49.809 \quad Ms = 4.395$
	$r = 16.114$
	$bp = 0$

goods market and the money market, the balance of payments is automatically determined from

$$bp = bp_0 + (f + g)R - my + v(r - r^*)$$

But this is a *short-run* result. Why? Because a deficit leads to a fall in the reserves and hence to a reduction in the money supply, while a surplus leads to a rise in the reserves and hence to an expansion in the money supply, as explained in sub-section 12.2.2. In the long run, with no sterilisation, interest rates and income will change until the deficit/surplus is eliminated. Geometrically, the LM curve will shift until it intersects the IS curve *on* the BP curve.

To see this adjustment consider the following numerical model outlined in table 12.2, where CBC_0 and IR_0 denote the initial level for Central Bank credit and international reserves, respectively.

In this model all three curves intersect at the same point, namely $(y, r) = (40.506, 14.253)$. The situation is shown in figure 12.7, in which it should be noted that the BP curve is less steep than the LM curve.

Consider a rise in autonomous spending by 10, e.g., because of a rise in government spending. The situation is shown in figure 12.8. In the short run the economy moves from equilibrium point E_0 to E_1. Since the money market always clears, or is very quick to clear, then the economy moves along either the LM curve or close to it. At E_1 the economy is in surplus. This follows from the new IS curve (whose

Figure 12.7.

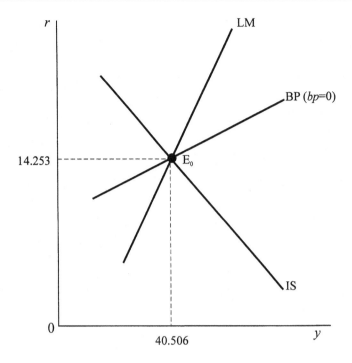

Figure 12.8.

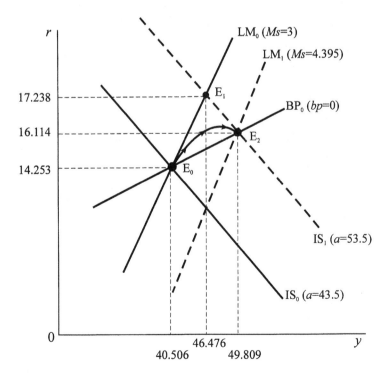

intercept and slope are indicated in the table 12.2), intersects the LM curve *above* the BP curve.

This must be a short-run result. Assuming no sterilisation, then the money supply must rise as the balance of payments surplus leads to a rise in international reserves. Of course, equilibrium E_1 will persist into the *medium* term if perfect sterilisation occurs and the money supply remains constant.[10] In the case of *no* sterilisation, then the money supply will rise, the LM curve will shift right, and this will continue until the balance of payments becomes zero once again. This requires the final LM curve to cut the BP curve *and* the IS curve *on* the BP curve. This is shown by LM_1 in figure 12.8, where all three curves (IS_1, LM_1 and BP_0) all intersect at point E_2. Given the fact that the money supply under these circumstances is endogenous, it is possible to establish that it must increase from $Ms = 3$ to $Ms = 4.395$.

We have so far concentrated on the comparative statics. But what type of trajectory will such an economy follow? From our analysis so far we know that the money market is quick to adjust and the initial movement will be close to the initial LM curve. But as the economy goes into surplus the money supply will rise so shifting the LM curve right, income will adjust and the interest rate will be brought down because of the monetary expansion. The expected trajectory, therefore, is shown by the path indicated in figure 12.8 on which the arrow heads are marked. To the extent that any sterilisation takes place, then the actual path the economy follows will deviate from the trajectory shown. For instance, with perfect sterilisation and instantaneous clearing in the money market, then the path will be along LM_0, between E_0 and E_1.

Under perfect capital mobility the BP curve is horizontal at $r = r^*$ ($v = \infty$). The qualitative results are similar. The fiscal expansion leads to a rise in interest rates, which in turn leads to an immediate capital inflow. This will continue until the interest rate is brought into line with the interest rate abroad. During this process the balance of payments is in surplus because of the favourable capital account. The resulting surplus on the balance of payments leads to a rise in the money supply. However, since adjustment is quite quick the trajectory is either *along* the BP curve or close to it, as shown in figure 12.9. This will occur, however, so long as no sterilisation takes place.

12.3.2   *Monetary expansion*

Consider next a monetary expansion for the model outlined in table 12.2. Suppose Central Bank credit is raised from zero to $CBC = 2$, raising the money supply from $Ms = 3$ to $Ms = 5$. This results in a new LM curve given by

$$LM_1 \quad r = -10 + 0.5y$$

This cuts IS_0 with solution values

$$y = 45.282 \qquad r = 12.641 \qquad bp = -2.567$$

---

[10] The situation is more serious where the BP curve is *steeper* than the LM curve, then the rise in autonomous spending leads to a deficit. Perfect sterilisation will eventually lead to a running out of gold and *overseas* currency.

Figure 12.9.

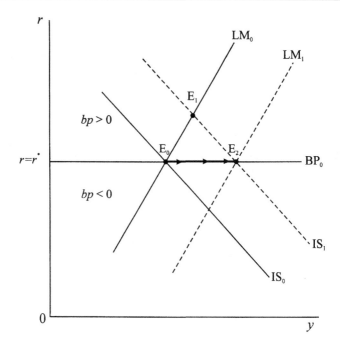

where the deficit on the balance of payments results because LM_1 cuts IS_0 below the BP curve, as shown in figure 12.10.

In the long run, however, the deficit leads to a fall in international reserves and a fall in the money supply, shifting the LM curve back to LM_0. The final equilibrium, E_2, is the same as E_0.

What about the dynamic path of this result? This is quite different from a situation of a fiscal expansion. To see this, consider a situation of instantaneous adjustment in the money market. The initial impact is a fall in the rate of interest to $r = 10.253$ (point A). This not only overshoots the short run equilibrium point E_1, but leads to a greater deficit because of the larger capital outflow. Two forces now come into operation. With a fall in the rate of interest investment rises which, through the multiplier, raises the level of income. Simultaneously, however, the deficit leads to a fall in international reserves and a fall in the money supply. The economy moves along a *shifting* LM curve, with a trajectory shown by the arrows pointing from position A to E_2. How 'bowed out' the trajectory is depends on the extent to which the money supply is slow to fall as a result of the deficit (i.e. as a consequence of the fall in the level of reserves). Also, the trajectory will be more bowed out the more the Central Bank engages in any sterilisation in an attempt to move (or keep) the economy at point E_1.

Perfect capital mobility does not change the qualitative nature of the results just discussed. The major difference is that the fall in the rate of interest below the world level r^* will lead to a rapid outflow of capital and a more immediate reduction in the money supply. The economy is more likely to return to E_0 more quickly, with a less 'bowed out' return trajectory.

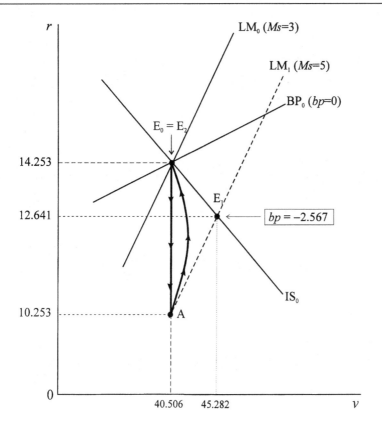

Figure 12.10.

This section verifies the Mundell–Fleming results:

PROPOSITION 2
Under fixed exchange rates, fiscal policy is effective at changing the level of income but monetary policy is totally ineffective.

Also, our analysis indicates three dynamic forces in operation:

(1) pressure on income to change whenever expenditure differs from income
(2) pressure on interest rates to change whenever the demand and supply of money are not equal
(3) pressure on the money supply to adjust whenever there is a balance of payments disequilibrium, and where the extent of this change depends on the degree of sterilisation being undertaken by the Central Bank.

The change in income is likely to be slow since the goods market takes time to adjust to any disequilibrium. On the other hand, interest rates are likely to adjust quite quickly. This supposition, however, assumes that the Central Bank is not attempting to control the rate of interest. The speed of the change in the money supply arising from changes in the balance of payments (the level of reserves) is likely to lie between that of the change in the rate of interest arising from capital flows and that of the level of income. What is being hinted at here is the need for another adjustment function: namely, the rate at which the authorities change the money supply in response to a change in the level of reserves. This is a much more sophisticated analysis than we propose to investigate in this book.

12.3.3   Rise in the foreign interest rate

A less frequently discussed shock, but an important one, arises from a change in the foreign interest rate. Consider a rise in the foreign interest rate, a rise in r^*. Such a rise shifts only the BP curve in the first instance. From equation (12.12) we note that a rise in r^* raises the intercept of the BP curve – in fact by exactly the rise in r^*. The situation is shown in figure 12.11, where we start from the same initial position. The rise in the foreign interest rate from $r^* = 15$ to $r^* = 18$ shifts the BP curve up to BP_1. Given this situation, the economy is still at E_0 and so experiences a deficit on the balance of payments, $bp = -3$. Under a fixed exchange rate and no sterilisation, the deficit leads to a capital outflow and a fall in the money supply. LM shifts left to LM_1 and the economy settles down at E_1. But what trajectory does the economy follow on its path to E_1?

The immediate impact of the deficit is a fall in the money supply. If the money market adjusts instantaneously to this fall in the money supply, then the economy moves vertically up to point B on LM_1. Thereafter, as income falls in response to the rise in the rate of interest, money demand falls putting pressure on the interest rate to fall until point E_1 is reached. In this scenario the trajectory of the economy is E_0->B->E_1, and labelled trajectory T_1. What we observe is an overshoot of the domestic interest rate. If the shift in the LM curve is not complete or not so immediate, and depending on income adjustment, another trajectory is possible, shown by T_2. Also note one other feature. The change in interest rate abroad is shown by the vertical distance between BP_0 and BP_1 while the rise in the domestic interest rate is less. Why is this? The fact that income is falling means a fall in imports and so net exports are rising. Hence the size of the capital outflow does not have to be as great.

Even with perfect capital mobility, the same basic logic holds. The only difference is that eventually the domestic interest rate will rise in line with the foreign interest rate. With instantaneous adjustment of money supply to the resulting deficit and instantaneous adjustment in the money market, the interest rate will once again overshoot the final rise.

In this section we have concentrated on the impact of changes in fiscal and monetary policy under a fixed exchange rate system – typical of the situation under Bretton Woods. However, since 1973 the exchange rate in most countries has been floating.[11] In the next section we consider the IS-LM-BP model under the assumption that the exchange rate is allowed to float. However, we retain the assumption that prices at home and abroad are constant. This reminder is important. A change in the exchange rate is most likely to lead to a change in the price level in the medium and longer term. We shall take up this question of the link between

---

[11] Britain floated its exchange rate in June 1972.

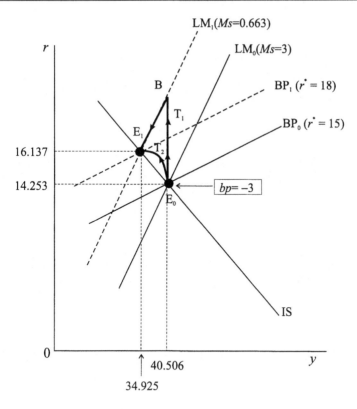

Figure 12.11.

the exchange rate and changes in the price level in chapter 13. Even so, what it does mean is that the real exchange rate, $R = SP^*/P$ is changing because of the change in S.

12.4   Fiscal and monetary expansion under flexible exchange rates

12.4.1   Fiscal expansion

In this section we shall consider monetary and fiscal policy under floating exchange rates. In doing this we need to be clear on the implications of floating. With the spot exchange rate floating, S variable, and with fixed prices at home and abroad (P and P^* constant), then the real exchange rate, R, will vary directly with S. Whatever is happening in the economy, the exchange rate will vary so that the balance of payments is always in equilibrium, $bp = 0$. If we assume instantaneous adjustment in the foreign exchange market and the money market, then the full impact of any change in the economy will initially fall on interest rates and the exchange rate. Only over time will the economy adjust to the situation as income changes. In terms of the diagrammatic treatment we have been using, the BP curve will shift continuously so that it always passes through the intersection between the IS and LM curves.

Consider the initial situation depicted in table 12.2. Once again let autonomous spending rise by 10. This shifts the IS curve to IS_1, as shown in figure 12.12, which

Figure 12.12.

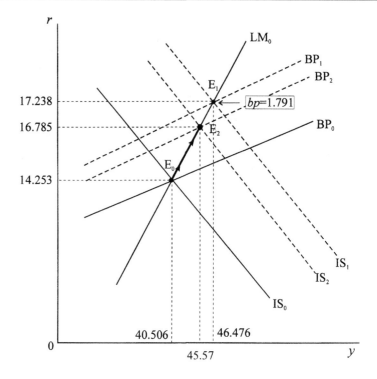

Table 12.3 Exchange rate values and equilibrium points for figure 12.12

$S = 1.764$		$S = 1.764$	
IS_0 $r = 27.924 - 0.3375y$		Point E_0	Point E_1
LM_0 $r = -6 + 0.5y$		$y = 40.506$	$y = 46.476$
BP_0 $r = 6.152 + 0.2y$		$r = 14.253$	$r = 17.238$
			$bp = 1.791$
IS_1 $r = 32.924 - 0.3375y$			
$S = 1.547$		$S = 1.547$	
IS_2 $r = 32.165 - 0.3375y$		Point E_2	
LM_0 $r = -6 + 0.5y$		$y = 45.57$	
BP_2 $r = 7.671 + 0.2y$		$r = 16.785$	

is the same IS_1 curve indicated in table 12.2. The resulting surplus on the balance of payments leads to an immediate appreciation of the domestic currency. The BP curve shifts up, and the resulting appreciation results in the IS curve shifting left to IS_2. The *final* results are set out in table 12.3 and illustrated in figure 12.12.

Our discussion, however, concentrates on the comparative statics. Let us for a moment turn to the dynamics of adjustment. In doing this we shall, as already indicated, assume instantaneous adjustment in all asset markets (money and foreign exchange), but slow adjustment in the goods market. The initial impact of the fiscal expansion is to move the economy to point E_1, with a trajectory moving *along* LM_0 from E_0 to E_1, as shown in figure 12.12. Because of the resulting surplus, the domestic currency appreciates shifting the BP curve up to BP_1. It should be noted

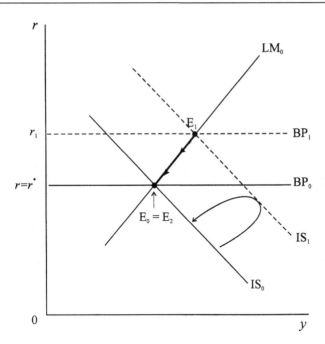

Figure 12.13.

that BP_1 passes through point E_1, which it must do to eliminate any surplus on the balance of payments. The appreciation, however, leads to an appreciation of the real exchange rate, a fall in R, which leads over time to a reduction in net exports. As net exports decline, so too does income through the multiplier impact. As income falls, so too does the demand for money, and this leads to a fall in the rate of interest. What we observe, since the money market is continuously in equilibrium, is a movement along LM_0 from E_1 to E_2. As the interest rate falls, however, the amount of net capital inflows declines and so the exchange rate must depreciate. This shifts the BP curve down from BP_1 to BP_2 which occurs as the IS curve shifts from IS_1 to IS_2. In other words, in the (y, r)-plane, the economy gradually moves down LM_0 from E_1 to E_2, establishing itself at the final equilibrium point E_2. The most likely trajectory, therefore, is a movement along LM_0 from E_0 to E_2 as all these forces take effect.

There is some difference in the results for the situation of perfect capital mobility. This is illustrated in figure 12.13. We can be brief because the formal analysis is similar. The fiscal expansion shifts IS to IS_1 and the economy from E_0 to E_1. The domestic currency appreciates as a result of the balance of payments surplus, shifting the BP line up to BP_1. The resulting appreciation leads to a fall in net exports shifting IS left. As this takes place, income falls, interest rates fall, and the exchange rate depreciates, with the economy moving down the LM curve from E_1 to $E_2 = E_0$, and with the situation returning to its initial position, with no impact on the level of income.

Two observations are worth noting about all these results, which we shall put in the form of two propositions. The first is the typical Mundell–Fleming result concerning a fiscal expansion under the assumption of a floating exchange rate; the second proposition is in the spirit of Dornbusch and overshooting.

PROPOSITION 3

Under flexible exchange rates, fiscal policy is effective in changing the level of income where there is some degree of capital mobility, but totally ineffective where there is perfect capital mobility.

PROPOSITION 4

Under flexible exchange rates, a fiscal expansion leads to an overshooting of interest rates and an overshooting of the exchange rate, and this result holds with some degree of capital mobility or with perfect capital mobility.

The important results are those with regard to some degree of capital mobility, since this is likely to capture the real world. A fiscal expansion would lead to a rise in income, a rise in interest rates and an appreciation of the domestic currency. This would be followed by interest rates falling, income falling and the exchange rate depreciating – but all such that the initial impact outweighs the secondary impacts.

12.4.2   Monetary expansion

A monetary expansion under imperfect capital mobility and under perfect capital mobility is illustrated in figures 12.14 and 12.15, respectively. The adjustment is similar in both cases. However, figure 12.14 illustrates a numerical example.

Figure 12.14.

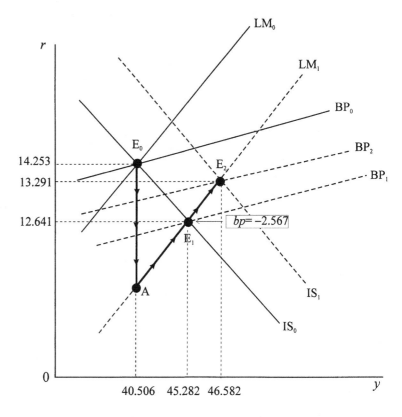

Figure 12.15.

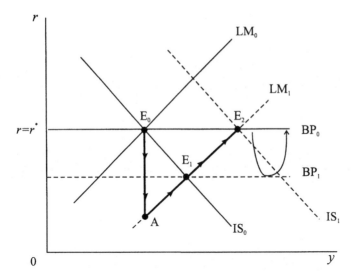

Table 12.4 Equilibrium points for figure 12.14

IS, LM and BP curves		Solution values			
IS_0	$r = 27.924 - 0.3375y$	E_0	$y = 40.506$	E_1	$y = 45.282$
LM_0	$r = -6 + 0.5y$		$r = 14.253$		$r = 12.641$
BP_0	$r = 6.152 + 0.2y$		$S = 1.764$		$bp = -2.567$
LM_1	$r = -10 + 0.5y$	E_2	$y = 46.582$		
IS_1	$r = 29.013 - 0.3375y$		$r = 13.291$		
BP_2	$r = 3.975 + 0.2y$		$S = 2.075$		

Which illustrates the result of increasing the money supply by 2. The relevant information is given in table 12.4

A rise in the money supply shifts the LM curve right to LM_1 and moves the economy from point E_0 to point E_1. At E_1 the balance of payments is in deficit. Since the exchange rate is flexible and adjusts instantaneously, it will depreciate, shifting the BP curve down from BP_0 to BP_1, where it intersects both the IS curve and LM curve at point E_1. The depreciation leads to a rise in the real exchange rate and hence to a stimulus to net exports. This leads to a shift right in the IS curve. In terms of figure 12.14, this will be to IS_1, and the resulting rise in the rate of interest leads to an appreciation of the exchange rate, but not enough to swamp the original depreciation. The economy accordingly moves to point E_2 (the intersection point between IS_1, LM_1 and BP_2). The situation in figure 12.15 is somewhat similar. The depreciation leads to a shift right in the IS curve to IS_1, but this will cut the LM_1 curve on the original BP curve because interest rates will have to be brought back into line with world interest rates, which is accomplished by an expected appreciation of the currency, which returns BP_1 to BP_0.

Again we have concentrated on the comparative statics. But what will the trajectory of the economy look like in the short run and in the long run? The analysis is similar for both figure 12.14 and figure 12.15. The immediate impact of the monetary expansion is a sharp drop in the rate of interest, to point A on LM_1. This is because the money market adjusts immediately, while the goods market is yet to alter. But there is another immediate result. The sharp fall in the rate of interest leads to a major depreciation of the exchange rate. There will be another BP curve (not shown) that passes through point A. As the goods market adjusts to the lower interest rate, stimulating investment, and through the multiplier stimulating the level of income, the economy will move to point E_1, the movement taking place along LM_1 and the BP curve continuously adjusting upwards until BP_1 is reached. In the longer run, however, the depreciation which originally occurred will begin to shift the IS curve because of the stimulus to net exports. This will lead to a further movement along LM_1 and a further shift up in the BP curve until the economy moves to point E_2.

Again we arrive at two propositions:

PROPOSITION 5
Under flexible exchange rates, monetary policy is effective in changing the level of income, and the effect is greater the greater the degree of capital mobility.

PROPOSITION 6
Under flexible exchange rates, a monetary expansion leads to overshooting of interest rates and overshooting of exchange rates, and the less the degree of capital mobility the greater the overshooting of the exchange rate.

The important results are those with regard to some degree of capital mobility, since this is likely to capture the real world. A monetary expansion would lead to a rise in income, a fall in interest rates and a depreciation of the domestic currency. This would be followed by interest rates rising, income rising and the exchange rate appreciating – but all such that the initial impact outweighs the secondary impacts.

12.4.3   A rise in the foreign interest rate

Finally, consider the situation where the foreign interest rate is increased under floating. As earlier, the initial impact is to raise the BP curve by the amount of the increase. The initial situation, point E_0 in figure 12.16, now represents a deficit on the balance of payments. This leads to a depreciation of the domestic currency, which improves competitiveness. The improvement in competitiveness stimulates net exports, so shifting IS to the right (to IS_1) and BP down to BP_2 in figure 12.16. The final equilibrium is at E_1. But what is the trajectory of the economy over the adjustment period? As the depreciation stimulates net exports shifting IS right and BP down, the economy will move along LM_0, since the money market clears in every period. The economy will have a trajectory along LM_0 between E_0 and E_1, shown by the arrows. We arrive, then, at the important conclusion that under a floating exchange rate the economy's adjustment exhibits *no* overshooting.

The same basic conclusion holds with perfect capital mobility, except that the final equilibrium must have the domestic interest rate equal to the new (higher) foreign interest rate. the trajectory remains along LM with *no* overshooting.

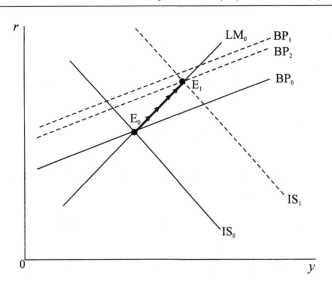

Figure 12.16.

12.5 Open economy dynamics under fixed prices and floating

So far we have concentrated on the comparative statics with some reference to the dynamics. Keeping within the simple linear model, let us consider the dynamics in more detail. We begin by stating the adjustment functions for the three markets explicitly, namely

Goods market $\dot{y} = \alpha(e - y)$ $\alpha > 0$

Money market $\dot{r} = \beta(m_d - m_s)$ $\beta > 0$ (12.20)

Foreign market $\dot{S} = \gamma(bp)$ $\gamma > 0$

To simplify we set $P = P^* = 1$ so that $R = S$ and hence

$$e = (a + nx_0) + [b(1 - t) + j - m]y - hr + (f + g)S$$

giving

$$\dot{y} = \alpha(a + nx_0) + \alpha[b(1 - t) + j - m - 1]y - \alpha hr + \alpha(f + g)S$$

or

$$\dot{y} = A_0 + A_1 y + A_2 r + A_3 S \tag{12.21}$$

where

$$A_0 = \alpha(a + nx_0)$$
$$A_1 = \alpha[b(1 - t) + j - m - 1]$$
$$A_2 = -\alpha h$$
$$A_3 = \alpha(f + g)$$

Equilibrium in the goods market is where $\dot{y} = 0$ which no more than traces out the IS curve in (y, r)-space. If $\dot{y} > 0$ then $e > y$ and r is below the value on the line $\dot{y} = 0$. Hence, below and to the left of $\dot{y} = 0$ then y is rising while above and to the right income is falling, as shown in figure 12.17(a).

Figure 12.17.

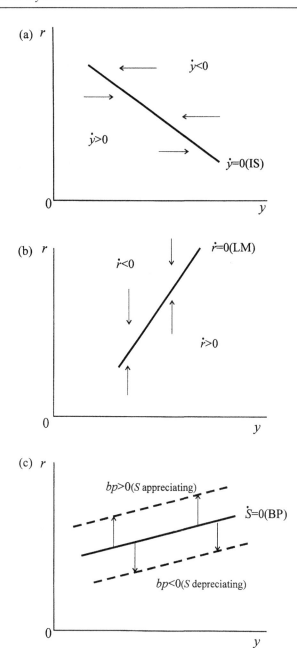

The money market is unchanged. Money market equilibrium is where $\dot{r} = 0$ which traces out the LM curve in (y, r)-space. If $\dot{r} > 0$ then $M_d/P > M_s/P$ and r is below and to the right of the value on the $\dot{r} = 0$ line. Hence, below and to the right of $\dot{r} = 0$ then r is rising, while above and to the left r is falling, as shown in figure 12.17(b). The greater the value of β the faster interest rates rise or fall to clear the money market.

Finally, the foreign exchange market is in equilibrium when $bp = 0$ or $\dot{S} = 0$, which simply traces out the BP curve in (y, r)-space. Here we need to be careful.

Below $\dot{S} = 0$ then $bp < 0$ and S is rising representing a depreciating of the domestic currency, resulting in the $\dot{S} = 0$ line shifting down, as shown in figure 12.17(c). The fact that the $\dot{S} = 0$ line shifts should be clear. The BP curve is drawn in (y, r)-space for a fixed exchange rate. When the exchange rate varies, which it will do for either a deficit or a surplus, then the result is a shift in the BP curve. However, there is also a shift in the IS curve. A depreciation of the domestic currency shifts IS right while an appreciation shifts it left – assuming the Marshall–Lerner conditions are satisfied.[12] The higher the value of γ, the more the BP curve shifts for any given deficit or surplus.

Turning to the money market we have

$$\dot{r} = \beta(m_d - m_s) \qquad \beta > 0$$
$$= \beta(ky - ur - m_0)$$
$$\text{i.e.} \quad \dot{r} = -\beta m_0 + \beta ky - \beta ur$$

or

$$\dot{r} = B_0 + B_1 y + B_2 r \tag{12.22}$$

where

$$B_0 = -\beta m_0$$
$$B_1 = \beta k$$
$$B_2 = -\beta u$$

Finally, for the foreign exchange market

$$\dot{S} = \gamma(bp) = \gamma[bp_0 + (f + g)S - my + v(r - r^*)]$$
$$= \gamma(bp_0 - vr^*) - \gamma my + \gamma vr + \gamma(f + g)S$$

or

$$\dot{S} = C_0 + C_1 y + C_2 r + C_3 S \tag{12.23}$$

where

$$C_0 = \gamma(bp_0 - vr^*)$$
$$C_1 = -\gamma m$$
$$C_2 = \gamma v$$
$$C_3 = \gamma(f + g)$$

Our model, then, amounts to three differential equations

$$\dot{y} = A_0 + A_1 y + A_2 r + A_3 S$$
$$\dot{r} = B_0 + B_1 y + B_2 r \tag{12.24}$$
$$\dot{S} = C_0 + C_1 y + C_2 r + C_3 S$$

The fixed point is where $\dot{y} = 0$, $\dot{r} = 0$ and $\dot{S} = 0$ and can be solved for the equilibrium values y^*, r^* (not the interest rate abroad)[13] and S^*.

---

[12] See n. 4, p. 526.
[13] There should be no confusion between the foreign interest rate and the equilibrium interest rate both being referred to as r^*.

It is clear from the specification of the initial adjustment functions that the three parameters α, β and γ have no bearing on the existence of a fixed point. What they do have a bearing on is the dynamic path or trajectory of the system from some initial value. Such a trajectory is less straightforward than any we have encountered so far because in (y, r)-space the trajectory is also governed by the movement of the exchange rate. The fiscal expansion we outlined in the previous section illustrates the problem.

Suppose we start from an equilibrium. A fiscal expansion will shift the $\dot{y} = 0$ line to the right. Interest rates will be pushed up and there will be a capital inflow resulting in a balance of payments surplus. The *extent* of the interest rate rise depends on the value of β. The resulting surplus on the balance of payments leads to an appreciation of the domestic currency. The *extent* of the appreciation depends on the value of γ, which in turn will influence the trajectory arising from changes in the rate of interest and changes in the level of income. Finally, the changes in income will be governed by the parameter α. The difficulty, of course, is that we are attempting to reduce a three-variable problem into a two-dimensional plane.

To appreciate some of the difficulties suppose we have the parameter values given in table 12.2 along with $\alpha = 0.05$, $\beta = 0.8$ and $\gamma = 0.0001$. The fixed point is

$$(y^*, r^*, S^*) = (40.506,\ 14.253,\ 1.764)$$

Now let autonomous spending rise by 10 as before. We have already established (see table 12.3) that the new fixed point is

$$(y^*, r^*, S^*) = (45.570,\ 16.785,\ 1.547)$$

But is this new fixed point attained?

The first thing we note is that E_0 becomes our initial position and the dynamics of the system are governed by point E_2. The differential equation system associated with point E_2 is

$$\dot{y} = 2.675 - 0.03375y - 0.1r + 0.35S$$
$$\dot{r} = -2.4 + 0.2y - 0.4r$$
$$\dot{S} = -0.00185 - 0.00002y + 0.0001r + 0.0007S$$

whose trajectory we can establish using a software package. One possible trajectory is shown in figure 12.18. The trajectory must begin in the shaded triangle and move anticlockwise. But there is nothing in the qualitative analysis precluding the system overshooting and spiralling towards E_2 (or even away from E_2!). Such a possibility is very dependent on the reaction coefficients α, β and γ.

For instance, with the same fiscal expansion but now $\alpha = 0.1$ (higher than before) then the trajectory lies *outside* that for $\alpha = 0.05$, as shown in figure 12.19. This should not be surprising because a higher α is indicating a greater response on income in the goods market for any given level of excess demand. On the other hand, a higher value for β (say $\beta = 1.5$ rather than 0.8) leads to a trajectory *inside* that for $\beta = 0.8$, as shown in figure 12.20. Again this should not be surprising

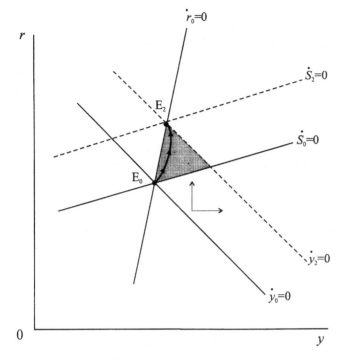

Figure 12.18.

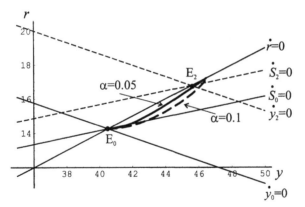

Figure 12.19.

since a higher value for β will push the trajectory towards the LM curve.[14] Notice, however, that the trajectory in figure 12.19 overshoots the equilibrium E_2 while it is difficult to see whether this is the case in figure 12.20.

We have not considered the reaction coefficient γ. The greater γ the more the BP curve and IS curve shift for any given level of balance of payments disequilibrium. The greater the value of γ the more likely the system over-reacts and equilibrium E_2 not attained. By way of example, compare the following two situations for a fiscal change. The first situation is as before, while situation II has a higher

---

[14] Recall that with instantaneous adjustment in the money market the system would move *along* the LM curve.

Figure 12.20.

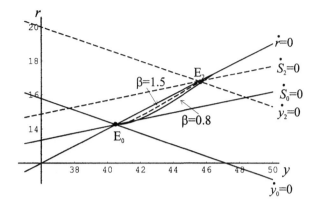

Figure 12.21.

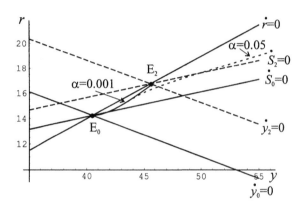

level of γ, with the exchange rate reacting significantly to balance of payments disequilibria.

Situation I $\alpha = 0.05, \beta = 0.8, \gamma = 0.0001$
$$\dot{y} = 2.675 - 0.03375y - 0.1r + 0.35S$$
$$\dot{r} = -2.4 + 0.2y - 0.4r$$
$$\dot{S} = -0.00185 - 0.00002y + 0.0001r + 0.0007S$$

Situation II $\alpha = 0.05, \beta = 0.8, \gamma = 0.05$
$$\dot{y} = 2.675 - 0.03375y - 0.1r + 0.35S$$
$$\dot{r} = -2.4 + 0.2y - 0.4r$$
$$\dot{S} = -0.925 - 0.01y + 0.05r + 0.35S$$

As can be seen from figure 12.21, the trajectories for these two situations are quite different. More significantly, although point E_2 exists, it is not attained in situation II. Why is this? We noted that the fiscal expansion led to a surplus and to an appreciation. The resulting rise in income led to a subsequent depreciation. But this is swamped in the present situation and the appreciation begins to dominate the dynamics pushing the system along the dotted line trajectory in figure 12.21.

Of course, these parameter values are purely illustrative. But they act as a warning in the present example that the comparative statics is not sufficient to establish the likely trajectory of the system. It also suggests that the larger γ the greater the possibility that the system is *dynamically* unstable.

Exercises

1.   Set up the same numerical model as in section 12.1, but have the adjustment lag $Y_t = E_{t-2}$. Compare your results for the time path of Y_t with that in table 12.1.

2.   Consider the simple dynamics of section 12.1 with exactly the same parameter values but with the following alternative lags for the import function (take each one separately):
     (i) $M_t = 10 + 0.2Y_{t-1}$
     (ii) $M_t = 10 + 0.2E_{t-1}$

3.   Show that

     $$\Delta NX_t = -mk_t \Delta G$$

     and that

     $$\lim_{t \to \infty} mk_t = mk$$

     where $X_t = X_0$ and $M_t = M_0 + mY_t$.

4.   Consider the numerical model in section 12.1 for three alternative marginal propensities to import: $m = 0.2$, $m = 0.3$ and $m = 0.4$, all other parameters constant.
     (i)   Show that the three total expenditure lines emanate from the same point on the vertical axis but that their slopes differ by deriving the equation for each total expenditure curve.
     (ii)   Obtain the equilibrium income in each case.
     (iii) Assuming income begins at $Y_0 = £2000$ million, plot on the same graph the path of income over 10 periods for each marginal propensity.
     (iv)   What conclusions do you draw from your analysis?

5.   Using the data in table 12.2, consider the new equilibrium income and interest rate for the following changes, assuming no sterilisation, constant prices and a fixed exchange rate. Draw each situation and the likely path to the new equilibrium.
     (i)   Rise in a from 43.5 to 50.0.
     (ii)   Fall in IR (hence fall in the money supply) from 3 to 2.
     (iii) Devaluation of the exchange rate from 1.764 to 2.

6.   Using the data in table 12.3, consider the new equilibrium income and interest rate for the following changes, assuming no sterilisation and that P and P^* are fixed. Draw each situation and the likely path to the new equilibrium.
     (i)   autonomous spending rises by 20 and under floating $S = 1.33$.
     (ii) Ms rises from 3 to 4, i.e., LM becomes $r = -8 + 0.5y$ and under floating $S = 1.92$.

7.   Consider the following discrete version of the numerical model of section 12.5, where again the figures refer to point E_2.

$$y_{t+1} - y_t = 2.675 - 0.03375y_t - 0.1r_t + 0.35S_t$$
$$r_{t+1} - r_t = -2.4 + 0.2y_t - 0.4r_t$$
$$S_{t+1} - S_t = -0.00185 - 0.00002y_t + 0.0001r_t + 0.0007S_t$$

(i) Set the system up on a spreadsheet and show that

$$(y^*, r^*, S^*) = (45.570, 16.785, 1.547)$$ is an equilibrium.

(ii) Show that this equilibrium is not attained from the initial position

$$(y_0, r_0, S_0) = (40.506, 14.253, 1.764).$$

(iii) Is the equilibrium attained for initial values *very close to* the equilibrium?

8.   For situation II in section 12.5, the equivalent discrete model is

$$y_{t+1} - y_t = 2.675 - 0.03375y_t - 0.1r_t + 0.35S_t$$
$$r_{t+1} - r_t = -2.4 + 0.2y_t - 0.4r_t$$
$$S_{t+1} - S_t = -0.925 - 0.01y_t + 0.05r_t + 0.35S_t$$

Given $(y_0, r_0, S_0) = (40.506, 14.253, 1.764)$ show that point E_2 represented by $(y^*, r^*, S^*) = (45.570, 16.785, 1.547)$ is *not* attained and that the system is explosive.

Additional reading

Additional material on the contents of this chapter can be obtained from Copeland (2000), Dernburg (1989), Gapinski (1982), Gärtner (1993), Karakitsos (1992), McCafferty (1990), Pilbeam (1998) and Shone (1989).

CHAPTER 13

Open economy dynamics: flexible price models

Since the advent of generalised floating in 1973 there have been a number of exchange rate models, most of which are dynamic. In this chapter we shall extend our discussion of the open economy to such models. Besides having the characteristic of a flexible exchange rate they also have the essential feature that the price level is also flexible, at least in the long run. This is in marked contrast to chapter 12 in which the price level was fixed. The models are often referred to, therefore, as fix-price models and flex-price models, respectively.

The majority of the flex-price models begin with the model presented by Dornbusch (1976). Although the model emphasised overshooting, what it did do was provide an alternative modelling procedure from the Mundell–Fleming model that had dominated international macroeconomic discourse for many years. It must be stressed, however, that the model and its variants are very monetarist in nature. Although the Mundell–Fleming model assumed prices fixed, which some saw as totally inappropriate, the models in the present chapter assume full employment, and hence a constant level of real income. This too may seem quite inappropriate. Looked at from a modelling perspective, it allows us to concentrate on the relationship between the price level and the exchange rate. Of particular importance, therefore, in such models is **purchasing power parity**. It does, of course, keep the analysis to just two main variables.

Purchasing power parity (PPP) indicates that prices in one country are equal to those in another after translating through the exchange market. There is a vast literature on this topic that we shall not go into here. All we shall do is stipulate that this is supposed to hold at the aggregate level. Hence, if P is the price level at home, P^* the price level abroad, and S the exchange rate (quoted in terms of domestic currency), then

$$SP^* = P$$

Taking natural logarithms, and setting the foreign price to unity (i.e. $P^* = 1$), which throughout is held constant, then

$$\ln S - \ln P^* = \ln P$$

i.e. $\quad s = p \quad$ since $\ln P^* = \ln 1 = 0$

where lower case letters denote natural logarithms. A rise in S (or s) is an appreciation of the foreign currency, i.e., a depreciation of the domestic currency.[1] For purchasing power parity to hold, therefore, we require $s = p$. So long as s differs from p, then purchasing power parity does not hold.[2] It is the purchasing power parity condition that drives the long-run result in the models to be discussed in this chapter. In other words, in the short run it is possible for the economy to deviate from purchasing power parity but in the long run purchasing power parity must hold.[3]

One of the essential differences between the present models and those of chapter 12 is that they are presented in terms of natural logarithms. Accordingly we shall denote all variables in natural logarithms with lower case letters. The exception is interest rates. These are percentages and the home interest rate will be denoted r and the foreign rate r^*, as in chapter 12.

In section 13.1 we consider a simplified Dornbusch model in which the goods market is independent of the rate of interest. This captures most of the characteristics of the original Dornbusch model but is easier to follow. In section 13.2 we consider Dornbusch's (1976) model. Both these models assume perfect capital mobility. In section 13.3 we consider what happens when capital is immobile (but not perfectly immobile). Next we consider the Dornbusch model under the assumption of perfect foresight, which gives a rational expectations solution (section 13.4). One of the main features of rational expectations modelling is the possibility of considering the impacts of government announcements. This topic we consider in section 13.5. The discovery of gas and then oil in the North Sea led to major impacts on the exchange rate, which in turn influenced adversely the non-oil sector. Section 13.6 presents a popular model for considering any resource discovery and its impact on the exchange rate. The final section 13.7 considers the dynamics of a simple monetarist model. Throughout we concentrate on the economic dynamics, illustrating this with many numerical examples.

13.1   A simplified Dornbusch model[4]

We begin with a simplified Dornbusch model that captures nearly all the features of the original but is more manageable. We can then go on to further complications once this is fully understood. All the Dornbusch models begin with three markets. There is the goods market, the money market and the foreign exchange market (or the balance of payments). The goods market reduces down to two simple relationships, a total expenditure equation and a price adjustment equation, where income is assumed constant at the full employed level. The money market is a

---

[1] The reader needs to be vigilant concerning which currency is appreciating and which depreciating. Since S (or s) is the price of overseas currency in terms of domestic currency (the European convention of quoting exchange rates, other than the UK), then a rise in the price is an appreciation of the foreign currency. However, most discussion takes place in terms of the price of *domestic* currency.

[2] In terms of the analysis of chapter 12 purchasing power parity requires the real exchange rate, R, to equal unity.

[3] There is something wholly unsatisfactory in this modelling. Although in the short run deviation from PPP is possible, but not in the long run, income cannot deviate from its full employment level either in the short run or in the long run, which is quite unrealistic.

[4] Based on a model presented in Gärtner (1993).

Table 13.1 Model 13.1

Goods market	$e = $ total expenditure
$e = cy + g + h(s - p)$ $0 < c < 1, h > 0$	$y = $ real income (exogenous)
$\dot{p} = a(e - y)$ $a > 0$	$g = $ government spending
	$s = $ spot exchange rate
	$p = $ domestic price level
	$\dot{p} = $ inflation rate (since $p = \ln P$)
Money market	$m_d = $ demand for money
$m_d = p + ky - ur$ $k > 0, u > 0$	$r = $ domestic interest rate
$m_s = m_d = m$	$m_s = $ supply of money
	$m = $ exogenous money balances
International asset market	$r^* = $ interest rate abroad
$r = r^* + \dot{s}^e$	$\dot{s}^e = $ change in expected spot rate
$\dot{s}^e = v(\bar{s} - s)$ $v > 0$	(expected depreciation/appreciation)
	$\bar{s} = $ purchasing power parity rate
	(equilibrium rate)

straightforward demand for money and a constant level of real money balances. The international asset market varies considerably from one model to another. Here we assume perfect capital mobility and therefore the domestic interest rate is equal to the foreign interest rate adjusted for any expected change in the exchange rate. The expected change in the exchange rate, in turn, depends on the extent of the deviation of the exchange rate from its purchasing power parity level. The model, then, is captured by the set of equations in table 13.1.

The model can be captured diagrammatically by deriving two equilibrium lines in (s,p)-space. A goods market equilibrium line, which denotes combinations of p and s for which the price level is not changing, i.e., $\dot{p} = 0$, which we shall denote GM; and an asset market line which denotes combinations of p and s which maintains equilibrium in the money market *and* satisfies the condition on the expected change in the exchange rate, which we shall denote AM.

Substituting the expenditure function into the price adjustment relation $\dot{p} = a(e - y)$, and setting $\dot{p}$ equal to zero, gives the following relationship between the price level and the exchange rate

$$p = s - \frac{(1 - c)y}{h} + \frac{g}{h} \tag{13.1}$$

Equation (13.1) is a positive relationship between p and s with a slope of unity. If we impose the condition of purchasing power parity, which we shall do, then in the long run $p = s$, and so the intercept of the GM line must be zero. Hence, in figure 13.1 we have drawn the GM line through the origin with a slope of unity. Furthermore, $\dot{p} > 0$ if $e > y$, i.e.

$$p < s - \frac{(1 - c)y}{h} + \frac{g}{h}$$

Hence, below the GM line expenditure exceeds income and there is pressure on prices to rise, while above the GM line expenditure is less than income, and there is pressure on prices to fall.

Figure 13.1.

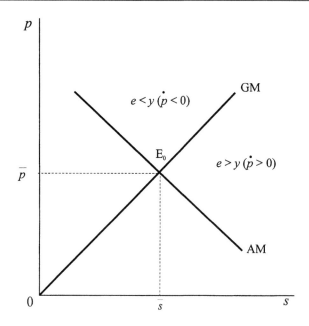

The asset market line, denoted AM in figure 13.1, is derived by substituting the condition on the expected exchange rate into the interest rate condition and substituting that into the money market equilibrium condition. Thus

(13.2)
$$m = p + ky - u[r^* + v(\bar{s} - s)]$$
$$\text{i.e.} \quad p = (m - ky + ur^* + uv\bar{s}) - uvs$$

which denotes a negative association between the price level, p, and the exchange rate, s. All markets are in equilibrium where the GM line intersects the AM line, at $(\bar{s}, \bar{p})$ in figure 13.1. From the asset market line we immediately have the condition

(13.3)
$$\bar{p} = m - ky + ur^*$$

while from the goods market condition we have

(13.4)
$$\bar{p} = \bar{s} - \frac{(1 - c)y}{h} + \frac{g}{h}$$

We are now in a position to consider some comparative statics and some dynamics. Consider an increase in the money supply from m_0 to m_1. This has no bearing on the goods market line, which remains unaffected. However, the rise in the money supply raises the intercept on the p-axis in terms of equation (13.2), and so shifts the AM line to the right, to AM_1 in figure 13.2. The equilibrium moves from E_0 to E_1, resulting in a rise in the price level and a depreciation of the domestic currency (a rise in s). But much more significant is the dynamic movement of the economy from E_0 to E_1. The rise in the money supply leads initially to a major depreciation of the domestic currency (rising from $\bar{s}_0$ to s_2). This is because the domestic interest rate falls below that abroad ($r < r^*$), resulting in an immediate capital outflow. This occurs because we have assumed that initially the goods market has not responded to the increase in the money supply, but the asset market can do so immediately. This is a basic behavioural assumption of all the models in

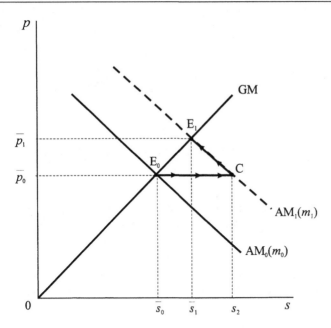

Figure 13.2.

this chapter: *the goods market is slow to adjust (there is price stickiness) while the asset market is very quick to adjust (here instantaneous).* Initially, therefore, the economy moves from point E_0 to point C. But at point C the goods market exhibits real expenditure in excess of real income. This puts pressure on prices to rise. As the price level rises this leads to a fall in real money balances. This reverses some of the capital outflow and so leads to an appreciation of the domestic currency (a fall in s). The economy accordingly moves up AM_1 from point C to point E_1. At E_1 not only are all markets in equilibrium, but purchasing power parity holds once more.

There are a number of characteristics of importance about this model:

(1)   The exchange rate initially **overshoots** its long-run result. Although there is an eventual depreciation of the domestic currency, it first depreciates by far too much, and then appreciates. This arises because the goods market is slow to adjust and the asset market is quick to adjust.

(2)   Because of the condition of purchasing power parity, $dp = ds = dm$ in moving from one equilibrium to the next. Geometrically it must be the case that $dp = ds$ because both E_0 and E_1 lie on the line GM, which has a slope of unity.

(3)   The speed of adjustment of prices towards the new equilibrium depends on the parameters, a, u, v and h. To see this we first note that

$$p = m - ky + ur^* - uv(s - \bar{s})$$
$$\bar{p} = m - ky + ur^*$$
$$\therefore \quad p = \bar{p} - uv(s - \bar{s})$$
$$\text{or} \quad s - \bar{s} = -\frac{1}{uv}(p - \bar{p})$$

Since $\dot{p} = a(e - y)$ then $0 = a(\bar{e} - y)$ and $\bar{e} = cy + g + h(\bar{s} - \bar{p})$. Subtracting we get

$$\dot{p} = a(e - \bar{e})$$
$$= a[h(s - \bar{s}) - h(p - \bar{p})]$$
$$= a\left[-\frac{h}{uv}(p - \bar{p}) - h(p - \bar{p})\right]$$

or

(13.5) $$\dot{p} = -ah\left(\frac{1}{uv} + 1\right)(p - \bar{p})$$

Which is a first-order autonomous homogeneous differential equation.

(4)   The model assumes perfect capital mobility. The domestic interest rate diverges from the foreign interest rate only to the extent of an expected change in the exchange rate. At equilibrium points E_0 and E_1, there is no expected change in the exchange rate and so the domestic rate of interest is equal to the foreign rate of interest. Since the foreign rate of interest is constant throughout, then *in the long run* there is no change in the domestic rate of interest. Although there is an initial fall in the rate of interest in response to the increase in the money supply, as prices begin to rise, real money balances fall and the rate of interest gradually returns to its former level. In other words, $r = r^*$ at point E_0 *and* point E_1.

Example 13.1, Model 13.1

We can explore the model by means of a numerical example. Namely

$$e = 0.8y + 4 + 0.01(s - p)$$
$$\dot{p} = 0.1(e - y)$$
$$m_d = p + 0.5y - 0.5r$$
$$m_s = m_d = 105$$
$$r = r^* + \dot{s}^e$$
$$\dot{s}^e = 0.2(\bar{s} - s)$$
$$y = 20, \qquad r^* = 10$$

This gives the GM line through the origin with unit slope and the AM line of $p = 110 - 0.1s$. The initial equilibrium, E_0, is therefore $\bar{p} = 100$ and $\bar{s} = 100$. A rise in the money supply from $m_0 = 105$ to $m_1 = 110$ shifts the AM line from AM_0 to AM_1 (with formula $p = 115.5 - 0.1s$), and new equilibrium, E_1, with $\bar{p} = 105$ and $\bar{s} = 105$, as shown in figure 13.3. The domestic currency initially depreciates from $\bar{s} = 100$ to $s_2 = 155$.

The adjustment coefficient for this model is

$$\lambda = ah\left(\frac{1}{uv} + 1\right) = 0.011$$

We have already shown that

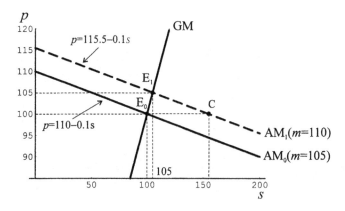

$$\dot{p} = -ah\left(\frac{1}{uv} + 1\right)(p - \bar{p})$$

$$= -\lambda(p - \bar{p})$$

This has the general solution

$$p(t) = \bar{p} + (p_0 - \bar{p})e^{-\lambda t}$$

For the numerical model $p_0 = 100, \bar{p} = 105$ and $\lambda = 0.011$. Hence

$$p(t) = 105 - 5e^{-0.011t}$$

Furthermore (see exercise 1)

$$s(t) = \bar{s} + (s_0 - \bar{s})e^{-\lambda t}$$

$$= 105 + 50e^{-0.011t}$$

and consequently both the price level and the exchange rate have the same adjustment coefficient. However, care must be exercised in interpreting these dynamic forces. What they represent is the movement along AM_1 from point C to equilibrium point E_1, in other words, the price level is rising from $p = 100$ to $p = 105$ while the domestic currency is *appreciating* from $s = 155$ to $s = 105$. The final result, however, is a depreciation of the domestic currency.

We can demonstrate that the trajectory is along AM_1 by eliminating $e^{-0.011t}$ in both $p(t)$ and $s(t)$. Thus

$$\frac{p(t) - 105}{-5} = \frac{s(t) - 105}{50}$$

i.e. $p(t) = 115.5 - 0.1s(t)$

which is the equation for AM_1.

13.2 The Dornbusch model

Having discussed a simplified version of the Dornbusch model we can now turn to his original formulation, shown in table 13.2. Although only one equation is

Table 13.2 Model 13.2

Goods market	e = total expenditure
$e = cy - dr + g + h(s - p)$ $0 < c < 1, d > 0, h > 0$	y = real income (exogenous)
$\dot{p} = a(e - y)$ $a > 0$	g = government spending
	s = spot exchange rate
	p = domestic price level
	$\dot{p}$ = inflation rate (since $p = \ln P$)
Money market	m_d = demand for money
$m_d = p + ky - ur$ $k > 0, u > 0$	r = domestic interest rate
$m_s = m_d = m$	m_s = supply of money
	m = exogenous money balances
International asset market	r^* = interest rate abroad
$r = r^* + \dot{s}^e$	$\dot{s}^e$ = change in expected spot rate
$\dot{s}^e = v(\bar{s} - s)$ $v > 0$	(expected depreciation/appreciation)
	$\bar{s}$ = purchasing power parity rate
	(equilibrium rate)

different, this does add a significant complication. The change is to the expenditure function, which now assumes that investment (a component of expenditure) is inversely related to the rate of interest; hence a component $-dr$ ($d > 0$) is added to the expenditure function. This has the immediate implication that the goods market and the asset market are interdependent, and this interdependence arises through the rate of interest.

The asset market line remains unaffected and therefore can be expressed as before, i.e., the AM line is

(13.6)
$$m = p + ky - u[r^* + v(\bar{s} - s)]$$
$$\text{i.e.}\quad p = (m - ky + ur^* + uv\bar{s}) - uvs$$

However, the goods market line, GM, now takes the form

(13.7)
$$p = \left\{ -\left[\frac{(1 - c) + (dk/u)}{h + (d/u)} \right] y + \left[\frac{g + (dm/u)}{h + (d/u)} \right] \right\} + \frac{hs}{h + (d/u)}$$

Notice in particular that the slope of the GM line (where p is on the vertical axis and s on the horizontal axis) is now

(13.8)
$$\text{slope GM} = \frac{h}{h + (d/u)} = \frac{1}{1 + (d/uh)} < 1$$

since d, v and h are all positive. It is also still the case that below the GM line the goods market has expenditure in excess of income, and so there is pressure on prices to rise. Above the GM line, expenditure is less than income, and there is pressure on prices to fall. The situation is illustrated in figure 13.4. In this figure we have both markets in equilibrium at point E, which in this instance is both a short-run equilibrium and a long-run equilibrium. It is a short-run equilibrium because the solution lies at the intersection of GM and AM, but it is also a long-run equilibrium because this also satisfies the purchasing power parity condition, which is given by the 45°-line, and denoted PPP. It is no longer the case, therefore, that the GM line coincides with the 45°-line.

Now consider a monetary expansion once again. This shifts the AM line to the right, as before. Since we have retained the assumption of an instantaneously adjusting asset market and a sluggish goods market adjustment, the economy

Figure 13.4.

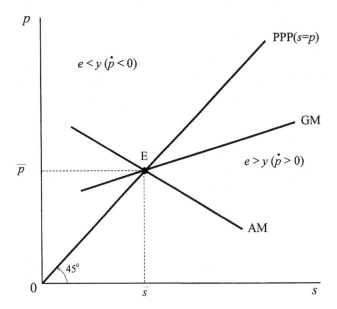

Figure 13.5.

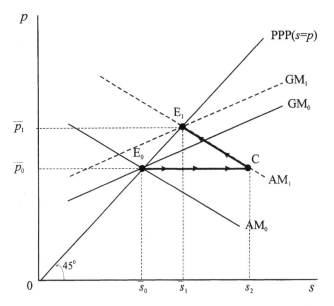

moves initially to point C on AM_1 in figure 13.5. This movement is because of
the immediate capital outflow. But now two responses come into play. At point C
expenditure is in excess of income and so there is pressure on prices to rise, so
moving the economy up AM_1. However, the rise in the nominal money supply has
initially led to a fall in the rate of interest. This fall in the rate of interest shifts the
GM curve to the left (it raises the intercept). One can think of the shift in the GM
line as follows. If the money supply rises, this puts pressure on domestic interest
rates to fall. This fall stimulates investment which increases expenditure. At the
existing exchange rate prices are now higher, and so the GM line has shifted up
(left) as a result of the impact on r from the rise in m. This result can be seen in

terms of equation (13.7). A rise in m leads to a rise in the intercept term, i.e., a shift up in the GM line. Expectations will change so long as the exchange rate differs from its purchasing power parity level. Hence, the system will come to a long-run equilibrium once the goods market line has shifted from GM_0 to GM_1, establishing a new equilibrium E_1 once again on the PPP line. Prices rise and the domestic currency depreciates. Because of our assumption about perfect capital mobility the rate of interest must return to its former level, which is equal to the foreign interest rate.

Consider the following numerical example.

Example 13.2, Model 13.2

$$e = 0.8y - 0.1r + 5 + 0.01(s - p)$$
$$\dot{p} = 0.1(e - y)$$
$$m_d = p + 0.5y - 0.5r$$
$$m_s = m_d = 105$$
$$r = r^* + \dot{s}^e$$
$$\dot{s}^e = 0.2(\bar{s} - s)$$
$$y = 20, \qquad r^* = 10$$

This gives the GM and AM lines as

$$\text{GM} \quad p = 95.2 + 0.0476s$$
$$\text{AM} \quad p = 110 - 0.1s$$

with equilibrium point E_0 given by $(\bar{s}_0, \bar{p}_0) = (100, 100)$, which satisfies the purchasing power parity condition, i.e., $s = p$. Furthermore, $r = r^* = 10$, as illustrated in figure 13.6.

Now consider an increase in the money supply from 105 to 110. As we indicated above, this shifts both the asset market line *and* the goods market line. The new lines are

$$\text{GM} \quad p = 100 + 0.0476s$$
$$\text{AM} \quad p = 115.5 - 0.1s$$

Figure 13.6.

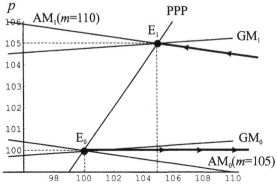

with the new equilibrium point, E_1, given by $(\bar{s}_1, \bar{p}_1) = (105, 105)$, which also satisfies the purchasing power parity condition and the condition that $r = r^* = 10$.

As in the previous model, comparing equilibrium point E_0 with E_1, we notice that

$$ds = dp = dm = 5$$

As we would expect with an unchanged AM line, point C has an exchange rate of $s = 155$ at the price level $p = 100$. Again there is overshooting of the exchange rate, first the domestic currency is depreciating and then appreciating, with an overall depreciation in the long run.

The fact that the interest rate affects the GM line must mean that although the system moves along AM, as in the previous model, it must do so at a different speed. We can establish this in the present example as follows. First we note (see exercise 3) that we can express the change in prices as a first-order autonomous homogeneous differential equation, i.e.

$$\dot{p} = -a\left(h + \frac{h}{uv} + \frac{d}{u}\right)(p - \bar{p})$$

This is consistent with our previous result. If $d = 0$, then this reduces to the same differential equation we considered in example 13.1. The adjustment coefficient

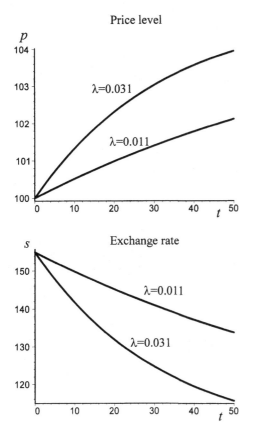

Price level

Figure 13.7.

is therefore

$$\lambda = a\left(h + \frac{h}{uv} + \frac{d}{u}\right) = 0.031$$

which is greater than 0.011 as we would expect.

In terms of the dynamics, the only essential difference is the adjustment coefficient λ. The price level and the exchange rate still adjust the same, since $e^{-\lambda t}$ applies to both, as in example 13.1, and so adjustment still takes place along a trajectory determined by the AM line. What makes the difference from example 13.1 is the change in the interest rate *during the adjustment period*. Although this moves the goods market line to the left, the change in the rate of interest speeds up the adjustment process. Eventually, however, the rate of interest returns to its former level of $r = r^* = 10$. This difference in the adjustment path for the exchange rate and the price level is illustrated in figure 13.7.

13.3 The Dornbusch model: capital immobility

The two versions of the Dornbusch model so far outlined assume that capital is perfectly mobile. This has the effect of leaving interest rates equal to the world level in long-run equilibrium. Furthermore, in the previous two models the exchange rate will always overshoot its long-run equilibrium when the money supply is changed. Allowing exchange rate immobility leads to the possibility of **undershooting** rather than overshooting.

To see this we need to change the relationship between the domestic interest rate and the foreign interest rate. In doing this we need to define the balance of payments. This is given by

(13.9)
$$bp = h(s - p) + b(r - r^* - \dot{s}^e) \quad h > 0, b > 0$$

Equation (13.9) says no more than the balance of payments is the sum of the current account and the net capital flow. The current account element is the same as that in the expenditure function,[5] while the second element denotes net capital flows which is responding to the difference between the two interest rates, adjusted for any expected change in the exchange rate. Perfect capital mobility implies $b = \infty$, while a value of b close to zero implies more extreme capital immobility. We need to make one further observation concerning this equation. Given a perfectly floating exchange rate, then the balance of payments is always in balance and so $bp = 0$. We retain the assumption about the expected change in the exchange rate, namely that it adjusts to the difference between the purchasing power parity level and the actual level. Since nothing else in the model is different, then there is no change in the goods market line. Only the specification of the asset market line is changed.

Consider example 13.1 again, which excludes any interest rate impact on the goods market, and so the GM line is the same as the purchasing power parity line, and is a 45°-line through the origin. The model is set out in detail below in table 13.3.

---

[5] Gärtner (1993) has a different coefficient on $(s - p)$ in the expenditure function and the balance of payments equation. There is no real need for this. Both arise from net exports, which occurs identically in both equations.

Table 13.3 Model 13.3

Goods market		e = total expenditure
$e = cy + g + h(s - p)$	$0 < c < 1, h > 0$	y = real income (exogenous)
$\dot{p} = a(e - y)$	$a > 0$	g = government spending
		s = spot exchange rate
		p = domestic price level
		$\dot{p}$ = inflation rate (since $p = \ln P$)
Money market		m_d = demand for money
$m_d = p + ky - ur$	$k > 0, u > 0$	r = domestic interest rate
$m_s = m_d = m$		m_s = supply of money
		m = exogenous money balances
International asset market		bp = balance of payments
$bp = h(s - p) + b(r - r^* - \dot{s}^e)$	$h > 0, b > 0$	r^* = interest rate abroad
$\dot{s}^e = v(\bar{s} - s)$	$v > 0$	$\dot{s}^e$ = change in expected spot rate
		(expected depreciation/appreciation)
		$\bar{s}$ = purchasing power parity rate
		(equilibrium rate)

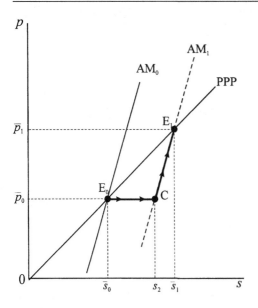

Figure 13.8.

As we have just indicated, the essential change is to the asset market line. This now takes the form

$$p = \frac{m - ky + ur^*}{1 - (uh/b)} + \frac{uv\bar{s}}{1 - (uh/b)} - \frac{[uv + (uh/b)]s}{1 - (uh/b)} \tag{13.10}$$

Notice that this is consistent with model 13.1. If $b \to \infty$ then this equation reduces to the asset market equation of section 13.1. Of particular importance in this model is the slope of the asset market line, which is

$$\text{slope of AM} = -\frac{uv + (uh/b)}{1 - (uh/b)} \tag{13.11}$$

A very high value of b, a high degree of capital mobility, will mean the typical negatively sloped asset market line, with analysis identical to that in section 13.1. However, with a very low degree of capital mobility, a value of b close to zero, can mean a positively sloped asset market line. The situation is illustrated in figure 13.8.

A rise in the money supply will shift the asset market line to the right, from AM_0 to AM_1, and the equilibrium will move from E_0 to E_1 on the goods market line, which coincides with the purchasing power parity condition. The movement of the economy now, however, is quite different. Although the trajectory is still along the new asset market line, with sticky prices initially the economy moves to point C on AM_1. Since again there is excess expenditure over income, prices will rise. The rise in the price level, although reducing real money balances and raising the rate of interest at home, will have only a small effect on capital inflows. In order, therefore, to maintain balance of payments equilibrium the domestic currency must also depreciate (s must rise). Hence, the economy moves along AM_1 from point C to point E_1. In this version of the model, therefore, the exchange rate **undershoots** its long-run equilibrium level. There is initially a rapid depreciation of the domestic currency (a movement from point E_0 to point C), followed by a further gradual depreciation in response to the price rise (a movement from point C to point E_1).

In this version of the model the rate of interest both before and after the change in the money supply will equal the interest rate abroad. Since purchasing power parity implies $s = p$, and since in long-run equilibrium $\dot{s}^e = 0$, then it follows that $r = r^*$ in long-run equilibrium.

Once again price movements and exchange rate movements can be expressed by the equations

(13.12)
$$p(t) = \bar{p} + (p_0 - \bar{p})e^{-\lambda t}$$
$$s(t) = \bar{s} + (s_0 - \bar{s})e^{-\lambda t}$$

but now

(13.13)
$$\lambda = ah \left(\frac{1 - (uh/b)}{uv + (uh/b)} + 1 \right)$$

Notice that for $b \to \infty$ this reduces to the adjustment coefficient of model 13.1 (see exercise 5 for a numerical example illustrating this model).

The analysis is very similar in the original Dornbusch model, but with capital immobility. This model, model 13.4, is presented in table 13.4.

Table 13.4 Model 13.4

Goods market	
$e = cy - dr + g + h(s - p)$ $0 < c < 1, d > 0, h > 0$	e = total expenditure
$\dot{p} = a(e - y)$ $a > 0$	y = real income (exogenous)
	g = government spending
	s = spot exchange rate
	p = domestic price level
	$\dot{p}$ = inflation rate (since $p = \ln P$)
Money market	m_d = demand for money
$m_d = p + ky - ur$ $k > 0, u > 0$	r = domestic interest rate
$m_s = m_d = m$	m_s = supply of money
	m = exogenous money balances
International asset market	bp = balance of payments
$bp = h(s - p) + b(r - r^* - \dot{s}^e)$ $h > 0, b > 0$	r^* = interest rate abroad
$\dot{s}^e = v(\bar{s} - s)$ $v > 0$	$\dot{s}^e$ = change in expected spot rate
	(expected depreciation/appreciation)
	$\bar{s}$ =purchasing power parity rate
	(equilibrium rate)

Figure 13.9.

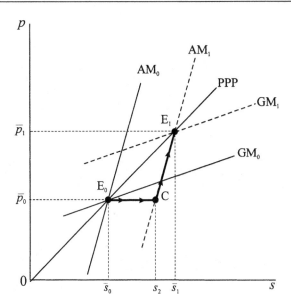

The situation is illustrated in figure 13.9. A rise in the money supply shifts both the asset market line and the goods market line. But because capital is very immobile, the exchange rate initially undershoots its long-run equilibrium value, $s_2 < \bar{s}_1$.

In this model we have (see exercise 6)

$$\dot{p} = -a \left[\frac{(h + dv)(1 - (uh/b))}{uv + (uh/b)} + h \right] (p - \bar{p}) \tag{13.14}$$

so prices and the exchange rate have the same adjustment coefficient

$$\lambda = a \left[\frac{(h + dv)(1 - (uh/b))}{uv + (uh/b)} + h \right] \tag{13.15}$$

This is consistent with all our previous results. If $d \to 0$ the model reduces to model 13.3; if $b \to \infty$ the model reduces to model 13.2; and if $d \to 0$ and $b \to \infty$ the model reduces to model 13.1.

13.4 The Dornbusch model under perfect foresight

One of the advantages of the Dornbusch model is that it readily lends itself to different specifications of exchange rate expectations. One such specification is perfect foresight. This model has a number of formal advantages. It can be shown that rational expectations is formally the same as expectations under perfect foresight, and since it is easier to handle models under the assumption of perfect foresight, then all the features of modelling rational expectations can be captured by this version. Second, the assumption that $\dot{s}^e = v(\bar{s} - s)$ with $v > 0$, is the same as the assumption of perfect foresight – so long as v is correctly chosen (see exercise 7).

Again we shall begin with the simplified Dornbusch model in which expenditure is independent of the rate of interest. The model is captured in model 13.5, and set out in table 13.5, where we have replaced the assumption about exchange

Table 13.5 Model 13.5

Goods market		e = total expenditure
$e = cy + g + h(s - p)$ $0 < c < 1, h > 0$		y = real income (exogenous)
$\dot{p} = a(e - y)$ $a > 0$		g = government spending
		s = spot exchange rate
		p = domestic price level
		$\dot{p}$ = inflation rate (since $p = \ln P$)
Money market		m_d = demand for money
$m_d = p + ky - ur$ $k > 0, u > 0$		r = domestic interest rate
$m_s = m_d = m$		m_s = supply of money
		m = exogenous money balances
International asset market		r^* = interest rate abroad
$r = r^* + \dot{s}^e$		$\dot{s}^e$ = change in expected spot rate
$\dot{s}^e = \dot{s}$		(expected depreciation/appreciation)
		$\dot{s}$ = change in spot exchange rate

rate expectations of model 13.1 with that of perfect foresight. This is the only difference from model 13.1, but it will be seen that it has significant implications for the dynamic behaviour of prices and exchange rates.

Since the formal algebraic manipulations are the same in deriving the goods market line and the asset market line, we shall be brief. There has been no change to the goods market, this remains the same as model 13.1, and under the assumption of purchasing power parity is a 45°-line through the origin. The dynamics of the goods market is still specified by the relationship

(13.16)
$$\dot{p} = a[h(s - p) - (1 - c)y + g] \qquad a > 0, h > 0, 0 < c < 1$$

The major change is in the foreign exchange market. Substituting the perfect foresight assumption into the interest rate condition, which retains the assumption of perfect capital mobility, and substituting this into the money market equilibrium, we obtain

$$m = p + ky - u(r^* + \dot{s})$$

(13.17)
$$\therefore \quad \dot{s} = \frac{1}{u}(p + ky - m) - r^*$$

We therefore have the following dynamic system

$$\dot{p} = a[g - (1 - c)y] - ahp + ahs$$

(13.18)
$$\dot{s} = \left[\frac{1}{u}(ky - m) - r^*\right] + \frac{1}{u}p$$

which is a differential equation system which can be solved for the two variables $p(t)$ and $s(t)$.

The critical point, stationary point, or equilibrium point of the system is where $\dot{p} = 0$ and $\dot{s} = 0$. Consider the second condition first. We immediately have no change in the exchange rate if

(13.19)
$$p = \bar{p} = m - ky + ur^*$$

which is a horizontal line in the phase plane, as shown in figure 13.10. Turning to the goods market, $\dot{p} = 0$ implies a straight line through the origin with slope 45°, as shown in figure 13.10.

Figure 13.10.

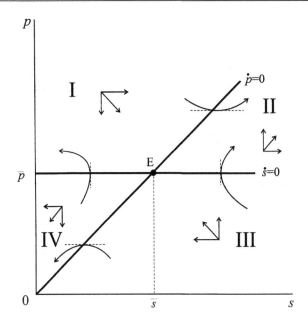

We are now in a position to consider the model's dynamics. Consider points either side of the $\dot{s} = 0$ line and $\dot{p} = 0$ line.

$$\dot{s} > 0 \text{ if } p > m - ky + ur^*$$
$$\dot{s} < 0 \text{ if } p < m - ky + ur^*$$

and

$$\dot{p} > 0 \text{ if } p < s + (g - (1 - c)y)/h$$
$$\dot{p} < 0 \text{ if } p > s + (g - (1 - c)y)/h$$

In other words, below the horizontal line the exchange rate is falling (the domestic currency is appreciating), while above the horizontal line the exchange rate is rising (the domestic currency is depreciating). On the other hand, below the goods market line prices are rising while above it prices are falling, consistent with our earlier analysis. The vector forces in figure 13.10 illustrate all this information.

What is quite clear from figure 13.10 is that we have a saddle point equilibrium. This can be established as follows. Consider the system in terms of deviations from equilibrium, which is particularly useful.

$$\dot{p} = a[h(s - p) - (1 - c)y + g]$$
$$0 = a[h(\bar{s} - \bar{p}) - (1 - c)y + g]$$
$$\therefore \quad \dot{p} = -ah(p - \bar{p}) + ah(s - \bar{s})$$

and

$$\dot{s} = \frac{1}{u}(p + ky - m) - r^*$$
$$0 = \frac{1}{u}(\bar{p} + ky - m) - r^*$$
$$\therefore \quad \dot{s} = \frac{1}{u}(p - \bar{p})$$

Hence, the system can be written in matrix form as follows.

(13.20)
$$\begin{bmatrix} \dot{p} \\ \dot{s} \end{bmatrix} = \begin{bmatrix} -ah & ah \\ 1/u & 0 \end{bmatrix} \begin{bmatrix} p - \bar{p} \\ s - \bar{s} \end{bmatrix}$$

Letting **A** denote the matrix of the system, then we immediately have

$$\mathbf{A} = \begin{bmatrix} -ah & ah \\ 1/u & 0 \end{bmatrix} \qquad \text{and} \qquad \det(\mathbf{A}) = \frac{-ah}{u} < 0$$

Since $\det(\mathbf{A}) < 0$ then the critical point, E in figure 13.10, is a saddle point.

What appears conspicuously absent from this analysis is any discussion of the asset market line, which was so prominent in model 13.1. But this is not the case. The saddle point solution along with the vector forces illustrated in figure 13.10 suggests there is one line through point E and passing through quadrants I and III which is a stable arm of the saddle. This is indeed the case. But more significantly, this stable arm is no more than the asset market line. We shall not prove this algebraically but rather show it is the case by means of a numerical example. Example 13.3 is a slight variant on example 13.1, where perfect foresight replaces the exchange rate expectation formation.

Example 13.3, Model 13.5

The model is

$$e = 0.8y + 4 + 0.01(s - p)$$
$$\dot{p} = 0.1(e - y)$$
$$m_d = p + 0.5y - 0.5r$$
$$m_s = m_d = 105$$
$$r = r^* + \dot{s}^e$$
$$\dot{s}^e = \dot{s}$$
$$y = 20, \qquad r^* = 10$$

We can express this in the form of deviations from equilibrium.

$$\dot{p} = -0.001(p - \bar{p}) + 0.001(s - \bar{s})$$
$$\dot{s} = 2(p - \bar{p})$$

The goods market line is the 45°-line through the origin as before. But this line simply denotes the condition $\dot{p} = 0$ while the horizontal line in figure 13.10 denotes the condition $\dot{s} = 0$. It is readily established that the equilibrium point is given by $(\bar{s}, \bar{p}) = (100, 100)$. In other words, the trajectories when passing over these lines do so with infinite slope and zero slope, respectively, in the phase plane. To establish the arms of the saddle point we need to consider the matrix of the system and its associated eigenvalues and eigenvectors.

The system can be written

$$\begin{bmatrix} \dot{p} \\ \dot{s} \end{bmatrix} = \begin{bmatrix} -0.001 & 0.001 \\ 2 & 0 \end{bmatrix} \begin{bmatrix} p - \bar{p} \\ s - \bar{s} \end{bmatrix}$$

with associated matrices

$$\mathbf{A} = \begin{bmatrix} -0.001 & 0.001 \\ 2 & 0 \end{bmatrix} \qquad \mathbf{A} - \lambda\mathbf{I} = \begin{bmatrix} -(0.001 + \lambda) & 0.001 \\ 2 & -\lambda \end{bmatrix}$$

Hence, $\det(\mathbf{A} - \lambda\mathbf{I}) = \lambda^2 + 0.001\lambda - 0.002 = 0$, with roots $r = 0.0442242$ and $s = -0.0452242$. The fact that the roots are of opposite sign verifies that the equilibrium point is a saddle point solution.

For $r = 0.0442242$ we have

$$(\mathbf{A} - r\mathbf{I})\mathbf{v}^r = \begin{bmatrix} -0.0452242 & 0.001 \\ 2 & 0.0442242 \end{bmatrix} \begin{bmatrix} p - \bar{p} \\ s - \bar{s} \end{bmatrix} = \begin{bmatrix} 0 \\ 0 \end{bmatrix}$$

This leads to the equation

$$-0.0452242(p - \bar{p}) + 0.001(s - \bar{s}) = 0$$

i.e. $p = 97.7888 + 0.0221s$

This is the line that would pass through the equivalent of quadrants II and IV in figure 13.10, and denotes the unstable arm of the saddle point. Or equivalently the eigenvector

$$\mathbf{v}^r = \begin{bmatrix} 1 \\ 45.2242 \end{bmatrix}$$

which emanates from point E_0. This solution is shown by the saddle path denoted SP^1 in figure 13.11. Similarly, using $s = -0.0452242$ we obtain

$$(\mathbf{A} - s\mathbf{I})\mathbf{v}^s = \begin{bmatrix} 0.0442242 & 0.001 \\ 2 & 0.0452242 \end{bmatrix} \begin{bmatrix} p - \bar{p} \\ s - \bar{s} \end{bmatrix} = \begin{bmatrix} 0 \\ 0 \end{bmatrix}$$

This leads to the equation

$$0.0442242(p - \bar{p}) + 0.001(s - \bar{s}) = 0$$

i.e. $p = 102.2612 - 0.0226s$

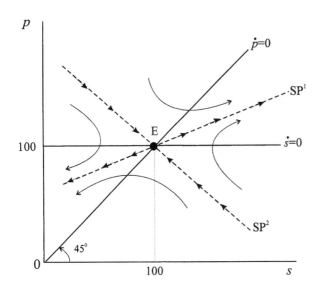

Figure 13.11.

Figure 13.12.

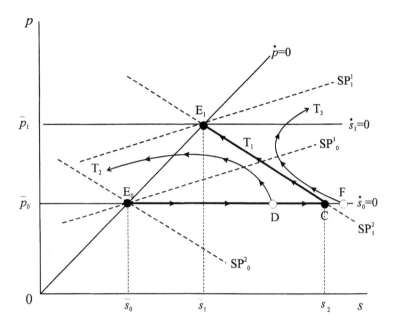

This is the line which would pass through the equivalent of quadrants I and III in figure 13.10, and denotes the stable arm of the saddle point, and is denoted SP^2 in figure 13.11. It leads to the eigenvector

$$\mathbf{v}^s = \begin{bmatrix} 1 \\ -44.2242 \end{bmatrix}$$

with the resulting general solution

$$\begin{bmatrix} p(t) \\ s(t) \end{bmatrix} = c_1 \begin{bmatrix} 1 \\ 45.2242 \end{bmatrix} e^{0.04422t} + c_2 \begin{bmatrix} 1 \\ -44.2242 \end{bmatrix} e^{-0.04522t}$$

The dynamics of the situation are revealed by considering an increase in the money supply. The initial equilibrium is at point E_0, with associated saddle paths SP_0^1 and SP_0^2. An increase in the money supply shifts the $\dot{s} = 0$ line up as shown in figure 13.12, from $\dot{s}_0 = 0$ to $\dot{s}_1 = 0$. There is a new equilibrium point E_1 with its associated saddle paths,[6] namely SP_1^1 and SP_1^2. But what is the trajectory of the economy in this situation? With perfect foresight the market knows that there is the saddle path through E_1, and so moves immediately to point C on this saddle path. At this stage prices have not moved and the domestic currency has depreciated to s_2. With excess demand in the goods market, the economy moves along the stable arm of the saddle path reaching point E_1 as prices begin to rise and the domestic currency appreciates, with the economy moving along trajectory T_1.

Unfortunately in this model, any lack of perfection will send the system away from point E_1. For example, if the market under-estimates the depreciation and the system moves to point D, then it will over time diverge and move along trajectory

---

[6] SP_1^2 has the equation $p = 107.3743 - 0.0226s$ for an increase in the money supply from $m = 105$ to $m = 110$.

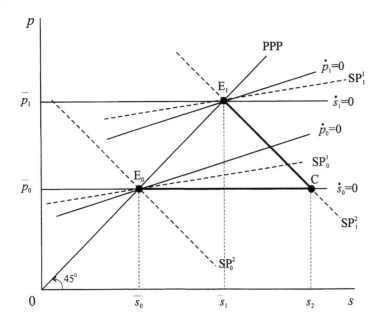

Figure 13.13.

T$_2$, with the economy heading into a major slump. Similarly, if the market over-adjusts and moves to point F, then the system will become explosive, with prices rising and the domestic currency depreciating, as shown by trajectory T$_3$.

Given all our previous analysis we can outline the original Dornbusch model under perfect foresight quite readily. All we need to recall is that the goods market line is positively sloped and with a slope less than unity, and that the 45°-line now indicates only purchasing power parity. The situation is captured in figure 13.13.

Again, an increase in the money supply moves the economy from point E$_0$ to point C as prices remain sticky. All adjustment initially falls on the exchange rate (and the rate of interest). There is a large depreciation of the domestic currency. As prices rise in response to excess demand in the goods market, the economy adjusts along the stable arm SP$_1^2$, eventually re-establishing purchasing power parity at the long-run equilibrium point E$_1$. Like the simpler version, any mis-judgement by the market will send the system away from point E$_1$ towards the unstable arm SP$_1^1$.

13.5 Announcement effects

This section has three objectives:

(i)   To present a discrete formulation of the Dornbusch model under perfect foresight.

(ii)   To deal with policy announcements which:

    (a) are actually carried out

    (b) are not carried out as promised.

(iii)   To provide some implications for price and exchange rate variability.

Table 13.6 Model 13.6

$$e_t = cy_t + g + h(s_t - p_t)$$
$$p_{t+1} - p_t = a(e_t - y)$$
$$m_t^d = p_t + ky - ur_t$$
$$m_t^d = m_t^s = m$$
$$r_t = r^* + (s_{t+1}^e - s_t^e)$$
$$s_{t+1}^e - s_t^e = s_{t+1} - s_t$$

We begin with a discrete version of the simple Dornbusch model under perfect foresight (model 13.6, table 13.6). All variables and parameters are as defined earlier in this chapter.

Define $\Delta p_{t+1} = p_{t+1} - p_t$ and $\Delta s_{t+1} = s_{t+1} - s_t$, then from the first two equations of table 13.6 we have

(13.21)
$$\Delta p_{t+1} = -ahp_t + ahs_t + a[g - (1 - c)y]$$

and from the asset market equations of table 13.6 we have

(13.22)
$$\Delta s_{t+1} = \frac{1}{u}p_t + \frac{1}{u}(ky - m - ur^*)$$

In equilibrium we have $\Delta p_{t+1} = \Delta s_{t+1} = 0$. Thus

$$0 = -ah\bar{p} + ah\bar{s} + a[g - (1 - c)y]$$
$$0 = \frac{1}{u}\bar{p} + \frac{1}{u}(ky - m - ur^*)$$

Hence, taking deviations from the equilibrium, we have

(13.23)
$$\Delta p_{t+1} = -ah(p_t - \bar{p}) + ah(s_t - \bar{s})$$
$$\Delta s_{t+1} = \frac{1}{u}(p_t - \bar{p})$$

Or in matrix notation

(13.24)
$$\begin{bmatrix} \Delta p_{t+1} \\ \Delta s_{t+1} \end{bmatrix} = \begin{bmatrix} -ah & ah \\ 1/u & 0 \end{bmatrix} \begin{bmatrix} p_t - \bar{p} \\ s_t - \bar{s} \end{bmatrix}$$

The system can be displayed in the form of a phase diagram, as shown in figure 13.14, where we once again illustrate the Dornbusch overshooting phenomenon. The vector forces are shown in relation to equilibrium point E_0.

It is clear from this result that the matrix of the system is identical with that of the continuous model. We shall use this fact in developing our numerical example. We shall now, therefore, pursue some of the properties and characteristics of this model by means of a numerical example, which follows closely that of example 13.3.

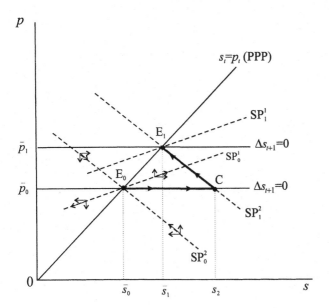

Example 13.4, Model 13.6

Our model is

$$e_t = 0.8y_t + 4 + 0.01(s_t - p_t)$$
$$p_{t+1} - p_t = 0.1(e_t - y)$$
$$m_t^d = p_t + 0.5y - 0.5r_t$$
$$m_t^d = m_t^s = 105$$
$$r_t = 10 + (s_{t+1}^e - s_t^e)$$
$$s_{t+1}^e - s_t^e = s_{t+1} - s_t$$

With $y = 20$ and setting $p_{t+1} = p_t = \bar{p}$ for all t and $s_{t+1} = s_t = \bar{s}$ for all t, then we readily establish the equilibrium as $(\bar{s}, \bar{p}) = (100, 100)$. Furthermore, the system is readily established to be

$$\begin{bmatrix} \Delta p_{t+1} \\ \Delta s_{t+1} \end{bmatrix} = \begin{bmatrix} -0.001 & 0.001 \\ 2 & 0 \end{bmatrix} \begin{bmatrix} p_t - 100 \\ s_t - 100 \end{bmatrix}$$

or

$$p_{t+1} = 0.999p_t + 0.001s_t$$
$$s_{t+1} = s_t + 2p_t - 200$$

Given p_0 and s_0, therefore, we can plot the path of p_t and s_t. Given these paths, we can also plot the path of r_t and e_t. All this can readily be accomplished by means of a spreadsheet.

In plotting trajectories, it is useful to establish the saddle paths. Since the matrix of the system is identical to that of the previous section, so are the saddle paths. The eigenvectors are $r = 0.0442242$ and $s = -0.0452242$. The two arms of the

Figure 13.15. *Note:*
Not to scale.

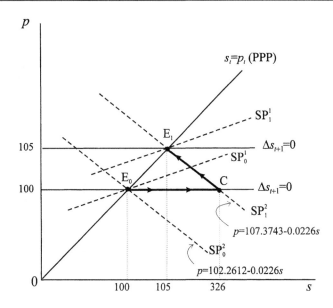

saddle point are

$$\text{SP}_0^1: \quad p = 97.788794 + 0.0221121s \quad \text{unstable arm}$$
$$\text{SP}_0^2: \quad p = 102.26121 - 0.0226121s \quad \text{stable arm}$$

for $m = 105$ and $E_0 = (100, 100)$, as shown in figure 13.15.

A rise in the money supply to $m = 110$ leads to a new long-run equilibrium point E_1, which is also a saddle point with arms

$$\text{SP}_1^1: \quad p = 102.67823 + 0.0221121s \quad \text{unstable arm}$$
$$\text{SP}_1^2: \quad p = 107.37427 - 0.0226121s \quad \text{stable arm}$$

If this were a totally unexpected change, then the domestic currency would depreciate sharply and the exchange rate would rise to

$$s = \frac{107.37427 - 100}{0.0226121} = 326.121$$

and will then appreciate as the economy moves along the asset market line given by SP_1^2 until point E_1 is reached, as shown in figure 13.15.

Now consider the implications of announcing a change in the money supply to take place in the future, say in one year's time. Market participants, having perfect foresight, will know two things. They will know that in the long run the price level and the exchange rate will increase by the same amount. Second, they will know that in the short run the domestic currency will sharply depreciate (since it will overshoot its long-run value), and will then begin to appreciate towards the long-run result. Given this knowledge transactors will attempt to move into real assets in order to preserve the value of their portfolio. Second, they will move out of domestic assets and into foreign assets. Although ideally this would take place just before the money supply is actually increased, in order to take advantage of

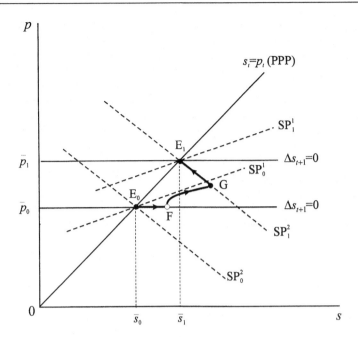

Figure 13.16.

the situation they would do it sooner. This line of reasoning will continue until the most sensible reaction is to move some funds immediately. This results in an immediate depreciation of the domestic currency. This moves the economy to the right, as shown in figure 13.16, but not as much as would have occurred with no announcement, i.e., the economy moves from point E_0 to point F. Prices have not yet changed. The dynamics is still governed by point E_0 because as yet the policy change has not taken place. Hence, the system will begin to diverge from E_0 towards the unstable arm SP_0^1. Given perfect foresight, the trajectory will coincide with the stable arm of the saddle point, namely SP_1^2 at the moment the policy change takes place, denoted by point G. Once this happens the economy will then move along this stable arm until point E_1 is reached in the long run.

We can establish such a trajectory with the help of our numerical example and a spreadsheet.[7] The situation is illustrated in figures 13.17 and 13.18. Figure 13.17 gives the main computations. Column (1) is simply the time period. Columns (2) and (3) are the price level and the exchange rate starting from a point such as F (i.e. a point to the right of E_0). In this example we have the point $(s,p) = (120, 100)$. The remaining computations are to establish the point where the trajectory cuts the asset market line (the line SP_1^2 of figure 13.16). First we compute points along the stable arm SP_1^2, as shown in columns (4) and (5), starting from the point $(s,p) = (100,326.121)$. We then compute, in column (6), the price level for each exchange rate given in column (3), but satisfying the formula

$$p_t = 107.37427 - 0.0226121s_t$$

This we have labelled SP[p(t)]. It is what the price would be on the stable arm of the saddle point through E_1. We then compute the difference between column (6)

---

[7] A more detailed explanation can be found in Shone (2001, section 8.6).

Figure 13.17.

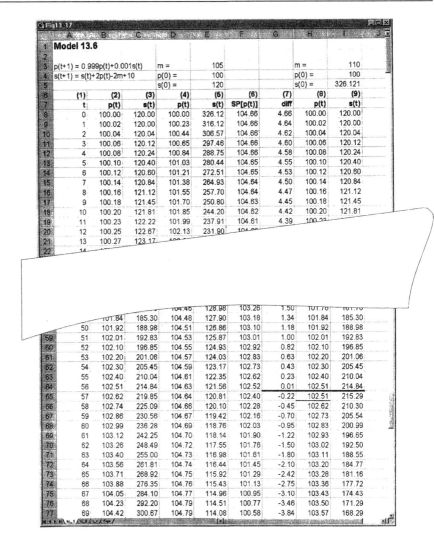

Figure 13.18.

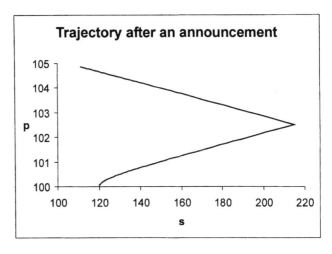

and column (2), to give column (7). When this difference is zero we have establish the point at which the economy begins to move along the stable arm of the saddle point associated with E_1. In other words, all the observations in columns (8) and (9) at or above where the difference column is positive are a copy of the observations in columns (2) and (3). After that point, shown by a bar across columns (8) and (9), we plot observations along the asset market line. We do this by first taking the price immediately above the bar and then using this to compute the corresponding point on SP_1^2. The remaining values in columns (8) and (9) then conform to the model with $m = 110$. Columns (8) and (9) constitute the observations for figure 13.18 for period 0 to 120.

This use of the spreadsheet allows us to consider different time periods of announcement. Columns (4) and (5) indicate the path of the economy where no announcement at all is made, and there is an unexpected increase in the money supply. This is the version first considered by Dornbusch. In terms of figure 13.19

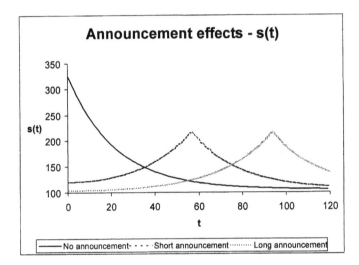

Figure 13.19.

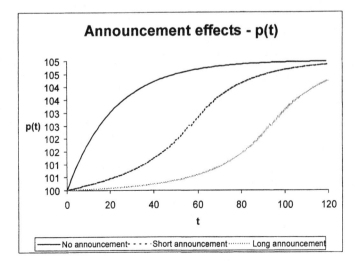

Table 13.7 Response periods

	Period ($s = 150$)	Period ($p = 102$)
No announcement	34	11
Short announcement	76	51
Long announcement	113	88

this gives the 'No announcement' path for the exchange rate and the price level, and is a plot of columns (5) and (4), respectively, of figure 13.17. A period that is relatively short in announcing government intentions will lead to a point like F, which is 'close to' the asset market line through point E_1. This is the trajectory computed in figure 13.17 and illustrated in figure 13.18. This leads to the path for the exchange rate and the price level marked 'Short announcement' in figure 13.19. A period of 'long announcement' will lead to a point F that is closer to point E_0. The computations of this are not given here, but follow exactly the same reasoning. This leads to the path for the exchange rate and the price level denoted 'Long announcement' in figure 13.19.

But we can go further in our analysis with this numerical example. Suppose we take a point of reference for the exchange rate, say $s = 150$. We now ask the question for each of these announcements, how long does it take the system to reach $s = 150$, when moving along the asset market line?[8] Similarly, how long does it take the exchange rate to reach $s = 150$ once the policy has actually been implemented? Similarly, how long does it take the price level to reach $p = 102$? The results are tabulated as shown in table 13.7.

What we observe from figure 13.19 and from table 13.7 is three important observations. First, the exchange rate varies less the longer the time period of the announcement. Second, the greater the time period for the announcement, the longer it takes for the exchange rate and the price level to reach the new equilibrium. Thus, *increasing the announcement period increases the adjustment period*. Policy-makers therefore need to weigh these two possibilities. Third, the price level gradually approaches its new level, with just a minor kink in the case of a short and long announcement. In other words, price changes do not show the same dramatic changes that can occur with the exchange rate.

But there is a further problem to consider. Policy-makers are often known to renege on their announcement. They may announce they will increase the money supply, but when the time comes, they decide not to do so! Does this in any way change the results? The situation is illustrated in figure 13.20. On the announcement of an increase in the money supply the economy immediately moves to point F in anticipation of the changes that are expected. As before, the economy then moves along the trajectory between F and G, which is dominated by the saddle path SP_0^1 which passes through equilibrium point E_0. At point G, the moment when the change should take place, the government announces that it does not intend to change the money supply after all! Given perfect foresight, and given instantaneous adjustment in the asset market, the economy will move immediately

---

[8] We cannot ask the time for it to reach point E_1, since this is at infinity. However, any *common* point of reference will do for this comparison.

Figure 13.20.

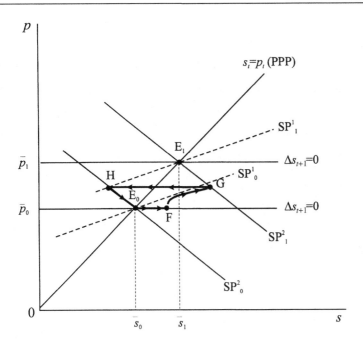

from point G to point H on SP_0^2 (since SP_0^2 is the asset market line through the original equilibrium point E_0). Since this is a stable arm of the saddle point E_0, the economy will accordingly move down this line approaching E_0 in the limit. Hence, the economy will have a trajectory E_0-F-G-H-E_0. Prices no longer show a gradual movement to the new equilibrium, but on the contrary rise and fall. But even more dramatic is the movement in the exchange rate.

We can illustrate the movement in prices and the exchange rate using the same technique we developed in relation to figure 13.19. We consider a short announcement period which positions F at $(s, p) = (100, 120)$, as before. Also as before, the economy moves along the same trajectory until point G is reached. Now, however, the situation changes, as shown in figure 13.21.[9] Realising the government has reneged on their decision, market participants move money back into the economy, leading to a sharp appreciation of the domestic currency. The economy is now above the PPP line, and income is in excess of expenditure. This leads to a gradual fall in prices, which in turn leads to a depreciation of the currency. The conclusion we come to, therefore, is that although policy announcements lead to less variation in prices and exchange rates, reneging on such policy announcements leads to more variation in prices and exchange rates than would have occurred without any such announcement.

13.6 Resource discovery and the exchange rate

The analysis so far presented, with some modification, allows us to consider some of the implications of a major resource discovery like North Sea Oil. We assume that

---

[9] Although in this numerical example the exchange rate becomes negative, which is not possible, the general path of the exchange rate, however, is as displayed in the figure.

Figure 13.21.

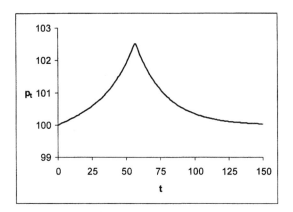

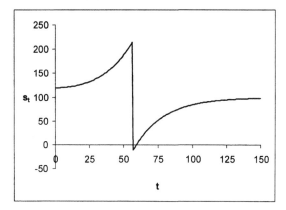

the discovery leads to an increase in wealth and hence to an increase in permanent income. We capture this effect by adding a term $f x_p (f > 0)$ to the expenditure equation, where x_p denotes the permanent income stream from the new wealth and f is a positive coefficient. Thus, our expenditure equation now takes the form

(13.25) $e = cy + g + h(s - p) + f x_p$

On the other hand, x is the current income from oil that adds additional demand for money balances, which is captured by a term $j x (j > 0)$ in the demand for money equation. But we need to make an additional change to the demand for money equation. To understand this, return to prices and exchange rates in unlogged form. We assume that the domestic price level (the RPI) is a weighted average of domestically produced goods, P, and imported goods, $P_f = SP^*$, i.e.

(13.26) $Q = P^\alpha (SP^*)^{1-\alpha}$

taking natural logarithms and denoting these by lower case letters, then

(13.27) $q = \alpha p + (1 - \alpha)(s + p^*)$

But if we set $P^* = 1$, then $p^* = 0$, hence

(13.28) $q = \alpha p + (1 - \alpha)s$

Table 13.8 Model 13.7

Goods market	e = total expenditure
$e = cy + g + h(s - p) + f x_p$	y = real income (exogenous)
$0 < c < 1, h > 0, f > 0$	g = government spending
$\dot{p} = a(e - y)$	s = spot exchange rate
	p = price of domestic goods
	$\dot{p}$ = inflation rate (since $p = \ln P$)
	m_d = demand for money
Money market	m_s = supply of money
$m_d = q + ky - ur + jx \quad k > 0, u > 0, j > 0$	r = domestic interest rate
$q = \alpha p + (1 - \alpha)s \quad 0 < \alpha < 1$	m = exogenous money balances
	q = domestic price level
	α = weight of domestic goods in q
International asset market	r^* = interest rate abroad
$r = r^* + \dot{s}^e$	$\dot{s}^e$ = change in expected spot rate
$\dot{s}^e = \dot{s}$	(expected depreciation/appreciation)
	$\dot{s}$ = change in spot exchange rate

Finally, we deflate money balances by the domestic price level Q. Thus the demand for money equation becomes

$$m_d = q + ky - ur + jx \tag{13.29}$$

where $q = \alpha p + (1 - \alpha)s$.

The complete model (model 13.7), under the assumption of perfect foresight and no interest rate effect on expenditure, is given in table 13.8. Carrying out the same manipulations as for model 13.5 we obtain

$$\dot{p} = a[g - (1 - c)y + f x_p] - ahp + ahs$$
$$\dot{s} = \left(\frac{\alpha}{u}\right)p + \left(\frac{1 - \alpha}{u}\right)s + \left[\frac{ky + jx - m}{u} - r^*\right] \tag{13.30}$$

In equilibrium $\dot{p} = 0$ and $\dot{s} = 0$, hence

$$0 = a[g - (1 - c)y + f x_p] - ah\bar{p} + ah\bar{s}$$
$$0 = \left(\frac{\alpha}{u}\right)\bar{p} + \left(\frac{1 - \alpha}{u}\right)\bar{s} + \left[\frac{ky + jx - m}{u} - r^*\right]$$

So taking deviations from the equilibrium we have

$$\dot{p} = -ah(p - \bar{p}) + ah(s - \bar{s})$$
$$\dot{s} = \left(\frac{\alpha}{u}\right)(p - \bar{p}) + \left(\frac{1 - \alpha}{u}\right)(s - \bar{s}) \tag{13.31}$$

Or in matrix notation

$$\begin{bmatrix} \dot{p} \\ \dot{s} \end{bmatrix} = \begin{bmatrix} -ah & ah \\ \dfrac{\alpha}{u} & \dfrac{1 - \alpha}{u} \end{bmatrix} \begin{bmatrix} p - \bar{p} \\ s - \bar{s} \end{bmatrix} \tag{13.32}$$

Hence, the matrix of this system is

$$\mathbf{A} = \begin{bmatrix} -ah & ah \\ \dfrac{\alpha}{u} & \dfrac{1 - \alpha}{u} \end{bmatrix}$$

Figure 13.22.

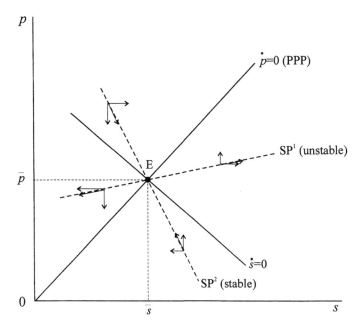

with $\det(\mathbf{A}) = -ah/u < 0$. Since $\det(\mathbf{A})$ is negative the equilibrium point is a saddle point.

From the conditions $\dot p = 0$ and $\dot s = 0$ given above, we can solve for $\bar p$ and $\bar s$ using Cramer's rule. These are

(13.33)

$$\bar p = m - \left[\frac{(1-c)(1-\alpha)}{h} + k\right]y + \frac{(1-\alpha)g}{h} + \frac{f(1-\alpha)x_p}{h} + ur^* - jx$$

$$\bar s = m + \left[\frac{\alpha(1-c)}{h} - k\right]y - \frac{\alpha g}{h} + \frac{\alpha f x_p}{h} + ur^* - jx$$

It is apparent, therefore, that the discovery of a major resource leading to terms x_p and x will influence the equilibrium price and exchange rate.[10] To see this more clearly we need to consider the model in more detail.

To do this we need to consider the equilibrium lines associated with $\dot p = 0$ and $\dot s = 0$. With some algebraic manipulation these are

(13.34)

$$p = s + \left[\frac{g - (1-c)y + f x_p}{h}\right] \qquad \text{for } \dot p = 0$$

$$p = \left(\frac{m - ky - jx + ur^*}{\alpha}\right) - \left(\frac{1-\alpha}{\alpha}\right)s \qquad \text{for } \dot s = 0$$

Consequently, the goods market line, the line associated with $\dot p = 0$, is a 45°-line. The second equilibrium line, that associated with $\dot s = 0$, is negatively sloped. Initially we assume that purchasing power parity is satisfied. This is best considered as the situation before any resource is discovered. Hence, the goods market line

---

[10] These results are consistent with those of model 13.5. If $\alpha = 1$ and $x = x_p = 0$, then we have the same equilibrium results as model 13.5.

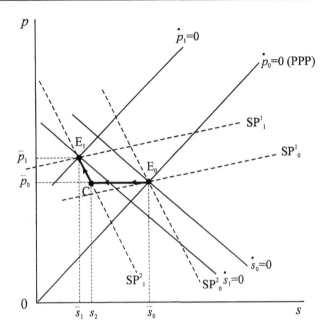

Figure 13.23.

passes through the origin, as shown in figure 13.22. This figure also shows the vector forces and the saddle paths associated with the equilibrium point E, and denoted SP^1 and SP^2. Note in particular that SP^2 denotes the asset market equilibrium. In this model, as in previous models, we assume asset markets are always clearing while the goods market takes time.

Now consider the discovery of a natural resource, such as oil, as shown in figure 13.23. The change in x_p (from zero to some positive amount) shifts the $\dot{p} = 0$ line *up* (i.e. leads to a rise in the intercept) to $\dot{p}_1 = 0$. But this will generate an income stream and so raise x (from zero to some positive amount). This in turn will shift the $\dot{s} = 0$ line left (i.e. will reduce the intercept) to $\dot{s}_1 = 0$. The economy will move from equilibrium point E_0 to equilibrium point E_1. But what trajectory will such an economy take? Initially prices do not change, and so the economy moves horizontally from point E_0 to point C, point C being on the new saddle path SP_1^2 through E_1. The domestic currency has accordingly appreciated taking the full impact of the adjustment in the short run. Point C is on the new asset market line. The resulting increase in permanent income raises consumers' expenditure. Since we have full employment this results in excess demand and hence to a rise in the price level. Accordingly the economy moves up the new asset market line from point C to point E_1. In this example there is no overshooting. This occurs, however, only where the goods market impact is greater than the money market impact.

To see this consider figure 13.24, which shows the situation where the money market impact exceeds that of the goods market. Again the economy moves horizontally from point E_0 to point C on SP_1^2, but then moves *down* the new asset market line until point E_1 is reached. This is because the significant effect of the current income stream on the demand for money leads to a significant rise in the rate of interest. In order to maintain the condition $r = r^* + \dot{s}^e$, the domestic

Figure 13.24.

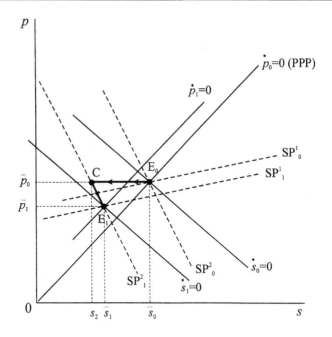

currency must depreciate, moving the economy along the path C to E_1 on SP_1^2. Although prices gradually fall, the home currency first appreciates, overshooting its long-run equilibrium value, and then depreciates but leading to an eventual appreciation of the exchange rate. The difference in the two results is determined by the *rate of resource depletion*. In figure 13.23 the rate of depletion is slow and so the permanent income stream outweighs the current income from the oil extraction. Figure 13.24, however, indicates that resource depletion is quick and there is a relatively large current income from resource sales. In either case, the discovery of a resource, although having ambiguous results on the price level, does lead to an appreciation of the home currency, with the possibility of overshooting the quicker the resource depletion.

Given the discovery of North Sea Oil, we may hypothesise that market participants with perfect foresight would know that the domestic currency would appreciate in the long run and would act accordingly. The situation is similar to the analysis in the previous section, and the result is shown in figure 13.25. Because of the anticipated appreciation, the economy moves to point F. We can think of this as the situation the moment the discovery is made. The economy then moves along the trajectory F to G, which is governed by the unstable arm SP_1^1, and where point G is determined by the point in time that the oil comes on-stream. The economy then moves along the asset market line, SP_1^2, from point G to point E_1.

13.7   The monetarist model

An early flex-price model of exchange rate determination was the simple monetarist model. The model is set out in table 13.9. All variables are in natural logarithms except for interest rates.[11]

---

[11] Since s is ln S, then $\dot{s}$ is the percentage change in the exchange rate.

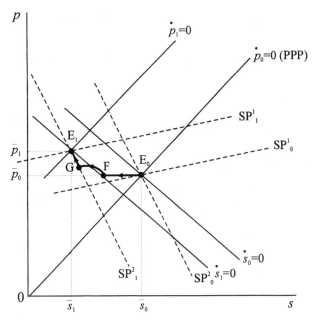

Figure 13.25.

Table 13.9 Monetarist model

$m - p = ky - ur$ $k > 0, u > 0$	m = nominal money supply
$r = r^* + \dot{s}^e$	y = real income
$p = s + p^*$	r = nominal interest rate at home
$\dot{s}^e = \dot{s}$	r^* = nominal interest rate abroad
	p = domestic price level
	p^* = foreign price level
	s = exchange rate

The first equation is no more than real money balances is equal to real demand for money balances, where we assume a simple demand for money equation. The second equation is the interest parity condition under perfect capital mobility, while the third equation is purchasing power parity. The final equation is rational expectations under perfect foresight. Real income is assumed constant at the natural level. Also m, r^* and p^* are assumed constant. Substituting, we have

$$m - s - p^* = ky - u(r^* + \dot{s}^e)$$

or

$$\dot{s} = \left(\frac{k}{u}\right)y - r^* - \frac{1}{u}(m - p^*) + \left(\frac{1}{u}\right)s \tag{13.35}$$

which is a first-order differential equation.

The dynamics of the model are illustrated in figure 13.26. Since m, y, r^* and p^* are constant, then so is

$$\left(\frac{k}{u}\right)y - r^* - \frac{1}{u}(m - p^*)$$

which is the intercept on the vertical axis. The slope is $1/u$. We have labelled the line A to denote asset market. The fixed point is readily established by setting

Figure 13.26.

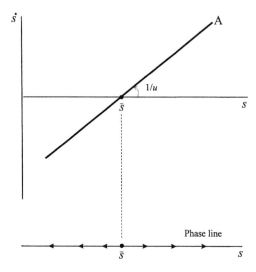

Figure 13.27.

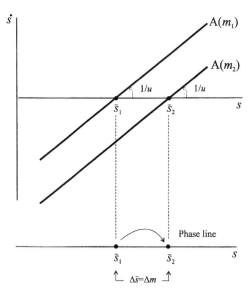

$\dot{s} = 0$, hence

$$0 = \left(\frac{k}{u}\right) y - r^* - \frac{1}{u}(m - p^*) + \left(\frac{1}{u}\right)\bar{s}$$

or

(13.36) $\bar{s} = (m - p^*) + ur^* - ky$

Since the slope of the asset market line is positive, the system is dynamically unstable. Also we have a linear differential equation, so the system is *globally* unstable.

To solve differential equation (13.35) we normally require an initial condition, say $s(0) = s_0$. But any $s_0 < \bar{s}$ leads the system to a continual appreciation of the home currency (fall in s); while for $s_0 > \bar{s}$ the home currency continually depreciates (s rises). Since in this rational expectations model market participants have perfect foresight, then s jumps immediately to $\bar{s}$.

The effect of a rise in nominal money balances is shown in figure 13.27. The asset market line shifts down (by $(1/u)\Delta m$) and the new equilibrium exchange rate increases to $\bar{s}_2$. From equation (13.36) it immediately follows that $\Delta \bar{s} = \Delta m$, i.e., the domestic currency depreciates by exactly the same percentage as the rise in nominal money balances. Under perfect foresight, expected depreciation and actual depreciation are identical and the system immediately jumps from $\bar{s}_1$ to $\bar{s}_2$.

Exercises

1. For the model outlined in table 13.1 we have the result

   $$p(t) = \bar{p} + (p_0 - \bar{p})e^{-\lambda t}$$

   (i) Show that

   $$s(t) = \bar{s} + (s_0 - \bar{s})e^{-\lambda t}$$

   where s_0 is the initial exchange rate after the shock, but associated with the price level p_0.

   (ii) In terms of example 13.1, show that point C is represented by

   $$(s,p) = (155, 100) \text{ and that}$$
   $$s(t) = 105 + 50e^{-0.011t}$$

   (iii) Plot on the same graph $p(t)$ and $s(t)$ for $\lambda = 0.011$ and $\lambda = 0.02$.

2. Given the model in section 13.1 (example 13.1), establish the comparative static and dynamics of a rise in the *foreign* interest rate from $r^* = 10$ to $r^* = 12$.

3. For the Dornbusch model given in table 13.2 (model 13.2), show that

   (i) $\quad s - \bar{s} = -\dfrac{1}{uv}(p - \bar{p})$

   (ii) hence show

   $$\dot{p} = -a\left(h + \frac{h}{uv} + \frac{d}{u}\right)(p - \bar{p})$$

   and

   $$\lambda = a\left(h + \frac{h}{uv} + \frac{d}{u}\right)$$

4. Consider the following discrete version of the Dornbusch model of table 13.2

   $$e_t = 0.8y - 0.1r_t + 5 + 0.01(s_t - p_t)$$
   $$p_{t+1} - p_t = 0.2(e_t - y)$$
   $$m_t^d = p_t + 0.5y - 0.25r_t$$
   $$m_t^d = m_t^s = 105$$
   $$r_t = r^* + s_{t+1}^e - s_t^e$$

$$s^e_{t+1} - s^e_t = 0.25(\bar{s} - s_t)$$

$$y = 20 \quad r^* = 10$$

(i) Derive an expression for the GM line and the AM line of the form $p_t = \phi(s_t)$ and establish the fixed point of the model.

(ii) Set up the model on a spreadsheet and establish its fixed point, starting from the initial value $p_t = 100$.

(iii) Let m_s rise from 105 to 110 establish the new equilibrium and demonstrate that $dm_t = ds_t = dp_t$.

5.   Given the numerical model based on table 13.3

$$e = 0.8y + 4 + 0.01(s - p)$$

$$\dot{p} = 0.2(e - y)$$

$$m_d = p + 0.5y - 0.5r$$

$$m_d = m_s = 105$$

$$bp = 0.01(s - p) + b(r - r^* - \dot{s}^e)$$

$$\dot{s}^e = 0.2(\bar{s} - s)$$

$$y = 20 \quad r^* = 10$$

(i) If $b = 0.0045$ establish that the initial equilibrium is $(s,p) = (100,100)$.

(ii) For a rise in the money supply to $m_s = 110$, establish that point C is represented by $(s,p) = (104.54128, 100)$.

(iii) Confirm that the new equilibrium satisfies $dp = ds = dm$.

6.   For the model in table 13.4

(i) Show that

$$\dot{p} = -a\left[\frac{(h + dv)(1 - (uh/b))}{uv + (uh/b)} + h\right](p - \bar{p})$$

and

$$\lambda = a\left[\frac{(h + dv)(1 - (uh/b))}{uv + (uh/b)} + h\right]$$

(ii) If $d \to 0$ then $\dot{p}$ and λ reduce to the values of model 13.3 (table 13.3).

(iii) If $b \to \infty$ then $\dot{p}$ and λ reduce to the values of model 13.2 (table 13.2).

(iv) If $d \to 0$ and $b \to \infty$ then $\dot{p}$ and λ reduce to the values of model 13.1 (table 13.1).

7.   A numerical version of model 13.4 (table 13.4) is

$$e = 0.8y - 0.1r + 5 + 0.01(s - p)$$

$$\dot{p} = 0.1(e - y)$$

$$m_d = p + 0.5y - 0.5r$$

$$m_d = m_s = 105$$

$$bp = 0.01(s - p) + 0.004(r - r^* - \dot{s}^e)$$

$\dot{s}^e = 0.2(\bar{s} - s)$

$y = 20 \quad r^* = 10$

(i) Establish the following at the initial equilibrium.
   (a) Equilibrium is $(s,p) = (100,100)$.
   (b) GM$_0$: $p = 95.238095 + 0.0476190s$
   (c) AM$_0$: $p = -440 + 5.4s$
(ii) Let m_s rise to 110. Find point C on AM$_1$ and establish that for the new equilibrium $dm = ds = dp$.

8.   Using the model in example 13.3, and assuming $r^* = 18$, all other parameters the same, then establish that

   (i) the initial equilibrium is $(s,p) = (104,104)$
   (ii) the characteristic roots are $r = 0.04422415$ and $s = -0.0452242$
   (iii) the saddle path equations are:
      (a) unstable arm: $p = 101.70034 + 0.02211208s$
      (b) stable arm: $p = 106.35166 - 0.0226121s$
   (iv) for a rise in the money supply to 110 the intercepts of the saddle paths only alter to 106.58978 for the unstable arm and to 111.46472 for the stable arm, respectively.

9.   In the model outlined in table 13.8 suppose we have the following numerical version of the model

$e = 0.8y + 4 + 0.01(s - p) + 2x_p$

$\dot{p} = 0.1(e - y)$

$m = q + 0.5y - 0.5r + x$

$q = \alpha p + (1 - \alpha)s$

$m_d = m_s = 105$

$r = r^* + \dot{s}^e$

$\dot{s}^e = \dot{s}$

$y = 20 \quad r^* = 10$

   (i) If initially $x_p = x = 0$ and $\alpha = 0.8$, show that the initial equilibrium, E_0, is given by $(s, p) = (100, 100)$.
   (ii) Show that the stable and unstable arms of the saddle point E_0 are:

   stable arm $p = 125.31 - 0.253s$

   unstable arm $p = 99.7531 + 0.002469s$

   (iii) Now assume a resource discovery which leads to $x_p = 0.5$ and $x = 0.3$. With $\alpha = 0.8$,
      (a) show that equilibrium $(s, p) = (19.7, 119.7)$
      (b) the unstable arm is given by $p = 119.65135 + 0.00246943s$
      (c) the stable arm is given by $p = 124.68608 - 0.2531005s$

10.   Use the model surrounding figure 13.25 to analyse the UK's position in 1979 when the Conservative government under Mrs Thatcher took office. The basic information at the time was as follows.

(a) Oil had been discovered in the North Sea, was being drilled around 1975 and was known to come on-stream in 1979.
(b) The Conservatives won the General Election in 1979 with Mrs Thatcher indicating:
    – removal of all UK exchange controls; and
    – a reduction in monetary growth to combat inflation.

Take as your starting date 1975 when oil was being drilled.

11.   For the monetarist model in table 13.8 let

$$y = 20, \quad m = 106, \quad p^* = 1, \quad k = 0.5, \quad u = 0.5, \quad r^* = 10$$

(i)   Derive the differential equation for this model.
(ii) Solve for equilibrium s.

12.   Suppose nominal money supply grows at a constant rate λ and inflation abroad is constant at π^*, i.e.

$$\dot{m} = \lambda \quad \text{and} \quad \dot{p}^* = \pi^*$$

Derive an expression for equilibrium s under the assumption that a stationary equilibrium is one in which real money balances are constant.

Additional reading

Additional material on the contents of this chapter can be obtained from Buiter and Miller (1981), Copeland (2000), Dornbusch (1976), Dernburg (1989), Ford (1990), Frenkel and Rodriguez (1982), Gärtner (1993), MacDonald (1988), Niehans (1984), Obstfeld and Rogoff (1999), Pilbeam (1998), Rødseth (2000), Shone (1989, 2001).

CHAPTER 14

Population models

14.1 Malthusian population growth

Population growth is frequently considered by means of differential equations, where the growth can be of persons, animal species, or bacteria. Although the increase in population is discontinuous, if the population is very large, then the additions to its size will be very small and so it can be considered as changing continuously. Hence, we assume population size, p, changes continuously over time and that $p(t)$ is differentiable. The simplest population growth model is to assume that population grows/declines at a constant rate. Thus

$$\frac{dp}{dt}\frac{1}{p} = k \tag{14.1}$$

this means that the change in the population is proportional to the size of the population

$$\frac{dp}{dt} = kp$$

where k is positive for a growth in the population and negative for a decline. The initial condition is that if at time t_0 the population is p_0 then

$$p(t_0) = p_0$$

Although (14.1) is a simple equation to solve, let us investigate its qualitative properties by means of phase-space.

For positive k the growth curve is linear, positively sloped, and passes through the origin, as shown in figure 14.1. It is clear, then, that the only equilibrium for this population is a population of zero, since this is the only value of p for which $dp/dt = 0$. Furthermore, for any population of size greater than zero, e.g., p_0, then dp/dt is positive and so population will be increasing over time. In other words, the arrows along the phase line indicate a continuously growing population. If, on the other hand, k is negative then equilibrium population size is still zero, but now for any population greater than zero means dp/dt is negative and so population will decrease over time until it is extinguished.

Although not wholly realistic, let us solve for the population size explicitly. To do this integrate both sides of the differential equation

Figure 14.1.

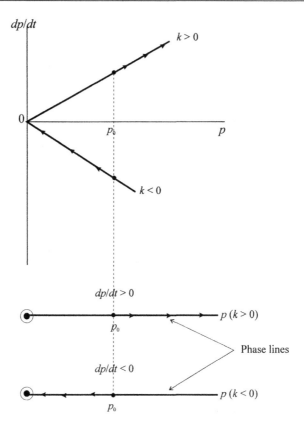

$$\frac{dp}{dt} = kp$$

$$\int \frac{dp}{dt} = \int k\,dt$$

$$\ln p = kt + c$$

$$p = c_0 e^{kt}$$

where c is the constant of integration. Applying the initial condition $p = p_0$ for $t = t_0$ we have

$$p = p_0 e^{kt_0}$$
$$\text{implying} \quad c_0 = p_0 e^{-kt_0}$$

Which leads to the result

(14.2) $$p = p_0 e^{-kt_0} e^{kt} = p_0 e^{k(t-t_0)}$$

and which clearly satisfies the initial condition.

In this model, population grows/declines exponentially, and is referred to as the *Malthusian model* of population growth.

Of interest in rapidly growing populations is the time necessary for the population to double in size.[1] It is readily shown that for the Malthusian model this

---

[1] Biologists refer to this as the **mean generation time**, i.e., the time necessary for a population to reproduce itself.

period depends only on the rate of growth, k. To show this let the population be p_0 initially at time t_0. Let the time period when the population has doubled be denoted t_1. Then the length of time for the population to double is $t_1 - t_0$. Furthermore, $p_1 = 2p_0$, hence

$$2p_0 = p_0 e^{k(t_1 - t_0)}$$
$$\ln 2 = k(t_1 - t_0)$$
$$\therefore \quad t_1 - t_0 = \frac{\ln 2}{k} = \frac{0.6931}{k}$$

For example, if a population is growing at 2% per annum, then it will double approximately every $0.6931/0.02 = 35$ years regardless of the initial population size.

Example 14.1

Table 14.1 gives the population of the UK from 1781 to 1931. Our first problem is to estimate the parameter k. Suppose we set $p_0 = 13$ million for the initial year 1781. Further, take the population in year 1791 to be as in the table, namely 14.5 million. This allows us to estimate the value of k. Letting $t_0 = 0$ to represent 1781, then $t_1 = 10$ for 1791, i.e., $t_1 - t_0 = 10$

$$p(0) = p_0 = 13$$
$$p(10) = p_0 e^{10k} = 13e^{10k} = 14.5$$
$$k = \frac{\ln 14.5 - \ln 13}{10} = \frac{2.6741 - 2.5649}{10}$$
$$k = 0.01092$$

Using this estimate of k we compute the Malthusian estimate of population growth, as shown in column (3) of table 14.1.

Table 14.1 UK Population, 1781–1931 (million)

Year	Actual	Malthusian	Logistic
1781	13.000	13.000	13.000
1791	14.500	14.500	14.996
1801	15.902	16.173	17.143
1811	18.103	18.039	19.410
1821	21.007	20.121	21.756
1831	24.135	22.442	24.135
1841	26.751	25.032	26.498
1851	27.393	27.920	28.799
1861	28.977	31.142	30.993
1871	31.556	34.735	33.046
1881	34.934	38.743	34.934
1891	37.802	43.213	36.641
1901	41.538	48.200	38.162
1911	45.299	53.761	39.500
1921	47.168	59.964	40.662
1931	49.007	66.883	41.662

Source: Deane and Cole (1962, table 3, p. 8).

A discrete version of the model may appear more appropriate. This takes the form

(14.3)
$$\Delta p_{t+1} = k p_t$$
$$\text{i.e.} \quad p_{t+1} = p_t + k p_t = (1 + k) p_t$$

Using the analysis of chapter 3, we have the general solution

(14.4)
$$p_t = (1 + k)^t p_0$$

Again, using $p_0 = 13$ and $p_{10} = (1 + k)^{10}(13) = 14.5$, we obtain

$$k = \left(\frac{14.5}{13} \right)^{\frac{1}{10}} - 1 = 0.0109798$$

Using this estimate of k, and the discrete solution, we compute an alternative series based on the Malthusian assumption. However, it is readily established that this gives exactly the same figures (to three places of decimal) as the continuous model.

The model is reasonably accurate up to 1851 but thereafter the error becomes not only quite large but increasing. This should not be surprising. In the first instance, k was estimated from the first two observations. Second, the population increases at an ever-increasing rate, which is unrealistic. Third, for distant population there is no account taken of competition of the population for the limited resources available.

It may be thought that the model is inappropriate because it does not take account of births and deaths. But this is not strictly true. If births are assumed to follow the Malthusian law as well as deaths, i.e., both grow at constant rates b and d, respectively, then

(14.5)
$$\frac{dp^b}{dt} = p_0 e^{bt} \quad \text{and} \quad \frac{dp^d}{dt} = p_0 e^{dt}$$
$$\frac{dp}{dt} = \frac{dp^b}{dt} - \frac{dp^d}{dt} = p_0 e^{(b-d)t} = p_0 e^{kt}$$

Hence, the k we estimated using data from 1781 and 1791 would account for both births and deaths. This means that the problem lies elsewhere.

Although we have considered births and deaths we have taken no account of immigration or emigration. Migration (immigration minus emigration), however, is usually fairly small relative to the total size of the population, or occurs only at specific times (most especially in human populations). This would suggest, therefore, that the exponential growth curve might not be the most appropriate specification of the growth process.

14.2 The logistic curve

An alternative approach is to assume that not only does population grow with population size, but that as it grows its members come into competition with each other for the food or limited resources. In order to capture this 'competition' it is assumed that there are $p(p - 1)/2$ interactions for a given population of size p. Assuming such interactions lead to additional deaths, for example because of disease or war, then we can assume that the growth in the population will also diminish in proportion to this element of interaction. In other words, population now changes by

$$\frac{dp}{dt} = kp - \frac{k_1 p(p-1)}{2}$$

$$= kp + \frac{k_1 p}{2} - \frac{k_1 p^2}{2}$$

$$= \left(k + \frac{k_1}{2}\right)p - \frac{k_1 p^2}{2}$$

Therefore

$$\frac{dp}{dt} = ap - bp^2 = p(a - bp) \quad a > 0, b > 0 \tag{14.6}$$

which is referred to as the *logistic growth equation*.

In general the parameter b is small relative to the parameter a, so that the second term is often negligible. However, as the population size grows and competition becomes greater, the second term $-bp^2$ becomes more significant. This is especially true as time moves further away from the initial level. As the second term becomes more significant, this dampens the growth in the population. This second formulation is referred to as the *logistic law* of growth.

Before solving for population explicitly, let us investigate the qualitative properties of the population by considering the phase-space. The logistic growth equation

$$\dot{p} = p(a - bp) \quad a > 0, b > 0$$

is an autonomous first-order differential equation. The qualitative properties of this equation are shown in the phase diagram in figure 14.2.

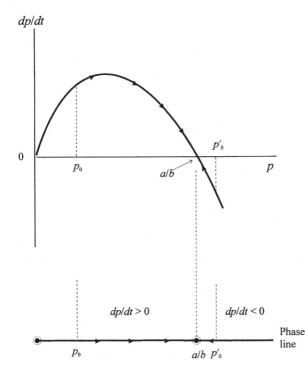

Figure 14.2.

The equilibrium population is where $\dot{p} = 0$, i.e., zero population growth, which occurs at

$$p_1^* = 0 \qquad \text{and} \qquad p_2^* = \frac{a}{b}$$

Since we are interested only in positive populations we can ignore $p_1^* = 0$ and so just refer to equilibrium rate p^*. For $p_0 < a/b$, where p_0 is the initial population, then $dp/dt > 0$, and so p rises over time. For $p_0 > a/b$ then $dp/dt < 0$, and p falls over time. The arrows in figure 14.2 show these properties. It is clear that $p^* = a/b$ is a (locally) stable equilibrium.[2] Although population approaches the limit a/b, this is never in fact achieved (see exercise 5).

We can solve for p explicitly as follows

$$\frac{dp}{dt} = ap - bp^2 = p(a - bp)$$

$$\int_{p_0}^{p} \frac{dp}{p(a - bp)} = \int_{p_0}^{p} dt$$

But

$$\frac{1}{p(a - bp)} = \frac{1}{a} \left(\frac{1}{p} - \frac{-b}{a - bp} \right)$$

$$\therefore \quad \frac{1}{a} \int_{p_0}^{p} \frac{dp}{p} - \frac{1}{a} \int_{p_0}^{p} \frac{-b dp}{(a - bp)} = \int_{t_0}^{t} dt$$

Solving we have

$$\left[\frac{1}{a} \ln p - \frac{1}{a}(-b) \ln(a - bp) \left(\frac{1}{-b} \right) \right]_{p_0}^{p} = t - t_0$$

$$\frac{1}{a} \ln \left(\frac{p}{p_0} \right) - \frac{1}{a} \ln \left(\frac{a - bp}{a - bp_0} \right) = t - t_0$$

$$\ln \left(\frac{p(a - bp_0)}{p_0(a - bp)} \right) = a(t - t_0)$$

$$\therefore \quad p_0(a - bp)e^{a(t - t_0)} = p(a - bp_0)$$

We can now solve for $p(t)$

$$p_0 a e^{a(t - t_0)} = p b p_0 e^{a(t - t_0)} + p(a - bp_0)$$
$$= p[b p_0 e^{a(t - t_0)} + (a - bp_0)]$$

i.e.

(14.7)
$$p(t) = \frac{a p_0}{b p_0 + (a - bp_0)e^{-a(t - t_0)}}$$

This represents the *logistic function*, which is sketched in figure 14.3, and shows the *logistic curve*. This curve depends on the three parameters a, b and p_0. It has an upper limit of

(14.8)
$$\lim_{t \to \infty} p(t) = \frac{a}{b}$$

---

[2] Expanding $\dot{p} = f(p)$ in a Taylor series around $p^* = a/b$ we obtain the following linear approximation $\dot{p} = -a\left(p - \frac{a}{b}\right)$, which has a positive intercept (a^2/b) and a negative slope $(-a)$.

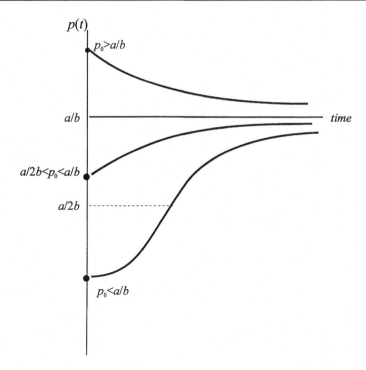

Figure 14.3.

The zero population growth is, however, never reached. (This result is also established in exercise 5 using a linear approximation around the equilibrium.) A second property of the logistic function is that it has an inflexion point at

$$p = \frac{a}{2b} \tag{14.9}$$

This is readily established from the logistic growth equation, since the inflexion point occurs where the logistic growth equation is at a maximum. Thus, if

$$f(p) = ap - bp^2$$
$$f'(p) = a - 2bp = 0$$
$$p = \frac{a}{2b}$$

The shape of the logistic curve depends on whether the initial population is below or above the inflexion value of p, or even above the limit value a/b. Figure 14.3 illustrates three different paths.

We can use the logistic function and the data provided in table 14.1 to compute the values of a and b for the logistic growth equation. Using figures for 1781, 1831 and 1881, respectively, for $t(0)$, $t(50)$ and $t(100)$, we have the following two equations

$$24.135 = \frac{13a}{13b + (a - 13b)e^{-50a}}$$

$$34.934 = \frac{13a}{13b + (a - 13b)e^{-100a}}$$

Figure 14.4.

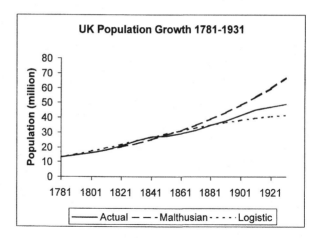

which provide two nonlinear equations in two unknowns. Using a mathematical software package for solving equations[3] (and using the Malthusian value of k for a first approximation for a), it can be established that

$$a = 0.02038302 \qquad b = 0.0004605$$

As indicated above, the value of b is very small and the population has to be large before this second term becomes significant. Even so, it implies an upper limit for the population of the UK of $a/b = 46.745186$ million. Using these values for a and b, we have the logistic results shown in column (4) of table 14.1. It is clear that these give significantly different results than those of the Malthusian growth law and that towards the end of the period they under-estimate the growth in the population of the UK. The different growth processors relative to the actual observations are illustrated in figure 14.4. This shows quite clearly that the Malthusian law grossly over-estimates the UK population in 1931, while the logistic growth equation under-estimates it. Of course, a possible reason for the under-estimate of the logistic growth equation is the choice of years to estimate the parameters a and b. We quite arbitrarily chose t_1 to be fifty years on from t_0 and t_2 to be 100 years on. A different choice of years would give different computed values of a and b, and hence different values in column (4) of table 14.1. It is even possible to estimate a and b using nonlinear statistical estimation, which would use all the available data in table 14.1. However, the point being emphasised is that the logistic calculations are sensitive to the computed/estimated values of a and b, and most especially the limit in the growth of the population.

We might, however, approach the logistic equation in terms of its discrete approximation we developed in chapter 3, section 3.7. It is assumed that the change in the population, Δp_{t+1} conforms to the rule

(14.10) $$\Delta p_{t+1} = ap_t - bp_t^2$$

---

[3] After defining the equations, *Mathematica* can solve these equations using the **FindRoot** command and using initial guesses for a and b. *Maple* can do the same using the **fsolve** command and giving ranges for a and b. The two programmes give the same results (see appendices 14.1 and 14.2). The same results can be established using *TK Solver*. With all programmes, care must be exercised in providing initial guesses.

which has the approximate solution

$$p_t = \frac{ap_0}{bp_0 + (1+a)^{-t}(a - bp_0)}$$

(14.11)

This too has the limit a/b. Again using the figures for 1781, 1831 and 1881 we obtain two equations

$$24.135 = \frac{13a}{13b + (1+10)^{-50}(a - 13b)}$$

$$34.934 = \frac{13a}{13b + (1+10)^{-100}(a - 13b)}$$

which gives two slightly different estimates for a and b, namely

$$a = 0.0205922 \qquad b = 0.00044052$$

However, once again using these estimates for a and b along with the discrete form for the population, we obtain exactly the same estimates as column (4) of table 14.1.

Although the discrete approximation is good for forecasting population, care must be exercised in its use. The original model is nonlinear. As we showed in chapter 3, for certain values of the parameters a and b the model leads to cyclical behaviour. *This is not true of the discrete approximation.* Regardless of the values of a and b the discrete approximation leads to an equilibrium value of a/b in the limit for some arbitrary population size which is nonzero.

For instance if we consider the two formulations[4]:

$$p_{t+1} = ap_t - bp_t^2 = 3.2p_t - 2.2p_t^2$$

$$p_{t+1} = \frac{(1+a)p_t}{1 + bp_t} = \frac{4.2p_t}{1 + 2.2p_t}$$

i.e. $a = 3.2$ and $b = 2.2$, then system (i) goes to a 2-cycle with values oscillating between 0.74625 and 1.16284. On the other hand, system (ii) converges very quickly on the limiting value of 1.45455. These quite different stability characteristics of the two systems are a warning about the use of approximations when dealing with nonlinear systems.

14.3   An alternative interpretation

In modelling population change it is useful to consider the process from a different perspective. Population at a point in time is a *stock*. This stock level will change depending on the difference between the inflow and the outflow. Depending on the population under investigation there will be different factors contributing to each of these flows. For example, a typical inflow will consist of births and immigration; while a typical outflow will consist of deaths and emigration. In the case of fish populations, however, there is also the extent of the harvesting over the period. We

---

[4] See chapter 3, section 3.9 for a derivation of the second equation above.

shall consider fisheries in chapter 15, and here we shall concentrate on 'natural' changes to population. We have then:

Net change in population = inflow − outflow
= (births + immigration) − (deaths + emigration)

But births and deaths can be considered as 'internal' to the population, while immigration and emigration can be considered as coming from outside the system, as 'external' influences on the population. We can, therefore, redefine the net change in the population as composed of internal change plus external change as follows:

Net change in population = internal change + external change
= (births − deaths) + migration

where, of course, migration is immigration less emigration. Notice that this interpretation is particularly useful for open systems, for it is only in such systems that migration can take place. For example, when considering the population of the UK we can consider the internal change in terms of births and deaths of UK citizens, and we can consider the external change in terms of the migration of the population in and out of the UK. On the other hand, if we are considering world population, then this is a closed system (at least until planetary movements of population take place!). There can be only births and deaths in a closed system.

Abstracting from the many characteristics that make up a population, like age, sex, density, fertility, etc., we can think of a representative unit that contributes a net amount to the internal change in the population, which we shall label n. The population size at a point in time is $p(t)$, and denotes the number of individuals at time t. Hence, the internal change in the population is $np(t)$. Letting $m(t)$ denote the migration (immigration less emigration) over the same interval of time as we are measuring the internal change, and measured at time t, then $m(t)$ denotes the external change. Accordingly, the change in the population, $dp(t)/dt$ is given by

(14.12)
$$\frac{dp}{dt} = np(t) + m(t)$$

Example 14.2 (Malthusian population growth)

In the case of the Malthusian population growth we considered earlier, there is no migration ($m(t) = 0$ for all t) and population is assumed to grow at a constant rate r. In other words, the net contribution of each member is assumed to be equal to r (i.e. $n = r$). Hence for $n = r$ and $m(t) = 0$ for all t

$$\frac{dp(t)}{dt} = rp(t)$$

with population at time t given by

$$p(t) = p_0 e^{rt}$$

Example 14.3 (Logistic growth curve)

Again there is assumed to be no migration and $m(t) = 0$ for all t. Assume, as in the Malthusian case, that a population which is not influenced by other factors grows at a constant rate r. But now further assume that there is a restraint on the growth process that is proportional to the size of the population. In other words, the growth process r is reduced by a factor $r_1 p(t)$. The net internal contribution is therefore given by

$$n(t) = r - r_1 p(t)$$

Notice in particular that the internal net contribution is a function of time since it is related to the stock size of the population. Under these two assumptions about migration and net internal change, we have for the growth of the population

$$\frac{dp}{dt} = (r - r_1 p(t)) p(t)$$

$$= r \left(1 - \frac{p(t)}{k} \right) p(t) \quad \text{where } k = \frac{r}{r_1}$$

(14.13)

which is the logistic growth equation we discussed earlier. Notice first that r is the Malthusian growth of population and k denotes the carrying capacity of the population. This version of the logistic equation will be found particularly useful when we discuss fisheries in chapter 15. For this population its size at time t is given by

$$p(t) = \frac{k}{1 + \left(\dfrac{k}{p_0} - 1 \right) e^{-rt}}$$

(14.14)

As we shall see in the next section, this alternative view of population change will be found very useful when considering multispecies populations that interact with each other in complex ways.

14.4 Multispecies population models: geometric analysis

Consider some closed system, a habitat, in which there are just two species. These two species can interact with each other in a variety of ways. They may be:

(1)   independent of each other,
(2)   in competition with each other,
(3)   one a predator and the other a prey,
(4)   both mutually supportive of each other.

If both are independent of each other then the populations will grow according to the type of laws we have already considered. In this section we are more concerned with interacting species. But before we consider each of the possible interactions in turn, we need to model the problem.

Let the two species be denoted $x(t)$ and $y(t)$, respectively. Then we can posit that the growth of the two species, with no migration for each species, as

(14.15)
$$\dot{x} = Rx(t)$$
$$\dot{y} = Qy(t)$$

where R denotes the net contribution of each individual in the x-population and Q the net contribution of each individual in the y-population. The extent to which a typical member of the x-population contributes to the stock depends not only on births and deaths, but also on its interaction with the y-population. The same holds for the y-population. Consider a very general interaction specification, namely

(14.16)
$$R = \alpha + \beta x(t) + \gamma y(t)$$
$$Q = \delta + \varepsilon y(t) + \zeta x(t)$$

For each population, α and δ denote the natural growth coefficient of the species. The second term denotes the over-crowding (or self-limiting) coefficient of the species. As with the logistic growth equation, if β and ε are negative, then over-crowding will occur and the species come into **competition** with *themselves*. On the other hand, if β and ε are positive, then growth expands as the population size increases, i.e., there is an increase in fertility as population expands. This we refer to as **mutualism**. If γ and ζ are both zero then the two species are **independent** of each other. If γ and ζ are both negative, then each is in competition for the limited resources of the habitat. The growth of one species is at the expense of the other. On the other hand, if γ and ζ are both positive, then we have a mutually supportive closed system: the growth of each species is mutually beneficial. Finally we have a **predatory–prey** relationship. If γ is positive and ζ is negative then x is the predator and y is the prey; if γ is negative and ζ is positive, then x is the prey and y is the predator. The predatory–prey model has been discussed in some detail in the literature, and much of it is the model of Lotka and Volterra or its extension. Given the general specifications here, then it is possible, for example, to consider models that combine over-crowding and have predatory–prey features or only predatory–prey characteristics.

We now turn to each of the various models to consider them in some detail. In doing this we shall employ *Mathematica* to illustrate, in particular, the numerical examples in the phase plane. Some of the basic instructions for doing this are provided in appendix 14.3, which also includes instructions for using *Maple*. Here we concentrate on the geometric features of the modelling, leaving the mathematical analysis of such models to the next section.

14.4.1 *Competition with no over-crowding*

Consider the following model

(14.17)
$$\dot{x} = [a - by]x \quad x(0) = x_0 \quad a > 0, b > 0$$
$$\dot{y} = [c - dx]y \quad y(0) = y_0 \quad c > 0, d > 0$$

The terms $-by$ and $-dx$ (where we suppress the time variable) show that each species is in competition for the limited resources of the habitat. We assume the habitat represents a closed system so there is no migration. Does such a system have an equilibrium? Stationary values occur when $\dot{x} = 0$ and $\dot{y} = 0$, i.e.

$$\dot{x} = [a - by(t)]x(t) = 0 \quad \text{implying} \quad y = a/b \text{ or } x = 0$$
$$\dot{y} = [c - dx(t)]y(t) = 0 \quad \text{implying} \quad x = c/d \text{ or } y = 0$$

Hence, there are two stationary points $(x_1^*, y_1^*) = (0, 0)$ and $(x_2^*, y_2^*) = (c/d, a/b)$, as shown by points E_0 and E_1, respectively, in figure 14.5.

Figure 14.5 also illustrates the qualitative nature of the trajectories. In this problem only nonnegative values of x and y are meaningful. Consider first the trajectories in the neighbourhood of the origin. Since $y < a/b$, then $0 < a - by$, and so $\dot{x} > 0$ and hence x is increasing. Similarly, $x < c/d$ means $0 < c - dx$, and so $\dot{y} > 0$ and hence y is increasing. In fact, this specifies the nature of trajectories in quadrant I in figure 14.5. Using the same reasoning, we can summarise the properties of the four quadrants as shown in table 14.2. The trajectories are looking complex. For some trajectories in quadrant I the system seems to tend towards the equilibrium point E_1. However, if it passes into quadrant II then it moves away from the equilibrium point E_1. This is because x dominates the habitat and fertility of y is now so low that it begins to decline. A similar problem occurs if the

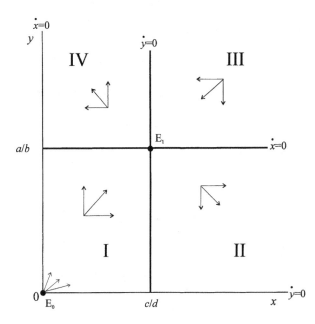

Figure 14.5.

Table 14.2 Vector properties for competition with no over-crowding

Quadrant I	**Quadrant II**
For $x < c/d$ then $c-dx < 0$, hence $\dot{y} > 0$	For $x > c/d$ then $0 > c-dx$, hence $\dot{y} < 0$
For $y < a/b$ then $0 < a-by$, hence $\dot{x} > 0$	For $y < a/b$ then $0 < a-by$, hence $\dot{x} > 0$
Quadrant III	**Quadrant IV**
For $x > c/d$ then $0 < c-dx$, hence $\dot{y} < 0$	For $x < c/d$ then $0 < c-dx$, hence $\dot{y} > 0$
For $y > a/b$ then $0 > a-by$, hence $\dot{x} < 0$	For $y > a/b$ then $0 > a-by$, hence $\dot{x} < 0$

trajectory moves from quadrant I into quadrant IV. In this instance, however, species y dominates the habitat and x declines to extinction. A similar logic holds if the system begins in quadrant III. An initial situation in either quadrant II or IV simply moves the system away from the equilibrium point E_1.

Example 14.4

We can try to see what is happening to this system by considering a numerical example. Consider the following competitive model

$$\dot{x} = [4 - 3y]x$$
$$\dot{y} = [3 - x]y$$

Equilibrium points can readily be found by setting $\dot{x} = 0$ and $\dot{y} = 0$, which gives two equilibrium points

$$E_0: (x_0^*, y_0^*) = (0, 0) \qquad E_1: (x_1^*, y_1^*) = (3, 4/3)$$

Point E_1, in particular, is the solution to the two equations

$$y = \frac{4}{3} \quad \dot{x} = 0$$
$$x = 3 \quad \dot{y} = 0$$

To highlight the stability/instability properties of equilibrium E_1 (here we ignore E_0), we can consider the direction field, which is illustrated in figure 14.6. This diagram illustrates a number of features. First, equilibrium E_1 appears to be a saddle path solution. Second, the possible trajectories of the system conform to those highlighted by the qualitative discussion of figure 14.5, in particular the movement of the system in the various quadrants, and the likely paths as trajectories move from one quadrant into another. Third, the movement of the system is from quadrant I into quadrants II and IV; and from quadrant III into quadrants II and IV. Fourth, it is not obvious whether any path will lead to the equilibrium point E_1.

Figure 14.6.

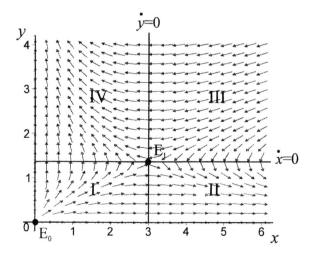

Although it was not possible to solve the nonlinear system given in the general specification of the system, we can obtain more detailed information on the properties of the trajectories in the phase-plane by noting[5]

$$\frac{dy}{dx} = \frac{dy/dt}{dx/dt} = \frac{(c - dx)y}{(a - by)x}$$

which uses the chain rule. We can re-arrange this expression as follows

$$\left(\frac{a}{y} - b\right)dy = \left(\frac{c}{x} - d\right)dx$$

Integrating both sides we have

$$\int \left(\frac{a}{y} - b\right)dy = \int \left(\frac{c}{x} - d\right)dx$$
$$a \ln y - by = c \ln x - dx + k_1$$
$$a \ln y - c \ln x = by - dx + k_1$$
$$y^a x^{-c} = ke^{by - dx} \quad k = e^{k_1}$$

where k_1 is the constant of integration. Hence

$$k = \frac{y^a x^{-c}}{e^{by - dx}}$$

where k is a constant. For a given value of k this solution gives the solution trajectory in the phase-plane.

Example 14. 4 (cont.)

Returning to our numerical example, we can use *Mathematica* or *Maple*, to plot the trajectories for various values of k. We do this using *Mathematica*'s **ContourPlot** command or *Maple*'s **contourplot** command (see appendix 14.3). Figure 14.7 shows a number of trajectories for different values of k. The trajectories in figure 14.7 verify the general features outlined in figures 14.5 and 14.6, most especially the saddle path nature of equilibrium E_1.

14.4.2 *Predatory–prey model with no over-crowding (Lotka–Volterra model)*

Consider the following model

$$\begin{aligned} \dot{x} &= (a - by)x = ax - bxy & a > 0, b > 0 \\ \dot{y} &= (-c + dx)y = -cy + dxy & c > 0, d > 0 \end{aligned} \tag{14.18}$$

In this model y is the predator and x is the prey. Notice that if the stock of x is zero, then the predator has no food and is assumed to die out, as indicated by $-c$. The greater the food stock, the greater the x-population, and hence the greater the growth in the predator. On the other hand, the natural growth of the x-stock does not depend on the predator for food and so a is positive, but it is subject to prey,

---

[5] This is possible only for autonomous systems, see chapter 4.

Figure 14.7.

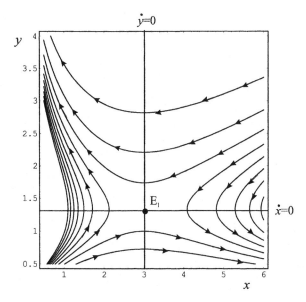

and so the greater the y-population, the more the x-population will be subject to prey, as indicated by $-b$.

Our first task is to establish the equilibrium of the system, to find the stationary points. We do this by setting $\dot{x} = 0$ and $\dot{y} = 0$ and solving for x and y. Thus

$$\dot{x} = (a - by)x = 0 \qquad \text{implying } y = a/b \text{ or } x = 0$$
$$\dot{y} = (-c + dx)y = 0 \qquad \text{implying } x = c/d \text{ or } y = 0$$

Hence, there are two stationary points: $(x_1^*, y_1^*) = (0, 0)$ and $(x_2^*, y_2^*) = (c/d, a/b)$, represented by points E_0 and E_1, respectively, in figure 14.8.

Figure 14.8 also illustrates the qualitative nature of the trajectories. We can summarise the properties of the four quadrants as shown in table 14.3.

It would appear, then, that the trajectories follow some sort of anticlockwise spiral.

Example 14.5

To see whether this is so, consider a numerical example at this stage, namely

$$\dot{x} = \left(2 - \frac{y}{100}\right)x$$
$$\dot{y} = \left(-2 + \frac{x}{50}\right)y$$

The equilibrium (other than the origin) is readily found to be $(x^*, y^*) = (100, 200)$. But the much more interesting question is what is happening to the species out of equilibrium. To obtain some initial insight into this obtain the direction field for this system. This is illustrated in figure 14.9. What is apparent from figure 14.9 is that the system has a cyclical pattern around the equilibrium point E_1, and that the movement of the system is anticlockwise.

Table 14.3 Vector properties for predatory–prey model

Quadrant I
For $x < c/d$ then $-c + dx < 0$, hence $\dot{y} < 0$
For $y < a/b$ then $0 < a - by$, hence $\dot{x} > 0$

Quadrant II
For $x > c/d$ then $-c + dx > 0$, hence $\dot{y} > 0$
For $y < a/b$ then $0 < a - by$, hence $\dot{x} > 0$

Quadrant III
2 For $x > c/d$ then $-c + dx > 0$, hence $\dot{y} > 0$
For $y > a/b$ then $0 > a-by$, hence $\dot{x} < 0$

Quadrant IV
For $x < c/d$ then $-c + dx < 0$, hence $\dot{y} < 0$
For $y > a/b$ then $0 > a-by$, hence $\dot{x} < 0$

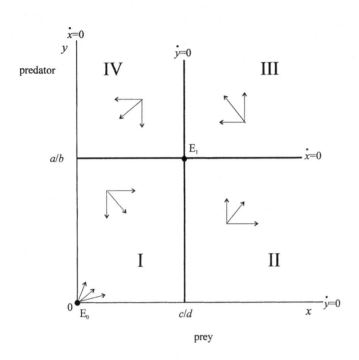

Figure 14.8.

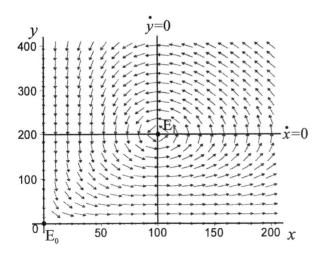

Figure 14.9.

However, we can go further into the trajectories by noting that the predator must be a function of the prey, i.e., $y = f(x)$. By the chain rule we have

$$\frac{dy}{dx} = \frac{dy/dt}{dx/dt}$$

Substituting the specific general equations, we have

$$\frac{dy}{dx} = \frac{(-c + dx)y}{(a - by)x}$$

or $$\left(\frac{a}{y} - b\right)dy = \left(\frac{-c}{x} + d\right)dx$$

Integrating both sides, we have

$$\int\left(\frac{a}{y} - b\right)dy = \int\left(\frac{-c}{x} + d\right)dx$$

$$a \ln y - by = -c \ln x + dx + k_1$$

$$a \ln y + c \ln x = by + dx + k_1$$

$$y^a x^c = ke^{by+dx} \quad k = e^{k_1}$$

where k_1 is the constant of integration. Hence,

$$k = \frac{y^a x^c}{e^{by+dx}}$$

where k is a constant. For a given value k this solution gives the solution trajectory in the phase-plane.

Once again, using *Mathematica*'s **ContourPlot** command or *Maple*'s **contourplot** command, we obtain typical trajectories shown in figure 14.10, which clearly illustrates the cyclical pattern of the solution. Using the information in figure 14.9 we further note that the system moves in an anticlockwise direction.

Suppose, however, we concentrate on just one trajectory with the initial situation shown by point P_0 in figure 14.11, where P_0 denotes the initial point $(x_0, y_0) = (50, 300)$. Point P_0 is in the northwest quadrant. In this situation the predator is in excess of its equilibrium level while the prey is below its equilibrium level. But because the number of predators is contracting, the number of prey will soon begin to rise as the system moves into the southwest quadrant. Once into the southwest quadrant, the number of prey begins to rise since the number of predators is too small to be a major threat. Eventually, this moves the system into the southeast quadrant, allowing sufficient prey for the predator once again to expand towards its equilibrium. However, too great an expansion in the predatory population diminishes the prey as the system moves into the northeast quadrant.

From figures 14.10 and 14.11 it is clear that the trajectories form *closed* curves. This means that neither the predator nor the prey becomes extinct. Each species cycles between its minimum and maximum level, as illustrated in figure 14.12. This figure plots the time path of the predator, y, and the prey, x. The starting point is represented by point P_0 (i.e. $x = 50$, $y = 300$), the point shown in figure 14.11.

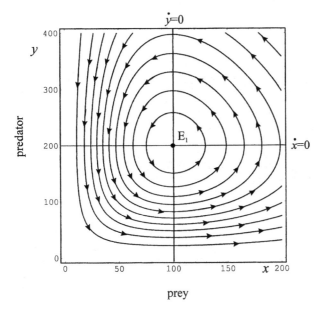

Figure 14.10.

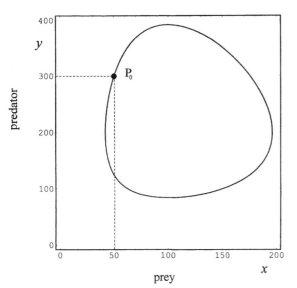

Figure 14.11.

What is also clear from figure 14.12 is that the predator lags behind the prey in a cyclic pattern, and because of this the stationary state is never attained.

14.4.3   *Competitive model with over-crowding*

In section 14.4.1 we considered a competitive model in which two species were in competition for the limited resources. But suppose there is also competition within each species as well; in other words, there is the possibility of over-crowding. We

Figure 14.12.

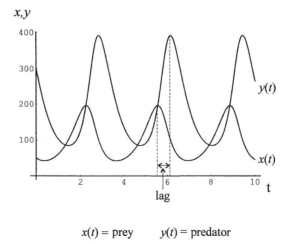

$$x(t) = \text{prey} \qquad y(t) = \text{predator}$$

can capture this situation in the following model

$$\dot{x} = (a - by - ux)x$$
$$\dot{y} = (c - dx - vy)y$$

where the terms $-ux^2$ and $-vy^2$ denote the over-crowding in the x-species, and y-species, respectively; while $-by$ and $-dx$ denote the interactive competition between the two species.

This system is nonlinear and much more complex than our earlier models. But we can still readily obtain the stationary points of the system by setting $\dot{x}$ and $\dot{y}$ equal to zero. This is certainly satisfied for $x = 0$ and $y = 0$, and so the origin denotes an equilibrium of the system, and the axes represent isoclines.

Once again we can use the chain rule to specify the situation in the phase-plane,

$$\frac{dy}{dx} = \frac{dy/dt}{dx/dt} = \frac{(c - dx - vy)y}{(a - by - ux)x}$$

We cannot solve this because the expression is not separable. We can, however, derive expressions for two further isoclines

$$\frac{dy}{dx} = 0 \text{ when } (c - dx - vy) = 0$$

$$\frac{dy}{dx} = 0 \text{ when } (a - by - ux) = 0$$

These represent two straight lines in the phase-plane, of which there are four configurations depending on the values of the six parameters, a, b, c, d, u, and v, as illustrated in figure 14.13. The markings along the isoclines indicate that

$\dot{x} = 0$ when $a - by - ux = 0$ implying $dy/dx = \infty$ and $y = (a/b) - (u/b)x$
$\dot{y} = 0$ when $c - bx - vy = 0$ implying $dy/dx = 0$ and $y = (c/v) - (d/v)x$

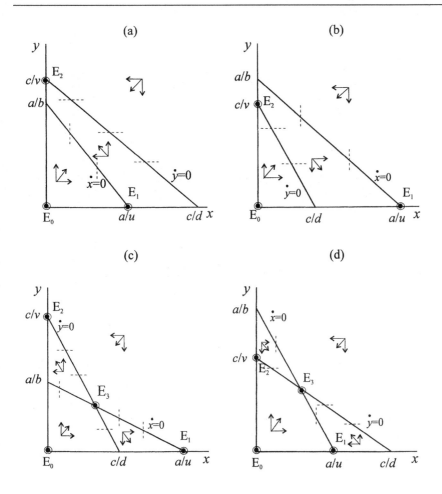

Figure 14.13.

while above and below the isoclines we have the properties

$\dot{x} > 0$ when $a - by - ux > 0$ implying $y < (a/b) - (u/b)x$ (below $\dot{x} = 0$)
$\dot{x} < 0$ when $a - by - ux < 0$ implying $y > (a/b) - (u/b)x$ (above $\dot{x} = 0$)
$\dot{y} > 0$ when $c - dx - vy > 0$ implying $y < (c/v) - (d/v)x$ (below $\dot{y} = 0$)
$\dot{y} < 0$ when $c - dx - vy < 0$ implying $y > (c/v) - (d/v)x$ (above $\dot{y} = 0$)

which are indicated by the vectors of force in figure 14.13.

In the upper diagrams in figure 14.13 extinction will occur in one of the species. So long as the system does not begin at the origin, then the system will either move to equilibrium point E_1, in which the y-species dies out, or to equilibrium point E_2, in which the x-species dies out. In the lower diagrams it is also possible for the two species to coexist. Such a situation occurs where the two isoclines intersect, and is given by the solution

$$(x^*, y^*) = \frac{av - bc}{uv - bd}$$

But an important question is whether such a coexisting equilibrium is a stable solution of the model. Figure 14.13(c) would suggest that E_3 is not a stable equilibrium,

Figure 14.14.

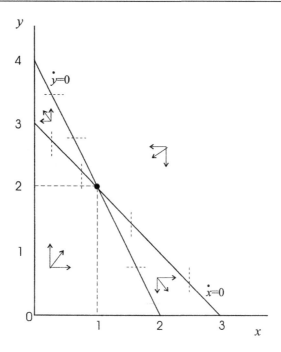

while in figure 14.13(d) E_3 appears a stable equilibrium. In order to verify these results we shall continue our discussion with two numerical examples. This not only allows us to compare the two diagrams in the lower part of figure 14.13 but also to consider some trajectories in the phase-plane. In order to show such trajectories, however, we need to solve the nonlinear system using numerical solutions. We do this within *Mathematica*, using the **NDSolve** command and the **ParametricPlot** command. Similar plots can be derived with *Maple*.[6]

Example 14.6

$$\dot{x} = (3 - y - x)x$$
$$\dot{y} = (4 - 2x - y)y$$

The basic properties of this system are illustrated in figure 14.14, which displays the isoclines and the vectors of force in the various quadrants. These forces are based on the following observations

$$\dot{x} = 0 \quad \text{when } 3 - y - x = 0 \text{ implying } y = 3 - x \text{ and } dy/dx = \infty$$
$$\dot{y} = 0 \quad \text{when } 4 - 2x - y = 0 \text{ implying } y = 4 - 2x \text{ and } dy/dx = 0$$
$$\dot{x} > 0 \quad \text{when } 3 - y - x > 0 \text{ implying } y < 3 - x \text{ (below } \dot{x})$$
$$\dot{x} < 0 \quad \text{when } 3 - y - x < 0 \text{ implying } y > 3 - x \text{ (above } \dot{x})$$
$$\dot{y} > 0 \quad \text{when } 4 - 2x - y > 0 \text{ implying } y < 4 - 2x \text{ (below } \dot{y})$$
$$\dot{y} < 0 \quad \text{when } 4 - 2x - y < 0 \text{ implying } y > 4 - 2x \text{ (above } \dot{y})$$

---

[6] See Lynch (2001) for plotting multispecies models with *Maple*.

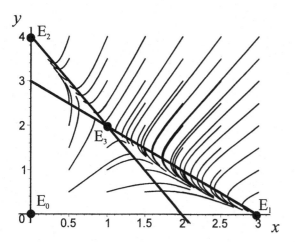

Figure 14.15.

This system in general leads to the extinction of one of the species, depending on the initial situation. This is clearly illustrated in figure 14.15. The trajectories in this figure required the use of a software package to solve numerically the nonlinear system of equations. What figure 14.15 clearly shows is that if the initial situation is not on the saddle path solution, then the system will tend either towards equilibrium E_1, where only the x-species survives, or equilibrium E_2, where only the y-species survives. Only in the unlikely event of the initial condition of the system being on the saddle path will the system converge to the coexistent equilibrium point E_3.

Example 14.7

$$\dot{x} = (4 - y - x)x$$
$$\dot{y} = (6 - x - 2y)y$$

The basic properties of this system are illustrated in figure 14.16, which displays the isoclines and the vectors of force in the various quadrants. These forces are based on the following observations

$\dot{x} = 0$ when $4 - y - x = 0$ implying $y = 4 - x$ and $dy/dx = \infty$

$\dot{y} = 0$ when $6 - x - 2y = 0$ implying $y = 3 - \frac{1}{2}x$ and $dy/dx = 0$

$\dot{x} > 0$ when $4 - y - x > 0$ implying $y < 4 - x$ (below $\dot{x}$)

$\dot{x} < 0$ when $4 - y - x < 0$ implying $y > 4 - x$ (above $\dot{x}$)

$\dot{y} > 0$ when $6 - x - 2y > 0$ implying $y < 3 - \frac{1}{2}x$ (below $\dot{y}$)

$\dot{y} < 0$ when $6 - x - 2y < 0$ implying $y > 3 - \frac{1}{2}x$ (above $\dot{y}$)

In this example, unlike the previous example, the system converges on the coexistent equilibrium point E_3, so long as the system does not have an initial point equal to the other stationary values. This is illustrated quite clearly in figure 14.17, which shows a number of trajectories for this nonlinear system. It is also quite clear from figure 14.17 that this system does not have a saddle path, except for the axes,

Figure 14.16.

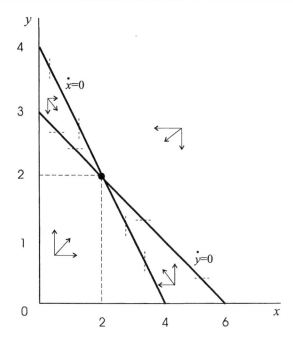

Figure 14.17.

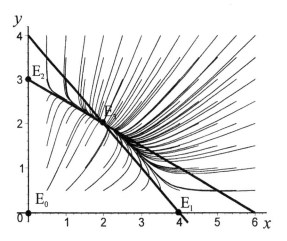

corresponding to the equilibrium point $(x^*, y^*) = (0, 0)$, which is an uninteresting case.

We can give another interpretation to our results. First we note that a denotes the natural growth of the x-species and c denotes the natural growth of the y-species. We can then make the following definitions:

u/a the competitive effect of x on itself relative to the natural growth of x
b/a the competitive effect of y on x relative to the natural growth of x
v/c the competitive effect of y on itself relative to the natural growth of y
d/c the competitive effect of x on y relative to the natural growth of y

Consider, then, figure 14.13(a). Here we have $c/v > a/b$ and $c/d > a/u$ or $b/a > v/c$ and $u/a > d/c$, i.e., the relative competitive effect of the y-species on x is greater than its relative competitive effect on itself; while the relative competitive effect of the x-species on itself is greater than its relative effect on the y-species. Depending, therefore, on the starting position, either the x-species will die out or the y-species will.

Turning to figure 14.13(b) we have $a/b > c/v$ and $a/u > c/d$ or $v/c > b/a$ and $d/c > u/a$, i.e., the relative competitive effect of the y-species on itself is greater than its effect on the x-species; while the relative impact of the x-species on the y-species is greater than the relative competitive effect on itself. Hence, depending on the starting position, one of the species will die out.

Next consider figure 14.3(c) where we have $c/v > a/b$ and $a/u > c/d$ or $b/a > v/c$ and $d/c > u/a$. In this instance the relative competitive effect of the y-species on x is greater than its relative competitive effect on itself; while the relative competitive effect of the x-species on y is greater than on itself. This is unstable, and which species wins out depends on the initial conditions, but E_3 cannot be attained unless the starting point lies on a saddle path.[7]

Finally, in figure 14.13(d) we have $a/b > c/v$ and $c/d > a/u$ or $v/c > b/a$ and $u/a > d/c$, i.e., the relative competitive effect of the y-species on itself is greater than the relative impact of the y-species on x; while the relative competitive effect of the x-species on itself is greater than the relative impact of the x-species on y. Accordingly, the species will settle to some mutually coexistent level – namely at E_3.

14.4.4   *Predatory–prey model with over-crowding*

In sub-section 14.4.2 we considered the predatory–prey model (often referred to as the Lotka–Volterra model), which involved no competition from *within* the species. But suppose there are many predators and so they are in competition with themselves for the prey. Suppose, too, that the prey, besides being under attack from the predator is also in competition for the resources of the habitat from members of its own species. Consider then the most general situation of predatory–prey with over-crowding of both species in the model

$$\dot{x} = (a - by - ux)x$$
$$\dot{y} = (-c + dx - vy)y$$

where the terms $-ux^2$ and $-vy^2$ denote the over-crowding in the prey (x-species), and the predator (y-species), respectively. The stationary points of the system are, once again, obtained by setting $\dot{x} = 0$ and $\dot{y} = 0$. This is certainly satisfied at the point $(x^*, y^*) = (0, 0)$. Hence the origin denotes one equilibrium solution, but an uninteresting one. The other solution is found by setting the terms in brackets to zero, which provides two isoclines.

$$\dot{x} = 0 \quad \text{when } a - by - ux = 0 \text{ implying } y = (a/b) - (u/b)x$$
$$\dot{y} = 0 \quad \text{when } -c + dx - vy = 0 \text{ implying } y = -(c/v) + (d/v)x$$

---

[7] We shall illustrate this in the next section.

which gives the nontrivial equilibrium

$$x^* = \frac{\left(\dfrac{a}{b} + \dfrac{c}{d}\right)}{\left(\dfrac{u}{b} + \dfrac{d}{v}\right)} \qquad y^* = \frac{\left(\dfrac{a}{b}\right)\left(\dfrac{d}{v}\right) - \left(\dfrac{u}{b}\right)\left(\dfrac{a}{v}\right)}{\left(\dfrac{u}{b} + \dfrac{d}{v}\right)}$$

Furthermore, we can use the chain rule to express the slope of the trajectory in the phase plane, i.e.

$$\frac{dy}{dx} = \frac{dy/dt}{dx/dt} = \frac{(-c + dx - vy)y}{(a - by - ux)x}$$

which is nonlinear and cannot be solved. Using the isoclines, however, we can get some insight into the possible trajectories. However, this is a much more complex system than the straight predatory–prey model, and so we shall continue our discussion with a numerical example.

Example 14.8

Let

$$\dot{x} = \left(2 - \frac{y}{100} - \frac{x}{75}\right)x$$
$$\dot{y} = \left(-2 + \frac{x}{50} - \frac{y}{200}\right)y$$

Then the nontrivial equilibrium point is $(x^*, y^*) = (112.5, 50)$. The question arises, however, as to whether, like the Lotka–Volterra model, a closed cycle occurs around the equilibrium point. In fact, this is not the case in the present model. The fact that there is competition from within each of the species leads the system towards the equilibrium point in the limit. This is illustrated in figure 14.18, which portrays the direction field along with a number of typical trajectories in the phase plane. It is quite clear that, given the parameter values, this system will always converge on the equilibrium in the limit. Hence, point $(x^*, y^*) = (112.5, 50)$ is asymptotically stable.

Figure 14.18.

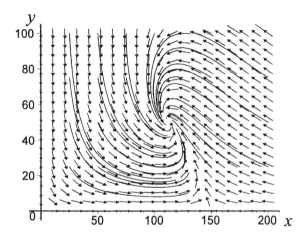

Of course, it is not always the situation that the equilibrium is asymptotically stable. For different parameter values the fixed point can be asymptotically unstable (see exercise 12), but once again does not converge on a closed orbit around the equilibrium, as in the Lotka–Volterra model.

This section has illustrated quite a variety of solution paths to systems involving the interaction between two species depending on whether the interaction is competitive, mutual or of the predatory–prey variety. With more than two species the variety of interactions becomes even more complex, but the nature of the solutions is basically similar. In the next section we shall consider the mathematical properties of these systems.

14.5 Multispecies population models: mathematical analysis[8]

In this section we shall set out the general approach, look at just two of the examples in the previous section in detail, and summarise all remaining examples. We shall then conclude with some general comments about such linear approximations to nonlinear systems.

Suppose we have a general nonlinear system denoting the interaction between two species of the form

$$\dot{x} = f(x, y)$$
$$\dot{y} = g(x, y)$$

Suppose further that this system has at least one fixed point, denoted (x^*, y^*), at which $\dot{x} = 0$ and $\dot{y} = 0$. If we wish to consider the stability of the system in the neighbourhood of the fixed point then, following our treatment in chapter 4, we can expand the system in a Taylor expansion around the fixed point. Thus

$$\dot{x} - x^* = \frac{\partial f(x^*, y^*)}{\partial x}(x - x^*) + \frac{\partial f(x^*, y^*)}{\partial y}(y - y^*)$$

$$\dot{y} - y^* = \frac{\partial g(x^*, y^*)}{\partial x}(x - x^*) + \frac{\partial g(x^*, y^*)}{\partial y}(y - y^*)$$

Let f_x, f_y, g_x and g_y denote the partial derivatives, each evaluated at the fixed point (x^*, y^*). Then

$$\dot{x} - x^* = f_x(x - x^*) + f_y(y - y^*)$$
$$\dot{y} - y^* = g_x(x - x^*) + g_y(y - y^*)$$

or, in matrix notation

$$\begin{bmatrix} \dot{x} - x^* \\ \dot{y} - y^* \end{bmatrix} = \begin{bmatrix} f_x & f_y \\ g_x & g_y \end{bmatrix} \begin{bmatrix} x - x^* \\ y - y^* \end{bmatrix}$$

The matrix composed of elements f_x, f_y, g_x and g_y are evaluated at the fixed point and this is a square matrix[9] and the system is a linear approximation of the original nonlinear system.

---

[8] This section requires knowledge of chapter 4.
[9] It is a Jacobian matrix.

Let

$$\mathbf{A} = \begin{bmatrix} f_x & f_y \\ g_x & g_y \end{bmatrix}$$

We have already shown in chapter 4 that all the stability properties of this linear system can be established from the eigenvalues and eigenvectors of $\mathbf{A}$, along with the trace and determinant of $\mathbf{A}$, where

$$\mathrm{tr}(\mathbf{A}) = f_x + g_y$$
$$\det(\mathbf{A}) = f_x g_y - f_y g_x$$

These properties, however, are only local and apply only for the neighbourhood of the fixed point under investigation. For nonlinear systems with more than one fixed point, as in all the examples in the previous section, then the neighbourhood of each fixed point must be investigated individually.

Example 14.4 (cont.)

Example 14.4 has the nonlinear system

$$\dot{x} = f(x, y) = 4x - 3xy$$
$$\dot{y} = g(x, y) = 3y - xy$$

Taking an arbitrary equilibrium point (x^*, y^*), then we can expand this system in a Taylor expansion around this value

$$\dot{x} - x^* = f_x(x - x^*) + f_y(y - y^*)$$
$$\dot{y} - y^* = g_x(x - x^*) + g_y(y - y^*)$$

where

$$f_x = 4 - 3y \text{ evaluated at } (x^*, y^*)$$
$$f_y = -3x \text{ evaluated at } (x^*, y^*)$$
$$g_x = -y \text{ evaluated at } (x^*, y^*)$$
$$g_y = 3 - x \text{ evaluated at } (x^*, y^*)$$

We have already established two fixed points

$$E_0 = (0, 0) \quad \text{and} \quad E_1 = (3, 4/3)$$

and we need to consider the system's behaviour in the neighbourhood of each. Take the point $E_0 = (0, 0)$. Then $f_x = 4, f_y = 0, g_x = 0$ and $g_y = 3$. Hence

$$\mathbf{A} = \begin{bmatrix} 4 & 0 \\ 0 & 3 \end{bmatrix}$$

and our system has the linear approximation

$$\begin{bmatrix} \dot{x} \\ \dot{y} \end{bmatrix} = \begin{bmatrix} 4 & 0 \\ 0 & 3 \end{bmatrix} \begin{bmatrix} x \\ y \end{bmatrix}$$

in the neighbourhood of the origin. The eigenvalues and eigenvectors are found from

$$\mathbf{A} - \lambda \mathbf{I} = \begin{bmatrix} 4 - \lambda & 0 \\ 0 & 3 - \lambda \end{bmatrix}$$

where $\det(\mathbf{A} - \lambda \mathbf{I}) = (4 - \lambda)(3 - \lambda) = 0$ with the two eigenvalues $r = 4$ and $s = 3$. Furthermore, $\text{tr}(\mathbf{A}) = 7$ and $\det(\mathbf{A}) = 12$. (Note that $\text{tr}(\mathbf{A})^2 > 4 \det(\mathbf{A})$).

For $r = 4$ then

$$\begin{bmatrix} 0 & 0 \\ 0 & -1 \end{bmatrix} \begin{bmatrix} x \\ y \end{bmatrix} = \begin{bmatrix} 0 \\ 0 \end{bmatrix}$$

Hence it does not matter what values x and y take in forming the eigenvector $\mathbf{v}^r$
Let

$$\mathbf{v}^r = \begin{bmatrix} 1 \\ 0 \end{bmatrix}$$

Next consider $s = 3$, then

$$\begin{bmatrix} 1 & 0 \\ 0 & 0 \end{bmatrix} \begin{bmatrix} x \\ y \end{bmatrix} = \begin{bmatrix} 0 \\ 0 \end{bmatrix}$$

and again it does not matter what values x and y take in forming the eigenvector $\mathbf{v}^s$. Since $\mathbf{v}^r$ must be linearly independent of $\mathbf{v}^s$, then let

$$\mathbf{v}^s = \begin{bmatrix} 0 \\ 1 \end{bmatrix}$$

The general solution is, therefore,

$$\begin{bmatrix} x(t) \\ y(t) \end{bmatrix} = c_1 \begin{bmatrix} 1 \\ 0 \end{bmatrix} e^{4t} + c_2 \begin{bmatrix} 0 \\ 1 \end{bmatrix} e^{3t}$$

and it is quite clear that this is asymptotically unstable. The situation is shown in figure 14.19, at the point E_0. For any value not the origin and in the positive quadrant will move the system away from the origin over time. (Also notice that the two independent eigenvectors form part of the axes.)

Next consider the point $E_1 = (3, 4/3)$. Then $f_x = 0$, $f_y = -9$, $g_x = -4/3$ and $g_y = 0$. Hence

$$\mathbf{A} = \begin{bmatrix} 0 & -9 \\ -4/3 & 0 \end{bmatrix}$$

and our system has the linear approximation

$$\begin{bmatrix} \dot{x} - x^* \\ \dot{y} - y^* \end{bmatrix} = \begin{bmatrix} 0 & -9 \\ -4/3 & 0 \end{bmatrix} \begin{bmatrix} x - x^* \\ y - y^* \end{bmatrix}$$

where $(x^*, y^*) = (3, 4/3)$. The eigenvalues and eigenvectors are found from

$$\mathbf{A} - \lambda \mathbf{I} = \begin{bmatrix} -\lambda & -9 \\ -4/3 & -\lambda \end{bmatrix}$$

where $\det(\mathbf{A} - \lambda \mathbf{I}) = \lambda^2 - 12 = 0$, with the two eigenvalues $r = \sqrt{12} = 2\sqrt{3}$ and $s = -\sqrt{12} = -2\sqrt{3}$. Furthermore, $\text{tr}(\mathbf{A}) = 0$ and $\det(\mathbf{A}) = -12$. From our analysis

Figure 14.19.

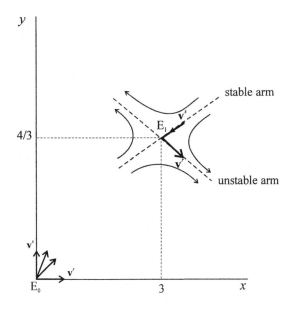

in chapter 4 we already know that these results identify a saddle point, since the eigenvalues are real and of opposite sign.[10]

For $r = 2\sqrt{3}$ then

$$\begin{bmatrix} -2\sqrt{3} & -9 \\ -4/3 & -2\sqrt{3} \end{bmatrix} \begin{bmatrix} x \\ y \end{bmatrix} = \begin{bmatrix} 0 \\ 0 \end{bmatrix}$$

giving

$$-2\sqrt{3}x - 9y = 0$$

Let $x = \sqrt{3}$ then $y = -2/3$, hence

$$\mathbf{v}^r = \begin{bmatrix} \sqrt{3} \\ -2/3 \end{bmatrix}$$

For $s = -2\sqrt{3}$ then

$$\begin{bmatrix} 2\sqrt{3} & -9 \\ -4/3 & 2\sqrt{3} \end{bmatrix} \begin{bmatrix} x \\ y \end{bmatrix} = \begin{bmatrix} 0 \\ 0 \end{bmatrix}$$

giving

$$2\sqrt{3}x - 9y = 0$$

Let $x = \sqrt{3}$ then $y = 2/3$, hence

$$\mathbf{v}^s = \begin{bmatrix} \sqrt{3} \\ 2/3 \end{bmatrix}$$

[10] Another identifying feature of the saddle point is that $\det(\mathbf{A}) < 0$.

The general solution is, therefore,

$$\begin{bmatrix} x - x^* \\ y - y^* \end{bmatrix} = c_1 \begin{bmatrix} \sqrt{3} \\ -2/3 \end{bmatrix} e^{(2\sqrt{3})t} + c_2 \begin{bmatrix} \sqrt{3} \\ 2/3 \end{bmatrix} e^{(-2\sqrt{3})t}$$

Suppose $c_2 = 0$ then

$$\begin{bmatrix} x - x^* \\ y - y^* \end{bmatrix} = c_1 \begin{bmatrix} \sqrt{3} \\ -2/3 \end{bmatrix} e^{(2\sqrt{3})t}$$

and so $\mathbf{v}^r$ represents an unstable arm because the system if perturbed will move over time away from (x^*, y^*) along the vector $\mathbf{v}^r$. On the other hand, if $c_1 = 0$ then

$$\begin{bmatrix} x - x^* \\ y - y^* \end{bmatrix} = c_2 \begin{bmatrix} \sqrt{3} \\ 2/3 \end{bmatrix} e^{(-2\sqrt{3})t}$$

which converges on (x^*, y^*) over time. Hence, $\mathbf{v}^s$ is a stable arm of the saddle point $E_1 = (3, 4/3)$. The behaviour of the system, therefore, in the neighbourhood of E_1 is illustrated in figure 14.19.

Unlike our analysis in the previous section, this present analysis indicates that if the system begins on the stable arm of the saddle point in the neighbourhood of the fixed point, then it will converge on the fixed point over time. However, for all other perturbations in the neighbourhood of the critical point, the system will diverge away from it. In which direction depends on how the system is disturbed, i.e., which of the four quadrants the system is moved into (but not along the arm through $\mathbf{v}^s$).

The next example has more equilibrium points to consider but the formal analysis is the same. Accordingly we shall be more succinct in our presentation.

Example 14.6 (cont.)

The system is

$$\dot{x} = f(x, y) = 3x - xy - x^2$$
$$\dot{y} = g(x, y) = 4y - 2xy - y^2$$

which has four equilibrium points:

$$E_0 = (0, 0), \qquad E_1 = (3, 0), \qquad E_2 = (0, 4), \qquad E_3 = (1, 2)$$

In each case we shall consider a linear approximation of the system in that neighbourhood.

The matrix of the linear system has elements

$$f_x = 3 - y - 2x \qquad f_y = -x$$
$$g_x = -2y \qquad g_y = 4 - 2x - 2y$$

$E_0 = (0,0)$

$$\mathbf{A} = \begin{bmatrix} 3 & 0 \\ 0 & 4 \end{bmatrix} \qquad \mathbf{A} - \lambda \mathbf{I} = \begin{bmatrix} 3 - \lambda & 0 \\ 0 & 4 - \lambda \end{bmatrix}$$

Figure 14.20.

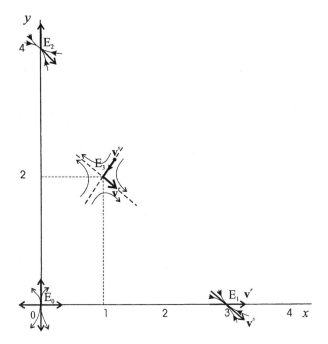

Hence $\det(\mathbf{A} - \lambda\mathbf{I}) = (3 - \lambda)(4 - \lambda) = 0$ with eigenvalues $r = 4$ and $s = 3$. The eigenvectors are

$$\mathbf{v}^r = \begin{bmatrix} 1 \\ 0 \end{bmatrix} \quad \text{and} \quad \mathbf{v}^s = \begin{bmatrix} 0 \\ 1 \end{bmatrix}$$

and the general solution is

$$\begin{bmatrix} x \\ y \end{bmatrix} = c_1 \begin{bmatrix} 1 \\ 0 \end{bmatrix} e^{4t} + c_2 \begin{bmatrix} 0 \\ 1 \end{bmatrix} e^{3t}$$

and is asymptotically unstable. The behaviour of the system in the neighbourhood of E_0 is shown in figure 14.20. In particular, since both x and y are positive then the system will move away from the origin.

$E_1 = (3,0)$

$$\mathbf{A} = \begin{bmatrix} -3 & -3 \\ 0 & -2 \end{bmatrix} \quad \mathbf{A} - \lambda\mathbf{I} = \begin{bmatrix} -(3 + \lambda) & -3 \\ 0 & -(2 + \lambda) \end{bmatrix}$$

Hence, $\det(\mathbf{A} - \lambda\mathbf{I}) = (3 + \lambda)(2 + \lambda) = 0$, with eigenvalues $r = -3$ and $s = -2$. Using $r = -3$ the associated eigenvector is

$$\mathbf{v}^r = \begin{bmatrix} 1 \\ 0 \end{bmatrix}$$

while for $s = -2$ the associated eigenvector is

$$\mathbf{v}^s = \begin{bmatrix} 3 \\ -1 \end{bmatrix}$$

and so the general solution in the neighbourhood of E_1 is

$$\begin{bmatrix} x - x^* \\ y - y^* \end{bmatrix} = c_1 \begin{bmatrix} 1 \\ 0 \end{bmatrix} e^{-3t} + c_2 \begin{bmatrix} 3 \\ -1 \end{bmatrix} e^{-2t}$$

Since both r and s are negative, then the system is asymptotically stable in the neighbourhood of E_1.

$E_2 = (0,4)$

$$A = \begin{bmatrix} -1 & 0 \\ -8 & -4 \end{bmatrix} \qquad A - \lambda I = \begin{bmatrix} -(1 + \lambda) & 0 \\ -8 & -(4 + \lambda) \end{bmatrix}$$

Hence, $\det(A - \lambda I) = (1 + \lambda)(4 + \lambda) = 0$, with eigenvalues $r = -4$ and $s = -1$. The associated eigenvectors are, respectively,

$$v^r = \begin{bmatrix} 0 \\ 1 \end{bmatrix} \qquad \text{and} \qquad v^s = \begin{bmatrix} 1 \\ -8/3 \end{bmatrix}$$

and the general solution in the neighbourhood of E_2 is

$$\begin{bmatrix} x - x^* \\ y - y^* \end{bmatrix} = c_1 \begin{bmatrix} 0 \\ 1 \end{bmatrix} e^{-4t} + c_2 \begin{bmatrix} 1 \\ -8/3 \end{bmatrix} e^{-t}$$

Since both r and s are negative, then the system is asymptotically stable in the neighbourhood of E_2.

$E_3 = (1,2)$

$$A = \begin{bmatrix} -1 & -1 \\ -4 & -2 \end{bmatrix} \qquad A - \lambda I = \begin{bmatrix} -(1 + \lambda) & -1 \\ -4 & -(2 + \lambda) \end{bmatrix}$$

Hence, $\det(A - \lambda I) = (1 + \lambda)(2 + \lambda) - 4 = \lambda^2 + 3\lambda - 2 = 0$, with eigenvalues

$$r = \frac{-3 + \sqrt{17}}{2} = 0.56155 \qquad \text{and} \qquad s = \frac{-3 - \sqrt{17}}{2} = -3.56155$$

The fact that the eigenvalues are of opposite sign indicates that E_3 is a local saddle point. The eigenvector associated with $r = 0.56155$ is

$$v^r = \begin{bmatrix} 1 \\ -1.5616 \end{bmatrix}$$

while that associated with $s = -3.56155$ is

$$v^s = \begin{bmatrix} 1 \\ 2.5616 \end{bmatrix}$$

and the general solution in the neighbourhood of E_3 is

$$\begin{bmatrix} x - x^* \\ y - y^* \end{bmatrix} = c_1 \begin{bmatrix} 1 \\ -1.5616 \end{bmatrix} e^{0.56155t} + c_2 \begin{bmatrix} 1 \\ 2.5616 \end{bmatrix} e^{-3.56155t}$$

It readily follows, therefore, that v^r is the unstable arm of the saddle point and v^s is the stable arm. Again the situation is illustrated in figure 14.20.

Although this second example involves more critical points, the linearisation of the nonlinear system enables us to investigate some useful properties of the system. Furthermore, it supports the analysis of the previous section.

Table 14.4 Eigenvalues and eigenvectors for examples 14.4–14.8

Ex	Points	Eigenvalues	Eigenvectors
14.4	$E_0 = (0,0)$	$r = 4$ $s = 3$	$\mathbf{v}^r = \begin{bmatrix} 1 \\ 0 \end{bmatrix},\ \mathbf{v}^s = \begin{bmatrix} 0 \\ 1 \end{bmatrix}$
	$E_1 = (3, 4/3)$	$r = +2\sqrt{3}$ $s = -2\sqrt{3}$	$\mathbf{v}^r = \begin{bmatrix} \sqrt{3} \\ -2/3 \end{bmatrix},\ \mathbf{v}^s = \begin{bmatrix} \sqrt{3} \\ 2/3 \end{bmatrix}$
14.5	$E_0 = (0,0)$	$r = 2$ $s = -2$	$\mathbf{v}^r = \begin{bmatrix} 1 \\ 0 \end{bmatrix},\ \mathbf{v}^s = \begin{bmatrix} 0 \\ 1 \end{bmatrix}$
	$E_1 = (100,200)$	$r = 2i$ $s = -2i$	$\mathbf{v}^r = \begin{bmatrix} 1 \\ 2i \end{bmatrix},\ \mathbf{v}^s = \begin{bmatrix} 1 \\ 2i \end{bmatrix}$
14.6	$E_0 = (0,0)$	$r = 4$ $s = 3$	$\mathbf{v}^r = \begin{bmatrix} 1 \\ 0 \end{bmatrix},\ \mathbf{v}^s = \begin{bmatrix} 0 \\ 1 \end{bmatrix}$
	$E_1 = (3,0)$	$r = -3$ $s = -2$	$\mathbf{v}^r = \begin{bmatrix} 1 \\ 0 \end{bmatrix},\ \mathbf{v}^s = \begin{bmatrix} 3 \\ -1 \end{bmatrix}$
	$E_2 = (0,4)$	$r = -4$ $s = -1$	$\mathbf{v}^r = \begin{bmatrix} 0 \\ 1 \end{bmatrix},\ \mathbf{v}^s = \begin{bmatrix} 1 \\ -8/3 \end{bmatrix}$
	$E_3 = (1,2)$	$r = 0.5616$ $s = -3.5616$	$\mathbf{v}^r = \begin{bmatrix} 1 \\ -1.5616 \end{bmatrix},\ \mathbf{v}^s = \begin{bmatrix} 1 \\ 2.5616 \end{bmatrix}$
14.7	$E_0 = (0,0)$	$r = 6$ $s = 4$	$\mathbf{v}^r = \begin{bmatrix} 0 \\ 1 \end{bmatrix},\ \mathbf{v}^s = \begin{bmatrix} 1 \\ 0 \end{bmatrix}$
	$E_1 = (4,0)$	$r = -4$ $s = 2$	$\mathbf{v}^r = \begin{bmatrix} 1 \\ 0 \end{bmatrix},\ \mathbf{v}^s = \begin{bmatrix} 2/3 \\ 1 \end{bmatrix}$
	$E_2 = (0,3)$	$r = 1$ $s = -6$	$\mathbf{v}^r = \begin{bmatrix} 1 \\ 3/7 \end{bmatrix},\ \mathbf{v}^s = \begin{bmatrix} 0 \\ 1 \end{bmatrix}$
	$E_3 = (2,2)$	$r = -0.7639$ $s = -5.2361$	$\mathbf{v}^r = \begin{bmatrix} 1 \\ 0.61805 \end{bmatrix},\ \mathbf{v}^s = \begin{bmatrix} 1 \\ 1.61805 \end{bmatrix}$
14.8	$E_1 = (0,0)$	$r = 2$ $s = -2$	$\mathbf{v}^r = \begin{bmatrix} 1 \\ 0 \end{bmatrix},\ \mathbf{v}^s = \begin{bmatrix} 0 \\ 1 \end{bmatrix}$
	$E_2 = (112.5,50)$	$r = 1.4375 + 1.0588i$ $s = -1.4375 - 1.0588i$	Complex conjugate vectors*

* If required they can be obtained using *Mathematica* or *Maple*. Obtain the matrix **A** and define it in *Mathematica* or *Maple* as a matrix, say m. Then use the **Eigenvectors[m]** command in *Mathematica* or **eigenvects(m)** command in *Maple*.

Before we comment generally on the linearisation of nonlinear systems, table 14.4 provides a summary of all the mathematical properties of examples 14.4–14.8 of the previous section.

14.5.1 *Some general remarks*

For linear systems there are general formulae for solutions. These general formulae include all solutions. Even where discontinuities exist, these can be located. Unfortunately, for nonlinear systems no such general formulae exist. This means that it is very difficult, or not even possible, to establish properties of solutions. Another difficulty with nonlinear systems is that of determining the interval in which a solution exist which satisfies an initial value.

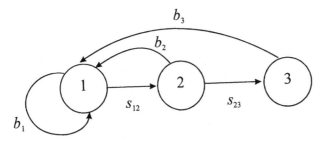

Figure 14.21.

14.6 Age classes and projection matrices

Since it is females that give birth, then a number of population models consider only the number of females. However, the probability of giving birth varies throughout the lifespan of the female – something that we have so far ignored. In any period there are two probabilities (events): (1) the probability of dying in that period, and (2) the probability of giving birth in that period. Put another way, there is a rate of survival and a reproduction rate for a given class. Many models, therefore, consider the population of women of childbearing age. In such models, equal class intervals are taken. If, for example, we assume women can bear children to age 45 and we have three class intervals, then we have the three classes: 0–15, 15–30 and 30–45. Let x denote the continuous variable 'age'. In general, if the terminal age is $N = 45$, and we have n age-classes, then N/n is the duration of the age class. In our present example this is $45/3 = 15$. Finally, let t denote the projection interval, which has the same duration as the age class (here 15 years). The population is observed at the end of each projection interval. Turning now to the characteristics of the female population, let b_i denote the birth rate for the ith-class ($i = 1, 2, 3$) and s_{ij} the survival rate from class i into class j. In our present example we have only s_{12} and s_{23}. The model can be captured in terms of a **state diagram**, presented in figure 14.21.

Let $x_i(t)$ denote the population of the ith-age class at the tth-time step. To be in class $i = 1$, age 0–15, then the female can be born from a woman of any of the three age classes. So

$$x_1(t + 1) = b_1 x_1(t) + b_2 x_2(t) + b_3 x_3(t)$$

But account must be taken of women in the population surviving into the second and third age class. The number surviving to the second age class is $x_2(t + 1) = s_{12} x_1(t)$; while the number surviving to the third age class is $x_3(t + 1) = s_{23} x_2(t)$. We have, then, the set of equations

$$x_1(t + 1) = b_1 x_1(t) + b_2 x_2(t) + b_3 x_3(t)$$
$$x_2(t + 1) = s_{12} x_1(t)$$
$$x_3(t + 1) = s_{23} x_2(t)$$

(14.19)

This can be written in the matrix form

$$\begin{bmatrix} x_1(t+1) \\ x_2(t+1) \\ x_3(t+1) \end{bmatrix} = \begin{bmatrix} b_1 & b_2 & b_3 \\ s_{12} & 0 & 0 \\ 0 & s_{23} & 0 \end{bmatrix} \begin{bmatrix} x_1(t) \\ x_2(t) \\ x_3(t) \end{bmatrix}$$

or more succinctly

$$\mathbf{x}(t+1) = \mathbf{A}\mathbf{x}(t) \tag{14.}$$

In general

(14.21)
$$\mathbf{A} = \begin{bmatrix} b_1 & b_2 & b_3 & \cdots & b_{n-1} & b_n \\ s_{12} & 0 & 0 & \cdots & 0 & 0 \\ \vdots & \vdots & \vdots & & \vdots & \vdots \\ 0 & 0 & 0 & \cdots & s_{n-1,n} & 0 \end{bmatrix}$$

The matrix $\mathbf{A}$ is often called a **Leslie matrix** after P. Leslie who first introduced them.

Of course (14.20) is just a recursive equation with solution

(14.22)
$$\mathbf{x}(t) = \mathbf{A}^t \mathbf{x}(0)$$

where $\mathbf{x}(0)$ denotes the vector of females in each ith-class in period 0.

Before continuing, consider the following simple numerical example.

Example 14.9

Let

$$b_1 = 0.4, \quad b_2 = 0.8, \quad b_3 = 0.2$$

$$s_{12} = 0.9, \quad s_{23} = 0.8$$

Suppose a population has 10 million females in each of the three age classes, giving a total female population of 30 million. Using the recursive relations specified in (14.19), by means of a spreadsheet we can derive the time profile of this population over, say, ten periods as shown in table 14.5(a). The ten periods cover 150 years, since the projection interval is 15 years. Figure 14.22 shows the time profile of this population in terms of the three classes.

Alternatively, using result (14.22) we could derive a particular row of the spreadsheet. For example, for $t = 4$ we have

$$\mathbf{x}(4) = \mathbf{A}^4 \mathbf{x}(0) = \begin{bmatrix} 1.0048 & .7680 & .1568 \\ .7056 & .6912 & .1584 \\ .6336 & .3456 & .0576 \end{bmatrix} \begin{bmatrix} 10 \\ 10 \\ 10 \end{bmatrix} = \begin{bmatrix} 19.2960 \\ 15.5520 \\ 10.3680 \end{bmatrix}$$

which is exactly the same as the row for $t = 4$ in table 14.5(a).

In table 14.5(b) we have computed the proportion of the total female population in each class. It should be noticed that these proportions are settling down to 42.7% in class 1, 33.7% in class 2 and 23.6% in class 3 by period 10.

What we shall now illustrate is that the dominant eigenvalue of the matrix $\mathbf{A}$ establishes the growth rate of the population, while the eigenvector associated with the dominant eigenvalue allows a computation of the proportion to which each class stabilises. Such results are highly significant. Once we know the matrix $\mathbf{A}$, it is relatively easy to establish with computer software the eigenvalues and eigenvectors.

To show these properties we utilise the following theorem.[11]

---

[11] This theorem itself utilises the Perron–Frobenious theorem.

Table 14.5 Age class projections
(a) Numbers

t	Years	$x_1(t)$	$x_2(t)$	$x_3(t)$	Total
0	0	10	10	10	30
1	15	14	9	8	31
2	30	14.4	12.6	7.2	34.2
3	45	17.28	12.96	10.08	40.32
4	60	19.296	15.552	10.368	45.216
5	75	22.237	17.366	12.442	52.042
6	90	25.275	20.010	13.893	59.178
7	105	28.897	22.747	16.008	67.652
8	120	32.958	26.007	18.198	77.163
9	135	37.629	29.662	20.806	88.097
10	150	42.943	33.866	23.730	100.538

(b) Per cent

t	Years	$x_1(t)$	$x_2(t)$	$x_3(t)$
0	0	33.3	33.3	33.3
1	15	45.2	29.0	25.8
2	30	42.1	36.8	21.1
3	45	42.9	32.1	25.0
4	60	42.7	34.4	22.9
5	75	42.7	33.4	23.9
6	90	42.7	33.8	23.5
7	105	42.7	33.6	23.7
8	120	42.7	33.7	23.6
9	135	42.7	33.7	23.6
10	150	42.7	33.7	23.6

THEOREM 14.1

If $\mathbf{A}$ *is a Leslie matrix of the form*

$$\mathbf{A} = \begin{bmatrix} b_1 & b_2 & b_3 & \cdots & b_{n-1} & b_n \\ s_{12} & 0 & 0 & \cdots & 0 & 0 \\ \vdots & \vdots & \vdots & & \vdots & \vdots \\ 0 & 0 & 0 & \cdots & s_{n-1,n} & 0 \end{bmatrix} \qquad \begin{array}{l} b_i \geq 0 \quad i = 1, \ldots n \\ 0 < s_{i-1,i} \leq 1 \quad i = 2, \ldots n \end{array}$$

then

(1)   *there exists a unique dominant eigenvalue,* λ_d, *which is positive,*
(2)   *the eigenvector associated with the dominant eigenvalue has positive components,*
(3)   *all other eigenvalues,* $\lambda_i \neq \lambda_d$ *satisfy* $|\lambda_i| < \lambda_d$.

Example 14.9 (cont.)

The Leslie matrix for example 14.9 is

$$\mathbf{A} = \begin{bmatrix} 0.4 & 0.8 & 0.2 \\ 0.9 & 0 & 0 \\ 0 & 0.8 & 0 \end{bmatrix}$$

Figure 14.22.

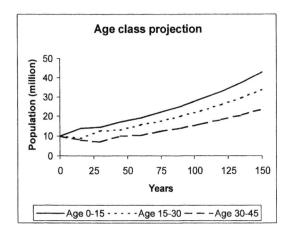

with eigenvalues

$$\lambda_1 = 1.14136 \qquad \lambda_2 = -0.4767 \qquad \lambda_3 = -0.26466$$

We see that λ_1 is the dominant eigenvalue and $|\lambda_2| < \lambda_1$ and $|\lambda_3| < \lambda_1$. The eigenvector, $\mathbf{v}^1$ associated with the eigenvalue λ_1 is

$$\mathbf{v}^1 = \begin{bmatrix} 0.72033 \\ 0.56800 \\ 0.39812 \end{bmatrix}$$

which clearly has all positive components.

Given the three eigenvalues, the system has the general solution

$$\mathbf{x}(t+1) = c_1 \lambda_1^t \mathbf{v}^1 + c_2 \lambda_2^t \mathbf{v}^2 + c_3 \lambda_3^t \mathbf{v}^3$$

which will be governed in the limit by the dominant root, λ_1. Since $\lambda_1 > 1$ then the system grows over time. This is clearly shown in figure 14.22. Furthermore, the growth of the system is given by $\lambda_1 - 1 = 0.14136$, which means a growth rate of 14.1%. Since the eigenvector $\mathbf{v}^1$ has elements $x_1(t) = 0.72033$, $x_2(t) = 0.56800$ and $x_3(t) = 0.39812$ then their sum is 1.68645 and so normalising the eigenvector by dividing each term by this sum, we arrive at the values

$$\begin{bmatrix} 0.42713 \\ 0.33680 \\ 0.23607 \end{bmatrix}$$

which in percentage terms are the values we obtained as the limiting values in table 14.5(b).

Appendix 14.1 Computing a and b for the logistic equation using *Mathematica*

When solving for a and b in the logistic growth equation do not use **Solve** or **Nsolve** command, rather use **FindRoot**. It is important to have 'good' initial estimates of *a* and *b*. First define the two equations:

$$In[1]:= \texttt{eq1} \; := \; 24.135 \; == \; \frac{13a}{13b \; + \; (a-13b) \quad e^{-50 \; a}}$$

$$In[2]:= \texttt{eq2} \; := \; 34.934 \; == \frac{13a}{13b \; + \; (a-13b) \quad e^{-100 \; a}}$$

Then use the **FindRoot** command using initial estimates for *a* and *b*.

$$In[3]:=\texttt{FindRoot[\{eq1, eq2\}, \{a, 0.02\}, \{b, 0.0004\}]}$$

$$Out[3]= \; \{a \; \rightarrow \; 0.020383, \; b \; \rightarrow \; 0.000436045\}$$

We do the same for the linear approximation

$$In[4]:= \texttt{eq3} \; := \; 24.135 \; == \; \frac{13a}{13b \; + \dfrac{a-13b}{(1+a)^{50}}}$$

$$In[5]:= \texttt{eq4} \; := \; 34.934 \; == \; \frac{13a}{13b \; + \dfrac{a-13b}{(1+a)^{100}}}$$

$$In[6]:= \; \texttt{FindRoot[\{eq3, eq4\}, \{a, 0.02\}, \{b, 0.0004\}]}$$

$$Out[6]= \; \{a \; \rightarrow \; 0.0205922, \; b \; \rightarrow \; 0.00044052\}$$

Appendix 14.2 Using *Maple* to compute *a* and *b* for the logistic equation

When solving for *a* and *b* in the logistic growth equation do not use the **solve** command, rather use the **fsolve** command. Because solving can be problematic, include ranges for *a* and *b*, e.g. $a = 0.02..0.03$ and $b = 0.0004..0.0005$.
  First define the two equations:

```
> eq1:=24.135=13*a/(13*b+(a-13*b)*exp(-50*a));
```
$$eq1 := 24.135 = 13\frac{a}{13b + (a - 13b)e^{(-50a)}}$$

```
> eq2:=34.934=13*a/(13*b+(a-13*b)*exp(-100*a));
```
$$eq2 := 34.934 = 13\frac{a}{13b + (a - 13b)e^{(-100a)}}$$

Then use the fsolve command using ranges for both *a* and *b*

```
> fsolve ({eq1,eq2},{a,b},
       {a=0.02..0.03,b=0.0004..0.0005});
```
$$\{a = .02038301946, b = .0004360453198\}$$

We do the same for the linear approximation

```
> eq3:=24.135=13*a/(13*b+((1+a)^(-50))*(a-13*b));
```
$$eq3 := 24.135 = 13\frac{a}{13b + \dfrac{a - 13b}{(1 + a)^{50}}}$$

```
> eq4:=34.934=13*a/(13*b+((1+a)^(-100))*(a-13*b));
```

$$eq4 := 34.934 = 13\frac{a}{13b + \dfrac{a - 13b}{(1 + a)^{100}}}$$

```
> fsolve ({eq3, eq4}, {a,b},
     {a=0.02..0.03, b=0.0004..0.0005});
```

$$\{a = .02059217184, b = .0004405196282\}$$

Appendix 14.3 Multispecies modelling with *Mathematica* and *Maple*

In this appendix we give detailed instructions for deriving direction fields and trajectories for example 14.4 employing both *Mathematica* and *Maple*. We also give some basic instructions for the linear approximation. All other problems in this chapter can be investigated in the same manner. Here we concentrate only on the input instructions.

The equation system we are to investigate is

$$\dot{x} = (4 - 3y)x$$
$$\dot{y} = (3 - x)y$$

This is a nonlinear system and cannot be solved directly by any known method. However, as we pointed out in sub-section 14.4.1, we can express the properties of

$$\dot{x} = (a - by)x \quad a > 0, b > 0$$
$$\dot{y} = (c - dx)y \quad c > 0, d > 0$$

in the phase plane by plotting the solution trajectories

$$k = \frac{y^a x^{-c}}{e^{by - dx}} \quad k \text{ a constant}$$

Alternatively for the nonlinear system

$$\dot{x} = f(x, y)$$
$$\dot{y} = g(x, y)$$

we can investigate the linear approximation

$$\begin{bmatrix} \dot{x} \\ \dot{y} \end{bmatrix} = \begin{bmatrix} f_x & f_y \\ g_x & g_y \end{bmatrix} \begin{bmatrix} x - x^* \\ y - y^* \end{bmatrix}$$

in the neighbourhood of a particular fixed point (x^*, y^*), and where f_x, f_y, g_x and g_y are evaluated at a fixed point.

14A.1 *Mathematica*

To derive the contour plot in *Mathematica* input the following instructions:

```
k[x_,y_]:=y^ a x^ (-c)/E^ (b y - d x)
{a=4, b=3, c=3, d=1}
graph1=ContourPlot[ k[x,y], {x,0.5,6}, {y,0.5,4},
      ContourShading->False,
      PlotPoints->50]
```

The contour plot, however, does not indicate in which direction the vector forces go. For this purpose we need to invoke the **PlotVectorField** command and then combine this with the contour plot. Thus

```
graph2=PlotVectorField[ {(4-3y)x,(3-x)y},
       {x,0.5,6}, {y,0.5,4}]
Show[graph1,graph2]
```

There may be memory problems with showing the two graphs together.

Turning to the linear approximation, the system can be investigated by means of the following input instructions

```
roots=Solve[ {(4-3y)x==0, (3-x)y==0}, {x,y} ]
eq3=(4-3y)x
eq4=(3-x)y
matrixA= { {D[eq3,x], D[eq3,y]},
          {D[eq4,x], D[eq4,y]} };
MatrixForm[matrixA]
matrixA1=matrixA /. roots[[1]]
Eigenvalues[matrixA1]
Eigenvectors[matrixA1]
matrixA2=matrixA /. roots[[2]]
Eigenvalues[matrixA2]
Eigenvectors[matrixA2]
```

Although *Mathematica* gives the eigenvectors for matrixA2 as

$$\mathbf{v}^r = \begin{bmatrix} \dfrac{-3\sqrt{3}}{2} \\ 1 \end{bmatrix} \quad \text{and} \quad \mathbf{v}^s = \begin{bmatrix} \dfrac{3\sqrt{3}}{2} \\ 1 \end{bmatrix}$$

these are, in fact, the same as those in the text.

14A.2 *Maple*

The equivalent in *Maple* is not as satisfactory. The contour plots can be obtained using the following input instructions.

```
with(plots):
equ:=y^e*x^(-3)/exp(3*y-x);
contourplot(equ, x=0.5..6, y=0.5..4, grid=[40,40]);
```

This plot has only contour lines to the left and right of the fixed point $(x^*, y^*) = (3, 4/3)$ and not above or below this value. A better rendition of the phase portrait is to utilise the following instructions.

```
with(plots):
with(DEtools):
seq1:=seq( [0,0.5,0.5+0.25*i], i=0..10);
seq2:=seq( [0, 6, 1+0.25*j], j=1..10);
seq3:=seq( [0,1,0.1+0.1*k], k=1..10)
```

```
inits:={seq1, seq2, seq3};
phaseportrait( equ, [x,y], 0..1, inits, x=0.5..6,
        y=0.5..4,arrows=THIN);
```

Turning to the linear approximation, the system can be investigated by means of the following input instructions

```
with(linalg):
sol1:=solve( {(4-3*y)*x=0, (3-x)*y=0} );
equ1:=(4-3*y)*x;
equ2:=(3-x)*y;
matrixA:=matrix( [ [diff(equ1,x), diff(equ1,y)],
[diff(equ2,x), diff(equ2,y)] ] );
matrixA1:=matrix( [ [ subs(sol1[1],diff(equ1,x) ),
        subs(sol1[1], diff(equ1,y) ) ],
        [subs(sol1[1], diff(equ2,x)),
        subs(sol1[1], diff (equ2,y)) ] ] );
eigenvals(matrixA1);
eigenvects(matrixA1);
matrixA2:=matrix( [ [ subs(sol1[2],diff(equ1,x) ),
        subs(sol1[2], diff(equ1,y) ) ],
        [subs(sol1[2], diff(equ2,x)),
        subs(sol1[2], diff (equ2,y)) ] ] );
eigenvals(matrixA2);
eigenvects(matrixA2);
```

These instructions produce the same results as with *Mathematica*, with the same eigenvectors that, as indicated above, are the same as those in the text – which can readily be verified.

Exercises

1. Given the following data for population in England and Wales over the period 1701–91, obtain the estimated population using the continuous Malthusian population model and compare your results with those provided. Why do you think the estimated population *under-estimates* the actual population in 1791?

Year	1701	1711	1721	1731	1741	1751	1761	1771	1781	1791
Population (million)	5.8	6.0	6.0	6.1	6.2	6.5	6.7	7.2	7.5	8.3

Source: Tranter (1973, table 1).

2. Two countries, A and B, have populations of equal size, p_0, and are growing at the same net rate of 2% per annum. However, population A has a birth rate of 3% per annum and a death rate of 1% per annum

while country B has a birth and death rate of 5% and 3%, respectively. Unfortunately, country A suffers a major spread of AIDS and its death rate rises to 2% per annum. Assuming both populations conform to the Malthusian model, how long will it take for the population of country B to be twice the size of country A?

3. A population has births b, deaths d and migration m each growing exponentially. If $b < (d + m)$, how long before the population is half its original size?

4. (i) If a population conforms to the Malthusian population model and is growing at 3% per annum, how long will it take for the population to treble in size?

   (ii) Derive a general formula for the time interval necessary for an increase in population to grow by λ times its initial size, assuming it is growing at some general rate $k\%$ per annum?

5. For the logistic equation

$$\dot{p} = p(a - bp) \qquad a > 0, b > 0$$

expand this as a Taylor series around the equilibrium a/b and hence show that the population in the neighbourhood of the equilibrium can be expressed

$$p - \frac{a}{b} = \left(p_0 - \frac{a}{b}\right) e^{at}$$

Show that as $t \to \infty$ then $p \to a/b$. What does this imply about the achievement of equilibrium?

6. Suppose

$$\dot{p} = p(a + cp) \qquad a > 0, c > 0$$

   (i) Explain this equation.
   (ii) Draw the phase line for this population and show that the population tends to infinity.
   (iii) Derive an explicit solution for the population and use this to show that an infinite population is reached at a *finite* point in time.

7. A population is thought to have the feature that if it falls below a minimum level, m, then it will die out and that there is a maximum carrying capacity of M for the same population.

   (i) Given an intrinsic growth rate of r, discuss the usefulness of

$$\dot{p} = r(M - p)(p - m)$$

   to describe this population.

   (ii) Compare
      (a) $\dot{p} = rp(M - p)$
      (b) $\dot{p} = r(M - p)(p - m)$

8. For the **Gompertz equation**

$$\dot{p} = rp(a - \ln p) \quad a > 0$$

   (i) Solve the equation subject to $p(0) = p_0$.
   (ii) Sketch this graph and its associated phase line.

(iii) Obtain the fixed points and establish their stability/instability.

(iv) What happens to p as $t \to \infty$?

9.   Solve the following system for two competing species x and y

$$\dot{x} = -3y(t)$$
$$\dot{y} = -9x(t)$$

and derive explicitly the phase line.

10.   Trout, species T, and bass, species B, are assumed to conform to the following model

$$\dot{T} = a\left(1 - \frac{T}{k_1}\right)T - bTB$$

$$\dot{B} = c\left(1 - \frac{B}{k_2}\right)B - dTB$$

Analyse this model in detail using a graphical analysis.

11.   Suppose $N(t)$ denotes the biomass of halibut in the Pacific Ocean. It has been estimated that for the equation

$$N(t) = \frac{N_0 K}{N_0 + (K - N_0)e^{-rt}}$$

Note: $N(t)/K = N_0/(N_0 + (K - N_0)e^{-rt}) = (N_0/K)/((N_0/K) + (1 - (N_0/K))e^{-rt})$ $r = 0.71$ per year and $K = 80.5 \times 10^6$ kg. If the initial biomass is one-quarter of the carrying capacity,

(i)   What is the biomass 2 years later?

(ii) What is the time at which the biomass is

(a) half the carrying capacity?

(b) three-quarters of the carrying capacity?

12.   In each of the following systems which describes the interaction between two species of population x and y,

(i)   Find the stationary values.

(ii) Linearise each system in the neighbourhood of all critical points.

(iii) Find the eigenvalues and eigenvectors for each linearisation and describe the nature of the critical point.

(iv) Try to establish the nature of the system by plotting sufficient trajectories.

(a) $\dot{x} = -x + \dfrac{xy}{100}$ $\dot{y} = 2y - \dfrac{2xy}{25}$

(b) $\dot{x} = -\tfrac{1}{2}x + \dfrac{xy}{(\tfrac{1}{4} + y)}$ $\dot{y} = y - y^2 - \dfrac{xy}{(\tfrac{1}{4} + y)}$

(c) $\dot{x} = x - x^2 - xy$ $\dot{y} = y - 2xy - 2y^2$

13.   Consider the following discrete numerical predatory–prey model, where x is the prey and y is the predator

$$x_{t+1} - x_t = 1.4(1 - y_t)x_t$$
$$y_{t+1} - y_t = 0.6(1 - 4y_t + x_t)y_t$$

(i)   Establish the critical points.

(ii) Find the linearisation coefficient matrix, $\mathbf{A}$, for each critical point.

(iii) Establish the eigenvalues and eigenvectors of **A**.

(iv) Set up the system on a spreadsheet and establish the limit value of x and y as $t \to \infty$.

14. Investigate fully the discrete dynamical system

$$x_{t+1} = 1.3x_t - 0.3x_t^2 - 0.15x_t y_t$$
$$y_{t+1} = 1.3y_t - 0.3y_t^2 - 0.15x_t y_t$$

(i) Showing in particular that *four* critical points exit.

(ii) Linearising the system about each critical point.

(iii) Establishing the behaviour of the system by considering sufficient trajectories in relation to (i)–(ii).

15. The American bison population can be sub-divided into three categories (Cullen 1985): calves, yearlings and adults. These are denoted $x_1(t)$, $x_2(t)$ and $x_3(t)$, respectively. In each year the number of newborns is 42% of the number of adults from the previous year. Each year 60% of the calves live to become yearlings, while 75% of yearlings become adults. Furthermore, 95% of adults survive to live to the following year.

(i) Write out the system as a set of difference equations.

(ii) Draw a state diagram for this population.

(iii) Show that this system has one real eigenvalue and two conjugate complex eigenvalues.

(iv) What is the eventual growth rate of the bison population?

(v) What proportion of calves, yearlings and adults does this system settle down to?

Additional reading

Additional material covered in this chapter can be found in Boyce and DiPrima (1997), Braun (1983), Caswell (2000), Deane and Cole (1962), Haberman (1977), Hoppensteadt (1992), Lynch (2001), Meyer (1985), Mooney and Swift (1999), Renshaw (1991), Sandefur (1990), Tranter (1973) and Vandermeer (1981).

CHAPTER 15

The dynamics of fisheries

In this chapter we consider a renewable resource. Although we shall concentrate on fishing, the same basic analysis applies to any biological species that involves births and deaths. A *fishery* consists of a number of different characteristics and activities that are associated with fishing. The type of fish to be harvested and the type of vessels used are the first obvious characteristics and activities. Trawlers fishing for herring are somewhat different from pelagic whaling.[1] In order to capture the nature of the problem we shall assume that there is just one type of fish in the region to be harvested and that the vessels used for harvesting are homogeneous and that harvesters have the same objective function.

Because fish reproduce, grow and die then they are a *renewable resource*. But one of the main characteristics of biological species is that for any given habitat there is a limit to what it can support. Of course, harvesting means removing fish from the stock of fish in the available habitat. Whether the stock is increasing, constant or decreasing, therefore, depends not only on the births and deaths but also on the quantity being harvested. The stock of fish at a moment of time denotes the total number of fish, and is referred to as the *biomass*. Although it is true that the biomass denotes fish of different sizes, different ages and different states of health, we ignore these facts and concentrate purely on the stock level of fish. But like any renewable resource, over an interval of time the stock level will change according to births, deaths and harvesting. We shall deal with harvesting later. For the moment we shall concentrate purely on the biological characteristics of the fish stock. Our first aim is to represent the biological growth curve of a fishery.

15.1 Biological growth curve of a fishery

We assume that the growth rate of the fish stock, denoted ds/dt, is related to the biomass (the stock level), denoted s. Although stock size and the growth in stock size are related to time, in what follows we shall suppress the time variable in the stock. Thus, the instantaneous growth process for fish can be represented by the equation

(15.1)
$$\frac{ds}{dt} = f(s)$$

---

[1] See Shone (1981, application 11) for a review of pelagic whaling.

which is a representation of the births and deaths of the species in the absence of harvesting.

In order to take the analysis further we need to assume something about the biological growth curve. A reasonable representation is given by the logistic equation, which we discussed in chapter 14. Thus

$$\frac{ds}{dt} = f(s) = rs\left(1 - \frac{s}{k}\right) \tag{15.2}$$

The coefficient r represents the intrinsic instantaneous growth rate of the biomass, i.e., it is equal to the rate of growth of the stock s when s is close to zero. More importantly, the coefficient k represents the *carrying capacity* (or saturation level) of the biomass, i.e., it represents the maximum population that the habitat can support. This follows immediately from the fact that the stock size will be a maximum when $ds/dt = 0$, i.e., when $s = k$. In what follows we assume that both r and k are constant. These, and other features of the logistic equation representing fish growth, are illustrated in figure 15.1.

In the upper section of the diagram we have the growth curve represented by the logistic equation, while in the lower section we draw the equation of the stock size against time, i.e., the solution equation

$$s = \frac{k}{1 + \left(\dfrac{k}{s_0} - 1\right)e^{-rt}} \tag{15.3}$$

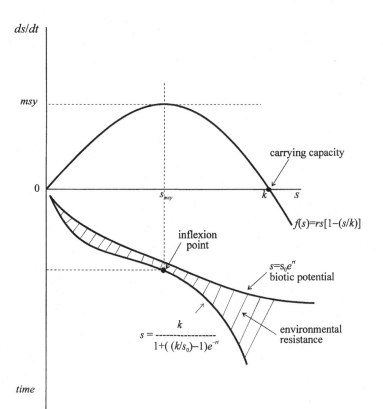

Figure 15.1.

time

In the lower section we also draw the curve denoting the *biotic potential*. This curve represents the growth of a species in which there is no negative feedback from over-crowding or environmental resistance. In other words, the biotic potential denotes the exponential growth curve

(15.4)
$$s = s_0 e^{rt}$$

The shaded region in the lower section of figure 15.1 shows the environmental resistance, which increases sharply after the inflexion point. The environmental resistance occurs because of the carrying capacity of the habitat.

From the upper diagram in figure 15.1 it is clear that the growth function has a maximum point. At the stock size denoted s_{msy} the growth of the fish stock is at a maximum, and is referred to as the *maximum sustainable yield*. The maximum sustainable yield is readily found. Since the growth curve is at a maximum, then we can establish this maximum by differentiating the growth curve and setting it equal to zero to solve for s_{msy} and then substituting this value into $f(s)$. Thus

$$f'(s) = rs\left(-\frac{1}{k}\right) + r\left(1 - \frac{s}{k}\right) = 0$$

$$-rs + r(k - s) = 0$$

(15.5)
$$s_{msy} = \frac{k}{2}$$

$$f\left(\frac{k}{2}\right) = \frac{rk}{4}$$

i.e. the stock level of fish at the maximum sustainable yield of a particular species is exactly half of its carrying capacity. Furthermore, given the logistic equation, equation (15.2), the growth function is symmetrical about s_{msy}.

The importance of the maximum sustainable yield is in relation to harvesting. The situation is shown in figure 15.2. With no harvesting, the species will be in

Figure 15.2.

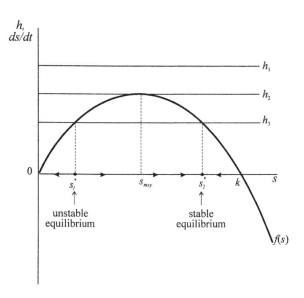

biological equilibrium when there is no growth, i.e., when $ds/dt = 0$. There are two biological equilibria, $s^* = 0$ and $s^* = k$, as shown in figure 15.2. Any stock size above zero and below the carrying capacity will lead to positive growth and hence an increase in the stock. Any stock level above the carrying capacity will lead to excessive environmental resistance, and hence to a decline in the stock size. (This naturally follows since above $s^* = k$, $ds/dt < 0$, and hence the stock size must be declining.)

Now consider three constant levels of harvesting, h_1, h_2 and h_3. Harvesting level h_1 is above the growth curve, which means that the fish are being extracted faster than they can reproduce. The fish will accordingly be harvested to extinction. At a harvest level of h_2, the harvest line just touches the growth curve at the maximum sustainable yield. What does this imply? Suppose the fish stock begins at the level of the carrying capacity. There will be no natural growth in the fish stock, but there will be a level of harvesting equal to h_2, which will result in the fish stock declining. When the fish stock declines to the maximum sustainable yield, then the natural growth in the fish population is just matched by the level of harvesting, and so this level of fish stock can be sustained perpetually. However, if the fish stock should fall below the maximum sustainable yield, then the rate of harvesting will exceed the natural population growth, and the fish stock will decline, and extinction will eventually result. This suggests that a management policy to harvest at the level h_2 is not necessarily a sensible one, especially with the uncertainty involved in estimating fish stocks.

If harvesting were at a level of h_3, there are two possible equilibria, s_1^* and s_2^*, given by the stock levels where the harvesting line cuts the growth curve. Both s_1^* and s_2^* represent sustainable yields. This is because at each of these stock levels the growth rate equals the rate of harvesting, and so the fish stock will remain constant. There are a number of characteristics of the fishery in this instance:

(1)   If $0 < s < s_1^*$ then harvesting exceeds natural fish growth, and the species will decline to extinction.
(2)   If $s_1^* < s < s_2^*$ then harvesting is less than the natural fish growth, and so the stock size will increase, and increase until s_2^* is reached.
(3)   If $s > s_2^*$ then again harvesting exceeds the natural fish growth and so the fish stock will decline until it reaches s_2^*.
(4)   Any deviation of the stock size away from s_1^* will lead to a further movement of the fish stock away from this level, either to extinction or to the level s_2^*. Accordingly, s_1^* denotes a *locally unstable* equilibrium.
(5)   Any deviation of the stock size around the level s_2^* will lead to the stock size changing until it reaches s_2^*. Hence, s_2^* denotes a *stable* equilibrium.

Consider the following discrete form of the model[2]

$$\Delta s_{t+1} = s_{t+1} - s_t = rs_t\left(1 - \frac{s_t}{k}\right) - h_t \tag{15.6}$$

which can readily be investigated by means of a spreadsheet. Let $r = 0.2$ and $k = 1000$; further assume $h = 20$ for all time periods. The results are shown

---

[2] It is well known that the discrete form of the model can produce far more complex behaviour than the continuous model depending on the value of r. See Sandefur (1990).

Figure 15.3.

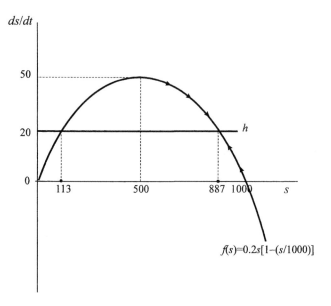

$f(s)=0.2s[1-(s/1000)]$

in figure 15.3. An initial stock size equal to the carrying capacity leads to an
equilibrium stock size of $s = 887$ approached from below (i.e. s falls). On the
other hand, an initial stock level equal to $s = 500$ (the *msy* stock level), leads to the
same equilibrium but approached from above (i.e. s increases). In fact any initial
stock in excess of $s = 113$ will lead to the stable equilibrium. An initial stock level
below $s = 113$ leads to extinction.[3] Any constant level of harvesting in excess of
50 will automatically lead to extinction.

We can generalise the problem by letting $h(t)$ denote the harvesting function,
then the net growth in the fish population is given by

$$\frac{ds(t)}{dt} = f(s(t)) - h(t)$$

$$= rs(t)\left(1 - \frac{s(t)}{k}\right) - h(t)$$

Suppressing the time variable for convenience, this can be expressed more simply
as

(15.7)
$$\frac{ds}{dt} = rs\left(1 - \frac{s}{k}\right) - h$$

Equilibrium is established by setting equation (15.7) equal to zero, which gives
the steady-state equilibrium. The steady-state equilibrium is at the maximum sustainable yield only if the harvest is at the level h_2.

One of the simplest models, developed by Crutchfield and Zellner (1962), is to
assume that the harvest level is partly determined in a demand and supply market.
Demand for fish is determined by price while the supply of fish is determined by
price and by fish stocks. The market is assumed to clear, which determines the

---

[3] Solving the quadratic $rs(1-s/k) = h$ gives $s_1^* = 112.702$ and $s_2^* = 887.298$.

harvest. Thus the model is

$$\frac{ds}{dt} = rs\left(1 - \frac{s}{k}\right) - h$$
$$q^d = a_0 - a_1 p \qquad a_0 > 0, a_1 > 0 \tag{15.8}$$
$$q^s = b_1 p + b_2 s \qquad b_1 > 0, b_2 > 0$$
$$q^d = q^s = h$$

From the market equations we can eliminate the price and solve for the harvest function in terms of stock levels. This gives

$$h = h(s) = \frac{a_0 b_1 + a_1 b_2 s}{b_1 + a_1} \tag{15.9}$$

which is linear with positive intercept and positive slope.

As before, the model is captured by superimposing the harvest function on the biological growth curve, as shown in figure 15.4.

Example 15.1

Using the following numerical discrete version of the model on a spreadsheet

$$s_{t+1} = s_t + 0.2\left(1 - \frac{s_t}{1000}\right)$$
$$q_t^d = 45 - p_t$$
$$q_t^s = 1.2p_t + 0.05s_t$$
$$q_t^d = q_t^s = h_t$$

the two equilibrium values are readily found to be $s_1^* = 172$ and $s_2^* = 715$. At the stable equilibrium value the price is found to be approximately $p^* = 4.2$, with

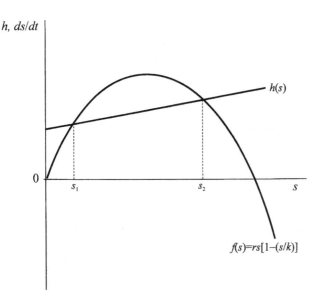

Figure 15.4.

Figure 15.5.

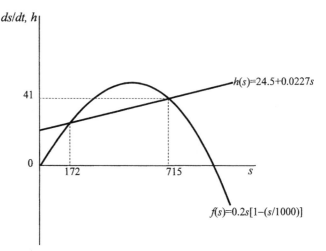

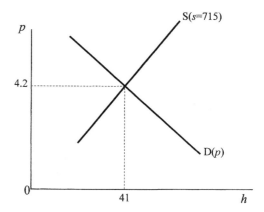

equilibrium harvest of $h^* = 41$.[4] The stable equilibrium of the model is illustrated in figure 15.5.

Although this model relates the harvest to the fish stock, through the supply equation, no account is taken of the number of vessels employed. A consequence of this is that no account is taken of the profitability of the fishing to the fishermen, and hence no account is taken of entry into and exit from the industry. In order to consider such possibilities we need to consider the harvesting function in more detail.

15.2   Harvesting function

The harvesting function, or catch locus, is a form of production function of the fishermen. Considered from this point of view, the harvest function is the catch at

---

[4] Using the continuous form of the model it is readily established, employing a software programme such as *Mathematica* or *Maple*, that $s_1^* = 171.736$, $s_2^* = 714.628$, $p(s_2^*) = 4.213$ and $h(s_2^*) = 40.787$.

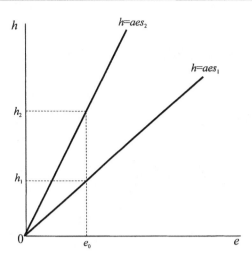

Figure 15.6.

time t, denoted $h(t)$, as a function of the inputs. We assume the inputs are of two kinds. First, the stock of fish available for catching, $s(t)$; and, second, the 'effort' expended by the fishermen, $e(t)$. Effort is here an index of all inputs commonly used for fishing – such as man-hours, trawlers, time spent at sea, nets, etc. Again we suppress the time variable and simply write the harvesting function as

$$h = h(e, s) \tag{15.10}$$

A common, and very simple, harvesting function used in the literature is

$$h = aes \qquad a > 0 \tag{15.11}$$

where a denotes the technical efficiency of the fishing fleet. This function is illustrated in figure 15.6, where we have drawn the harvesting (measured in terms of numbers of fish) against effort. For a given stock size, harvesting is a constant fraction of effort. It follows therefore that the marginal product to effort is constant and equal to the average product with respect to effort. Also shown in figure 15.6 is that for a higher stock size, the harvesting function is to the left, i.e., for given effort (e_0 say) the catch size is greater the greater the stock of fish in the habitat ($h_2 > h_1$ if $s_2 > s_1$).

Although a common harvesting function, this is but a special case of the Cobb–Douglas type harvesting function that allows for a diminishing marginal product to effort and to stock size. Such a function would be

$$h = ae^{\alpha} s^{\beta} \qquad a > 0, \qquad 0 < \alpha \le 1, \qquad 0 < \beta \le 1 \tag{15.12}$$

Diminishing returns to stock size seem sensible if effort is constant. With diminishing returns, stocks may be reasonably maintained until the level falls below a critical size. This appears to be the situation with pelagic species, such as herring and anchovy, that exhibit schooling behaviour. It appears that predation is a decreasing function of school size. Where heavy fishing reduces the school size below a critical level then the fish stock may be in danger of collapse as it finds the school is unable to handle the level of predation or major adverse environmental change. Such diminishing return to stock size has been one reason advanced for

Figure 15.7.

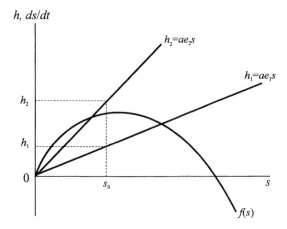

h, ds/dt

$h_2 = ae_2 s$

$h_1 = ae_1 s$

h_2

h_1

0

s_0

s

$f(s)$

the collapse of the Peruvian anchoveta fisheries and the North Sea herring fisheries in the 1970s. It is even more likely that there are diminishing returns to effort. In the short run stock size is undoubtedly limited, and it is quite unrealistic to assume that yield will double or triple with a doubling or tripling of effort.

In many studies diminishing returns is usually ignored because it cannot be handled formally. We shall do the same in the body of this text, but in using spreadsheets and some of the more popular software packages now available, there is no great difficulty in handling diminishing returns. We shall pursue this aspect, however, in the exercises at the end of this chapter.

We can illustrate the harvesting function given by $\alpha = \beta = 1$ in equation (15.12) on the biological growth diagram. In figure 15.7 we have the growth function, relating the growth in the fish stock to the stock level; and the harvesting function, which relates the fish harvest to the stock level. In figure 15.7, therefore, any particular harvesting function is drawn under the assumption of a fixed effort. The greater the effort the further the harvesting function is to the left, i.e., for a given fish stock (s_0 say), the greater the effort the more fish are harvested ($h_2 > h_1$ if $e_2 > e_1$). Second, as drawn in figure 15.7, we have a constant marginal product with respect to fish stock (in terms of the Cobb–Douglas function this means $\beta = 1$).

Now that we have outlined the harvesting function we can return to consider equilibria. Steady-state equilibria requires that $ds/dt = 0$, hence it requires the condition

(15.13) $f(s) = h(s)$

where we have suppressed the time variable. The situation is illustrated in figure 15.8. First consider effort at level e_1 with a corresponding harvesting function h_1. There are two equilibria, an unstable equilibrium at $s = 0$ and a stable equilibrium at $s = s_1$. On the other hand, if effort is raised to the level e_2, with the corresponding harvesting function h_2, then the stable stock equilibrium falls to s_2. But another feature is illustrated in figure 15.8. As drawn the harvesting function h_1 and h_2 both yield the *same* level of harvest at the respective equilibrium stock sizes. Economic efficiency would imply that the same harvest level would always

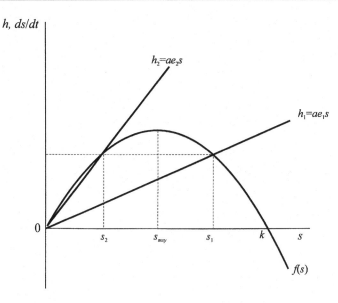

Figure 15.8.

be undertaken at the lowest effort. This means that harvest function h_1 would be chosen over harvest function h_2. In fact, on the grounds of economic efficiency, no effort would be employed which led to a harvesting function resulting in an equilibrium fish stock size *less than* the maximum sustainable yield. However, we have so far assumed *open access* to the fishery by all companies.

But are there any circumstances where an equilibrium in open access to the fishery would be at a stock level below the maximum sustainable yield? To answer this question it must be recalled that open access involves *no* restrictions on companies harvesting in the locality under study or of new firms entering the industry (or firms leaving the industry). What is clearly missing from the analysis so far is any consideration of profits to the industry.

15.3 Industry profits and free access

We simplify our analysis by assuming that the unit cost of effort expended is constant. Let this be denoted w, and can be considered as the 'wage' for effort. Then the total cost is given by

$$TC = we \qquad (15.14)$$

Turning to revenue, we assume that all fish are sold at the same price, denoted p. Hence, with the total fish caught being h, it follows that total revenue is

$$TR = ph = paes \qquad (15.15)$$

It follows, then, that profits for the industry are

$$\begin{aligned} \pi &= TR - TC \\ &= paes - we \qquad (15.16) \\ &= (pas - w)e \end{aligned}$$

What is the shape of the TR and TC functions? We wish to construct TR and TC against effort. TC is linear since TC $= we$ and w is assumed constant. TR is less straightforward. As effort rises we have already established that the stock size in equilibrium falls.

Return to figure 15.7. At zero effort the harvesting function lies along the horizontal axis and the stock size is at the level k, but total revenue is zero. As effort rises the harvesting line shifts left, h rises and, with p constant, total revenue rises. Once effort has risen to a level such that $s = s_{msy}$, then total revenue must be at a maximum since the harvest is at the maximum level. Effort beyond this means a fall in harvesting and a fall in total revenue. Hence, TR takes a similar shape to $f(s)$, adjusted by the factor p. More formally TR $= ph$. But in equilibrium

$$rs\left(1 - \frac{s}{k}\right) - aes = 0$$

$$\text{or } s = k\left(1 - \frac{ae}{r}\right)$$

Hence we can express $h = aes$ as a function of e

$$h = aek\left(1 - \frac{ae}{r}\right)$$

$$= \frac{ak}{r}(r - ae)e$$

Hence

(15.17)
$$TR = ph = \frac{pak}{r}(r - ae)e$$

which is quadratic in e. It is readily established that for this TR function:

(1)   TR $= 0$ at $e = 0$ and $e = r/a$
(2)   TR is a maximum at $e = r/2a$.

The situation is shown in figure 15.9.

Figure 15.9 highlights two other features. A rise in the 'wage' to effort shifts the total cost function to the left. Second, a rise in the price of fish shifts the total revenue function up, but still passing through the points $e = 0$ and $e = e_m$. The results on the profits function are illustrated in figure 15.10.

In figure 15.11(a) assume effort is at the level e_2. At this level of effort TR exceeds total cost (TR$_2 >$ TC$_2$). There are excess profits in the industry and there will be entry by firms to take advantage of the excess profits. The increase in firms is captured in this model by an increase in effort. Entry will continue in open access while total revenue exceeds total cost. As effort rises with entry, total revenue will rise initially beyond TR$_2$ but will then fall. Furthermore, as effort rises we move along both TC and TR. Effort will rise (entry will continue) until effort level e_1 is reached, where TR $=$ TC. In figure 15.11(b) we note that at effort level e_1 we have the harvest function h_1 and the equilibrium stock is s_1 which is *less* than s_{msy}.

What we have established here is that although for the same harvest lower effort would be the most efficient, with open access and free entry, effort would be established at level e_1 and the equilibrium stock size $s_1 < s_{msy}$. In other words, effort will always be adjusted until profits reduce to zero because only then will

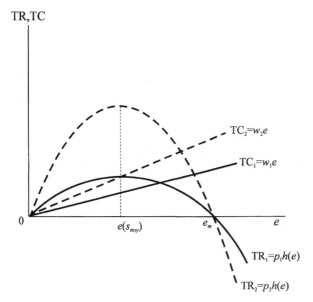

Figure 15.9.

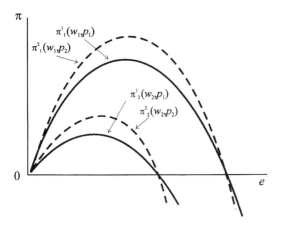

Figure 15.10.

there be no further entry into the industry. But at effort e_1, MR is negative as shown by the slope of the TR curve at $e = e_1$, and MC is constant (and equal to w). Hence, at $e = e_1$ MR < MC, which is economically inefficient. It is also biologically inefficient in that it leads to a stock size *below* the maximum sustainable yield. What we have illustrated is that with free access, entry will continue until profits are reduced to zero. This leads to excess effort (over fishing) and hence to a stock size below the maximum sustainable yield. It is, however, sustainable in the sense that the level of harvesting equals the level of natural population growth.

It readily follows in the case of open access that depending on the price of fish and the wage rate to effort, it is possible that effort is such that the harvesting function in figure 15.11(b) lies wholly above the growth function $f(s)$ and so the catch is to extinction. This has been argued to be the case for a number of species, including the blue whale (see Shone 1981, application 11).

Figure 15.11.

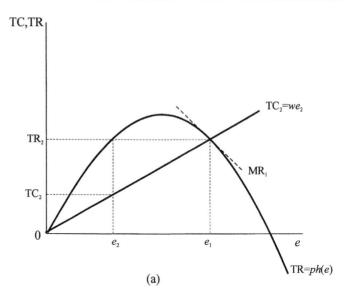

(a)

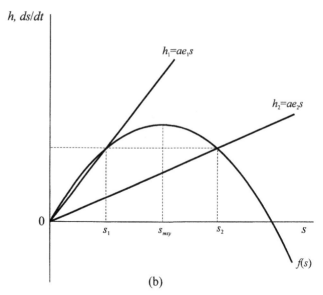

(b)

15.4 The dynamics of open access fishery

So far we have concentrated on the equilibrium situation. However, it is necessary to consider what happens to the fish stock when it is *out of equilibrium*. To do this we need to consider the model in terms of phase space. In order to do this we shall assume that effort changes according to a fraction of the profits. In other words, if profits are positive then effort will rise, and the greater the profits the more entry will occur and the more effort expended. Similarly, if profits are negative, then some firms will leave the industry and effort will fall. The greater the loss, the greater the number of firms leaving the industry. We can capture this change in effort over time quite simply as follows

$$\frac{de}{dt} = v\pi \qquad v > 0$$
$$= v(pas - w)e$$

(15.18)

Our fisheries model with open access can therefore be captured by means of two dynamic equations

$$\dot{s} = rs\left(1 - \frac{s}{k}\right) - aes$$
$$\dot{e} = v(pas - w)e$$

(15.19)

where we have used the dot notation to denote the derivative with respect to time. The two variables under consideration are the stock size, s, and the amount of effort, e. In equilibrium both variables must be jointly determined. When out of equilibrium, equations for $\dot{s}$ and $\dot{e}$ will determine the dynamic path taken. To this we now turn.

The situation is shown in figure 15.12. We measure the stock size on the horizontal axis and effort on the vertical axis. Our first problem is to determine the equilibrium paths. In equilibrium we know that

$$\dot{s} = 0 \text{ for equilibrium stock size}$$
$$\dot{e} = 0 \text{ for equilibrium effort}$$

First consider the effort equilibrium. Entry will occur until profits are zero, at which point effort is zero. There is only one stock size consistent with this result,

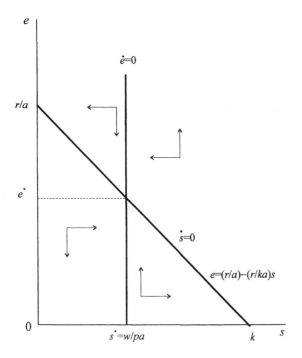

Figure 15.12.

namely

(15.20) $$s^* = \frac{w}{ap}$$

This is shown by the vertical line in figure 15.12. Now consider a stock size less than w/ap. In this case $pas < w$ (or $pas - w < 0$), and so losses are being made. Firms leave the industry and so effort is reduced. In other words, to the left of the vertical line there is a force on effort to fall. Similarly, to the right of the vertical line $pas - w > 0$ and so profits are being made and firms enter the industry with a resulting increase in effort. Hence, to the right of the vertical line there is a force on effort to rise. These forces are shown by the vertical arrows in figure 15.12.

Now consider the stock equilibrium. We derive this as follows

(15.21)
$$\dot{s} = rs\left(1 - \frac{s}{k}\right) - aes = 0$$
$$r(k - s) = kae$$
$$e = \frac{r}{a} - \left(\frac{r}{ka}\right)s$$

Result (15.21) indicates that the equilibrium situation for stock size is linear with a negative slope. The intercept on the effort axis is given by (r/a), the slope is given by $-(r/ka)$ and the intercept on the stock axis is k. Consider next points either side of this equilibrium line. Above the stock equilibrium line we have the condition

$$e > \frac{r}{a} - \left(\frac{r}{ka}\right)s$$
$$aes > rs\left(1 - \frac{s}{k}\right)$$

which means the harvest exceeds the natural stock growth for a given stock size. This, in turn, means that the stock size will fall over time. Hence, above the stock equilibrium line the forces are shown by arrows pointing to the left. By similar reasoning, points below the stock equilibrium line lead to growth in excess of harvesting for any stock size, and so the stock size will increase over time. Hence, below the stock equilibrium line the forces are shown by arrows pointing to the right. All these vectors of forces are illustrated in figure 15.12.

Finally, we can readily establish the equilibrium stock size and effort level by solving the two linear equations. The equilibrium stock size is given immediately as $s^* = w/pa$ and the equilibrium effort is readily found to be equal to

(15.22) $$e^* = \frac{r}{a}\left(1 - \frac{w}{kap}\right)$$

One final observation to make concerning the dynamics is the slope of the path when it crosses either equilibrium line. In the case of the vertical line at any point on this line effort is unchanging and so the trajectory must have a zero slope when crossing the vertical line. Similarly, a trajectory crossing the stock equilibrium line must have the stock size unchanging; hence the trajectory must have no slope when crossing this line.

The trajectory over time must depend on the starting position of the species. Suppose, for illustrative purposes, that the species is at the level of its carrying

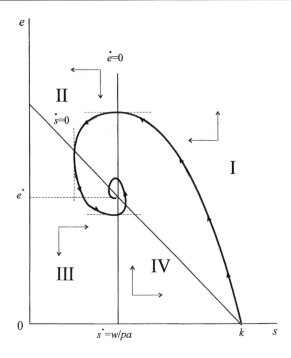

Figure 15.13.

capacity, i.e., $s = k$, as shown in figure 15.13. At this stock level profits are to be had and entry will occur. This entry will raise the effort of the industry and will simultaneously reduce the fish stock. Because profits are initially large there is a sizable entry into the industry that pushes effort beyond its eventual equilibrium. As a result, the path must cross the vertical line (which it does with a zero slope). In other words, the system moves from quadrant I into quadrant II. In this quadrant harvesting is still above the natural growth level and so the stock size is continuing to fall. On the other hand, profits are now negative and some firms will be leaving the industry, resulting in a reduction in effort. However, the reduction in effort results in the system moving from quadrant II into quadrant III (cutting the stock equilibrium line with a zero slope). In quadrant III losses are still being made and so effort is falling, but the reduction in effort leads to less harvesting and a rise in the stock of fish. This pushes the system into quadrant IV. Now profits are again positive and firms will enter the industry resulting in increased effort. Furthermore, the harvesting is less than the natural growth and so the stock size will be rising. It follows, then, that the trajectory of the system over time is shown by the heavy line, showing a counter-clockwise spiralling path.

Although figure 15.13 illustrates a stable spiral we have implicitly assumed certain values on the parameters in the construction of the diagram. This can best be noted by considering the mathematical properties of the system (equations (15.19)). In order to do this, however, we need to make two adjustments to the dynamical system. First, we consider percentage changes rather than simply changes. Hence, we need to divide the first equation by the stock size, s, and the second equation by the effort, e. Using hats to denote percentage changes, then our dynamic system takes the form

(15.23)

$$\hat{s} = r\left(1 - \frac{s}{k}\right) - ae$$

$$\hat{e} = v(pas - w)$$

Next we note that in equilibrium the percentage changes are zero, hence

$$0 = r\left(1 - \frac{\bar{s}}{k}\right) - a\bar{e}$$

$$0 = v(pa\bar{s} - w)$$

Subtracting the equilibrium conditions from these equations gives

(15.24)

$$\hat{s} = -\left(\frac{r}{k}\right)(s - \bar{s}) - a(e - \bar{e})$$

$$\hat{e} = vpa(s - \bar{s})$$

The matrix of this system is

$$\mathbf{A} = \begin{bmatrix} -\left(\frac{r}{k}\right) & -a \\ vpa & 0 \end{bmatrix}$$

where the trace and determinant of $\mathbf{A}$ are

$$\text{tr}(\mathbf{A}) = -\frac{r}{k}$$

$$\det(\mathbf{A}) = a^2 vp$$

A stable spiral, as indicated in table 4.1 (p. 180), requires three conditions to be met

(1) $\text{tr}(\mathbf{A}) < 0$ i.e. $\text{tr}(\mathbf{A}) = -(r/k) < 0$
(2) $\det(\mathbf{A}) > 0$ i.e. $\det(\mathbf{A}) = a^2 vp > 0$
(3) $[\text{tr}(\mathbf{A})]^2 < 4\det(\mathbf{A})$

It is the third condition that we have *implicitly* assumed in graphing figure 15.15. This requires the condition

$$\left(\frac{r}{k}\right)^2 < 4a^2 vp$$

to be met. In order to see this issue, we shall now consider a numerical example.

15.5   The dynamics of open access fishery: a numerical example

Example 15.2

Consider the following numerical example of the open access fishery

$$\dot{s} = 0.5s\left(1 - \frac{s}{200}\right) - 0.005es$$

$$p = 25, \qquad w = 4, \qquad v = 0.02$$

The two dynamic equations are, then

$$\dot{s} = 0.5s \left(1 - \frac{s}{200} \right) - 0.005es$$

$$\dot{e} = 0.02(0.125es - 4e)$$

Which gives the two equilibrium lines

$$s = 32$$
$$e = 100 - 0.5s$$

and the equilibrium solutions $s^* = 32$ and $e^* = 84$. The diagrams consistent with these results are illustrated in figure 15.14.

The stable spiral in this example is readily established. The matrix $\mathbf{A}$, its trace and determinant are

$$\mathbf{A} = \begin{bmatrix} -0.0025 & -0.005 \\ 0.0375 & 0 \end{bmatrix}$$

$$\text{tr}(\mathbf{A}) = -0.0025$$
$$\det(\mathbf{A}) = 0.0001875$$

from which it readily follows that not only are the first two conditions for a stable spiral met, but so is the third condition, since $[\text{tr}(\mathbf{A})]^2 < 4\det(\mathbf{A})$.

A change in **p** or **w**

The model readily illustrates the result of either a change in the wage rate or a change in the price level. Neither of these changes does anything to the stock equilibrium line. Only the effort equilibrium is altered. Thus, a rise in the price of fish will result in the effort equilibrium line shifting to the left. Assuming the system was initially in equilibrium, the result is shown in figure 15.15, where effort rises and the fish stock falls. The assumed trajectory is shown by T_1. For example, in our numerical example if the price of fish rises from $p = 25$ to $p = 32$, then the system will settle down at $s^* = 25$ and $e^* = 87.5$.

On the other hand, a rise in the wage paid to effort will shift the effort equilibrium line to the right. The situation is shown in figure 15.16, where effort falls and the fish stock rises. The assumed trajectory is shown by T_1. For example, in our numerical example, if the wage rate rises from $w = 4$ to $w = 10$, then the system will settle down at $s^* = 80$ and $e^* = 60$.

Figure 15.15 and 15.16 highlight a potential misleading result if concentration is paid only to equilibrium values. The *equilibrium* stock size will lead to extinction only if the price rises infinitely. But this ignores the dynamic behaviour out of equilibrium. If the trajectory of the system is that shown by T_2 in figure 15.15, then extinction occurs before some positive equilibrium stock size can occur. In the case of trajectory T_2, the rise in the price of fish leads to a glut of firms entering the industry. The rise in effort that results leads to excess harvesting and fish harvested faster than they can reproduce, so leading to extinction. The system never reaches its eventual equilibrium!

Figure 15.14.

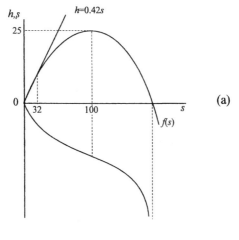

(a)

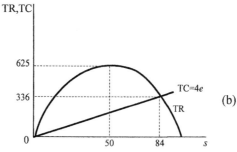

(b)

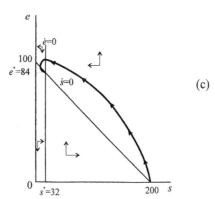

(c)

The same issue can arise with a rise in the wage rate. This is shown by trajectory T_2 in figure 15.16. Effort is reduced to zero and the fishing industry effectively collapses before the new equilibrium can be reached.

One of the parameters of significance in these last two results is v, which is a *reaction coefficient* of the industry to profits and losses. The larger v, then the more likely are the results shown by trajectory T_2 in figures 15.15 and 15.16. This is because the larger v, then the more firms will enter the industry when profits are positive. This means that effort rises more for any given size of fish stock, hence, the more steep the trajectory resulting from a rise in the price of fish. Similarly, if wages rise, then the resulting losses lead to a more rapid exit from the

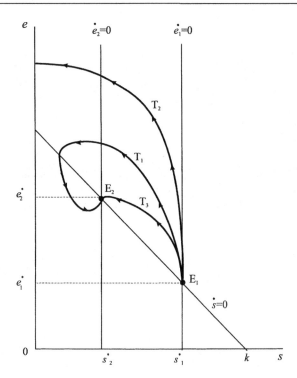

Figure 15.15.

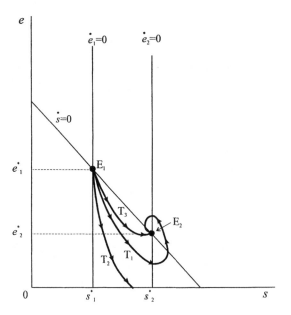

Figure 15.16.

industry and a relatively greater reduction in effort. The resulting trajectory is fairly steep.

The converse of these results is that the *smaller* the value of the reaction coefficient, v, the more likely the system will converge to its equilibrium without oscillations, shown by trajectory T_3 in figures 15.15 and 15.16.

15.6   The fisheries control problem

In the next section we shall discuss school fisheries, i.e., fish populations that shoal in large numbers. However, before we can do this we need to consider the optimal control problem more closely. So far we have ignored the facts that profits are spread over time, they need discounting, and fish left in the sea is forgone revenue for the fisherman. In this section we shall consider only a continuous model formulation, leaving the discrete form as exercises.

Since the aim of the fisherman or agency is to maximise discounted profits subject to the biological growth function, we have a typical control problem as outlined in chapter 6, sections 6.1–6.3. Knowledge of these sections is required for the present section and the next one. To recap before we consider fisheries, a typical maximisation principle problem is to[5]

$$\max_{\{u\}} \int_{t_0}^{t_1} V(x, u, t)dt + F(x^1, t_1)$$

(15.25)

$$\text{s.t. } \dot{x} = f(x, u, t)$$

$$x(t_0) = x^0$$

$$x(t_1) = x^1$$

by a suitable choice of the control variable u. Here $V(x, u, t)$ is the objective function, $F(x^1)$ is the value of the terminal state, $\dot{x} = f(x, u, t)$ denotes how the state variable changes over time, while $x(t_0) = x^0$ and $x(t_1) = x^1$ denote the initial and final values of the state variable. In solving this maximisation principle problem, we form the dynamic Lagrangian.

$$L = \int_{t_0}^{t_1} V(x, u, t)dt + F(x^1) + \int_{t_0}^{t_1} \lambda[f(x, u, t) - \dot{x}]dt$$

$$= \int_{t_0}^{t_1} [V(x, u, t) + \lambda f(x, u, t) - \lambda\dot{x}]dt + F(x^1)$$

We further define the Hamiltonian function

$$H(x, u, t) = V(x, u, t) + \lambda f(x, u, t)$$

which implies

$$L = \int_{t_0}^{t_1} [H(x, u, t) - \lambda\dot{x}]dt + F(x^1)$$

and using

$$-\int_{t_0}^{t_1} \lambda\dot{x}dt = \int_{t_0}^{t_1} x\dot{\lambda}dt - [\lambda(t_1)x(t_1) - \lambda(t_0)x(t_0)]$$

(see exercise 2, chapter 6) then

$$L = \int_{t_0}^{t_1} [H(x, u, t) + \dot{\lambda}x]dt + F(x^1) - [\lambda(t_1)x(t_1) - \lambda(t_0)x(t_0)]$$

---

[5] In chapter 6 we assumed $F(x^1, t_1) = 0$ and so $\lambda(t_1) = 0$. Here we assume a nonzero terminal state $x(t_1) = x^1$ with value $F(x^1)$.

The necessary conditions for an (interior) solution are, then,

(i) $\quad \dfrac{\partial H}{\partial u} = 0 \qquad t_0 \leq t \leq t_1$

(ii) $\quad \dot{\lambda} = -\dfrac{\partial H}{\partial x} \qquad t_0 \leq t \leq t_1$

(iii) $\quad \dot{x} = \dfrac{\partial H}{\partial \lambda} = f(x, u, t)$ $\qquad\qquad\qquad\qquad$ (15.26)

(iv) $\quad \lambda(t_1) = \dfrac{\partial F}{\partial x^1}$

(v) $\quad x(t_0) = x^0$

Our first task, therefore, is to appropriately define the objective function $V(x, u, t)$. Returning to our fisheries question, the profit at time t is total revenue less total cost. We continue to assume the following relationships:

(i) $\quad \dot{s} = f(s) - h(e, s)$
(ii) $\quad TR = ph = ph(e, s) \quad p$ is a constant
(iii) $\quad TC = we \quad w$ is a constant

where $f(s)$ is the biological growth function and $h = h(e, s)$ is the harvesting function; and where TR = total revenue and TC = total cost. The price of fish, p, and, w, the 'wage' to effort are both assumed constant. Since profits are defined as total revenue minus total cost, then

$$\pi = TR - TC = ph(e, s) - we$$

where we have suppressed the time variable.

One possible objective function is to let $V(s, e, t)$ be given by the profits function $\pi(e, s, t)$ which can be maximised over the interval $t_0 \leq t \leq t_1$. But this is not appropriate for two reasons:

(i) It does not allow discounting either of profits, or of the terminal state $F(s^1)$.
(ii) It ignores the fact that stock that is left in the sea will lead to a capital gain or loss if the shadow price of fish should rise or fall, respectively.

This extreme problem with no discounting is left as an exercise (see exercise 8).

Now consider the objective function when profits are discounted between $0 \leq t \leq T$. Letting $E^{-\delta t}$ denote the discount factor and δ the discount rate, then the objective is

$$\max_{\{e\}} \int_0^T E^{-\delta t} V(s, e, t)dt + E^{-\delta t} F(s^1) =$$
$$\qquad\qquad\qquad\qquad\qquad\qquad\qquad (15.27)$$
$$\max_{\{e\}} \int_0^T E^{-\delta t}(ph(e, s) - we)dt + E^{-\delta t} F(s^1)$$

subject to the growth function and the terminal condition. Our problem, then, is

$$\max_{\{e\}} \int_0^T E^{-\delta t}(ph(e, s) - we)dt + E^{-\delta t}F(s^1)$$

(15.28)

$$\text{s.t.} \quad \dot{s} = f(s) - h(e, s)$$

$$s(T) = s^1$$

Hence

$$L = \int_0^T E^{-\delta t}[ph(e, s) - we]dt$$

$$+ \int_0^T \lambda[f(s) - h(e, s) - \dot{s}]dt + E^{-\delta t}F(s^1) - \lambda(T)s(T)$$

The Hamiltonian function associated with this is

$$H(e, s, t) = E^{-\delta t}[ph(e, s) - we] + \lambda[f(s) - h(e, s)]$$

with first-order necessary conditions

(i) $\dfrac{\partial H}{\partial e} = 0$ or $E^{-\delta t}p\dfrac{\partial h}{\partial e} - w - \lambda\dfrac{\partial h}{\partial e} = 0$

i.e. $(p - \lambda E^{\delta t})\dfrac{\partial h}{\partial e} = w$

$\dot{\lambda} = -\dfrac{\partial H}{\partial s}$ or $\dot{\lambda} = -\left[E^{-\delta t}p\dfrac{\partial h}{\partial s} + \lambda f'(s) - \lambda\dfrac{\partial h}{\partial s}\right]$

(ii) $\dot{\lambda} = -(E^{-\delta t}p - \lambda)\dfrac{\partial h}{\partial s} - \lambda f'(s)$

i.e. $\dot{\lambda} = (\lambda - E^{-\delta t}p)\dfrac{\partial h}{\partial s} - \lambda f'(s)$

(iii) $\dot{s} = \dfrac{\partial H}{\partial \lambda} = f(s) - h(e, s)$

(iv) $\lambda(T) = \dfrac{\partial F}{\partial s^T} = 0$

(v) $s(0) = 0$

Now define

$$\mu(t) = E^{\delta t}\lambda(t) \quad \text{or} \quad \mu = E^{\delta t}\lambda$$

Then $\lambda = E^{-\delta t}\mu$ and

$$\dot{\lambda} = E^{-\delta t}\dot{\mu} - \delta E^{-\delta t}\mu$$

Condition (i) then becomes

$$(p - \mu)\dfrac{\partial h}{\partial e} = w$$

while condition (ii) becomes

$$E^{-\delta t}\dot\mu - \delta E^{-\delta t}\mu = (\lambda - E^{-\delta t}p)\frac{\partial h}{\partial s} - \lambda f'(s)$$

or $\quad \dot\mu = \delta\mu + \mu\dfrac{\partial h}{\partial s} - p\dfrac{\partial h}{\partial s} - \mu f'(s)$

i.e. $\quad \dot\mu = [\delta - f'(s)]\mu - (p - \mu)\dfrac{\partial h}{\partial s}$

The three necessary conditions can now be summarised

(i) $\quad (p - \mu)\dfrac{\partial h}{\partial e} = w$

(ii) $\quad \dot\mu = [\delta - f'(s)]\mu - (p - \mu)\dfrac{\partial h}{\partial s}$ (15.29)

(iii) $\quad \dot s = f(s) - h(e, s)$

These three conditions are known, respectively, as the maximum principle, the portfolio balance condition and the dynamic constraint.[6] The maximum principle indicates that the current value Hamiltonian is maximised if the marginal net revenue from effort equals the marginal cost of that effort – the typical marginal revenue equals marginal cost condition. Since p is the market price of fish sold and μ is the resource price of fish in the sea (the shadow price) then $(p - \mu)$ can be considered as the net price of a caught fish. Hence, $(p - \mu)\partial h/\partial e$ is the marginal net revenue of fish caught. Now consider condition (ii). On the right-hand side of condition (ii), the first term denotes the net interest from selling the fish and investing the proceeds. The second term denotes the net revenue from holding fish. Thus, the first term denotes the net interest forgone, while the second term is the net benefit from holding fish. If

$$[\delta - f'(s)]\mu - (p - \mu)\frac{\partial h}{\partial s} > 0 \qquad \text{then} \qquad \dot\mu > 0$$

i.e. there is need of a capital gain to compensate for the loss of interest forgone. The third equation is simply the constraint.

A steady state requires

$$\dot e = 0, \qquad \dot s = 0 \qquad \text{and} \qquad \dot\mu = 0$$

15.7 Schooling fishery

It is well known that some fish move in shoals for purposes of migration, reproduction or to fend off predators. Although schooling activity is a defence against natural predators, it makes them especially vulnerable to human predation. Modern equipment means shoals are easy to locate and the fish easy to catch. This means that the stock size has little impact on the catch so $\partial h/\partial s = 0$. We can, therefore, define the catch function as $h = h(e, s) = h(e)$ and the three necessary conditions

[6] See Neher (1990, chapter 9).

as

(15.30)
(i) $(p - \mu)h'(e) = w$
(ii) $\dot{\mu} = [\delta - f'(s)]\mu$
(iii) $\dot{s} = f(s) - h(e)$

where we retain the assumption that the fish sell at a constant price p and the 'wage' per unit of effort, w, is constant.

The steady state requires three conditions to be met

$$\dot{e} = 0, \qquad \dot{s} = 0 \qquad \text{and} \qquad \dot{\mu} = 0$$

The dynamics of the problem is solved in stages. First, two variables are chosen whose dynamics are 'solved' in terms of the phase-plane. Both the steady state (equilibrium) and out-of-equilibrium situations can be depicted. The third variable is then considered in the light of what is occurring with these two. The common approach is to consider the phase-plane in terms of fish stock, s, and its shadow price μ.[7]

In continuing our analysis we shall assume some *specific* functional forms. The catch locus we shall assume is

(15.31) $h = ae^b \qquad a > 0, 0 < b < 1$

while the biological growth $f(s)$ we shall assume is logistic

(15.32) $f(s) = rs \left(1 - \dfrac{s}{k}\right)$

where k is the carrying capacity and r is the intrinsic growth. Using these specifications

$$h'(e) = abe^{b-1}$$
$$f'(s) = r - \frac{2rs}{k}$$

and the three necessary conditions are

(15.33)
(i) $(p - \mu)abe^{b-1} = w$

(ii) $\dot{\mu} = \left[\delta - \left(r - \dfrac{2rs}{k}\right)\right]\mu$

(iii) $\dot{s} = rs\left(1 - \dfrac{s}{k}\right) - ae^b$

If $\dot{\mu} = 0$ then

(15.34)
$$\delta - \left(r - \frac{2rs}{k}\right) = 0$$
$$s^* = \frac{k(r - \delta)}{2r}$$

which is shown by the vertical line in figure 15.17. If $\mu > 0$ then $s > k(r - \delta)/2r$, and μ is rising. Similarly, when $s < k(r - \delta)/2r$ then μ is falling. We can conclude

---

[7] This is the *resource cost* of the fish caught as distinct from the price at which the fish sells on the market.

Figure 15.17.

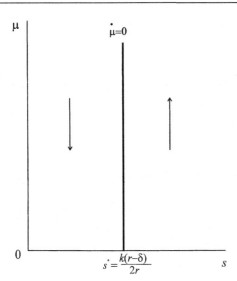

that for $s < s^*$ then μ is falling[8] while for $s > s^*$ then μ is rising. These results are shown by the vector forces in figure 15.17.

In order to derive the second isocline $\dot{s} = 0$, we first need to eliminate effort, e. From (15.33)(i) we have

$$b(p - \mu)ae^{b-1} = w$$

$$\therefore e = \left[\frac{w}{ab(p - \mu)}\right]^{\frac{1}{b-1}}$$

Substituting this into (15.33)(iii) gives

$$\dot{s} = rs\left(1 - \frac{s}{k}\right) - a\left[\frac{w}{ab(p - \mu)}\right]^{\frac{b}{b-1}} \tag{15.35}$$

If $\dot{s} = 0$, then the above expression is equal to zero, which is a quadratic in s. There is little gain in solving this for μ in terms of s explicitly. We can, however, express it implicitly. Define

$$\phi(s, \mu) = -rs\left(1 - \frac{s}{k}\right) + a\left[\frac{w}{ab(p - \mu)}\right]^{\frac{b}{b-1}} \tag{15.36}$$

Then for a turning point

$$\frac{\partial\phi}{\partial s} = -r + \frac{2rs}{k} = 0$$

$$\text{i.e.} \quad s^* = \frac{k}{2}$$

$$\frac{\partial^2\phi}{\partial s^2} = \frac{2r}{k} > 0$$

[8] For $s^* > 0$ then δ must be less than r, i.e., the discount rate must be less than the intrinsic growth rate.

Figure 15.18.

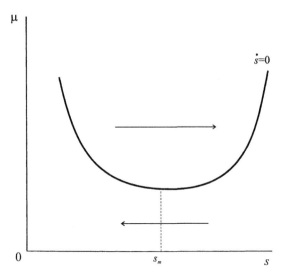

Figure 15.18.

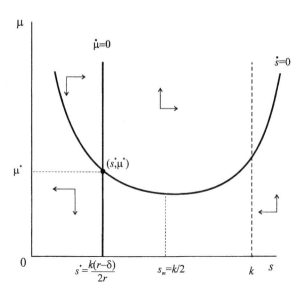

Figure 15.19.

hence it is a minimum. The relationship between μ and s for $\dot{s} = 0$ is shown in figure 15.18.

If $\dot{s} > 0$ then $\phi(s, \mu)$ is above the curve, i.e., above $\dot{s} = 0$ and s is rising; while below $\dot{s} = 0$, s is falling. These forces are represented by the arrows in figure 15.18.

We can now combine all the results, as shown in figure 15.19. The fixed point, the equilibrium point, is given by (s^*, μ^*), which occurs at the intersection of the two steady-state conditions $\dot{\mu} = 0$ and $\dot{s} = 0$. They lead to four quadrants with vector forces illustrated by the arrows.

The typical trajectories arising from this problem are illustrated in figure 15.20, indicating the presence of a stable saddle path $S_1 S_1'$ and an unstable saddle path $S_2 S_2'$.

Figure 15.20.

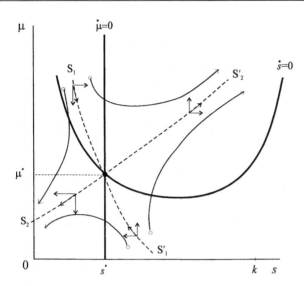

Example 15.3

Let

$$f(s) = 0.2s\left(1 - \frac{s}{100}\right) \qquad \text{i.e. } r = 0.2, k = 100$$

$$h(e) = 5e^{0.5} \qquad\qquad \text{i.e. } a = 5, b = 0.5$$

$$p = 10, \qquad w = 8, \qquad \delta = 0.1$$

Our three maximisation conditions are, then

(i) $\quad (10 - \mu)(2.5)e^{-0.5} = 8$

(ii) $\quad \dot{\mu} = \left[0.1 - \left(0.2 - \frac{0.4s}{100}\right)\right]\mu$

(iii) $\quad \dot{s} = 0.2s\left(1 - \frac{s}{100}\right) - 5e^{0.5}$

which can be solved for e, s and μ once the steady-state conditions $\dot{\mu} = 0$ and $\dot{s} = 0$ are imposed. For this example

$$e^* = 0.5625, \qquad s^* = 25, \qquad \mu^* = 7.6$$

The curve denoting $\dot{s} = 0$ is given by

$$0.2s\left(1 - \frac{s}{100}\right) - 1.5625(10 - \mu) = 0$$

i.e. $\quad \mu = 10 - 0.128s + 0.00128s^2$

with minimum point at $s_m = 50$.

This example is nonlinear but we can investigate the stability of the equilibrium point $(s^*, \mu^*) = (25, 7.6)$ using a linear approximation.[9] Let $\dot{\mu} = g(s, \mu)$ and

---

[9] See chapter 4.

$\dot{s} = v(s, \mu)$, then

$$\dot{s} = \frac{\partial v(s^*, \mu^*)}{\partial s}(s - s^*) + \frac{\partial v(s^*, \mu^*)}{\partial \mu}(\mu - \mu^*)$$

$$\dot{\mu} = \frac{\partial g(s^*, \mu^*)}{\partial s}(s - s^*) + \frac{\partial g(s^*, \mu^*)}{\partial \mu}(\mu - \mu^*)$$

Or

$$\dot{s} = (0.2 - 0.004s^*)(s - s^*) + 0.97652(10 - \mu^*)(\mu - \mu^*)$$
$$\dot{\mu} = 0.004\mu^*(s - s^*) + (-0.1 + 0.004s^*)(\mu - \mu^*)$$

i.e.

$$\dot{s} = 0.1(s - s^*) + 2.34375(\mu - \mu^*)$$
$$\dot{\mu} = 0.0304(s - s^*)$$

Writing the equations in matrix form, we have

$$\begin{bmatrix} \dot{s} \\ \dot{\mu} \end{bmatrix} = \begin{bmatrix} 0.1 & 2.34375 \\ 0.0304 & 0 \end{bmatrix} \begin{bmatrix} s - s^* \\ \mu - \mu^* \end{bmatrix}$$

where the matrix of the system, $\mathbf{A}$, is given by

$$\mathbf{A} = \begin{bmatrix} 0.1 & 2.34375 \\ 0.0304 & 0 \end{bmatrix}$$

from which we can readily compute

$$\text{tr}(\mathbf{A}) = 0.1$$
$$\det(\mathbf{A}) = -(0.0304)(2.34375) = -0.07125$$

Since $\det(\mathbf{A}) < 0$, we know from chapter 4 that we must have a saddle point. This is also verified if the characteristic roots are of opposite sign. The roots of the characteristic equation are

$$\lambda_1, \lambda_2 = \frac{\text{tr}(\mathbf{A}) \pm \sqrt{\text{tr}(\mathbf{A}) - 4\det(\mathbf{A})}}{2}$$

$$= \frac{0.1 \pm \sqrt{(0.1)^2 - 4(-0.07125)}}{2}$$

$$\lambda_1 = 0.32157 \quad \lambda_2 = -0.22157$$

Using the first solution we have

$$\begin{bmatrix} 0.1 & 2.34375 \\ 0.0304 & 0 \end{bmatrix} \begin{bmatrix} s - s^* \\ \mu - \mu^* \end{bmatrix} = 0.32157 \begin{bmatrix} s - s^* \\ \mu - \mu^* \end{bmatrix}$$

which leads to the relationship

$$\mu = 5.2375 + 0.0945s$$

Using the second solution we have

$$\begin{bmatrix} 0.1 & 2.34375 \\ 0.0304 & 0 \end{bmatrix} \begin{bmatrix} s - s^* \\ \mu - \mu^* \end{bmatrix} = -0.22157 \begin{bmatrix} s - s^* \\ \mu - \mu^* \end{bmatrix}$$

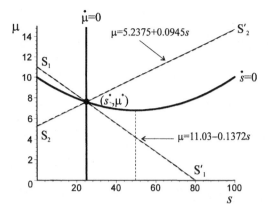

Figure 15.21.

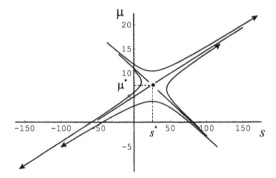

Figure 15.22.

which leads to the relationship

$$\mu = 11.03 - 0.1372s$$

These saddle path solutions, along with the isoclines $\dot{s} = 0$ and $\dot{\mu} = 0$ are shown in figure 15.21.

Finally *Mathematica* was used to produce a number of trajectories, as shown in figure 15.22. In doing this we employed the linear approximation results, i.e., we used the **NDSolve** command on the simultaneous linear differential equations

$$\dot{s} = 0.1(s - s^*) + 2.34375(\mu - \mu^*)$$
$$\dot{\mu} = 0.0304(s - s^*)$$

where $(s^*, \mu^*) = (25, 7.6)$. Notice that this linear approximation was reasonable. The stable and unstable saddle paths are given by

$$\mu = 11.03 - 0.1372s$$
$$\mu = 5.2375 + 0.0945s,$$

respectively. Given $s = 10$, then the corresponding points on the saddle paths are $\mu_0 = 9.658$ and $\mu_0 = 6.1825$, respectively. Taking the trajectory through the point (10,9.658) did indeed lead to a trajectory straight towards the equilibrium (s^*, μ^*). Similarly, for the point (10,6.1825) the trajectory moved directly away

Figure 15.23.

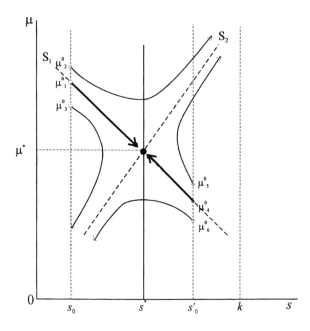

from (s^*, μ^*). The same is true for $\mu_0 = 4.17$ and $\mu_0 = 9.9625$ on the stable and unstable saddle paths for $s = 50$. All other initial points were taken *off* the saddle paths. It is quite clear from figure 15.22 that the numerical results support our earlier *qualitative* results.

What meaning can we give to these results? All the trajectories in figure 15.22 represent solution paths, in the sense that each satisfies the three conditions listed above. The decision-maker, whether it be the fishery manager or the manager of an agency, begins with a stock size s_0 at time $t = 0$. Suppose this is below s^*, as shown in figure 15.23. The manager has control over effort, $e(t)$, and by implication over the shadow price μ. In particular, the manager can control the initial shadow price $\mu_0 = \mu(0)$. Given (s_0, μ_0) then the particular trajectory starting at this point will move the system to reach s^T. If the terminal time T is also a choice variable, then the manager has to choose both μ_0 and T.

Consider first the choice of T. If T is finite, then s^T would be a target. But this implies that net benefits beyond s^T are of no concern to the manager. Since, under free choice, this is unlikely, then the only logical possibility is for T to be infinite.

Now consider all infinite planning horizons and the choice of μ_0. With an initial stock s_0, three possible choices are shown by μ_0^1, μ_0^2 and μ_0^3. μ_0^1 belongs to the stable arm of the saddle path $S_1 S_1'$. Hence, the trajectory is along this path tending to (s^*, μ^*) in the limit.[10] A choice of μ_0^2 (above $S_1 S_1'$) implies a shadow price of fish in the sea higher than μ_0^1. Fishing effort is not so great and the fish stock rises until it reaches its own biological carrying capacity of k. On the other hand, an initial shadow price of μ_0^3 leads to increased effort and to eventual extinction. The trajectories emanating from μ_0^2 and μ_0^3 cannot, therefore, be maximising paths.

---

[10] Since the paths are infinite, the trajectory never actually reaches μ^*.

Only μ_0^1 is optimal. The same logic holds if s_0 is initially above s^*, at $s_0 = s_0'$, μ_0^4 is the only optimal path.

The conclusion we arrive at is that the optimal path is to choose an initial point on the stable arm of the saddle path. Although this result is appealing, there is here a warning. If the shadow price is incorrectly estimated, then a *divergent* path is the most likely outcome – either raising the stock size to its carrying capacity or diminishing the species to extinction. This is certainly the problem facing a fishing agency which is attempting to balance profit and conservation.

15.8   Harvesting and age classes[11]

So far we have assumed the fish are homogeneous and in particular have not made any distinction between males and females or age composition. As we pointed out in chapter 14, section 14.6, we can model female populations in terms of age classes. In doing this here for fish populations, we shall simplify drastically and concentrate on sustainable harvesting.

Let $x_i(t)$ denote the population of fish in the ith-age class just before harvesting and assume harvesting takes place at discrete time intervals. Throughout we will consider just three age classes. As in section 14.6, let b_i denote the birth rate for the ith-class and s_{ij} the survival rate from class i to class j. This gives the Leslie matrix in the present example for $i = 1, 2, 3$ of

$$\mathbf{L} = \begin{bmatrix} b_1 & b_2 & b_3 \\ s_{12} & 0 & 0 \\ 0 & s_{23} & 0 \end{bmatrix}$$

and without harvesting we have

$$\begin{bmatrix} x_1(t+1) \\ x_2(t+1) \\ x_3(t+1) \end{bmatrix} = \begin{bmatrix} b_1 & b_2 & b_3 \\ s_{12} & 0 & 0 \\ 0 & s_{23} & 0 \end{bmatrix} \begin{bmatrix} x_1(t) \\ x_2(t) \\ x_3(t) \end{bmatrix}$$

or

$$\mathbf{x}(t+1) = \mathbf{L}\mathbf{x}(t) \tag{15.37}$$

Now suppose h_i are harvested (killed) for the age class i ($i = 1, 2, 3$). Then the number of females harvested is

$$h_1 x_1(t)$$
$$h_2 x_2(t) \quad \text{or} \quad \mathbf{H}\mathbf{x}(t)$$
$$h_3 x_3(t)$$

where

$$\mathbf{H} = \begin{bmatrix} h_1 & 0 & 0 \\ 0 & h_2 & 0 \\ 0 & 0 & h_3 \end{bmatrix}$$

[11] This section is based on the analysis in Lynch (2001, chapter 13).

This means that $\mathbf{HLx}(t)$ will be the total harvested and the remaining population will be

$$\mathbf{x}(t+1) = \mathbf{Lx}(t) - \mathbf{HLx}(t) = (\mathbf{I} - \mathbf{H})\mathbf{Lx}(t)$$

If harvesting is to be sustainable *across the age classes*, then we require $\mathbf{x}(t+1) = \mathbf{x}(t)$, i.e.

(15.38)
$$\mathbf{x}(t) = (\mathbf{I} - \mathbf{H})\mathbf{Lx}(t)$$

Let $\mathbf{M} = (\mathbf{I} - \mathbf{H})\mathbf{L}$, then $\mathbf{M}$ is also a Leslie matrix, and by theorem 14.1 (p. 629) there is a unique dominant eigenvalue λ_d which is positive. Also recall from section 14.6 that the population will then grow at a rate $\lambda_d - 1$. If we require the population to stabilise (no growth), then we require $\lambda_d = 1$ and there is a nonzero vector solution of

$$(\mathbf{I} - \mathbf{H})\mathbf{Lx}(t) = \lambda_d \mathbf{x}(t) = \mathbf{x}(t)$$

where $\mathbf{x}(t)$ is the eigenvector associated with $\lambda_d = 1$. This means that we require the dominant eigenvalue of the matrix $\mathbf{M} = (\mathbf{I} - \mathbf{H})\mathbf{L}$ to equal unity. In our present example of $i = 1, 2, 3$ we have

(15.39)
$$\mathbf{M} = (\mathbf{I} - \mathbf{H})\mathbf{L} = \begin{bmatrix} 1 - h_1 & 0 & 0 \\ 0 & 1 - h_2 & 0 \\ 0 & 0 & 1 - h_3 \end{bmatrix} \begin{bmatrix} b_1 & b_2 & b_3 \\ s_{12} & 0 & 0 \\ 0 & s_{23} & 0 \end{bmatrix}$$

$$= \begin{bmatrix} (1 - h_1)b_1 & (1 - h_1)b_2 & (1 - h_1)b_3 \\ (1 - h_2)s_{12} & 0 & 0 \\ 0 & (1 - h_3)s_{23} & 0 \end{bmatrix}$$

Since $\lambda_d = 1$ is to be the dominant root, then we require

$$|\mathbf{M} - \lambda_d \mathbf{I}| = |\mathbf{M} - \mathbf{I}| = 0$$

which will impose restrictions on the h-values. We have

$$|\mathbf{M} - \mathbf{I}| = \begin{vmatrix} (1 - h_1)b_1 - 1 & (1 - h_1)b_2 & (1 - h_1)b_3 \\ (1 - h_2)s_{12} & -1 & 0 \\ 0 & (1 - h_3)s_{23} & -1 \end{vmatrix} = 0$$

i.e.

$$[(1 - h_1)b_1 - 1] + (1 - h_1)b_2(1 - h_2)s_{12}$$
$$+ (1 - h_1)b_3[(1 - h_2)(1 - h_3)s_{12}s_{23}] = 0$$

or

(15.40)
$$(1 - h_1)b_1 + (1 - h_1)(1 - h_2)b_2 s_{12}$$
$$+ (1 - h_1)(1 - h_2)(1 - h_3)b_3 s_{12} s_{23} = 1$$

Only values of $h_i(i = 1, 2, 3)$ lying in the range $0 \le h_i \le 1$ will satisfy (15.40) in order to produce a sustainable policy. Once $h_i(i = 1, 2, 3)$ are found, the eigenvector of $\mathbf{M}$ associated with $\lambda_d = 1$ can be computed. Finally, from this the normalised vector can be obtained.

Example 15.4

A fish species is divided into three age classes with a Leslie matrix

$$\mathbf{L} = \begin{bmatrix} 0.4 & 0.8 & 0.2 \\ 0.9 & 0 & 0 \\ 0 & 0.8 & 0 \end{bmatrix}$$

We have already solved for the eigenvalues of this in example 14.9, where we found

$$\lambda_1 = 1.14136, \qquad \lambda_2 = -0.4767, \qquad \lambda_3 = -0.26466$$

with dominant root $\lambda_1 = 1.14136$ and associated eigenvector

$$\mathbf{v}^1 = \begin{bmatrix} 0.72033 \\ 0.56800 \\ 0.39812 \end{bmatrix}$$

and associated normalised eigenvector

$$\mathbf{x}_n^1 = \begin{bmatrix} 0.42713 \\ 0.33680 \\ 0.23607 \end{bmatrix}$$

If no harvesting takes place, therefore, the fish population grows at $\lambda_d - 1 = 0.14136$ or about 14% every period. Furthermore, the female population will settle down at 42.7% in age group 1, 33.7% in age group 2 and 23.6% in age group 3.
Now consider four harvesting policies:

(i)   Uniform harvesting $h_1 = h_2 = h_3 = h$
(ii) Harvesting only the youngest age class $h_1 \neq 0$, $h_2 = 0$, $h_3 = 0$
(iii) Harvesting only the middle age class $h_1 = 0$, $h_2 \neq 0$, $h_3 = 0$
(iv) Harvesting only the oldest age class $h_1 = 0$, $h_2 = 0$, $h_3 \neq 0$

(i) Uniform harvesting $h_1 = h_2 = h_3 = h$
Under this policy, and given the Leslie matrix above, equation (15.40) becomes

$$(1 - h)(0.4) + (1 - h)^2(0.8)(0.9) + (1 - h)^3(0.2)(0.9)(0.8) = 1$$

with solution $h = 0.123855$. Given this value for h, the matrix $\mathbf{M}$ takes the form

$$\mathbf{M}_u = \begin{bmatrix} 0.350458 & 0.700916 & 0.175229 \\ 0.788531 & 0 & 0 \\ 0 & 0.700916 & 0 \end{bmatrix}$$

and the associated eigenvector is

$$\mathbf{v}^1 = \begin{bmatrix} 0.720329 \\ 0.568001 \\ 0.398121 \end{bmatrix}$$

while the normalised eigenvector is

$$\mathbf{x}_u = \begin{bmatrix} 0.427127 \\ 0.336803 \\ 0.236070 \end{bmatrix}$$

(ii) Harvesting the youngest age class $h_1 \neq 0, h_2 = 0, h_3 = 0$
Under this policy, and given the Leslie matrix above, equation (15.40) becomes

$$(1 - h_1)(0.4) + (1 - h_1)(0.8)(0.9) + (1 - h_1)(0.2)(0.9)(0.8) = 1$$

with solution $h_1 = 0.208861$. Given this value for h_1, the matrix $\mathbf{M}$ takes the form

$$\mathbf{M}_1 = \begin{bmatrix} 0.316456 & 0.632911 & 0.158228 \\ 0.9 & 0 & 0 \\ 0 & 0.8 & 0 \end{bmatrix}$$

and the associated eigenvector is

$$\mathbf{v}^1 = \begin{bmatrix} 0.655347 \\ 0.589812 \\ 0.471850 \end{bmatrix}$$

while the normalised eigenvector is

$$\mathbf{x}_{n1} = \begin{bmatrix} 0.381679 \\ 0.343511 \\ 0.274809 \end{bmatrix}$$

(iii) Harvesting the middle age class $h_1 = 0, h_2 \neq 0, h_3 = 0$
Under this policy, and given the Leslie matrix above, equation (15.40) becomes

$$(1)(0.4) + (1 - h_2)(0.8)(0.9) + (1 - h_3)(0.2)(0.9)(0.8) = 1$$

with solution $h_2 = 0.305556$. Given this value for h_2, the matrix $\mathbf{M}$ takes the form

$$\mathbf{M}_2 = \begin{bmatrix} 0.4 & 0.8 & 0.2 \\ 0.625 & 0 & 0 \\ 0 & 0.8 & 0 \end{bmatrix}$$

and the associated eigenvector is

$$\mathbf{v}^1 = \begin{bmatrix} 0.78072 \\ 0.48795 \\ 0.39036 \end{bmatrix}$$

while the normalised eigenvector is

$$\mathbf{x}_{n2} = \begin{bmatrix} 0.470588 \\ 0.294118 \\ 0.235294 \end{bmatrix}$$

(iv) Harvesting the oldest age class $h_1 = 0, h_2 = 0, h_3 \neq 0$
Under this policy, and given the Leslie matrix above, equation (15.40) becomes

$$(1)(0.4) + (1)(0.8)(0.9) + (1 - h_3)(0.2)(0.9)(0.8) = 1$$

There is no solution for h_3 that lies in the range $0 \leq h_3 \leq 1$.

The normalised vectors $\mathbf{x}_u$, $\mathbf{x}_{n1}$ and $\mathbf{x}_{n2}$ determine the long-term distribution of the fish in the different age categories. If, however, it was considered beneficial to leave as many of the young age fish in the sea as possible, then pursuing a policy of catching middle age fish should be undertaken. In this case, the female population of the youngest age class would settle down at about 47%.

Exercises

1. A discrete-time production function takes the form

    $$h_t = s_t(1 - E^{ae_t})$$

    where E is the exponential term. Show that this function exhibits diminishing returns to effort and constant returns with respect to stock size.

2. For the **Gompertz growth function**

    $$f(s) = rs \ln \left(\frac{k}{s} \right)$$

    derive the s_m level and the growth at this level.

3. Given the following two growth functions, $f(s)$ and $g(s)$, respectively, and the same harvest function $h(e, s)$,

    $$f(s) = rs \left(1 - \frac{s}{k} \right)$$
    $$g(s) = rs \ln \left(\frac{k}{s} \right)$$
    $$h(e, s) = aes$$

    (i) Show, after eliminating the stock size, that the yield to effort (h/e) is linear and log-linear, respectively.
    (ii) Demonstrate that ordinary least squares estimates of the parameters in (i) are not sufficient to determine the three parameters a, r and k.

4. In the following numerical model

    $$\dot{s} = 0.2s \left(1 - \frac{s}{1000} \right) - h$$
    $$q^d = 45 - p$$
    $$q^s = 1.2p + 0.05s$$
    $$q^d = q^s = h$$

    establish whether it is possible for a regulatory authority to set the price to clear the market at a stable equilibrium which has a yield equal to the maximum sustainable yield.

5. A typical fisheries problem can be captured by the following three fundamental relationships, where the first denotes the biological growth process of a fish stock; the second a harvesting function (or catch function); while the third denotes the profits of a fishing agency.

    $$g = ks(s_u - s)$$
    $$h = aes$$
    $$\pi = ph - we$$

where:

$g = $ growth of fish stock
$k = $ stock-specific parameter
$s = $ fish stock
$s_u = $ maximum sustainable fish population
$h = $ harvest level
$a = $ technology efficiency parameter
$e = $ per unit of 'effort' expended in fishing
$p = $ price per unit of fish
$w = $ "wage" rate

(i) Interpret these three equations in detail using sketches where possible.

For the remaining questions assume:

$$g = 0.5s(25 - s)$$
$$h = 2.5es$$

(ii) Given the level of effort is $e = 2$.
   (a) Establish the maximum sustainable yield (*msy*) and the stock size at this level.
   (b) Establish the steady-state value of the stock size.
   (c) Explain why the steady-state value of s exceeds the *msy* value.

(iii) Now assume that 'effort' is not known and must be determined along with the stock size. Assume $p = 0.6$ and $w = 12$.
   (a) Establish the equilibrium values of stock size and effort that maximise profits. What is this level of profits? What is the growth rate?
   (b) Under the same price and wage levels, calculate the profits under the condition $e = 2$ (i.e. use your answers in (ii)) and compare them with the present level of maximum profits.
   (c) Explain why the stock size in this maximisation problem is greater than under (ii)(b).

(iv) Undertake the calculations in question (iii) (a) with the following values for the respective parameters:
   (a) $p = 0.8$, $w = 12$ and $a = 2.5$
   (b) $p = 0.6$, $w = 15$ and $a = 2.5$
   (c) $p = 0.6$, $w = 12$ and $a = 3$
   Discuss the implications of these results.

(v) Suppose entry and exit occurs according to the following rule:

$$\dot{e} = v\pi = v(ph - we)$$

where the parameter v denotes the speed of entry and exit in response to profits. For $v = 5$, $p = 0.6$ and $w = 12$, establish the stock level associated with equilibrium (i.e. no entry or exit). Establish the vector of forces each side of the $\dot{s} = 0$ phase line drawn with e on the vertical axis and s on the horizontal axis.

(vi) For a steady-state solution $\dot{s} = 0$, and using $p = 0.6$ and $w = 12$, show that e is a linear function of s, and hence establish the vector of forces either side of this phase line.

(vii) Using the results in (v) and (vi), establish the equilibrium for stock size and effort. Show that for a starting stock size of $s_0 = 25$, the dynamic path gives a stable oscillation to equilibrium. Verify this result by establishing the characteristic roots of the dynamic system and the trace and determinant.

(viii) Discuss this fisheries model with entry and exit commenting, in particular, on the importance of the parameter v.

6. (i) In the following model

$$\dot{s} = 0.2s \left(1 - \frac{s}{1000} \right) - h$$

$$h = 0.125es$$

what is the level of effort that should be set by the regulatory authority to have a stable equilibrium with the maximum sustainable yield?

(ii) Show that the level of effort obtained in (i) is the level that maximises

$$\frac{125}{0.2}(0.2 - 0.125e)e$$

(iii) What is the stock size which maximises profits in equilibrium if $TR = ph$ and $TC = we$, with $p = 0.4$ and $w = 10$?

7. Show that in the case of open access fishery, a rise in either the price of fish or the productivity of the fishing industry leads to an increase in effort and a reduction in fish stocks.

8. Show that if the aim is to

$$\max_{\{u\}} \int_0^T \pi \, dt$$

$$\dot{s} = f(s) - h$$

where $\pi = ph - we$, and p and w are constant and $h = h(e, s)$. Then the first-order conditions for an interior maximum are:

(i) $(p - \lambda)\dfrac{\partial h}{\partial e} = w$

(ii) $\dot{\lambda} = (\lambda - p)\dfrac{\partial h}{\partial s} - \lambda f'(s)$

(iii) $\dot{s} = f(s) - h(e, s)$

where λ is the Lagrangian multiplier (the shadow price of the resource).

9. In a fishery the fish can be divided into three age groups, each one a year long. The Leslie matrix for this population is

$$\mathbf{L} = \begin{bmatrix} 0 & 3 & 40 \\ 0.1 & 0 & 0 \\ 0 & 0.5 & 0 \end{bmatrix}$$

(i) What is the growth rate of the fish population if no harvesting takes place?

(ii) What is the long-run behaviour of the system if 25% of each age class is harvested?

10.   What is the optimal sustainable harvesting policy for the system in question 9, given the youngest age class is not harvested and groups two and three are harvested to the same extent?

Additional reading

Additional material on the contents of this chapter can be obtained from Conrad (1999), Conrad and Clark (1987), Crutchfield and Zellner (1962), Cunningham, Dunn and Whitmarsh (1985), Dasgupta and Heal (1979), Fisher (1981), Hamilton (1948), Hartwick and Olewiler (1986), Hilborn and Walters (1992), Lynch (2001), McVay (1966), Neher (1990), Peterson and Fisher (1987), Shone (1981) and Smith *et al.* (1977).

Answers to selected exercises

Chapter 2

2    $p(t) = p_0 e^{-tk} e^{-a(e^{tk}-1)}$

     $p(0) = p_0$ and $p \to e^a$ as $t \to \infty$

3   (i) $y = \dfrac{ce^{x^2} - 1}{ce^{x^2} + 1}$ (ii) $y = \dfrac{x - 1 - c}{x - c}$

     (iii) $y = \dfrac{x}{1 - cx}$

4   (i) $y = \dfrac{x^3}{3} - x^2 + x + 1$ (ii) $y = 1 \pm \sqrt{4 + x^3 + 2x^2 + 2x}$

5   (i) $y = \dfrac{e^{-x}}{e^{-x} + c}$ (ii) $y = \dfrac{1}{-x + 1 + ce^{-x}}$

     (iii) $\dfrac{1}{y} = \dfrac{e^x}{3} + ce^{-2x}$

7   Table about 1220AD

8   1990BC

11   (i) r (ii) $P(t) = P_0 e^{rt}$ (iii) £2,910

12   14 years

13   (i) $x = 3$ (repellor), $x = -5$ (attractor)

14   (ii) $k^* = 0.908$

15   (ii) $Y(t) = Y_0 e^{(s/v)t}$

16   $D(t) = D_0 + \dfrac{k}{r} Y_0 (e^{rt} - 1)$

17   7.77%

18   (a)

'Rich' countries	Years to double	'Poor' countries	Years to double
France	26	China	29
Japan	14	India	35
West Germany	28	Uganda	−347
UK	35	Zimbabwe	347
USA	50		

     (b) Years for the population to halve.

19   (a) 23.32%

(b) 3 years (2.97)

(c) 0.7506×10^{10}

20   £292,507.52

Chapter 3

1   (i) second-order, linear, autonomous, nonhomogeneous
(ii) second-order, linear, autonomous, nonhomogeneous
(iii) first-order, linear, autonomous, homogeneous
(iv) second-order, linear, non-autonomous, nonhomogeneous

2    $P_t = (1 + r)P_{t-1} - R$

$$P_n = (1 + r)^n \left(P_0 - \frac{R}{r} \right) + \frac{R}{r}$$

3    $P_n = (1 + r)^n P_0 - (1 + r)^{n-1} R_1 - (1 + r)^{n-2} R_2 - \ldots$

$- (1 + r)R_{n-1} - R_n$

4   (i) $y_n = y_0 \left(-\frac{1}{2} \right)^n - 2 \left(-\frac{1}{2} \right)^n + 2$, stable

(ii) $y_n = y_0 \left(-\frac{3}{2} \right)^n - \frac{4}{5} \left(-\frac{3}{2} \right)^n + \frac{4}{5}$, unstable

(iii) $y_n = y_0(-1)^n - 3(-1)^n + 3$, cyclical

(iv) $y_n = y_0 \left(\frac{1}{2} \right)^n - 6 \left(\frac{1}{2} \right)^n + 6$, stable

(v) $y_n = y_0 (-1)^n - \frac{1}{4}(-1)^n + \frac{1}{4}$, cyclical

5   (i) $a^3 - a^2 - a + 1 = (a + 1)(a - 1)^2$

7   (i) $p_t = \frac{8}{3} - \frac{1}{3}p_{t-1}$, stable

(ii) $p_t = 5.5 - p_{t-1}$, oscillatory

(iii) $p_t = 16 - 3p_{t-1}$, unstable

8    $Y_n = \left(\frac{a + I + G}{1 - b} \right) + b^n \left[Y_0 - \left(\frac{a + I + G}{1 - b} \right) \right]$, stable if $0 < b < 1$

10   (i) $p_t = \left(\frac{a - c}{b} \right) - \left(\frac{d}{b} \right)(1 - e)p_{t-1} - \left(\frac{de}{b} \right)p_{t-2}$

16   (i) $p_t = \left[1 - \frac{\lambda(b + d)}{b} \right]p_{t-1} + \frac{\lambda(a - c)}{b}$

(ii) $\bar{p} = \frac{a - c}{b + d}$, $\bar{q} = \frac{ad + bc}{b + d}$

17   £248.85

18   22.25 minutes

19     $x_n = \dfrac{x_0}{1 + nx_0}$

20   (ii) *Mathematica* $x_n = \dfrac{2^{-1-n}[-(1-\sqrt{5})^{1+n} + (1+\sqrt{5})^{1+n}]}{\sqrt{5}}$

      (ii) *Maple* $x_n = -\dfrac{2}{5}\dfrac{\sqrt{5}\left(-2\dfrac{1}{1-\sqrt{5}}\right)^n}{1-\sqrt{5}} + \dfrac{\dfrac{2}{5}\sqrt{5}\left(-2\dfrac{1}{1+\sqrt{5}}\right)^n}{1+\sqrt{5}}$

Chapter 4

1     $y = \sqrt{\dfrac{9x}{2}}$

5     $\mathbf{v}^1 = \begin{bmatrix} 1 \\ 1 \end{bmatrix}, \quad \mathbf{v}^2 = \begin{bmatrix} 1 \\ -1 \end{bmatrix}$

7     $\mathbf{W} = 4$

8   (i) $\lambda_1 = 1, \quad \lambda_2 = 2, \quad \lambda_3 = 5$

$$\mathbf{v}^1 = \begin{bmatrix} 1 \\ -3/2 \\ 1 \end{bmatrix}, \quad \mathbf{v}^2 = \begin{bmatrix} 0 \\ 1 \\ -1 \end{bmatrix}, \quad \mathbf{v}^3 = \begin{bmatrix} 0 \\ 1 \\ 2 \end{bmatrix}$$

$x(t) = c_1 e^t$

(ii) $y(t) = -\dfrac{3}{2}c_1 e^t + c_2 e^{2t} + c_3 e^{5t}$

$z(t) = c_1 e^t - c_2 e^{2t} + 2c_3 e^{5t}$

(iii) $\mathbf{W} = 3$

9   (i) $(r, s) = (-2, -4), \quad \mathbf{v}^r = \begin{bmatrix} 1 \\ 1 \end{bmatrix}, \quad \mathbf{v}^s = \begin{bmatrix} -1 \\ 1 \end{bmatrix}$

$x(t) = c_1 e^{-2t} - c_2 e^{-4t} \quad$ improper node

$y(t) = c_1 e^{-2t} + c_2 e^{-4t}$

(ii) $(r, s) = (1, -2), \quad \mathbf{v}^r = \begin{bmatrix} 4 \\ 1 \end{bmatrix}, \quad \mathbf{v}^s = \begin{bmatrix} 1 \\ 1 \end{bmatrix}$

$x(t) = 4c_1 e^t + c_2 e^{-2t} \quad$ saddle point

$y(t) = c_1 e^t + c_2 e^{-2t}$

(iii) $(r, s) = (2i, -2i), \quad \mathbf{v}^r = \begin{bmatrix} -i/2 \\ 1 \end{bmatrix}, \quad \mathbf{v}^s = \begin{bmatrix} i/2 \\ 1 \end{bmatrix}$

$x(t) = c_1 \sin(2t) + c_2 \cos(2t) \quad$ centre

$y(t) = 2c_1 \cos(2t) - 2c_2 \sin(2t)$

(iv) $(r, s) = (-1 + i, -1 - i), \quad \mathbf{v}^r = \begin{bmatrix} -i \\ 1 \end{bmatrix}, \quad \mathbf{v}^s = \begin{bmatrix} i \\ 1 \end{bmatrix}$

$x(t) = c_2 e^{-t} \sin(t) - c_1 e^{-t} \cos(t) \quad$ spiral

$y(t) = c_1 e^{-t} \sin(t) + c_2 e^{-t} \cos(t)$

10   (i) $P_1 = (6,0)$ and $P_2 = (0.846, 2.114)$.

(ii) Fixed point P_2, exhibits a stable limit cycle

12   (i) $(p^*, Y^*) = (7.055, 26.221)$

(ii) Yes.

13   System has limit cycles that shrinks as β rises.

14   System has limit cycles that expand as α rises.

Chapter 5

7   (i) (a) $(r, s) = (i, -i)$ (b) $\mathbf{v}^r = \begin{bmatrix} -i \\ 1 \end{bmatrix}$, $\mathbf{v}^s = \begin{bmatrix} i \\ 1 \end{bmatrix}$

(c) $\mathbf{D} = \begin{bmatrix} i & 0 \\ 0 & -i \end{bmatrix}$

(ii) (a) $(r, s) = (-3, -1)$ (b) $\mathbf{v}^r = \begin{bmatrix} -1 \\ 1 \end{bmatrix}$, $\mathbf{v}^s = \begin{bmatrix} 1 \\ 1 \end{bmatrix}$

(c) $\mathbf{D} = \begin{bmatrix} -3 & 0 \\ 0 & -1 \end{bmatrix}$

(iii) (a) $(r, s) = (2, -1)$ (b) $\mathbf{v}^r = \begin{bmatrix} 4 \\ 1 \end{bmatrix}$, $\mathbf{v}^s = \begin{bmatrix} 1 \\ 1 \end{bmatrix}$

(c) $\mathbf{D} = \begin{bmatrix} 2 & 0 \\ 0 & -1 \end{bmatrix}$

11   (i) trace $= 11$, determinant $= 14$

(ii) $\begin{bmatrix} 3 & 5 \\ 4 & 2 \\ 11 & -5 \end{bmatrix}$

(iii) $\begin{bmatrix} 1/2 & -1 \\ 1/2 & -2 \end{bmatrix}$

(iv) $r = \sqrt{7}, \qquad s = -\sqrt{7}$ for mA

$r = \dfrac{3}{2} + \dfrac{1}{2}\sqrt{17}, \qquad s = \dfrac{3}{2} - \dfrac{1}{2}\sqrt{17}$ for mB

$\mathbf{v}^r = \begin{bmatrix} 1 \\ \dfrac{1}{3}\sqrt{7} - \dfrac{2}{3} \end{bmatrix}$, $\mathbf{v}^s = \begin{bmatrix} 1 \\ -\dfrac{1}{3}\sqrt{7} - \dfrac{2}{3} \end{bmatrix}$ for mA

$\mathbf{v}^r = \begin{bmatrix} 1 \\ \dfrac{5}{4} - \dfrac{1}{4}\sqrt{17} \end{bmatrix}$, $\mathbf{v}^s = \begin{bmatrix} 1 \\ \dfrac{5}{4} + \dfrac{1}{4}\sqrt{17} \end{bmatrix}$ for mB

(v) $\lambda^2 - 7$

12   *Mathematica* $x_t = -9 + \left(5 + \dfrac{i}{2}\right)(-i)^t + \left(5 - \dfrac{i}{2}\right)i^t$

$y_t = \left(\dfrac{1}{4} + \dfrac{i}{4}\right)((-5 + 5i) + (10 + i)(-i)^t - (1 + 10i)i^t)$

Maple 　$x_t = -9 + 5(-i)^t + 5i^t + \dfrac{1}{2}i(-i)^t - \dfrac{1}{2}i\,i^t$

$$y_t = -\frac{5}{2} + \frac{9}{4}(-i)^t + \frac{11}{4}i(-i)^t + \frac{9}{4}i^t - \frac{11}{4}i\,i^t$$

13 　$\mathbf{J} = \begin{bmatrix} -i & 0 \\ 0 & i \end{bmatrix}, \quad \mathbf{V} = \begin{bmatrix} 1-i & 1+i \\ 1 & 1 \end{bmatrix}$

14 　(i) $(x^*, y^*) = (-9, -\dfrac{5}{2})$, 4-period cycle results

15 　$\mathbf{J} = \begin{bmatrix} -0.5 & 0 \\ 0 & -0.4 \end{bmatrix}, \quad \mathbf{V} = \begin{bmatrix} 0 & 1 \\ -4 & 4 \end{bmatrix}$

Chapter 6

1 　(i) Minimum ABEHJ $= 12$, 　　(ii) JHEBA, hence same.
8 　$x(t) = 5\cos(1.11803t) + 8.68811\sin(1.11803t)$
　　$y(t) = 3.2697\cos(1.11803t) + 0.688441\sin(1.11803t)$

9 　$x(t) = \dfrac{5e^{-t}(-3e + 2e^{-2} - 2e^{2t} + 3e^{1+2t})}{e^2 - 1}$

　　$y(t) = \dfrac{10e^{-t}(-9e + 6e^2 - 2e^{2t} + 3e^{1+2t})}{1 - e^2}$

10 　$\dot{c} = (0.4k^{-0.7} - 0.1067)c$
　　$\dot{k} = k^{0.3} - 0.05k - c$
　　$k^* = 6.6047, \quad c^* = 1.4316$

Chapter 7

1 　$\lambda_2 = 3.5458$

2 　$\lambda_k = \left(\dfrac{\lambda_1 - \lambda_0}{\delta}\right)\left(\dfrac{1}{\delta^{k-2}} + \dfrac{1}{\delta^{k-1}} + \cdots - 1\right) + \lambda_1$

　　$\displaystyle\lim_{k\to\infty} \lambda_k = \dfrac{\lambda_1 - \lambda_0}{\delta} + \lambda_1$

Chapter 8

2 　(i) $p_t = 60 - 1.5p_{t-1}$, 　　oscillatory and divergent
　　(ii) $p_t = 15 + 0.5p_{t-1}$, 　　convergent
　　(iii) $p_t = 60 - p_{t-1}$, 　　cyclical

　　(iv) $p_t = \dfrac{28}{3} - \dfrac{4}{3}p_{t-1}$, 　　oscillatory and divergent

3 　(i) $p_t = 24 - 14(-0.25)^t$
　　(ii) $p_t = 30 - 20(-0.9)^t$

4 　(i) $p_t = 4.5 - 0.2p_{t-1}$, 　　cyclical and convergent
　　(ii) $p_t = 100 + 0.2p_{t-1}$, 　　convergent

5   (i) $p^* = 4$, $p_t = 4 - 0.5(p_{t-1} - 4)$,   stable
          $p^* = 10$, $p_t = 10 + 2.5(p_{t-1} - 10)$,   unstable
     (ii) $p^* = 6$, $p_t = 6 + 0.5(p_{t-1} - 6)$,   stable
          $p^* = 8$, $p_t = 8 + 1.5(p_{t-1} - 8)$,   unstable

6   (i) $p^* = 3.5$, $q^* = 20.5$ (ii) 4 periods

7    $p_t = \dfrac{49\lambda}{9} + \left(1 - \dfrac{14\lambda}{9}\right)p_{t-1}$

     (i) 4 periods,   (ii) 2 periods,
     (iii) 2 periods,   (iv) 5 periods.

8   (i) $p(t) = 3 + c_1 e^{-37.5t}$ (ii) stable

9   (i) $w^* = 4$, (ii) Investigate $f(w) = \begin{cases} 10 - 1.5w & w \leq 14/3 \\ 3 & w > 14/3 \end{cases}$

12   $p_t = 1 + \left(-\dfrac{2}{3}\right)^t (p_0 - 1)$,   stable

13   $p_t = \dfrac{28\lambda}{5} + \left(1 - \dfrac{7\lambda}{5}\right)p_{t-1}$

14   (i) $\dot{P} = r(P - P^*) - R'(h^*)(h - h^*)$
          $\dot{h} = g'(P^*)(P - P^*) - (d + n)(h - h^*)$

Chapter 9

4   (i) $q_1^* = \dfrac{9 - 2a_1 + a_2}{3}$

     $q_2^* = \dfrac{9 + a_1 - 2a_2}{3}$

     (ii) Cournot solution $(q_1^*, q_2^*) = \left(\frac{8}{3}, \frac{2}{3}\right)$ Firm 1 monopolist.

5   (i) $(q_1^*, q_2^*, q_3^*) = (1, 1, 1)$

     (ii) $q_{1,t} = 2 - \frac{1}{2}q_{2,t-1} - \frac{1}{2}q_{3,t-1}$

     $q_{2,t} = 2 - \frac{1}{2}q_{1,t-1} - \frac{1}{2}q_{3,t-1}$

     $q_{3,t} = 2 - \frac{1}{2}q_{1,t-1} - \frac{1}{2}q_{2,t-1}$

     (iii) Yes.

6   (i) $(q_1^*, q_2^*, q_3^*) = \left(\frac{3}{4}, \frac{7}{4}, \frac{11}{4}\right)$

     (ii) $q_{1t} = \dfrac{3}{4} - \dfrac{7}{4}(-1)^t + \dfrac{1}{3}(-1)^t(q_{10} + q_{20} + q_{30})$

     $+ \dfrac{1}{3}\left(\dfrac{1}{2}\right)^t (2q_{10} - q_{20} - q_{30})$

     $q_{2t} = \dfrac{7}{4} - \dfrac{7}{4}(-1)^t + \dfrac{1}{3}(-1)^t(q_{10} + q_{20} + q_{30})$

     $+ \dfrac{1}{3}\left(\dfrac{1}{2}\right)^t (-q_{10} + 2q_{20} - q_{30})$

$$q_{3t} = \frac{11}{4} - \frac{7}{4}(-1)^t + \frac{1}{3}(-1)^t(q_{10} + q_{20} + q_{30})$$

$$+ \frac{1}{3}\left(\frac{1}{2}\right)^t (-q_{10} - q_{20} + 2q_{30})$$

7   (i) $(q_1^*, q_2^*, q_3^*) = \left(\frac{5}{8}, \frac{13}{8}, \frac{17}{8}\right)$

    (iii) $q_{1t} = \frac{5}{8} - \frac{35}{24}(-1)^t + \frac{1}{3}(-1)^t(q_{10} + q_{20} + q_{30})$

$$+ \frac{1}{3}\left(\frac{1}{2}\right)^t (2q_{10} - q_{20} - q_{30})$$

$$q_{2t} = \frac{13}{8} - \frac{35}{24}(-1)^t + \frac{1}{3}(-1)^t(q_{10} + q_{20} + q_{30})$$

$$+ \frac{1}{3}\left(\frac{1}{2}\right)^t (-q_{10} + 2q_{20} - q_{30})$$

$$q_{3t} = \frac{17}{8} - \frac{35}{24}(-1)^t + \frac{1}{3}(-1)^t(q_{10} + q_{20} + q_{30})$$

$$+ \frac{1}{3}\left(\frac{1}{2}\right)^t (-q_{10} - q_{20} + 2q_{30})$$

8   (i)   (a) $(q_1^*, q_2^*) = (1.778, 1.778)$ (b) $(q_1^*, q_2^*, q_3^*) = \left(\frac{4}{3}, \frac{4}{3}, \frac{4}{3}\right)$
       (c) $(q_1^*, q_2^*) = (1.176, 1.176)$ (d) $(q_1^*, q_2^*, q_3^*) = (1, 1, 1)$

9   (i) $(q_1^*, q_2^*) = \left(\frac{16}{9}, \frac{16}{9}\right)$
    (ii) Yes.

10   Cournot solution $(q_1^*, q_2^*) = \left(\frac{16}{9}, \frac{16}{9}\right)$. Yes, all paths converge on Cournot solution.

Chapter 10

2    $y_t = 1000 + 0.6y_{t-1} - 0.1y_{t-2}$

3   Smaller for any given time period.

4   (i) $Y_t = 110 + 4.75Y_{t-1} - 4Y_{t-2}$,   explosive
    (ii) $Y_t = 110 + 3.75Y_{t-1} - 3Y_{t-2}$,   explosive

6   (i) Change in a, b or t.
    (ii) Change in k, u or m_0.

12   No. Roots are $(r, s) = (0.22984, -0.5715)$ with
    $r - r^* = 0.2825(y - y^*)$ associated with r
    $r - r^* = 0.2298(y - y^*)$ associated with s

14   (i) $(y^*, r^*) = (27.907, 13.178)$
    (ii) IS curve: $r = 16.6667 - 0.125y$
           LM curve: $r = -33.3333 + 1.6667y$
    (iii) trace $= -0.129$, determinant $= 0.016$, stable spiral.

15   (i) $(y^*, q^*) = (35.720, 0.720)$
    (iii) $q = 6.5498 - 0.1632y$

Chapter 11

1   (i) $\pi(t) = \dfrac{f(u)}{1-\delta} + e^{-\beta(1-\delta)t}\left(1 - \dfrac{f(u)}{1-\delta}\right)$

3   $(r, s) = (-0.925 + 1.464i, -0.925 - 1.464i)$

11   (i) $(m_s^*, \pi^{e*}) = (700, 0)$
    (ii) $\dot{m}_s = 0$ gives $\pi^e = 68.29 - 0.098m_s$
      $\dot{\pi}^e = 0$ gives $\pi^e = 140 - 0.2m_s$
    (iii) $\pi^e = -488.125 + 0.625m_s$

12   (i) $\ln S = \ln \lambda - \alpha\lambda$

Chapter 12

1   $Y_t = 1320 - 0.5Y_{t-2}$

2   (i) $Y_t = 1320 - 0.7Y_{t-1} - 0.2Y_{t-2}$
    (ii) $Y_t = 1320 + 0.5Y_{t-1}$

4   (i) $Y_t = 1250 + 0.5Y_{t-1},\qquad Y_t = 1250 + 0.4Y_{t-1},$
      $Y_t = 1250 + 0.3Y_{t-1}$
    (ii) $Y^*(m = 0.2) = 2500,\qquad Y^*(m = 0.3) = 2083.3,$
      $Y^*(m = 0.4) = 1785.7$

5   (i) $(y, r) = (44.39, 16.19)$
    (ii) $(y, r) = (38.12, 15.06)$
    (iii) $(y, r) = (41.49, 14.75)$

6   (i) $(y, r) = (52.447, 20.223)$ s fixed, $s = 1.7640145$
      $(y, r) = (50.663, 19.316)$ s variable, $s = 1.33$
    (ii) $(y, r) = (42.894, 13.447)$ s fixed, $s = 1.7640145$
      $(y, r) = (43.544, 13.772)$ s variable, $s = 1.9195$

Chapter 13

2   $AM(r^* = 12)$ $p = 111.1 - 0.1s$

4   (i) $GM_0:$ $p_t = 95.122 + 0.0244s_t$
      $AM_0:$ $p_t = 103.5938 - 0.0625s_t$
      $(s^*, p^*) = (97.5, 97.5)$
    (ii) $GM_1:$ $p_t = 100 + 0.0244s_t$
      $AM_1:$ $p_t = 108.90625 - 0.0625s_t$
      $(s^*, p^*) = (102.5, 102.5)$

7   (ii) $C(s, p) = (104.07407, 100)$

11   (i) $\dot{s} = -200 + 2s$ (ii) $\bar{s} = 100$

12   $\bar{s} = (m - p^*) - ky + u(r^* + \lambda - \pi^*)$

Chapter 14

2   69 years

3   $\dfrac{-\ln 2}{b - (d + m)}$ years

4   (i) 37 years   (ii) $\dfrac{\ln \lambda}{k}$ years

5    $\dot{p} \simeq -a\left(p - \dfrac{a}{b}\right)$ $p(t) = \dfrac{a}{b} + \left(p_0 - \dfrac{a}{b}\right)e^{-at}$

$\lim\limits_{t \to \infty} p(t) = \dfrac{a}{b}$, hence equilibrium never achieved in finite time period.

6   (iii) $p(t) = \dfrac{-a}{c - kae^{-at}}$ $k =$ constant of integration

$p(t) = \infty$ at $t = \dfrac{\ln(c/ak)}{-a}$ which is finite

8   (i) $p(t) = p_0^{e^{-rt}} e^{-a(e^{-rt} - 1)}$

(iii) $p = 0$, unstable; $p = e^a$, stable

(iv) $\lim\limits_{t \to \infty} p(t) = e^a$

9    $y = \sqrt{3x^2 + c}$

10    $B = \dfrac{a}{b} - \left(\dfrac{a}{bk_1}\right)T$ for $\dot{T} = 0$

$B = k_2 - \left(\dfrac{dk_2}{c}\right)T$ for $\dot{B} = 0$

11   (i) 46.67×10^6 kg   (ii) (a) 1.27 years   (b) 3.095 years

12   (i) (a) $E_1 = (0, 0)$, $E_2 = (25, 100)$
       (b) $E_1 = (0, 0)$, $E_2 = (0, 1)$, $E_3 = (0.375, 0.25)$
       (c) $E_1 = (0, 0)$, $E_2 = (1, 0)$, $E_3 = (0, 0.5)$

(ii) (a) oscillations around $E_2 = (25, 100)$
       (b) limit cycle around $E_3 = (0.375, 0.25)$
       (c) competing predators at $E_2 = (1, 0)$

13   (i) $E_1 = (0, 0)$ $E_2 = (3, 1)$ $E_3 = (0, \frac{1}{4})$

(ii) $\mathbf{A}_1 = \begin{bmatrix} 1.4 & 0 \\ 0 & 0.6 \end{bmatrix}$, $\mathbf{A}_2 = \begin{bmatrix} 0 & -4.2 \\ 0.6 & -2.4 \end{bmatrix}$,

$\mathbf{A}_3 = \begin{bmatrix} 1.05 & 0 \\ 0.15 & -0.6 \end{bmatrix}$

(iii) $E_1 = (0, 0)$, $(r, s) = (0.6, 1.4)$

$\mathbf{v}^r = \begin{bmatrix} 0 \\ 1 \end{bmatrix}$, $\mathbf{v}^s = \begin{bmatrix} 1 \\ 0 \end{bmatrix}$

$E_2 = (3, 1)$, $(r, s) = (-1.2 + 1.039i, -1.2 - 1.039i)$

$\mathbf{v}^r = \begin{bmatrix} -1.732 + 2i \\ i \end{bmatrix}$, $\mathbf{v}^s = \begin{bmatrix} -1.732 - 2i \\ -i \end{bmatrix}$

$E_3 = (0, \frac{1}{4})$, $(r, s) = (-0.6, 1.5)$

$\mathbf{v}^r = \begin{bmatrix} 0 \\ 1 \end{bmatrix}$, $\mathbf{v}^s = \begin{bmatrix} 1 \\ 0.09 \end{bmatrix}$

14   (i) $E_1 = (0,0)$ $E_2 = (1,0)$ $E_3 = (0,1)$ $E_4 = \left(\frac{2}{3}, \frac{2}{3}\right)$

(ii) $\mathbf{A}_1 = \begin{bmatrix} \dfrac{3}{10} & 0 \\ 0 & \dfrac{3}{10} \end{bmatrix}$, $\mathbf{A}_2 = \begin{bmatrix} \dfrac{-3}{10} & \dfrac{-3}{20} \\ 0 & \dfrac{3}{20} \end{bmatrix}$,

$\mathbf{A}_3 = \begin{bmatrix} \dfrac{3}{20} & 0 \\ \dfrac{-3}{20} & \dfrac{-3}{10} \end{bmatrix}$, $\mathbf{A}_4 = \begin{bmatrix} \dfrac{-1}{5} & \dfrac{-1}{10} \\ \dfrac{-1}{10} & \dfrac{-1}{5} \end{bmatrix}$

15   (i) $x_1(t+1) = 0.4x_3(t)$
$x_2(t+1) = 0.6x_1(t)$
$x_3(t+1) = 0.95x_2(t) + 0.75x_3(t)$

(iv) 10.5%
(v) 24%, 13% and 63%

Chapter 15

1    $\dfrac{\partial h_t}{\partial e_t} = s_t(aE^{-ae_t}) > 0,$ $\dfrac{\partial^2 h_t}{\partial e_t^2} = -a^2 s_t E^{-ae_t} < 0$

$\dfrac{\partial h_t}{\partial s_t} = 1 - E^{-ae_t},$ $\dfrac{\partial^2 h_t}{\partial s_t^2} = 0$

2    $s_m = \dfrac{k}{E},$ $f(s_m) = \dfrac{rk}{E}$ where E is the exponential

3   (i) $\dfrac{h}{e} = ak - \left(\dfrac{a^2 k}{r}\right)e$ for $f(s)$

$\ln\left(\dfrac{h}{e}\right) = \ln(ak) - \left(\dfrac{a}{r}\right)e$ for $g(s)$

(ii) Use $h/e = \hat{\alpha} + \hat{\beta}e$ and $\ln(h/e) = \hat{\alpha} + \hat{\beta}e$. In each case $\hat{\alpha}$ and $\hat{\beta}$ are insufficient to identify all parameters.

4   No.
5   (ii) (a) $s_m = 12.5,$ $g(s_m) = 78.125,$ (b) $s = 15$
(iii) (a) $s_m = 16.5,$ $e = 17,$ $\pi = 21.675,$ $g = 70.125$ (b) $\pi = 21$
(iv)

	$p = 0.8$ $w = 12$ $a = 2.5$	$p = 0.6$ $w = 15$ $a = 2.5$	$p = 0.6$ $w = 12$ $a = 3$
s	15.5	17.5	15.83
e	1.9	1.5	1.53
π	36.1	16.875	25.21
g	73.625	65.625	72.57

(v) $s^* = 8$
(vi) $e = 5 - 0.2s$

(vii) $s^* = 8, \quad e^* = 3.4$

$$\mathbf{A} = \begin{bmatrix} -0.5 & -2.5 \\ 7.5 & 0 \end{bmatrix}, \qquad (r, s) = (-0.25 + 4.32i, -0.25 - 4.32i)$$

$\text{tr}(\mathbf{A}) = -0.5, \qquad \det(\mathbf{A}) = 18.75$

6   (i) $e = 0.8$ (iii) $s = 600$

9   (i) 34%

     (ii) group one, 90.7%; group two, 6.8%; group three, 2.5%

10    $h = 0.7192$ with group 1, 94.5%; group 2, 4.5%; group 3, 1.0%

Bibliography

Abell, M.L. and Braselton, J.P. (1992) *The Mathematica Handbook*, Boston: Academic Press

(1993) *Differential Equations with Mathematica*, Boston: Academic Press

(1994a) *Differential Equations with Maple V*, Boston: AP Professional

(1994b) *The Maple V Handbook*, Boston: AP Professional

(1997a) *Mathematica by Example*, 2nd edn., San Diego: Academic Press

(1997b) *Differential Equations with Mathematica*, 2nd edn., San Diego: Academic Press

(1999) *Maple V by Example*, 2nd edn., Boston: AP Professional

Allen, R.G.D. (1965) *Mathematical Economics*, 2nd edn., London: Macmillan

Arrowsmith, D.K. and Place, C.M. (1992) *Dynamical Systems*, London: Chapman & Hall

Attfield, C.L.F., Demery, D. and Duck, N.W. (1985) *Rational Expectations in Macroeconomics*, Oxford: Blackwell

Azariadis, C. (1993) *Intertemporal Macroeconomics*, Oxford: Blackwell

Baker, G.L. and Gollub, J.P. (1990) *Chaotic Dynamics: An Introduction*, Cambridge: Cambridge University Press

Barro, R.J. and Grilli, V. (1994) *European Macroeconomics*, London: Macmillan

Barro, R.J. and Sala-i-Martin, X. (1995) *Economic Growth*, New York: McGraw-Hill

Baumol, W.J. (1959) *Economic Dynamics*, 2nd edn., New York: Macmillan

Baumol, W.J. and Benhabib, J. (1989) Chaos: significance, mechanism and economic applications, *Journal of Economic Perspectives*, 3, 77–105

Baumol, W.J. and Wolff, E.N. (1991) Feedback between R & D and productivity growth: a chaos model, in Benhabib, J. (ed.), *Cycles and Chaos in Economic Equilibrium*, Princeton: Princeton University Press

Beavis, B. and Dobbs, I. (1990) *Optimization and Stability Theory for Economic Analysis*, Cambridge: Cambridge University Press

Benhabib, J. and Day, R.H. (1981) Rational choice and erratic behaviour, *Review of Economic Studies*, 48, 459–471

Benhabib, J. and *et al.* (1992) *Cycles and Chaos in Economic Equilibrium*, Princeton: Princeton University Press

Berry, J. (1996) *Introduction to Non-Linear Systems*, London: Arnold

Blachman, N. (1992) *Mathematica: A Practical Approach*, Englewood Cliffs: Prentice-Hall

Blackburn, K. (1987) Macroeconomic policy evaluation and optimal control theory: a critical review of some recent developments, *Journal of Economic Surveys*, 1(2), 111–148

Blanchard, O.J. (1981) Output, the stock market and interest rates, *American Economic Review*, 71, 132–143

Blanchard, O.J. and Fischer, S. (1989) *Lectures on Macroeconomics*, Cambridge, Mass.: MIT Press

Blatt, J.M. (1983) *Dynamic Economic Systems*, New York: M.E. Sharpe

Boldrin, M. and Woodford, M. (1990) Equilibrium models displaying endogenous fluctuations and chaos: a survey, *Journal of Monetary Economics*, 25, 189–222

Borrelli, R.L., Coleman, C. and Boyce, W.E. (1992) *Differential Equations Laboratory Workbook*, New York: John Wiley

Boyce, W.E. and DiPrima, R.C. (1997) *Elementary Differential Equations and Boundary Value Problems*, 6th edn., New York: John Wiley

Brauer, F. and Nohel, J.A. (1969) *The Qualitative Theory of Ordinary Differential Equations: An Introduction*, New York: Dover Publications

Braun, M. (1983) *Differential Equations and Their Application*, 3rd edn., short version, New York: Springer-Verlag

Brock, W.A. (1986) Distinguishing random and deterministic systems, *Journal of Economic Theory*, 40, 168–195

Brock, W.A. and Malliaris, A.G. (1989) *Differential Equations, Stability and Chaos in Dynamic Economics*, Amsterdam: North-Holland

Brown, D.P., Porta, H. and Uhl, J.J. (1991) *Calculus & Mathematica*, Redwood City, Cal.: Addison-Wesley

Bryson, A.E., Jr. and Ho, Y. (1975) *Applied Optimal Control*, New York: John Wiley

Buchanan, N.S. (1939) A reconsideration of the cobweb theorem, *Journal of Political Economy*, 47, 67–81

Buiter, W.H. and Miller, M.H. (1981) Monetary policy and international competitiveness: the problem of adjustment, *Oxford Economic Papers*, 33, 143–175

Bullard, J. and Butler, A. (1993) Nonlinearity and chaos in economic models: implications for policy decisions, *Economic Journal*, 103(419), 849–867

Burbulla, D.C.M. and Dodson, C.T.J. (1992) *Self-Tutor for Computer Calculus Using Mathematica 2.0*, Scarborough, Ontario: Prentice-Hall Canada

Burghes, D.N., Huntley, I. and McDonald, J. (1982) *Applying Mathematics: A Course in Mathematical Modelling*, Chichester: Ellis Horwood Ltd

Burmeister, E. and Dobell, A.R. (1970) *Mathematical Theories of Economic Growth*, London: Macmillan

Cagan, P. (1956) The monetary dynamics of hyperinflation, in Friedman, M. (ed.), *Studies in the Quantity Theory of Money*, Chicago: University of Chicago Press

Carter, M. and Maddock, R. (1984) *Rational Expectations*, London: Macmillan

Cass, D. (1965) Optimum growth in an aggregate model of capital accumulation, *Review of Economic Studies*, 32, 233–240

(1992) Sunspots and incomplete financial markets: the general case, *Economic Theory*, 2, 341–358

Cass, D. and Shell, K. (1983) Do sunspots matter?, *Journal of Political Economy*, 91, 193–227

Caswell, H. (2000) *Matrix Population Models*, 2nd edn., Sunderland, Mass.: Sinauer Associates

Chappell, D. (1997) Chaotic behaviour in a simple model of inflation, *The Manchester School*, 65(3), 259–279

Chiang, A.C. (1984) *Fundamental Methods of Mathematical Economics*, 2nd edn., New York: McGraw-Hill

(1992) *Elements of Dynamic Optimization*, New York: McGraw-Hill

Conrad, J.M. (1999) *Resource Economics*, Cambridge: Cambridge University Press

Conrad, J.M. and Clark, C.W. (1987) *Natural Resource Economics*, Cambridge: Cambridge University Press

Coombes, K.R. and et al. (1998) *Differential Equations with Mathematica*, New York: John Wiley

Copeland, L.S. (2000) *Exchange Rates and International Finance*, 3rd edn., Workingham: Addison-Wesley

Crandall, R.E. (1991) *Mathematica for the Sciences*, Redwood City, Cal.: Addison-Wesley

Crutchfield, J.A. and Zellner, A. (1962) Economic aspects of the Pacific halibut fishery, *Fishery Industrial Research*, 1, 1–173

Cullen, M. (1985) *Linear Models in Biology*, Chichester: Ellis Horwood Ltd

Cunningham, S., Dunn, M.R. and Whitmarsh, D. (1985) *Fisheries Economics: An Introduction*, London: Mansell Publishing

Dasgupta, P.S. and Heal, G.M. (1979) *Economic Theory and Exhaustive Resources*, Cambridge: Cambridge University Press

Davies, S. (1979) *The Diffusion of Process Innovations*, Cambridge: Cambridge University Press

Day, R.H. and Shafer, W. (1992) Keynesian chaos, in Benhabib, J. (ed.), *Cycles and Chaos in Economic Equilibrium*, Princeton: Princeton University Press

Deane, P. and Cole, W.A. (1962) *British Economic Growth 1688–1959*, Cambridge: Cambridge University Press

Dernburg, T.F. (1989) *Global Macroeconomics*, New York: Harper & Row

Devitt, J.S. (1993) *Calculus with Maple V*, Pacific Grove, Cal.: Brooks/Cole

Diamond, P.A. (1971) A model of price adjustment, *Journal of Economic Theory*, 3, 156–168

(1982) Wage determination and efficiency in search equilibrium, *Review of Economic Studies*, 49, 761–782

Domar, E.D. (1944) The burden of debt and the national income, *American Economic Review*, 34, 798–827

Don, E. (2001) *Mathematica*, New York: McGraw-Hill

Dornbusch, R. (1976) Expectations and exchange rate dynamics, *Journal of Political Economy*, 84, 1161–1176

Eckalbar, J.C. (1993) Economic dynamics, in Varian, H.R. (ed.), *Economic and Financial Modeling with Mathematica*, New York: Springer-Verlag

Elaydi, S.N. (1996) *An Introduction to Difference Equations*, New York: Springer-Verlag

Ellis, W.J., Johnson, E.W., Lodi, E. and Schwalbe, D. (1992) *Maple V Flight Manual*, Pacific Grove, Cal.: Brooks/Cole

Ezekiel, M. (1938) The cobweb theorem, *Quarterly Journal of Economics*, 52, 255–280

Farmer, R.E.A. (1999) *The Macroeconomics of Self-Fulfilling Prophecies*, 2nd edn., Cambridge, Mass.: MIT Press

Ferguson, B.S. and Lim, G.C. (1998) *Introduction to Dynamic Economic Models*, Manchester: Manchester University Press

Fischer, R.D. and Mirman, L.J. (1992) Strategic dynamic interaction: fish wars, *Journal of Economic Dynamics and Control*, 16(2), 267–287

Fischer, S. (1990) Rules versus discretion in monetary policy, in Friedman, B.J. and Hahn, F.H. (eds.), *Handbook of Monetary Economics, II*, Amsterdam: North-Holland, 1155–1184

Fisher, C.A. (1981) *Resource and Environmental Economics*, Cambridge: Cambridge University Press

Flaschel, P., Franke, R. and Semmler, W. (1997) *Dynamic Macroeconomics*, Cambridge, Mass.: MIT Press

Ford, J.L. (1990) Macroeconomic policy effectiveness in the open economy: the Niehans paradox re-visited, in Ford, J.L. (ed.), *Current Issues in Open Economy Macroeconomics*, Aldershot: Edward Elgar

Frank, M.Z. and Stengos, T. (1988) Chaotic dynamics in economic time series, *Journal of Economic Surveys*, 2(2), 103–133

Frenkel, R. and Rodriguez, C.A. (1982) Exchange rate dynamics and the overshooting hypothesis, *International Monetary Fund Staff Papers*, 29, 1, 1–30

Friedman, B.M. (1990) Targets and instruments of monetary policy, in Friedman, B.J. and Hahn, F.H. (eds.), *Handbook of Monetary Economics, II*, Amsterdam: North-Holland, 1185–1230

Friedman, J. (1983) *Oligopoly Theory*, Cambridge: Cambridge University Press

Frisch, H. (1983) *Theories of Inflation*, Cambridge: Cambridge University Press

Frisch, R. (1936) On the notion of equilibrium and disequilibrium, *Review of Economic Studies*, 3, 100–105

Fryer, M.J. and Greenman, J.V. (1987) *Optimization Theory: Applications in OR and Economics*, London: Edward Arnold

Fuente, A. de la (2000) *Mathematical Methods and Models for Economists*, Cambridge: Cambridge University Press

Gander, W. and Hrebicek, J. (1991) *Solving Problems in Scientific Computing Using Maple and MATLAB*, New York: Springer-Verlag

Gandolfo, G. (1971) *Mathematical Methods and Models in Economic Dynamics*, Amsterdam: North-Holland

   (1997) *Economic Dynamics*, Berlin: Springer

Gapinski, J.H. (1982) *Macroeconomic Theory*, New York: McGraw-Hill

Gärtner, M. (1993) *Macroeconomics under Flexible Exchange Rates*, London: Harvester Wheatsheaf

Gehrig, W. (1981) On the complete solution of the linear Cournot oligopoly model, *Review of Economic Studies*, 48, 667–670

George, D.A.R. and Oxley, L. (1991) Fixed money growth rules and the rate of inflation, *Scottish Journal of Political Economy*, 38(3), 209–226

Giordano, F.R. and Weir, M.D. (1991) *Differential Equations: A Modeling Approach*, Reading, Mass.: Addison-Wesley

Gleick, J. (1988) *Chaos*, London: Heinemann

Goldberg, S. (1961) *Introduction to Differential Equations*, New York: John Wiley

Goodwin, R.M. (1947) Dynamic coupling with especial reference to markets having production lags, *Econometrica*, 15, 181–204

Gray, T.W. and Glynn, J. (1991) *Exploring Mathematics with Mathematica*, Redwood City, Cal. Addison-Wesley

Griffiths, H.B. and Oldknow, A. (1993) *Mathematics of Models: Continuous and Discrete Dynamical Systems*, New York: Ellis Horwood Ltd

Groth, C. (1993) Some unfamiliar dynamics of a familiar macro model: a note, *Journal of Economics*, 58(3), 293–305.

Gulick, D. (1992) *Encounters with Chaos*, New York: McGraw-Hill

Haberman, R. (1977) *Mathematical Models*, Englewood Cliffs: Prentice-Hall

Hamilton, J.E. (1948) Effect of present-day whaling on the stock of whales, *Nature*, 161, 12 June, 913–914

Harris, M. (1987) *Dynamic Economic Analysis*, Oxford: Oxford University Press

Hartwick, J.M. and Olewiler, N.D. (1986) *The Economics of Natural Resource Use*, New York: Harper & Row

Heck, A. (1993) *Introduction to Maple*, New York: Springer-Verlag

Henderson, J.M. and Quandt, R.E. (1971) *Microeconomic Theory: A Mathematical Approach*, 2nd edn., New York: McGraw-Hill

Hicks, J.R. (1950) *A Contribution to the Theory of the Trade Cycle*, Oxford: Oxford University Press

Hilborn, R. and Walters, C.J. (1992) *Quantitative Fisheries Stock Assessment*, London: Chapman & Hall

Hilborn, R.C. (1994) *Chaos and Nonlinear Dynamics*, Oxford: Oxford University Press

Holden, K., Peel, D.A. and Thompson, J.L. (1985) *Expectations: Theory and Evidence*, London: Macmillan

Holmgren, R.A. (1994) *A First Course in Discrete Dynamical Systems*, New York: Springer-Verlag

Hommes, C.H. (1991) *Chaotic Dynamics in Economic Models: Some Simple Case-Studies*, Groningen: Wolters-Noordhoff

Honkapohja, S. (ed.) (1990) *The State of Macroeconomics*, Oxford: Basil Blackwell

Hoppensteadt, F.C. (1992) *Mathematical Methods of Population Biology*, Cambridge: Cambridge University Press

Huang, C.J. and Crooke, P.S. (1997) *Mathematics and Mathematica for Economists*, Oxford: Blackwell

Humphrey, T.M. (1992) Price-level stabilization rules in a Wicksellian model of the cumulative process, *Scandinavian Journal of Economics*, 94(3), 509–518

Intriligator, M.D. (1971) *Mathematical Optimization and Economic Theory*, Englewood Cliffs: Prentice-Hall

Jeffrey, A. (1990) *Linear Algebra and Ordinary Differential Equations*, Oxford: Blackwell Scientific

Jones, C.I. (1998) *Introduction to Economic Growth*, New York: W.W. Norton

Jong, F.J. de (1967) *Dimensional Analysis for Economists*, Amsterdam: North-Holland

Judge, G. (2000) *Computing Skills for Economists*, Chichester: John Wiley

Kajii, A. (1997) On the role of options in sunspot equilibria, *Econometrica*, 65(4), 977–986

Kamien, M.I. and Schwartz, N.L. (1991) *Dynamic Optimization. The Calculus of Variations and Optimal Control in Economics and Management*, 2nd edn., Amsterdam: North-Holland

Karakitsos, E. (1992) *Macrosystems*, Oxford: Blackwell

Keeler, E., Spence, M. and Zeckhauser, R. (1977) The optimal control of pollution, in Smith, V.L. (ed.), *Economics of Natural & Environmental Resources*, New York: Gordon & Breach, 409–439

Kelley, W.G. and Peterson, A.C. (2001) *Difference Equations*, 2nd edn., San Diego: Academic Press,

Kenkel, J.L. (1974) *Dynamic Linear Economic Models*, New York: Gordon & Breach

Kesley, D. (1988) The chaos of economics, *Oxford Economic Papers*, 40, 1–31

Kirk, D.E. (1970) *Optimal Control Theory, An Introduction*, Englewood Cliffs: Prentice-Hall

Kofler, M. (1997) *Maple: An Introduction and Reference*, New York: Addison-Wesley

Kreyszig, E. and Norminton, E.J. (1994) *Maple Computer Manual for Advanced Engineering Mathematics*, New York: John Wiley

Krugman, P. (1999) *Deflationary spirals*, web site: http://web.mit.edu/krugman/www/spirals.html

Lai, C., Hu, S. and Wang, V. (1996) Commodity price dynamics and anticipated shocks, *American Journal of Agricultural Economics*, 78(4), 982–990

Lawler, P. (1994) Monetary policy and asymmetrical fiscal policy in a jointly floating currency area, *Scottish Journal of Political Economy*, 41, 142–162

Léonard, D. and Long, N.V. (1992) *Optimal Control Theory and Static Optimization in Economics*, Cambridge: Cambridge University Press

Leslie, D. (1993) *Advanced Macroeconomics: Beyond IS/LM*, London: McGraw-Hill

Lynch, S. (2001) *Dynamical Systems with Applications using Maple*, Boston: Birkhäuser

MacDonald, R. (1988) *Floating Exchange Rates*, London: Unwin Hyman

Machlup, F. (1959) Statics and dynamics: kaleidoscopic words, *Southern Economic Journal*, 26, 91–110

Mahajan, V. and Peterson, R.A. (1985) *Models for Innovation Diffusion*, Beverly Hills: Sage

Mahajan, V. and Wind, Y. (eds.) (1986) *Innovation Diffusion Models of New Product Acceptance*, Cambridge, Mass.: Ballinger

Mandelbrot, B. (1987) Towards a second stage of determinism in science, *Interdisciplinary Science Review*, 12, 117–127

Mankiw, N.G. and Weil, D.N. (1989) The baby boom, the baby bust, and the housing market, *Regional Science and Urban Economics*, 19(2), 235–258

Manning, A. (1990) Imperfect competition, multiple equilibria and unemployment policy, *Economic Journal*, 100(400) Supplement, 151–162

Mas-Colell, A. (1986) Notes on price and quantity tâtonnement dynamics, in Sonnenschein, H. (ed.), *Models of Economic Dynamics*, New York: Springer

May, R.M. (1976) Simple mathematical models with very complicated dynamics, *Nature*, 261, 10 June, 459–467

McCafferty, S. (1990) *Macroeconomic Theory*, New York: Harper & Row

McMannus, M. (1962) Dynamic Cournot-type oligopoly models: a correction, *Review of Economic Studies*, 29, 337–339

McVay, S. (1966) The last of the great whales., *Scientific America*, August

Medio, A. (1992) *Chaotic Dynamics*, Cambridge: Cambridge University Press

Meyer, G.E. (1993) *SPSS: A Minimalist Approach*, New York: Harcourt Brace Jovanovich

Meyer, W.J. (1985) *Concepts of Mathematical Modeling*, New York: McGraw-Hill

Mirowski, P. (1986) From Mandelbrot to chaos in economic theory, *Southern Economic Journal*, 57, 289–307

Mizrach, B. (1992) The state of economic dynamics, *Journal of Economic Dynamics and Control*, 16(1), 175–190

Mooney, D. and Swift, R. (1999) *A Course in Mathematical Modelling*, The Mathematical Association of America

Mortensen, D.T. (1990) The persistence and indeterminacy of unemployment in search equilibrium, in Honkapohja, S. (ed.), *The State of Macroeconomics*, Oxford: Basil Blackwell

Mullineux, A. and Peng, W. (1993) Nonlinear business cycle modelling, *Journal of Economic Surveys*, 7(1), 41–83

Mundell, R.A. (1962) The appropriate use of monetary and fiscal policy for internal and external stability, *International Monetary Fund Staff Papers*, 9, 70–77

Munro, G.R. and Scott, A.D. (1985) The economics of fisheries management, in Kneese, A.V. and Sweeney, J.L. (eds.), *Handbook of Natural Resource and Energy Economics, II*, Amsterdam: North-Holland

Neal, F. and Shone, R. (1976) *Economic Model Building*, London: Macmillan

Neher, P.A. (1990) *Natural Resource Economics: Conservation and Exploitation*, Cambridge: Cambridge University Press

Nerlov, M. (1958) Adaptive expectations and cobweb phenomena, *Quarterly Journal of Economics*, 72, 227–240

Nicolaides, R. and Walkington, N. (1996) *Maple. A Comprehensive Introduction*, Cambridge: Cambridge University Press

Niehans, J. (1984) *International Monetary Economics*, Oxford: Philip Allan

Obstfeld, M. and Rogoff, K. (1999) *Foundations of International Macroeconomics*, Cambridge, Mass.: MIT Press

Okuguchi, K. (1970) Adaptive expectations in an oligopoly model, *Review of Economic Studies*, 37, 233–237

(1976) *Expectations and Stability in Oligopoly Models*, Berlin: Springer-Verlag

Okuguchi, K. and Szidarovsky, F. (1988) A linear oligopoly model with adaptive expectations: stability reconsidered, *Journal of Economics*, 48, 79–82

(1990) *The Theory of Oligopoly with Multi-Product Firms*, Berlin: Springer-Verlag

Orphanides, A. and Solow, R.M. (1990) Money, inflation and growth, in Friedman, B.J. and Hahn, F.H. (eds.), *Handbook of Monetary Economics, I*, Amsterdam: North-Holland, 213–261

Parker, D., Whitby, S. and Tobias, A. (2000) Improving our understanding of competitive dynamics: a nonlinear model of duopolistic competition, *Economic Issues*, 5, part 3, 27–44

Parkin, M. and King, D.N. (1995) *Economics*, 2nd edn., Wokingam: Addison-Wesley

Percival, I. and Richards, D. (1982) *Introduction to Dynamics*, Cambridge: Cambridge University Press

Peterson, F.M. and Fisher, A.C. (1987) The exploitation of extractive resources: a survey, *Economic Journal*, 87, 681–721

Pietra, T. (1992) The structure of the set of sunspot equilibria in economics with incomplete financial markets, *Economic Theory*, 2, 321–340

Pilbeam, K. (1998) *International Finance*, 2nd edn., London: Macmillan

Pissarides, C.A. (1976) *Labour Market Adjustment*, Cambridge: Cambridge University Press

(1985) Short-run equilibrium dynamics of unemployment, vacancies, and real wages, *American Economic Review*, 75(4), 676–690

Pitchford, J.D. (1974) *Population in Economic Growth*, Amsterdam: North Holland

Pontryagin, L.S., Boltyanskii, V.G., Gamkredlidze, R.V. and Mishchenko, E.F. (1962) *The Mathematical Theory of Optimization*, New York: Interscience Publishers

Pratt, J.W. (1964) Risk aversion in the small and in the large, *Econometrica*, 32, 122–136

Ramsey, F.P. (1928) A mathematical theory of saving, *Economic Journal*, 38, 543–559

Renshaw, E. (1991) *Modelling Biological Populations in Space and Time*, Cambridge: Cambridge University Press

Rocheteau, G. (1999) Balanced-budget rules and indeterminacy of the equilibrium unemployment rate, *Oxford Economic Papers*, 51, 399–409

Rødseth, A. (2000) *Open Economy Macroeconomics*, Cambridge: Cambridge University Press

Romer, D. (2001) *Advanced Macroeconomics*, 2nd edn., New York: McGraw-Hill

Ross, S.L. (1980) *Introduction to Ordinary Differential Equations*, 3rd edn., New York: John Wiley

Royama, T. (1992) *Analytical Population Dynamics*, London: Chapman & Hall

Ruskeepaa, H. (1999) *Mathematica Navigator*, San Diego: Academic Press

Samuelson, P.A. (1939) Interaction between the multiplier analysis and principle of acceleration, *Review of Economic Statistics*, 21, 75–78

Sandefur, J.T. (1990) *Discrete Dynamical Systems*, Oxford: Clarendon Press

Sargent, T.J. and Wallace, N. (1981) Some unpleasant monetarist arithmetic, *Federal Reserve Bank of Minneapolis Quarterly Review*, 5, 1–17.

Scarth, W.M. (1996) *Macroeconomics. An Introduction to Advanced Methods*, 2nd edn., New York: Harcourt Brace Jovanovich

Scheinkman, J.A. (1990) Nonlinearities in economic dynamics, *Economic Journal*, 100 (400) Supplement, 33–48

Schwalbe, D. and Wagon, S. (1996) *VisualDSolve*, New York: Springer-Verlag

Shaw, W.T. and Tigg, J. (1994) *Applied Mathematica*, Reading, Mass.: Addison-Wesley

Sheffrin, S.M. (1983) *Rational Expectations*, Cambridge: Cambridge University Press

Shone, R. (1975) *Microeconomics: A Modern Treatment*, London: Macmillan

(1979) Internal and external balance – problems of interpretation, *Journal of Economic Studies*, 6(2), 216–226

(1980) The monetary approach to the balance of payments: stock–flow equilibria, *Oxford Economic Papers*, 32(2), 200–209

(1981) *Applications in Intermediate Microeconomics*, Oxford: Martin Robertson

(1989) *Open Economy Macroeconomics*, London: Harvester Wheatsheaf

(2001) *An Introduction to Economic Dynamics*, Cambridge: Cambridge University Press

Simon, C.P. and Blume, L. (1994) *Mathematics for Economists*, New York: W.W. Norton

Sinclair, P.J.N. (1992) The scope and nature of monetary economics, *Journal of Economic Surveys*, 6(1), 63–82

Skeel, R.D. and Keiper, J.B. (1993) *Elementary Numerical Computing with Mathematica*, New York: McGraw-Hill

Smith, V.L. and et al. (1977) *Economics of Natural and Environmental Resources*, New York: Gordon & Breach

Solow, R.M. (1956) A contribution to the theory of economic growth, *Quarterly Journal of Economics*, 70, 65–94

Sonnenschein, H. (ed.) (1986) *Models of Economic Dynamics*, New York: Springer

Staver, I.van (1999) Chaos theory and institutional economics: metaphor or model, *Journal of Economic Issues*, 33(1), 141–167

Stevenson, A., Muscatelli, V. and Gregory, M. (1988) *Macroeconomic Theory and Stabilisation Policy*, Oxford: Philip Allan

Suda, S., Tallon, J.-M. and Villanacci, A. (1992) Real indeterminacy in equilibria in a sunspot economy, *Economic Theory*, 2, 309–319

Takayama, A. (1994) *Analytical Methods in Economics*, London: Harvester Wheatsheaf

Teigen, R.L. (1978) The theory of income determination, in Teigen, R.L. (ed.), *Readings in Money, National Income, and Stabilization Policy*, 4th edn., Homewood II: Richard D. Irwin

Teigen, R.L. and *et al.* (1978) *Readings in Money, National Income, and Stabilization Policy*, 4th edn., Homewood Ill.: Richard D. Irwin

Theocharis, R.D. (1960) On the stability of the Cournot solution on the oligopoly problem, *Review of Economic Studies*, 27, 133–134

Tinbergen, J. (1956) *Economic Policy: Principles and Design*, Amsterdam: North-Holland

Tobin, J. (1969) A general equilibrium approach to monetary theory, *Journal of Money, Credit and Banking*, 1, 15–29

Tranter, N. (1973) *Population Since the Industrial Revolution: The Case of England and Wales*, London: Croom Helm

Tu, P.N.V. (1994) *Dynamical Systems*, 2nd edn., Berlin: Springer-Verlag

Turnovsky, S.J. (1995) *Methods of Macroeconomic Dynamics*, Cambridge, Mass.: MIT Press

Vandermeer, J. (1981) *Elementary Mathematical Ecology*, New York: John Wiley

Varian, J.R., Kaplan, T., Mukherji, A., Eckalbar, J.C., Judd, K.L., Guu, S., Noguchi, A., Anderson, G.S., Dickhaut, J., Carter, M., Steele, J.M., Stine, R.A., Kendall, W.S., Rose, C., Miller, R.M., Brown, S.J., Belsley, D.A., Ley, E., Steel, F.J. and Korsan, R.J. (1993) *Economic and Financial Modeling with Mathematica*, New York: Springer-Verlag

Wagon, S. (1991) *Mathematica in Action*, New York: W.H. Freeman

Waugh, F.V. (1964) Cobweb models, *Journal of Farm Economics*, 46(4), 732–750

Whigham, D. (1998) *Qualitative Business Methods Using Excel*, Oxford: Oxford University Press

Wolfram, S. (1999) *Mathematica: A System for Doing Mathematics by Computer*, 4th edn., Redwood City: Addison-Wesley

Author index

Subject index